Fodor's 2002

W9-CED-560

Hawai'i

Fodor's Travel Publications • New York, Toronto, London, Sydney, Auckland
www.fodors.com

CONTENTS

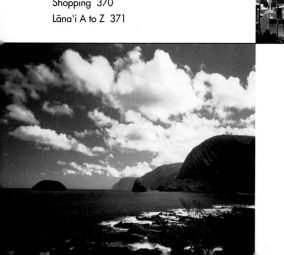

MAPS

Circled letters in text correspond to letters on the photographs. For more information on the sights pictured, turn to the indicated page number **Ⓐ** on each photograph.

DESTINATION
HAWAI'I

Just try to describe Hawai'i without saying "paradise." It's nearly impossible. In this place of ineffable beauty, the word is not cliché but a fact, even an understatement. Eden may greet you on a heroic scale, as at Waimea Canyon on Kaua'i, or may appear in the palm of your hand, as when you hold a native Lokelani rose. The pleasures come in forms that are material and sensual, as well—consider the beguiling shopping and the inspired cuisine created in kitchens energized by world-class chefs. You can also get physical. Go birding, hiking, swimming, or waterskiing, or pursue almost any other outdoor sport known to man—even snow skiing or snowboarding. Or simply head for the nearest perfect crescent of palm-shaded beach and do nothing at all.

O‘AHU

O'ahu is the most visited Hawaiian island, yet even here grandeur reveals itself at every turn. The landscape is so rugged and mountainous that many a developer has just shrugged his shoulders and walked away, mumbling in frustration. The monster winter waves along Ⓐ**O'ahu's North Shore** are worth driving from Honolulu to see. Inside the "tube," time stands still: master surfers experience a space like the inside of a glass cathedral, a roar like a jet engine's, and unparalleled exhilaration. Novice-friendly waves roll in at Honolulu's famous Ⓑ**Waikīkī Beach,** where just about anyone can hang ten on a rented surfboard under the supervision of an experienced instructor. The neighborhood nearby, with its sprawling malls and many diverse boutiques, is a reminder that this Hawaiian Eden has more than one face. Ⓒ**King Kamehameha I,** who united the islands in the 1790s, could never have anticipated the busy, modern neighborhood inland from his roost in the capital's Ⓓ**'Iolani Palace.** Hawaiian royalty called this

Ⓑ▷59

Ⓒ▷50

Victorian structure home between 1882 and 1893, when, on the heels of the uncongenial arrival of 160 U.S. Marines, Queen Lili'uokalani ended the monarchy once and for all. The chill thrown over Hawaiian culture by this event lingered for years.

Ⓓ▷49

O'AHU

Today a cultural renaissance is under way in Hawai'i, and the lively entertainment accompanying the revival of interest in ancient ways will educate, sensitize, and broaden you—particularly as it's on view in Lā'ie at the 40-acre ⒺⒾ**Polynesian Cultural Center.** Here, amid re-created villages from Tahiti and Samoa, Fiji and the Marquesas, Tonga, and other countries all over the Pacific, you can marvel at the hula and the Samoan Fireknife Dance, both carefully explained. More Hawaiiana is on view at the fine Bishop Museum. Or head for the Waimea Valley in search of the Hawaiian nēnē, the state bird, and to watch an exhibition of cliff-diving. You can also explore waterfalls or just sun yourself on any number of beaches. But it is Pearl Harbor that is, without a doubt, O'ahu's most moving sight. A surprise Japanese air attack on December 7, 1941, crippled the U.S. Navy's Pacific Fleet and prompted America's entry into World War II. Walk the paths lined with memorial stones that front

Ⓔ❯**59**

Ⓕ❯**57**

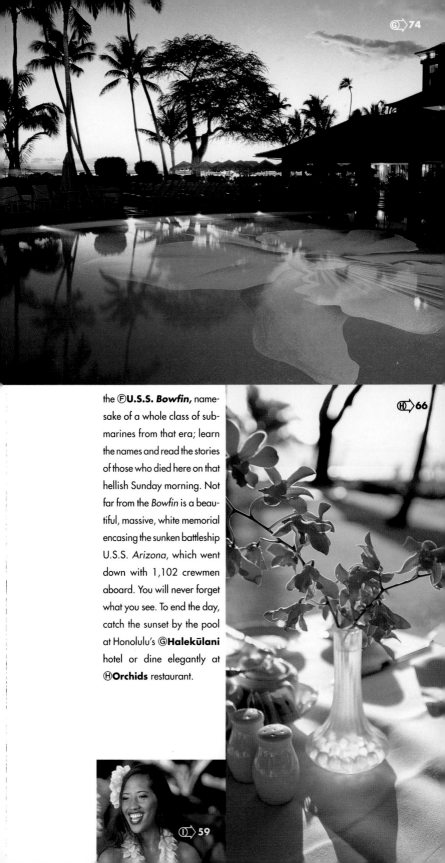

Ⓖ➤74

the Ⓕ**U.S.S. *Bowfin*,** namesake of a whole class of submarines from that era; learn the names and read the stories of those who died here on that hellish Sunday morning. Not far from the *Bowfin* is a beautiful, massive, white memorial encasing the sunken battleship U.S.S. *Arizona*, which went down with 1,102 crewmen aboard. You will never forget what you see. To end the day, catch the sunset by the pool at Honolulu's Ⓖ**Halekūlani** hotel or dine elegantly at Ⓗ**Orchids** restaurant.

Ⓗ➤66

Ⓘ➤59

The last two decades have brought golf courses and luxurious hotels, tourists and traffic to the second-largest Hawaiian isle. But the landscape surrounding ⒶⒸ**Haleakalā,** the world's largest dormant volcano, remains preternatural in its loveliness. If you wanted to ruin the view, you could fit Manhattan inside its great volcanic bowl. All over the island, but particularly here, lush forests keep company with strikingly red and desertlike terrain, and some of the flora and fauna are rare even in Hawai'i. The stunning silversword plant grows only here and at high elevations on the Big Island. It will bloom just once in its life, near the end of its days. At Ⓑ**ʻĪao Valley State Park,** wind and water have sculpted impressive rock spires.

MAUI

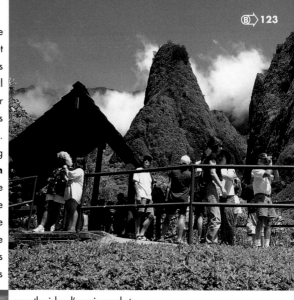

Mark Twain may not have thought much of Venice, but he was captivated by this place—and no wonder. All over Maui, rainbows hover over the mists and waterfalls shower the mountainsides. Hop aboard the charming 1890s Ⓓ**Sugarcane Train** and take a ride through the magnificent, lush landscape between Kāʻanapali, on the west coast, and Lahaina, the former whaling town that was once Hawaiʻi's capital and is

Ⓒ⟩ 128

now the island's main market center. Sugarcane, a mainstay of Maui's economy for years, was a powerful influence on the island's history. Production ceased in 1999, but the train has happily outlived the crop. For local farmers the soil yields other bounties, among them grapes for wine and rich pasture-lands where horses graze. The vineyards and grasslands create another kind of landscape on Maui, one that's intimate, charming, and a perfect counterpoint to nature's grandstanding.

Ⓓ⟩ 120

MAUI

Ⓔ▷133

For 19th-century missionaries from New England, Hawai'i represented a golden opportunity to save souls—not just Hawaiian souls but those of fellow New Englanders, whalers drawn to the Pacific by the big profits to be made on whalebone and whale oil. For these roistering mainlanders, Maui and its port of ⒻⒽ**Lahaina** were a red-light district where the bars never closed. The 19th-century buildings where they took their rowdy R&R have been renovated, and much of the town is now a National Historic Landmark. As for the North Pacific's humpback whale population, which once numbered many thousands, only about 1,500

Ⓕ▷115

remain. On winter whale-watching tours from Lahaina you can see them spectacularly breaching and blowing offshore. Under water, along the western and southwestern coasts, the sea yields still other spectacular sights. In the Molokini Crater area, a marine preserve, fish are so tame that they eat right out of a diver's hand. If you're not certified to dive, you can get an idea of the island's submarine wonders at the Ⓙ**Maui Ocean Center** in Mā'alaea. Back on land, West Maui's so-called Golf Coast, north of Lahaina, calls relentlessly to

Ⓖ▷131

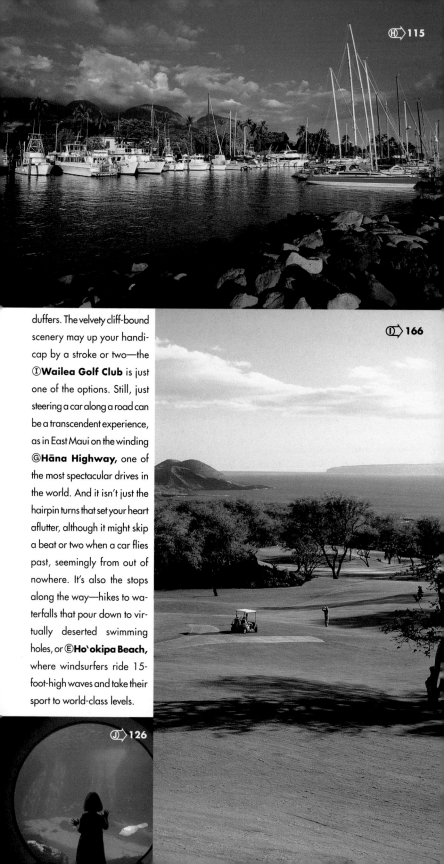

①⟩ 166

duffers. The velvety cliff-bound scenery may up your handicap by a stroke or two—the ①**Wailea Golf Club** is just one of the options. Still, just steering a car along a road can be a transcendent experience, as in East Maui on the winding ⑥**Hāna Highway,** one of the most spectacular drives in the world. And it isn't just the hairpin turns that set your heart aflutter, although it might skip a beat or two when a car flies past, seemingly from out of nowhere. It's also the stops along the way—hikes to waterfalls that pour down to virtually deserted swimming holes, or ⑤**Ho'okipa Beach,** where windsurfers ride 15-foot-high waves and take their sport to world-class levels.

①⟩ 126

BIG ISLAND

Ⓐ 201

If you like your paradises un-crowded, you'll like the Big Island. (Its formal name, *Hawai'i*, is also the name of the *state*—and something had to give.) Of all the Hawaiian Islands, it's the youngest. Inland, ancient Hawaiian ruins and sleepy and not-so-sleepy towns with melodic names punctuate a landscape of tropical forests, lush pasturelands, and barren lava fields. Rainbows arch over gorges and shimmer near sparkling cascades as at Ⓓ**Rainbow Falls,** outside Hilo, the county seat.

Ⓑ 204

©⟩ 204

Here and there you'll see ancient stone *heiau* and statues, perhaps of the war god Ku. And the volcanic activity that created the entire chain still percolates impressively—over the last 10 years, lava on the coast has added some 70 acres to the Island. Ⓐ**Hawai'i Volcanoes National Park** is the site of Kīlauea, one of the world's most active volcanoes and the only one in the state that's not currently dormant; fireworks displays pale by comparison. The park's bleakly beautiful ©**Devastation Trail** demonstrates what happens when lava gets a bit too frisky: The forest that covered the land in 1959 is completely gone, even some 40 years later. Lava tubes, cinder cones, and barren craters create an otherworldly landscape along Chain of Craters Road. In the park's coastal section, near Ⓑ**Kalapana,** lava flows into the sea—slowly enough for you to get a good close look at it through the steam. Lava flows have even blocked portions of the roads here.

Ⓓ⟩200

BIG ISLAND

On the Big Island you find occasional sparkling white crescents of sand, but many beaches come in colors. Here olive-green, there golden, they are sometimes as black as the lava that formed them, especially on the Ⓖ**South Kohala Coast.** Eruptions of Mt. Hualālai 200 years ago created moonscapes that extend to the sea all through the island's northwest corner.

Ⓔ▷210

Palm trees shading these strands and golf courses at nearby luxury resorts glow especially green against the inky sands and vivid blue waters. The volcanic wonderland extends offshore, where sea turtles and bright fish such as butterfly fish, damselfish, and false moorish idols swim among lava towers, tubes, and caves, as you'll see on trips with organizers like Ⓗ**Red Sail Sports** and at snorkeling destinations such as Punaluʻu Beach Park. Experts can explore a wrecked plane off Keāhole Point. On land, hike along trails blazed by ancient Hawaiians. The hike up

Ⓕ▷246

ⓖ⟩216

ⓗ⟩252

13,680-foot Mauna Loa is one of the state's best-kept secrets. If your timing is right, try to see October's ①**Ironman Triathlon,** a 2.4-mile open-ocean swim and a 112-mile bike ride capped with a full 26.2-mile marathon. Try to catch a local hula school rehearsing at the 19th-century Ⓔ**Hulihe'e Palace** in Kailua-Kona weekday afternoons— Hawaiian culture flourishes here as well. Lodging options range from small B&Bs to hotel complexes like the Ⓕ**Kona Village Resort.** Wherever you stay, don't check out without acquiring some rich, smooth macadamia nuts, grown on the Big Island. Or pick up 100% pure Kona coffee, grown just upland of the south Kona shore. The world-famous brews of Kona begin life not as beans but as berries called "cherries." Many of Kona's 600-plus coffee farms permit you to sip their blends gratis, and in a twist that will be novel if you've been to California's wine country, tasting tours in Kona keep you *sober.* These guided visits end, of course, at the plantation's gift shop, and you'll be glad: Some good coffee will help ease the symptoms of "paradise withdrawal" back home.

①⟩259

KAUA'I

They call it the Garden Isle, which is saying a lot when you consider the floral splendor of Hawai'i in general. Kaua'i more than lives up to its sobriquet. Then again, as the oldest of the main Hawaiian islands, it's had a few more million years to become splendid. The elemental forces of nature, given a few extra aeons, have given much of Kaua'i a chiseled beauty, including the coastline up north, around the Ⓓ**Hanalei Valley.** Pure glorious scenery is the result—and the reason that many a visitor is drawn to Kaua'i. Yes, you can golf on fine courses here. And yes, there are lovely places to eat, fun places to shop, and varied hostelries, from luxurious resorts to rustic cabins. But Kaua'i is not really about those things. It's about *grandeur,* about

Ⓑ 293

Creation outdoing itself. The stunning vistas of the ocean and a mountain named Bali Hai from the Ⓐ**Limahuli Garden,** part of the National Tropical Botanical Garden on the northern coast, will teach you that lesson. So will viewpoints like Canyon Lookout and Kalalau Lookout, with their panorama of jagged moun-

Ⓒ 289

18

Ⓓ 283

tains and lacy cascades, not to mention the natural water show on the south shore at the Ⓒ**Spouting Horn** and the perfect dunes and spectacular sunsets of the west at Ⓑ**Polihale Beach.** If Hawai'i is paradise, then Kaua'i may be paradise's prettiest subdivision.

KAUA'I

Ⓔ➤283

On Kaua'i, mountain bikers assault the 12-mile-long Power Line Trail, hikers tackle the twisting Kalalau Trail, golfers and tennis players test their skills on any number of resort layouts, outrigger canoeists race offshore, and snorkelers and scuba divers explore the bounty of submarine wonders. Nature lovers have a field day as well. They search for nests of endangered seabirds on the cliffs below the bright white Ⓔ**Kīlauea Lighthouse,** a National Historic Landmark on Kaua'i's north coast, or, in the heart of the island in Kōke'e State Park's Ⓖ**Waimea Canyon,** try to spot the rare jungle fowl, whose ancestors ar-

Ⓕ➤285

Ⓖ 292

rived with the Polynesians. (If Mark Twain hadn't called this gorge the "Grand Canyon of the Pacific," someone else would have.) Cascades like Ⓕ **ʻŌpaekaʻa Falls,** to the east, aren't hard to find either.

Ⓗ 308

Obeying gravity over time, these 40 feet of water have carved out many a breathtaking vista on Kauaʻi. Volcanic Mount Waiʻaleʻale, towering over the island's center, is known as the "wettest spot on earth," with almost 500 inches of rain annually. The clever planners of the Ⓗ **Princeville Hotel** made sure that its Horizon Pool appears to flow seamlessly into Hanalei Bay. The Clever Planner of Kauaʻi's west-coast beaches made sure that every day ends with a spectacle.

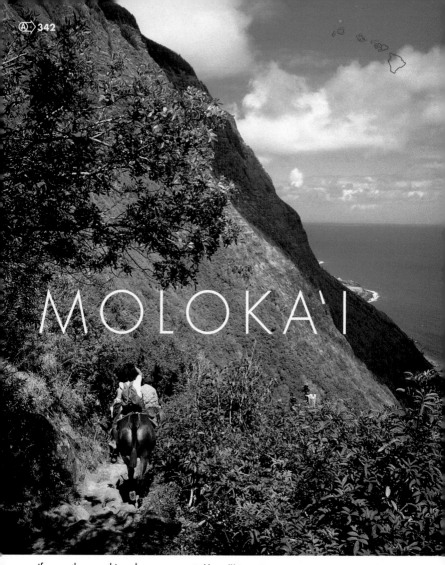

MOLOKAʻI

If, more than anything else, you come to Hawaiʻi to rest your body and soul, give serious consideration to basing yourself on the "Friendly Isle." This is where Hawaiians themselves vacation, drawn by the island's peace and quiet and its great beauty. It is also where people with Hansen's disease were exiled, beginning in the 1860s, back in the days that its sufferers, then known as lepers, were feared and before drugs could arrest the disease's course. It is a deeply moving experience to visit the settlement, known as Kalaupapa, which is accessible from Pālāʻau State Park via

Ⓑ 344

(C) 344

the Ⓐ**Moloka'i Mule Ride.** Moloka'i is so mellow that few other sights are musts. But most visitors do take in at least part of the 53,000-acre Moloka'i Ranch for horseback riding and cultural walks, and Ⓑ**Kaloko'eli Fishpond** near Kaunakakai, a distinctive structure built by the earliest Hawaiians. Many endangered species survive at

(D) 348

the Nature Conservancy's lush, wet Ⓒ**Kamakou Preserve;** reserve ahead for the rare guided hikes. The low-key island lifestyle means that your lodging will in all likelihood be understated; you even have the option of sleeping under canvas at Ⓓ**Paniolo Camp.** The showers there are warmed by the Hawaiian sun, and the proprietors are accommodating about packing box lunches for your day trips to splendid beaches such as Ⓔ**Hālawa Beach Park,** where ancient chieftains once surfed to unwind.

(E) 346

LĀNA'I

A little more than a decade ago, the planting, growing, and harvesting of pineapples were the major preoccupation on warm, arid Lāna'i. Things changed fast after the Great Hawaiian Pineapple Crash of the 1980s. Suddenly, Lāna'i needed a new economic base. Castle & Cooke, Inc. (formerly Dole), which owns almost all of the island, is pinning its hopes on the two luxury resorts the company created in 1990 to join the venerable, and still charming, Hotel Lāna'i. Many of the new visitors check out the Ⓐ**Garden of the Gods,**

© 370

Ⓓ 364

north of Lāna'i City. The strewn boulders look merely curious at midday, but as the shadows lengthen, the place becomes eerily beautiful. More poignant than spooky is once prosperous and lovely Ⓑ**Keōmuku,** laid low by an economic crisis in 1901 and finally abandoned in 1954. The Ⓓ**Munro Trail** will take you to Lāna'i's highest point, whose commanding view encompasses most of Hawai'i's other islands. Or sign up with ©Ⓔ**Trilogy Oceansports Lāna'i** for a trip to sea—for snorkeling lessons, or just some old-fashioned horsing around.

Ⓔ 370

GREAT ITINERARIES

The map shows the following locations on Kaua'i:
Kīlauea Lighthouse and Kīlauea Point National Wildlife Refuge, Hanalei Bay, Hanalei Valley Overlook, Waimea Canyon, Wailua River, Fern Grotto, National Tropical Botanical Gardens, Līhu'e, Kilohana, Po'ipū Beach.

KAUA`I

NI`IHAU

10 miles

Highlights of Hawai'i
14 days

Many Hawai'i visitors simply loll in a chaise longue during their stay. If you would prefer to take a peek at several islands, to get a better feeling for the world's most isolated archipelago, let this itinerary be your guide. You'll travel from O'ahu to Kaua'i, with stops at Moloka'i, Maui, and the Big Island.

O'ahu
3 days

The third largest of the Hawaiian Islands, 608-square-mi O'ahu is a good place to start your tour, with its frequent air service from the mainland and its scores of restaurants and hotels and seemingly endless shopping. It's a lush and beautiful place. Wind and weather have carved dramatic valleys between steep cliffs across the middle of the island, and the temperate, forgiving climate and abundant rainfall keep things a vivid shade of green. On the first morning, rise early to make the steep walk to Diamond Head, the summit of an extinct volcano, for a panorama of the city and the beaches. Once you've soaked up the vista, take in a bit of history at the U.S.S. *Bowfin,* a World War

II submarine; the U.S.S. *Missouri,* which saw action from World War II to the Persian Gulf War; and the *Arizona* Memorial, commemorating the sinking of this ship on December 7, 1941, with more than a thousand men aboard. Then spend some time exploring the shops, restaurants, and other attractions of Waikīkī—including the Waikīkī Aquarium, which spotlights marine life of Hawai'i and the South Pacific, and the Bishop Museum, which started out as a home for the possessions of King Kamehameha the Great's last direct descendant and is now known for its collection of Polynesiana. On day two, drive around Diamond Head to watch the windsurfers, then follow the coast to ⒷHanauma Bay and the windward town of Kailua. Take side trips to the Nu'uanu Pali Lookout, where the view is spectacular, and the Byodo-In Temple, a replica of the Kyoto original, on your way to the ⒶPolynesian Cultural Center, with its Polynesian villages and demonstrations. Pick up a souvenir or two in

its open-air shopping village—it has a good selection of Polynesian handicrafts. It's a long, dark drive back to Waikīkī after the show, so you might want to stay at a local B&B. On your third day continue along the North Shore, stopping at Waimea Valley and Waimea Bay, a popular picnic spot, en route back to Waikīkī. In Honolulu, explore the lei stands and herb shops in the city's Chinatown. Then take a guided tour of America's only royal residence, 'Iolani Palace, and stroll around Mission Houses Museum, the homes of Hawai'i's first missionaries (who arrived in 1820), and Kawaiaha'o Church, built out of local coral blocks and used for royal ceremonies.

D▷292

Kaua'i
2 days

On the Garden Isle, begin by making the 90-minute drive from Līhu'e around the south shore of the island and up to spectacular ⒹWaimea Canyon, nicknamed the "Grand Canyon of the Pacific." Lookouts en route give you wonderful views of the entire panorama. Kōke'e State Park is at the northern end of the canyon, a true wilderness full of colorful flowers. Return the way you came, stopping en route as time permits to visit the National Tropical Botanical Gardens and the eclectic shops at Kilohana. Plan your trip to allow time to arrive at Po'ipū Beach and catch the sunset over the Pacific—a sight you won't soon forget. On your final day, cruise up the Wailua River to the Fern Grotto, take a flightseeing tour, and stop at Kīlauea Lighthouse, built in 1913 and towering over the Kīlauea Point National Wildlife Refuge, and the Hanalei Valley Overlook, where fields of taro stretch before you almost as far as you can see. Spend your last evening watching the sun set at Hanalei Bay, a spectacular way to bring your island sojourn to a close.

Moloka'i
2 days

This long, small island doesn't take long to explore. The best strategy is to see just a little each day to allow time to nearby Lodge at Moloka'i Ranch. Its restaurant, although the most formal on the island, is casual and comfortable, and if you eat before the sun goes down you can marvel at the spectacular ocean vista through the big picture windows. The next day—and it will be a full

Waimea Bay
12 mi
Polynesian Cultural Center
10 miles
Waimea Valley
83
83
99
28 mi
O`AHU
32 mi
USS *Bowfin*/ USS *Missouri*/ *Arizona* Memorial
H2
Byodo-In Temple
83
Kailua
Bishop Museum
H1
Honolulu
61
Nu'uanu Pali Lookout
72
Chinatown
'Iolani Palace
1.3 mi
Waīkīki
H1
72
Mission Houses Museum
Waīkīki Aquarium
Hanauma Bay
Kawaiaha'o Church
Diamond Head
21 mi

©▷346

kick back and relax. West Moloka'i is mostly given over to 53,000-acre Moloka'i Ranch, the largest local landholder. In tiny Maunaloa, which anchors the area, start by stopping at the old market and kite shop, on the brief main street. Later head for wide ©Pāpōhaku Beach, the island's nicest and most private strand and one of the state's most sensational, with its stunning white sand. At dinnertime head for the

one—reserve ahead to tour Kalaupapa, to which people afflicted with Hansen's disease were once relegated; make the tortuous 2-mi trip via the Moloka'i Mule Ride. Father Damien, a Catholic priest, cared for the community's residents until he succumbed to the disease in 1889. Before you catch an evening flight to Maui, take in the stupendous view of the peninsula from Pālā'au State Park.

27

(F) 122

Lodge at
Molokai
Ranch
Mule Ride
Kalaupapa
470
Pālāau
State Park
460
MOLOKA'I
Maunaloa
Pāpōhaku
Beach

Bailey
House
Kā`anapali
'Īao Valley
State Park
Wailuku
36
Lahaina
LĀNA'I
55 mi
24 mi
30
Hāna Hwy
440
30
Alexander
& Baldwin
Sugar
Museum
360
Hāna
10 miles
21 mi
377
Maui
Tropical
Plantation
Haleakalā
National
Park
10 mi
'Ohe'o
Gulch
KAHOOLAWE
MAUI

(E) 128

Maui
4 days

Maui, which inspires people to call it the Valley Isle, is the second-largest landfall in the state. Start your Maui sojourn in 'Īao Valley State Park, where a 2,000-ft-high spire known as the 'Īao Needle rises astonishingly from the valley floor and easy hikes lead through jungly forests. The peripatetic Mark Twain, stopping in the area during his peregrinations through the islands, dubbed it the Yosemite of the Pacific. Nothing less did justice to its charismatic grandeur. Afterward take 'Īao Valley Road into Wailuku, where it becomes Main Street. Many of the old buildings in this dozy little town are on the National Register of Historic Places. Bailey House, former home of prominent 19th-century missionaries Edward and Caroline Bailey, displays period furniture and artifacts. Then follow Highway 30 south a couple of miles to the 120-acre Maui Tropical Plantation, a sort of agricultural theme park, to tour former sugarcane fields, get an overview of the growing processes, and catch lively demonstrations of activities like lei-making and coconut-husking. Then head over to the (F)Alexander & Baldwin Sugar Museum in Kahului. The next day, if it's sunny, make the fabulous 4-hr drive to Hāna. It's a spectacular 55 mi of bridges and turns and vistas showcasing classic Hawaiian scenery. Keep an eye out en route for waterfalls, pools, swimming holes, hiking trails, lookout points, and other stopping places. Overnight in Hāna, a onetime company town devoted to the sugar industry that's now almost entirely focused on tourism.
In the morning visit aviator Charles Lindbergh's grave and 'Ohe'o Gulch, where there are many waterfalls more than 100 ft high with idyllic pools at the bottom. The place is perfect for picnicking and sunbathing and can get very crowded. Backtracking along the Hāna Highway, end the day exploring historic Lahaina, the famous restored former whaling town where crusty sailors just back from many months at sea clashed with New England missionaries whose single-minded goal was to save the men's souls. After you've explored its antique buildings, go on to Kā`anapali to spend the night. The next morning, get up early for a sailing-and-snorkeling cruise out of Lahaina to Lāna'i. Then get to bed early, because the following day you'll rise before dawn to see the sun rise over the immense crater of (E)Haleakalā, the volcano whose lava flow created all of East Maui. The crater is now the centerpiece of Haleakalā National Park, which is full of hiking trails. At lovely Hosmer Grove, a forested area, you can pick up a trail map. The Sliding Sands trail off the top of the crater shows off some amazingly colorful scenery that's almost lunar.

Big Island
3 days

After arriving in Hilo, the county seat of the island and the fourth-largest city in the state, drive up Waiānuenue Avenue about a mile (stay to the right) as far as exquisite (H)Rainbow Falls. It's beautiful when the sun is shining, and rainbows form above the mist if the sun is right in the morning. Then travel north of Hilo for 7 mi along Highway 19, and turn right onto the 4-mi scenic bypass that skirts Hawai'i Tropical Botanical Garden, 17 acres crowded with exotic species like ginger and heliconia, before rejoining the highway. Next turn left inland toward the small and unprepossessing town of Honomū and drive 4 mi to 'Akaka Falls State Park, where a 20-min walk yields the rewarding sight of the park's two cascades—the 100-ft Kahuna Falls and the 420-ft 'Akaka Falls. Spend the afternoon in (G)Hawai'i Volcanoes National Park, exploring its lava tubes and mineral formations, steam vents and tropical plants—and, if you're lucky, to catch the sight of lava flowing from Kīlauea Volcano. It would take years to see everything in this 359-square-mi preserve, but you can get a feel for the volcanic terrain in just a short time with a visit to Halema'uma'u Crater, a steam-clouded pit inside the Kīlauea Caldera, or with a hike along the blackened Devastation Trail. Begin the next day with a drive up the Hāmākua Coast to Waimea, to see the Hawaiiana in the Kamuela Museum and tour the Parker Ranch Visitor Center. The ranch was founded in 1847 and grew up around 2 acres of land given to John Palmer Parker by King Kamehameha I; one of Parker's descendants collected some very fine art, and a Utrillo and Renoir are on display. En route to the Kohala Coast resorts—don't miss the nearby petroglyph carvings—look for the snow-capped summit of Mauna Ke'a. (The next morning head south through Hōlualoa, Kealakekua, and Captain Cook, stopping for a bit at Pu'uhonua o Hōnaunau National Historic Park, about 20 mi south of Kailua-Kona. Games and crafts demonstra-tions, among other activities there, teach you a lot about Hawaiian history. If you have time, continue on to Ka Lae, the southernmost point in the United States. This windswept and grassy area gives a realistic glimpse of Hawai'i's past. When you've seen it all, head back to Kailua-Kona and the Astronaut Ellison S. Onizuka Space Center, a tribute to Hawai'i's first astronaut. Spend the rest of the day sightseeing, shopping, and relaxing in Kailua-Kona.

Kamuela Museum

19 41 mi 19 Hāmākua Coast

10 mi

Kohala Coast Waimea Parker Ranch Visitor Center

Petroglyph Carvings

19

Honomū

`Akaka Falls State Park 4 mi Scenic Drive

19

Mauna Ke'a

32 mi

Hawai'i Tropical Botanical Garden 7 mi Airport

Rainbow Falls Hilo 1 mi

Astronaut Ellison S. Onizuka Space Center

HAWAI'I

Kailua-Kona

11

Hōlualoa 20 mi

Kealakekua

Captain Cook

Hawai'i Volcanoes National Park/ Kīlauea Volcano

27 mi 11

Pu'uhonua o Hōnaunau National Historic Park

Halema'uma'u Crater Devastation Trail

10 miles

Ⓗ>200

Ka Lae

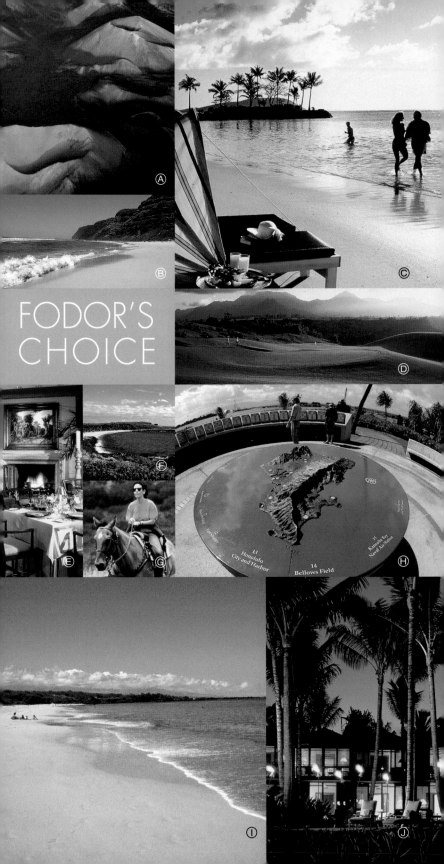

FODOR'S
CHOICE

Even with so many special places in Hawai'i, Fodor's writers and editors have their favorites. Here are a few that stand out.

QUINTESSENTIAL HAWAI'I

Ⓗ ***Arizona* Memorial, O'ahu.** For practically every visitor this is a must-see, with its gleaming white memorial and powerful presentation. ☞ p. 57

Big Island sunsets. On the Kohala Coast, the sun consistently sets as a blazing red orb, casting fiery orange and magenta hues across an ocean view broken only by an occasional billowing sail. ☞ p. 219

Garden of the Gods, Lāna'i. For photography it's hard to top this surreal landscape scattered with red and black lava formations and rocks, with the blue Pacific in the background. ☞ p. 363

Hiking on the Big Island. In Hawai'i Volcanoes National Park, trek through fern forests to watch fresh lava hit the Pacific amid billowing steam—and new land being created. ☞ p. 255

Ⓐ **Maui and Kaua'i flight-seeing.** Gaze down on the moonscape craters of Maui's Haleakalā volcano or zoom over rain forests, waterfalls, beaches, and emerald-green carpeted canyons. ☞ p. 166

Road to Hāna, Maui. Fifty-five mi of curvy road and one-lane bridges forge a path through Maui's rain forest, passing spectacular waterfalls and secluded beaches. ☞ p. 131

Surfing O'ahu's North Shore. Winter brings giant waves to Sunset Beach and Waimea Bay, and the world's top pros and hundreds of spectators gather for surfing's major competitions. ☞ p. 97

Whale-watching off Maui. Humpback whales breach and blow right offshore between November and May. ☞ p. 112

BEACHES

Ⓘ **Hāpuna Beach, Big Island.** In summer this clean, wide white-sand beach is perfect for snorkeling and scuba-diving. Kids can romp alongside the tidal pools in a cove at the north end. ☞ p. 221

Ⓕ **Hulopo'e Beach, Lāna'i.** The island's only swimming beach is great for snorkeling. ☞ p. 365

Kahaloa and Ulukou Beaches, O'ahu. The swimming stands out at these strands fronting Waikīkī's Royal Hawaiian and Sheraton Moana Surfrider hotels. ☞ p. 60

Nāpili Beach, Maui. This sparkling white beach forms a secluded cove that's tailor-made for romantics. ☞ p. 137

Ⓑ **Pāpōhaku Beach, Moloka'i.** You can always find a private section of glorious white sand on the island's longest beach. ☞ p. 346

Polihale Beach Park, Kaua'i. Come for the breathtaking views of rugged cliffs; surf and currents make swimming dangerous. ☞ p. 293

DINING

Ⓙ **Pahu i'a at Four Seasons Resort Huālalai, Big Island.** Meals are imaginative and beautifully presented; at night, spotlights illuminate the surf just feet from your table. $$$–$$$$ ☞ p. 233

Formal Dining Room, Lodge at Kō'ele, Lāna'i. Fresh local ingredients create an inventive island cuisine in this elegant Upcountry restaurant. $$$ ☞ p. 365

A Pacific Cafe, Maui. Hawaiian Regional cuisine is at its best here. Rather than simply adding a tropical flourish to traditional fare, these chefs create new flavors with innovative combinations that reflect Hawai'i's cultural diversity. $$–$$$ ☞ p. 146

A Pacific Cafe O'ahu, at Ward Centre, O'ahu. Chef Jean-Marie Josselin's splendidly creative cuisine is served up in a setting that's modern and whimsical. $$ ☞ p. 70

Hamura Saimin, Līhu'e, Kaua'i. Do as approximately 999 other diners do each day: Order a steaming bowl of *saimin* (broth and noodle soup with pork, fish cake, wonton, or other ingredients)—and enjoy. $ ☞ p. 288

Kanemitsu Bakery and Restaurant, Kaunakakai, Moloka'i. Don't miss the round Moloka'i bread baked on the premises. $ ☞ p. 342

LODGING

Ⓖ **The Camps at Moloka'i Ranch, Moloka'i.** Moloka'i Ranch's three upscale camps offer meals, many activities, and evening entertainment by the local paniolo. City slickers never had it this good. $$$$ ☞ p. 348

Four Seasons Resort Huālalai, Big Island. This is a resort that movie moguls only dream of, with accommodations in two-story bungalows arranged around swimming pools by the ocean's edge and connected by torch-lit paths. $$$$ ☞ p. 245

Halekūlani, O'ahu. The gorgeous setting, top-rated service, spectacular dining, and beautiful guest rooms (every one with a lānai) make this retreat one of the world's most sumptuous resorts. $$$$ ☞ p. 74

Ⓒ **Kāhala Mandarin Oriental, O'ahu.** For luxurious privacy, great food, and lovely rooms near Waikīkī shopping and attractions, this hotel fills the bill—beautifully. $$$$ ☞ p. 81

Ⓔ **Lodge at Kō'ele, Lāna'i City, Lāna'i.** Fireplaces warm this sprawling mountain retreat in the cool highlands; local artwork and rare Pacific artifacts embellish the interiors. $$$$ ☞ p. 367

Ⓓ **Princeville Hotel, Kaua'i.** In Kaua'i's most romantic retreat, a spectacular cliffside property, mountain peaks frame breathtaking views across Hanalei Bay and the Pacific. Service and facilities are unrivaled, the golf course world-class. $$$$ ☞ p. 308

Ritz-Carlton, Kapalua, Maui. A magnificent setting, terraced swimming pools, refined cuisine, exemplary service, and beautifully appointed rooms (most with ocean views over landscaped golf courses) make for an island idyll. $$$$ ☞ p. 152

1 O'AHU

THE GATHERING PLACE

O'ahu is where the spirit of Aloha was born, and it's still Hawai'i's most exciting, cosmopolitan gathering place with an eclectic blend of people, customs, and cuisines. Here's all the tropical splendor for which the Islands are famous, plus the urbanity of Honolulu. O'ahu may be the seat of government and the commercial center for the Hawaiian Islands, but those who live here know that in a matter of minutes you can leave urban life behind and wander through some of Hawai'i's most beautiful forest reserves, mountain areas, and beach parks.

Updated by
Maggie
Wunsch

F**OR THOSE WHO LOVE** the sophistication of the city but yearn for the pleasures of nature's most abundant beauty, O'ahu has become the island to return to again and again. Part of its dramatic appearance lies in its majestic highlands: the western Wai'anae Mountains rise 4,000 ft above sea level, and the verdant Ko'olau Mountains cross the island's midsection at elevations of more than 3,000 ft. Eons of erosion by wind and weather have carved these ranges' sculptured, jagged peaks, deep valleys, sheer green cliffs, and dynamic vistas. At the base of these mountains more than 50 beach parks lie draped like a beautiful lei, each known for a different activity, be it snorkeling, surfing, swimming, or sunbathing.

Third-largest of the Hawaiian Islands and covering 608 square mi, O'ahu was formed by two volcanoes that erupted 4 to 6 million years ago. Honolulu, the nation's eleventh-largest city, is here, and 75% of Hawai'i's 1.1 million residents call the island home. Somehow, amid all this urban development, you are never more than a glimpse away from an ocean or mountain view that can take your breath away.

Hawai'i's last kings and queens ruled from Honolulu's 'Iolani Palace, near the present downtown. It was at 'Iolani that the American flag first flew over the Islands. Even in those days of royalty, the virtues of Waikīkī as a vacation destination were recognized. Long processions of *ali'i* (nobility) made their way across streams and swamps, past the duck ponds, to the coconut groves and the beach.

By the 1880s guest houses were scattered along the south shore like so many seashells. The first hotel, the Moana (now the Sheraton Moana Surfrider), was built at the turn of the 20th century and christened "The First Lady of Waikīkī." The Moana's inaugural room rates of $1.50 per night were the talk of the town. At that time Waikīkī was connected to the rest of Honolulu by tram, which brought townspeople to the shore. In 1927 the "Pink Palace of the Pacific," the Royal Hawaiian Hotel, was built by the Matson Navigation Company to accommodate travelers arriving on luxury liners. It was opened with a grand ball, and Waikīkī was launched as a first-class tourist destination—duck ponds, taro patches, and all.

December 7, 1941, brought that era to a close, with the bombing of Pearl Harbor and America's entry into the war in the Pacific. The Royal Hawaiian was turned over to American military forces and became a respite for war-weary soldiers and sailors. But with victory came the postwar boom, and by 1952 Waikīkī had 2,000 hotel rooms. Today, hundreds of thousands of visitors sleep in the more than 31,000 rooms of Waikīkī's nearly 120 hotels and condominiums. As this new millennium began, Waikīkī received a makeover to ensure that it would remain a top destination for fun and tropical enchantment. You can now stroll along a new and improved Kūhiō Beach and find wider beach expanses, extensive new beach services, and a historic Waikīkī walking trail, along with free nightly Hawaiian music and dance performances on the Kūhiō Beach stage. With Waikīkī leading the way, O'ahu maintains its status as an exciting destination, with more things to see, more places to eat, and more things to do than on all the other Hawaiian Islands combined.

Pleasures and Pastimes

Dining

O'ahu's cuisines are as diverse as its population, with Asian, European, and Pacific flavors most prevalent. Here, the Asian influence can even be found at the corner fast-food restaurant, where the McDonald's menu is posted in both English and kanji. In addition to its regular fare, McDonald's serves saimin, the Hawaiian version of Japanese ramen that ranks as the local favorite snack. While you're exploring O'ahu's banquet of choices, be sure to sample Hawai'i regional cuisine, also known variously as Euro-Asian or Pacific Rim. Created by a new generation of Hawai'i chefs, it marries European culinary influences with "local kine" foods—flavors and products that are the tradition of the Islands.

Driving

A walk on the sand at sunset may epitomize the romance of O'ahu, but a drive around the island brings you face-to-face with its sheer natural beauty. Roll past the wave-dashed coastline of the eastern shore, with its photogenic beaches, islands, and cliffs. Drive through the central plains past acres of red soil, once rich in pineapple and now supporting diversified crops, such as coffee. Head to the North Shore, a reflection of old O'ahu with its rickety storefronts and trees hanging heavy with bananas and papaya. Forget the air-conditioning, roll down the windows, and smell the salt air along the windward coast, where the view is dominated by mountains chiseled by centuries of winds, rains, and waterfalls.

Lodging

O'ahu's lodgings range from sprawling resorts that seem to be cities unto themselves to intimate, low-rise hideaways. First-time visitors who wish to be in the heart of the island's activity can find it all in Waikīkī. Guests do well by this south shore tourist mecca, since shops, restaurants, nightlife, and the beach are all just a stroll away. Business travelers prefer to stay on the eastern edge of Waikīkī, near the Hawai'i Convention Center, or in downtown Honolulu's sole hotel. Windward and North Shore digs are casual and shorter on amenities but have charms all their own.

Shopping

From top designer couture to casual island wear, O'ahu has the ultimate shopping venues for trinkets and treasures. What makes shopping on O'ahu additionally interesting is the rich cultural diversity of its products and the many items unique to Hawai'i, such as bowls made of koa wood and jewelry fashioned from rare shells from the island of Ni'ihau. Waikīkī, Honolulu proper, and Hale'iwa on the North Shore are particularly good places to find handmade Hawaiian souvenirs. Honolulu, with unique boutiques and sprawling malls such as Ala Moana Shopping Center, is a shopper's paradise. DFS Galleria Waikīkī unveiled its new multilevel complex, designed to be reminiscent of the "Old Hawai'i style," in 2001 in Waikīkī on the corner of Royal Hawaiian and Kalakaua avenues.

Water Sports

Whether you soar above them, sail on them, or dive into them, the waters surrounding O'ahu are an ocean lover's dream. The seas off Waikīkī call to those looking for a surfing lesson and outrigger canoe ride, while the North Shore is the headquarters for accomplished wave riders. Snorkeling and scuba diving at Hanauma Bay, on the island's eastern tip, bring you face-to-face with a rainbow of sea creatures. Honolulu's Kewalo Basin is the starting point for most fishing charters and the Honolulu harborfront piers serve as home port for many of the new luxury cruise excursions. Windsurfers and ocean kayakers head to the beaches of the windward side, Lanikai in particular. Year-round and island wide, the water temperature is conducive to a dip, but don't so much as wade if the waves and currents are threatening.

EXPLORING O'AHU

O'ahu is a mixed bag, with enough attractions and adventures to fill an entire vacation. Waikīkī is the center of the island's visitor industry and home to its largest concentration of accommodations, stores, restaurants, and nightclubs. Dominated by Diamond Head crater, Waikīkī's less populated eastern end includes a zoo, an aquarium, and a beautiful park designed for sports from jogging to kite-flying. West of Waikīkī is Honolulu, Hawai'i's capital city, a bustling blend of history and modern-day commerce. The photogenic East O'ahu coast is fringed with white-sand beaches and turquoise seas, and you can drive right over the top of the Ko'olau Mountains. Finally, a circle-island tour takes you to central, northern, and windward O'ahu, where shoes and cell phones give way to sandy toes and Hawaiian time.

To stay oriented on the island, keep in mind that directions on O'ahu are often given as *mauka* (toward the mountains) or *makai* (toward the ocean). In Honolulu and Waikīkī, you may also hear people referring to "Diamond Head" (toward that landmark) and *'ewa*—away from Diamond Head.

Numbers in the text correspond to numbers in the margin and on the Waikīkī, Downtown Honolulu, and O'ahu maps.

Great Itineraries

IF YOU HAVE 1 DAY

If you have a short layover on your way to another island or if you can tear yourself away from a convention (or a honeymoon resort) for just one day of sightseeing, the first thing you should do is treat yourself to a dawn hike up **Diamond Head** ⑳, then have breakfast at one of Waikīkī's beachfront restaurants. Next, take the bus or drive to nearby Ala Moana Shopping Center, which has stores to satisfy all souvenir needs. Buy a carryout lunch from its eclectic, international food court, cross Ala Moana Boulevard, and picnic, sun, and swim at Ala Moana Beach Park. Go on a late-afternoon outrigger canoe ride with one of Waikīkī's beach attendants, followed by *mai tais* (potent rum drinks with orange and lime juice) and Hawaiian music at sunset at the **Halekūlani** ⑦ or **Royal Hawaiian Hotel** ⑧.

IF YOU HAVE 3 DAYS

On your first day, dig in by following the Waikīkī and/or Kapi'olani Park tours described below. Start the second day at the **Hawai'i Maritime Center** ㉑ in downtown Honolulu, followed by shopping and lunch at the adjacent **Aloha Tower Marketplace** ㉒. For a view from atop the building that was once the tallest structure in Honolulu, go next door for a short elevator ride to the Aloha Tower's observation deck. Explore historic downtown Honolulu before heading back to Waikīkī for sunset and dinner. On day three, get an early start so you arrive at **Hanauma Bay** ㊵ by 7:30, before the crowds. Get a break from the sun with a stop a little farther north along the coast at **Sea Life Park** ㊲, which features some splashy marine shows. From here, follow the East O'ahu Ring tour in reverse, back to Waikīkī.

IF YOU HAVE 5 DAYS

Devote the first day to Waikīkī, the second to downtown Honolulu, and the third to East O'ahu. On the fourth day, get an early start in order to see the **Arizona Memorial** and **Battleship *Missouri* Memorial** ㊹, since the waiting lines lengthen throughout the morning. Or take the early morning boat tour to Pearl Harbor. From there, drive to the **Bishop Museum** ㊷ and spend some time immersed in Hawaiiana. Keep the rest of the day low-key until evening, when you can take in a cocktail or dinner show followed by dancing. Devote the fifth day to the

North Shore. Drive to **Hale'iwa** ㊼ for breakfast and shopping, then tour **Waimea Valley and Adventures Park** ㊽, and finish with a late-afternoon or early evening visit to the **Polynesian Cultural Center** ㊿.

When to Tour O'ahu

The ideal seasons to visit O'ahu are spring and fall, when fewer tourists are around and the weather is warm, but not too warm. Fall is additionally fun thanks to the Aloha Festivals, a monthlong program of free Hawaiian-style celebrations and special events. Festival highlights on O'ahu include a floral parade and evening block parties downtown and in Waikīkī. Because many families travel in the summer, most O'ahu hotels offer children's programs from June through August. Come December, downtown Honolulu is a veritable wonderland during its holiday festival of lights.

Waikīkī

If Hawai'i is America's most exotic, most unique state, then Waikīkī is its generator, keeping everything humming. On the dry, sunny side of O'ahu, it incorporates all the natural splendors of the Islands and synthesizes them with elegance and daring into an international playground in the middle of the vast blue Pacific.

A tropical retreat since the days of Hawai'i's kings and queens, Waikīkī sparkles along 2½ mi of spangled sea from the famous Diamond Head crater on the east to the Ala Wai Yacht Harbor on the west. Separated on its northern boundary from the sprawling city of Honolulu by the broad Ala Wai Canal, Waikīkī is 3½ mi from downtown Honolulu and worlds apart from any other city in the world. Nowhere else is there such a salad of cultures so artfully tossed, each one retaining its distinct flavor. You may find yourself saying things like *aloha* and *mahalo* (thank you), and don't be surprised if you find yourself planning your next trip back as you laze on its sunny, hypnotic shores.

A Good Walk

A good place to start a Waikīkī walking tour is the **Ala Wai Yacht Harbor** ①, home to an armada of pleasure boats and two members-only yacht clubs. It's just makai of the Renaissance 'Ilikai Waikīkī at 1777 Ala Moana Boulevard. From here head toward the main intersection of Ala Moana Boulevard and Kālia Road, turn right at the big sign to **Hilton Hawaiian Village** ②, and wander through this lush, 20-acre resort complex past gardens and waterfalls.

Continue makai on Kālia Road to Ft. DeRussy, home of the **U.S. Army Museum** ③. Across the street, on Saratoga Road, nestled snugly amid the commerce of Waikīkī, is an oasis of tranquillity: the tea house at **The Urasenke Foundation** ④, where the art of Hawaiian hospitality bows to the art of the centuries-old Japanese tea ceremony.

With a little taste of Asia and some Zen for the road, head mauka on Saratoga Road until you reach Kalākaua Avenue. Then turn right toward Diamond Head. At the intersection with Lewers Street, stop and peer into the lobby of the **First Hawaiian Bank** ⑤ for a quick view of the island's history in six massive wall murals. Diagonally across Kalākaua Avenue is one of Waikīkī's architectural landmarks, the **Gump Building** ⑥.

Walk down Lewers Street toward the ocean. It dead-ends at the impressive **Halekūlani** ⑦, one of Waikīkī's most prestigious hotels, famed for its elegant hospitality. From the Halekūlani stroll toward Diamond Head along the paved oceanside walkway. It leads past the Sheraton Waikīkī to the gracious, historic, and very pink **Royal Hawaiian Hotel** ⑧. Back on the mauka side of Kalākaua Avenue, walk two blocks

Honolulu Including Waikīkī

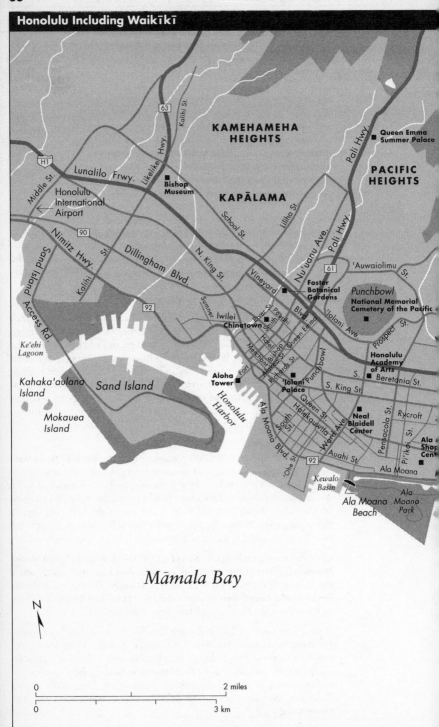

KAMEHAMEHA
HEIGHTS

Queen Emma
Summer Palace

PACIFIC
HEIGHTS

63

Kalihi St.

H1

Lunalilo Frwy.

Middle St.

Likelike Hwy.

Pali Hwy.

Bishop
Museum

KAPĀLAMA

Honolulu
International
Airport

School St.

Liliha St.

Nu'uanu Ave.

Pali Hwy.

90

Nimitz Hwy.

Kalihi St.

Dillingham Blvd.

N. King St.

Vineyard

61

'Auwaiolimu St.

Foster
Botanical
Gardens

Punchbowl

National Memorial
Cemetery of the Pacific

92

Sand Island Access Rd.

Ke'ehi
Lagoon

Iwilei

Chinatown

Sumner

River St. Patch

Nu'uanu Blvd.

Maunakea St.

Hotel

Smith

Iolani Ave.

Prospect St.

Honolulu
Academy
of Arts

Kahaka'aulana
Island

Sand Island

Aloha
Tower

Honolulu
Harbor

Fort

Merchant St.

Bishop

Alakea St.

Richards St.

Queen Emma

Beretania St.

Mokauea
Island

'Iolani
Palace

Queen St.

S. King St.

Punchbowl

Rycroft

Neal
Blaidell
Center

Pensacola St.

Pi'ikoi St.

Ala
Shop
Cen

South St.

Ho'okauwila

Ward Ave.

Auahi St.

Ala Moana Blvd.

'Ohe St.

92

Ala Moana

Kewalo
Basin

Ala Moana
Beach

Ala
Moana
Park

Māmala Bay

N

0   2 miles

0   3 km

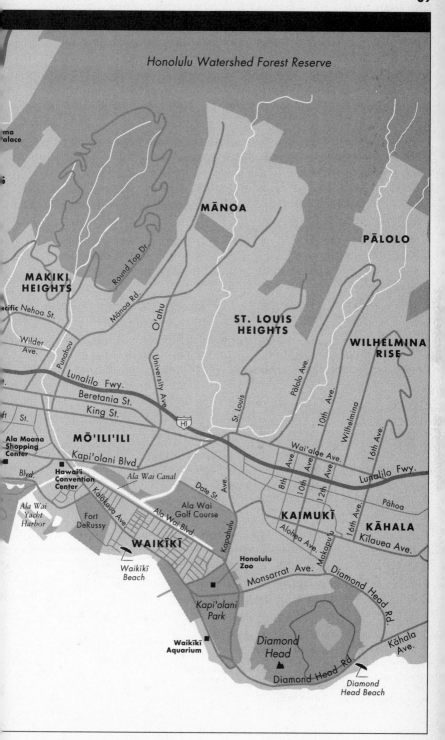

Honolulu Watershed Forest Reserve

MĀNOA

PĀLOLO

MAKIKI
HEIGHTS

ST. LOUIS
HEIGHTS

WILHELMINA
RISE

...ma
...alace

...cific Nehoa St.

Round Top Dr.

Mānoa Rd.

O'ahu

University Ave.

St. Louis

Pālolo Ave.

10th Ave.

Wilhelmina

16th Ave.

Wilder
Ave.

Punahou

Lunalilo Fwy.

Beretania St.

King St.

H1

...ft   St.

Ala Moana
Shopping
Center

MŌ'ILI'ILI

Kapi'olani Blvd.

Wai'alae Ave.

8th Ave.

10th Ave.

12th Ave.

Lunalilo Fwy.

Pāhoa

...Blvd.

Hawai'i
Convention
Center

Ala Wai Canal

Date St

Ala Wai
Golf Course

Ave.

16th Ave.

Ala Wai
Yacht
Harbor

Fort
DeRussy

Kalākaua Ave.

Ala Wai Blvd.

Kapahulu

Alohea Ave.

Makapu'u

KAIMUKĪ

16th Ave.

KĀHALA

Kīlauea Ave.

WAIKĪKĪ

Waikīkī
Beach

Honolulu
Zoo

Monsarrat Ave.

Diamond Head Rd.

Kapi'olani
Park

Kāhala
Ave.

Waikīkī
Aquarium

Diamond
Head

Diamond Head Rd.

Diamond
Head Beach

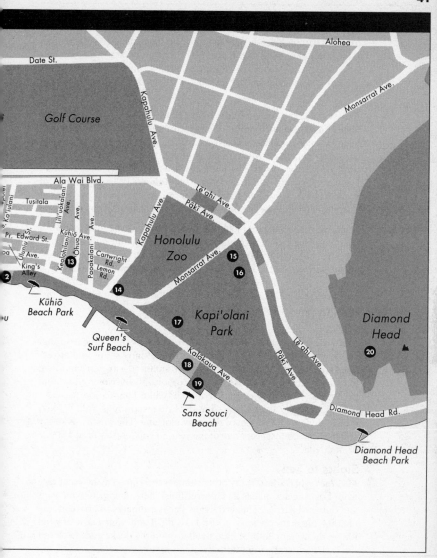

Alohea

Date St.

Monsarrat Ave.

Golf Course

Kapahulu Ave.

Ala Wai Blvd.

Tusitala

Lili'uokalani Ave.

Kūhiō Ave.

Le'ahi Ave.

Pāki Ave.

Pr. Edward St.

Kealohilani Ave.

'Ōhua Ave.

Paoakalani

Honolulu Zoo

Monsarrat Ave.

15

16

Cartwright Rd.

Lemon Rd.

Kūhiō Ave.

King's Alley

2

13

14

Kūhiō Beach Park

Queen's Surf Beach

17

Kapi'olani Park

Diamond Head

20

Kalākaua Ave.

Pāki Ave.

Le'ahi Ave.

18

19

Sans Souci Beach

Diamond Head Rd.

Diamond Head Beach Park

'ewa and one block mauka to the **IMAX Waikīkī Theater** ⑨, home of continuous huge-screen films. Return to Kalākaua Avenue and walk toward Diamond Head. Your next stop on the mauka side of the street is the **International Market Place** ⑩, home to shops, stalls, and artisans who display their wares in an open-air bazaar setting. Catch some shade beneath the banyan tree that features its very own Swiss Family Robinson–style tree house.

Across Kalākaua Avenue is the oldest hotel in Waikīkī, the venerable **Sheraton Moana Surfrider** ⑪. Wander through the breezy lobby to the wide back porch, called the Banyan Veranda, or take a quick tour through tourism history in the Moana's second-floor historical room. From here, walk down the beach and head toward Diamond Head. Next to Kalakaua Avenue you'll find the four **Kahuna (Wizard) Stones of Waikīkī** ⑫. Said to hold magical powers, they are often overlooked and, more often than not, irreverently draped with wet towels.

Continue your walk four blocks farther down Kalākaua Avenue toward Diamond Head, then turn mauka onto 'Ōhua Avenue and you'll find the only church in Waikīkī with its own building, the Roman Catholic St. Augustine's. In the back of the church is the **Damien Museum** ⑬, a small but fascinating exhibition on the life of Father Damien, a Belgian priest who died while ministering to the victims of Hansen's disease (leprosy) on the island of Moloka'i.

TIMING

Allow yourself at least one full day for this walk, and time it so that you'll wind up on Waikīkī Beach at sunset. Many shops and attractions are open every day of the year from sunup to way past sundown, to cater to the body clocks and pocketbooks of tourists from around the world. Note, however, that the Urasenke Foundation tea ceremonies only take place Wednesday and Friday mornings. Still, Waikīkī is most inviting in the cool of the early morning. The weather is sunny and pleasant almost every day of the year, so you'll rarely need a jacket or umbrella.

Sights to See

❶ **Ala Wai Yacht Harbor.** Every other summer the Trans-Pacific yacht race from Los Angeles makes its colorful finish here, complete with flags and onboard parties. The next Trans-Pac is estimated to arrive in July of 2003. No matter when you visit Hawai'i, if you want a taste of what life on the water could be like, stroll around the docks and check out the variety of craft, from houseboats to luxury cruisers. ✉ *1777 Ala Moana Blvd., oceanside across from Renaissance'Ilikai Waikīkī.*

❸ **Damien Museum.** This tiny two-room museum behind St. Augustine's Church contains low-key exhibits about Father Damien, the Belgian priest who worked with those afflicted with Hansen's disease (leprosy) and exiled to the Hawaiian island of Moloka'i during the late 1800s. Ask to see the museum's 20-minute videotape. It's low-budget but well done and emotionally gripping. ✉ *130 'Ōhua Ave.,* ☎ *808/923–2690.* ✁ *Free.* ☼ *Weekdays 9–3.*

❺ **First Hawaiian Bank.** Get a glimpse of Hawaiian history kept safe in this Waikīkī bank, where half a dozen murals depict the evolution of Hawaiian culture. The impressive panels were painted between 1951 and 1952 by Jean Charlot (1898–1979), whose work is represented in Florence at the Uffizi Gallery and in New York at both the Metropolitan Museum and the Museum of Modern Art. The murals are beautifully lit at night, with some panels visible from the street. ✉ *2181 Kalākaua Ave.,* ☎ *808/943–4670.* ✁ *Free.* ☼ *Mon.–Thurs. 8:30–4, Fri. 8:30–6.*

6 Gump Building. Built in 1929 in Hawaiian-colonial style, with Asian architectural motifs and a blue-tile roof, this structure once housed Hawai'i's premier store, Gump's, which was known for high-quality Asian and Hawaiian objects. It's now home to a Louis Vuitton boutique. ⊠ *2200 Kalākaua Ave.*

7 Halekūlani. Maintaining an air of mystery within its tranquil setting, the modern Halekūlani is centered around a portion of its original (1917) beachfront estate, immortalized as the setting for the first of the Charlie Chan detective novels, *The House Without a Key.* For a view of an orchid blossom unlike any other, take a peek at the swimming pool with its huge orchid mosaic on the bottom. ⊠ *2199 Kālia Rd.,* ☎ *808/923–2311.*

NEED A BREAK?

If it's lunchtime or close to sunset, linger at the Halekulani and get a table at **House Without a Key** (⊠ 2199 Kālia Rd., ☎ 808/923–2311), where nearly every table affords a view of Diamond Head. The restaurant has a light lunch menu and serves wonderful tropical drinks and *pūpū* (appetizers) before dinner. Enjoy the view and the sounds of the Hawaiian steel guitar, and watch graceful hula performed nightly beneath the centuries-old *kiawe* tree (kiawe is a mesquite-type wood).

2 Hilton Hawaiian Village. With a little island in Kahanamoku Lagoon and palm trees all around, this 20-acre Waikīkī resort is the quintessential tropical getaway. The village is a hodgepodge of Asian architecture, with a Chinese moon gate, a pagoda, and a Japanese farmhouse with a waterwheel, all dominated by a tall mosaic mural of the hotel's Rainbow Tower. You can browse for souvenirs in all price ranges at the **Rainbow Bazaar**, which has 90 different specialty stores. Check out the penguin pond in the back of the main lobby. ⊠ *2005 Kālia Rd.,* ☎ *808/949–4321.*

☾ 9 IMAX Waikīkī Theater. Immerse yourself in whatever is being shown on a screen five stories high and 70 ft wide; digital surround sound completes the experience. Call or consult local newspapers for shows and times. ⊠ *325 Seaside Ave.,* ☎ *808/923–4629,* WEB *www.imaxwaikiki.com.* ☜ *$9.75, $13.75 for double feature.* ☉ *Daily, call for show times.*

10 International Market Place. The tropical open-air setting is fun to wander through, with wood-carvers, basket-weavers, and other artisans from various Pacific islands hawking their handicrafts. Intrepid shoppers find fun souvenirs here, and at the adjacent Duke's Lane. ⊠ *2330 Kalākaua Ave.,* ☎ *808/923–9871.*

12 Kahuna (Wizard) Stones of Waikīkī. According to legend, these boulders preserve the magnetic legacy of four sorcerers—Kapaemahu, Kinohi, Kapuni, and Kahaloa—who came here from Tahiti. Legend has it that these healers transferred their powers to these rock-solid totems. Just to the west of these revered rocks is the **Duke Kahanamoku Statue**, erected in honor of Hawai'i's celebrated surfer and swimmer. Known as the "father of modern surfing," Duke won his first gold medal for the 100-m freestyle at the 1912 Olympics. When the bronze statue was first placed here, it caused a wave of controversy, as the Duke is facing away from the water with his back to the ocean, something no safety-conscious surfer would ever do. Check out the standing bronze surfboard next to the statue; it's one of several markers that can be found throughout Waikīkī's part of the new historic Waikīkī walking trail. ⊠ *Waikīkī Beach, Diamond Head side of Sheraton Moana Surfrider.*

8 Royal Hawaiian Hotel. This legendary hotel sticks out amid the highrises on Waikīkī Beach like a candy confection. Affectionately nicknamed the Pink Palace, the Royal Hawaiian opened in 1927, and the lobby, with its pink decor, is reminiscent of an era when visitors to the Islands arrived on luxury liners. A stroll through the Royal's coconut grove garden is like a walk back to a time when Waikīkī was still a sleepy, tropical paradise. ⊠ *2259 Kalākaua Ave.,* ☎ *808/923–7311.*

NEED A BREAK? The **Island Snow** kiosk (⊠ Royal Hawaiian Shopping Center, 2201 Kalākaua Ave.) serves shave ice—a local favorite and the Hawaiian version of a snow cone. It comes in such exotic fruit flavors as guava, coconut, banana, litchi, and mango. To really go local, try it with ice cream and adzuki beans.

★ ⑪ **Sheraton Moana Surfrider.** Listed on the National Register of Historic Places, this intricate beaux arts–style hotel was christened "The First Lady of Waikīkī" when she opened her doors at the turn of the 20th century. With period furnishings and historical exhibits, this landmark holds plenty of Hawai'i nostalgia. Visit the **Historical Room** in the rotunda above the main entrance to see the collection of old photographs and memorabilia dating from the opening of the hotel. Then take afternoon high tea on the **Banyan Veranda.** ⊠ *2365 Kalākaua Ave.,* ☎ *808/922–3111.*

❹ **The Urasenke Foundation.** The teahouse here was the first of its kind to be built outside Japan and provides an excellent introduction to Japanese culture. If you are looking for a slice of serenity in Waikīkī, this is a good place to find it. The meditative ceremony reflects the influences of centuries of Zen Buddhism and an appreciation of the simplicity of nature. Each ceremony lasts approximately 30 minutes. Visitors can either watch or be actual participants in the ceremony. Wear something comfortable enough for sitting on the floor (but no shorts, please). ⊠ *245 Saratoga Rd.,* ☎ *808/923–3059.* ▣ *Minimum donation $2.* ☉ *Wed. and Fri. 10–noon.*

☾ ❸ **U.S. Army Museum.** This museum at Ft. DeRussy houses an intimidating collection of war paraphernalia. The major focus is on World War II memorabilia, but exhibits range from ancient Hawaiian weaponry to displays relating to the Vietnam War. It's within Battery Randolf (Building 32), a bunker built in 1911 as a key to the defense of Pearl Harbor and Honolulu. Some of its walls are 22 ft thick. Guided group tours can be arranged. ⊠ *Ft. DeRussy, Bldg. 32, Kālia Rd.,* ☎ *808/438–2822.* ▣ *Free.* ☉ *Tues.–Sun. 10–4:30.*

Kapi'olani Park and Diamond Head

Kapi'olani Park, established during the late 1800s by King Kalākaua and named after his queen, is a 500-acre expanse where you can play all sorts of sports, enjoy a picnic, see wild animals, or hear live music. It lies in the shadow of Diamond Head crater, perhaps Hawai'i's most famous natural landmark. Diamond Head got its name from sailors who thought they had found precious gems on its slopes. The diamonds proved to be volcanic refuse.

A Good Walk

The 'ewa end of Kapi'olani Park is occupied by the **Honolulu Zoo** ⑭, on the corner of Kalākaua and Kapahulu avenues. Its 40 acres are home to 2,000 furry and finned creatures. On weekends look for the Zoo Fence Art Mart, on Monsarrat Avenue outside the zoo, on the Diamond Head side. You might find some affordable works by contemporary artists and craftspeople that make better Hawai'i keepsakes than the ashtrays and monkeypod bowls carved in the Philippines.

Across Monsarrat Avenue, between Kalākaua Avenue and Pākī Avenue in Kapi'olani Park, is the **Waikīkī Shell** ⑮, Honolulu's outdoor concert arena. Next to the Shell is the site of the **Kodak Hula Show** ⑯. Cut across the park toward the ocean to the **Kapi'olani Bandstand** ⑰, where you'll hear more free island tunes on days when community events are taking place.

Cross Kalākaua Avenue toward the ocean to the **Waikīkī Aquarium** ⑱ and its neighbor, the **Waikīkī War Memorial Natatorium** ⑲, an open-air swimming stadium built in 1927 to commemorate lives lost in World War I.

As it leaves Kapi'olani Park, Kalākaua Avenue forks into Diamond Head Road, a scenic 2-mi stretch popular with walkers and joggers, and winds around the base of Diamond Head alongside the ocean, passing handsome Diamond Head Lighthouse (not open to the public). Lookout areas offer views of the surfers and windsurfers below. The hike to the summit of **Diamond Head** ⑳ affords a marvelous view, but requires strenuous walking. To save time and energy, drive, don't walk, along Diamond Head Road, turn left at Monsarrat Avenue, head a mile up the hill, and look for a sign on the right to the entrance to the crater. Drive through the tunnel to the inside of the crater. The trail begins at the parking lot.

TIMING

Budget a full day to see Kapi'olani Park and Diamond Head. If you want to hike up to the crater's summit, do it before breakfast. That way you beat not only the heat but the crowds. Hiking Diamond Head takes an hour round-trip, but factor in some extra time to enjoy the views from the top. Keep an eye on your watch if you're there at day's end, because the gates close promptly at 6. If you want to see the Honolulu Zoo, it's best to get there right when it opens, since the animals are livelier in the cool of the morning. Give the aquarium an hour, including 10 minutes in its Sea Vision Theater. For the best seats at the 10 AM Kodak Hula Show, get there by 8 or so.

Sights to See

★ ⑳ **Diamond Head.** Panoramas from this 760-ft extinct volcanic peak, once used as a military fortification, sweep from across Waikīkī and Honolulu in one direction and out to Koko Head in the other, with surfers and windsurfers scattered like confetti on the cresting waves below. This ideal 360-degree O'ahu perspective is great for first-time visitors. Most guidebooks say there are 99 steps on the trail to the top. That's true of one flight, but there are four flights altogether. Bring a flashlight to see your way through a narrow tunnel and up a very dark flight of winding stairs. And take bottled water with you to ensure that you stay hydrated under the tropical sun. ⊠ *Monsarrat Ave. at 18th Ave.* ☞ *$1.* ☉ *Daily 6–6.*

☺ ⑭ **Honolulu Zoo.** There are bigger and better zoos, but this one is pretty, and on Wednesday evening in summer, the zoo puts on "The Wildest Show in Town," a free program of song, dance, and island entertainment. The best part of the zoo is its 7½-acre African savanna, where animals roam freely on the other side of hidden rails and moats. If you're visiting during a full moon, check out the zoo's Night Walks. Call or check the local newspaper for information about other special events. ⊠ *151 Kapahulu Ave.,* ☎ *808/971–7171.* ☞ *$6.* ☉ *Daily 9–4:30.*

⑰ **Kapi'olani Bandstand.** A replica of the Victorian Kapi'olani Bandstand, which was originally built in the late 1890s, is Kapi'olani Park's new centerpiece for community entertainment and concerts. Check out the "Bandstand Jams," held at 5:30 every Friday, with concert performances ranging from contemporary Hawaiian to jazz to reggae. The local newspapers list entertainment information. ⊠ *'Ewa end of Kapi'olani Park, mauka side of Kalākaua Ave.*

★ ⓰ **Kodak Hula Show.** This one-hour show, in the bleachers adjacent to the Waikīkī Shell, is colorful, lively, and fun. It has been wowing crowds since 1937. For the best viewpoints, come early for good seating. It's a great opportunity to take photographs. ⊠ *2805 Monsarrat Ave.,* ☎ *808/627–3379.* ☒ *Free.* ☉ *Tues.–Thurs. at 10.*

★ ☾ ⓲ **Waikīkī Aquarium.** This amazing little attraction harbors more than 300 species of Hawaiian and South Pacific marine life, including the giant clam, the only chambered nautilus living in captivity, and sharks. The Edge of the Reef exhibit showcases five different types of reef environments found along Hawai'i's shorelines. Check out the Sea Visions Theater and the new educational audio tour. ⊠ *2777 Kalākaua Ave.,* ☎ *808/923–9741,* WEB *www.mic.hawaii.edu/aquarium/.* ☒ *$7.* ☉ *Daily 9–5.*

⓯ **Waikīkī Shell.** Local people bring a picnic and get "grass seats" (lawn seating). Here's a chance to enjoy a magical night underneath the stars with some of Hawai'i's best musicians as well as visiting guest artists. Concerts are held May 1 to Labor Day. Check the newspapers to see what's playing. ⊠ *2805 Monsarrat Ave.,* ☎ *808/924–8934.*

⓳ **Waikīkī War Memorial Natatorium.** This 1927 World War I monument stands proudly, its outer wall lighted at night, showing off a newly restored entrance facade. The 100-m saltwater swimming pool is closed to the public. ⊠ *2777 Kalākaua Ave.*

NEED A
BREAK?   You can enjoy breakfast, lunch, or dinner outdoors beneath the shade of a hau tree at the New Otani Kaimana Beach Hotel, next to the Waikīkī War Memorial Natatorium. Dubbed the **Hau Tree Lānai** (⊠ 2863 Kalākaua Ave., ☎ 808/921–7066), it's a little jewel if you want oceanfront refreshment.

Downtown Honolulu

Honolulu's past and present play a delightful counterpoint throughout the downtown sector. Modern skyscrapers stand directly across from the Aloha Tower, which was built in 1926 and was, until the early 1960s, the tallest structure in Honolulu. Old structures have found new meaning here. For instance, today's governor's mansion, built in 1846, was the home of Queen Lili'uokalani until her death in 1917.

To reach downtown Honolulu from Waikīkī by car, take Ala Moana Boulevard to Alakea Street. There are public parking lots (50¢ per half hour for the first two hours) in buildings along Alakea Street and Bethel Street, two blocks 'ewa. Keep in mind that parking in most downtown lots is expensive ($3 per half hour).

A Good Walk

Begin at the **Hawai'i Maritime Center** ㉑ at the harbor front, across Ala Moana Boulevard from Alakea Street in downtown Honolulu. This museum traces the history of Hawai'i's love affair with the sea. Just 'ewa of the Hawai'i Maritime Center is **Aloha Tower Marketplace** ㉒, a complex of harborside shops and restaurants where you can also view the luxury cruise liners in port and the traditional Hawaiian Boat Days celebrations that greet each arrival.

Cross Ala Moana Boulevard, walk a block 'ewa, and turn mauka on Ft. Street Mall, a pedestrian walkway, until you reach King Street. Turn

Downtown Honolulu

left, and in a few blocks you'll reach **Chinatown** ㉓, the old section of downtown Honolulu. Here you can find a Buddhist temple, a Japanese shrine, shops, art galleries, ethnic restaurants, and a big open market.

Walk back toward Diamond Head along King Street until it intersects with Bishop Street. On the mauka side is lovely **Tamarind Park** ㉔, a popular lunchtime picnic spot for Honolulu's workforce, which gathers under its shady plumeria, kukui, and monkeypod trees—and one tamarind. Continue down King Street until you reach **'Iolani Palace** ㉕, on the mauka side. This graceful Victorian structure was built by King David Kalākaua in 1882. Also on the palace grounds is the Kalākaua Coronation Bandstand, where the Royal Hawaiian Band performs at noon most Fridays.

Across King Street from 'Iolani Palace is Ali'iōlani Hale, the judiciary building that once served as the parliament hall during the kingship era. In front of it is the gilded **Kamehameha I Statue** ㉖, which honors Hawai'i's greatest monarch. Walk one block mauka up Richards Street to tour the **Hawai'i State Capitol** ㉗. Almost across the street from the state capitol is Washington Place, the home of Hawai'i's governor.

Return to King Street via Punchbowl Street, stay on the mauka side, and proceed in a Diamond Head direction. Walk past the palace again till you come to the massive stone **Hawai'i State Library** ㉘, a showcase of architectural restoration. At Punchbowl Street is **Honolulu Hale** ㉙, or City Hall. Across the street is the **Kawaiaha'o Church** ㉚, perhaps Hawai'i's most famous religious structure. On the Diamond Head side of the Kawaiaha'o Church is the **Mission Houses Museum** ㉛, where the first American missionaries in Hawai'i lived. From here it's three long blocks toward Diamond Head to Ward Avenue and one block mauka to Beretania Street, but the **Honolulu Academy of Arts** ㉜ is worth the extra mileage (you might choose to drive there instead). It houses a world-class collection of Western and Asian art.

TIMING

Downtown Honolulu merits a full day of your time. Be sure to stop by the palace Tuesday through Saturday, the only days tours are offered. Remember that the Mission Houses Museum is closed Sunday and Monday and the Honolulu Academy of Arts is closed Monday. Saturday morning is the best time to walk through Chinatown. That's when the open-air markets do their biggest business with local families. A walk through Chinatown can take an hour, as can tours of the Mission Houses and 'Iolani Palace. Wrap up your day at sunset with refreshments or dinner back at the Aloha Tower Marketplace, which stays open late into the evening, with live entertainment on the harbor front.

Sights to See

🖑 ㉒ **Aloha Tower Marketplace.** Two stories of shops, kiosks, indoor and outdoor restaurants, and live entertainment are here at the Honolulu Harbor with Aloha Tower as its anchor. For a bird's-eye view of this working harbor, take the free ride up to the tower's observation deck. The Marketplace's location makes it an ideal spot for watching the arrival of cruise ships. On Hawaiian Boat Days, the waterfront comes alive with entertainment and hula dancers who greet the arriving ships. ✉ *1 Aloha Tower Dr., at Piers 8, 9, and 10,* ☎ *808/528–5700.* ☉ *Daily 9–9, restaurants 9 am–2 am.*

㉓ **Chinatown.** Noodle factories and herb shops, lei stands and acupuncture studios, art galleries and Chinese and Thai restaurants comprise this historic neighborhood, which has experienced a recent surge in restoration. A major highlight is the colorful O'ahu Market, an open-air emporium with hanging pigs' heads, display cases of fresh fish, row after row of exotic fruits and vegetables, and vendors of all ethnic backgrounds. Check out the Chinese Cultural Plaza's Moongate stage for cultural events, especially around the Chinese New Year. ⊠ *King St. between Smith and River Sts.*

NEED A
BREAK?

There are Chinese, Thai, Japanese, Korean, and Italian food stalls at **Maunakea Marketplace** (⊠ 1120 Maunakea St., ☎ 808/524–3409), one block mauka of King Street. The food offerings are usually flavorful and reasonably priced. A courtyard has some seating.

🄲 ㉑ **Hawai'i Maritime Center.** The main exhibits, some of which are interactive, at this maritime museum are in the **Kalākaua Boat House,** where you can learn about Hawai'i's whaling days, the history of Honolulu Harbor, the Clipper seaplane, and surfing and windsurfing in Hawai'i. Moored next to the Boat House are the *Falls of Clyde,* a century-old, four-masted, square-rigged ship now used as a museum; and the *Hōkūle'a,* a reproduction of an ancient Polynesian double-hull voyaging canoe. The *Hōkūle'a* has completed several journeys throughout the Pacific, during which the crew used only the stars and the sea as a navigational guide. ⊠ *Ala Moana Blvd., at Pier 7,* ☎ *808/536–6373.* 🖾 *$7.50.* ☉ *Daily 8:30–5.*

㉗ **Hawai'i State Capitol.** The capitol's architecture is richly symbolic: the columns look like palm trees, the legislative chambers are shaped like volcanic cinder cones, and the central court is open to the sky, representing Hawai'i's open society. The building is surrounded by reflecting pools, just as the Islands are embraced by water. ⊠ *215 S. Beretania St.,* ☎ *808/586–0178.* 🖾 *Free.* ☉ *Guided tour weekdays at 1:30.*

㉘ **Hawai'i State Library.** This beautifully renovated main library, originally built in 1913 and restored in 1992, is wonderful to explore. Its "Asia and the Pacific" room has a fascinating collection of books old and new about Hawai'i. The center courtyard offers a respite from busy downtown. ⊠ *478 King St.,* ☎ *808/586–3500.* 🖾 *Free.* ☉ *Mon. and Fri.–Sat. 9–5, Tues. and Thurs. 9–8, Wed. 10–5.*

㉜ **Honolulu Academy of Arts.** The Academy dates to 1927 and has an impressive permanent collection that includes Hiroshige's ukiyo-e Japanese prints, donated by James Michener; Italian Renaissance paintings; and American and European art. Six open-air courtyards provide a casual counterpart to the more formal interior galleries. The new Luce Pavilion complex houses a traveling-exhibit gallery, a Hawaiian gallery, a café, and a gift shop. Call about special exhibits, concerts, and films. ⊠ *900 S. Beretania St.,* ☎ *808/532–8700,* ᴡᴇʙ *www.honoluluacademy.org.* 🖾 *$7.* ☉ *Tues.–Sat. 10–4:30, Sun. 1–5.*

㉙ **Honolulu Hale.** This Mediterranean Renaissance–style building was constructed in 1929 and serves as the center of city government. Stroll through the cool, open-ceiling lobby with exhibits of local artists, and time your visit to coincide with one of the free concerts sometimes offered in the evening, when the building stays open late. During the winter holiday season, the Hale becomes the focal point for the annual Honolulu City Lights Festival program. ⊠ *530 S. King St.,* ☎ *808/527–5666 for concert information.* 🖾 *Free.* ☉ *Weekdays 8–4:30.*

㉕ **'Iolani Palace.** Built in 1882 on the site of an earlier palace and beautifully restored, this is America's only royal residence. It contains the thrones of King Kalākaua and his successor (and sister) Queen Lili'uokalani. The palace is open for guided tours only, and reservations are essential. Take a look at the gift shop, formerly the 'Iolani

Barracks, built to house the Royal Guard. ⊠ *King and Richards Sts.,* ☎ *808/522–0832.* ⊡ *$15.* ⊙ *Tues.–Sat. 9–2:15.*

NEED A
BREAK?

For a quick pick-me-up, stop by **Lion Coffee** (⊠ 222 Merchant St., between Alakea and Richards Sts., ☎ 808/521–5466) for an espresso, cappuccino, latte, or plain ol' cuppa joe along with a fresh-baked muffin, scone, or cookie. Lion Coffee shares space with Native Books & Beautiful Things, a lovely shop selling Hawaiian crafts and publications.

㉖ Kamehameha I Statue. This downtown landmark pays tribute to the Big Island chieftain who united all the warring Hawaiian Islands into one kingdom at the turn of the 18th century. He stands with one arm outstretched in welcome. The original version is in Kapa'au, on the Big Island, near the king's birthplace. Each year on June 11, his birthday, the statue is draped in leis. ⊠ *417 S. King St., outside Ali'iōlani Hale.*

㉚ Kawaiaha'o Church. Fancifully called Hawai'i's Westminster Abbey, this 14,000-coral-block house of worship witnessed the coronations, weddings, and funerals of generations of Hawaiian royalty. The graves of missionaries and of King Lunalilo are in the yard. The upper gallery has an exhibit of paintings of the royal families. Services in English and Hawaiian are held each Sunday. Although there are no guided tours, you can look around the church at no cost. ⊠ *957 Punchbowl St., at King St.,* ☎ *808/522–1333.* ⊡ *Free.* ⊙ *Service Sun. at 8 am, in Hawaiian at 10:30 am, Wed. at 6 pm.*

㉛ Mission Houses Museum. The stalwart Hawai'i missionaries arrived in 1820, gaining royal favor and influencing every aspect of island life. Their descendants became leaders in government and business. You can walk through their original dwellings, including a white-frame house that was prefabricated in New England, shipped around the Horn, and is Hawai'i's oldest wooden structure. The museum hosts living history programs, candlelight museum tours, and crafts fairs. Certain areas of the museum may be seen only on a one-hour guided tour. ⊠ *553 S. King St.,* ☎ *808/531–0481.* ⊡ *$8.* ⊙ *Tues.–Sat. 9–4; guided tours at 9:45, 11:15, 1, and 2:30.*

㉔ Tamarind Park. From jazz and Hawaiian tunes to the strains of the U.S. Marine Band, music fills this pretty park at noon on Friday. Do as the locals do: pick up lunch at one of the many carryout restaurants and find a bench or patch of grass. ⊠ *S. King St. between Bishop and Alakea Sts.,* ☎ *808/527–5666 for concert information.* ⊡ *Free.*

The East O'ahu Ring

At once historic and contemporary, serene and active, the east end of O'ahu holds within its relatively small area remarkable variety and picture-perfect scenery featuring windswept cliffs and wave-dashed shores.

A Good Drive

From Waikīkī there are two routes to Lunalilo Freeway (H-1). On the Diamond Head end, go mauka on Kapahulu Avenue and follow the signs to the freeway. On the 'ewa end, take Ala Wai Boulevard and turn mauka at Kalākaua Avenue, staying on it until it ends at Beretania Street, which is one-way going left. Turn right off Beretania Street at Pi'ikoi Street, and the signs will direct you onto the freeway heading west.

Take the freeway exit marked Pali Highway (Highway 61), one of three roads that cut through the Ko'olau Mountains. On the right is the **Queen Emma Summer Palace** ㉝. The colonial-style white mansion, which once served as the summer retreat of King Kamehameha IV and his wife, Queen Emma, is now a museum.

As you drive toward the summit of the highway, the road is lined with sweet ginger in summer and red poinsettias in winter. If it has been raining, waterfalls will be tumbling down the chiseled cliffs of the Koʻolau. If it is very windy, those waterfalls can look as if they are traveling up the cliffs, not down, making them a sight to behold.

Watch for the turn to the **Nuʻuanu Pali Lookout** ㉞. There is a small parking lot and a lookout wall from which you can see all the way up and down the windward coast—a view that Mark Twain called the most beautiful in the world.

As you follow the highway down the other side of the mountain, continue straight along what becomes Kailua Road. If you're interested in Hawaiian history, look for the YMCA at the Castle Hospital junction of Kalanianaʻole Highway and Kailua Road. Behind it is **Ulupō Heiau** ㉟, an ancient outdoor shrine. Ready for a detour? Head straight on Kailua Road to Kailua Beach Park, which many people consider the best on the island. The road twists and turns, so watch the signs.

Retracing your route back to Castle Junction, turn left at the intersection onto Kalanianaʻole Highway. Soon you will come to the small town of **Waimānalo** ㊱. Waimānalo's two beaches are Bellows Beach, great for swimming and bodysurfing, and Waimānalo Beach Park, also safe for swimming.

Another mile along the highway, on the right, is **Sea Life Park** ㊲, home to the world's only "wholphin," the offspring of a whale and a dolphin. Across the highway from Sea Life Park is Makapuʻu Beach, a beautiful cove that is great for seasoned bodysurfers but treacherous for weak swimmers. The road winds up a hill, at the top of which is a turnoff on the makai side to **Makapuʻu Point** ㊳, a fabulous photo opportunity.

Next you'll see a long stretch of inviting sand called Sandy Beach. Tempting as this beach looks, it is not advisable to swim here because the waves are powerful and the rip currents more than tricky. From here the road twists and turns next to steep cliffs along the Koko Head shoreline. Offshore, the islands of Molokaʻi and Lānaʻi call like distant sirens, and every once in a while Maui is visible in blue silhouette. For the best photos, pull into the parking lot at **Hālona Blowhole** ㊴. At the top of the hill on the makai side of the road is the entrance to **Hanauma Bay** ㊵, one of Oʻahu's most famous snorkeling destinations.

From here back to Waikīkī the highway passes several residential communities called Hawaiʻi Kai, Niu Valley, and ʻĀina Haina, each of which has a small shopping center where you can pick up a soda or a snack. Right before you turn off from Kalanianaʻole Highway there's a long stretch of green on the makai side. This is the private Waiʻalae Country Club, scene of the televised annual Sony Hawaiian Open Golf Tournament.

Take the Kīlauea Avenue exit. Turn left at the stoplight onto Kīlauea Avenue. Here you'll see Kāhala Mall, an upscale shopping complex with yuppie eateries, high-fashion stores, and eight movie theaters. A few blocks past the mall, take a left on Hunakai Street and follow it until it dead-ends at Kāhala Avenue. Turn right and drive through **Kāhala** ㊶, Oʻahu's wealthiest neighborhood. Kāhala Avenue becomes Diamond Head Road. Follow it straight to Kapiʻolani Park. Stay on the right side of the park until you hit Kapahulu Avenue. Take a left, and you're back in Waikīkī.

TIMING

Take your time, take all day, and enjoy a few beaches along the way. The weather is sunny and warm year-round, and the scenery of Oʻahu's

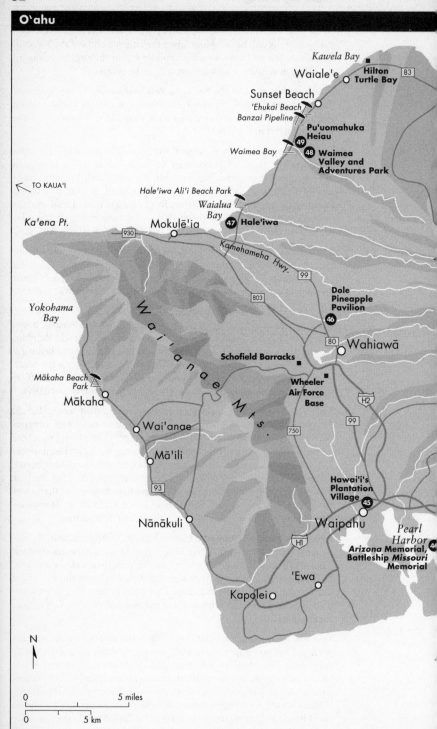

Kawela Bay

Waiale'e

**Hilton
Turtle Bay** 83

Sunset Beach

'Ehukai Beach
Banzai Pipeline

**Pu'uomahuka
Heiau**

49

Waimea Bay 48 **Waimea
Valley and
Adventures Park**

← TO KAUA'I

Hale'iwa Ali'i Beach Park

Ka'ena Pt.

*Waialua
Bay*

Mokulē'ia 930 47 **Hale'iwa**

Kamehameha Hwy.

99

803

**Dole
Pineapple
Pavilion**

*Yokohama
Bay*

46

80 **Wahiawā**

Schofield Barracks

*Mākaha Beach
Park*

**Wheeler
Air Force
Base**

Mākaha

750

H2

99

Wai'anae

Mā'ili

93

**Hawai'i's
Plantation
Village**

45

Nānākuli

Waipahu

*Pearl
Harbor*

H1

44

***Arizona* Memorial,
Battleship *Missouri*
Memorial**

'Ewa

Kapolei

N

0   5 miles

0   5 km

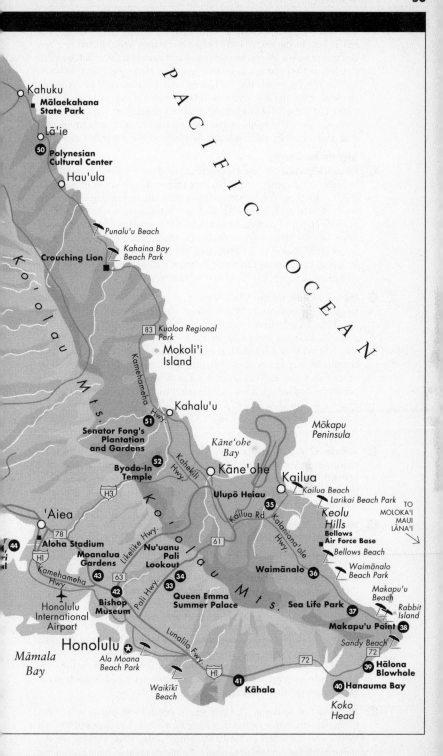

PACIFIC OCEAN

Kahuku
Mālaekahana State Park

Lāʻie

50 **Polynesian Cultural Center**

Hauʻula

Punaluʻu Beach

Crouching Lion
Kahaina Bay Beach Park

83 Kualoa Regional Park

Mokoliʻi Island

Kahaluʻu

51
Senator Fong's Plantation and Gardens

52
Byodo-In Temple

Kāneʻohe Bay

Mōkapu Peninsula

H3

Ulupō Heiau

Kāneʻohe

Kailua

Kailua Beach

Larikai Beach Park

TO MOLOKAʻI MAUI LĀNAʻI

Koʻolau Mts.

35

Keolu Hills

Bellows Air Force Base

Kailua Rd.

ʻAiea

78

44

Aloha Stadium

Moanalua Gardens

Nuʻuanu Pali Lookout

43

63

42

Bishop Museum

Pali Hwy.

H1

Kamehameha Hwy.

61

Bellows Beach

Waimānalo Beach Park

Waimānalo

36

Kalanianaʻole Hwy.

Sea Life Park

Makapuʻu Beach

37

Rabbit Island

Makapuʻu Point 38

Queen Emma Summer Palace

34

33

Lunalilo Hwy.

Honolulu International Airport

Honolulu

Māmala Bay

Ala Moana Beach Park

Waikīkī Beach

Sandy Beach

72

72

39 **Hālona Blowhole**

H1

41 **Kāhala**

72

40 **Hanauma Bay**

Koko Head

Kamehameha Hwy.

east side is too miraculous to rush through. If Hanauma Bay is your main focus, avoid Tuesday, when the park is closed. Also note that the bay is best in the early hours before the waters are churned up. You could reverse the above directions and get there first thing in the morning, before the crowds. Allow two hours for Hanauma Bay, two hours for Sea Life Park, and one for Queen Emma Summer Palace. Another tip: look up to the top of the mountains and, if it's clear, head directly to the Nuʻuanu Pali Lookout. It's a shame to get there only to find the view obscured by clouds or fog. Temperatures at the summit are several degrees cooler than in warm Waikīkī, so bring a jacket along.

Sights to See

㊲ Hālona Blowhole. Below a scenic turnout along the Koko Head shoreline, this oft-photographed lava tube that sucks the ocean in and spits it out in lofty plumes may or may not perform, depending on the currents. Nearby is the tiny beach used to film the wave-washed love scene in *From Here to Eternity*. As you face the blowhole and the ocean, look down to your far right to see the beach. This beach is not recommended for swimming or even wading. Also, take your valuables with you and lock your car, because this scenic location is a hot spot for petty thieves. ⊠ *Kalanianaʻole Hwy., 1 mi east of Hanauma Bay.*

㊵ Hanauma Bay. One of Oʻahu's most famous snorkeling destinations, this partially collapsed volcanic crater is home to more than 50 species of Hawaiian fish. Even from the overlook, the horseshoe-shape bay is a beauty, and you can easily see the reefs through the clear aqua waters. The wide beach is a great place for sunbathing and picnics. This is a marine conservation district, and regulations prohibit the feeding of the fish. Come early to get parking as the number of visitors allowed per day is limited. Call for current conditions. The beach is closed to visitors on Tuesday. ⊠ *7455 Kalanianaʻole Hwy.,* ☎ *808/396–4229.* ⊡ *Donation $3; parking $1; mask, fins, and snorkel rental $6.* ⊙ *Wed.– Mon. 6–6.*

㊶ Kāhala. Oʻahu's wealthiest neighborhood has streets lined with multimillion-dollar homes, and the classy Kāhala Mandarin Oriental Hawaiʻi hotel attracts a prestigious clientele. At intervals along tree-lined Kāhala Avenue are narrow lanes that provide public access to **Kāhala Beach.** ⊠ *East of Diamond Head.*

㊳ Makapuʻu Point. This spot has breathtaking views of the ocean, mountains, and the windward islands. The peninsula jutting out in the distance is **Mōkapu,** site of a U.S. Marine base. The spired mountain peak is **Mt. Olomana.** In front of you on the long pier is part of the **Makai Undersea Test Range,** a research facility that is closed to the public. Offshore is **Rabbit Island,** a picturesque cay so named because some think it looks like a swimming bunny.

Nestled in the cliff face is the **Makapuʻu Lighthouse,** which is closed to the public. Near the Makapuʻu Point turnout, you'll find the start of a mile-long paved road (closed to traffic). Hike up it to the top of the 647-ft bluff for a closer view of the lighthouse and, during the winter months, a great whale-watching vantage point. ⊠ *Kalanianaʻole Hwy., turnout above Makapuʻu Beach.*

㉞ Nuʻuanu Pali Lookout. This panoramic perch looks out to windward Oʻahu. It was in this region that King Kamehameha I drove defending forces over the edges of the 1,000-ft-high cliffs, thus winning the decisive battle for control of Oʻahu. It's a windy spot, so hang on to your hat. Lock your car if you get out, because break-ins have occurred here. ⊠ *Top of Pali Hwy.*

③ **Queen Emma Summer Palace.** Queen Emma and her family used this stately white home, built in 1848, as a retreat from the rigors of court life in hot and dusty Honolulu during the mid-1800s. It has an eclectic mix of European, Victorian, and Hawaiian furnishings and has excellent examples of Hawaiian quilts and koa-wood furniture as well as the queen's wedding dress and other memorabilia. ⊠ *2913 Pali Hwy.,* ☎ *808/595–3167.* ☞ *$5.* ⊙ *Guided tours daily 9–4.*

🐢 ③ **Sea Life Park.** Dolphins leap and spin, penguins frolic, and a killer whale performs impressive tricks at the shows in this marine-life attraction. In addition to a 300,000-gallon Hawaiian reef tank, the Pacific Whaling Museum, the Hawaiian Monk Seal Care Center, and Sea Turtle Lagoon, there are several interactive activities such as a stingray encounter, an underwater photo safari, and a "Splash University" dolphin training session. Sea Life Park is home to the world's only "wholphin," the offspring of a whale and a dolphin. ⊠ *Kalanianaʻole Hwy., Waimānalo,* ☎ *808/259–7933.* ☞ *$25.* ⊙ *Daily 9:30–5.*

③ **Ulupō Heiau.** Though they may look like piles of rocks to the uninitiated, *heiau* are sacred stone platforms for the worship of the gods and date from ancient times. *Ulupō* means "night inspiration," referring to the legendary *menehune,* a mythical race of diminutive people who supposedly built the heiau under the cloak of darkness. ⊠ *Behind YMCA at Kalanianaʻole Hwy. and Kailua Rd.*

. . . .

NEED A BREAK? Generations of children have purchased their beach snacks and sodas at **Kalapawai Market** (⊠ 306 S. Kalāheo Ave.), near Kailua Beach. A windward landmark since 1932, the green-and-white market has distinctive charm. It's a good source for your carryout lunch, since there's no concession stand at the beach.

. . . .

③ **Waimānalo.** This modest little seaside town flanked by chiseled cliffs is worth a visit. Its biggest draw is its beautiful beach, offering glorious views to the windward side. Down the side roads, heading mauka, are little farms that grow a variety of fruits and flowers. Toward the back of the valley are small ranches with grazing horses. If you see any trucks selling corn and you're staying at a place where you can cook it, be sure to get some in Waimānalo. It may be the sweetest you'll ever eat, and the price is the lowest on Oʻahu. ⊠ *Kalanianaʻole Hwy.*

Around the Island

After visiting three historic attractions in populated West Honolulu, you'll find that the Oʻahu landscape turns increasingly rural as you head north. Once carpeted in pineapple and sugarcane plantations, the central plains and the North Shore are now home to ranches, banana farms, and fields of exotic flowers and coffee grown for export. The plantation towns are small. Some have become cute with boutiques and little art galleries. Others are just themselves—old, wooden, and picturesque—the small homes surrounded by a riot of flowers and tropical-fruit trees.

A Good Drive

Follow H-1 Freeway heading west. Take the exit for Likelike Highway. Stay in the right lane and look for signs to the **Bishop Museum** ④. Once you're back on the freeway heading west, the road merges into the Moanalua Freeway (Route 78). Stay on this past the Puʻuloa Road–Tripler Hospital exit for **Moanalua Gardens** ④, a lovely park with huge, spreading monkeypod trees.

Continuing on the freeway, up over what is known as "Red Hill," you'll pass Aloha Stadium, a 50,000-seat arena that hosts the annual NFL Pro Bowl, local football and baseball games, and big-name rock concerts. The Aloha Flea Market is also held here. As you approach the stadium on the freeway, bear right at the sign to ʻAiea, and then merge left onto Kamehameha Highway (Route 99), going south to Pearl Harbor. Turn right at the Hālawa Gate for a tour of the **Arizona Memorial, Battleship *Missouri* Memorial** ㊹, and the U.S.S. *Bowfin*.

Follow H-1 west to Waipahu (Exit 8B) and onto Farrington Highway. Turn right at Waipahu Depot Road and left onto Waipahu Street to reach **Hawaiʻi's Plantation Village** ㊺, a collection of restored original and replicated homes from a 19th-century plantation town.

Take H-1 to H-2 to Highway 80 (Kamehameha Highway), heading to Wahiawā, home of the U.S. Army base at Schofield Barracks. Head north until Highway 80 meets Highway 99, where you'll see a scrubby patch called the Del Monte Pineapple Variety Garden. Unpromising as it looks, it's actually quite interesting, with varieties of the ubiquitous fruit ranging from thumb-size pink ones to big golden ones.

Merge left on Kamehameha Highway and you'll see the **Dole Pineapple Pavilion** ㊻. From here, Kamehameha Highway cuts through pineapple and sugarcane fields. Close to the bottom of the hill, a traffic-light intersection invites you to take the Haleʻiwa bypass road to save time. Don't. Turn left instead and drive to the traffic circle. Go around the circle and continue 7 mi to Mokulēʻia on Route 930. Soon you'll come to Dillingham Airfield, where you can fly in a glider.

Back at the traffic circle, follow the signs to **Haleʻiwa** ㊼, a sleepy plantation town with fashion boutiques, surf shops, restaurants, and the best grilled mahimahi sandwich on the North Shore at Kua ʻAina Sandwich. Leaving Haleʻiwa and continuing along Kamehameha Highway (Route 83), you'll pass the famous North Shore beaches, where the winter surf comes in size extra extra large. The first of these is the famous big surf spot Waimea Bay. Across the street, on the mauka side of the road, is **Waimea Valley and Adventures Park** ㊽. If you're interested in seeing a fine example of an ancient Hawaiian heiau, turn mauka at the Foodland store and take Pūpūkea Road up the steep climb, not quite a mile, to the dirt road on the right, leading to the **Puʻuomahuka Heiau** ㊾.

Continue along the coastal road past more famous surfing beaches, including ʻEhukai and Sunset. If it's wintertime, keep clear of those waves, which sometimes rise as high as 30 ft. Leave the sea to the daring (some say crazy) surfers who ride the towering waves with astounding grace. The only hotel of any consequence in these parts is your next landmark: the Hilton Turtle Bay Resort. If it's Sunday between 10 and 2, you might want to stop for its incredibly extensive champagne brunch, served in a pretty oceanside dining room.

As you approach the town of Lāʻie, there is a long stretch of pine trees on the makai side. Look for the entrance to Mālaekahana State Park. Coming up on the mauka side is the sprawling **Polynesian Cultural Center** ㊿.

As you continue driving along the shoreline, notice the picturesque little island of Mokoliʻi ("little lizard"), a 208-ft-high sea stack. According to Hawaiian legend, the goddess Hiʻiaka, sister of Pele, slew the dragon Mokoliʻi and flung its tail into the sea, forming the distinct islet. Other dragon body parts—in the form of rocks, of course—were scattered along the base of nearby Kualoa Ridge.

Continue straight on Kahekili Highway (Route 83) and look on your right for **Senator Fong's Plantation and Gardens** ⑤. Two miles farther on the right is the Valley of the Temples and its lovely **Byodo-In Temple** ㉒, a replica of a 900-year-old temple outside of Kyoto, Japan.

Follow Kahekili Highway to Likelike Highway (Highway 63), where you turn mauka and head back toward Honolulu through the Wilson Tunnel. The highway leads to Lunalilo Freeway going east. Exit at Pali Highway and go south through downtown Honolulu on Bishop Street. Then turn left on Ala Moana Boulevard, which leads to Kalākaua Avenue in Waikīkī.

TIMING

Unless you don't plan on stopping at any of the sights, allot nothing less than a day to circle the island. Try to factor in two or three different excursions and time-outs along this scenic North Shore. Don't rush through the Polynesian Cultural Center, because you'll miss much of what makes it so well done. Instead, devote an afternoon and evening to the center, perhaps stopping first for a morning at Waimea Valley. Note that the center is closed Sunday.

On another day, allow a full afternoon for the Bishop Museum. Inquire also about the "Behind-the-Scenes" museum tour. Afternoons, you may have to wait as long as two hours to see the *Arizona* Memorial. The best bet is to head out there early in the day. Hale'iwa deserves two hours: factor in some extra North Shore time for hiking, relaxing on a beach, kayaking, taking a glider ride, and having a snack. Wear flip-flops but bring a pair of walking shoes as well.

The weather is mercurial on the North Shore. It can be sunny and clear in Waikīkī and cloudy in the country. Carry along a light jacket, a hat, and sunscreen. Then you'll be ready for anything.

Sights to See

★ ㊸ ***Arizona* Memorial.** A simple, gleaming white structure shields the hulk of the U.S.S. *Arizona,* which sank with 1,102 men aboard when the Japanese attacked Pearl Harbor on December 7, 1941. The tour includes a 20-minute documentary with actual news footage from the day of the attack and a shuttle-boat ride to the memorial. Appropriate dress is required (no bathing suits, slippers, or bare feet). ✉ *National Park Service, Pearl Harbor,* ☎ *808/422–0561,* WEB *www.nps.gov/usar.* ⬚ *Free. Tour tickets distributed on a first-come, first-served basis, with 1- to 3-hr waits common.* ☉ *Daily 8–3.*

㊸ **Battleship *Missouri* Memorial.** The U.S.S. *Missouri,* which saw action from World War II to the Persian Gulf War, and on whose decks the agreement for Japanese surrender to end World War II was signed, was towed from Bremerton, Washington, to Pearl Harbor in 1998. The famed battleship, now moored about 1,000 ft from the *Arizona,* opened as a museum and interactive educational center in 1999. Tours start at the visitor center located between the *Arizona* and U.S.S. *Bowfin* Memorial. A trolley transports you to the Navy's Ford Island, where you can board the "Mighty Mo," tour the educational exhibits, and see how 2,400 sailors lived and worked together in the shadow of its 16-inch guns. ✉ *Pearl Harbor,* ☎ *808/545–2263 or 888/877–6477,* WEB *www.ussmissouri.com.* ⬚ *$14, guided tours $20.* ☉ *Daily 9–5.*

OFF THE
BEATEN PATH

U.S.S. *BOWFIN* – Dubbed "the Pearl Harbor Avenger" and moored near the *Arizona* Memorial visitor center, the *Bowfin* is one of only 15 World War II subs in existence. Children under four are not admitted. ✉ *11 Arizona Memorial Dr., at Pearl Harbor,* ☎ *808/423–1342,* WEB *www.aloha.net/bowfin.* ⬚ *$8.* ☉ *Daily 9–5.*

42 Bishop Museum. Founded in 1889 by Charles R. Bishop as a memorial to his wife, Princess Bernice Pauahi, the museum began as a repository for the royal possessions of this last direct descendant of King Kamehameha the Great. Today it is the Hawai'i State Museum of Natural and Cultural History, with world-famous displays of Polynesian artifacts: lustrous feather capes; the skeleton of a giant sperm whale; an authentic, well-preserved grass house; and photography and crafts displays. Also visit the planetarium, hula and Hawaiian craft demonstrations, and special exhibits. The building alone, with its huge Victorian turrets and immense stone walls, is worth seeing. ⊠ *1525 Bernice St.,* ☎ *808/847–3511,* WEB *www.bishopmuseum.org.* ☞ *$14.95.* ☉ *Daily 9–5.*

52 Byodo-In Temple. Tucked away in the back of the Valley of the Temples cemetery is a replica of the 11th-century Temple at Uji in Japan. A 2-ton statue of the Buddha presides inside the main temple building and alongside a meditation house and gardens set dramatically against the sheer, green cliffs of the Ko'olau Mountains. Visitors have the opportunity to ring the 5-ft, 3-ton brass bell for good luck and may also feed some 10,000 carp that inhabit the garden's ponds. ⊠ *47-200 Kahekili Hwy., Kāne'ohe,* ☎ *808/239–8811.* ☞ *$2.* ☉ *Daily 8–4:30.*

46 Dole Pineapple Pavilion. Celebrate Hawai'i's famous golden fruit at this promotional, tourist-oriented center with exhibits, a huge gift shop, snack concession, educational displays, and the world's largest maze. Although much more sophisticated than its original 1950 fruit stand, the Pavilion is filled with souvenir options galore, and kids love the 1.7-mi Pineapple Garden Maze made up of 11,400 colorful Hawaiian plants. ⊠ *64-1550 Kamehameha Hwy.,* ☎ *808/621–8408,* WEB *www.doleplantation.com.* ☞ *Pavilion free, maze $4.50.* ☉ *Daily 9–6.*

47 Hale'iwa. During the 1920s this seaside hamlet was a trendy retreat at the end of a railroad line. During the '60s hippies gathered here, followed by surfers. Today Hale'iwa is a fun mix, with old general stores and contemporary boutiques, galleries, and eateries. Be sure to stop in at **Lili'uokalani Protestant Church,** founded by missionaries in the 1830s. It's fronted by a large, stone archway built in 1910 and covered with night-blooming cereus. ⊠ *Follow H-1 west from Honolulu to H-2 north, exit at Wahiawā, follow Kamehameha Hwy. 6 mi, turn left at signaled intersection, then right into Hale'iwa.*

NEED A
BREAK?

For a real slice of Hale'iwa life, stop at **Matsumoto's** (⊠ 66-087 Kamehameha Hwy.), a family-run business in a building dating from 1910. It sells shaved ice, a tropical snow cone that costs about $1. They shave the ice right before your eyes and offer every flavor imaginable, including banana, mango, papaya, coconut, and strawberry.

45 Hawai'i's Plantation Village. Displays and authentically furnished buildings, both original and replicated, re-create Hawai'i's sugar plantation era. Tour a Chinese social hall, Japanese shrine, sumo ring, saimin stand, dental office, and historic homes at this "living museum" 30 minutes from downtown Honolulu. ⊠ *Waipahu Cultural Gardens Park, 94-695 Waipahu St., Waipahu,* ☎ *808/677–0110.* ☞ *$5.* ☉ *Mon.–Fri. 9–4, Sat. 10–4 with guided tours hourly.*

43 Moanalua Gardens. This lovely park is the site of a major hula festival on the third weekend in July. Throughout the year, the Moanalua Gardens Foundation sponsors hikes that leave from here to Moanalua Valley. Call for specific times. ⊠ *1401 Mahiole St., Honolulu,* ☎ *808/839–5334.* ☞ *Free.* ☉ *Weekdays 8–4.*

🕐 ⑤⓪ **Polynesian Cultural Center.** Re-created, individual villages showcase the lifestyles and traditions of Hawai'i, Tahiti, Samoa, Fiji, the Marquesas Islands, New Zealand, and Tonga. This 45-acre center, founded in 1963 by the Church of Jesus Christ of Latter-day Saints, also houses restaurants and lū'aus, and shares cultural traditions such as tribal tattooing, fire dancing, and ancient customs and ceremonies. The expansive open-air shopping village carries Polynesian handicrafts. If you're staying in Honolulu, see the center as part of a van tour so you won't have to drive home late at night after the two-hour evening show. Various packages are available, from basic admission with no transportation to an all-inclusive deal. ⊠ *55-370 Kamehameha Hwy., Lā'ie,* ☏ *808/ 293–3333 or 808/923–1861,* WEB *www.polynesia.com.* ⊠ *$27–$95.* ☉ *Mon.–Sat. 12:30–9:30.*

⑨ **Pu'uomahuka Heiau.** Worth a stop for its spectacular views from a bluff high above the ocean overlooking Waimea Bay, this sacred spot was once the site of human sacrifices. It's now on the National Register of Historic Places. ⊠ *½ mi north of Waimea Bay on Rte. 83, turn right on Pūpūkea Rd. and drive 1 mi uphill.*

⑤① **Senator Fong's Plantation and Gardens.** Hiram Fong, the first Asian-American to be elected to Congress, shares his love of Hawaiian flora and fauna by allowing tours of his 700-acre plantation estate. A 45-minute guided tram tour takes you through the landscaped grounds, which include human-made ponds fed by natural springs. The visitor center has a snack bar and gift shop. ⊠ *47-285 Pūlama Rd., off Kahekili Hwy., 2 mi north of Byodo-In Temple, Kahalu'u,* ☏ *808/239– 6775.* ⊠ *$10.* ☉ *Tram tours daily 9–4.*

🕐 ⑧ **Waimea Valley and Adventures Park.** At this 1,800-acre attraction, remnants of an early Hawaiian civilization are surrounded by more than 2,500 tropical plants and trees. The garden trails are well marked, and the plants are labeled. You might spot a Hawaiian nēnē, the state bird. There's a spectacular show of cliff-diving from 45-ft-high falls, and you can take part in Hawaiian games and dances. Tour the backcountry on horseback or by kayak, mountain bike, or all-terrain vehicle. Free "moonwalks" are held two nights at the time of each full moon. ⊠ *59-864 Kamehameha Hwy., Hale'iwa,* ☏ *808/638–8511.* ⊠ *$24.* ☉ *Daily 10–5:30.*

BEACHES

For South Seas sun, fun, and surf, O'ahu is a dream destination, but first some words of caution: when approaching any Hawaiian beach, heed signs indicating current surf conditions. If they warn of dangerous surf or currents, pay attention. Most beaches have lifeguards, although two exceptions are Kahana and Mālaekahano. Waikīkī is only 21 degrees north of the equator, so the sun here is very strong. No alcoholic beverages are allowed, and no matter which beach you choose, lock your car and never, ever leave your valuables unattended.

Waikīkī Beaches

The 2½-mi strand called **Waikīkī Beach** actually extends from Hilton Hawaiian Village on one end to Kapi'olani Park and Diamond Head on the other. Areas along this sandy strip have separate names but subtle differences. Beach areas are listed here from west to east.

Kahanamoku Beach. Named for Hawai'i's famous Olympic swimming champion, Duke Kahanamoku, this beach has decent snorkeling and swimming and a gentle surf. Its sandy bottom slopes gradually. The area has a snack concession, showers, a beach-gear and surfboard rental shop, catamaran cruises, and a sand volleyball court. ⊠ *In front of Hilton Hawaiian Village.*

★ **Ft. DeRussy Beach.** Sunbathers, swimmers, and windsurfers enjoy this beach, one of the widest in Waikīkī, fronting the military hotel, the Hale Koa, and the U.S. Army Museum. It trails off to a coral ocean bottom with fairly good snorkeling sights. The beach is frequented by military personnel but is open to everyone. There are volleyball courts, food stands, picnic tables, dressing rooms, and showers. ⊠ *In front of Ft. DeRussy and Hale Koa Hotel.*

Gray's Beach. Named for a little lodging house called Gray's-by-the-Sea, which stood here in the 1920s, this beach is known for two good surfing spots called Paradise and Number Threes just beyond its reef. High tides often cover the narrow beach. You'll find food stands, surfboard and beach-gear rental, and canoe and catamaran rides. ⊠ *In front of Halekūlani.*

★ **Kahaloa and Ulukou Beaches.** Possibly the best swimming and lots of activities are available along this little stretch of Waikīkī Beach. Take a catamaran or outrigger canoe ride out into the bay, unless you're ready to try your skill at surfing. ⊠ *In front of Royal Hawaiian Hotel and Sheraton Moana Surfrider.*

★ **Kūhiō Beach Park.** This beach is a hotspot for shoreline and beach activities. Check out the Kūhiō Beach stage nightly at 6:30 for free hula and Hawaiian-music performances; weekends there's a torchlighting ceremony at sunset as well. Surf lessons for beginners are available from the beach center here every half hour. The beach is named for Prince Jonah Kūhiō Kalaniana'ole, a distinguished native statesman who once had his home here on Waikīkī's shore. ⊠ *Past the Sheraton Moana Surfrider Hotel to Kapahulu Ave. pier.*

Queen's Surf. A great place for a sunset picnic, this beach is beyond the seawall, toward Diamond Head, at what's known as the "other end of Waikīkī." It was once the site of Queen Lili'uokalani's beach house. A mix of families and gays gather here, and it seems as if someone is always playing a bongo drum. There are good shade trees, picnic tables, and a changing house with showers. ⊠ *Across from entrance to Honolulu Zoo.*

Sans Souci. Nicknamed Dig-Me Beach because of its outlandish display of skimpy bathing suits, this small rectangle of sand is nonetheless a good sunning spot for all ages. Children enjoy its shallow, safe waters, and the shore draws many ocean kayakers and outrigger canoeists. Serious swimmers and triathletes also swim in the channel here, beyond the reef. There's no food concession, but near one end is the Hau Tree Lānai restaurant. ⊠ *Makai side of Kapi'olani Park, between New Otani Kaimana Beach Hotel and Waikīkī War Memorial Natatorium.*

Beaches Around O'ahu

Hanauma Bay. The main attraction here is snorkeling. The coral reefs are clearly visible through the turquoise waters of this sunken volcanic crater half open to the ocean. It is a designated marine preserve and closed one day a week to the public. Although the fish are the tamest you'll view while snorkeling, feeding them is not allowed. The bay is best early in the morning (around 7), before the crowds arrive. It can be difficult to park later in the day. There is a busy food and snorkel-equipment concession on the beach, plus changing rooms and showers. No smoking is allowed on the beach. **Hanauma Bay Snorkeling Excursions** (☎ 808/373–5060) run to and from Waikīkī. ⊠ *7455 Kalaniana'ole Hwy.,* ☎ *808/396–4229.* ☞ *Donation $3; parking $1; mask, snorkel, and fins rental $6.* ☾ *Wed.–Mon. 6–6.*

Sandy Beach. Strong, steady winds make "Sandy's" a kite-flyer's paradise. But the shore break is vicious here, and this beach has a reputation as one of the leading sites for injury to those who lack knowledge of how to handle rough surf. Do not swim here. Sandy's is a popular spot for the high school and college crowd. There's a changing house with indoor and outdoor showers but no food concessions. ⊠ *Makai of Kalaniana'ole Hwy., 2 mi east of Hanauma Bay.*

Makapu'u Beach. Swimming at Makapu'u should be attempted only by strong strokers and bodysurfers, because the swells can be overwhelmingly big and powerful. Instead, consider this tiny crescent cove—popular with locals—as a prime sunbathing spot. Finding parking in the small lot can be tricky. In a pinch, try parking on the narrow shoulder and walking down to the beach. There is a changing house with indoor and outdoor showers. ⊠ *Makai of Kalaniana'ole Hwy., across from Sea Life Park, 2 mi south of Waimānalo.*

★ **Waimānalo Beach Park.** This is a "local" beach busy with picnicking families and active sports fields. Sometimes, folks are not very friendly to tourists here, but the beach itself is one of the island's most beautiful. Expect a wide stretch of sand; turquoise, emerald, and deep-blue seas; and waves full of boogie boarders. ⊠ *Windward side, look for signs makai of Kalaniana'ole Hwy., south of Waimānalo town.*

Bellows Beach. The waves here are great for bodysurfing. Locals come for the fine swimming on weekends and holidays, when the Air Force opens the beach to civilians. There are showers, abundant parking, and plenty of spots for picnicking underneath shady ironwood trees. There is no food concession, but McDonald's and other take-out fare is available right outside the entrance gate. ⊠ *Entrance on Kalaniana'ole Hwy. near Waimānalo town center, signs on makai side of road.*

★ **Kailua Beach Park.** Steady breezes attract windsurfers by the dozens to this long, palm-fringed beach with gently sloping sands. You can rent equipment in Kailua and try it yourself. This is a local favorite, so if you want the beach to yourself, head here on a weekday. There are showers, changing rooms, picnic areas, and a concession stand. Buy your picnic provisions at the Kalapawai Market nearby. ⊠ *Windward side, makai of Kailua town, turn right on Kailua Rd. at market, cross bridge, then turn left into beach parking lot.*

Lanikai Beach Park. A mile of buttery sand is ideal for a beach stroll, with views of water the color of turquoise. The beach fronts some of the most expensive real estate on the windward side. When the trade winds are active, look for windsurfers. Early birds can watch some spectacular sunrises. ⊠ *Windward side, past Kailua Beach Park, street parking on Mokulua Dr. for various public access points to beach.*

Kahana Bay Beach Park. Local parents often bring their children to wade in safety at this pretty beach cove with very shallow, protected waters. A grove of tall ironwood and pandanus trees keeps the area cool, shady, and ideal for a picnic. An ancient Hawaiian fishpond, which was in use until the '20s, is visible nearby. There are changing houses, showers, and picnic tables. Across the highway is Kahana Valley, burgeoning with banana, breadfruit, and mango trees. ⊠ *Windward side of island, makai of Kamehameha Hwy., north of Kualoa Park.*

Kualoa Regional Park. This is one of the island's most beautiful picnic, camping, and beach areas. Grassy expanses border a long, narrow stretch of beach with spectacular views of Kāne'ohe Bay and the Ko'olau Mountains. Dominating the view is an islet called Mokoli'i, which rises 206 ft above the water. You can swim in the shallow areas year-round. The one drawback is that it's usually windy. Bring a cooler because no refreshments are sold here. There are places to shower, change, and picnic in the shade of palm trees. ⊠ *Windward side, makai of Kamehameha Hwy., north of Waiāhole.*

Mālaekahana Beach Park. The big attraction here is tiny Goat Island, a bird sanctuary just offshore. At low tide the water is shallow enough—never more than waist high—so that you can wade out to it. Wear sneakers so you don't cut yourself on the coral. Families love to camp in the groves of ironwood trees at Mālaekahana State Park. The beach itself is fairly narrow but long enough for a 20-minute stroll, one-way. The waves are never too big, and sometimes they're just right for the beginning bodysurfer. There are changing houses, showers, and picnic tables. Note that the entrance gates are easy to miss because you can't see the beach from the road. ⊠ *Windward side, entrance gates are makai of Kamehameha Hwy., ½ mi north of Lā'ie.*

Sunset Beach. This is one link in the chain of North Shore beaches that extends for miles. It's popular for its gentle summer waves and crashing winter surf. The beach is broad, and the sand is soft. Lining the adjacent highway there are usually carryout truck stands selling shave ice, plate lunches, and sodas. ⊠ *North shore, 1 mi north of 'Ehukai Beach Park on makai side of Kamehameha Hwy.*

'Ehukai Beach Park. 'Ehukai is part of a series of beaches running for many miles along the North Shore. What sets it apart is the view of the famous Banzai Pipeline, where the waves curl into magnificent tubes making it an experienced wave-rider's dream. In spring and summer, the waves are more accommodating to the average swimmer. The long, wide, and generally uncrowded beach has a changing house with toilets and an outdoor shower and water fountain. Bring along drinks because there is very little shade here, and the nearest store is a mile away. ⊠ *North Shore, 1 mi north of Foodland store at Pūpūkea, turn makai off Kamehameha Hwy. directly into the small parking lot bordering highway.*

★ **Waimea Bay.** Made popular in that old Beach Boys song "Surfin' U.S.A.," Waimea Bay is a slice of hang-ten heaven and home to the king-size 25- to 30-ft winter waves. Summer is the time to swim and snorkel in the calm waters. The beach is a broad crescent of soft sand backed by a shady area with tables, a changing house, and showers. Parking is almost impossible in the lot on weekends, so folks just park along the road and walk down. ⊠ *North shore across from Waimea Valley, 3 mi north of Hale'iwa on makai side of Kamehameha Hwy.*

Hale'iwa Ali'i Beach Park. The winter waves are impressive here, but in summer the ocean is like a lake, ideal for family swimming. The beach itself is big and often full of locals. Its broad lawns off the highway invite volleyball and Frisbee games and groups of barbecuers. *Baywatch* fans take note: the beach here serves as the home base for *Baywatch in Hawaii*. There is a changing house with showers but no food concessions. Hale'iwa has everything you need for provisions. ⊠ *North Shore, makai side of Kamehameha Hwy., north of Hale'iwa town center and past harbor.*

Yokohama Bay. You'll be one of the few outsiders at this Wai'anae Coast beach at the very end of the road. It feels and looks remote and untouched, which may explain the lack of crowds. Locals come here to fish and swim in waters that are calm enough for children in summer. The beach is narrow and rocky in places. Bring provisions, because the nearest town is a 15-minute drive away. There's a changing house and showers, plus a small parking lot, but most folks just pull over and park on the side of the bumpy road. ⊠ *Wai'anae Coast, northern end of Farrington Hwy. about 7 mi north of Mākaha.*

Mākaha Beach Park. This beach provides a slice of local life most visitors don't see. Families string up tarps for the day, fire up hibachis, set up lawn chairs, get out the fishing gear, and strum 'ukulele while they "talk story" (chat). The swimming is generally decent in the summer, but avoid the big winter waves. This was home to the island's first professional surf meet, in 1952. The ¼-mi beach has a changing house and showers and is the site of a yearly big-board surf meet. ⊠ *Wai'anae Coast, 1½ hrs west of Honolulu on H-1 Fwy. and Farrington Hwy., makai side of hwy.*

★ **Ala Moana Beach Park.** Ala Moana has a protective reef, which keeps the waters calm and perfect for swimming. After Waikīkī, this is the most popular beach among visitors. To the Waikīkī side is a peninsula called Magic Island, with picnic tables, shady trees, and paved sidewalks ideal for jogging. Ala Moana also has playing fields, changing houses, indoor and outdoor showers, lifeguards, concession stands, and tennis courts. This beach is for everyone, but only in the daytime. It's a high-crime area after dark. ⊠ *Honolulu, makai side of Ala Moana Shopping Center and Ala Moana Blvd.; from Waikīkī take Bus 8 to shopping center and cross Ala Moana Blvd.*

DINING

If you're looking for a meal with a view, explore the restaurants at the upscale hotels and resorts that line O'ahu's shores. Settings can be as casual as a "barefoot bar" or as elegant as a romantic dinner for two under the stars. Beyond Waikīkī are culinary jewels tucked away in shopping centers and residential neighborhoods that specialize in ethnic cuisines. You'll almost never go wrong if you sample the offerings at any establishment whose name ends in the words "Drive Inn." Here you will find the local grinds, which are the staples of the Hawaiian diet: seafood plate lunches and noodle saimin soups. For snacks and fast food around the island, look for the lunch wagons, usually parked roadside near the beaches. For an explanation of price categories, *see* Dining *in* Smart Travel Tips.

Waikīkī

Chinese

$–$$ ✕ **Golden Dragon.** Nearly 65 à la carte dishes and a six-course Sig-
★ nature Selection dinner make up the menu of fine Cantonese, Szechuan, and nouvelle-Chinese dishes prepared by chef Steve Chiang. The restaurant, overlooking the lagoon on the mezzanine of the Hilton Hawaiian Village's Rainbow Tower, has lazy Susans on each table for easy sampling. Signature dishes include stir-fried lobster with curry sauce and Szechuan beef. Two of the house specialties—the Imperial Peking duck and Imperial beggar's chicken (whole chicken wrapped in lotus leaves and baked in a clay pot)—must be ordered 24 hours in advance. ⊠ *Hilton Hawaiian Village, 2005 Kālia Rd.,* ☎ *808/946–5336. Reservations essential. AE, D, DC, MC, V. No lunch.*

Contemporary

$$–$$$ ✕ **Bali by the Sea.** In the Hilton Hawaiian Village, this restaurant is
★ breeze-swept and pretty, with an oceanside setting offering glorious views of Waikīkī Beach. Chef Jean-Luc Voegele's menu is a blend of French and Asian influences, with such entrées as casserole of Hawaiian lobster and 'ōpakapaka (blue snapper) with Kaffir lime sauce. Another favorite is the rack of lamb crusted with macadamia nuts and herbs. ⊠ *Hilton Hawaiian Village, 2005 Kālia Rd.,* ☎ *808/941–2254. Reservations essential. AE, D, DC, MC, V. No dinner Sun.*

$$–$$$ ✕ **Cascada.** This Waikīkī hideaway restaurant, in the Royal Garden at Waikīkī hotel, was designed in the style of dining terraces found in the villas of Southern Italy and France. The dining room has a hand-painted trompe l'oeil ceiling and tables spilling out onto a marble terrace with tropical gardens and a cascading waterfall. Island flair goes into the Mediterranean dishes created by Chef Matt Stephenson. Grilled prawns, royal crab cake served with Asian pesto aioli and

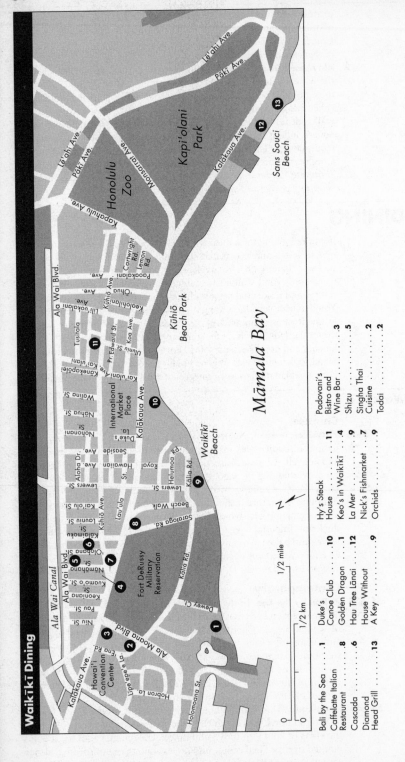

Waikīkī Dining

HOW TO USE THIS GUIDE

Great trips begin with great planning, and this guide makes planning easy. It's packed with everything you need—insider advice on hotels and restaurants, cool tools, practical tips, essential maps, and much more.

COOL TOOLS

Fodor's Choice Top picks are marked throughout with a star.

Great Itineraries These tours, planned by Fodor's experts, give you the skinny on what you can see and do in the time you have.

Smart Travel Tips A to Z This special section is packed with important contacts and advice on everything from how to get around to what to pack.

Good Walks You won't miss a thing if you follow the numbered bullets on our maps.

Need a Break? Looking for a quick bite to eat or a spot to rest? These sure bets are along the way.

Off the Beaten Path Some lesser-known sights are worth a detour. We've marked those you should make time for.

POST-IT® FLAGS

Dog-ear no more!

"Post-it" is a registered trademark of 3M.

Favorite restaurants • Essential maps •
Frequently used numbers • Walking tours
• Can't-miss sights • Smart Travel
Tips • Web sites • Top shops • Hot

nightclubs • Addresses • Smart contacts •
Events • Off-the-beaten-path spots • Favorite
restaurants • Essential maps • Frequently
used numbers • Walking tours •

ICONS AND SYMBOLS

Watch for these symbols throughout:

★ Our special recommendations

✕ Restaurant

🏠 Lodging establishment

✕🏠 Lodging establishment whose restaurant warrants
a special trip

🍼 Good for kids

☞ Sends you to another section of the guide for
more information

✉ Address

☎ Telephone number

FAX Fax number

WEB Web site

💳 Admission price

🕗 Opening hours

$-$$$$ Lodging and dining price categories, keyed to strategically
sited price charts. Check the index for locations.

①❶ Numbers in white and black circles on the maps, in the
margins, and within tours correspond to one another.

ON THE WEB

Continue your planning with these useful tools found at
www.fodors.com, the Web's best source for travel information.

"Rich with resources." —*New York Times*

"Navigation is a cinch." —*Forbes* "Best of the Web" list

"Put together by people bursting with know-how."
—*Sunday Times* (London)

Create a Miniguide Pinpoint hotels, restaurants, and attractions that have what you want at the price you want to pay.

Rants and Raves Find out what readers say about Fodor's picks—or write your own reviews of hotels and restaurants you've just visited.

Travel Talk Post your questions and get answers from fellow travelers, or share your own experiences.

On-Line Booking Find the best prices on airline tickets, rental cars, cruises, or vacations, and book them on the spot.

About our Books Learn about other Fodor's guides to your destination and many others.

Expert Advice and Trip Ideas From what to tip to how to take great photos, from the national parks to Nepal, Fodors.com has suggestions that'll make your trip a breeze. Log on and get informed and inspired.

Smart Resources Check the weather in your destination or convert your currency. Learn the local language or link to the latest event listings. Or consult hundreds of detailed maps—all in one place.

rouille, veal Milanese with arugula and mozzarella, and chicken Napoleon saltimbocca style are a few of the popular choices. ✉ *Royal Garden at Waikīkī, 440 'Olohana St., ☎ 808/943–0202. AE, D, DC, MC, V.*

$$–$$$ ✕ **Diamond Head Grill.** The grill caters to business travelers staying at the W Honolulu–Diamond Head Hotel, where this restaurant is located. Among the breakfast choices are macadamia-and-ginger waffles with *pohā*-berry butter (pohā is Hawaiian for cape gooseberry), crab and egg crepes, and local-style fried rice with Portuguese sausage and two fried eggs. Lunch and dinner appetizers include a *kālua* (roasted) pork *lumpia* (spring roll) with mango guacamole and spicy mustard sauce and a coconut curry seafood chowder. Entrées such as grilled yellowfin tuna with hot-and-sour lobster soy broth, sweet Kahuku corn-and-carrot risotto, and guava-and-mustard-crusted rack of lamb round out the menu. There's a serpentine martini bar, and a baby grand piano provides live evening entertainment. ✉ *W Honolulu–Diamond Head Hotel, 2885 Kalākaua Ave., ☎ 808/922–3734. Reservations essential. AE, D, MC, V. No lunch weekends.*

$$–$$$ ✕ **Hau Tree Lānai.** Dining out of doors is how it should be done in Hawai'i. At breakfast, lunch, or dinner you can eat under graceful hau trees, so close to Kaimana Beach you can hear the whisper of the waves. Breakfast offerings include a huge helping of eggs Benedict, poi pancakes, or a delicious salmon omelet. For dinner, get fresh with moonfish or snapper, or try the popular sesame-crusted hoisin rack of lamb. ✉ *New Otani Kaimana Beach Hotel, 2863 Kalākaua Ave., ☎ 808/ 921–7066. Reservations essential. AE, D, DC, MC, V.*

$–$$ ✕ **Duke's Canoe Club.** Beachfront in the Outrigger Waikīkī, and named after Hawai'i's famous surfer Duke Kahanamoku, this eatery is casual and usually crowded (reserve ahead or you'll probably have to wait for a table). Weekend evenings the restaurant hosts sunset "concerts on the beach" on its outdoor terrace. Seafood and steak are at the heart of the menu, and prices are moderate. Fish can be served up Duke's style, which is baked in a garlic, lemon, and sweet basil glaze to keep it tender and moist. The chef will also grill, sauté, roast, or hibachi your fish selection. Other Duke's specialties include Caesar salad, macadamia-and-crab wontons, and the decadent Hula Pie. ✉ *Outrigger Waikīkī on the Beach, 2335 Kalākaua Ave., ☎ 808/922–2268. AE, D, DC, MC, V.*

$–$$ ✕ **House Without a Key.** This is one of the jewels of Waikīkī, a casual seaside spot in the serene Halekūlani hotel serving salads, sandwiches, and hearty meals. Favorites include Joy's Sandwich (crabmeat salad, bacon, and avocado on whole wheat bread) and the beef burger on a kaiser roll. With the ocean and Diamond Head in view, this is a mesmerizing place at sunset, when hula dancing and Hawaiian music say "aloha" to the day's end. A breakfast buffet is served daily between 7 and 10:30. ✉ *Halekūlani, 2199 Kālia Rd., ☎ 808/923–2311. Reservations not accepted. AE, MC, V.*

French

$$$ ✕ **La Mer.** In the exotic, oceanfront atmosphere of a Mandalay man-
★ sion, you'll be served neoclassic French cuisine that many consider to be the finest in Hawai'i. Here, on the grounds of the Halekūlani, is a room—open to the ocean, and with sweeping views of Diamond Head—as luscious as its menu. La Mer celebrates the marriage of French and Island cuisines. Begin your meal with tartares of *hamachi* (yellowtail), *'ahi* (yellowfin tuna), and salmon with three caviars. Entrées include *onaga* (pink or red snapper) fillet cooked skin-side crisp with confit of tomato, truffle juice, and fried basil, and *kumu* (goatfish) in a rosemary-salt crust. A favorite sweet is the symphony of four desserts. In addition to à la carte selections, there are two complete din-

ner menus: four courses for $85 and six courses for $105. ⊠ *Halekūlani, 2199 Kālia Rd.,* ☎ *808/923–2311. Reservations essential. Jacket required. AE, MC, V. No lunch.*

$$–$$$ ✕ **Padovani's Bistro and Wine Bar.** Philippe Padovani gained fame at
★ three top Hawai'i hotels (Halekūlani, Ritz-Carlton, and Mānele Bay) and as a founding member of the Hawai'i Regional Cuisine Council. Now, at his own place in the Doubletree Alana Waikīkī, he presents French food that spotlights local seafood, greens, herbs, fruits, and other Hawaiian products. The chef's specialties include an appetizer of pan-fried duck liver and a tart of onion marmalade and mushrooms. For entrées, venison loin is paired with ginger plum sauce and sweet-potato purée, and sautéed tiger shrimp is served with mushroom-herb polenta and tomato and basil sauce. The room is small and romantic, and an upstairs wine bar offers 50 varietals by the glass, single-malt Scotches, live music on weekend evenings, and an enclosed cigar room. Padovani's also features a prix-fixe menu for $45 and a tasting menu for $85. ⊠ *Doubletree Alana Waikīkī, 1956 Ala Moana Blvd.,* ☎ *808/946–3456 or 808/947–1236. Reservations essential. AE, D, DC, MC, V.*

Italian

$$$ ✕ **Caffelatte Italian Restaurant.** Every dish at this tiny trattoria is worth ordering, from the gnocchi in a thick, rich sauce of Gorgonzola cheese to the veal scallopini in a light white wine sauce sprinkled with parsley. The tiramisù is the best in town. A family from Milan operates this restaurant with limited seating inside and a few tables outside on the narrow lānai. Be aware that each person must order three courses (appetizer, main course, and dessert), a rule that keeps the tab on the high side. The chef will prepare a special mystery dinner for two for $60. There's no parking, so walk here if you can. ⊠ *339 Saratoga Rd., 2nd level,* ☎ *808/924–1414. AE, DC, MC, V. Closed Tues.*

Japanese

$$–$$$ ✕ **Shizu.** Sample the Japanese cooking styles of *teishoku* (traditional Japanese preparation of fish, rice, soup, and more, served in lacquer bowls) and tableside *teppanyaki* in a contemporary setting overlooking a Zen-style rock garden. The two teppanyaki rooms have spectacular stained-glass windows with vibrant irises. Here, diners sit around a massive iron grill on which a dexterous chef slices and cooks sizzling meats and vegetables. An elaborate 10-course teppanyaki dinner is one of the offerings. There's also a sushi bar and traditional dishes such as tempura. Try green-tea cheesecake for dessert. ⊠ *Royal Garden at Waikīkī, 440 'Olohana St., 4th floor,* ☎ *808/943–0202. AE, D, DC, MC, V.*

Seafood

$$–$$$ ✕ **Nick's Fishmarket.** The decor is a little old-fashioned perhaps—black
★ booths, candlelight, and formal table settings—but it's hard to beat Nick's seafood. The bouillabaisse is an outstanding combination of lobster, crab, prawns, mussels, clams, and fish. This is one of the few places with abalone on the menu; it's sautéed and served with lobster risotto. Nick's is also the place for *imu*-style seafood: ti leaves and hot lava rocks line the cooking pot to steam such delicacies as Tristan lobster tail, scallops, and salmon. Leave room for Vanbana Pie, a decadent combination of bananas, vanilla Swiss-almond ice cream, and hot caramel sauce. ⊠ *Waikīkī Gateway Hotel, 2070 Kalākaua Ave.,* ☎ *808/955–6333. Reservations essential. AE, D, DC, MC, V.*

$$–$$$ ✕ **Orchids.** It seems only fitting that you can hear the waves from this
★ oceanfront dining room that lays out the best seafood bar in town, including sashimi, *poke* (marinated raw fish), and shellfish. Try the pistachio-crusted *hapuʻupuʻu* (sea bass) and a hearty paella that combines fresh-caught fish, mussels, jumbo shrimp, squid, and saffron rice. Meat

and poultry dishes include a mustard-herb roasted Colorado lamb rack and tandoori-roasted island chicken. Outdoor and indoor seating is available, with the best views from the lānai. ⊠ *Halekūlani, 2199 Kālia Rd., ☎ 808/923–2311. Reservations essential. AE, MC, V.*

$–$$ ✕ **Todai.** You know a restaurant is doing something right if it's located ★ in tourist-heavy Waikīkī and has become a favorite of local residents. This recent addition to the dining scene has the longest seafood buffet in Hawai'i: 180 ft long, and with 40 different kinds of sushi. You'll also find lobster, shrimp tempura, Alaskan snow crab, salad, barbecued ribs, and much more on the buffet. Todai is long on seafood, but short on elegant decor. ⊠ *1910 Ala Moana Blvd., ☎ 808/947–1000. Reservations essential. AE, D, DC, MC, V.*

Steak

$$–$$$$ ✕ **Hy's Steak House.** Things always seem to go well at Hy's, from the filet mignon tartare and oysters Rockefeller right through to the flaming desserts. The atmosphere is snug and librarylike, and you can watch the chef perform behind glass. Tuxedoed waiters make helpful suggestions about the menu. Hy's is famous for its kiawe-broiled New York strip steak, cold-water lobster tail, and rack of lamb. The Caesar salad is excellent, as are the panfried O'Brien potatoes. ⊠ *Waikīkī Park Heights Hotel, 2440 Kūhiō Ave., ☎ 808/922–5555. Reservations essential. AE, DC, MC, V. No lunch.*

Thai

$–$$ ✕ **Singha Thai Cuisine.** Dishes here are prepared in traditional Thai ★ fashion, with just a sprinkling of Hawaiian regional flavorings. Seafood, vegetarian curry dishes, and the Thai chili are wonderful. Singha's beautiful Royal Thai dancers dressed in traditional costume add to the occasion, performing nightly center stage in the restaurant. ⊠ *1910 Ala Moana Blvd., ☎ 808/941–2898. Reservations essential. AE, D, DC, MC, V. No lunch.*

$ ✕ **Keo's in Waikīkī.** Hollywood celebrities have discovered this twin- ★ kling nook with tables set amid lighted trees, big paper umbrellas, and sprays of orchids everywhere. What many may not know is that many of the herbs, vegetables, fruits, and flowers found here are grown on owner Keo Sananikone's North Shore farm. Favorite dishes include Evil Jungle Prince (shrimp, vegetables, or chicken in a sauce flavored with basil, coconut milk, and red chili) and *chiang mai* salad (chicken salad seasoned with lemongrass, red chili, mint, and fish sauce). Consider ordering your food mild or medium. It'll still be hot, but not as hot as it *could* be. For dessert, the apple bananas (small, tart bananas grown in Hawai'i) in coconut milk are wonderful. ⊠ *2028 Kūhiō Ave., ☎ 808/951–9355. Reservations essential. AE, D, DC, MC, V. No lunch.*

Honolulu

American/Casual

$–$$ ✕ **California Pizza Kitchen.** This trio of dining and watering holes for young fast-trackers is worth the likely wait for a table. The pizzas have unusual toppings, such as Thai chicken, Peking duck, and Caribbean shrimp. The pastas are made fresh daily. At the Kāhala site, a glass atrium with tiled and mirrored walls and one side open to the shopping mall creates a sidewalk-café effect. The location on the top level of the Ala Moana Center offers a great respite for the weary shopper. ⊠ *Kāhala Mall, 4211 Wai'alae Ave., ☎ 808/737–9446; ⊠ Ala Moana Shopping Center, 1450 Ala Moana Blvd., ☎ 808/941–7715; ⊠ 554 Pearlridge Center Downtown, 'Aiea, ☎ 808/487–7741. Reservations not accepted. AE, D, DC, MC, V.*

$–$$ ✕ **Hard Rock Cafe.** The Honolulu branch of this international chain has its trademark rock-and-roll memorabilia on display along with

68

Honolulu Dining

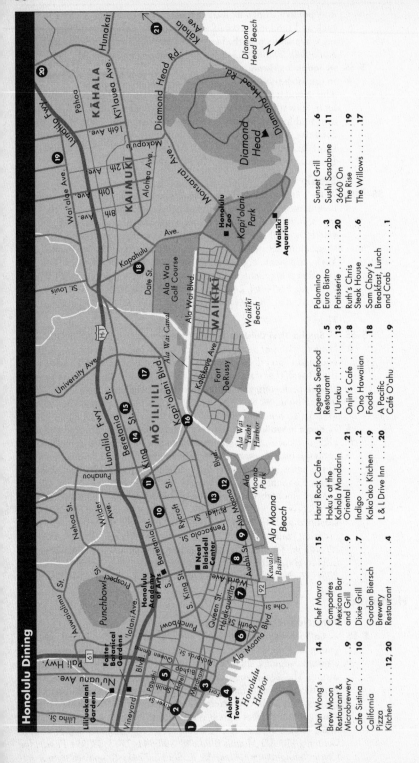

Alan Wong's **15**
Brew Moon
Restaurant &
Microbrewery **9**
Cafe Sistina **10**
California
Pizza
Kitchen **12, 20**

Chef Mavro **14**
Compadres
Mexican Bar
and Grill **9**
Dixie Grill **7**
Gordon Biersch
Brewery
Restaurant **4**

Hard Rock Cafe . . **16**
Hoku's at the
Kahala Mandarin
Oriental **21**
Indigo **2**
Kaka'ako Kitchen . . **9**
L & L Drive Inn . . **20**

Legends Seafood
Restaurant **5**
L'Uraku **13**
Onjin's Cafe **8**
'Ono Hawaiian
Foods **18**
A Pacific
Cafe O'ahu **9**

Palomino
Euro Bistro **3**
Patisserie **20**
Ruth's Chris
Steak House **6**
Sam Choy's
Breakfast, Lunch
and Crab **1**

Sunset Grill **6**
Sushi Sasabune . . **11**
3660 On **19**
The Rise **19**
The Willows **17**

Hawaiian surfboards and aloha shirts for added local flavor. Hard Rock has always sold more T-shirts than T-bones, so don't expect culinary surprises on its formula menu. The portion-controlled quarter-pound burgers hold sway, but don't overlook the 'ahi steak sandwiches or the watermelon baby-back ribs. French fries are, of course, a must. You can count on the sound system being loud, the energy being high, and waiting for a table during peak hours. ⊠ *1837 Kapi'olani Blvd.,* ☏ *808/955–7383. Reservations not accepted. AE, MC, V.*

$ ✕ **L & L Drive Inn.** In the Kāhala Mall, and at more than 40 neighborhood locations throughout the island, the "drive inn" serves up an impressive mix of Asian-American and Hawaiian-style plate lunches. Chicken *katsu* (cutlet), beef curry, and seafood mix plates include two scoops of rice and macaroni salad. There are also "mini" versions of the large-portion plates that include just one scoop of starch. This is great casual island dining, with prices that are very affordable. It's also a good place to pick up lunch before heading to the nearest beach park. ⊠ *Kāhala Mall, 4211 Waialae Ave.,* ☏ *808/732–4042. Reservations not accepted. No credit cards.*

Barbecue

$–$$ ✕ **Dixie Grill.** This southern-inspired eatery emphasizes just how much fun food can be. Why, there's even an outdoor sandbox for the kids! Dixie Grill specializes in baby-back ribs, smoked barbecue chicken, whole Dungeness crab, campfire steak, and fried catfish. Recipes for the barbecue sauces come from Memphis, the Carolinas, Georgia, and Texas. Save room for the Georgia peach cobbler. ⊠ *404 Ward Ave.,* ☏ *808/ 596–8359. AE, D, DC, MC, V.*

Chinese

$ ✕ **Legends Seafood Restaurant.** When touring Chinatown, take time out and do dim sum for lunch at this restaurant, where you'll hear Chinese spoken as often as English. With dim sum you'll have to attract the attention of the servers, who whip by tables with serving carts full of delectable goodies. Try the prawn dumplings and fresh vegetables, and note the Hawaiian influence on the food in the form of deep-fried taro puffs. (Taro is the root from which poi is made.) ⊠ *Chinese Cultural Plaza, 100 N. Beretania St.,* ☏ *808/532–1868. AE, D, DC, MC, V.*

Contemporary

$$–$$$ ✕ **Chef Mavro.** Named for chef-owner George Mavrothalassitis, for-
★ merly of the Four Seasons Maui and Halekūlani, this high-end bistro marries island ingredients with contemporary French techniques. The chef bakes onaga in a crust of Hawaiian salt, herbs, and *ogo* (seaweed), and his terrine of marinated Waimānalo vegetables comes with diced Japanese pickles. Three prix-fixe menus are accompanied by suggested wines available by the glass. The menu changes every six weeks, a testament to Chef Mavro's creativity and commitment to local, seasonal ingredients. ⊠ *1969 S. King St.,* ☏ *808/944–4714. Reservations essential. AE, DC, MC, V. No lunch.*

$$–$$$ ✕ **Hoku's at the Kahala Mandarin Oriental.** Hoku's is earning raves and plenty of awards for its ambience, menu, and service. Here you can sample a world of cuisines from Indian nan bread baked in a tandoori oven to wok-fried Szechuan shrimp. The presentation of items is as innovative as the decor, which features a bamboo floor. The restaurant is on the lobby level of the hotel, front and center overlooking Kahala Beach. ⊠ *Kāhala Mandarin Oriental, 5000 Kāhala Ave.,* ☏ *808/739–8777. AE, D, MC, V.*

$$ ✕ **Alan Wong's.** Chef-owner Alan Wong focuses heavily on Hawai-
★ ian-grown products to keep the flavors super fresh, and he's utterly creative, turning local grinds into beautifully presented epicurean

treats. For starters, get Da Bag, a puffed-up foil bag that's punctured at the table, revealing steamed clams, kālua pork, spinach, and shiitake mushrooms. Garlic mashed potatoes come with a black bean salsa, grilled pork chops with a coconut-ginger sweet potato puree. Don't miss the coconut sorbet served in a chocolate-and-macadamia-nut shell and surrounded by exotic fruits. The dining room is low-key, and there's a display kitchen. ⊠ *McCully Court, 1857 S. King St., 3rd floor,* ☎ *808/ 949-2526. AE, MC, V. No lunch.*

$$ ✕ **L'Uraku.** If you like a little whimsy with your wasabi, then you'll appreciate the decor of this Japanese-European fusion restaurant, which stays sunny with its collection of bright, patterned umbrellas hanging from the ceiling. On the menu are roasted-garlic-crusted 'ahi, *miyosaki* butterfish (prepared with miso and sake), and accompaniments such as miso osso buco and macadamia-nut pesto. ⊠ *1341 Kapi'olani Blvd.,* ☎ *808/955-0552. AE, D, MC, V.*

$$ ✕ **A Pacific Café O'ahu.** Take Asian, Mediterranean, and Indian cuisines
★ and combine them with a love of Hawai'i's homegrown products. The result: chef Jean-Marie Josselin's wonderful menu, a true O'ahu standout. Lunch highlights include a shiitake-mushroom sandwich with mozzarella, and a mixed green salad with grilled Japanese eggplant, goat cheese, and chili vinaigrette. At dinner the wok-charred mahimahi with a garlic-sesame crust and lime-ginger beurre blanc is superb. ⊠ *Ward Centre, 1200 Ala Moana Blvd.,* ☎ *808/593-0035. AE, DC, MC, V.*

$$ ✕ **3660 on the Rise.** Light hardwoods, frosted glass, green marble, and
★ black granite mix in a leisurely fashion here, and there's almost always a full house. Homegrown ingredients are combined with European flavors: Dungeness crab cakes are prepared in a nest of angel hair and served with a ginger-cilantro aioli, and *pūlehu* (broiled) lamb chops are intensified by garlic, pepper, rosemary, and thyme. The restaurant is known for its spectacular desserts, so save room for the warm chocolate soufflé cake with espresso sauce and vanilla ice cream. This stellar eatery is a 10-minute drive from Waikīkī in the up-and-coming culinary mecca of Kaimukī. ⊠ *3660 Wai'alae Ave.,* ☎ *808/737-1177. AE, DC, MC, V.*

$-$$ ✕ **Brew Moon Restaurant & Microbrewery.** The menu states "A vision for food, a passion for beer," and Brew Moon lives up to both promises. Entrées are varied and creative, from sesame-seared 'ahi to fire-roasted ribs and grilled pizzas. The molasses and cumin-charred pork tenderloin comes with garlic mashed potatoes, and there's a spicy curry chicken. Large picture windows proudly display the brewery and fermentation room where six beers are crafted, including a low-calorie light-alcohol brew and a rich copper-color ale. The dessert specialty is a float made with fresh-brewed root beer. This is a favorite spot for business lunches and after-work drinks, so expect a high-energy atmosphere. Vie for a table on the 150-seat lānai if you want a more relaxed setting for cocktails and conversation. ⊠ *Ward Centre, 1200 Ala Moana Blvd.,* ☎ *808/593-0088. AE, D, DC, MC, V.*

$-$$ ✕ **Gordon Biersch Brewery Restaurant.** Snuggling up to Honolulu
★ Harbor, this indoor-outdoor eatery, part of a West Coast–based chain of microbreweries, is Aloha Tower Marketplace's busiest. The menu is American with an island twist, from chicken skewers in a hot peanut-coconut sauce to fresh-seared 'ahi in a *sansho* (Japanese pepper) crust. There is also a variety of pastas and pizzas. You can smell the garlic fries the moment you walk in. All that spicy food goes well with the beer. Ask for tastes of the dark, medium, and light brews before choosing your favorite. ⊠ *Aloha Tower Marketplace, 1 Aloha Tower Dr.,* ☎ *808/599-4877. AE, D, DC, MC, V.*

$-$$ ✕ **Indigo.** Indigo set the pace for a new generation of downtown Honolulu eateries. The decor emphasizes wicker and track lighting, and there's a charming back lānai that shields you from the downtown hubbub. Owner Glenn Chu's variations on foods from his Chinese heritage include crispy wontons stuffed with hot goat cheese, Szechuan peppered beef loin in black bean sauce, and *bao* buns (steamed wheat-flour buns). The restaurant is within walking distance of the Hawai'i Theatre. ✉ *1121 Nu'uanu Ave.,* ☎ *808/521–2900. AE, D, DC, MC, V.*

$–$$ ✕ **Onjin's Cafe.** Chef Onjin Kim's newest venture is this cafe' near Victoria Ward Centers in Kaka'ako. At lunchtime, sit at the counter and
★ order fresh seafood dishes with a touch of Asian influence, such as the crispy *moi* (threadfish) with ginger and soy sauce. Evenings, dine on crab in almond flour, charred 'ahi, or roasted duck for your entrée. ✉ *1225 Hopaka St.,* ☎ *808/591–0253. AE, MC, V. Closed Sun.*

$–$$ ✕ **Palomino Euro-Bistro.** Palomino's menu fuses French, Spanish, and Ital-
★ ian cuisines. Entrées from the wood-burning oven include mahimahi with creamy polenta, fig-caper-olive relish, and mussels, and Basque-style chicken. For seafood, consider the cedar-roasted salmon, seafood ravioli, or the crab cakes with pesto beurre blanc. This downtown Honolulu restaurant has art deco decor, with handblown glass chandeliers, a grand staircase, and a 50-ft marble-and-mahogany bar. ✉ *Harbor Court, 66 Queen St., 3rd floor,* ☎ *808/528–2400. AE, D, DC, MC, V.*

$–$$ ✕ **Sunset Grill.** The sweet smell of wood smoke greets you as you enter the sleek Sunset Grill, which specializes in kiawe-broiled bistro cuisine. Choose from salmon cakes; kiawe-grilled ribs; or the salade niçoise, served with marinated grilled 'ahi and big enough for a whole dinner. The trout and scallops, cooked in a wood oven, are both very good. Accompany your meal with a selection from an extensive 400-bottle wine list. ✉ *Restaurant Row, 500 Ala Moana Blvd.,* ☎ *808/521–4409. AE, DC, MC, V.*

$ ✕ **Kaka'ako Kitchen.** This is where the owners of the restaurant 3660 on the Rise turned their talents to perfecting the art of "plate lunch." Fresh fish entrées mix with pan-seared chicken salad, teriyaki chicken sandwich, sautéed mahimahi, and vegetarian offerings such as tofu burgers. You can even order brown rice and a side of mesclun greens. If you're fond of bread pudding, make this your dessert order. Best yet, you can order takeout and head across the street to Ala Moana Beach Park for a meal with a view. ✉ *Ward Centre, 1200 Ala Moana Blvd.,* ☎ *808/596–7488. Reservations not accepted. No credit cards. Closed Sun. No dinner.*

German

$–$$ ✕ **Patisserie.** By day, this bakery in the Kāhala Mall is a deli, but five nights a week it turns into a 24-seat restaurant with great German food, a rarity in Hawai'i. The menu is small—only 10 entrées—but any choice is a good one. The Wiener schnitzel is juicy within its crispy crust, and veal ribs are garnished with a sprig of rosemary. Try the potato pancakes, crisp outside and soft inside, joined by a healthy spoonful of applesauce. The carrot salad is as delicious as the pastries. ✉ *Kāhala Mall, 4211 Wai'alae Ave.,* ☎ *808/735–4402. Reservations not accepted. MC, V. Closed Sun.–Mon.*

Hawaiian

$$–$$$ ✕ **The Willows.** Tucked away amid low-rise apartment buildings, this restaurant gives little clue from the outside as to the wonderful ambience that awaits within its walls. Human-made ponds are sprinkled among the thatched dining pavilions, and you'll also find a tiny wedding chapel and a gallery gift shop. The food, served buffet-style, includes the trademark Willows' curry along with roasted portobello mushrooms, *laulau* (a steamed bundle of ti leaves containing pork, butterfish, and taro tops), and pineapple-mango barbecued ribs. Willows,

opened in 1944 and closed for much of the '90s, was bought, restored, and reopened in 1999 with a renewed reputation for historic Hawaiian hospitality. ✉ *901 Hausten St.,* ☎ *808/952–9200. Reservations essential. AE, D, MC, V.*

$　✗ **'Ono Hawaiian Foods.** The adventurous in search of a real "local food" experience should head to this no-frills hangout. You know it has to be good if residents are waiting in line to get in. Here you can sample poi, *lomilomi* salmon (salmon massaged until tender and served with minced onions and tomatoes), laulau, kālua pork, and *haupia* (a light, gelatinlike dessert made from coconut). Appropriately enough, the Hawaiian word *'ono* means delicious. ✉ *726 Kapahulu Ave.,* ☎ *808/737–2275. Reservations not accepted. No credit cards. Closed Sun.*

Italian

$–$$　✗ **Cafe Sistina.** Step off a busy Honolulu street and right into this tiny, artistic café. Sergio Mitrotti has gained quite a following with his inventive Italian-Mediterranean cuisine. He's concocted an appetizer of goat cheese, chili peppers, garlic, prosciutto, and Greek olives, and he fills ravioli with such delights as Gorgonzola, porcini mushrooms, red peppers, and pancetta cream. Linguine *alla puttanesca* comes alive with tomatoes, onions, capers, and kalamata olives. Fresh chewy bread comes with a pesto butter to die for. A graphic artist by training, Mitrotti has painted the café's walls with Italianesque scenes. ✉ *1314 S. King St.,* ☎ *808/596–0061. AE, MC, V.*

Japanese

$–$$　✗ **Sushi Sasabune.** This tiny sushi bar is the home of the island's most famous "trust me" sushi. Sit at the bar, and eat what the chef chooses for you. And don't expect a California roll. It might be something as exotic as teriyaki octopus. Sasabune's sushi specials also include crab, salmon, and tuna, and come with miso soup, seaweed salad, and adzuki bean ice cream. The sushi is authentically Japanese, with fish and seafood flown in from around the globe. ✉ *1419 S. King St.,* ☎ *808/947–3800. Reservations essential. AE, D, DC, MC, V.*

Mexican

$–$$　✗ **Compadres Mexican Bar and Grill.** The after-work crowd gathers here for potent margaritas and yummy pūpū. An outdoor terrace is best for cocktails and chips. Inside, the wooden floors, colorful photographs, and lively paintings create a festive setting for imaginative Mexican specialties. Fajitas, baby-back ribs, *huevos rancheros* (eggs with salsa, beans, and guacamole and served on a tortilla), and grilled shrimp are just a few of the many offerings. ✉ *Ward Centre, 1200 Ala Moana Blvd.,* ☎ *808/591–8307. D, MC, V.*

Seafood

$$–$$$　✗ **Sam Choy's Breakfast, Lunch and Crab.** In this casual setting, great
★　　for families, diners can get crackin' with crab, friendly with fried rice, and filled up with an abundance of both seafood and landlubber fare. This eatery's warehouse size sets the tone for its large portions. An on-site microbrewery brews eight varieties of Big Aloha beer. Sam Choy's is located in downtown Honolulu's more industrial area, on the highway heading toward Honolulu International Airport. ✉ *580 Nimitz Hwy.,* ☎ *808/545–7979. AE, D, DC, MC, V.*

Steak

$$–$$$　✗ **Ruth's Chris Steak House.** Here's a steak joint that doesn't look like one. This pastel-hue dining room on Restaurant Row caters to meat lovers by serving top-of-the-line steak cuts. The portions are large, so bring an appetite. Side orders include generous salads and an ultracreamy

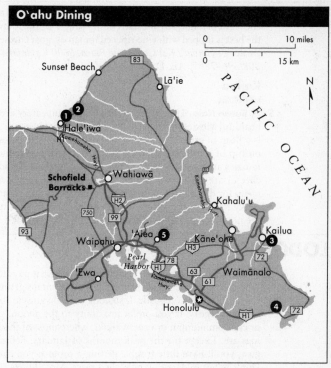

O'ahu Dining

spinach au gratin. Charbroiled fish, veal, and lamb chops provide nice alternatives to the steaks. For dessert, try the house special, a bread pudding happily soaked in whiskey sauce. ⊠ *Restaurant Row, 500 Ala Moana Ave.,* ☎ *808/599–3860. AE, DC, MC, V.*

Around the Island

Hale'iwa

AMERICAN/CASUAL

$–$$ ✕ **Haleiwa Joe's.** A day of surfing or just watching the big wave riders can work up an appetite. Haleiwa Joe's, located just past the Hale'iwa Bridge, serves up steaks, prime rib, and seafood in sauces ranging from coconut to sweet-and-sour. Come in time to watch the sun set over Hale'iwa Harbor; windows overlook the harbor, or you can watch from the lānai. ⊠ *66-0011 Kamehameha Hwy.,* ☎ *808/637–8005. Reservations not accepted. AE, DC, MC, V.*

$ ✕ **Kua 'Aina Sandwich.** A must-stop spot during a drive around the island, this tiny North Shore eatery has a few tables inside and a few more on the lānai next to the road. Burgers are heaped with bacon, cheese, salsa, or pineapple, and the grilled mahimahi sandwich comes with a homemade tartar sauce. Do try the French fries. You can also check out Kua 'Aina's newest location across from the Ward Centre in Honolulu (⊠ 1116 Auahi St., 808/591–9133). ⊠ *66-214 Kamehameha Hwy.,* ☎ *808/637–6067. Reservations not accepted. No credit cards.*

Hawai'i Kai

CONTEMPORARY

$–$$ ✕ **Roy's.** Two walls of windows offer views of Maunalua Bay and Diamond Head in the distance, and a glassed-in kitchen affords views of what's cooking at Roy Yamaguchi's Hawai'i Kai venture. This is a noisy two-story restaurant with a devoted following. The menu matches

Hawai'i flavors with Euro-Asian accents. It's hard to find a better blackened 'ahi in a hot, soy-mustard butter sauce. Of the individual pizzas, the best is topped with vine-ripened tomatoes, goat cheese, and roasted garlic. ⊠ *Hawai'i Kai Corporate Plaza, 6600 Kalaniana'ole Hwy.,* ☎ *808/396–7697. AE, D, DC, MC, V.*

Kailua

MEXICAN

$ ✕ **Bueno Nalo.** The owners of this family-run eatery are dedicated to healthful Mexican cuisine, and the food is reliably good. *Topopo* salad is a heap of greens, tomatoes, onions, tuna, olives, cheese, and beans on top of a tortilla. Combination plates with tacos, enchiladas, and tamales are bargains, and the chiles *rellenos* (roasted and stuffed with cheese) are expertly seasoned. Families appreciate the *keiki* (child's) menu for diners 10 and under. Velvet paintings and piñatas add a fun, funky flavor to the setting. Reservations for parties of fewer than six are not accepted. ⊠ *20 Kainehe St.,* ☎ *808/263–1999. AE, MC, V.*

LODGING

O'ahu has a wide range of accommodations, so it pays to plan ahead. First consider whether your dream vacation entails getting away from the usual hustle and bustle. If so, look at the listings in the Around the Island category. If you prefer proximity to the action, go for a hotel or condominium in or near Waikīkī, where most of the island's lodgings are. Except for the peak months of January, February, and August, you'll have little trouble getting a room if you call in advance. Don't be intimidated by published rates. Most hotels offer a variety of package options and special deals, such as sports, honeymoon, room and car, and kids stay/eat free promotions. These extras can make vacations even more affordable, so ask about them when you book.

Below is a selective list of lodging choices in each price category. For an explanation of price categories, *see* Lodging *in* Smart Travel Tips. For a complete list of every hotel and condominium on the island, write or call the Hawai'i Visitors & Convention Bureau for a free *Accommodation Guide*. It details amenities and lists each hotel's proximity to the beach.

Waikīkī

$$$$ 🏨 **Aston Waikīkī Beach Tower.** On Kalākaua Avenue, but set back from the street on the mauka side, this 39-story luxury condominium resort has the atmosphere of an intimate vest-pocket hotel. The property has the usual amenities, oversize rooms, and views of Waikīkī that you'd expect from a larger beachfront resort. Stylish one- and two-bedroom suites have complete kitchens, washer-dryers, and private lānai. There is twice-daily maid service, and a heated swimming pool is on the recreation deck. ⊠ *2470 Kalākaua Ave., Honolulu 96815,* ☎ *808/926–6400 or 800/922–7866,* FAX *808/926–7380,* WEB *www.aston-hotels.com. 140 suites. Kitchenettes, minibars, room service, pool, sauna, concierge. AE, D, DC, MC, V.*

$$$$ 🏨 **Halekūlani.** Today's sleek, modern, and luxurious oceanside
★ Halekūlani exemplifies the translation of its name—the "house befitting heaven." A masterful blend of the past and present is set within an architectural design that incorporates the original estate's main building. The service is impeccable, and the mood is tranquil amid the frenetic activity of Waikīkī. Guest rooms are spacious, artfully appointed in marble and wood. Ninety percent have ocean views, and each has its own lānai. Dozens of little touches, such as fruit baskets, bathrobes,

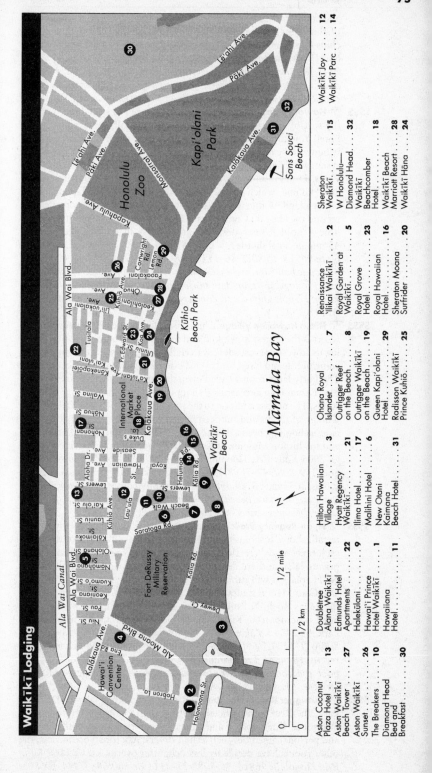

Waikīkī Lodging

Sans Souci
Beach

Kapi'olani
Park

Honolulu
Zoo

Kūhio
Beach Park

Waikīkī
Beach

International
Market
Place

Duke's

Māmala Bay

Fort DeRussy
Military
Reservation

Hawai'i
Convention
Center

Ala Wai Canal

0   1/2 mile
0   1/2 km

and complimentary newspapers, are sure to please. The hotel has three of the finest restaurants—House Without a Key, La Mer, and Orchids—in Honolulu and an oceanside pool with a giant orchid mosaic. ⊠ *2199 Kālia Rd., Honolulu 96815,* ☎ *808/923–2311 or 800/367–2343,* ℻ *808/926–8004,* WEB *www.halekulani.com. 412 rooms, 44 suites. 3 restaurants, 3 bars, minibars, room service, pool, exercise room, beach, concierge, business services, meeting room. AE, DC, MC, V.*

$$$$ 🏨 **Hawaiʻi Prince Hotel Waikīkī.** The Prince is a sleek high-rise with the sort of sophisticated interior design generally reserved for a city hotel. You know you're in Waikīkī, however, when you look out your window at the Ala Wai Yacht Harbor. Guest rooms have high-tech phone systems and data ports along with floor-to-ceiling windows with ocean views. Hotel restaurants include the elegant Prince Court restaurant and Hakone, which serves some of the best authentic Japanese food on the island. Within walking distance to the Ala Moana Shopping Center and the Hawaiʻi Convention Center, this hotel also has its own 27-hole Arnold Palmer–designed golf course in Ewa Beach, about a 45-minute hotel shuttle ride from Waikīki. ⊠ *100 Holomoana St., Honolulu 96815,* ☎ *808/956–1111 or 800/321–6248,* ℻ *808/946–0811,* WEB *www.hawaiiprincehotel.com. 467 rooms, 54 suites. 3 restaurants, lobby lounge, in-room data ports, minibars, room service, pool, hair salon, 27-hole golf course, concierge, business services, meeting room. AE, DC, MC, V.*

$$$$ 🏨 **Hilton Hawaiian Village.** This lavishly landscaped 20-acre oceanfront
★ resort is the largest in Waikīkī and a destination unto itself. Surrounding its towers are cascading waterfalls, a 10,000-square-ft super pool, colorful fish and birds, and even a botanical garden with labeled flora. The fairly large rooms have Polynesian-style decor. The hotel's Rainbow Bazaar is an international shopping arcade with dozens of specialty stores. The newest addition to the property is the 24-story Kalia Tower, with guest rooms and suites equipped with work spaces to accommodate technology needs. The tower also houses a multilevel health spa and the Bishop Museum at Kalia Hawaiian Cultural Activities Center. ⊠ *2005 Kālia Rd., Honolulu 96815,* ☎ *808/949–4321 or 800/445–8667,* ℻ *808/947–7898,* WEB *www.hawaiianvillage.hilton.com. 2,180 rooms, 365 suites. 6 restaurants, lounges, minibars, room service, 3 pools, spa, exercise room, beach, shops, children's programs (ages 5–12), concierge, business services, meeting room. AE, D, DC, MC, V.*

$$$$ 🏨 **Hyatt Regency Waikīkī.** An open-air atrium with a two-story waterfall, shops, live music, and Harry's Bar make this one of the liveliest lobbies anywhere, though you may get lost in it. Guest rooms have private lānai and are decorated in soft creams and ocean blues. The Na Hoʻola Spa will pamper you, and poolside massages are available. The Ciao Mein restaurant serves both Italian and Chinese food, and the Texas Rock 'N Roll Sushi Bar is where East meets western. The hotel is across from Kūhiō Beach and a short walk from Kapiʻolani Park. ⊠ *2424 Kalākaua Ave., Honolulu 96815,* ☎ *808/923–1234 or 800/233–1234,* ℻ *808/923–7839,* WEB *www.hyattwaikiki.com. 1,212 rooms, 18 suites. 4 restaurants, lobby lounges, minibars, room service, pool, spa, shops, children's programs (ages 5–12), concierge, business services. AE, D, DC, MC, V.*

$$$$ 🏨 **Outrigger Reef on the Beach.** Right on the beach near Ft. DeRussy Park, the Reef is the official hotel for the Honolulu Marathon each December. Guest rooms and suites have refrigerators, coffeemakers, and personal amenities such as hair dryers. Ask for an ocean view; the other rooms have decidedly less delightful overlooks. ⊠ *2169 Kālia Rd., Honolulu 96815,* ☎ *808/923–3111 or 800/688–7444,* ℻ *808/ 924–4957,* WEB *www.outrigger.com. 846 rooms, 39 suites. 2 restaurants, 4 bars, no-smoking rooms, refrigerators, room service, pool, exercise* *room, beach, nightclub, children's programs (ages 5–12), meeting room. AE, D, DC, MC, V.*

$$$$ ⊞ **Outrigger Waikīkī on the Beach.** Outrigger Hotels & Resorts' star property, on Kalākaua Avenue stands next to some of the nicest sands in Waikīkī. Rooms have a Polynesian motif, and each has a lānai. The top four floors are for members of the Voyager Club and include a guest lounge that serves Continental breakfast and sunset appetizers daily. For more than 25 years, the main ballroom has been home to the sizzling Society of Seven entertainers. The beachfront Duke's Canoe Club is a dining hot spot. ⊠ *2335 Kalākaua Ave., Honolulu 96815, ☎ 808/923–0711 or 800/688–7444, 𝖥𝖠𝖷 800/622–4852, 𝖶𝖤𝖡 www.outrigger.com. 500 rooms, 30 suites. 6 restaurants, 5 bars, lobby lounge, kitchenettes, minibars, room service, pool. AE, D, DC, MC, V.*

$$$$ ⊞ **Renaissance 'Ilikai Waikīkī.** At press time this hotel was undergoing a renaissance of its own with a major renovation of its guest rooms and public spaces; the goal is to restore the feeling of the Hawaiian experience that made this place a favorite when it first opened in the mid-1960s. Guest rooms are spacious, with kitchenettes, and offer Internet access via television screens and cordless keyboards. Crowds gather at sunset on the lobby-level deck for the torchlighting ceremony, hula dancing, and live Hawaiian music. For sky-high dining, there's Sarento's Top of the 'I' Italian restaurant. ⊠ *1777 Ala Moana Blvd., Honolulu 96815, ☎ 808/949–3811 or 800/645–5687, 𝖥𝖠𝖷 808/947–0892, 𝖶𝖤𝖡 www.ilikaihotel.com. 728 rooms, 51 suites. 4 restaurants, 2 lobby lounges, minibars, room service, 2 pools, 7 tennis courts, business services, meeting room. AE, D, DC, MC, V.*

$$$$ ⊞ **Royal Hawaiian Hotel.** One of the hotels that made Waikīkī famous,
★ the Royal Hawaiian has been host to movie stars, royalty, and some of the world's wealthiest travelers. Called the "Pink Palace of the Pacific" due to its architecture and pink exterior, the Royal was built in 1927 by Matson Navigation Company to accommodate its luxury-cruise passengers. The hotel retains the feel of that historic time with its high ceilings and period furniture. Pink telephones in each room and corridors of pink carpeting add a dreamy quality. The modern wing is more expensive, but for charm, the rooms in the Historic Wing are a treasure. You can dine by the water's edge at the Surf Room, sip a mai tai at the bar that made that drink famous, or lounge on the sand on the hotel's private beach. ⊠ *2259 Kalākaua Ave., Honolulu 96815, ☎ 808/923–7311 or 800/782–9488, 𝖥𝖠𝖷 808/924–7098, 𝖶𝖤𝖡 www.royal-hawaiian.com. 472 rooms, 53 suites. 3 restaurants, bar, minibars, room service, pool, concierge, business services, meeting room. AE, DC, MC, V.*

$$$$ ⊞ **Sheraton Moana Surfrider.** The first hotel built on Waikīkī Beach and now listed on the National Register of Historic Places, the Moana opened its doors in 1901. The hotel has since merged with the newer Surfrider next door, but you can appreciate the history of the place by requesting a room in the Moana Banyan Wing. These rooms are small by today's standards, but are well-appointed and charming. For more spacious accommodations with a modern feel, the Diamond and Tower wings are a better choice. The Banyan Court is the focal point for beachfront activity, and you can relax on the gracious veranda for high tea. ⊠ *2365 Kalākaua Ave., Honolulu 96815, ☎ 808/922–3111 or 800/782–9488, 𝖥𝖠𝖷 808/923–0308. 750 rooms, 41 suites. 3 restaurants, bar, lobby lounges, snack bar, minibars, room service, pool, beach, concierge, meeting room. AE, DC, MC, V.*

$$$$ ⊞ **Sheraton Waikīkī.** Towering over its neighbors, the Sheraton takes center stage on Waikīkī Beach. If you like constant activity, the Sheraton Waikīkī has it: entertainment venues, poolside hula, year-round children's programs, and the host of many meetings and conventions. Guest rooms are spacious, and many have grand views of Diamond

Head. The hotel is just steps away from the multilevel Royal Hawaiian Shopping Center and next to the Royal Hawaiian Hotel. Be sure to take the glass-walled elevator up to the Hanohano Room, an elegant dining room with breathtaking panoramas of the ocean and Waikīkī. The hotel conducts historical and nature tours, one of which spotlights the Honu sea turtles that can be viewed in the Pacific waters at the hotel's edge. ⊠ *2255 Kalākaua Ave., Honolulu 96815,* ☎ *808/922–4422 or 800/325–3535,* FAX *808/923–8785,* WEB *www.sheraton-hawaii.com. 1,709 rooms, 130 suites. 5 restaurants, lobby lounges, minibars, room service, 2 pools, health club, beach, shops, dance club, children's programs (ages 5–12), concierge, business services, meeting rooms. AE, DC, MC, V.*

$$$$ **W Honolulu—Diamond Head.** Created with the business traveler in mind, W Honolulu offers 24-hour concierge and room service, and each guest room has a private balcony and amenities such as in-room data ports, CD players, and VCRs with video library. The luxurious trademark W beds wrap you in 250-thread-count sheets, and rooms are elegantly appointed with teak furnishings, a Balinese island motif, and spectacular oceanfront views. The hotel's signature restaurant is the Diamond Head Grill. This Starwood Resort property is located beachfront on the quiet edge of Waikīkī across from Kapi'olani Park. ⊠ *2885 Kalākaua Ave., Honolulu 96815,* ☎ *808/922–1700 or 888/528–9465,* FAX *808/923–2249. 44 rooms, 4 suites. Restaurant, room service, in-room data ports, in-room VCRs, beach, dry cleaning, laundry service, concierge, business services. AE, D, DC, MC, V.*

$$$–$$$$ **Aston Waikīkī Sunset.** Families enjoy this high-rise condominium resort near Diamond Head, one block from Waikīkī Beach and two blocks from the Honolulu Zoo. One-bedroom suites have complete kitchens, daily maid service, and private lānai. There are a guest activities deck, tennis, outdoor barbecues, a children's playground, and an on-site store. ⊠ *229 Paoakalani Ave., Honolulu 96815,* ☎ *808/ 922–0511 or 800/922–7866,* FAX *808/922–8580,* WEB *www.aston-hotels. com. 307 suites. Snack bar, kitchenettes, pool, sauna, tennis court, playground. AE, D, DC, MC, V.*

$$$–$$$$ **Doubletree Alana Waikīkī.** Leisure and business travelers appreciate this hotel's location on the west edge of Waikīkī, two blocks from Ala Moana Shopping Center, Ala Moana Beach Park, and the Hawai'i Convention Center. The lobby of this 19-story high-rise is modern and attractive, with rotating exhibits of local artists' work. Guest rooms have private lānai with panoramic views of Waikīkī, the ocean, or the mountains. The staff of this boutique property has a reputation for hospitality, and service is attentive, plus you get the trademark Doubletree chocolate-chip cookies upon arrival. Those doing business globally like the 24-hour business-center services. Also open round-the-clock is the fitness center. ⊠ *1956 Ala Moana Blvd., Honolulu 96815,* ☎ *808/941–7275 or 800/367–6070,* FAX *808/949–0996. 268 rooms, 45 suites. Restaurant, lobby lounge, minibars, room service, pool, exercise room, concierge, business services. AE, D, MC, V.*

$$$–$$$$ **New Otani Kaimana Beach Hotel.** Polished to a shine, this hotel is ★   open to the trade winds and furnished with big, comfortable chairs. The ambience is cheerful and charming, and the lobby has a happy, unpretentious feel. Best of all, it's right on the beach at the quiet end of Waikīkī, practically at the foot of Diamond Head. Rooms are smallish but very nicely appointed, with soothing pastel decor and off-white furnishings. ⊠ *2863 Kalākaua Ave., Honolulu 96815,* ☎ *808/923– 1555 or 800/356–8264,* FAX *808/922–9404,* WEB *www.kaimana.com. 119 rooms, 6 suites. 2 restaurants, lobby lounge, minibars, room service, meeting room. AE, D, DC, MC, V.*

$$$-$$$$ ⊞ **Radisson Waikīkī Prince Kūhiō.** Two blocks from Kūhiō Beach, this 37-story high-rise is on the Diamond Head end of Waikīkī. Hawaiian-print bedspreads and artwork in sepia, cream, and earth tones decorate the rooms, which also have coffeemakers, tiny refrigerators, hair dryers, and data ports. Cupid's, the lobby lounge, plays Hawaiian music, and two restaurants serve contemporary or Chinese cuisine. ⊠ *2500 Kūhiō Ave., Honolulu 96815,* ☎ *808/922–8811 or 800/557–4422,* ℻ *808/923–0330. 620 rooms. 2 restaurants, lobby lounge, in-room data ports, room service, pool, hot tub, exercise room, business services. AE, D, DC, MC, V.*

$$$-$$$$ ⊞ **Waikīkī Beach Marriott Resort.** On the eastern edge of Waikīkī, the hotel is across from Kūhiō Beach and close to Kapiʻolani Park, the zoo, and the aquarium. Formerly the Hawaiian Regent Hotel, the resort was recently acquired by Marriott International, who at press time was planning a major renovation intended to restore the hotel's reputation as a showplace for Hawaiian hospitality. Its two towers, two lobbies, and courtyards are open to ocean breezes and sunlight. The Kalākaua Tower's spacious guest rooms are some of the largest in Waikīkī, and offer unparalleled views of the Waikīkī strip or Diamond Head. Family rooms can accommodate sleeping for six and have two bathrooms. ⊠ *2552 Kalākaua Ave., Honolulu 96815,* ☎ *808/922–6611 or 800/ 367–5370,* ℻ *808/921–5222,* ⊞ *www.marriotthotels.com. 1,337 rooms, 9 suites. 5 restaurants, lobby lounges, minibars, room service, 2 pools, tennis court, exercise room, dance club, concierge, business services, meeting room. AE, D, MC, V.*

$$$-$$$$ ⊞ **Waikīkī Beachcomber Hotel.** With an excellent location right across
★ the street from Waikīkī Beach, the Beachcomber is also a short walk from the Royal Hawaiian Shopping Center and the International Market Place. Rooms have contemporary furnishings, prints by local artists, and private lānai. Two evening shows are presented here: the venerable "Don Ho" and "The Magic of Polynesia." ⊠ *2300 Kalākaua Ave., Honolulu 96815,* ☎ *808/922–4646 or 800/622–4646,* ℻ *808/923– 4889,* ⊞ *www.waikikibeachcomber.com. 487 rooms, 11 suites. Restaurant, lobby lounge, snack bar, no-smoking rooms, minibars, refrigerators, room service, pool. AE, DC, MC, V.*

$$$-$$$$ ⊞ **Waikīkī Parc.** Billed as an executive boutique hotel and owned and
★ managed by the same group that manages the Halekūlani across the street, where guests have signing privileges, the Parc offers the same attention to detail in service and architectural design but lacks a beach-front location. The lobby is light and airy, and guest rooms are done in cool blues and whites and lots of rattan. The hotel has a fine Japanese restaurant called Kacho, and the lovely Parc Café is known for its sumptuous buffets. Business travelers can depend on the 24-hour services of the business center, which includes a boardroom. ⊠ *2233 Helumoa Rd., Honolulu 96815,* ☎ *808/921–7272 or 800/422–0450,* ℻ *808/931–6638,* ⊞ *www.waikikiparc.com. 298 rooms. 2 restaurants, in-room safes, minibars, room service, pool, exercise room, concierge, business services. AE, D, DC, MC, V.*

$$$ ⊞ **Royal Garden at Waikīkī.** From the outside, this 25-story boutique hotel looks like the average Waikīkī high-rise. But step inside and it whispers elegance, from the marble and etched glass in the lobby to the genuine graciousness of the staff. Guest rooms have sitting areas, private lānai, and marble and brass baths. There's a free shuttle service to and from Kapiʻolani Park, Ala Moana Shopping Center, Royal Hawaiian Shopping Center, and duty-free shops. ⊠ *440 ʻOlohana St., Honolulu 96815,* ☎ *808/943–0202 or 800/367–5666,* ℻ *808/946–8777,* ⊞ *www. royalgardens.com. 202 rooms, 18 suites. 2 restaurants, lobby lounge, in-room safes, refrigerators, room service, 2 pools, exercise room, business services, meeting room. AE, D, DC, MC, V.*

$$$ ⊞ **Waikīkī Joy.** This boutique hotel is a lesser-known gem. The location is great, tucked away on a quiet side street yet still close to Waikīkī's restaurants, shops, and entertainment. One tower has all suites, and another has standard hotel rooms. Units have either ocean or partial ocean views. Each has a lānai, a whirlpool bath, a deluxe stereo system, and a control panel by the bed. ⊠ *320 Lewers St., Honolulu 96815,* ☎ *808/923–2300 or 800/922–7866,* ℻ *808/924–4010,* WEB *www.aston-hotels.com. 50 rooms, 44 suites. Lobby lounge, kitchenettes, minibars, pool, sauna. AE, D, DC, MC, V.*

$$–$$$ ⊞ **Ohana Royal Islander.** Outrigger's Ohana hotels promise clean, comfortable accommodations, with conveniences such as refrigerators and laundry services, at a value price. The Royal Islander is just a two-minute walk from a very nice section of Waikīkī Beach. Each unit has a private lānai, and you can choose from studios, one-bedroom apartments, or suites. Guests have access to pools at other Outrigger hotels. ⊠ *2164 Kālia Rd., Honolulu 96815,* ☎ *808/922–1961 or 800/462–6262,* ℻ *808/923–4632,* WEB *www.ohanahotels.com. 94 rooms, 7 suites. In-room safes, coin laundry. AE, D, DC, MC, V.*

$$–$$$ ⊞ **Queen Kapi'olani Hotel.** This 19-story hotel a half-block from the beach appeals to those in search of clean, basic accommodations within walking distance of the water and Waikīkī's main attractions. Some rooms have kitchenettes, and there's a large pool and sundeck on the third floor. ⊠ *150 Kapahulu Ave., Honolulu 96815,* ☎ *808/922–1941 or 800/367–5004,* ℻ *808/922–2694,* WEB *www.castle-group.com. 308 rooms, 7 suites. 2 restaurants, bar, refrigerators, room service, pool, meeting room. AE, D, DC, MC, V.*

$$ ⊞ **Aston Coconut Plaza Hotel.** With its intimate size and service, Coconut Plaza, on the Ala Wai Canal and three blocks from the beach, is a true boutique hotel. Tropical plantation decor features rattan furnishings and floral bedspreads. Guest rooms have private lānai, and all except standard-view rooms come with kitchenettes. Free Continental breakfast is served daily on the lobby veranda. ⊠ *450 Lewers St., Honolulu 96815,* ☎ *808/923–8828 or 800/882–9696,* ℻ *808/923–3473,* WEB *www.aston-hotels.com. 70 rooms, 11 suites. Kitchenettes, pool, coin laundry, meeting room. AE, D, DC, MC, V.*

$$ ⊞ **The Breakers.** The Breakers' two-story buildings surround the pool and overlook gardens filled with exotic tropical flowers. A throwback to the early 1960s, guest rooms have Japanese-style shoji doors and carefully chosen decor. Rooms come with kitchenettes, bath with shower only, and lānai. Guests return here year after year to soak up the laid-back Old Hawai'i atmosphere. It's a couple blocks from the beach and from Waikīkī restaurants. ⊠ *250 Beach Walk, Honolulu 96815,* ☎ *808/923–3181,* ℻ *808/923–7174,* WEB *www.breakers-hawaii.com. 64 units. Kitchenettes, pool. AE, DC, MC, V.*

$$ ⊞ **Diamond Head Bed and Breakfast.** The two guest rooms at this bed-and-breakfast on the southeastern edge of Kapi'olani Park are big, have private bath, are tropical in style, and open to a lānai and large backyard that makes the hustle and bustle of Waikīkī seem light years away. Hostess Joanne Trotter has filled the large living spaces with modern artwork and furnishings created for tropical comfort. ⊠ *3240 Noela Dr., Honolulu 96815,* ☎ *808/885–4550,* ℻ *808/885–0559. Reservations: Hawai'i's Best Bed and Breakfasts, Box 563, Kamuela, 96743,* ☎ *808/885–4550 or 800/262–9912,* ℻ *808/885–0559,* WEB *www.bestbnb.com. 2 rooms. No credit cards.*

$$ ⊞ **Hawaiiana Hotel.** Step back in time to Old Hawai'i at this intimate,
★   low-rise hideaway a few blocks from the beach. The Hawaiiana is surrounded by a garden of lush tropical plants, and a giant tiki god carving greets you at the entry. Hawaiian musical entertainment is featured each week. The hotel's centerpiece is the pool, and every morning guests

are served Kona coffee here. Each room has both a double and single bed as well as a kitchenette and view of the gardens below. ⊠ *260 Beach Walk, Honolulu 96815,* ☏ *808/923–3811,* FAX *808/926–5728. 95 rooms. Pool, coin laundry. AE, D, DC, MC, V.*

$$ ▦ **Ilima Hotel.** This 17-story condominium-style hotel has large studios with two double beds, full kitchens, and spacious lānai. Centrally located on a side street near the Ala Wai Canal, the Ilima is a short walk away from the International Market Place and the Royal Hawaiian Shopping Center. Amenities include 24-hour front-desk service, a pool, and a sauna. ⊠ *445 Nohonai St., Honolulu 96815,* ☏ *808/923– 1877,* FAX *808/924–8371,* WEB *www.ilima.com. 99 units. Kitchenettes, pool, sauna. AE, DC, MC, V.*

$–$$ ▦ **Malihini Hotel.** There's no pool, it's not on the beach, none of the units have a TV or air-conditioning, and the rooms are spartan. Still, the atmosphere of this low-rise complex is cool and pleasant, and the gardens are well maintained. All rooms are either studios or one-bedrooms, with kitchenettes and daily maid service. The low prices and decent location make this a popular place, so be sure to book well in advance. ⊠ *217 Saratoga Rd., Honolulu 96815,* ☏ *808/923–9644. 21 rooms, 9 suites. Kitchenettes. No credit cards.*

$–$$ ▦ **Waikīkī Hāna.** Smack dab in the middle of Waikīkī and a block away from the beach, this eight-story hotel is convenient for exploring just about every shop, restaurant, and activity in Oʻahu's tourist hub. Accommodations are clean and plain. Many rooms have their own lānai. Pay a little extra per day and you can rent a refrigerator. ⊠ *2424 Koa Ave., Honolulu 96815,* ☏ *808/926–8841 or 800/367–5004,* FAX *808/596–0158. 70 rooms, 2 suites. Restaurant, lobby lounge, in-room safes, kitchenettes, coin laundry. AE, DC, MC, V.*

$ ▦ **Edmunds Hotel Apartments.** Long lānai wrap around the building, so each room has its own view of the pretty Ala Wai Canal and glorious Mānoa Valley beyond—views that look especially lovely at night, when lights are twinkling up the mountain ridges. This has been a budget alternative for decades, and if you can put up with the constant sounds of traffic on the boulevard this is a real bargain. The ocean is four blocks away. ⊠ *2411 Ala Wai Blvd., Honolulu 96815,* ☏ *808/ 923–8381 or 808/732–5169. 8 rooms. Kitchenettes. No credit cards.*

$ ▦ **Royal Grove Hotel.** This flamingo-pink family-oriented hotel is reminiscent of Miami. With just six floors, it is one of Waikīkī's smaller hotels. The lobby is comfortable; the rooms, though agreeably furnished, have neither themes nor views. Go for the high-end rooms if possible, because the economy rooms have no air-conditioning and more street noise. The hotel is about two blocks from the beach, and the pool area is bright with tropical flowers. ⊠ *15 Uluniu Ave., Honolulu 96815,* ☏ *808/923–7691,* FAX *808/922–7508. 78 rooms, 7 suites. Kitchenettes, pool. AE, D, DC, MC, V.*

Honolulu

$$$$ ▦ **Kāhala Mandarin Oriental Hawaiʻi.** Minutes away from Waikīkī, ★ on the quiet side of Diamond Head, this elegant oceanfront hotel is hidden in the wealthy neighborhood of Kāhala. Rooms combine touches of Asia and Old Hawaiʻi, with mahogany furniture, teak parquet floors, hand-loomed area rugs, local art, and grass-cloth wall coverings. If you're adventurous, you may want to reserve ahead to interact with dolphins in the hotel's impressive 26,000-square-ft lagoon. ⊠ *5000 Kāhala Ave., 96816,* ☏ *808/739–8888 or 800/367–2525,* FAX *808/ 739–8800,* WEB *www.mandarin-oriental.com. 341 rooms, 29 suites. 3 restaurants, lobby lounges, minibars, room service, pool, outdoor hot tub, sauna, steam room, exercise room, beach, dive shop, snorkeling, concierge, business services, meeting room. AE, D, DC, MC, V.*

$$$–$$$$ 🖼 **Ala Moana Hotel.** This long-standing landmark has an excellent location near the popular Ala Moana Shopping Center (they're connected by a pedestrian ramp), the Hawai'i Convention Center, and Ala Moana Beach Park. Each room in this 36-story high-rise has a lānai with a view of Ala Moana Beach, the ocean, or the mountains. Rooms on the 29th to 35th floors provide concierge service, in-room whirlpool baths, and free use of the conference room. The hotel's nightclub, Rumours, is popular with the after-work crowd. ✉ *410 Atkinson Dr., 96814,* ☎ *808/955–4811 or 800/367–6025,* ℻ *808/944–6839,* WEB *www.alamoanahotel.com. 1,102 rooms, 67 suites. 4 restaurants, bar, 2 lobby lounges, in-room safes, minibars, room service, pool, exercise room, dance club, nightclub, meeting room. AE, DC, MC, V.*

$$$ 🖼 **Aston at the Executive Centre Hotel.** Here's a great option for the corporate traveler who wants to avoid Waikīkī. Downtown Honolulu's only hotel is an all-suite high-rise in the center of the business district, within walking distance of the Aloha Tower Marketplace and 10 minutes from Honolulu International Airport. Suites are on the top 10 floors of a 40-story glass-walled tower, providing views of downtown and Honolulu Harbor. Each unit has a separate living area and kitchenette stocked with cold beverages. Some units have washer-dryers. Continental breakfast is included. ✉ *1088 Bishop St., 96813,* ☎ *808/539–3000 or 800/922–7866,* ℻ *808/523–1088,* WEB *www. aston-hotels.com. 116 suites. Restaurant, in-room safes, kitchenettes, pool, exercise room, business services, meeting room. AE, DC, MC, V.*

$$$ 🖼 **Mānoa Valley Inn.** An intimate surprise is tucked away in Mānoa Valley, just 2 mi from Waikīkī. Built in 1919, this stately home is on the National Register of Historic Places. Linger over the complimentary Continental breakfast buffet on the shady backyard lānai each morning and enjoy tropical fruit and cheese in the afternoon. Rooms are furnished in country-inn style, with antique four-poster beds, marble-top dressers, patterned wallpaper, and fresh flowers. There's a reading room with a TV and VCR. ✉ *2001 Vancouver Dr., Honolulu 96822,* ☎ *808/947–6019 or 800/535–0085,* ℻ *808/922–2421. 8 rooms, 4 with bath; 1 cottage. AE, DC, MC, V.*

$$ 🖼 **Pagoda Hotel.** Minutes away from Ala Moana Shopping Center and Ala Moana Beach Park, the Pagoda is well placed. The location and moderate rates make this a good choice if you're simply looking for a place to sleep and catch a couple of meals. Studios include a full-size refrigerator, a stove, and cooking utensils. There are no memorable views because the hotel is surrounded by high-rises. The floating restaurant is notable for its Japanese gardens and carp-filled waterways. ✉ *1525 Rycroft St., Honolulu 96814,* ☎ *808/941–6611 or 800/472–4632,* ℻ *808/955–5067. 364 rooms. 2 restaurants, refrigerators, pool. AE, D, DC, MC, V.*

Around the Island

$$$$ 🖼 **Hilton Turtle Bay Resort.** At press time, this oceanside retreat was in the midst of a much-needed exterior and interior renovation, but it continues to offer an abundance of activities and a relaxing stay away from town. Guests can participate in numerous water sports, horseback ride along the spectacular shoreline, play golf and tennis, or relax by either of the hotel's two pools. Check out the mammoth Sunday champagne brunch, and dine next to huge windows with views of the crashing surf. The resort's cabanas offer more privacy, but the main building rooms afford better views. ✉ *57-091 Kamehameha Hwy. (Box 187), Kahuku 96731,* ☎ *808/293–8811 or 800/445–8667,* ℻ *808/293–9147,* WEB *www.turtlebayresort.hilton.com. 450 rooms, 30 suites, 86*

O'ahu Lodging

cabanas. 2 restaurants, lobby lounge, refrigerators, room service, pool, 2 18-hole golf courses, 10 tennis courts, exercise room, horseback riding, beach, children's programs (ages 5–12), meeting room. AE, D, DC, MC, V.

$$$$ ☆ **J. W. Marriott 'Ihilani Resort & Spa.** Only the 10th Marriott hotel to carry the exclusive J. W. Marriott designation, the 'Ihilani is in a sleek 15-story building illuminated by a glass-dome atrium. Guest rooms have marble bathrooms with deep soaking tubs, private lānai, teak furnishings, in-room CD players with a selection of CDs, and a high-tech control system (lights, temperature controls, and more) built into the telephones. Most rooms have ocean views. The 35,000-square-ft 'Ihilani Spa has everything from seaweed baths to stair-climbers, and there's a Ted Robinson–designed 18-hole championship golf facility. Located on O'ahu's western shore, the hotel is a 25-minute drive from Honolulu International Airport. ✉ *92-1001 'Ōlani St., Kapolei 96707,* ☎ *808/679–0079 or 800/626–4446,* FAX *808/679–0295,* WEB *www.ihilani.com. 333 rooms, 54 suites. 4 restaurants, minibars, room service, 2 pools, spa, 18-hole golf course, 6 tennis courts, baby-sitting, children's programs (ages 5–12), concierge, meeting room. AE, DC, MC, V.*

$–$$ ☷ **Backpackers Vacation Inn and Plantation Village.** Spartan in furnishings and definitely very casual in spirit, Backpackers is a surfer's kind of place to catch some sleep between wave sets. It's near Waimea Bay on the North Shore and offers double rooms (some with a double bed, others with two single beds), hostel accommodations, and cottages. Some accommodations have kitchenettes. It's a three-minute walk to the supermarket. ✉ *59-788 Kamehameha Hwy., Hale'iwa 96712,* ☎ *808/638–7838,* FAX *808/638–7515. 25 rooms. MC, V.*

$–$$ ☷ **Schrader's Windward Marine Resort.** In a setting that is more roadside motel than resort, Schrader's provides a moderately priced lodging alternative. You'll find fewer amenities than you would in Waikīkī, but perhaps a little more personalized attention. Schrader's proximity to the U.S. Marine base makes it popular with military families. Some rooms open onto Kāne'ohe Bay; others face the Ko'olau Mountains. One-, two-, and three-bedroom accommodations are available. This is a popular spot for water activities. ⊠ *47-039 Lihikai Dr., Kāne'ohe 96744,* ☎ *808/239–5711 or 800/735–5711,* 𝖥𝖠𝖷 *808/239–6658,* 𝖶𝖤𝖡 *www.hawaiiscene.com/schrader. 57 rooms. Kitchenettes, pool. AE, D, DC, MC, V.*

$ ⊡ **Breck's on the Beach Hostel.** Just north of Sunset Beach Park, Breck's offers a great location, with rooms ranging from basic dormitory to ocean-view balcony apartments that sleep eight people. Guests, usually surfer types from many continents, have access to free body boards and snorkeling equipment. Bicycles and surfboards are also available. Studio apartments have refrigerators and private bath, and the larger balcony apartments include kitchens. Airport pickup is available. A three-night minimum stay is required. ⊠ *59-043 Huelo St., Sunset Beach 96712,* ☎ *808/638–7873. 21 units. No credit cards.*

NIGHTLIFE AND THE ARTS

Nightlife on O'ahu can be as simple as a barefoot stroll in the sand or as elaborate as a dinner show with all the glitter of a Las Vegas production. You can view the vibrant hues of a Honolulu sunset during a cocktail cruise or hear the melodies of ancient chants at a lūau on a remote west-shore beach.

Waikīkī's Kalākaua and Kūhiō avenues come to life when the sun goes down and the lights go on. Outside Honolulu, offerings are slimmer but equally diverse. Wafting through the night air of O'ahu is the sound of music of every kind—from classical to contemporary. Music has been the language of Hawai'i from the beginning, and O'ahu has the best selection. Everywhere there is hula, whether dancers wear sequin skirts in Waikīkī or authentic ti-leaf skirts at Paradise Cove.

The arts thrive alongside the tourist industry in the island's balmy climate. O'ahu has an established symphony, a thriving opera company, chamber music groups, and community theaters. Major Broadway shows, dance companies, and rock stars also make their way to Honolulu. Check the local newspapers—the morning *Honolulu Advertiser,* the afternoon *Honolulu Star-Bulletin,* or the *Honolulu Weekly*—for the latest events.

Bars, Cabarets, and Clubs

Drinking age is 21 on O'ahu and throughout Hawai'i. Many bars will admit younger people but will not serve them alcohol. By law, all establishments that serve alcoholic beverages must close at 2 AM. The only exceptions are those with a cabaret license, which have a 4 AM curfew. Most places have a cover charge of $2 to $5.

Waikīkī

Banyan Veranda. Home to many of Hawaii's most talented entertainers, Banyan Veranda is steeped in history. From this location the radio program *Hawaii Calls* first broadcast the sounds of Hawaiian music and the rolling surf to a U.S. mainland audience. ⊠ *Sheraton Moana Surfrider, 2365 Kalākaua Ave.,* ☎ *808/922–3111.* ⊙ *Nightly 5:30–11.*

Chai's Bistro. Chai's welcomes some of Hawaii's top entertainers, such as the Brothers Cazimero, Hapa, and the Makaha Sons. There's also a Pacific Rim–cuisine menu with a twist of Thai to go with the contemporary Hawaiian music. ⊠ *Aloha Tower Marketplace, 1 Aloha*

Tower Dr., ☎ *808/585–0011.* ⊘ *Nightly from 4; music performances nightly at 7.*

Esprit. Honolulu, an all-male octet, performs music from the big-band era of the 1930s up through current pop hits, with Broadway numbers, too. This club, in the heart of Waikīkī, is a popular dance spot, and also features the high-energy singers, The Krush. ⊠ *Sheraton Waikīkī, 2255 Kalākaua Ave.,* ☎ *808/922–4422.* ⊘ *Sat.–Mon. 8:30–2.*

Hanohano Room. World-class views 30 stories above Waikīkī, combined with late-night jazz and weekly jam sessions by some of Hawai'i's best musicians, make this a romantic spot for those who like to dance close and slow. ⊠ *Sheraton Waikīkī, 2255 Kalākaua Ave., 30th floor,* ☎ *808/922–4422.* ⊘ *Sat. 11–1.*

Lewers Lounge. Bruce Hamada and friends perform contemporary jazz and standards here at Halekūlani hotel Tuesday through Saturday evenings. A vocalist-pianist sits in Sunday and Monday. A dessert menu is offered. ⊠ *Halekūlani, 2199 Kālia Rd.,* ☎ *808/923–2311.* ⊘ *Entertainment nightly 10:30–midnight.*

Lobby Bar. The open-air lobby lounge of the Waikīkī Beach Marriott Resort is home to the legendary Hawaiian musical treasure Aunty Genoa Keawe. Slack-key guitar can also be heard here. ⊠ *Waikīkī Beach Marriott Resort, 2552 Kalākaua Ave.,* ☎ *808/922–6611.* ⊘ *Nightly from 5:30.*

Mai Tai Bar. Keith and Carmen Haugen sing island duets at this open-air Waikīkī Beach bar. Carmen's hula is a thing of beauty. Catch them in the early evenings Tuesday and Wednesday. Entertainers vary on other nights. ⊠ *Royal Hawaiian Hotel, 2259 Kalākaua Ave.,* ☎ *808/923–7311.* ⊘ *Entertainment nightly 5:30–7:30.*

Moose McGillycuddy's Pub and Cafe. Loud bands play for the beach-and-beer gang in a blue-jeans-and-T-shirt setting. ⊠ *310 Lewers St.,* ☎ *808/923–0751.* ⊘ *Nightly 9–1:30.*

Nashville Waikīkī. Country music in the tropics? You bet! Put on your *paniolo* (Hawaiian cowboy) duds and mosey on out to the giant dance floor. There are pool tables, dart boards, line dancing, and free dance lessons to boot. ⊠ *Ohana Waikīkī West Hotel, 2330 Kūhiō Ave.,* ☎ *808/926–7911.* ⊘ *Daily 4–4; dance lessons nightly at 7.*

Nick's Fishmarket. This is probably the most comfortable of Waikīkī's upscale dance lounges, with an elegant crowd, smooth music, and an intimate atmosphere. ⊠ *Waikīkī Gateway Motel, 2070 Kalākaua Ave.,* ☎ *808/955–6333.* ⊘ *Nightly 10–2.*

Paradise Lounge. Several contemporary Hawaiian acts, including the longtime band Olomana, perform in this pretty outdoor club. ⊠ *Hilton Hawaiian Village, 2005 Kālia Rd.,* ☎ *808/949–4321.* ⊘ *Fri.–Sat. 8–midnight.*

Pipeline Cafe and Sports Bar. This is two stories of fun with pool, darts, and more. The upstairs sports bar is for watching sports on TV; dancing takes place downstairs to both live musical acts and DJs. ⊠ *805 Pohukaina St.,* ☎ *808/589–1999.* ⊘ *Nightly 8–4.*

Pool Stage. Various local performers present Hawaiian song and dance by the Sheraton Waikīkī's oceanfront pool. One of the most popular is 'ukulele wizard Moe Keale, familiar to TV viewers from his roles on *Hawai'i Five-O.* ⊠ *Sheraton Waikīkī, 2255 Kalākaua Ave.,* ☎ *808/922–4422.* ⊘ *Nightly 6–8:30.*

Royal Garden at Waikīkī. Some of O'ahu's top jazz stylists perform in the elegant, intimate lobby lounge of this sophisticated hotel. ⊠ *Royal Garden at Waikīkī, 444 'Olohana St.,* ☎ *808/943–0202.* ⊘ *Tues.–Sun. 8–11.*

Rumours. The after-work crowd loves this spot, which has dance videos, disco, and throbbing lights. On Saturday "Little Chill" nights, the club plays oldies from the '70s and '80s and serves free pūpū. There is ballroom dancing Sunday evening from 5 to 9. ✉ *Ala Moana Hotel, 410 Atkinson St.,* ☎ *808/955–4811.* �l *Wed.–Fri. 5–2, Sat. 8–4, Sun. 5–9 (for ballroom dance).*

Shore Bird Beach Broiler. This Waikīkī beachfront disco spills right out onto the sand. It has a large dance floor and a 10-ft video screen. Karaoke sing-alongs are held nightly. ✉ *Outrigger Reef Hotel on the Beach, 2169 Kālia Rd.,* ☎ *808/922–2887.* �l *Nightly 9–2.*

Virtual Experience. Calling itself a place to escape, this posh, high-tech club has 12 oversize screens for exploring computerized worlds, an atmosphere conducive to quiet conversation, and drinks and pūpū to heighten the experience. ✉ *311 Lewers St.,* ☎ *808/847–8825.* �l *Nightly 6–4. Live entertainment Tues. and Thurs.*

Wave Waikīkī. Dance to live rock and roll until 1:30 and recorded music after that. It can be a rough scene, but the bands are tops. ✉ *1877 Kalākaua Ave.,* ☎ *808/941–0424.* �l *Nightly 9–4.*

Zanzabar. DJ's spin top hits, from hip-hop to soul, at this elegant and high-energy nightspot in the Waikīkī Trade Center. ✉ *2255 Kūhiō Ave.,* ☎ *808/924–3939.* �l *Nightly 9–4.*

Honolulu

Aaron's at the Top of the Ala Moana. A splendid view, good contemporary dance music, and a well-dressed crowd come together at this Honolulu nightclub. ✉ *Ala Moana Hotel, 410 Atkinson Dr.,* ☎ *808/955–4466.* �l *Dancing Sun.–Thurs. 9:30–2, Fri.–Sat. 10–2.*

Anna Bannana's. Generations of Hawaiʻi college students have spent more than an evening or two at this legendary two-story, smoky dive. Here, the music is fresh, loud, and sometimes experimental. Local favorites deliver ultracreative dance music, and the likes of blues singer Taj Mahal have been known to perform. ✉ *2440 S. Beretania St.,* ☎ *808/946–5190.* �l *Nightly 11:30–2, live music Thurs.–Sat. 9–2.*

Gordon Biersch Brewery Restaurant. Live duos and trios serenade patrons of the outside bar that flanks Honolulu Harbor. While there's no dancing, this is the place in Honolulu to see and be seen. ✉ *Aloha Tower Marketplace, 1 Aloha Tower Dr.,* ☎ *808/599–4877.* �l *Wed.–Sat. 7–1.*

Honu Bar and Terrace. Sophisticated and swank, this lobby lounge presents light jazz and island ensembles during the cocktail and sunset hours. ✉ *Kāhala Mandarin Oriental Hawaiʻi, 5000 Kāhala Ave.,* ☎ *808/739–8888.* �l *Mon.–Thurs. 4:30–6:30, Fri.–Sun. 5–7.*

Pier Bar. Here's one of the few places in Honolulu where you can hear live music outdoors and dance underneath the stars. It attracts a grab bag of groups; call ahead to find out who's playing. ✉ *Aloha Tower Marketplace, 1 Aloha Tower Dr.,* ☎ *808/536–2166.* �l *Nightly 6:30–4.*

Venus Nightclub. This high-energy social bar features pūpū and dancing nightly, with live entertainment five nights a week. Attention, ladies: the male dance revue is definitely a Honolulu experience. ✉ *1349 Kapiʻolani Blvd.,* ☎ *808/955–2640.* �l *Nightly 8–4.*

World Cafe. Honolulu's only upscale billiards nightclub also has a sports bar and dancing to Top 40 tunes. ✉ *500 Ala Moana Blvd.,* ☎ *808/599–4450.* �l *Mon.–Thurs. 11:30 pm–2 am, Fri.–Sat. 11:30 pm–4 am, Sun. 3 pm–2 am.*

Kahuku

Bayview Lounge. A beautiful place to watch the sun set over the North Shore water, this lounge inside the Hilton Turtle Bay hosts a variety of local bands that play contemporary Hawaiian tunes. ✉ *Hilton Turtle Bay Resort, 57-091 Kamehameha Hwy.,* ☎ *808/293–8811.* �l *Nightly 6–9.*

Cocktail and Dinner Cruises

Dinner cruises depart either from the piers adjacent to the Aloha Tower Marketplace in downtown Honolulu or from Kewalo Basin, just 'ewa of Ala Moana Beach Park, and head along the coast toward Diamond Head. There's usually dinner, dancing, drinks, and a sensational sunset. Except as noted, dinner cruises cost approximately $50–$60, cocktail cruises $20 to $30. Most major credit cards are accepted.

Ali`i Kai Catamaran. Patterned after an ancient Polynesian vessel, this huge catamaran casts off from historic Aloha Tower with 1,000 passengers. The deluxe dinner cruise has two open bars, a huge dinner, and an authentic Polynesian show with colorful hula music. The food is good, the after-dinner show loud and fun, and everyone dances on the way back to shore. ✉ *Pier 5, street level, Honolulu,* ☎ *808/539–9495.*

Dream Cruises. The 100-ft motor yacht *American Dream* handles up to 225 guests for evening cruises off the shores of Waikīkī. Decks have plenty of outdoor space for views of the twinkling city lights. The dinner cruise includes one mai tai, buffet, and soft drinks. You pay for extra drinks. After a hula demonstration with audience participation, a disc jockey spins dancing tunes from the '50s through the '70s. ✉ *1020 Auahi St., Honolulu,* ☎ *808/592–5200,* WEB *www.dream-cruises.com.*

Navatek Cruises. The sleek *Navatek* is a revolutionary craft designed to sail smoothly in rough waters. That allows it to power farther along Waikīkī's coastline than its competitors. Choose from sunset dinner or moonlight cruises, or daytime breakfast and lunch whale-watch cruises December through mid-April. ✉ *Honolulu Harbor,* ☎ *808/973–1311,* WEB *goatlantis.com.*

Paradise Cruises. Prices vary depending on which deck you choose on the 1,600-passenger, four-deck *Star of Honolulu.* For instance, a seven-course French dinner on the top costs $199. A steak and crab feast on level two costs $72. Evening excursions also take place on the 340-passenger *Starlet I* and 230-passenger *Starlet II.* ✉ *1540 S. King St., Honolulu,* ☎ *808/983–7827.*

Cocktail and Dinner Shows

Some Oʻahu entertainers have been around for years, and others have just arrived on the scene. Either way, the dinner-show food is usually buffet-style with a definite local accent. Dinner shows are all in the $45 to $60 range. Cocktail shows run $30 to $35. The prices usually include one cocktail, tax, and gratuity. In all cases, reservations are essential, and most major credit cards are accepted. Be sure to call in advance. You never know when an artist may have switched venues.

Creation: A Polynesian Odyssey. This show traces Hawaiʻi's culture and history, from its origins to statehood. The highlight is a daring Samoan fire knife dancer. ✉ *ʻĀinahau Showroom, Sheraton Princess Kaʻiulani Hotel, 120 Kaʻiulani Ave., Waikīkī,* ☎ *808/931–4660.* ☉ *Dinner seatings nightly at 5:15 and 8, cocktail seatings nightly at 5:45 and 8:15, shows nightly at 6 and 8:30.*

Don Ho. The singer who made tiny bubbles famous, he is the entertainer visitors ask about first when it comes to Waikīkī entertainment. His show, a Polynesian revue (with a cast of young and attractive Hawaiian performers), has found the perfect home in this intimate club setting inside the Waikīkī Beachcomber Hotel. ✉ *Waikīkī Beachcomber Hotel, 2300 Kalākaua Ave., Waikīkī,* ☎ *808/923–3981.* ☉ *Shows Sun.–Thurs. at 7, with cocktail and dinner seatings.*

Magic of Polynesia. Hawaiʻi's top illusionist, John Hirokawa, displays mystifying sleight of hand in this highly entertaining show, which also includes the requisite hula and island music. ✉ *Waikīkī Beachcomber Hotel, 2300 Kalākaua Ave., Waikīkī,* ☎ *808/971–4321.* ⊙ *Nightly at 6:30 and 8:45.*

Polynesian Cultural Center. Easily one of the best on the Islands, this show has soaring moments and an "erupting volcano." The performers are students from Brigham Young University's Hawaiʻi campus. ✉ *55-370 Kamehameha Hwy., Lāʻie,* ☎ *808/293–3333,* ⅦEB *www.polynesia.com.* ⊙ *Dinner seating Mon.–Sat. at 4:30; show Apr.–May and Sept.–Dec. 25, Mon.–Sat. at 7:30, and Dec. 25–Mar. and June–Aug., Mon.–Sat. at 6 and 7:45.*

Society of Seven. This lively, popular septet has great staying power and, after more than 25 years, continues to put on one of the best shows in Waikīkī. They sing, dance, do impersonations, play instruments, and, above all, entertain with their contemporary sound. ✉ *Outrigger Waikīkī on the Beach, 2335 Kalākaua Ave., Waikīkī,* ☎ *808/923–7469.* ⊙ *Mon. at 8:30; Tues.–Sat. at 6:30 and 8:30.*

Yes! An Encore. Acrobats, magicians, clowns, mimes, and dancers gather onstage in this international nightclub revue. Highlights include tumblers clad in gold from head to toe, a life-size Raggedy Ann, exotic birds, and a giant slinky flipping and sliding across the stage. It's a one-of-a-kind act in Waikīkī. ✉ *Polynesian Palace, Outrigger Reef Towers Hotel, 227 Lewers St., Waikīkī,* ☎ *808/923–7469.* ⊙ *Tues.– Sun. at 6:30 and 8:30.*

Dance

Every year at least one of mainland America's finer ballet troupes makes the trip to Honolulu for a series of dance performances at the **Neal Blaisdell Center Concert Hall** (✉ Ward Ave. at King St., Honolulu, ☎ 808/591–2211). A local company, **Ballet Hawaiʻi** (☎ 808/988–7578), is active during the holiday season with its annual production of *The Nutcracker,* which is usually held at the Mamiya Theater (✉ 3142 Waiʻalae Ave., Chaminade University, Honolulu).

Film

Art, international, classic, and silent films are screened at the little theater at the **Honolulu Academy of Arts** (✉ 900 S. Beretania St., Honolulu, ☎ 808/532–8768). **Kāhala Mall** (✉ 4211 Waiʻalae Ave., Honolulu, ☎ 808/733–6233) has eight movie theaters showing a diverse range of films. It's a 10-minute drive from Waikīkī. **Varsity Theater** (✉ 1106 University Ave., Honolulu, ☎ 808/973–5834) is a two-theater art house that brings internationally acclaimed motion pictures to Honolulu. Waikīkī generally gets the first-run films at its trio of theaters dubbed, appropriately, **Waikīkī 1, Waikīkī 2** (✉ 333 Seaside Ave., ☎ 808/971–5033) and **Waikīkī 3** (✉ 2284 Kalakaua Ave., ☎ 808/ 971–5033). Check newspapers for what's playing.

The **Hawaiʻi International Film Festival** (☎ 808/528–3456) may not be Cannes, but it is unique and exciting. During the weeklong festival, held from the end of November to early December, top films from the United States, Asia, and the Pacific are screened day and night at several theaters on Oʻahu.

Lūʻau

These are some good lūʻau that emphasize fun over strict adherence to tradition. They generally cost $40–$75. Reservations are essential, and most major credit cards are accepted.

HAWAIIAN MUSIC

ASK MOST VISITORS about Hawaiian music and they'll likely break into a lighthearted rendition of "Little Grass Shack." When they're done, lead them directly to a stereo.

First, play them a recording of singer Kekuhi Kanahele, whose compositions combine ancient Hawaiian chants with modern melodies. Then ask them to listen to a CD by guitarist Keola Beamer, who loosens his strings and plays slack-key tunings dating back to the 1830s. Share a recording by falsetto virtuoso Amy Hanaiali'i Gilliom, one of the very few singers perpetuating the upper-register vocal style.

These artists, like many others, are proving just how multifaceted Hawaiian music has become. They're unearthing their island roots in the form of revered songs and chants, and they're reinterpreting them for today's audiences. It's "chicken-skin" (goose-bumps) stuff, to be sure, and it's made only in Hawai'i.

Granted, "Little Grass Shack" does have its place in the history books. After Hawai'i became a U.S. territory in 1900, the world discovered its music thanks to touring ensembles who turned heads with swaying hips, steel guitars, and pseudo-Hawaiian lyrics. Once radio and movies got into the act, dreams of Hawai'i came with a saccharine Hollywood sound track.

But Hawaiian music is far more complex. It harks back to the sounds of the ancient Islanders who beat rough-hewn drums, blew haunting calls on conch shells, and intoned repetitive chants for their gods. It recalls the voices of 19th-century Christian missionaries who taught Islanders how to sing in four-part harmony, a style that's still popular today.

The music takes on international overtones thanks to gifts from foreign immigrants: the 'ukulele from Portuguese laborers, for instance, and the guitar from Mexican traders. And it's enlivened by a million renderings of "Tiny Bubbles," as mainstream entertainers like Don Ho croon Hawaiian-pop hits for Waikīkī tourists.

Island music came full circle in the late 1960s and '70s, a time termed the Hawaiian Renaissance. While the rest of the world was rocking 'n' rolling, a few dedicated artists began giving voice to a resurgence of interest in Hawaiian culture, history, and traditions.

Today's artistic trailblazers are digging deep to explore their heritage, and their music reflects that thoughtful search. They go one step further by incorporating such time-honored instruments as nose flutes and gourds, helping them keep pace with the past.

Why is Hawaiian music such a well-kept secret? Simply put, it's rarely played outside of the Islands. A handful of local performers are making their mark on the mainland and in Japan. But if you want to experience the true essence of Hawaiian music, you must come to Hawai'i. Check ads and listings in local papers for information on concerts, which take place in indoor and outdoor theaters, hotel ballrooms, and cozy nightclubs. When you hear the sound, you'll know it's Hawaiian because it'll make you feel right at home.

Germaine's Lū'au. This lū'au is billed as being "100 years away from Waikīkī." Expect a lively crowd as you are bused to a private beach 35 minutes from Waikīkī. The bus ride is actually a lot of fun, and the beach and the sunset are pleasant. The service is brisk in order to feed everyone on time, and the food is the usual multicourse, all-you-can-eat buffet, but the show is warm and friendly. ☎ 808/941–3338. ☉ *Tues.–Sun. at 6.*

Paradise Cove Lū'au. There are palms and a glorious sunset, and the pageantry is fun, even informative. The food—well, you didn't come for the food, did you? This is another mass-produced event for 1,000 or so. A bus takes you from one of six Waikīkī hotel pickup points to a remote beachfront estate beside a picturesque cove on the western side of the island, 27 mi from Waikīkī. ☎ *808/973–5828.* ☉ *Daily at 5:30, doors open at 5.*

Polynesian Cultural Center Ali'i Lū'au. An hour's drive from Honolulu, this North Shore O'ahu lū'au is set amid seven re-created villages of Polynesia. Dinner is all-you-can-eat, followed by a world-class revue. ☎ *808/923–1861.* ☉ *Mon.–Sat. at 5:30.*

Royal Hawaiian Lū'au. Waikīkī's only oceanfront lū'au offers an exotic, upscale menu and entertainment. With the setting sun, Diamond Head, the Pacific Ocean, and the legendary Pink Palace in the background, who cares if the lū'au isn't totally authentic? ☎ *808/923–7311.* ☉ *Mon. at 6.*

Music

Chamber Music Hawai'i (☎ 808/947–1975) gives 25 concerts a year at the **Honolulu Lutheran Church** (✉ 1730 Punahou St., Honolulu), **Honolulu Academy of Arts** (✉ 900 S. Beretania St., Honolulu), and other locations around the island.

Hawai'i Opera Theater's season spans from January through March and includes such works as *The Barber of Seville, Tristan,* and *Madame Butterfly.* All are performed in their original language with projected English translation. ✉ *Neal Blaisdell Concert Hall, Ward Ave. and King St., Honolulu,* ☎ *808/596–7858.* ☲ *$23–$77 at box office.*

The **Honolulu Symphony Orchestra** performs at the Neil Blaisdell Concert Hall and is led by the young, dynamic Samuel Wong. The Honolulu Pops series, with some performances underneath the stars summer nights at the Waikīkī Shell, features top local and national artists under the direction of talented conductor-composer Matt Catingub. ✉ *677 Ala Moana Blvd., Honolulu,* ☎ *808/792–2000,* WEB *www. honolulusymphony.com.* ☲ *$10–$50.*

Rock concerts are usually performed at the cavernous **Neal Blaisdell Center Arena** (☎ 808/591–2211). Internationally famous performers pack them in at **Aloha Stadium** (☎ 808/486–9300).

Theater

Because many of today's touring shows and music artists depend on major theatrical sets, lighting, and sound, Hawai'i, already pricey, can be an expensive gig. As a result, major touring companies rarely come here. But there is strong community support for local performing arts companies. O'ahu has developed several excellent local theater troupes, which present first-rate entertainment on an amateur and semiprofessional level all year long.

Army Community Theatre. This is a favorite for its revivals of musical theater classics, presented in an 800-seat house. The casts are talented, and the fare is great for families. ⊠ *Richardson Theater, Fort Shafter, Honolulu,* ☎ *808/438–4480.* ☜ *$12–$15.*

Diamond Head Theater. The repertoire includes a little of everything: musicals, dramas, experimental productions, and classics. This company is in residence five minutes from Waikīkī, right next to Diamond Head. ⊠ *520 Makapuʻu Ave., Honolulu,* ☎ *808/734–0274.* ☜ *$10–$40.*

Hawaiʻi Theatre Center. Beautifully restored, this downtown Honolulu theater built in the 1920s hosts a wide range of unique events, including theatrical productions. Historic tours of the theater are offered Tuesdays at 11. ⊠ *1130 Bethel St., Honolulu,* ☎ *808/528–0506.* ☜ *Prices vary.*

☾ **Honolulu Theater for Youth.** This group stages delightful productions for children around the Islands from July through May. Call for a schedule. ⊠ *2846 Ualena St., Honolulu,* ☎ *808/839–9885.* ☜ *$10.*

John F. Kennedy Theater. Eclectic dramatic offerings—everything from musical theater to Kabuki, Nō, and Chinese opera—are performed at this space at the University of Hawaiʻi's Manoa campus. ⊠ *1770 East–West Rd., Honolulu,* ☎ *808/956–7655.* ☜ *$9–$12.*

Kumu Kahua. This is the only troupe presenting shows and plays written on and about the Islands. It stages five or six productions a year. ⊠ *46 Merchant St., Honolulu,* ☎ *808/536–4441.* ☜ *$12–$15.*

Mānoa Valley Theater. Wonderful nonprofessional performances are put on in this intimate theater in Mānoa Valley from September through July. ⊠ *2833 E. Mānoa Rd., Honolulu,* ☎ *808/988–6131.* ☜ *$17–$20.*

OUTDOOR ACTIVITIES AND SPORTS

Participant Sports

Biking

The good news is that the coastal roads are flat and well paved. On the downside, they're also awash in vehicular traffic. Frankly, biking is no fun in either Waikīkī or Honolulu, but things are a bit better outside the city. Be sure to take along a nylon jacket for the frequent showers on the windward side and remember that Hawaiʻi is Paradise after the Fall: lock up your bike.

Mountain bikes are available for rent at **Blue Sky Rentals & Sports Center** (⊠ 1920 Ala Moana Blvd., across from the Hilton Hawaiian Village, Waikīkī, ☎ 808/947–0101). Rates are $15 a day (from 8 to 6), $20 for 24 hours, and $75 per week, plus a $25 deposit. This price includes a bike, a helmet, a lock, and a water bottle.

If you want to find some biking buddies, write ahead to the **Hawaiʻi Bicycling League** (⊠ Box 4403, Honolulu 96813, ☎ 808/735–5756, WEB www.bikehawaii.com), which can tell you about upcoming races and club rides (frequent on all the Islands).

For biking information and maps, contact the **Honolulu City and County Bike Coordinator** (☎ 808/527–5044).

Tour Oʻahu's North Shore by bike with guided tours from **Waimea Valley Adventure Park** (⊠ 59-864 Kamehameha Hwy., Haleʻiwa, ☎ 808/638–5300); rides are $59 per 45 minutes, and include admission into the park.

Camping and Hiking

For a free Oʻahu recreation map that outlines the island's 33 major trails, including the visitor-friendly Mānoa Falls Trail, Makapuʻu Lighthouse Trail, Waʻahila Ridge Trail, and Leeward's Oʻahu's Kaena Point, contact the **Hawaiʻi State Department of Land and Natural Resources**

(✉ 1151 Punchbowl St., Room 130, Honolulu 96813, ☎ 808/587–030, WEB www.hawaii.gov).

For a complimentary hiking safety guide, contact the City and County of Honolulu's **Trails and Access Manager** (☎ 808/973–9782). Ask for a copy of "Hiking on O'ahu: The Official Guide."

For families, the **Hawai'i Nature Center** (✉ 2131 Makiki Heights Dr., Honolulu, 96822, ☎ 808/955–0100) in upper Makiki Valley conducts a number of programs for both adults and children. The center conducts guided hikes into tropical settings that reveal hidden waterfalls and protected forest reserves. **O'ahu Nature Tours** (☎ 800/861–6018 or 808/924–2473; WEB www.oahunaturetours.com) offers glorious sunrise, rain forest, and volcanic walking tours with an escort who will explain the wealth of native flora and fauna that is your companion along the way.

Camping on O'ahu is available at 4 state parks, 12 county beach parks, and within the grounds of one county botanic garden. Stays are restricted to five nights per month in all beach and state recreation areas, and parks are closed to campers on Wednesday and Thursday evenings. To obtain a free camping permit for state parks, write to **Department of Land and Natural Resources, State Parks Division** (✉ Box 621, Honolulu, 96809, ☎ 808/587–0300). For county and beach parks, contact the **Honolulu Department of Parks and Recreation** (✉ 650 S. King St., Honolulu 96813, ☎ 808/523–4525). A word of caution: although some O'ahu recreation areas have caretakers and gates that close in the evening for your safety, many others can be quite isolated at night.

Mālaekahana State Park on the North Shore is a local favorite camping spot and offers a beachfront setting with two areas that include rest rooms, showers, picnic tables, and drinking water. It's on Kamehameha Highway between Lā'ie and Kahuku. On the windward coast, **Hoomaluhia Botanic Gardens,** (✉ 45-680 Luluku Rd., Kaneohe, ☎ 808/523–4525) provides a safe, scenic camping setting at the base of the majestic Ko'olau Mountains. Five grassy camping areas with rest rooms, showers, and drinking water are available on Friday, Saturday, and Sunday evenings only. Permits are free and are issued at the garden daily between 9 and 4.

You can rent everything from tents to backpacks at **The Bike Shop** (✉ 1149 S. King St., Honolulu, ☎ 808/595–0588).

Fitness Centers and Spas

Ampy's European Facials and Body Spa. This spa is famous for its European-style facials; massages; and spa packages, including a Gentlemen's Retreat. It's located in the Ala Moana Building, adjacent to Ala Moana Shopping Center. ✉ *1441 Kapiolani Blvd., Honolulu,* ☎ *808/946–3838.*

Clark Hatch Physical Fitness Center. Weight-training facilities, an indoor pool, a racquetball court, aerobics classes, and treadmills are all available at this club. ✉ *745 Fort St., Honolulu,* ☎ *808/536–7205.* ▣ *About $10 per day.* ☉ *Weekdays 6 am–8 pm, Sat. 7:30–5:30.*

Hawaiian Rainforest Salon and Spa. Vichy showers; a sauna; facial and massage treatments; and complete hair, nail, and makeup services are available here. ✉ *Pacific Beach Hotel, 5th floor, 2490 Kalākaua Ave., Waikīkī,* ☎ *808/922–1233.*

'Ihilani Resort & Spa. About 25 minutes from the airport is O'ahu's largest health and fitness center. There's 35,000 square ft of space for classes, weight rooms, relaxation programs, hydrotherapies—you name it. Call for prices and to arrange nonguest privileges. ✉ *J. W.*

Marriott 'Ihilani Resort & Spa, 92-1001 Olani St., Kapolei, ☎ *808/ 679–0079.*

Malama Salon Spas. Malama has two locations, one on the third level of Ala Moana Shopping Center adjacent to Neiman Marcus, and the other in Mānoa Valley, about 15 minutes from Waikīkī. These Aveda Lifestyle Salons offer massages, facials, and body and beauty treatments in settings so serene and elegant you may forget just how busy the world is outside the front doors. ⊠ *Ala Moana Shopping Center, 3rd level, 1450 Ala Moana Blvd., Honolulu;* ⊠ *2801 East Mānoa Rd., Honolulu,* ☎ *808/988–0101 for both locations.*

Mandara Spa and Holistica Hawaii Wellness Center. This 42,000-square-ft spa and wellness center spans two floors of the Hilton Hawaiian Village's Kalia Tower. You'll find a cardiovascular fitness center, outdoor lānai and spa suites, and a wealth of spa treatments and salon services that incorporate Hawaiian, Asian, European, and Polynesian techniques. Holistica Hawaii will guide you in your quest for a healthy lifestyle. ⊠ *Hilton Hawaiian Village, 2005 Kālia Rd., Waikīkī,* ☎ *808/949–4321.*

Na Ho'ola at the Hyatt Waikīkī. Come here for an authentic Hawaiian spa experience with *lomi lomi* (Hawaiian massage) and poolside massages, body wraps, thalasso therapies, and fitness facilities with cardio-workout equipment. ⊠ *2424 Kalākaua Ave., Waikīkī,* ☎ *808/921– 1234).*

Paul Brown Salon and Day Spa. Indulge in a tropical-fruit facial or mineral body wrap followed by an aromatherapy massage. Paul Brown offers spa pampering and complete hair-salon services. ⊠ *Ward Centre, 1200 Ala Moana Blvd., Honolulu, P 808/591–1881.*

24-Hour Fitness. Waikīkī's most accessible fitness center has weight-training machines, cardiovascular equipment, free weights, and a pro shop. ⊠ *Pacific Beach Hotel, 2nd floor, 2490 Kalākaua Ave., Waikīkī, P 808/971–4653.* ☜ *$10 per day for guests of many Waikīkī hotels (call for list), $20 for nonguests.* ☼ *Daily.*

Golf

O'ahu has more than three dozen public and private golf courses, 10 of which were first built in the 1990s. Hotel concierges can assist with tee times and transportation. To get a preview before you arrive, check out www.808golf.com, which offers a comprehensive on-line guide to Hawai'i golf, including course descriptions and tee-time reservations.

Ala Wai Golf Course. One of the most popular municipal 18-hole courses is on Waikīkī's mauka end, across the Ala Wai Canal. It's par 70 on 6,424 yards and has a pro shop and a restaurant. There's always a waiting list for tee times, so if you plan to play, call the minute you land. ⊠ *404 Kapahulu Ave., Waikīkī,* ☎ *808/733–7387.* ☜ *Greens fee $40, cart $12.*

Hawai'i Kai Championship Course. Advance reservations are recommended at this 18-hole, 6,222-yard course and the neighboring 18-hole, 2,386-yard Hawai'i Kai Executive Course. ⊠ *8902 Kalaniana'ole Hwy., Honolulu,* ☎ *808/395–2358.* ☜ *Greens fee weekdays $90 for Championship Course and $37 for Executive Course; weekends and holidays $100 and $42, respectively; cart included.*

Hawai'i Prince Golf Club. This 27-hole Arnold Palmer–designed course welcomes visiting players. ⊠ *91-1200 Ft. Weaver Rd., 'Ewa Beach,* ☎ *808/944–4567.* ☜ *Greens fee $90 guests, $135 nonguests; cart included.*

Kahuku Golf Course. The 9-hole walking-only course is played more by locals than by visitors, but serves up some stunning North Shore natural beauty. ⊠ *56-501 Kamehameha Hwy., Kahuku,* ☎ *808/293– 5842.* ☜ *Greens fee $20 for nonresidents.*

Ko Olina Golf Club. Affiliated with the 'Ihilani Resort is this club on O'ahu's west side. Its 18 holes are beautifully landscaped with waterfalls and ponds where black and white swans serve as your gallery. ⊠ *Ko Olina Resort, 92-1220 Ali'inui Dr., Kapolei,* ☎ *808/676–5300.* ⚑ *Greens fee $145, cart included.*

Ko'olau Golf Club. This 18-hole, par-72 course on O'ahu's windward side in Kaneohe is officially rated by the United States Golf Association as the most difficult golf course in the country. Up for the challenge? ⊠ *45-550 Kionaole Rd., Kaneohe,* ☎ *808/236–4653.* ⚑ *Greens fee $100, cart included.*

Links at Kuilima at Hilton Turtle Bay Resort. The 18 holes here were designed by Arnold Palmer and Ed Seay around Punahoolapa March, a protected wetland for the endangered Hawaiian waterfowl. ⊠ *Hilton Turtle Bay Resort, 57-091 Kamehameha Hwy., Kahuku,* ☎ *808/293–8574.* ⚑ *Greens fee $75 guests, $125 nonguests; separate 9-hole course $25; cart included.*

Luana Hills Country Club. The front nine of this 18-hole, par-72 course is carved in the slopes of Mount Olomana. ⊠ *770 Auloa Rd., Kailua,* ☎ *808/262–2139.* ⚑ *Greens fee $80, cart included.*

Mililani Golf Club. The tree-lined greens at this par-72, 6,455-yard course affords magnificent views of the Ko'olau and Wai'anae mountain ranges around it. ⊠ *95-176 Kuahelani Ave., Mililani,* ☎ *808/623–2222.* ⚑ *Greens fee $95, cart included.*

Olomana Golf Links. This par-72, 6,326-yard course features hills and some interesting water hazards, not to mention a backdrop of the sheer cliffs of the Ko'olau Mountains. ⊠ *41-1801 Kalanianaole Hwy., Waimānalo,* ☎ *808/259–7626.* ⚑ *Greens fee $60, cart included.*

Sheraton Mākaha Country Club. Two exceptional 18-hole courses here offer a beautiful valley setting. ⊠ *84-626 Mākaha Valley Rd., Wai'anae,* ☎ *808/695–9544.* ⚑ *Greens fee $125 until noon, $90 noon–2:30, $50 2:30–closing; cart included.*

Horseback Riding

Correa Trails Hawaii. Ride along trails that hug the Ko'olau Mountain range and offer ocean views of the spectacular Waimānalo coast. Rates are $35 for a one-hour ride and $60 for a two-hour trek. ⊠ *41-050 Kalanianaole Hwy., Waimānalo,* ☎ *808/259–9005.*

Hilton Turtle Bay Resort. Seventy-five acres of hotel property, including a private beach, are accessible for exploring on horseback at a cost of $35 for 45 minutes. ⊠ *57-091 Kamehameha Hwy., Kahuku,* ☎ *808/293–8811.*

Kualoa Ranch. This ranch across from Kualoa Beach Park leads trail rides in Ka'a'awa, one of the most beautiful valleys in all Hawai'i. Trail rides cost between $35 and $99. Kualoa has other activities as well, such as windsurfing, Jet Skiing, all-terrain-vehicle trail rides, and children's activities. ⊠ *49-560 Kamehameha Hwy., Ka'a'awa,* ☎ *808/237–8515; 808/538–7636 in Honolulu.*

Waimea Valley Adventure Park. Take a guided horseback trail ride through the verdant Waimea Valley. Prices start at $35 per hour. ⊠ *59-864 Kamehameha Hwy., Haliewa,* ☎ *808/638–5300.*

Jogging

In Honolulu, the most popular places are the two parks, **Kapi'olani** and **Ala Moana,** at either end of Waikīkī. In both cases, the loop around the park is just under 2 mi. You can run a 4½-mi ring around **Diamond Head crater,** past scenic views, luxurious homes, and herds of other joggers. If you're looking for jogging companions, show up for the free **Honolulu Marathon Clinic,** which starts at the Kapi'olani Bandstand from March through November, Sunday at 7:30 AM.

Once you leave Honolulu, it gets trickier to find places to jog that are scenic as well as safe. It's best to stick to the well-traveled routes, or ask the experienced folks at the **Running Room** (⊠ 819 Kapahulu Ave., Honolulu, ☎ 808/737–2422) for advice.

The "Honolulu Walking Map" and "The Fitness Fun Map" are free from the **Hawai'i State Department of Health** (⊠ 1250 Punchbowl St., Room 217, Honolulu, ☎ 808/586–4661). These list more than two dozen routes and suggested itineraries for seeing O'ahu on foot.

Rock Climbing

The Mokulē'ia Wall 900-ft vertical trail on the North Shore is one of the world's best venues for rock climbing. Those skilled enough to make it to the top get glorious views of the coastline. From Farrington Highway (Highway 930), west of Hale'iwa, there is a trail leading to the base of the Mokulē'ia Wall, but the trailhead is poorly marked and easy to miss. For help in finding it, call or visit the experts at **Climbers Paradise** (⊠ 214 Sand Island Rd., Honolulu, ☎ 808/842–7625), an indoor climbing center that also rents gear and offers lessons.

Tennis

O'ahu has 181 public tennis courts that are free and open for play on a first-come, first-served basis; you're limited to 45 minutes of court time if others are waiting to play. A complete listing is available free of charge from the **Department of Parks and Recreation** (⊠ Tennis Unit, 650 S. King St., Honolulu 96813, ☎ 808/971–7150, WEB www.co. honolulu.hi.us).

Kapi'olani Park, on the Diamond Head end of Waikīkī, has two tennis locations. The **Diamond Head Tennis Center,** (⊠ 3908 Pākī Ave., ☎ 808/971–7150) on the mauka side of Kapi'olani Park, has nine courts open to the public. There are more than a dozen courts for play at **Kapi'olani Tennis Courts** (⊠ 2748 Kalākaua Ave., ☎ 808/971–2525). The closest public courts to the ewa end of Waikiki are in **Ala Moana Park** (⊠ Makai side of Ala Moana Blvd., ☎ 808/522–7031).

A few Waikīkī hotels have tennis courts that are open to nonguests for a fee. The **Renaissance 'Ilikai Waikīkī** (⊠ 1777 Ala Moana Blvd., ☎ 808/949–3811) has only one court available for play. There's one championship tennis court located on the third-floor recreation deck of the **Waikīkī Beach Marriott Resort** (⊠ 2552 Kalākaua Ave., ☎ 808/ 922–6611). Two tennis courts and tennis lessons are available at the **Pacific Beach Hotel** (⊠ 2490 Kalākaua Ave., ☎ 808/922–1233).

Forty-five minutes from Waikīkī, on O'ahu's Ewa Plain, are two championship tennis courts at the **Hawai'i Prince Golf Club** (⊠ 91-1200 Ft. Weaver Rd., 'Ewa Beach, ☎ 808/944–4567); shuttle service is available from the Hawai'i Prince Hotel Waikīkī for hotel guests.

Water Park

Hawaiian Adventures Water Park. Get wet and wild at this 25-acre water-theme park with a football field–size wave pool, inner tube cruising, and multistory waterslides. A children's water land of delight has a kiddie pool, waterfalls, minislides, and animal floaties. A food court, gift shop, and locker rentals are also here. It's in Kapolei, mauka of the H-1 Freeway on Farrington Highway, 15 minutes from the Honolulu International Airport. ⊠ *400 Farrington Hwy., Kapolei,* ☎ *808/674–9283,* WEB *www.hawaiianwaters.com.* ☞ *$30.* ☉ *10:30–5:30, longer hours in summer.*

Water Sports

The seemingly endless ocean options can be arranged through any hotel travel desk or beach concession. Try the **Waikīkī Beach Center,** next

to the Sheraton Moana Surfrider, or the **C & K Beach Service,** by the
Hilton Hawaiian Village (no telephones).

DEEP-SEA FISHING

Inter-Island Sportfishing (☎ 808/591–8888) operates four vessels available for exclusive or shared deep-sea fishing charters. Rates range from $135–$750 per day. If the "big one" doesn't get away, Inter-Island will arrange to have your trophy fish mounted and sent to you. Departures for charters are from Kewalo Basin. **Magic Sportfishing** (☎ 808/596–2998) offers shared and private charters; rates range from $120 to $650 per day.

OCEAN KAYAKING

This dynamic sport is catching on fast in the Islands. On the North Shore, kayak lessons are available from **Kayak O'ahu Adventures** (⊠ Waimea Valley Adventures Park, 59-894 Kamehameha Hwy., ☎ 808/638–8189). You can kayak the "surfing waters of the kings" off Waikīkī with assistance from **Prime Time Sports** (⊠ Ft. DeRussy Beach, ☎ 808/949–8952). Bob Twogood, a name that is synonymous with O'ahu kayaking, runs a shop called **Twogood Kayaks Hawai'i** (⊠ 345 Hahani St., Kailua, ☎ 808/262–5656), which makes, rents, and sells the fiberglass craft. Twogood rents solo kayaks for $25 a half day, and $32 for a full day. Tandems are $32 a half day and $42 for a full day, including kayak delivery and pickup across from Kailua Beach.

SAILING

Honolulu Sailing Company (☎ 808/239–3900, WEB www.honsail.com) offers a variety of sailing options as well as sailing instruction. Departures are from Pier 2, Honolulu Harbor.

SCUBA DIVING AND SNORKELING

Captain Bruce's Scuba Charters (☎ 808/395–3590) focuses on intimate trips for experienced divers. Led by a naturalist guide, charters run out of O'ahu's west coast, known for its great scuba sites. A two-tank dive costs $96 including transportation from Waikīkī, equipment, and refreshments. **South Seas Aquatics** (☎ 808/922–0852) offers two-tank boat dives at various sites for $75. Several certification courses are available; call for rates. On the North Shore, **Surf-N-Sea** (☎ 808/637–9887) conducts a variety of dive excursions, including night dives. A two-tank excursion starts at $65. Night dives begin at $80.

The most famous snorkeling spot in Hawai'i is Hanauma Bay. You can get masks, fins, and snorkels at the **rental stand** (☎ 808/395–4725) right at the park. **Hanauma Bay Snorkeling Excursions** (☎ 808/373–5060) provides transport from Waikīkī and costs $20 round-trip, including park admission, snorkeling gear, and lessons. You can pick up snorkeling equipment and site advice from **Snorkel Bob's** (⊠ 700 Kapahulu Avenue (☎ 808/735–7944), conveniently located on the way to Hanauma Bay.

Hale'iwa Surf Center (⊠ 66-167 Hale'iwa Rd., Hale'iwa, ☎ 808/637–5051) rents snorkeling equipment and offers guided tours of the North Shore's best sites.

Area dive sites include the following:

Hanauma Bay. East of Koko Head, this bay is an underwater state park and a popular dive site. The shallow inner reef gradually drops from 10 ft to 70 ft at the outer reef. Expect to see butterfly fish, goatfish, parrot fish, surgeon fish, and sea turtles.

Mahi Wai'anae. This 165-ft minesweeper was sunk in 1982 to create an artificial reef. It's intact and penetrable. Goatfish, tame lemon butterfly fish, blue-striped snapper, and 6-ft moray eels can be seen hanging out here. Depths are from 50 ft to 90 ft.

Maunalua Bay. East of Diamond Head, Maunalua Bay has several sites, including Turtle Canyon, with lava flow ridges and sandy canyons teeming with green sea turtles of all sizes; *Kāhala Barge,* a penetrable, 200-ft sunken vessel; Big Eel Reef, with many varieties of moray eels; and Fantasy Reef, a series of lava ledges and archways populated with barracuda and eels.

Shark's Cove. This North Shore site is diveable in the summer months only and should be explored only by experienced divers. Sunlight from above creates a stained-glass effect in the large, roomy caverns. Easily accessible from shore, the cove's depths range from 15 ft to 45 ft. This is the most popular cavern dive on the island.

Three Tables. Named for the trio of flat rocks that break the surface near the beach, this North Shore site has easy access from the shore. Beneath the waves are large rock formations, caverns, and ledges. It's diveable only in the summer months.

SURFING

To rent a board in Waikīkī, visit **C&K Beach Service** (☎ no phone), on the beach fronting the Hilton Hawaiian Village. Rentals cost $8 to $10 per hour, depending on the size of the board, and $12 for two hours. Lessons are $30 per hour with board, and they promise to have you riding the waves by lesson's end.

Novice surfers can meet with guaranteed success with lessons from the **Palakaiko Beach Boys Club** (☎ no phone) who have lessons available every half hour on famous Kūhiō Beach.

On the North Shore, rent a short board for $5 an hour or a long board for $7 from a shop called **Surf 'N' Sea** (☎ 808/637–9887). Its surfing lessons cost $65 for three hours and start daily at 1 PM.

WATERSKIING

Snyderhoud Water Sports and Water Ski Center (✉ Koko Marina Shopping Center, 7192 Kalaniana'ole Hwy., Hawai'i Kai, ☎ 808/395–3773) has a package with round-trip transportation from Waikīkī and a half day of waterskiing in Hawai'i Kai Marina for $110 per hour per person (two-person minimum), with lessons. There are also rides in inflatable banana boats and bumper tubes for kids of all ages.

Waterskiing, jet skiing, powerboating, and parasailing are just some of the sports available in the **AquaZone,** which also features PADI certificate courses for scuba diving. (✉ Koko Marina Shopping Center, 7192 Kalaniana'ole Hwy., Hawai'i Kai, ☎ 808/366–7353).

WINDSURFING

This sport was born in Hawai'i, and O'ahu's Kailua Beach is its cradle. World champion Robby Naish and his family build and sell boards, rent equipment, provide accommodation referrals, and offer windsurfing instruction out of **Naish Hawai'i** (✉ 155A Hāmākua Dr., Kailua, ☎ 808/261–6067, WEB www.niash.com). A four-hour package, including 90 minutes of instruction, costs $55.

Kailua Sailboard and Kayaks Company (✉ 130 Kailua Rd., Kailua, ☎ 808/262–2555) offers small group lessons, rents equipment and transports it to the waterfront five minutes away. On the North Shore, **Surf 'N' Sea** (✉ Hale'iwa, ☎ 808/637–9887) rents windsurfing gear for $12 per hour; a two-hour windsurfing lesson costs $58. Or try **Windsurfing School North Shore,** which offers expert instruction, but you have to bring your own board. (✉ 59-452 Makana Rd., Hale'iwa, ☎ 808/638–8198).

Spectator Sports

Football

The nationally televised **Jeep Aloha Bowl Football Classic** (☎ 808/486–9300), held on Christmas Day at Aloha Stadium in Honolulu, is a sports tradition bringing together powerhouse college teams from the PAC-10 and BIG-12 conferences. For local action the **University of Hawai'i Rainbows** take to the field at Aloha Stadium in season, with a big local following. There are often express buses to games from Kapi'olani Park (☎ 808/956–6508 for details).

Golf

The giants of the greens return to Hawai'i every January or February (depending on the TV scheduling) to compete in the **Sony Hawaiian Open Golf Tournament** (☎ 808/831–5400), a PGA tour regular with a $1 million purse. It's held at the exclusive Wai'alae Country Club in Kahala, and it's always a crowd pleaser.

Mountain Biking

Professional mountain bikers come to O'ahu each year for the **Outrigger Hotels Hawaiian Mountain Tour** (☎ 808/921–6941), a four-day, five-stage race across the most rugged terrain of the windward coast.

Running

The **Honolulu Marathon** is a thrilling event to watch as well as to participate in. Join the throngs who cheer at the finish line at Kapi'olani Park as internationally famous and local runners tackle the 26.2-mi challenge. It's held on the second Sunday in December and is sponsored by the Honolulu Marathon Association (☎ 808/734–7200).

Surfing

For two weekends each March **Buffalo's Annual Big-Board Surfing Classic** (☎ 808/696–3878) fills Mākaha Beach with Hawaiian entertainment, food booths, and the best in big-board surfing. In winter head out to the North Shore to watch the best surfers in the world hang ten during the **Triple Crown Hawaiian Pro Surfing Championships** (☎ 808/638–7266). This two-day event, scheduled according to wave conditions, is generally held at the Banzai Pipeline and Sunset Beach during November and December.

Triathlon

Swim-bike-run events are gaining in popularity and number in Hawai'i. Most fun to watch (or compete in) is the **Tinman Triathlon** (☎ 808/732–7311), held in mid-July in Waikīkī.

Volleyball

Volleyball is extremely popular on the Islands, and no wonder. Both the men's and women's teams of the **University of Hawai'i** have blasted to a number-one ranking in years past. Crowded, noisy, and very exciting home games are played from September through December (women's) and from January through April (men's) in the university's 10,000-seat Stan Sheriff Arena. ⊠ *Lower Campus Rd., Honolulu,* ☎ *808/956–4481.* ✇ *$8.*

Windsurfing

Watch the pros jump and spin on the waves during July's **Pan Am Hawaiian Windsurfing World Cup** (☎ 808/734–6999) off Kailua Beach. For windsurfing competitions off Diamond Head point, check out August's **Wahine Classic** (808/521–4322), featuring the world's best female boardsailors.

SHOPPING

Honolulu is the number-one shopping spot in the Islands and an international crossroads of the shopping scene. It has sprawling shopping malls, unique boutiques, hotel arcades, neighborhood businesses, and a variety of other enterprises. Major shopping malls are generally open daily from 10 to 9; smaller neighborhood boutiques are usually 9-to-5 operations.

Shopping Centers

In Waikīkī

DFS Galleria Waikīkī (⊠ Corner of Kalākaua and Royal Hawaiian Aves., ☎ 808/931–2655) has boutiques of world-class designers—such as Hermes, Cartier, and Calvin Klein—as well as Hawai'i's largest beauty and cosmetic store. An "Old Hawai'i" atmosphere is created by a three-story replica of a 1920s luxury cruise liner; daily Hawaiian music and dance performances; and the Waikīkī Walk, with authentic fashions, arts and crafts, and gifts of the Hawaiian islands. There is also an exclusive boutique floor available to duty-free shoppers only.

The fashionable **King Kalākaua Plaza** (⊠ 2080 Kalākaua Ave.), one of Waikīkī's newer shopping destinations, offers flagship stores Banana Republic and Nike Town as well as the All Sports Hawaii Cafe.

The **Royal Hawaiian Shopping Center** (2201 Kalākaua Ave., ☎ 808/922–0588, WEB www.shopwaikiki.com), fronting the Royal Hawaiian and Sheraton Waikīkī hotels, is three blocks long and contains 150 stores on four levels. There are such upscale establishments as Chanel and Cartier, as well as the Hawaiian Heirloom Jewelry Factory by Philip Rickard, which also has a museum with Victorian jewelry pieces. Bike buffs may want to check out the Harley-Davidson MotorClothes and Collectibles Boutique. The center houses 15 restaurants, including the Paradiso Seafood Grill and Villa Paradiso, and even has a post office.

Waikīkī Shopping Plaza (⊠ 2270 Kalākaua Ave.) is across the street from the Royal Hawaiian Shopping Center. Its landmark is a 75-ft-high water-sculpture gizmo, which looks great when it's working. Sawada Pro Golf Shop, Armani Exchange, and Tanaka of Tokyo Restaurant are some of the 50 shops and restaurants on six floors.

Waikīkī has three theme park–style shopping centers. Right in the heart of the area is the **International Market Place** (⊠ 2330 Kalākaua Ave.), a tangle of 200 souvenir shops and stalls under a giant banyan tree. **Waikīkī Town Center** (⊠ 2301 Kūhiō Ave.) is an open-air complex with a variety of shops ranging from fashions to jewelry. There are free hula shows here Monday, Wednesday, Friday, and Saturday at 7 PM. The **King's Village** shopping complex (⊠ 131 Ka'iulani Ave., ☎ 808/944–6855) looks like a Hollywood stage set of monarchy-era Honolulu, complete with a changing-of-the-guard ceremony every evening at 6:15; shops include Hawaiian Island Creations Jewelry, Swim City USA Swimwear, and Pipeline Leather Fashions.

Around Honolulu

Ala Moana Shopping Center (⊠ 1450 Ala Moana Blvd., ☎ 808/955–9517 for special-events information and information about shuttle service) is one of the nation's largest open-air malls and just five minutes from Waikīkī by bus. More than 200 stores, restaurants, and services make up this 50-acre complex. All of Hawai'i's major department stores are here, including Neiman Marcus, Sears, JCPenney, and Liberty House. Palm Boulevard features upscale designer fashions, such as Gucci, Louis Vuitton, Gianni Versace, and Emporio Armani.

Ala Moana has a huge assortment of local-style souvenir shops, such as Hawaiian Island Creations, Irene's Hawaiian Gifts, and Products of Hawai'i. Makai Market is a large international food bazaar representing a range of cuisines, from Hawaiian to Cajun. Center Stage hosts free daily musical entertainment. Shuttle service is provided between many Waikīkī hotels and the Center.

Aloha Flea Market (⊠ 99-500 Salt Lake Blvd., ☎ 808/732–9611) is a thrice-weekly outdoor bazaar that attracts hundreds of vendors and even more bargain hunters. Operations range from slick tents with rows of neatly stacked, new wares to blankets spread on the pavement, covered with garage-sale treasures. You'll find gold trinkets, antique furniture, Japanese fishing floats, T-shirts, mu'umu'u, and palm-frond hats. The flea market takes place in the Aloha Stadium parking lot Wednesday and weekends from 6 to 3; the $6 admission fee includes round-trip shuttle service from Waikīkī.

Aloha Tower Marketplace (⊠ 1 Aloha Tower Dr., at Piers 8, 9, and 10, ☎ 808/566–2337, WEB www.alohatower.com/atm for special-events information) cozies up to Honolulu Harbor and bills itself as a festival marketplace. Along with restaurants and entertainment venues, it has 80 shops and kiosks selling mostly visitor-oriented merchandise, from expensive sunglasses to souvenir refrigerator magnets. It's also home to Don Ho's Island Grill, with Hawaiian entertainment and food harborside.

Kāhala Mall (⊠ 4211 Wai'alae Ave., ☎ 808/732–7736) has 90 retail outlets and such clothing stores as Liberty House and Gap. Reyn's is the acknowledged place to go for men's resort wear. Its aloha shirts have muted colors and button-down collars, suitable for most social occasions. Along with an assortment of gift shops, Kāhala Mall also has eight movie theaters (☎ 808/733–6233) for post-shopping entertainment. The mall is 10 minutes by car from Waikīkī in the chic residential neighborhood of Kāhala, near the slopes of Diamond Head.

Heading west from Waikīkī toward downtown Honolulu, you'll run into a section of town with five distinct shopping-complex areas known as the **Victoria Ward Centers;** there are more than 100 specialty shops and 17 restaurants here. Two of the largest and most popular complexes are Ward Warehouse (⊠ 1050 Ala Moana Blvd.) and Ward Centre (⊠ 1200 Ala Moana Blvd.).

The **Waikele Premium Outlets** (⊠ H-1 Fwy., Waikele, 30 minutes west of downtown Honolulu) reflects Hawai'i's latest craze: warehouse shopping at discount prices. Among its occupants are the Anne Klein Factory, Donna Karan Company Store, Villeroy & Boch, and Saks Fifth Avenue.

Specialty Stores

Clothing

HIGH FASHION

Neiman Marcus (⊠ Ala Moana Shopping Center, 1450 Ala Moana Blvd., Honolulu, ☎ 808/951–8887) is the trendy end of the high-fashion scene. For the latest in footwear, **Nordstrom Shoes** (⊠ Ala Moana Shopping Center, 1450 Ala Moana Blvd., Honolulu, ☎ 808/973–4620) displays an elegant array of pricey styles. Top-of-the-line international fashions for men and women are available at **Mandalay Imports** (⊠ Halekūlani, 2199 Kālia Rd., Waikīkī, ☎ 808/922–7766), home of Star of Siam silks and cottons, Anne Namba couture, and designs by Choisy, who works out of Bangkok. **Pzazz** (⊠ 1419 Kalākaua Ave., Waikīkī, ☎ 808/955–

5800), nicknamed the Ann Taylor of consignment shops, sells high fashion at low prices.

ISLAND WEAR

For stylish Hawaiian wear, the kind worn by local men and women, look in one of the **Liberty House** branches at Ala Moana Shopping Center, Kāhala Mall, or in downtown Honolulu (⊠ 2314 Kalākaua Ave., Waikīkī, ☎ 808/941–2345 for all stores). **Native Books and Beautiful Things** (⊠ Ward Warehouse, 1050 Ala Moana Blvd., Honolulu, ☎ 808/537–2926) sells handpainted, one-of-a-kind clothing created by local artisans. **Ohelo Road** (⊠ Kāhala Mall, 4211 Wai'alae Ave., Honolulu, ☎ 808/735–5525) carries island print dresses in materials that make living in the tropics cool year-round. For menswear, try **Reyn's** (⊠ Ala Moana Shopping Center, 1450 Ala Moana Blvd., Honolulu, ☎ 808/949–5929; ⊠ Kāhala Mall, 4211 Wai'alae Ave., Honolulu, ☎ 808/737–8313; ⊠ Sheraton Waikīkī, 2255 Kalākaua Ave., Waikīkī, ☎ 808/923–0331).

If you're looking for aloha wear that ranges from the bright-and-bold to the cool-and-classy, try **Hilo Hattie** (⊠ 700 N. Nimitz Hwy., Honolulu, ☎ 808/537–2926), the world's largest manufacturer of Hawaiian and tropical fashions; it's also a good source for island souvenirs. Free shuttle service is available from Waikīkī. For vintage aloha shirts, try **Bailey's Antique Clothing and Thrift Shop** (⊠ 517 Kapahulu Ave., ☎ 808/734–7628), on the edge of Waikīkī.

Food

Bring home fresh pineapple, papaya, or coconut to savor or share with friends and family. Jam comes in flavors such as pohā, passion fruit, and guava. Kona- and O'ahu-grown Waialua coffee beans have an international following. There are dried-food products such as saimin, haupia, and teriyaki barbecue sauce. All kinds of cookies are available, as well as exotic teas, drink mixes, and pancake syrups. And don't forget the macadamia nuts, from plain to chocolate-covered and brittled. By law, all fresh-fruit products must be inspected by the Department of Agriculture before export. For cheap prices on local delicacies, try one of the many **Long's Drugs** stores (⊠ Ala Moana Shopping Center, 1450 Ala Moana Blvd., 2nd level, Honolulu, ☎ 808/941–4433; ⊠ Kāhala Mall, 4211 Wai'alae Ave., Honolulu, ☎ 808/732–0784; ⊠ 1088 Bishop Street Mall, downtown Honolulu, ☎ 808/536–4551). **Tropical Fruits Distributors of Hawai'i** (⊠ 651 Ilalo St., Honolulu, ☎ 808/874–3234) specializes in packing inspected pineapple and papaya; it will deliver to your hotel and to the airport baggage check-in counter or ship to the mainland United States and Canada.

Gifts

Following Sea (⊠ Kāhala Mall, 4211 Wai'alae Ave., Honolulu, ☎ 808/734–4425) sells beautiful handmade jewelry and pottery.

To send home tropical flowers, contact **Hawaiian Greenhouse** (☎ 888/965–8351, WEB www.hawaiiangreenhouse.com). **Robyn Buntin Galleries** (⊠ 820 S. Beretania St., Honolulu, ☎ 808/545–5572) presents Chinese nephrite jade carvings, Japanese lacquer and screens, Buddhist sculptures, and other international pieces. **Takenoya Arts** (⊠ Halekūlani, 2199 Kālia Rd., Waikīkī, ☎ 808/926–1939) specializes in intricately carved *netsuke* (toggles used to fasten containers to kimonos), both antique and contemporary, and one-of-a-kind necklaces.

Hawaiian Art and Crafts

Items handcrafted of native Hawaiian wood make lovely gifts. Koa and milo each have a beautiful color and grain. The great koa forests are disappearing because of environmental factors, so the wood is becoming valuable; most koa products you'll encounter are produced from wood grown on commercial farms.

A wonderful selection of Hawaiian arts, crafts, and children's toys can be found at **My Little Secret** (⊠ Ward Warehouse, 1050 Ala Moana Blvd., ☎ 808/596–2990).

For hula costumes and instruments, try **Hula Supply Center** (⊠ 2346 S. King St., ☎ 808/941–5379). You can purchase traditional island comforters at **Quilts Hawaiʻi** (⊠ 2338 S. King St., ☎ 808/942–3195). For high-end collector's items, head to **Martin & MacArthur** (⊠ Aloha Tower Marketplace, 1 Aloha Tower Dr., ☎ 808/524–6066), specialists in koa furniture.

Jewelry
Bernard Hurtig's (⊠ Hilton Hawaiian Village Aliʻi Tower, 2005 Kālia Rd., ☎ 808/947–9399) sells fine jewelry with an emphasis on 18-karat gold and antique jade. **Haimoff & Haimoff Creations in Gold** (⊠ Halekūlani, 2199 Kālia Rd., ☎ 808/923–8777) sells the work of award-winning jewelry designer Harry Haimoff.

Coral and pearl jewelry is popular, stunning, and fairly affordable. To see where it comes from and how jewelry is designed using these treasures from the sea, take a tour of the **Maui Divers Jewelry Design Center** (⊠ 1520 Liona St., Honolulu, ☎ 808/943–8383).

OʻAHU A TO Z

To research prices, get advice from other travelers, and book travel arrangements, visit www.fodors.com.

AIR TRAVEL
Most flights to Honolulu International originate in Los Angeles or San Francisco, which means they are nonstop. Flying time from the West Coast is 4½–5 hours. Honolulu also has a number of carriers routing to the islands from the United Kingdom.

CARRIERS

Carriers flying into Honolulu from the mainland United States include American, Continental, Delta, Hawaiian, Northwest, and United. Carriers flying from the United Kingdom to Honolulu include Air New Zealand, American, Continental, Delta, and United. Rates for an APEX ticket vary. Check around for the best offer.

Charter flights are the least expensive and the least reliable—with chronically late departures and occasional cancellations. They also tend to depart less frequently (usually once a week) than do regularly scheduled flights. The savings may be worth the potential annoyance, however. Charter flights serving Honolulu International Airport are available from American Trans Air and Hawaiian Airlines.
➤ AIRLINES & CONTACTS: **Air New Zealand** (☎ 800/262–1234). **American** (☎ 808/833–7600 or 800/433–7300). **American Trans Air** (☎ 800/435–9282). **Continental** (☎ 800/525–0280). **Delta** (☎ 800/221–1212). **Hawaiian Airlines** (☎ 808/838–1555 or 800/367–5320). **Northwest** (☎ 808/955–2255 or 800/225–2525). **United** (☎ 800/241–6522).

AIRPORT
More direct flights, by more domestic and international air carriers, arrive and depart from Honolulu International than at any other airport in Hawaiʻi. If you find yourself waiting at the airport with extra time on your hands, be sure to visit the Pacific Aerospace Museum, open daily from 8:30 to 6, in the main terminal. It includes a 1,700-

square-ft, three-dimensional, multimedia theater presenting the history of flight in Hawai'i, and a full-scale space shuttle flight deck. Hands-on exhibits include a mission-control computer program tracing flights in the Pacific.

➤ AIRPORT INFORMATION: **Honolulu International Airport** (☎ 808/ 836–6413). **Pacific Aerospace Museum** (☎ 808/839–0777, ✉ $3).

AIRPORT TRANSFERS

There are taxis right at the airport baggage-claim exit. At $1.50 start-up plus $1.50 for each mile, the fare to Waikīkī will run approximately $20, plus tip. Drivers are also allowed to charge 30¢ per suitcase. Trans Hawaiian Services runs an airport shuttle service to Waikīkī. Fare is $7 one-way, $13 round-trip. The municipal bus (TheBus) will take you into Waikīkī for only $1.50, but you are allowed only one bag, which must fit on your lap. Some hotels have their own pickup service. Check when you book.

➤ TAXIS & SHUTTLES: **TheBus** (☎ 808/848–5555). **Trans Hawaiian Services** (☎ 808/566–7333).

BOAT & FERRY TRAVEL

Boat Day used to be the biggest day of the week. Jet travel once obscured that custom, but arriving in Hawai'i by ship is making a comeback. If you have the time, it is one sure way to unwind. Many cruises are planned a year or more in advance and fill up fast. Most cruise-ship companies offer a fare that includes round-trip air travel to the point of embarkation.

Cunard/N.A.C. Line, Royal Cruises, Princess Cruises, and Royal Caribbean have cruise ships passing through Honolulu once or twice a year. There are currently two interisland cruise vessels based in Hawaiian waters. The S.S. *Independence* is based in Kahalui, Maui, and its weekly interisland cruises include ports of call at O'ahu, Kaua'i, and the Big Island of Hawai'i. The newest addition to the Hawai'i cruise industry is the M.S. *Patriot,* which is home-ported in Honolulu Harbor and departs each Saturday on a weeklong interisland cruise. You can also book three- and four-day packages on the Hawai'i-based luxury liner.

➤ BOAT & FERRY INFORMATION: **American Hawai'i Cruises** (✉ 1380 Port of New Orleans Pl., Robin St. Wharf, New Orleans, LA 70130, ☎ 504/586–0631 or 800/543–7637, WEB www.cruisehawaii.com).

BIKE & MOPED TRAVEL

Blue Sky Rentals & Sports Center rents mopeds for $20 a day (8–6) and $25 for 24 hours. Mountain bikes from Blue Sky Rentals cost $15 a day, $20 for 24 hours, and $75 for the week, plus a $25 deposit. Island Motorcycle rents a variety of motorcycles for $129 to $149 a day.

➤ BIKE RENTALS: **Blue Sky Rentals & Sports Center** (✉ 1920 Ala Moana Blvd., across from Hilton Hawaiian Village, Waikīkī, ☎ 808/ 947–0101). **Island Motorcycle** (✉ Kalakaua Ave., Waikīkī, ☎ 808/957–0517).

BUS TRAVEL

You can go all around the island or just down Kalākaua Avenue for $1.50 on Honolulu's municipal transportation system, affectionately known as TheBus and voted the "Best Transit System in America for 2000–2001" by the American Public Transit Association. You're entitled to one free transfer per fare if you ask for it when boarding. Exact change is required, and dollar bills are accepted. A four-day pass for visitors costs $10 and is sold at the more than 30 ABC stores (Hawaiian chain stores that sell sundries and are geared to tourists) in Waikīkī. Monthly passes cost $25.

There are no official bus-route maps, but you can find privately published booklets at most drugstores and other convenience outlets. The important route numbers for Waikīkī are 2, 4, 8, 19, 20, and 58. If you venture afield, you can always get back on one of these.

There's also a number of brightly painted private buses, many free, that will take you to such commercial attractions as dinner cruises, garment factories, and the like.

➤ BUS INFORMATION: **TheBus** (☎ 808/848–5555).

CAR RENTAL

If you plan to go beyond the limits of Waikīkī to tour Oʻahu itself, renting a car is essential. During peak seasons—summer, Christmas vacations, and February—reservations are necessary. Rental agencies abound in and around the Honolulu International Airport and in Waikīkī. Local agencies rent everything from used cars to classics and pickup trucks.

Cloud Nine Limousine Service provides red-carpet treatment in its chauffeur-driven superstretch limousines. Rates are $60 an hour, plus tax and tip, with a two-hour minimum. Another reliable company is Lowy Limousine Service, which specializes in Lincoln stretch limos starting at $50 per hour, with a two-hour minimum.

➤ MAJOR AGENCIES: **Avis** (☎ 808/834–5524 or 800/333–1212). **Budget** (☎ 808/838–1111 or 800/527–0700). **Dollar** (☎ 800/367–7006). **Hertz** (☎ 808/523–5176 or 800/654–8200). **National** (☎ 808/831–0270 or 800/227–7368). **Thrifty** (☎ 808/733–5188 or 800/367–2277).

➤ LOCAL AGENCIES: **JN Car and Truck Rentals** (☎ 808/831–2724). **VIP** (☎ 808/922–4605).

➤ LIMOUSINE RENTALS: **Cloud Nine Limousine Service** (☎ 808/524–7999 or 800/524–7999). **Lowy Limousine Service** (☎ 808/455–2444).

CAR TRAVEL

Oʻahu's drivers are generally courteous, and you rarely hear a horn. People will slow down and let you into traffic with a wave of the hand. A friendly wave back is customary. If a driver sticks a hand out the window in a fist with the thumb and pinky sticking straight out, this is a good thing: the Hawaiian symbol for "hang loose," it's called the *shaka* and is often used to say "thanks," as well.

Hawaiʻi has a seat-belt law for front-seat passengers and those under the age of 18 in the back seats. Children under 40 pounds must be in a car seat, available from your car-rental agency.

It's hard to get lost on Oʻahu. Roads and streets, although perhaps unpronounceable to visitors, are at least well marked. Major attractions and scenic spots are marked by the distinctive HVCB sign with its red-caped warrior. Although it's hard to get lost, driving in Honolulu can be frustrating, as many streets are one-way.

Driving in rush-hour traffic (6:30–8:30 and 3:30–5:30) can be exasperating, because left turns are prohibited at many intersections. Parking along many streets is curtailed during these hours, and towing is strictly enforced. Read the curbside parking signs before leaving your vehicle, even at a meter. Remember not to leave valuables in your car. Rental cars are often targets for thieves.

EMERGENCIES

To reach the police, fire department, or an ambulance in an emergency, dial **911.**

A doctor, laboratory-radiology technician, and nurses are always on duty at Doctors on Call. Appointments are recommended but not necessary. Services include diagnosis and treatment of illness and injury, laboratory testing, X ray on-site, and referral, when necessary. Dozens of kinds of medical insurance are accepted, including Medicare, Medicaid, and most kinds of travel insurance.

Kūhiō Pharmacy is Waikīkī's only pharmacy and handles prescription requests until 4:30 PM. Long's Drugs is open evenings at its Ala Moana location and 24 hours at its South King Street location (15 minutes from Waikīkī by car).

➤ DOCTORS & DENTISTS: **Doctors on Call** (⊠ Nicos Bldg., 2222 Kalākaua Ave., 2nd floor, Waikīkī, ☎ 808/971–6000).

➤ EMERGENCY SERVICES: **Coast Guard Rescue Center** (☎ 800/552–6458).

➤ HOSPITALS: **Castle Medical Center** (⊠ 640 Ulukahiki, Kailua, ☎ 808/263–5500). **Kapiolani Medical Center for Women and Children** (⊠ 1319 Punahou St., Honolulu, ☎ 808/973–8511). **Queen's Medical Center** (⊠ 1301 Punchbowl St., Honolulu, ☎ 808/538–9011). **Saint Francis Medical Center–West** (⊠ 91-2141 Ft. Weaver Rd., 'Ewa Beach, ☎ 808/678–7000). **Straub Clinic** (⊠ 888 S. King St., Honolulu, ☎ 808/522–4000).

➤ PHARMACIES: **Kūhiō Pharmacy** (⊠ Outrigger West Hotel, 2330 Kūhiō Ave., Waikīkī, ☎ 808/923–4466). **Long's Drugs** (⊠ Ala Moana Shopping Center, 1450 Ala Moana Blvd., 2nd level, Honolulu, ☎ 808/949–4010; ⊠ 2220 S. King St., Honolulu, ☎ 808/947–2651).

SIGHTSEEING TOURS

AERIAL TOURS

After suiting up with the goggles and leather helmets of Biplane Rides, you can climb into an open cockpit of a restored Stearman biplane for loops, rolls, hammer heads, and other aerobatic maneuvers above O'ahu's North Shore. Only one person can go up at a time—20 minutes cost $125, 40 minutes cost $175.

Through the bubble top of Glider Rides' sleek sail plane you get aerial views of O'ahu's North Shore with its coral pools, sugarcane fields, windsurfers, and, in winter, humpback whales. On-board live video-taping is available. Reservations are not accepted; 20- and 30-minute flights leave every 20 minutes daily 10–5. The charge for one passenger is $90, two people fly for $120.

Island Seaplane Service takes off from Keahi Lagoon and sets you soaring on an aerial tour that is either a half-hour South and Eastern O'ahu shoreline tour or an hour Circle Island tour. Get the feel of what Hawai'i air transportation was like during the Pan Am Clipper days, for $79–$129.

Makani Kai Helicopters departs from Honolulu International Airport for helicopter tours of O'ahu by daylight or at sunset. A Waikiki By Night excursion sends you soaring by the breathtaking Honolulu city lights.

➤ TOUR OPERATORS: **Biplane Rides** (⊠ Dillingham Airfield, Mokulē'ia, ☎ 808/637–4461). **Glider Rides** (⊠ Dillingham Airfield, Mokulē'ia, ☎ 808/677–3404). **Island Seaplane Service** (⊠ Keahi Lagoon, Honolulu, ☎ 808/836–6273). **Makani Kai Helicopters** (⊠ Honolulu International Airport, Honolulu, ☎ 808/834–5813).

BOAT TOURS

Dream Cruises offers tours of Pearl Harbor aboard the 100-ft motor yacht *American Dream*. The trip takes place in the early morning—from 7:30 to 10:30—to coincide with the time that Pearl Harbor was attacked on December 7, 1941. It includes a stop near the *Arizona* Memorial, where the captain conducts a brief memorial service and lei placement ceremony. Narration and videos help describe the sights. In winter, this cruise is paired with a whale-watch. The cost is $21.95.

Tradewind Charters is a good bet for half-day private charter tours for sailing, snorkeling, and whale-watching. These luxury yachts not only eliminate crowds, but you also have the opportunity to "take the helm" if you wish. The cruise also includes snorkeling at an exclusive anchorage as well as hands-on snorkeling and sailing instruction. Charter prices are approximately $495 for up to six passengers.

➤ Tour Operators: **Dream Cruises** (✉ 1020 Auahi St., Honolulu, ☎ 808/592–5200). **Tradewind Charters** (✉ 796 Kalanipuu St., Honolulu 96825, ☎ 800/829–4899).

BUS & VAN TOURS

There are many ground-tour companies in O'ahu that handle day-long sightseeing excursions. Depending on the size of the tour, travel may be by air-conditioned bus or smaller vans. Vans are recommended because less time is spent picking up passengers, and you get to know your fellow passengers and your tour guide. Ask exactly what the tour includes in the way of actual "get-off-the-bus" stops and "window sights." Most of the tour guides have taken special Hawaiiana classes to learn their history and lore, and many are certified by the State of Hawai'i. Tipping ($2 per person at least) is customary.

American Express Tours and Activities Center books through several tour companies and can help you choose which tour best suits your needs. E Noa Tours uses minibuses and trolleys and likes to get you into the great outdoors. Polynesian Adventure Tours has motorcoaches, vans, and minicoaches. Polynesian Hospitality provides narrated tours. Roberts Hawai'i has equipment ranging from vans to presidential limousines. Trans Hawaiian Services offers multilingual tours.

Most tour companies offer some version of the following standard O'ahu tours listed below:

There are several variations on the Circle Island Tour theme. Some of these all-day tours, ranging from $45–$65, include lunch. Little Circle tours cover East O'ahu. This is a half-day tour and costs between $25–$40.

The comprehensive Pearl Harbor and City tour includes the boat tour to Pearl Harbor run by the National Park Service. These tours cost between $35–$40.

One of the advantages of the Polynesian Cultural Center tour is that you don't have to drive yourself back to Waikīkī after dark if you take in the evening show. The tour is $70–$80 per person.

➤ Tour Operators: **American Express Tours and Activities Center** (☎ 808/521–7283). **E Noa Tours** (☎ 808/591–2561, WEB www.enoa.com). **National Park Service** (☎ 808/422–0561). **Polynesian Adventure Tours** (☎ 808/833–3000). **Polynesian Cultural Center** (☎ 808/293–3333 or 808/923–1861). **Polynesian Hospitality** (☎ 808/526–3565). **Roberts Hawai'i** (☎ 808/539–9400). **Trans Hawaiian Services** (☎ 808/566–7420).

THEME TOURS

E Noa Tours has certified tour guides who conduct not only Circle Island and Pearl Harbor tours, but also shopping tours to the Waikele Premium Outlets.

Hawaiian Island Eco-tours, Ltd.'s experienced guides take nature lovers and hikers on limited access trails to some of O'ahu's most splendid waterfalls, rain forests, and coastlines.

Home of the Brave offers military-history buffs a narrated tour of military bases plus a drive through the National Memorial Cemetary of the Pacific.

Mauka Makai Excursions takes visitors to visit some of the ancient Hawaiian archeological, legendary, and nature sites that islanders hold sacred.

➤ TOUR OPERATORS: **E Noa Tours** (☎ 808/591–2561, WEB www. enoa.com). **Hawaiian Island Eco-tours, Ltd.** (☎ 808/236–7766). **Home of the Brave** (☎ 808/396–8112). **Mauka Makai Excursions** (☎ 808/ 593–3525).

UNDERWATER TOURS

Atlantis Submarines operates two vessels off Waikīkī: a 65-ft, 80-ton sub carrying up to 48 passengers for $89 per person, and a newer 102-ft, 64-passenger craft, which costs $99 per person. The subs dive up to 100 ft to see a sunken navy-yard oiler and an artificial reef populated by brilliant fish. The dive itself lasts about one hour, and you get a one-hour cruise with informative narration. Rides are popular with children, who must be at least 3-ft tall to board. Note: Flash photography will not work; use film speed ASA 200 or above without flash.

Voyager Submarines' roomy, air-conditioned yellow submarine takes you to the depths of the sea for a view of submerged lava flows, coral reef gardens, and Hawai'i's marine world of reef shark, angelfish, and parrot fish. The cost is $89. For the more adventurous, the company also operates Hawaii Ocean Thrills, offering extreme marine sports including Jet Skis and jet-propelled Formula One racing boats.

➤ TOUR OPERATORS: *Atlantis* Submarines (⊠ 1600 Kapi'olani Blvd., Suite 1630, Honolulu 96814, ☎ 808/973–9811). *Voyager* Submarines (⊠ 1085 Ala Moana Blvd., Honolulu 96814, ☎ 808/592–7850, WEB www.robertshawaii.com).

WALKING TOURS

Meet at the Chinese Chamber of Commerce for a fascinating peek into herbal shops, an acupuncturist's office, open-air markets, and specialty stores. The 2½-hour tour sponsored by the Chinese Chamber of Commerce costs $5 and is available every Tuesday at 9:30. Reservations are required.

Volunteers from the Mission Houses Museum take you on a two-hour walk through Honolulu, where historic sites stand side by side with modern business towers. During the first hour, you get a tour of the Mission Houses themselves. Reservations are required. Tours, which cost $8, are available Thursday and Friday between 9:30 AM–12:30 PM.

History springs to life for young and old alike during Honolulu Time Walks, which come with appropriately costumed narrators and cost $7–$45. Tours include "Haunted Honolulu," "Honolulu's Crime Beat," "Mysteries of Mō'ili'ili," "Mark Twain's Honolulu," and the "Old Hawai'i Saloon Walk." The company also presents theater shows and films about the Islands.

➤ TOUR OPERATORS: **Chinatown Walking Tour** (⊠ Chinese Chamber of Commerce, 42 N. King St., Honolulu, ☎ 808/533–3181). **Historic Downtown Walking Tour.** (⊠ 553 S. King St., Honolulu, ☎ 808/531–0481). **Honolulu Time Walks** (⊠ 2634 S. King St., Suite 3, Honolulu, ☎ 808/943–0371).

TAXIS

You can usually get a taxi right outside your hotel. Most restaurants will call a taxi for you. Rates are $1.50 at the drop of the flag, plus $1.50 per mile. Drivers are generally courteous, and the cars are in good condition, many of them air-conditioned. For transportation throughout the island, try Charley's Taxi & Tours. SIDA of Hawai'i Taxis, Inc. offers 24-hour island wide transportation service and multilingual drivers.

➤ TAXI COMPANIES: **Charley's Taxi & Tours** (☎ 808/531–1333). **SIDA of Hawai'i Taxis Inc.** (☎ 808/836–0011).

TRANSPORTATION AROUND O'AHU

Waikīkī is only 2½ mi long and ½ mi wide, which means you can usually walk to where you are going. However, if you plan to venture outside of Waikīkī, it's best to rent a car.

TROLLEY TRAVEL

The Waikīkī Trolley has three lines that allow you to design your own itinerary. The Red Line cruises around Waikīkī, Ala Moana, and downtown Honolulu. The Yellow Line hits major shopping centers and restaurant locations. The Blue Line provides a tour of O'ahu's southeastern coastline, including Hanauma Bay and Sea Life Park. The trolleys depart from the Royal Hawaiian Shopping Center in Waikīkī every 15 minutes daily from 8–4:30. Buy an all-day pass from the conductor for $18.

➤ CONTACT: **Waikīkī Trolley** (☎ 808/596–2199).

VISITOR INFORMATION

➤ TOURIST INFORMATION: **Hawai'i Attractions Association** (☎ 808/596–7733, WEB www.hawaiiattractions.com). **Hawai'i Visitors & Convention Bureau** (✉ Waikīkī Business Plaza, 2270 Kalākaua Ave., Suite 801, Honolulu 96815, ☎ 808/923–1811 or 800/464–2924, WEB www.gohawaii.com). **O'ahu Visitor Bureau** (☎ 877/525–6248, WEB www.visit-oahu.com). **Surf Report** (☎ 808/596–7873). **Weather** (☎ 808/973–4381).

2 MAUI
THE VALLEY ISLE

The three planned resort communities along Maui's lee shore—Kapalua, Kāʻanapali, and Wailea—are self-contained environments of such luxury and beauty that the effect is almost surreal. With its golf courses, beaches, glorious sunsets, and (in winter) leaping humpback whales, leeward Maui is justifiably one of the top beach-vacation spots in the world. But there's more to the story—the curious history of Lahaina, the national park at Haleakalā, the towns and ranches Upcountry, and the dramatic rain forest drive to Hāna.

Updated by
Kim
Westerman

MAUI NŌ KA ʻOI IS WHAT THE LOCALS SAY—it's the best, the most, the top of the heap. To those who know Maui well, there's good reason for the superlatives. The second-largest island in the Hawaiian chain, Maui has made an international name for itself with its tropical allure, its arts and cultural activities, and miles of perfect-tan beaches. Maui weaves a spell over the more than 2 million people who visit its shores each year, and many visitors decide to return for good.

Maui residents have quite a bit to do with their island's successful tourism story. In the mid-1970s, savvy marketers on Maui saw a way to increase their sleepy island's economy by positioning it as an island apart. Community leaders started promoting their Valley Isle separately from the rest of the state. They nicknamed West Maui "the Golf Coast," luring in heavyweight tournaments that, in turn, would bring more visitors. They attracted some of the finest resorts and hotels in the world, and they became the state's condominium experts, emphasizing the luxurious privacy these accommodations can provide. Maui's visitor count swelled, putting it far ahead of that of the other Neighbor Islands.

Quick growth has led to its share of problems. During the busy seasons—from Christmas to Easter and then again during the summer— West Maui can be overly crowded. Although Maui has widened the road that connects Lahaina and Kāʻanapali, the occasional traffic congestion here might not be what you bargained for. And East Maui's Kīhei still has trouble keeping traffic in motion along its one seaside main drive.

But then consider Maui's natural resources. The island is made up of two volcanoes, one now extinct and the other dormant, that both erupted long ago and joined into one island. The resulting depression between the two is what gives Maui its nickname, the Valley Isle. West Maui's 5,788-ft Puʻu Kukui was the first volcano to form, a distinction that gives that area's mountainous topography a more weathered look. Rainbows seem to grow wild over this terrain as gentle mists fill the deeply eroded canyons.

The Valley Isle's second volcano is the 10,023-ft Haleakalā, a mammoth mountain. If you hike its slopes or peer into its enormous crater, you'll witness an impressive variety of nature, with desertlike terrain butted up against tropical forests.

The island's volcanic history gives Maui much of its beauty. The roads around the island are lined with rich red soil, the fertile foothold for sugarcane. Sugar has disappeared from West Maui, as it has nearly everywhere in the state. But Central Maui is still carpeted with grassy green, thanks to HC&S with its working mills at Puʻunēnē and Pāʻia. As the deep blue of ocean and sky mingles with the red and green of Maui's topography, it looks as though an artist has been busy painting the landscape. Indeed, visual artists love Maui.

Farmers also appreciate the Valley Isle. On the slopes of Haleakalā, the volcanic richness of the soil has yielded lush results. Sweetly scented flowers bloom large and healthy. Grapes cultivated on Haleakalā's slopes are squeezed for wine and champagne. Horses graze languidly on rolling meadows of the best Upcountry grasses, while jacaranda trees dot the hillsides with spurts of luscious lavender. As the big brute of a volcano slides east and becomes the town of Hāna, the rains that lavishly fall there turn the soil into a jungle and waterfalls cascade down the crags.

Pleasures and Pastimes

Beaches

Maui's beaches win awards for being the best in the world. (Yes, there are awards for beaches.) Those of Wailea and Kapalua lead the pack. Residents particularly revere Mākena Beach, beyond Wailea—so much so that they launched a successful grassroots campaign to have it preserved as a state park. Don't expect to find the island ringed with sand. In fact, most of the coastline is dramatically craggy. Beaches tend to be pockets. Each one has a personality of its own and can be completely explored in a half day. The thin, clean strand of Kā'anapali, though, goes on for 3 miles, past resort after resort. Offshore here, yachts, catamarans, and parasail riders drift across brilliant porcelain-blue water. Many of Maui's beaches are a little difficult to spot from the road, especially where homes and hotels have taken up shoreline property. Just remember that you can go to any beach you want. Access to the sea is a sacred trust in Hawai'i, preserved from ancient times. Sometimes you have to poke around to find the beach. Then again, maybe those are the ones you want.

Culture

Maui residents like the arts so much that they built the Maui Arts & Cultural Center, with its well-designed 1,200-seat Castle Theater and its Schaefer International Art Gallery. The island also has one of the oldest community-theater groups in the country and one of the highest per capita populations of painters anywhere. Friday night is Art Night in Lahaina, where commercial galleries line Front Street. But many artists have retreated to the Upcountry region, making Makawao their hub. Up here, Hui No'eau Visual Arts Center has been providing classes, studios, and exhibits since the 1930s. The resorts, too, are lined with splendid art collections. The hotels also perpetuate Hawaiian culture. The best at this are the Ritz-Carlton, Kapalua and the Kā'anapali Beach Hotel. The best way to explore Maui's curious history and mixed cultures is to tour the small museums—Baldwin Home in Lahaina, Bailey House in Wailuku, the Alexander & Baldwin (A&B) Sugar Museum in Pu'unēnē, the Hāna Cultural Center Museum, and the 'Ulupalakua Ranch History Room at the Tedeschi Vineyards and Winery, to name a handful. Or go to the local events, the festivals and benefit concerts, a Japanese o-bon dance or a Portuguese church bazaar. There's always something going on. Check *The Maui News* on Thursday ("The Scene") and Sunday ("Currents").

Dining

You can eat a great meal every night for a month on Maui without ever dining twice in the same place. The resorts set very high standards, and restaurants elsewhere have risen to the challenge. Maui continues to attract fine chefs, several of whom are known for their trendsetting Hawai'i regional cuisine. This growing movement uses fruits and vegetables unique to Hawai'i in classic European or Asian ways—spawning such dishes as 'ahi (yellowfin tuna) carpaccio, breadfruit soufflé, and papaya cheesecake. Of course, you can find plain old local-style cooking here—particularly if you wander into the less-touristy areas of Wailuku or Kahului, for example. A good "plate lunch" will fulfill your daily requirement of carbohydrates: macaroni salad, two scoops of rice, and an entrée of, say, curry stew, teriyaki beef, or *kālua* (roasted in an underground oven) pig and cabbage.

Driving

Maui has bad roads in beautiful places. Lots of visitors take a break from the beach and just go driving, usually taking day trips from their lodgings around Lahaina or Kīhei. Maui's landscape is extraordinarily diverse for such a small island. Your sense of place (and the weather) will seem to change every few miles. If you drive to the top of Haleakalā you rise from palm-lined beaches to the rare world inhabited by airplanes in only an hour and a half. The road to Hāna takes you into the tropical rain forest, testing your reflexes behind the wheel on the rain-gouged windward side. Upcountry—around Makawao and Haʻikū—you can drive into and out of the rain, with rainbows that seem to land on the hood of your car. Older, smaller West Maui has its own moods. ʻĪao Valley in Wailuku captures the spirit of these mountains best.

Lodging

The resorts here re-create whatever is beautiful about Maui on the premises, doing their best to improve on nature. And their best is pretty amazing—opulent gardens, fantasy swimming pools with slide-down waterfalls and hidden grottoes (sometimes with swim-up bars in them), spas, cultural events, championship golf courses, priceless art collections, tennis clubs. . . . They make it hard to work up the willpower to leave the resort and go see the real thing. Kāʻanapali, the grande dame, sits next to Lahaina's action. Kapalua, farther north, is more private and serene—and catches a bit more wind and rain. Sprawling Wailea on the South Shore has excellent beaches and designer golf courses, each with a distinct personality. Resort prices are not for everyone. Many visitors compromise on the luxury and find condominium apartments in Nāpili and Kahana (for West Maui) or in Kīhei (East Maui). With a few exceptions, you'll find that accommodations are all clustered along these leeward shores. If you want to stay elsewhere on the island—say, Upcountry or in Hāna (without using the Hotel Hāna-Maui)—seek out a bed-and-breakfast or a rental property.

Water Sports

The West Maui vacation coast (from Lahaina to Kapalua) centers on Lahaina Harbor, where you can find boats for snorkeling, scuba diving, deep-sea fishing, whale-watching, parasailing, and sunset cocktail–partying. At the harbor, you can learn to surf or you can ride a submarine; catch a ferry ride to Lānaʻi or grab a seat on a fast inflatable and explore all the way around it. The East Maui vacation coast has Māʻalaea Harbor and the great snorkeling beaches of Kīhei and Wailea. If you want to walk through the ocean without getting wet, visit the top-notch aquarium in Māʻalaea. If you'd rather watch, drive to Hoʻokipa, near Pāʻia, for surfers and windsurfers.

Whale-Watching

One of the best signs of the high intelligence of humpback whales is that they return to Maui every year. Having fattened themselves in subarctic waters all summer, they migrate south in the winter to breed, and thousands of them cruise the Lahaina Roadstead (that is, the leeward Maui sea channel) in particular. From December 15 to May 1 the Pacific Whale Foundation has naturalists stationed in two places—on the rooftop of their headquarters and at the scenic viewpoint on the *pali*, or cliffside stretch, of the highway into Lahaina. The foundation also runs whale-watch boats that depart every hour of the day. In fact, every boat on the island will go out of its way to watch humpbacks when the opportunity arises—which it does often, as the whales themselves seem to have a penchant for people-watching.

EXPLORING MAUI

There is plenty to see and do on the Valley Isle besides spending time on the beach. The island can be split up into five exploring areas—West Maui, Central Maui, the South Shore, Upcountry (including Haleakalā), and the Road to Hāna (East Maui). You can spend a half day to a full day or more in each area, depending on how long you have to visit. The best way to see the whole island is by car, but there are opportunities for good walking tours.

To get yourself oriented, first look at a map of the island. You will notice two distinct circular landmasses. These are volcanic in origin. The smaller landmass, on the western part of the island, consists of 5,788-ft Puʻu Kukui and the West Maui Mountains. The interior of these mountains is one of the earth's wettest spots. Annual rainfall of 400 inches has sliced the land into impassable gorges and razor-sharp ridges. Oddly enough, the area's leeward shore—what most people mean when they say "West Maui"—is sunny and warm year-round.

The large landmass on the eastern portion of Maui was created by Haleakalā, the cloud-wreathed volcanic peak at its center. One of the best-known mountains in the world, Haleakalā is popular with hikers and sightseers. This larger region of the island is called East Maui. Its dry, leeward South Shore is flanked with resorts, condominiums, beaches, and the busy town of Kīhei. Its windward shore, largely one great rain forest, is traversed by the Road to Hāna.

Between the two mountain areas is Central Maui, the location of the county seat of Wailuku, from which the islands of Maui, Lānaʻi, Molokaʻi, and Kahoʻolawe are governed. It's also the base for much of the island's commerce and industry.

In the Islands, the directions *mauka* (toward the mountains) and *makai* (toward the ocean) are often used.

Great Itineraries

Many visitors never get over the spell of the sea, and never go inland to explore the island and its people. Those who do, though, launch out early from their beachside hotel or condo, loop through a district, then wind up back "home" for sunsets and *mai tais* (potent rum drinks with orange and lime juice). When you live on an island, you get used to going in circles. Don't be too goal-oriented as you travel around. If you rush to "get there," you might find you've missed the point of going, which is to encounter one of the most beautiful islands in the world, still largely unpopulated.

Numbers in the text correspond to numbers in the margin and on the Maui, Lahaina, and Kahului-Wailuku maps.

IF YOU HAVE 1 DAY

This is a tough choice. But how can you miss the opportunity to see **Haleakalā National Park** ㊳ and the volcano's enormous, otherworldly crater? Sunrise at the summit has become the thing to do. It's quite dramatic (and chilly), but there are drawbacks. Namely, you miss seeing the landscape and views on the way up in the dark. You also have to get up early. How early? You'll need an hour and a half from the bottom of **Haleakalā Highway** (Highway 37) ㊲ to the summit. Add to that the time of travel to the highway—at least 45 minutes from Lahaina or Kīhei. *The Maui News* posts the hour of sunrise every day. The best experience of the crater takes all day and good legs. Start at the summit, hike down Sliding Sands trail, cross the crater floor, and come back up the Halemau'u switchbacks. (This works out best if you leave your car at the Halemau'u trailhead parking lot and get a lift for the last 20-minute drive to the mountaintop.) All you need is a packed lunch, water, and decent walking shoes. If you don't hike, leave the mountain early enough to go explore **ʻIao Valley State Park** ㉙ above Wailuku. This will show you the island's jungle landscape and will compensate for the fact that you're missing the drive to Hāna.

IF YOU HAVE 3 DAYS

Give yourself the Haleakalā volcano experience one day, and then rest up a little with a beach-snorkel-exploring jaunt on either East or West Maui. The East Maui trip will have to include the **Maui Ocean Center** ㉜ at Māʻalaea. Then drive the South Shore, sampling the little beaches in **Wailea** ㉞ and getting a good dose of big, golden **Mākena Beach State Park** ㉟. Be sure to drive on past Mākena into the rough lava fields, the site of Maui's last lava flows, which formed rugged **La Pérouse Bay** ㊱. The ʻĀhihi-Kīnaʻu Marine Preserve has no beach, but it's a rich spot for snorkeling.

Or take the West Maui trip over the pali through Olowalu, **Lahaina** ④– ⑰, and **Kāʻanapali** ③, and dodge off the highway to find small beaches in Nāpili, Kahana, **Kapalua** ①, and beyond. The road gets narrow and sensational around **Kahakuloa** ②. If you're enjoying it, keep circling West Maui and return through the Central Valley.

On your third day, explore **Hāna** ㊺. Stop in **Pāʻia** ㊹ for a meal, pause at **Hoʻokipa Beach** ㊺ for the surf action, and savor the sight of the taro fields of **Keʻanae Arboretum** �51 and **Wailua Overlook** �53. Nearly everyone keeps going past Hāna town to **ʻOheʻo Gulch** ㊿, the "seven pools."

IF YOU HAVE 5 DAYS

After you've completed the three-day itinerary above, explore Upcountry. Get to the town of **Makawao** ㊷ and use it as your pivot point. Head north at the town's crossroads and drive around **Haʻikū** ㊻ by turning left at the first street (Kokomo Road), right at Haʻikū Road, then coming back uphill on any of those leafy, twisting gulch-country roads. After you've explored Makawao town, drive out to Kula on the Kula Highway. This is farmland, with fields of flowers and vegetables and small ranches with well-nourished cattle. Stop in little Kēōkea for coffee, and keep driving on Kula Highway to the ʻUlupalakua Ranch History Room at the **Tedeschi Vineyards and Winery** ㊵. Add some time in Central Maui to really get to the heart of things, especially **Wailuku** ㉓– ㉘, with its old buildings and curious shops. From here you can loop out to **Pāʻia** ㊹ and spend some time enjoying beaches in the Spreckelsville area and poking around the shops of this old plantation town.

When to Tour Maui

Although Maui has the usual temperate-zone shift of seasons—a bit rainier in the winter, hotter and drier in the summer—these seasonal changes are negligible on the leeward coasts, where most visitors stay. The only season worth mentioning is tourist season, when the roads around Lahaina and Kīhei get crowded. Peak visitor activity occurs from December through March and picks up again in summer. If traffic is bothering you, get out of town and explore the countryside. During high season, the Road to Hāna tends to clog—well, not clog exactly, but develop little choo-choo trains of cars, with everyone in a line of six or a dozen driving as slowly as the first car. The solution: leave early (dawn) and return late (dusk). And if you find yourself playing the role of locomotive, pull over and let the other drivers pass.

West Maui

West Maui, anchored by the amusing old whaling town of Lahaina, was the focus of development when Maui set out to become a premier tourist destination. The condo-filled beach towns of Nāpili, Kahana, and Honokōwai are arrayed between the stunning resorts of Kapalua and Kāʻanapali, north of Lahaina.

Lahaina itself has a notorious past. There are stories of lusty whalers who met head-on with missionaries bent on saving souls. Both groups journeyed to Lahaina from New England in the early 1800s. At first, Lahaina might look touristy, but there's a lot that's genuine here as well. The town has renovated most of its old buildings, which date from the time when it was Hawaiʻi's capital. Much of the town has been designated a National Historic Landmark, and any new buildings must conform in style to those built before 1920.

A Good Drive

Begin this tour in **Kapalua** ①. Even if you're not staying there, you'll want to have a look around the renowned Kapalua Bay Hotel and enjoy a meal or snack before you begin exploring. From Kapalua drive north on the Honoapiʻilani Highway (Highway 30). This road is paved, but storms now and then make it partly impassable, especially on the winding 8-mi stretch that is only one lane wide, with no shoulder and a sheer drop-off into the ocean. However, you'll discover some gorgeous photo opportunities along the road, and if you go far enough, you'll come to **Kahakuloa** ②, a sleepy fishing village tucked into a cleft in the mountain. The road pushes on to Wailuku, but you may be tired of the narrow and precipitously winding course you have to take.

From Kahakuloa turn around and go back in the direction from which you came—south toward Kāʻanapali and Lahaina, past the beach towns of Nāpili, Kahana, and Honokōwai. If you wish to explore these towns, get off the Upper Honoapiʻilani Highway and drive closer to the water. If you're not staying there, you may want to visit the planned resort community of **Kāʻanapali** ③, especially the Hyatt Regency Maui and the Westin Maui. To reach them, turn right onto Kāʻanapali Parkway. Next, head for Lahaina. Before you start your Lahaina trek, take a short detour by turning left from Honoapiʻilani Highway onto Lahainaluna Road, and stop at the **Hale Paʻi** ④, the printing shop built by Protestant missionaries in 1837. Return down Lahainaluna Road until you reach Front Street and turn left.

Since Lahaina is best explored on foot, use the drive along Front Street to get oriented and then park at or near **505 Front Street** ⑤, at the south end of the town's historic and colorful commercial area. Heading back into town, turn right onto Prison Street and you'll come to **Hale Paʻahao** ⑥, which was built from coral blocks. Return to Front Street, where it's a short stroll north to the **Banyan Tree** ⑦, one of the town's best-known landmarks, and behind it, the old **Court House** ⑧. Next door, also in Banyan Park, stand the reconstructed remains of the waterfront **Fort** ⑨. About a half block northwest, you'll find the site of Kamehameha's **Brick Palace** ⑩. **Brig *Carthaginian II*** ⑪ is anchored at the dock nearby and is open to visitors. If you walk from the brig to the corner of Front and Dickenson streets, you'll find the **Baldwin Home** ⑫, restored to reflect the decor of the early 19th century and now home to the Lahaina Restoration Foundation. Next door is the **Master's Reading Room** ⑬, Maui's oldest building.

Wander north or south on Front Street to explore Lahaina's commercial side. At the Wharf Cinema Center, you can see the **Spring House** ⑭, built over a freshwater spring. If you head north on Front Street, you'll

Maui

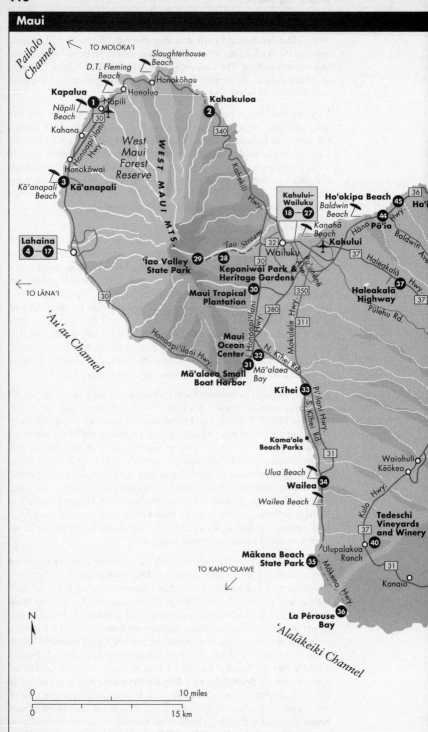

Pailolo Channel

TO MOLOKA'I

Slaughterhouse Beach

D.T. Fleming Beach

Honokōhau

Kapalua ❶ Nāpili

Honolua

Kahakuloa ❷

Nāpili Beach

30

Kahana

Honoapi'ilani Hwy.

340

West Maui Forest Reserve

Honokōwai

WEST MAUI MTS.

Kahekili Hwy.

Kā'anapali Beach

❸ **Kā'anapali**

Kahului–Wailuku 18 27

Ho'okipa Beach 45

Baldwin Beach

36

Hā'

Kanahā Beach

44 **Pā'ia**

Hāna Hwy.

Baldwin Ave.

Lahaina 4 17

'Īao Stream

32 **Wailuku**

Kahului

37

Pu'unēnē

Haleakalā

TO LĀNA'I

'Īao Valley State Park ❷❾ ❷❽

Kepaniwai Park & Heritage Gardens

30

Haleakalā Highway 37

37

350

Pūlehu Rd.

Maui Tropical Plantation

30

380

311

Mokulele Hwy.

N. Kīhei Rd.

Honoapi'ilani Hwy.

Honoapi'ilani Hwy.

Maui Ocean Center 32

Mā'alaea Small Boat Harbor 31

Mā'alaea Bay

Kīhei 33

Pi'ilani Hwy.

S. Kīhei Rd.

Waiohuli

Kēōkea

Kama'ole Beach Parks

31

Ulua Beach

Wailea 34

Wailea Beach

Kula Hwy.

Tedeschi Vineyards and Winery 40

Mākena Beach State Park 35

Ulupalakua Ranch

37

31

Kanaio

Mākena Hwy.

TO KAHO'OLAWE

La Pérouse Bay 36

'Au'au Channel

'Alalākeiki Channel

N

0 — 10 miles

0 — 15 km

PACIFIC OCEAN

iku
46
Ulumalu
Rd.
365
Kaupakalua Rd.
Huelo
Kailua
360
47

390
Kokomo
43
42
Makawao
Hui No'eau
Visual Arts
Center
Pukalani
Enchanting
Floral Gardens
41
377
Haleakalā
National Park
Headquarters/
Visitor Center
37
Haleakalā Hwy.
Kula
378
38
Leleiwi
Overlook
39
Kula Botanical
Gardens
Kalahaku
Overlook
Haleakalā
Pu'u 'Ula'ula
Overlook
Haleakalā Visitor
Center

Puahokamoa
Stream
Kaumahina State
Wayside Park
48
49
Honomanū
Bay
50
51
Ke'anae Arboretum
52
Wailua
Ke'anae Overlook
53
Wailua Overlook
54
Waikāne
Falls
55
Nāhiku

Haleakalā
Crater Rd.
Pi'ina'au Stream
Kōolau
Forest
Reserve
360
Hāna Hwy.
Hāna
Airport
Pi'ilanihale
Heiau
56
Wai'ānapanapa
State Park
57

Halemau'u Trail
Haleakalā
National Park
Hāna Forest Reserve
59
58
Hāna
Pi'ilani Hwy.
Kōkī Beach
Hāmoa
Beach

Kahikinui
Forest
Reserve
Kaupō Trail
Mū'olea
60
'Ohe'o Gulch
Kipahulu
31
61
Grave of
Charles Lindbergh
Kaupō

Pi'ilani Hwy.
31

'Alenuihāhā Channel

TO THE BIG ISLAND OF HAWAI'I

come to the **Wo Hing Museum** ⑮ on the right. Walk another two blocks north, and you'll find the **Seamen's Hospital** ⑯. If it's before dusk and you still have a hankering for just one more stop, try the **Waiola Church and Cemetery** ⑰. Walk south down Front Street, make a left onto Dickenson Street, and then make a right onto Waine'e Street and walk another few blocks.

TIMING

You can walk the length of Lahaina's Front Street in less than 30 minutes if you don't stop along the way. Just *try* not to be intrigued by the town's colorful shops and historic sites. Realistically, you'll need at least a half day—and can easily spend a full day—to check out the area's coastal beaches, towns, and resorts. The Banyan Tree in Lahaina is a terrific spot to be when the sun sets—mynah birds settle in here for a screeching symphony, which can be an event in itself. If you arrange to spend a Friday afternoon exploring Front Street, you can dine in town and hang around for Art Night, when the galleries stay open into the evening and entertainment fills the streets.

Sights to See

★ ⑫ **Baldwin Home.** In 1835 an early missionary to Lahaina, Ephraim Spaulding, built this attractive thick-walled house of coral and stone. In 1836 Dr. Dwight Baldwin—also a missionary—moved in with his family. The home has been restored and furnished to reflect the period. You can view the living room, with the family's grand piano; the dining room; and Dr. Baldwin's dispensary. The Lahaina Restoration Foundation occupies the building, and its knowledgeable staff is here to answer almost any question about historic sites in town. Ask for its walking-tour brochure. ⊠ *696 Front St., Lahaina,* ☎ *808/661–3262.* ☞ *$3.* ⊙ *Daily 10–4.*

7 Banyan Tree. This massive tree, a popular and hard-to-miss meeting place if your party splits up for independent exploring, was planted in 1873. It's the largest of its kind in the state and provides a welcome retreat for the weary who come to sit under its awesome branches. ✉ *Front St., between Hotel and Canal Sts., Lahaina.*

10 Brick Palace. All that's left of the palace built by King Kamehameha I around 1802 to welcome the captains of visiting ships are the excavated cornerstones and foundation in front of the Pioneer Inn. Hawaiʻi's first king lived only one year in the palace because his favorite wife, Kaʻahumanu, refused to stay here. It was then used as a warehouse, storeroom, and meeting house for 70 years, until it collapsed. ✉ *Makai end of Market St., Lahaina.*

★ **11 Brig *Carthaginian II.*** This vessel's sailing days are over, but it makes an interesting museum. It was built in Germany in the 1920s and is a replica of the type of ship that brought the New England missionaries around Cape Horn to Hawaiʻi in the early 1800s. A small museum belowdecks features the "World of the Whale," a colorful multimedia exhibit about whaling and local sea life. ✉ *At dock opposite north end of Wharf St., Lahaina,* ☎ *808/661–3262.* 🎟 *$3.* ☉ *Daily 10–4.*

8 Court House. This old civic building was erected in 1859, rebuilt in 1925, and restored to its 1925 condition in 1999. At one time or another it served as a customs house, post office, vault and collector's office, governor's office, police court, and courtroom. Now it houses museum displays, the Lahaina Arts Society, a visitor center—where volunteers will answer your questions—and, perhaps best of all, a water cooler. ✉ *649 Wharf St., Lahaina,* ☎ *808/661–0111.* 🎟 *Free.* ☉ *Daily 9–5.*

5 505 Front Street. Quaint New England–style architecture characterizes this mall, which houses small shops and casual restaurants connected by a wooden sidewalk. It isn't as crowded as some other areas in Lahaina, probably because between here and the nearby Banyan Tree the town turns into a sleepy residential neighborhood and some people, walking from the more bustling center of Front Street, give up before they reach the mall. ✉ *South end of Front St. near Shaw St., Lahaina.*

9 Fort. Used mostly as a prison, this fortress was positioned so that it could police the whaling ships that crowded the harbor. It was built from 1831 to 1832 after sailors, angered by a law forbidding local women from swimming out to ships, lobbed cannonballs at the town. Cannons raised from the wreck of a warship in Honolulu Harbor were brought to Lahaina and placed in front of the fort, where they still sit today. The building itself is an eloquent ruin. ✉ *Canal and Wharf Sts., Lahaina.*

6 Hale Paʻahao (Old Prison). This jailhouse dates to rowdy whaling days. Its name means "stuck-in-irons house," referring to the wall shackles and ball-and-chain restraints. The compound was built in the 1850s by convict laborers out of blocks of coral that had been salvaged from the demolished waterfront Fort. Most prisoners were sent here for desertion, drunkenness, or reckless horse riding. Today, a wax figure representing an imprisoned old sailor tells visitors his recorded tale of woe. ✉ *Waineʻe and Prison Sts., Lahaina.* 🎟 *Free.* ☉ *Daily 8–5.*

4 Hale Paʻi. Six years after Protestant missionaries established Lahainaluna Seminary as a center of learning and enlightenment in 1831, they built this printing shop. Here at the press, they and their young Hawaiian scholars created a written Hawaiian language and used it to produce a Bible, history texts, and a newspaper. An exhibit displays a replica of the original Rampage press and facsimiles of early printing. The oldest

U.S. educational institution west of the Rockies, the seminary now serves as Lahaina's public high school. ⊠ *980 Lahainaluna Rd., Lahaina,* ☎ *808/661–3262.* ▭ *Donation.* ☉ *Weekdays 10–3.*

❸ Kāʻanapali. The theatrical look of Hawaiʻi tourism—planned resort communities where luxury homes mix with high-rise hotels, fantasy swimming pools, and a theme-park landscape—all began right here in the 1960s. Three miles of uninterrupted white beach and placid water form the front yard for this artificial utopia, with its 40 tennis courts and two championship golf courses. The six major hotels here are all worth visiting just for a look around, especially the Hyatt Regency Maui, which has a multimillion-dollar art collection. At the Whalers Village shopping complex, a small **Whaling Museum** (⊠ Kāʻanapali Pkwy., Suite H16, ☎ 808/661–5992; ▭ Donation) tells the story of the 19th-century *Moby-Dick* era; it's open daily from 9:30 AM to 10 PM. ⊠ *2435 Kāʻanapali Pkwy.*

❷ Kahakuloa. Untouched by progress, this tiny village is a relic of pre-jet travel Maui. Many remote villages similar to Kahakuloa used to be tucked away in the valleys of this area. This is the wild side of West Maui. True adventurers will find terrific snorkeling and swimming along this coast, as well as some good hiking trails. ⊠ *North end of Honoapiʻilani Hwy.*

❶ Kapalua. Set in a beautiful secluded spot surrounded by pineapple fields, this resort got its first big boost in 1978, when the Maui Land & Pineapple Company built the luxurious Kapalua Bay Hotel. It was joined in 1992 by a dazzling Ritz-Carlton. The hotels host dedicated golfers, celebrities who want to be left alone, and some of the world's richest folks. Kapalua's shops and restaurants are among Maui's finest, but expect to pay high prices. By contrast, the old **Honolua Store** serves informal plate lunches, popular with locals. ⊠ *Bay Dr., Kapalua.*

☾ Lahaina–Kāʻanapali & Pacific Railroad. Affectionately called the Sugarcane Train, this is Maui's only passenger train. It's an 1890s-vintage railway that once shuttled sugar but now moves sightseers between Kāʻanapali and Lahaina. This quaint little attraction with its singing conductor is a big deal for Hawaiʻi but probably not much of a thrill for those more accustomed to trains. The kids will like it. ⊠ *1½ blocks north of the Lahainaluna Rd. stoplight on Honoapiʻilani Hwy., Lahaina,* ☎ *808/661–0089.* ▭ *$15 round-trip, $11 one-way.* ☉ *Train departs from Lahaina at 9:45, 11:05, 12:50, 2:10, 3:30, and 4:50 (4:50 is one-way only).*

⑬ Master's Reading Room. This could be Maui's oldest residential building, constructed in 1834. In those days the ground floor was a mission's storeroom, and the reading room upstairs was for sailors. ⊠ *Front and Dickenson Sts., Lahaina,* ☎ *808/661–3262.*

⑯ Seamen's Hospital. Built in the 1830s to house King Kamehameha III's royal court, this property was later turned over to the U.S. government, which used it as a hospital for whalers. Next door is a typical **sugar plantation camp residence,** circa 1900. ⊠ *1024 Front St., Lahaina,* ☎ *808/661–3262.*

⑭ Spring House. Built by missionaries to shelter a freshwater spring, this historic structure is now home to a huge Fresnel lens, once used in a local lighthouse that guided ships to Lahaina. ⊠ *Wharf Cinema Center, 658 Front St., Lahaina.*

NEED A BREAK?   The sandwiches have real Gruyère and Emmentaler cheese at **Maui Swiss Cafe** (⊠ 640 Front St., Lahaina, ☎ 808/661–6776)—expensive ingredients with affordable results. The friendly owner scoops the best and cheapest locally made ice cream in Lahaina. Daily lunch specials are less than $6. Courtyard tables are set back from Front Street at this informal local favorite.

⑰ **Waiola Church and Cemetery.** The Waiola Cemetery is actually older than the neighboring church; it dates from the time when Kamehameha's sacred wife, Queen Keōpūolani, died and was buried here in 1823. The first church here was erected in 1832 by Hawaiian chiefs and was originally named Ebenezer by the queen's second husband and widower, Governor Hoapili. Aptly immortalized in James Michener's *Hawai'i* as the church that wouldn't stand, it was burned down twice and demolished in two windstorms. The present structure was put up in 1953 and named Waiola (water of life). ⊠ *535 Waine'e St., Lahaina,* ☎ *808/661–4349.*

⑮ **Wo Hing Museum.** Built by the Wo Hing Society in 1912 as a fraternal society for Chinese residents, this eye-catching building now contains Chinese artifacts and a historic theater that features Thomas Edison's films of Hawai'i, circa 1898. Upstairs is the only public Taoist altar on Maui. ⊠ *858 Front St., Lahaina,* ☎ *808/661–5553.* ⊡ *Donation.* ☉ *Daily 10–4.*

Central Maui

Kahului, an industrial and commercial town in the center of the island, is home to many of Maui's permanent residents, who find their jobs close by. The area was developed in the early '50s to meet the housing needs of workers for the large sugarcane interests here, specifically those of Alexander & Baldwin. The large company was tired of playing landlord to its many plantation workers and sold land to a developer who promised to create affordable housing. The scheme worked, and Kahului became the first planned city in Hawai'i. Ka'ahumanu Avenue (Highway 32), Kahului's main street, runs from the harbor to the hills. It's the logical place to begin your exploration of Central Maui.

A Good Tour

Begin at the **Alexander & Baldwin Sugar Museum** ⑱ in Pu'unēnē, directly across from the HC&S sugar mill. The mill has been processing cane and belching steam and smoke since it opened in 1902. For a while it was the biggest sugar mill in the world. By 1930 Pu'unēnē had a population of 10,000 workers and families living in "camps" around the mill, and it had a school, churches, and a bowling alley. All of that is gone today, but the museum tells the story of these people and of the industry they helped create.

From here, explore **Kahului,** which looks nothing like the lush tropical paradise most people envision as Hawai'i. Head northwest on Pu'unēnē Avenue all the way to its end at Ka'ahumanu Avenue and turn left. Three blocks ahead you'll see the sputniklike canvas domes of Ka'ahumanu Center, Maui's largest shopping center. If you turn right at the signal just before that, you'll follow the curve of Kahului Beach Road and see many ships in port at **Kahului Harbor** ⑲. On your left are the cream-and-brown buildings of **Maui Arts & Cultural Center** ⑳. Continue past the harbor, turn right at Waiehu Beach Road, and about a mile later as you cross the 'Īao Stream you'll see **Haleki'i-Pihana Heiau State Monument** ㉑ on the hilltop to your left. Return along the harbor road and make a right turn at Kanaloa Avenue. Return to Ka'ahumanu Avenue on this road, passing **Keōpūolani Park** ㉒ and the War Memorial Stadium, site of the annual Hula Bowl game. Turn right to reach Wailuku (Ka'ahumanu Avenue eventually becomes Wailuku's Main

122

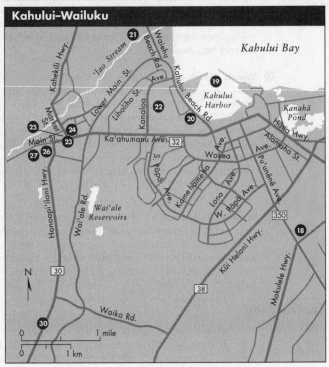

Street). To get a closer look at **Wailuku's Historic District** ㉓, turn right from Main Street onto Market Street, where you can park for free within view of the landmark '**Iao Theater** ㉔. The theater is a good place to begin your walking tour. Many amusing shops line **Market Street** ㉕ between Vineyard and Main streets. From here, it's a short walk along Main Street to **Ka'ahumanu Church** ㉖ on High Street, just around the corner from Main and across the way from the County Court House. Retrieve your car and turn a right onto Main Street. After a few blocks, on your left, you'll see **Bailey House** ㉗.

Continue driving uphill, into the mountains. Main Street turns into 'Iao Valley Road, the air cools, and the hilly terrain gets more lush. Soon you'll come to **Kepaniwai Park & Heritage Gardens** ㉘. 'Iao Valley Road ends at '**Iao Valley State Park** ㉙, home of the erosion-formed gray and moss-green rock called 'Iao Needle. This is a great place to picnic, wade in the stream, and explore the paths. Then return to Wailuku and, at the traffic light, turn right onto Highway 30. Drive south a couple of miles to the **Maui Tropical Plantation & Country Store** ㉚.

TIMING

The complete itinerary will take a full day. But you can explore Central Maui comfortably in little more than a half day if you whiz through the Maui Tropical Plantation, or save it for another day. If you want to combine sightseeing with shopping, this is a good itinerary for it, but you'll need more time. Hikers may want to expand their outing to a full day to explore 'Iao Valley State Park.

Sights to See

★ ⑱ **Alexander & Baldwin Sugar Museum.** "A&B," Maui's largest landowner, was one of five companies known collectively as the Big Five that spearheaded the planting, harvesting, and processing of the valuable agricultural product sugarcane. Although Hawaiian cane sugar is now being supplanted by cheaper foreign versions—as well as by sugar derived from inexpensive sugar beets—the crop was for many years the mainstay of the Hawaiian economy. You'll find the museum in a small, restored plantation manager's house next to the post office and the still-operating sugar refinery (black smoke billows up when cane is burning). Historic photos, artifacts, and documents explain the introduction of sugarcane to Hawai'i and how plantation managers brought in laborers from other countries, thereby changing the Islands' ethnic mix. Exhibits also describe the sugar-making process. ⊠ *3957 Hansen Rd., Pu'unēnē,* ☎ *808/871–8058.* ⊡ *$5.* ⊙ *Mon.–Sat. 9:30–4:30 (last admission at 4).*

★ ㉗ **Bailey House.** This was the home of Edward and Caroline Bailey, two prominent missionaries who came to Wailuku to run the first Hawaiian girls' school on the island, the Wailuku Female Seminary. The school's main function was to train the girls in the "feminine arts." It once stood next door to the Baileys' home, which they called Halehō'ike'ike (House of Display), but locals always called it the Bailey House, and the sign painters eventually gave in. Construction of the house, between 1833 and 1850, was supervised by Edward Bailey himself. The Maui Historical Society runs a museum in the plastered stone house, with a small collection of artifacts from before and after the missionaries' arrival and with Mr. Bailey's paintings of Wailuku. Some rooms have missionary-period furniture. The Hawaiian Room has exhibits on the making of tapa cloth, as well as samples of pre–Captain Cook weaponry. ⊠ *2375A Main St., Wailuku,* ☎ *808/244–3326,* 𝖶𝖤𝖡 *www.mauimuseum.org.* ⊡ *$5.* ⊙ *Mon.–Sat. 10–4.*

㉑ **Haleki'i-Pihana Heiau State Monument.** Stand here at either of the two heiau and imagine the king of Maui surveying his domain. That's what Kahekili, Maui's last fierce king, did, and so did Kamehameha the Great after he defeated Kahekili's soldiers. Today the view is most instructive. Below, the once-powerful 'Iao Stream has been sucked dry and boxed in by concrete. Before you is the urban heart of the island. The suburban community behind you is all Hawaiian Homelands. ⊠ *End of Hea Pl., off Kuhio Pl. from Waiehu Beach Rd. (Hwy. 340), Kahului.* ⊡ *Free.* ⊙ *Daily 7–7.*

㉔ **'Iao Theater.** One of Wailuku's most-photographed landmarks, this charming movie house went up in 1927 and served as a community gathering spot. When restoration work was completed in 1996, the Maui Community Theatre resumed its longtime residence here in its historic Wailuku headquarters. The Art Deco building is now the showpiece of Wailuku's Main Street. ⊠ *68 N. Market St., Wailuku,* ☎ *808/242–6969.*

NEED A BREAK? | **Maui Bake Shop & Deli Ltd.** (⊠ 2092 Vineyard St., Wailuku, ☎ 808/242–0064) serves salads, sandwiches, and a variety of light entrées, but what you're really going to crave are the pastries—a feast for the eyes as well as the palate. The pastel-frosted frogs, chicks, rabbits, and mice, made of orange butter-cream cookie dough, are irresistible.

★ ㉙ **'Iao Valley State Park.** When Mark Twain saw this park, he dubbed it the Yosemite of the Pacific. Yosemite it's not, but it is a lovely deep valley with the curious 'Iao Needle, a spire that rises more than 2,000 ft from the valley floor. You can take one of several easy hikes from the parking lot across 'Iao Stream and explore the junglelike area. This park has a beautiful network of well-maintained walks, where you can stop and meditate by the edge of a stream or marvel at the native plants and flowers. Mist occasionally rises if there has been a rain, which makes

being here even more magical. ⊠ *Western end of Hwy. 32.* 🏷 *Free.*
🕙 *Daily 7–7.*

㉖ Ka'ahumanu Church. It's said that Queen Ka'ahumanu attended services on this site in 1832 and requested that a permanent structure be erected. Builders first tried adobe, which dissolved in the rain, then stone. The present wooden structure, built in 1876, is classic New England style, with white exterior walls and striking green trim. You won't be able to see the interior, however, unless you attend Sunday services. There's a service entirely in the Hawaiian language each Sunday morning at 9:30. ⊠ *Main and High Sts., Wailuku,* ☎ *808/244–5189.*

Kahului. The town of Kahului is the industrial and commercial center for Maui's year-round residents, as close to a bustling urban center as Maui gets. Most visitors arrive at the airport here and see all they will see of the town as they drive on to their hotels. But this is the home of Maui's largest mall, Ka'ahumanu Center, which is virtually the social center of island life. It's also the site of the Maui Mall (with a 12-theater megaplex) and the island's big mainland-style box stores, which are all visible on the main road from the airport.

㉙ Kahului Harbor. The island's only deep-draft harbor, Kahului Harbor is Maui's chief port. American Hawaii's 800-passenger S.S. *Independence* and S.S. *Constitution* each stop here once a week, as do cargo ships and smaller vessels, including the occasional yacht. Surfers sometimes use this spot to catch some good waves, but it's not a good swimming beach. ⊠ *Kahului Beach Rd., Kahului.*

㉒ Keōpūolani Park. Maui's "Central Park" covers 101 acres, and—reflecting Maui residents' traditional love of sports—it has seven playing fields. Named for the great Maui queen who was born near here and is buried in Lahaina's Waiola Church cemetery, the park is planted with native species that are still growing to reach their potential. The park also includes a native-plant botanical garden and a 3-mi walking path. ⊠ *Kanaloa Ave. next to the YMCA.*

👋 **㉘ Kepaniwai Park & Heritage Gardens.** This county park is a memorial to Maui's cultural roots, with picnic facilities and ethnic displays dotting the landscape. There's an early Hawaiian shack, a New England–style saltbox, a Portuguese-style villa with gardens, and dwellings from such other cultures as China and the Philippines. Next door the **Hawai'i Nature Center** has an interactive exhibit and hikes good for children.

The peacefulness here belies the history of the area. During his quest for domination, King Kamehameha I brought his troops from the Big Island of Hawai'i to the Valley Isle in 1790 and engaged in a successful and particularly bloody battle against the son of Maui's chief, Kahekili, near Kepaniwai Park. An earlier battle at the site had pitted Kahekili himself against an older Big Island chief, Kalani'ōpu'u. Kahekili prevailed, but the carnage was so great that the nearby stream became known as Wailuku (water of destruction) and the place where fallen warriors choked the stream's flow was called Kepaniwai (the water dam). ⊠ *'Īao Valley Rd., Wailuku.* 🏷 *Free.* 🕙 *Daily 7–7.*

NEED A BREAK?	If you're in Central Maui at lunchtime, try local favorite **Cafe O'Lei** (⊠ 2051 Main St., Wailuku, ☎ 808/244–6816), right in downtown Wailuku. The food is healthful, fresh, and tasty; the prices are great; and the people are friendly.

㉕ Market Street. An idiosyncratic assortment of shops—with proprietors to match—makes Wailuku's Market Street a delightful place for a stroll. Shops like the Good Fortune Trading Company and Brown-

Kobayashi have affordable antiques and home furnishings. Merchants are happy to recommend a restaurant and offer advice or directions. ⊠ *Wailuku.*

★ ⑳ **Maui Arts & Cultural Center.** An epic fund drive by the citizens of Maui led to the creation of this $32-million facility, which opened in 1994. The top-of-the-line Castle Theater seats 1,200 people on orchestra, mez-zanine, and balcony levels. Rock stars play the A&B Amphitheater. The Center (as it's called) also includes a small black box theater, an art gallery with interesting exhibits, and classrooms. The building itself is worth the visit: it incorporates work by Maui artists, and its signature lava-rock wall pays tribute to the skills of the Hawaiians. ⊠ *Above the harbor on Kahului Beach Rd., Kahului,* ☎ *808/242–2787; 808/ 242–7469 box office.* ☉ *Weekdays 9–5.*

☝ ㉚ **Maui Tropical Plantation & Country Store.** When Maui's once-paramount crop declined in importance, a group of visionaries decided to open an agricultural theme park on the site of this former sugarcane field. The 60-acre preserve, on Highway 30 just outside Wailuku, offers a 30-minute tram ride through its fields with an informative narration covering growing processes and plant types. Children will probably enjoy the historical-characters exhibit as well as fruit-testing, coconut-husk-ing, and lei-making demonstrations, not to mention some entertain-ing spider monkeys. There's a restaurant on the property and a "country store" specializing in Made In Maui products. ⊠ *Honoapi'ilani Hwy. (Hwy. 30), Waikapu,* ☎ *808/244–7643.* ☎ *Free; tram ride with nar-rated tour $9.50.* ☉ *Daily 9–5.*

㉓ **Wailuku's Historic District.** The National Register of Historic Places lists many of the old buildings here. You can pick up a free brochure that describes a self-guided walking tour at **Wailuku Main Street Associa-tion** (2062 Main St., ☎ 808/244–3888). Over all, the little town is sleepy, and one wouldn't guess that it's Maui's county seat. The mayor sits on the top floor of the tallest building in town, on the corner of Main and High streets. ⊠ *High, Vineyard, and Market Sts., Wailuku.*

The South Shore

Twenty years ago almost no one lived in Kīhei. Now about one-third of the Maui population lives here in what was, for a while, one of the fastest-growing towns in America. Traffic lights and mini-malls may not fit your notion of tropical paradise, but Kīhei does offer sun, heat, and excellent beaches. Besides that, the town's relatively inexpensive condos and small hotels make this a home base for many Maui visi-tors. At one end of this populous strip, you have Mā'alaea Small Boat Harbor and the Maui Ocean Center, a world-class seawater aquarium. At the other end, lovely Wailea—a resort community to rival those on West Maui—gives way to truly unspoiled coastline.

A Good Drive

Start with a look at **Mā'alaea Small Boat Harbor** ㉛, the setting-out place for many whale-watching trips, snorkel excursions (often out to the tiny crescent island Molokini), and sunset dinner cruises. Then tour the **Maui Ocean Center** ㉜, an aquarium dedicated to the sea life of the North Pacific. When you leave the aquarium, turn right onto High-way 30 and then turn right again at the first traffic signal onto North Kīhei Road (Highway 31). You're headed toward the town of **Kīhei** ㉝ on a straight road following the long sandy coastline of Mā'alaea Bay. On your left is marshy Keālia Pond, a state-managed wildlife sanctu-ary. On your right, ecologically fragile dunes run between the road and the sea. A turnout provides some parking stalls, information about the dunes, and a boardwalk so you can cross the dunes and use the beach. When you get to the long, thin town of Kīhei, you have a choice. You can turn right at the fork in the road and experience the colorful stop-and-go beach route of South Kīhei Road. Or you can turn left and by-pass the town on the Pi'ilani Highway, hastening to the resort community of **Wailea** ㉞. If you're looking for the best beach, you might as well flip a coin. There are great beaches all along this coast. At Wailea, you'll drive past grand resorts interspersed with stretches of golf courses and access roads leading down to small but excellent beaches. As you head south on Wailea Alanui Drive, the manicured look of Wailea gives way to wildness and, after a couple of miles, to **Mākena Beach State Park** ㉟. Mākena is such a big beach that it has two paved parking areas. Beyond this point the landscape gets wilder and the road gradually fades away in black fields of cracked lava. This is **La Pérouse Bay** ㊱.

TIMING

Because it includes so many fine beach choices, this is definitely an all-day excursion—especially if you include a visit to the aquarium. A good way to do this trip is to get active in the morning with exploring and snorkeling, then shower in a beach park, dress up a little, and enjoy the cool luxury of the Wailea resorts. At sunset, settle in for dinner at one of the area's many fine restaurants.

Sights to See

㉝ **Kīhei.** This is a community that's still discovering itself. Much of it is less than a decade old, inhabited by recent Maui immigrants. An abundance of condos, moderately priced hotels, and sprawl-malls makes the town convenient for visitors. The beaches and the reliably sunny weather are added attractions. The county beach parks such as Kama'ole I, II, and III have lawns, showers, and picnic tables. Remember: Beach park or no beach park, the public has a right to the entire coastal strand, and this one in Kīhei has many off-road delights.

㊱ **La Pérouse Bay.** Beyond Mākena Beach, the road fades away into a vast territory of black lava flows, the result of Haleakalā's last eruption some 200 years ago. This is where Maui received its first official visit by a European explorer—the French admiral Jean-François de Galaup, Comte de La Pérouse, in 1786. Before it ends, the road passes through 'Āhihi-Kīna'u Marine Preserve, an excellent place for morning snorkel adventures.

㉛ **Mā'alaea Small Boat Harbor.** With only 89 slips and so many good reasons to take people out on the water, this active little harbor needs to be expanded. The Army Corps of Engineers has a plan to do so, but harbor users are fighting it—particularly the surfers, who say the plan would destroy their surf breaks. In fact, the surf here is world renowned, especially the break to the left of the harbor called "freight train," said to be the fastest anywhere. ⊠ *Off Honoapi'ilani Hwy. (Hwy. 30).*

★ ㉟ **Mākena Beach State Park.** "Big Beach" they call it—a huge stretch of coarse golden sand without a house or hotel for miles. A decade ago, Maui citizens campaigned successfully to preserve this beloved beach from development. At the right-hand end of the beach rises the beautiful hill called Pu'u 'Ōla'i, a perfect cinder cone. A climb over the rocks at this end leads to "Little Beach," where the (technically illegal) clothing-optional attitude prevails.

★ ㉜ **Maui Ocean Center.** You'll feel as though you're walking from the seashore down to the bottom of the reef, and then through an acrylic tunnel in the middle of the sea at this aquarium, which focuses on Hawaii and the Pacific. Special tanks get you close up with turtles, rays, and the unusual creatures of the tide pools. The center is part of a growing complex of retail shops and restaurants overlooking the harbor. ✉ *Enter from Honoapiʻilani Hwy. (Hwy. 30) as it curves past Māʻalaea Harbor, Māʻalaea,* ☎ *808/270–7000.* 💵 *$18.50.* ☉ *June–Aug., daily 9–6; Sept.–May, daily 9–5.*

★ ㉞ **Wailea.** Wailea is to Kīhei as Kāʻanapali—Maui's original fantasy resort development—is to the town of Lahaina. In both cases, the town is real and the resort community is ideal. The luxury of the Grand Wailea, the Moorish near-silliness of the Kea Lani, the simple grandeur of the Four Seasons, the public displays of fine art and architecture make Wailea a unique Maui attraction. A handful of perfect little beaches all have public access, and a paved beach walk allows you to stroll among all the properties, restaurants, and sandy coves.

Haleakalā and Upcountry

The west-facing upper slopes of Haleakalā are locally called "Upcountry." This region is responsible for much of Hawaiʻi's produce—lettuce, tomatoes, and sweet Maui onions—but the area is also a big flower producer. As you drive along you'll notice cactus thickets mingled with purple jacaranda, wild hibiscus, and towering eucalyptus trees. Upcountry is also fertile ranch land, with such spreads as the historic 20,000-acre ʻUlupalakua Ranch and 32,000-acre Haleakalā Ranch. In Makawao each July 4, the Maui Roping Club throws its annual rodeo and parade.

A Good Drive

Take the **Haleakalā Highway** ㊲ (Highway 37) to **Haleakalā National Park** ㊳ and the mountain's breathtaking summit. Make sure you have a full tank of gas. There are no service stations above Kula. Watch the signs: Haleakalā Highway divides. If you go straight it becomes Kula Highway, which is still Highway 37. If you veer to the left it becomes Highway 377, the road you want. After about 6 mi, make a left onto Highway 378. The switchbacks begin here. Near the top of the mountain is the Park Headquarters/Visitor Center, a good spot to stretch your legs and learn a little bit about the park.

Continuing up the mountain, you'll come to several overlooks, including Leleiwi Overlook and Kalahaku Overlook, both with views into the crater. Not far from Kalahaku Overlook you'll find the Haleakalā Visitor Center. Eventually you'll reach the highest point on Maui, the Puʻu ʻUlaʻula Overlook.

On the return trip, turn left when you reach Highway 377. Drive about 2 mi, and you'll come to **Kula Botanical Gardens** ㊴ on your left. It's worth a stop here to admire the abundant tropical flora. Continue south on Highway 377 and you'll soon join Highway 37 again. Turn left and, about 8 mi farther on, you'll reach ʻUlupalakua Ranch headquarters and **Tedeschi Vineyards and Winery** ㊵, where you can sample Maui's only homemade wines.

Return toward Kahului on Highway 37, the Kula Highway. **Enchanting Floral Gardens** ㊶ is clearly visible on the right side of the road near Mile Marker 10, about 2 mi before the Highway 37/377 junction. If you're pressed for time you can take Highway 37 from here back to Kahului. Otherwise, head north on Highway 365 toward **Makawao** ㊷, a classic old Hawaiian town. The **Hui Noʻeau Visual Arts Center** ㊸ is about a mile from the Makawao crossroads as you head down Baldwin Avenue. From here it's a 7-mi drive down toward the ocean to the Hāna Highway at the town of Pāʻia. Make a left on the Hāna Highway to return to Kahului.

TIMING

This can be an all-day outing even without the detours to Tedeschi Vineyards and Makawao. If you start early enough to catch the sunrise from Haleakalā's summit, you'll have plenty of time to explore the mountain, have lunch in Kula or at 'Ulupalakua Ranch, and end your day with dinner in Makawao or Ha'ikū.

Sights to See

㊶ **Enchanting Floral Gardens.** This eight-acre flower garden shines with blooms from every part of the globe. There are excellent collections of bromeliads and proteas, but this garden doesn't specialize. You'll find some of everything, and the signage is very good. A paved path winds through the display, under blooming arbors, and past three colorful gazebos that are often used for weddings. ⊠ *Hwy. 37 near Omaopio Rd., Kula,* ☎ *808/878–2531.* ➪ *$5.* ☉ *Daily 9–5.*

�37 **Haleakalā Highway.** On this road, you'll travel from sea level to an elevation of 10,023 ft in only 38 mi—a feat you won't be able to repeat on any other car route in the world. It's not a quick drive, however. It'll take you about two hours—longer if you can't resist the temptation to stop and enjoy the spectacular views. ⊠ *Hwy. 37.*

★ ㊳ **Haleakalā National Park.** Haleakalā Crater is the centerpiece of this 27,284-acre national park, first established in 1916. The crater is actually an "erosional valley," flushed out by water pouring from the summit through two enormous "gaps." The small hills within the crater are volcanic cinder cones (called *pu'u* in Hawaiian), each with a small crater at its top, and each the site of a former eruption. The mountain has terrific camping and hiking opportunities, including a trail that loops through the crater.

Before you head up Haleakalā, call for the latest **park weather conditions** (☎ 808/871–5054). Extreme gusty winds, heavy rain, and even snow in winter are not uncommon—even if it's paradise as usual down at beach level. Because of the high altitude, the mountaintop temperature is often as much as 30 degrees cooler than that at sea level. Be sure to pack an extra jacket.

You can learn something of the volcano's origins and eruption history at the **Park Headquarters/Visitor Center,** at a 7,000-ft elevation on Haleakalā Highway. Maps, posters, and other memorabilia are available at the gift shop here.

Leleiwi Overlook, at about an 8,800-ft elevation on Haleakalā, is one of several lookout areas in the park. If you're here in the late afternoon, it's possible you'll experience a phenomenon called the Brocken Specter. Named after a similar occurrence in East Germany's Harz Mountains, the "specter" allows you to see yourself reflected on the clouds and encircled by a rainbow. Don't wait all day for this, because it's not a daily occurrence.

The famous silversword plant grows amid the desertlike surroundings at **Kalahaku Overlook,** at the 9,000-ft level on Haleakalā. This endangered flowering plant grows only here in the crater at the summit of this mountain. The silversword looks like a member of the yucca family and produces a 3- to 8-ft-tall stalk with several hundred purple sunflowers. At this lookout the silversword is kept in an enclosure to protect it from souvenir hunters and nibbling wildlife.

The **Haleakalā Visitor Center,** at an elevation of 9,740 ft, has exhibits inside, and a trail from here leads to White Hill—a short, easy walk that will give you an even better view of the valley. Hosmer Grove, just off the highway before you get to the visitor center, has campsites and interpretive trails. Park rangers maintain a changing schedule of talks and hikes both here and at the top of the mountain. Call the park for current schedules.

Just before the summit, the **Crater Observatory** offers warmth and shelter, informative displays, and an eye-popping view of the cinder-cone-studded, 7-mi by 3-mi crater. The highest point on Maui is the **Pu'u 'Ula'ula Overlook,** at the 10,023-ft summit. Here you'll find a glass-enclosed lookout with a 360-degree view. The building is open 24 hours a day, and this is where visitors gather for the best sunrise view. Dawn begins between 5:45 and 7, depending on the time of year. On a clear day you can see the islands of Moloka'i, Lāna'i, Kaho'olawe, and Hawai'i (the Big Island). On a *really* clear day you can even spot O'ahu glimmering in the distance.

On a small hill nearby, you'll see **Science City,** a research and communications center straight out of an espionage thriller. The University of Hawai'i and the Department of Defense don't allow visitors to enter the facility. The university maintains an observatory here, and the Department of Defense tracks satellites. ⊠ *Haleakalā Crater Rd. (Hwy. 378), Makawao,* ☎ *808/572–4400.* ⊡ *$10 per car.* ☉ *Park Headquarters/Visitor Center daily 7:30–4; Haleakalā visitor center daily sunrise–3.*

NEED A
BREAK?

Kula Lodge (⊠ Haleakalā Hwy., Kula, ☎ 808/878–2517) serves hearty breakfasts from 6:30 to 11:15, a favorite with visitors coming down from a sunrise visit to Haleakalā's summit, as well as those on their way up for a late-morning tramp in the crater. Spectacular ocean views fill the windows of this mountainside lodge.

---

43 **Hui No'eau Visual Arts Center.** The main house of this nonprofit cultural center on the old Baldwin estate, just outside the town of Makawaoan, is an elegant two-story Mediterranean-style villa designed in the 1920s by the defining Hawai'i architect C. W. Dickey. "The Hui" is the grande dame of Maui's well-known arts scene. The acreage seems like a botanical garden, and the nonstop exhibits are always satisfying. The Hui also offers classes and maintains working artists' studios. ⊠ *2841 Baldwin Ave., Makawao,* ☎ *808/572–6560.* ⊡ *Free.* ☉ *Tues.–Sun. 10–4.*

39 **Kula Botanical Gardens.** This well-kept garden has assimilated itself naturally into its craggy six-acre habitat. There are beautiful trees here, including native koa (prized by woodworkers) and kukui (the state tree, a symbol of enlightenment). There's also a good selection of proteas, the flowering shrubs that have become a signature flower crop of Upcountry Maui. A natural stream feeds into a koi pond, which is also home to a pair of African cranes. ⊠ *R.R. 2, Upper Kula Rd., Kula,* ☎ *808/878–1715.* ⊡ *$5.* ☉ *Daily 9–4.*

42 **Makawao.** This once-tiny town has managed to hang on to its country charm (and eccentricity) as it has grown in popularity. The district was settled originally by Portuguese and Japanese immigrants, who came to Maui to work the sugar plantations and then moved "Upcountry" to establish small farms, ranches, and stores. Descendants now work the neighboring Haleakalā and 'Ulupalakua ranches. Every July 4 the *paniolo* (Hawaiian cowboy) set comes out in force for the Makawao Rodeo. The crossroads of town—lined with places to shop, view the work of local artists, and dine—reflects a growing population of people who came here just because they liked it. ⊠ *Hwy. 365, East Maui.*

HAWAI'I'S FLORA AND FAUNA

HAWAI'I HAS the dubious distinction of claiming more extinct and endangered animal species than all of the North American continent. The Hawaiian crow, or 'alalā, for example, has been reduced to a population of only about 15 birds, and most of these have been raised in captivity on the Big Island. The 'alalā is now facing a serious threat from another endangered bird—the 'io, or Hawaiian hawk. Still "protected" although making a comeback from its former endangered status, the nēnē goose, Hawai'i's state bird, roams freely in parts of Maui, Kaua'i, and the Big Island, where mating pairs are often spotted ambling across roads in Hawai'i Volcanoes National Park.

The mongoose is not endangered, although some residents wish it were. Alert drivers can catch a glimpse of the ferretlike animal darting across country roads. The mongoose was brought to Hawai'i in 1883 in an attempt to control the rat population, but the plan had only limited success, because the hunter and hunted rarely met: mongooses are active during the day, rats at night. Another creature, the rock wallaby, arrived in Honolulu in 1916 after being purchased from the Sydney Zoological Garden. Two escaped, and today about 50 of the small, reclusive marsupials live in remote areas of Kalihi Valley on O'ahu.

At the Kīlauea Point National Wildlife Refuge on Kauai'i, hundreds of Laysan albatross, wedge-tail shearwaters, red-footed boobies, and other marine birds glide and soar within photo-op distance of visitors to Kīlauea Lighthouse. Boobie chicks hatch in the fall and emerge from nests burrowed into cliffside dirt banks and even under stairs—any launching pad from which the fledgling flyer can catch the nearest air current.

Hawai'i has only two native mammals. Threatened with extinction, the rare Hawaiian bat hangs out primarily at Kealakekua Bay on the Big Island. Also on the endangered species list, doe-eyed Hawaiian monk seals breed in the northwestern Islands. With only 1,500 left in the wild, you won't catch many lounging on the beaches of Hawai'i's populated islands, but you can see rescued pups and adults along with "threatened" Hawaiian green sea turtles at Sea Life Park and the Waikīkī Aquarium on O'ahu.

Tropical flowers such as plumeria, orchids, hibiscus, red ginger, heliconia, and anthuriums grow wild on all islands. Pīkake blossoms make the most fragrant leis, and fragile orange 'ilima (once reserved only for royalty) the most elegant leis. The lovely wood rose is actually the dried seedpod of a species of morning glory. Mountain apple, Hawaiian raspberry, thimbleberry, and strawberry guava provide refreshing snacks for hikers; and giant banyan trees, hundreds of years old, spread their canopies over families picnicking in parks, inviting youngsters to swing from their hanging vines.

Sprouting ruby pom-pom-like lehua blossoms—thought to be the favorite flower of Pele, the volcano goddess—'ōhi'a trees bury their roots in fields of once-molten lava. Also growing on the Big Island as well as the outer slopes of Maui's Haleakalā, exotic protea flourish only at an elevation of 4,000 ft; within Haleakalā's moonscape crater, the rare and otherworldly silversword—a 7-ft stalk with a single white spike and pale yellow flower found nowhere else on earth—blooms once and then dies.

NEED A
BREAK?

One of Makawao's most famous landmarks is **Komoda Store & Bakery** (⊠ 3674 Baldwin Ave., ☎ 808/572–7261)—a classic mom-and-pop store that has changed little in three-quarters of a century—where you can get a delicious cream puff if you arrive early enough. They make hundreds, but sell out each day.

★ ⓜ **Tedeschi Vineyards and Winery.** You can take a tour of the winery and its historic grounds, the former Rose Ranch, and sample the island's only wines: a pleasant Maui Blush, the Maui Brut-Blanc de Noirs Hawaiian Champagne, and Tedeschi's annual Maui Nouveau. The top-selling products, however, are pineapple wines. The tasting room is a cottage built in the late 1800s for the frequent visits of King Kalākaua. The cottage also contains the 'Ulupalakua Ranch History Room, which tells colorful stories of the ranch's owners, the paniolo tradition that developed here, and Maui's polo teams. The old General Store may look like a museum, but in fact it's an excellent pit stop. The ranch and winery are not too out of the way when you're returning from a visit to Haleakalā, and they're definitely worth a stop. ⊠ *Kula Hwy.,* *'Ulupalakua Ranch,* ☎ 808/878–6058. ☒ *Free.* ☉ *Daily 9–5, tours at 10:30 and 1:30.*

The Road to Hāna

Don't let anyone tell you Hāna Highway is impassable, frightening, or otherwise unadvisable. Because of all the hype, you're bound to be a little nervous approaching it for the first time. But once you try it, you'll wonder if maybe there's somebody out there making it sound tough just to keep out the hordes. The 55-mi road begins in Kahului, where it is a well-paved highway. The eastern half of the road, riddled with turns and bridges, is challenging, and you'll want to stop often so the driver can enjoy the view, too. But it's not a grueling all-day drive. The challenging part of the road takes only an hour and a half. Don't expect a booming city when you get to Hāna. It's the road, which meanders past lush scenery and waterfalls, that's the draw.

A Good Drive

Hāna Highway is the main street in the little town of **Pā'ia** ⑭. You'll want to begin with a full tank of gas. There are no gas stations along Hāna Highway, and the stations in Hāna close by 6 PM. You can also pick up a picnic lunch here. Lunch and snack choices along the way are limited to local fare from rustic fruit stands. Once the road gets twisty, remember that many residents make this trip frequently. You'll recognize them because they're the ones who'll be zipping around every curve. They've seen this so many times before that they don't care to linger. Pull over to let them pass.

Two miles east of Pā'ia you'll see **Ho'okipa Beach** ⑮, arguably the windsurfing capital of the world. Two miles later the bottom of Ha'ikū Road offers a right-turn side trip to **Ha'ikū** ⑯, Maui's verdant gulch country. About 6 mi later, at the bottom of Kaupakalua Road, the roadside mileposts begin measuring the 36 mi to Hāna town. The road's trademark noodling starts about 3 mi after that. All along this stretch of road, waterfalls are abundant. Open the windows to enjoy the sounds and smells. There are plenty of places to pull off and park. You'll want to plan on doing this a few times, since the road's curves make driving without a break difficult. When it's raining (which is often), the drive is particularly beautiful.

As you drive on you'll pass the sleepy country villages of **Huelo** ⑰ and Kailua. At about Mile Marker 11 you can stop at the bridge over **Puahokamoa Stream** ⑱, where there are more pools and waterfalls. If you'd rather stretch your legs and use a flush toilet, continue another mile to the **Kaumahina State Wayside Park** ㊾. Near Mile Marker 14 you'll find yourself driving along a cliffside down into deep, lush **Honomanū Bay** ㊿. Another 4 mi brings you to the **Ke'anae Arboretum** �51, where you can add to your botanical education or enjoy a challenging hike into a forest. Nearby you'll find the **Ke'anae Overlook** �52. Coming up is the halfway mark to Hāna. If you've had enough scenery, this is as good a time as any to turn around and head back to civilization.

Continue from Mile Marker 20 for about ¾ mi to **Wailua Overlook** �53. After another ½ mi you'll hit the best falls on the entire drive to Hāna, **Waikāne Falls** �54. At about Mile Marker 25 you'll see a road that heads down toward the ocean and the village of **Nāhiku** �55, once a populous ancient settlement. Just after Mile Marker 31, the left turn at 'Ula'ino Road doubles back for a mile, loses its pavement, and even crosses a streambed just before Kahanu Garden and **Pi'ilanihale Heiau** �56, the largest in the state. Back on the road and less than ½ mi farther is the turnoff for Hāna Airport. Just beyond Mile Marker 32 you'll pass **Wai'ānapanapa State Park** �57. Stop at the black-sand beach for a swim. **Hāna** �58 is just minutes away from here. **Hotel Hāna-Maui** �59, with its surrounding ranch, is the mainstay of Hāna's economy.

Once you've seen Hāna, you might want to drive 10 mi past the town to the pools at **'Ohe'o Gulch** �60. Many people travel the mile past 'Ohe'o Gulch to see the **Grave of Charles Lindbergh** �61. You'll see a ruined sugar mill with a big chimney on the right side of the road and then, on the left, a rutted track leading to Palapala Ho'omau Congregational Church. The simple one-room church sits on a bluff over the sea, with the small graveyard on the ocean side. From here, you'll want to return the way you came. The road ahead is quite rough and not recommended for rental cars.

TIMING

With stops, the drive from Pā'ia to Hāna should take you between two and three hours. Lunching in Hāna, hiking, and swimming can easily turn the round-trip into a full-day outing. Since there's so much lush scenery to take in, try to plan your Road to Hāna drive for a day that promises fair, sunny weather, though the drive can be beautiful when it's raining. And be prepared for car trains that form spontaneously during the busier tourist seasons. (If you find one forming behind you, pull over and let the other drivers pass.)

Sights to See

�61 **Grave of Charles Lindbergh.** The world-renowned aviator chose to be buried here because he and his wife, writer Anne Morrow Lindbergh, spent a lot of time living in the area in a home they'd built. He was buried here in 1974, next to Palapala Ho'omau Congregational Church. Since this is a churchyard, be considerate and leave everything exactly as you found it. Next to the churchyard on the ocean side is a small county park, a good place for a peaceful picnic. ⊠ *Palapala Ho'omau Congregational Church, Pi'ilani Hwy., Kīpahulu.*

OFF THE BEATEN PATH

KAUPŌ ROAD – The road to Hāna continues all the way around Haleakalā's "back side" through 'Ulupalakua Ranch and into Kula. The desertlike area, with its grand vistas, is unlike anything else on the island, but the road itself is bad, sometimes impassable in winter. The car-rental agencies are smart to call it off-limits to their passenger cars. Most of the residents along the road in these wild reaches also prefer that you stick to the windward side of the mountain. The danger and dust from increasing numbers of speeding jeep drivers are making life tough for the residents, especially in Kaupō, with its 4 mi of unpaved road. The small communities around East Maui cling tenuously to the old ways. Please keep them in mind if you do pass this way.

㊻ Haʻikū. At one time this town vibrated around a couple of enormous pineapple canneries. Now the place is reawakening and becoming a self-reliant community. At the town center, the old cannery has been turned into a rustic mall. Nearby warehouses are following suit. Continue 2 mi up Kokomo Road to see a large puʻu capped with a grove of columnar pines, and the 4th Marine Division Memorial Park. During World War II American GIs trained here for battles on Iwo Jima and Saipan. Locals have nicknamed the cinder cone "Giggle Hill," because it was a popular hangout for Maui women and their favorite servicemen. You might want to return to Hāna Highway by following Haʻikū Road east. This is one of Maui's prettiest drives, and it passes West Kuiaha Road, where a left turn will bring you to a second renovated cannery. ⊠ *Intersection of Haʻikū and Kokomo Rds.*

★ **㊹ Hāna.** The town centers on its lovely circular bay, dominated on the right-hand shore by a puʻu called Kaʻuiki. A short trail here leads to a cave, the birthplace of Queen Kāʻahumanu. Two miles beyond town another puʻu presides over a loop road that passes Hāna's two best beaches—Koki and Hāmoa. The hill is called Ka Iwi O Pele (Pele's Bone). This area is rich in Hawaiian history and legend. Offshore here, at tiny ʻĀlau Island, the demigod Maui supposedly fished up the Hawaiian islands.

Keep in mind that this is a company town. Although sugar was once the mainstay of Hāna's economy, the last plantation shut down in the '40s. In 1946 rancher Paul Fagan built the **Hotel Hāna-Maui** and stocked the surrounding pastureland with cattle. Suddenly, it was the ranch and its hotel that were putting food on most tables. The cross you'll see on the hill above the hotel was put there in memory of Fagan.

For many years, the Hotel Hāna-Maui was the only attraction for diners and shoppers determined to spend some time and money in Hāna after their long drive. The **Hāna Cultural Center Museum** (⊠ Ukea St., ☏ 808/248–8622) helps to meet that need. Besides operating a well-stocked gift shop, it displays artifacts, quilts, a replica of an authentic *kauhale* (an ancient Hawaiian living complex, with thatched huts and food gardens), and other Hawaiiana. The knowledgeable staff can explain it all to you. ⊠ *Hāna Hwy., Mile Marker 35.*

Hāna Airport. Think of Amelia Earhart. Think of Waldo Pepper. If these picket-fence runways don't turn your thoughts to the derring-do of barnstorming pilots, you haven't seen enough old movies. Only the smallest planes can land and depart here, and when none of them happen to be around, the lonely wind sock is the only evidence that this is a working airfield. ⊠ *Hāna Hwy. past Mile Marker 30,* ☏ *808/248–8208.*

㊿ Honomanū Bay. At Mile Marker 14 the Hāna Highway drops into and out of this enormous valley, with its rocky black-sand beach. The Honomanū Valley was carved by erosion during Haleakalā's first dormant period. At the canyon's head there are 3,000-ft cliffs and a 1,000-ft waterfall, but don't try to reach them. There's not much of a trail, and what does exist is practically impassable. ⊠ *Hāna Hwy. before Keʻanae.*

★ **㊺ Hoʻokipa Beach.** There is no better place on this or any other island to watch the world's best windsurfers in action. The surfers know five different surf breaks here by name. Unless it's a rare day without wind or waves, you're sure to get a show. It's not safe to park on the shoulder. Use the ample parking lot at the county park entrance. ⊠ *2 mi past Pā'ia on Hwy. 36.*

⑤ Hotel Hāna-Maui. It's pleasant to stroll around the lobby of this low-key but beautiful property, perhaps on the way to dinner at the restaurant, drinks at the bar, or shopping in the gift stores. The newer Sea Ranch cottages, built to look like authentic plantation housing from the outside, across the road are also part of the hotel. ⊠ *Hāna Hwy., Hāna,* ☎ *808/248–8211.*

㊼ Huelo. This sleepy little farm town has two quaint churches and several lovely B&B's. It's a good place to stay if you value privacy, but it also provides an opportunity to meet local residents and learn about a rural lifestyle you might not have expected to find in the Islands. The same can be said for nearby **Kailua** (Mile Marker 6), home to Alexander & Baldwin's irrigation employees. ⊠ *Hāna Hwy. near Mile Marker 5.*

㊾ Kaumahina State Wayside Park. The park has a picnic area, rest rooms, and a lovely overlook to the Ke'anae Peninsula. Hardier souls can camp here, with a permit. ⊠ *Hāna Hwy., Mile Marker 12, Kailua,* ☎ *808/984–8109.* ☜ *Free.* ☉ *Weekdays 8–4.*

㊿ Ke'anae Arboretum. Here's a place to learn the names of the many plants and trees now considered native to Hawai'i. The meandering Pi'ina'au Stream adds a graceful touch to the arboretum and provides a swimming pond besides. You can take a fairly rigorous hike from the arboretum, if you can find the trail at one side of the large taro patch. Be careful not to lose the trail once you're on it. A lovely forest waits at the end of the hike. ⊠ *Hāna Hwy., Mile Marker 17, Ke'anae.* ☜ *Free.* ☉ *Daily 24 hrs.*

㊾ Ke'anae Overlook. From this observation point, you can take in the patchwork-quilt effect the taro farms create below. The people of Ke'anae are working hard to revive this Hawaiian agricultural art and the traditional cultural values that the crop represents. The ocean provides a dramatic backdrop for the farms. In the other direction there are awesome views of Haleakalā through the foliage. This is a great spot for photos. ⊠ *Hāna Hwy. near Mile Marker 17, Ke'anae.*

⑤ Nāhiku. In ancient times this was a busy settlement with hundreds of residents. Now only about 80 people live in Nāhiku, mostly native Hawaiians and some back-to-the-land types. A rubber grower planted trees here in the early 1900s. The experiment didn't work out, so Nāhiku was essentially abandoned. The road ends at the sea in a pretty landing. This is the rainiest, densest part of the East Maui rain forest. ⊠ *Makai side of Hāna Hwy., Mile Marker 25.*

★ ⑥ 'Ohe'o Gulch. One branch of Haleakalā National Park runs down the mountain from the crater and reaches the sea here, where a basalt-lined stream cascades from one pool to the next. Some tour guides still call this area "Seven Sacred Pools," but in truth there are more than seven, and they've never been considered sacred. You can park here and walk to the lowest pools for a cool swim. The place gets crowded, though, since most people who drive the Hāna Road make this their last stop. If you can hike at all, go up the stream on the 2-mi hike to **Waimoku Falls.** The trail crosses a spectacular gorge, then turns into a boardwalk that takes you through an amazing bamboo forest. You can pitch a tent in the grassy campground down by the sea. *Pi'ilani Hwy., 10 mi south of Hāna.*

★ ㊹ Pā'ia. This little town on Maui's north shore was once a sugarcane enclave, with a mill and plantation camps. Astute immigrants quickly opened shops to serve the workers, who probably found it easier to buy supplies near home. The town boomed during World War II when the marines set up camp in nearby Ha'ikū. The HC&S sugar mill, on Baldwin Avenue about a mile above the traffic light at Hāna Highway, is still in full production. After the war, however, workers moved to other parts of Maui, and the town's population began to dwindle. In the '70s Pā'ia became a hippie town as dropouts headed for Maui to open boutiques, galleries, and unusual eateries. In the '80s windsurfers discovered nearby Ho'okipa Beach and brought an international flavor to Pā'ia. You can see this in the youth of the town and in the budget inns that have cropped up to offer accommodations to those who windsurf for a living. Currently, there's a political controversy about continuing development, which has the surfers and other residents, both native and adopted, up in arms.

Pā'ia is still a tourist-friendly town, though. If you want to do some shopping, you can find clothing and handcrafted keepsakes or snacks and sweets in abundance. Pā'ia is also home to Lama Tenzin, a Tibetan monk who lives and teaches at a small open temple called **Karma Rimay O Sal Ling**, on Baldwin Avenue a half mile from the traffic light. ⊠ *Hwys. 390 and 36, north shore.*

NEED A BREAK?	Pā'ia has become a great place to find food. Picnics and Charley's Saloon used to be the two big eateries in town. Now, right near the intersection of Baldwin Avenue and Hāna Road, you have a number of choices. **Picnics** (☎ 808/579–8021) is the best place to get takeout on Baldwin Avenue. **Charley's Saloon** (☎ 808/579–8085), on Hāna Road, is an easygoing local hangout with pool tables. **Pā'ia Fishmarket** (☎ 808/579–8030) specializes in fresh island fish both by the pound and served as tasty lunches and dinners. **Anthony's Coffee Company** (☎ 808/579–8340) serves ice cream, smoothies, and picnic lunches. The little town has an excellent wine store, **The Wine Corner** (☎ 808/579–8940). **Mana Foods** (☎ 808/579–8078) is an admirable natural-foods store.

★ ❺❻ **Pi'ilanihale Heiau.** The largest prehistoric monument in Hawai'i, this temple platform was built for a great 16th-century Maui king named Pi'ilani and his heirs. This king also supervised the construction of a 10-ft-wide road that completely encircled the island. (That's why his name is part of most of Maui's highway titles.) Hawaiian families continue to maintain and protect this sacred site as they have for centuries, and they have not been eager to turn it into a tourist attraction. However, they now offer a brochure so you can tour the property yourself. Parties of four or more can reserve a guided tour by calling 48 hours in advance. Tours include 122-acre **Kahanu Garden**, a federally funded research center focusing on the ethnobotany of the Pacific. ⊠ *Left on 'Ula'ino Rd. at Mile Marker 31 of Hāna Hwy.; the road turns to gravel; continue 1½ mi,* ☎ *808/248–8912.* 🏷 *$5 self-guided tours, $10 guided tours.* ⊙ *Weekdays 9–3.*

❹❽ **Puahokamoa Stream.** The bridge over Puahokamoa Stream is one of many you'll cross en route from Pā'ia to Hāna. It spans pools and waterfalls. Picnic tables are available, so many people favor this as a stopping point, but there are no rest rooms. ⊠ *Hāna Hwy. near Mile Marker 11.*

★ ❺❼ **Wai'ānapanapa State Park.** The park is right on the ocean, and it's a lovely spot to picnic, hike, or swim. An ancient burial site is nearby, as well as a heiau. Wai'ānapanapa also has one of Maui's only black-sand beaches and some freshwater caves for adventurous swimmers to explore. The water in the tide pools here turns red several times a year. Scientists say it's explained by the arrival of small shrimp, but locals claim the color represents the blood of Popoalaea, whom legend says was murdered in one of the caves by her husband, Chief Kaakea. In either case, the dramatic contrast between the rain forest green of the cliffs and the black volcanic rock is not to be missed. With a permit you can stay in state-run (and rather shabby) cabins here for less than $30 a night—the price varies depending on the number of people—but reserve early. They often book up a year in advance. ⊠ *Hāna Hwy. near Mile Marker 32, Hāna,* ☏ *808/984–8109.* ⊠ *Free.*

54 Waikāne Falls. Though not necessarily bigger or taller than the other falls, these are the most dramatic—some say the best—falls you'll find on the road to Hāna. That's partly because the water is not diverted for sugar irrigation. The taro farmers in Wailua need all the runoff. This is a particularly good spot for photos. ⊠ *Hāna Hwy. past Mile Marker 21, Wailua.*

53 Wailua Overlook. From the parking lot you can see Wailua Canyon, but you'll have to walk up steps to get a view of Wailua Village. The landmark in Wailua Village is a church made of coral, built in 1860. Once called St. Gabriel's Catholic Church, the current Our Lady of Fatima Shrine has an interesting legend surrounding it. As the story goes, a storm washed just enough coral up onto the shore to build the church but then took any extra coral back to sea. ⊠ *Hāna Hwy. near Mile Marker 21, Wailua.*

BEACHES

All of Hawai'i's beaches are free and open to the public—even those that grace the front yards of fancy hotels—so you can make yourself at home on any one of them. Blue beach-access signs indicate rights-of-way through condominium and resort properties.

Although they don't appear often, be sure to pay attention to any signs or warning flags on the beaches. Warnings of high surf or rough currents should be taken seriously. Before you seek shade under a coconut palm, be aware that the trade winds are strong enough to knock fruit off the trees and onto your head. Drinking alcoholic beverages on beaches in Hawai'i is prohibited.

West Maui

"Slaughterhouse" (Mokuleia) Beach. The island's northernmost beach is part of the Honolua-Mokuleia Marine Life Conservation District. "Slaughterhouse" is the surfers' nickname for what is officially Mokuleia. When the weather permits, this is a great place for bodysurfing and sunbathing. Concrete steps and a green railing help you get down the sheer cliff to the sand. The next bay over, Honolua, has no beach but offers one of the best surf breaks in Hawai'i. Often you'll see competitions happening there, with cars pulled off the road and parked in the pineapple field. There are no facilities at this wild area. ⊠ *Mile Marker 32 on the road past Kapalua.*

D. T. Fleming Beach. Because the current can be quite strong, this charming, mile-long sandy cove is better for sunbathing than for swimming. Still it's one of the island's most popular beaches, and there are rest rooms, showers, picnic tables, grills, and paved parking. Part of the beach runs along the front of the Ritz-Carlton, Kapalua. ⊠ *Hwy. 30, 1 mi north of Kapalua Resort.*

Kapalua Beach. On the northern side of Nāpili Bay is small, pristine Kapalua Beach. You may have to share sand space with a number of other beachgoers, however, because the area is quite popular for lazing, swimming, and snorkeling. There are showers, rest rooms, and a paved parking lot. ⊠ *Past Bay Club restaurant off Lower Honoapiʻilani Hwy., before Kapalua Bay Hotel.*

★ **Nāpili Beach.** A sparkling white crescent makes a perfect cove for strolling and sunbathing. It's right outside the Nāpili Kai Beach Club, a popular little resort for honeymooners, but despite this and other condominiums and development around the bay, the facilities here are minimal. There are showers at the far right end of the beach and a tap by the beach-access entrance, where you can wash the sand off your feet, and you're only a few miles south of Kapalua. ⊠ *5900 Lower Honoapiʻilani Hwy.; from upper highway follow cutoff road closest to Kapalua Resort and look for Nāpili Pl. or Hui Dr.*

★ **Kāʻanapali Beach.** If you're looking for peace and quiet, this is not the beach for you. But if you want lots of action, lay out your towel here. The beach fronts the big hotels at Kāʻanapali and is one of Maui's best people-watching spots: cruises, windsurfers, and parasailers head out from here while the beautiful people take in the scenery. The area around Black Rock is a snorkeler's paradise, and the bravest of the brave dive off the imposing rock into the calm water below. Although no facilities are available, the nearby hotels have rest rooms and some, like the Marriott, have outdoor showers. You're also close to plenty of shops and concession stands. ⊠ *Follow any of 3 Kāʻanapali exits from Honoapiʻilani Hwy. and park at any of the hotels.*

The South Shore

Kīhei has excellent beaches right in town, including three beach parks called **Kamaʻole I, II,** and **III,** which have showers, rest rooms, picnic tables, and barbecues. Good snorkeling can be done along the rocky borders of the parks. If Kīhei is excellent, though, Wailea is even better. Look for a little road and parking lot between the first two big resorts—the Renaissance and the Outrigger. This gets you to **Mōkapu** and **Ulua beaches.** A road just after the Grand Wailea takes you to ★**Wailea Beach.** Near the Kea Lani resort, you'll find **Polo Beach.** Each beach is a pocket-size beauty with wonderful snorkeling, as well as showers and rest rooms.

★ **Mākena.** Just south of Wailea is the state park at Mākena, with two good beaches. Big Beach is 3,000 ft long and 100 ft wide. The water off Big Beach is fine for swimming and snorkeling, and you'll find showers, rest rooms, and paved parking here. If you walk over the cinder cone at Big Beach, you'll reach Little Beach, which is clothing-optional by popular practice. Officially, nude sunbathing is illegal in Hawaiʻi, but several bathers who've pushed their arrests through the courts have found their cases dismissed. On Sunday, New Age hippies, gay couples, and free spirits of all kinds crowd the shoreline. At 4 PM on Sunday there's a drumming circle and bonfire. ⊠ *Off Wailea Alanui Dr.*

The North Shore

Kanahā Beach. Local folk and windsurfers like this long golden strip of sand bordered by a wide grassy area. This is a popular Kahului spot for joggers and picnicking Maui families. Kanahā Beach has toilets, showers, picnic tables, and grills. ⊠ *Drive through airport and back out to car-rental road (Koeheke), turn right, and keep going.*

★ **Baldwin Beach.** Another local favorite, just west of Pāʻia town, this beach is a big body of comfortable sand. There's not much wave action for bodysurfing, but this is a good place to stretch out and swim or jog. The county park at the right side of the beach has picnic areas, rest rooms, showers, and sometimes even a lifeguard. ⊠ *Hāna Rd., 1 mi west of Baldwin Ave.*

★ **Hoʻokipa Beach.** If you want to see some of the world's finest windsurfers, stop at this beach along Hāna Highway. The sport has become an art—and a career, to some—and its popularity was largely developed right at Ho'okipa. It's also one of Maui's hottest surfing spots, with waves as high as 15 ft. This is not a good swimming beach, nor the place to learn windsurfing yourself, but plenty of picnic tables and barbecue grills are available for hanging out. ⊠ *2 mi past Pā'ia on Hwy. 36.*

Hāna

Kōkī Beach. This beach in Hāna offers unusually good bodysurfing because the sandy bottom stays shallow for a long way out. On the down side, there are no facilities here. But this is a wild place rich in Hawaiian lore. Watch conditions because the riptides here can be mean. Just down the road is the beach James Michener called the best in the Pacific—crescent-shape Hāmoa Beach. Park on the roadside and walk down either one of the steep paths. Hotel Hāna-Maui keeps facilities here for its guests but has politely included a shower and rest room for the public. ⊠ *Haneo'o Loop Rd., 2 mi east of Hāna town.*

DINING

In the resorts you'll find some of Maui's finest Continental restaurants and some good cafés and bistros as well. In addition, because many of the upscale hotels sit right on the beach, you'll often have the benefit of an oceanfront ambience. Outside the resorts, you'll find great places to dine formally or grab a bite informally (to use the pidgin term, "grind").

Except as noted, reservations are not required, but it's never a bad idea to phone ahead to book a table. Restaurants are open daily unless otherwise noted. Few restaurants on Maui require jackets. An aloha shirt and pants for men and a simple dress or pants for women are acceptable in all but the most upscale establishments. For price category explanations, *see* Dining *in* Smart Travel Tips.

West Maui

American

$$ ✕ **Longhi's.** A Lahaina establishment, Longhi's has been around since 1976, serving great Italian pasta as well as sandwiches, seafood, beef, and chicken dishes. All the pasta is homemade, and the in-house bakery turns out breakfast pastries, desserts, and fresh bread. Even on a warm day, you won't need air-conditioning here with two spacious, breezy, open-air levels to choose from. The black-and-white tile floors are a nice touch. ⊠ *888 Front St., Lahaina,* ☎ *808/667–2288. AE, D, DC, MC, V.*

$–$$ ✕ **Lahaina Coolers.** This breezy little café with a surfboard hanging
★ from its ceiling serves such tantalizing fare as Evil Jungle Pasta (with grilled chicken in spicy Thai peanut sauce) and linguine with prawns, basil, garlic, and cream. It also has pizzas, steaks, burgers, and such desserts as a chocolate taco filled with tropical fruit and berry salsa. Pastas are made fresh in-house. Don't be surprised to see a local fisherman walk through the dining area with a freshly caught snapper, or a harbor captain reeling in a hearty breakfast. ⊠ *180 Dickenson St., Lahaina,* ☎ *808/661–7082. AE, MC, V.*

$ ✕ **The Gazebo Restaurant.** Even locals will stand in line upwards of a half hour for a table overlooking the beach at this restaurant, an actual open-air gazebo. The food is standard diner fare, but it's thoughtfully prepared. Breakfast choices include macadamia-nut pancakes and Portuguese-sausage omelets. There are satisfying burgers and salads at lunch. The friendly hotel staff puts out coffee for those waiting in line. ⊠ *Nāpili Shores Resort, 5315 Lower Honoapi'ilani Hwy., Nāpili,*

☎ *808/669–5621. No credit cards. No dinner.*

Continental

$$$–$$$$ ✕ **Bay Club.** A candlelit dinner at this spot on a rocky promontory over-
★ looking the ocean is a romantic way to cap off a day in the sun, espe-
cially if you've been swimming at Kapalua Beach just a few yards from
the door. You won't want to walk through the richly paneled, elegant
interior with sandy feet, however. For a truly relaxing evening, shower
and dress first and then lean back, sip a glass of cabernet or Riesling
from the excellent wine list, and watch the sun slip gloriously past the
Maui horizon. Island seafood is the emphasis here, starting with ap-
petizers such as the seared 'ahi tartare and foie gras and building to
main courses such as the Hawaiian seafood pan roast of prawns, lob-
ster, and scallops cooked in sweet basil broth. ⊠ *Kapalua Bay Hotel,
1 Bay Dr., Kapalua,* ☎ *808/669–5656. AE, D, DC, MC, V.*

$$–$$$ ✕ **Swan Court.** You enter this elegant eatery via a grand staircase and
what seems like a tropical, cathedral-ceiling ballroom, where black and
white swans glide across a waterfall-fed lagoon. The menu applies Eu-
ropean and Pacific Rim flavors to fresh, locally grown vegetables,
seafood, and meats. Try the crispy scallop dim sum in plum sauce; creamy
lobster-coconut bisque brimming with chunks of fish, lobster, shrimp,
and button mushrooms; or charbroiled lamb chops in macadamia
satay sauce. Arrive early and ask for a table on the left side, where the
swans linger in the evening. The restaurant serves a breakfast buffet.
⊠ *Hyatt Regency Maui, Kā'anapali Beach Resort, 200 Nohea Kai Dr.,
Lahaina,* ☎ *808/661–1234. AE, D, DC, MC, V.*

French

$$–$$$$ ✕ **Chez Paul.** Since 1975 this tiny roadside restaurant between Lahaina
★ and Mā'alaea in Olowalu has been serving excellent French cuisine to
a packed house of repeat customers. Such dishes as fresh local fish
poached in white wine with shallots, cream, and capers typify the classical menu with island touches. The restaurant's nondescript exterior
belies the fine art, 14 linen-draped tables, 22-seat private dining room,
wine cellar, and charming atmosphere inside. Don't blink or you'll miss
this small group of buildings huddled in the middle of nowhere. ⊠
Honoapi'ilani Hwy., 4 mi south of Lahaina, Olowalu, ☎ *808/661–
3843. Reservations essential. AE, D, MC, V. No lunch.*

$$–$$$ ✕ **Gerard's.** Owner and celebrated chef Gerard Reversade started
★ cooking at the age of 10, and at 12 he was baking croissants. Since
1982 he has been honoring the French tradition at this charming
restaurant with such exquisitely prepared dishes as rack of lamb in mint
crust with thyme jus; venison cutlets in a port sauce with confit of chest-
nuts, walnuts, fennel, and pearl onions; and impeccably fresh fish. The
menu changes once a year, but many favorites—such as the sinfully good
crème brûlée—remain. A first-class wine list, a lovely room, and
celebrity-spotting round out the experience. ⊠ *Plantation Inn, 174 Lahainaluna Rd., Lahaina,* ☎ *808/661–8939. AE, D, DC, MC, V. No
lunch.*

Hawaiian/Pacific Rim

$$$–$$$$ ✕ **'Ānuenue Room.** In Hawaiian, *'ānuenue* means rainbow. The name,
★ however, doesn't really characterize the Ritz-Carlton's elegant signa-
ture restaurant, with its dark-wood walls and massive chandeliers. The
cuisine is pure Hawaiian, inventively elevated. Appetizers include *opihi*
(sea snail) with island goat cheese in pastry, and crispy corn-and-sea-
urchin fritters served with shrimp, seaweed, and Hawaiian chili-lob-
ster sauce. For the main course, how about kālua suckling pig served
with Hawaiian sticky rice, cabbage, port wine, and *'ohelo* berries (the
island equivalent of cranberries)? Service is excellent, as you might ex-

Maui Dining

Honokōhau

Kapalua

Honolua

③ ②

①

④ 30

Nāpili

Kahakuloa

Kahana

⑤

⑥

⑦

WEST MAUI MTS.

340

Honokōwai

⑧ ⑨ Kā'anapali

LAHAINA

⑩ – ⑭

'Īao Valley
State Park

⑮ ⑯

30

⑰

Olowalu

Honoapi'ilani Hwy.

N

0   5 miles

0   5 km

PACIFIC OCEAN

Paʻuwela **39**

Haʻikū

Ulumalu

WAILUKU

32–**37**

Pāʻia **38**

Hāna Hwy.

Kahakili Hwy.

Iao Stream

36

Baldwin Ave.

Kaupakalua Rd.

365

31

KAHULUI

37

Haleakalā Hwy.

Hāliʻimaile Rd.

390

Kokomo

30

30

Puʻunēnē

40

41

42–**44**

Makawao

350

45

380

Honoapiʻilani Hwy.

18–**20**

Pukalani

N. Kihei Rd.

Mokulele Hwy.

377

Māʻalaea
Harbor

Kula Hwy.

Haleakalā Hwy.

Kīhei

21

Piʻilani Hwy.

37

378

S. Kihei Rd.

22

31

23

Waiohuli

24 **25**

Keōkea

27

WAILEA

28

26

29

Kula Hwy.

pect at the Ritz. ✉ *Ritz-Carlton, Kapalua, 1 Ritz-Carlton Dr., Kapalua,* ☎ *808/669–1665. AE, D, DC, MC, V.*

$$–$$$$ ✕ **David Paul's Lahaina Grill.** This beautifully designed restaurant sits
★   arm in arm with the elegant Lahaina Inn in a historic, creaky building
         on Lahainaluna Road. It's won numerous awards since it opened in
         1990, including *Honolulu* magazine's selection as "Best Restaurant on
         Maui" seven years in a row. The chef's celebrated menu is revised sea-
         sonally, but you can count on finding the signature tequila shrimp and
         firecracker rice along with such scrumptious desserts as triple-berry pie.
         The restaurant has an extensive wine cellar, an in-house bakery, and
         a baby grand in the lounge. ✉ *127 Lahainaluna Rd., Lahaina,* ☎ *808/
         667–5117. AE, DC, MC, V.*

$$–$$$ ✕ **Hula Grill.** The food at genial chef-restaurateur Peter Merriman's
         bustling, family-oriented restaurant is every bit as good as the cuisine
         at his first popular eatery, the more formal Merriman's, on the Big Is-
         land. South Pacific snapper is baked with tomato, chili, and cumin aioli
         and served with black bean, Maui onion, and avocado relish. Spare
         ribs are steamed in banana leaves, then grilled with mango barbecue
         sauce over mesquite-like *kiawe* wood. The restaurant is set in a re-cre-
         ated 1930s Hawaiian beach house, and every table has an ocean-beach
         view. Or you can actually dine on the beach, toes in the sand, at the
         Barefoot Bar, where Hawaiian entertainment is presented every evening.
         ✉ *Whalers Village, 2435 Kā'anapali Pkwy., Kā'anapali,* ☎ *808/667–
         6636. AE, DC, MC, V.*

$$–$$$ ✕ **I'o.** Right from its opening in 1999, this restaurant immediately es-
★   tablished itself as the hippest place in Lahaina—both for its theatrical,
         sculpted interior designed by the artist Dado and for its eclectic menu
         of contemporary Pacific cuisine. The most popular appetizer is the Silken
         Purse—steamed wontons stuffed with roasted peppers, mushrooms,
         macadamia nuts, and tofu and served with jalapeño-scented tomato
         sauce and yogurt puree. Favorite dinners include the crispy 'ahi, sashimi-
         grade tuna wrapped in nori and served with a salad of green papaya
         and sweet peppers; and lemongrass-coconut fish served with fresh
         hearts-of-palm salad and chilled spicy *soba* noodles. Desserts to look
         for are the Hawaiian Vintage Chocolate Mousse and the chocolate pâté
         with Kula strawberries. ✉ *505 Front St., Lahaina,* ☎ *808/661–8422.
         AE, D, DC, MC, V. No lunch.*

$$–$$$ ✕ **Plantation House Restaurant.** It's hard to decide which is best here,
         the food or the view. Rolling hills, grassy volcanic ridges lined with
         pine trees, and fairways that appear to drop off into the ocean pro-
         vide an idyllic setting. The specialty is fresh island fish prepared ac-
         cording to different "tastes"—Upcountry Maui, Asian-Pacific, Provence,
         and others. The Taste of the Rich Forest includes roasted wild mush-
         rooms served on tender tot soi greens and garlic mashed potatoes with
         a Maui onion meunière. The breeze through the large shuttered win-
         dows can be cool, so you may want to bring a sweater or sit by the
         fireplace. ✉ *Plantation Course Clubhouse, 2000 Plantation Club Dr.,
         past Kapalua,* ☎ *808/669–6299. AE, MC, V.*

$$–$$$ ✕ **Roy's Kahana Bar & Grill.** Anyone who's ever eaten at one of Roy
         Yamaguchi's restaurants knows how good the food is, and this Roy's
         is no exception. Such Asian-Pacific specialties as shrimp with sweet-and-
         spicy chili sauce keep regulars returning for more. Locals find this is a
         great place to get together with friends for fun and good food. Next
         door is the somewhat quieter Roy Yamaguchi's Nicolina, which caters
         to a spice-loving crowd with grilled Southwestern-style chicken with chili
         hash and smoked tomato sauce, and smoked-and-peppered duck with
         gingered sweet potatoes and Szechuan-Mandarin sauce. ✉ *Kahana
         Gateway Shopping Center, 4405 Honoapi'ilani Hwy., Kahana,* ☎ *808/
         669–6999 (Roy's); 808/669–5000 (Nicolina). AE, D, DC, MC, V.*

Japanese

$$ **★** ✕ **Sansei.** One of the best restaurants on the island, Sansei is Japanese with a Hawaiian twist. Inspired dishes include *panko*-crusted 'ahi (panko are Japanese bread crumbs), spicy fried calamari, mango-and-crab-salad roll, and a decadent foie gras *nigiri* sushi. Don't miss the Asian rock-shrimp cakes, a signature dish. Desserts, equally inventive, often use local fruit; the Kula-persimmon crème brûlée is stunning. ✉ *Kapalua Shops, 115 Bay Dr., Kapalua,* ☎ *808/666–6286. AE, D, MC, V. No lunch.*

Seafood

$$–$$$ ✕ **Erik's Seafood Grotto.** This seafood diner is so proud of its large selection of fresh fish that it displays the whole offering nightly as a photo opportunity. Additional house specialties include bouillabaisse brimming with clams, scallops, lobster, shrimp, and fish and served with toasted garlic bread; and cioppino served over homemade fettuccine. A stop at the oyster bar is a worthwhile detour. Try half shells topped with horseradish mayonnaise and baked with Gruyère cheese. Come to this nautical spot between 5 and 6 and catch the $12.95–$13.95 early bird specials. ✉ *Kahana Villas, 4242 Lower Honoapi'ilani Hwy., Kahana,* ☎ *808/669–4806. AE, D, DC, MC, V.*

$$–$$$ ✕ **Pacific'O.** You can sit outdoors at umbrella-shaded tables near the water's edge, or find a spot in the breezy, marble-floor interior. The menu is exciting, with the likes of fresh 'ahi-and-*ono* tempura (ono is a makerel-like fish), in which the two kinds of fish are wrapped around *tobiko* (flying-fish roe), then in nori, and wok-fried. There's a great lamb dish, too—a whole rack of sweet New Zealand lamb, sesame-crusted and served with roasted macadamia sauce and Hawaiian chutney. Live jazz is played Thursday through Saturday nights from 9 to midnight. Guitarist George Benson likes to sit in. ✉ *505 Front St., Lahaina,* ☎ *808/667–4341. AE, D, DC, MC, V.*

$–$$$ ✕ **Kimo's.** Outstanding seafood is just one of the options here. Also good are Hawaiian-style chicken and pork dishes, burgers, sandwiches, vegetarian pasta, and sashimi. The smoked marlin appetizer is especially good. On a warm Lahaina summer day, it's a treat to relax at an umbrella-shaded table on the open-air lānai, sip a pineapple-passion-fruit-guava drink, and watch sailboats and parasailers glide in and out of the harbor. Try the signature dessert, Hula Pie: vanilla–macadamia-nut ice cream topped with chocolate fudge and whipped cream in an Oreo-cookie crust. ✉ *845 Front St., Lahaina,* ☎ *808/661–4811. AE, DC, MC, V.*

Central Maui

American

$ ✕ **Maui Bake Shop.** Wonderful breads baked in brick ovens from 1935, hearty lunch fare, and irresistible desserts make this a popular spot in Central Maui. Baker José Krall was trained in France, and his wife, Claire, is a Maui native whose friendly face you'll often see when you walk in. Standouts include the focaccia and homemade soups. ✉ *2092 Vineyard St., Wailuku,* ☎ *808/242–0064. AE, D, MC, V. Closed Sun. No dinner.*

Eclectic

$$ ✕ **Class Act.** This little-known place offers one of the best values on Maui, as well as a chance to see rising chefs in action. Run by the esteemed Food Service Department at Maui Community College, the restaurant features student chefs in every position, from the kitchen to the waitstaff. The cuisine changes weekly, so you might find Thai, Moroccan, Austrian, Japanese, or Italian on the menu. No alcohol is served, but you're welcome to bring your own. ✉ *Maui Community College, 310 Ka'ahumanu Ave., Wailuku,* ☎ *808/984–3480. No credit cards. No dinner.*

Hawaiian

$ ✕ **Sam Sato's.** Locals and tourists sit elbow to elbow at the counter for cheap, delicious saimin and *manju* (pastries with sweetened adzuki beans). The plate lunch of barbecued pork is also popular. Don't miss the fantastic pineapple turnovers. ✉ *1750 Wili Pa Loop, Wailuku,* ☎ *808/244–7124. No credit cards. Closed Sun. No dinner.*

Italian

$–$$ ✕ **Marco's Grill & Deli.** This convenient eatery outside Kahului Airport (look for the green awning) serves reliable Italian food that's slightly overpriced. Homemade pastas appear on the extensive menu, along with an unforgettably good Reuben sandwich and the best Greek salad on the island. The local business crowd fills the place for breakfast, lunch, and dinner. ✉ *444 Hāna Hwy., Kahului,* ☎ *808/877–4446. AE, D, DC, MC, V.*

Japanese

$ ✕ **Restaurant Matsu.** Sit at a common table and eat authentic Japanese fare along with the locals—*katsu* (cutlet) dishes and curries served with white rice, or bowls of saimin or *udon* noodles with tempura. ✉ *161 Ala Maha St., Kahului,* ☎ *808/871–0822. No credit cards.*

Thai

$–$$ ✕ **Saeng's Thai Cuisine.** Choosing a dish from the six-page menu here requires determination, but the food is worth the effort, and most dishes can be tailored to your taste buds: hot, medium, or mild. Begin with spring rolls and a dipping sauce, move on to such entrées as Evil Prince Chicken (cooked in coconut sauce with Thai herbs) or red curry shrimp, and finish up with tea and tapioca pudding. Asian artifacts, flowers, and a waterfall decorate the dining room, and tables on a veranda will satisfy outdoors lovers. ✉ *2119 Vineyard St., Wailuku,* ☎ *808/244–1567. AE, MC, V.*

$–$$ ✕ **Siam Thai.** Behind a slightly weathered storefront you'll find some of the best Thai food on Maui. This local favorite serves traditional chicken-coconut soup, beef and chicken sautéed with ginger and bamboo shoots, curries, and vegetarian dishes—about 60 selections in all. The food tends to be spicy, the portions small, and huge crowds arrive at lunchtime. Some patrons opt for takeout because there's not much in the way of decor. ✉ *123 Market St., Wailuku,* ☎ *808/244–3817. AE, D, DC, MC, V.*

Vietnamese

$–$$ ✕ **A Saigon Café.** The only storefront sign announcing this small, delightful hideaway is one reading OPEN. Once you find it, treat yourself to *banh hoi chao tom,* more commonly known as "shrimp pops burritos" (ground marinated shrimp, steamed and grilled on a stick of sugarcane). It's fun and messy. Vegetarian fare is also well represented here; try the green-papaya salad. A variety of fresh island fish is always available. The white interior serves as a backdrop for Vietnamese carvings in this otherwise unadorned space. Background music includes one-hit wonders from the early '70s. ✉ *1792 Main St., Wailuku,* ☎ *808/243–9560. D, MC, V.*

The South Shore

American

$–$$ ✕ **Hapa's Brewhaus & Restaurant.** This friendly place has an assort-
ment of great eats that includes pizza, calzones, pastas, chicken-teriyaki
burgers, vegetarian stir-fry, sashimi, and lobster bisque. There are
seven kinds of beer on tap, including Kona Longboard Lager. The adjoining room, Hapa's Rockin' Sushi, is open 'til 1 AM. ⊠ *Lipoa Center, 41 E. Lipoa St., Kīhei,* ☎ *808/879–9001. D, DC, MC, V.*

$–$$ ✕ **Joe's Bar & Grill.** With friendly service; a great view of Lāna'i; and
such dishes as New York strip steak with caramelized onions, wild mushrooms, and Gorgonzola cheese crumble, there are lots of reasons to
stop in at this spacious, breezy spot. Owners Joe and Bev Gannon, who
run the immensely popular Hāli'imaile General Store, have brought
their flair for food home to roost in this comfortable treetop-level restaurant at the Wailea Tennis Club, where you can dine while watching
court action from a balcony seat. ⊠ *131 Wailea Ike Pl., Wailea,* ☎
808/875–7767. AE, MC, V.

$–$$ ✕ **Maui Onion.** Forget the overrated Cheeseburger in Paradise in La-
★ haina. Maui Onion has the best burgers on the island, hands down,
and phenomenal onion rings as well. They coat the onions in pancake
batter, then dip them in panko, then fry them 'til they're golden brown.
⊠ *Renaissance Wailea, 3550 Wailea Alanui Dr., Wailea,* ☎ *808/879–
4900. AE, D, DC, MC, V.*

Eclectic

$$$–$$$$ ✕ **Seasons.** Acclaimed executive chef George Mavrothalassitis prepares
standout dishes that marry fresh island ingredients with flavors from
his native Provence as well as from China, Japan, Thailand, and the
Pacific islands. Consider, for example, *onaga* (pink or red snapper) and
summer truffles with braised leeks, or shaved *hamachi* (yellowtail)
sashimi served with a tomato and peppercorn gelée and citrus *shoyu*
(sweet soy sauce). As befits the Four Seasons Resort, this is a restau-
rant of understated elegance, with tables set with white linen and
French china and decor that emphasizes natural materials. A trio of
island musicians and sensational ocean vistas add to the delicious am-
bience. ⊠ *Four Seasons Resort Maui, 3900 Wailea Alanui Dr., Wailea,*
☎ *808/874–8000. AE, D, DC, MC, V. No lunch.*

Hawaiian/Pacific Rim

$$–$$$ ✕ **Hula Moons.** This delightful oceanside spot is full of memorabilia
chronicling the island life of Don Blanding, a writer, artist, and poet
who became Hawai'i's unofficial ambassador of aloha in the 1930s.
The outstanding menu blends locally grown produce with Pacific Rim
and European preparations. Don't miss the fabulous vegetarian appetizer
of fresh pohole ferns, Hana tomatoes, and Kula onions. Try the bam-
boo-steamed whole *moi,* a fish once reserved for Hawaiian royalty, or
the tangy braised short ribs. The Sunday brunch is one of the most lav-
ish on the island, and the wine list is extensive. You can dine inside,
poolside, or outside on the terrace. ⊠ *Outrigger Wailea Resort, 3700
Wailea Alanui Dr., Wailea,* ☎ *808/879–1922. AE, D, DC, MC, V.*

$$–$$$ ✕ **Humuhumunukunukuāpua'a.** Your waiter will ask you to pronounce
★ the restaurant's name by the end of the evening, but after a few glasses
of wine you might just prefer to call it "humu." Whether you succeed
or fail, you'll have one of the best meals of your vacation in Maui's most
romantic spot. The open-air restaurant actually floats on a lagoon, and
the thatched roof and tiki torches give it a Polynesian feel. You can fetch
your own spiny lobster (which is best simply grilled) from a cage below
the water's surface or order from the exciting menu. Sweet-corn and
lobster soup with poached rock shrimp and basil puree is a standout,

as is the sesame-crusted mahimahi with coconut rice, baby bok choy, and black bean miso sauce. Humuhumunukunukuāpuaʻa, by the way, is the state fish. ⊠ *Grand Wailea Resort, 3850 Wailea Alanui Dr., Wailea,* ☎ *808/875–1234. AE, D, DC, MC, V.*

$$–$$$ ✕ **Merriman's Bamboo Bistro.** Peter Merriman's fusion "bistro," the newest addition to the growing dining scene at the Maui Ocean Center, serves tapas-style small plates meant for sharing. Among the best are sesame-crusted island fish, kiawe-grilled beef, and salads made from local produce. ⊠ *Māʻalaea Harbor Village, corner of Old Māʻalaea Rd. and Honoapiʻilani Hwy., next to the Maui Ocean Center, Māʻalaea,* ☎ *808/243–7374. AE, D, DC, MC, V.*

$$–$$$ ✕ **A Pacific Café.** Hawaiʻi regional cuisine began with a few innova-
★   tive island chefs, including Jean-Marie Josselin. With the assistance of corporate chef George Gomes, Jr., who was born and raised in the Islands, Josselin now serves this innovative cuisine in five island locations, two on Maui. Flavorful combinations include pan-seared mahimahi with a garlic sesame crust and ginger-lime sauce; Chinese roasted duck with baked sour-cherry *manapua* (dough wrapped around diced pork), charred baby eggplant, and *likoʻi*–star anise sauce ("likoʻi" is Hawaiian for passion fruit); and "the original" tiger-eye ʻahi sushi tempura with pear tomato salad and Chinese-mustard sauce. The restaurant's tropical, whimsical decor has been described as "the Flintstones meet the Jetsons." The Kīhei location is more consistent than the Honōkowai restaurant. ⊠ *Azeka Place II Shopping Center, 1279 S. Kīhei Rd., Kīhei,* ☎ *808/879–0069;* ⊠ *3350 Lower Honoapiʻilani Hwy., Honōkowai,* ☎ *808/669–2800. AE, D, DC, MC, V. No lunch.*

Italian

$–$$ ✕ **Bella Luna Ristorante.** Best sunset view on the island—who would dare to claim such a title? Bella Luna does, and deservedly so. This is a small place (40 seats), where you dine looking out over a golf course and the open sea at the very quiet, off-the-beaten-path Diamond Resort. It's an informal and friendly place, with seafood, Italian dishes, and a wine list with decent, affordable selections. It's a great place for a date. The owners also serve three meals a day out of the Wailea Blue Clubhouse just down the street. ⊠ *Diamond Resort, 555 Kaukahi St., Wailea,* ☎ *808/879–8255. AE, DC, MC, V. No lunch.*

Japanese

$$–$$$$ ✕ **Hakone.** The best Japanese food on the south side of the island is served at this restaurant in the Maui Prince hotel, at the end of the strip of Wailea resorts. A full six-course *kaiseki* meal—with small dishes of raw, cooked, hot, cold, sweet, and savory items—is $58, a good value for the quality of food presented. Impeccably fresh sushi, traditional cooked dishes, and an impressive sake list round out the menu. The Sunday-night sushi buffet is popular. ⊠ *Maui Prince hotel, 5400 Mākena Alanui Rd., Mākena,* ☎ *808/874–1111. AE, MC, V. No lunch.*

Seafood

$$ ✕ **Māʻalaea Waterfront Restaurant.** At this harborside establishment fresh fish is prepared in a host of sumptuous ways: baked in buttered parchment paper; imprisoned in ribbons of angel-hair potato; or topped with tomato salsa, smoked chili pepper, and avocado. The varied menu also lists an outstanding rack of lamb and veal scallopini. Tourists come early to dine at sunset on the outdoor patio. Enter Māʻalaea at the Maui Ocean Center and then follow the blue WATERFRONT RESTAURANT signs to the third condominium. ⊠ *50 Hauʻoli St., Māʻalaea,* ☎ *808/244–9028. AE, D, DC, MC, V.*

$–$$ ✕ **Blue Marlin Harborfront Grill & Bar.** This is a casual, less expensive alternative to the Māʻalaea Waterfront Restaurant. It's as much a bar as it is a grill, but the kitchen nonetheless sends out well-prepared, substantial servings of fresh fish, burgers, and salads. The sidewalk tables have a lovely view of the harbor. ⊠ *Māʻalaea Harbor Village, corner of Old Māʻalaea Rd. and Honoapiilani Hwy., next to the Maui Ocean Center, Māʻalaea,* ☎ *808/244–8844. AE, MC, V.*

East Maui

American

$ ✕ **Café O Lei.** Puns notwithstanding, this is your best bet for a casual
★ lunch in Makawao. Especially recommended are the quinoa salad and the snow-crab-and-avocado sandwich on focaccia. Seating is outdoors only. ⊠ *Paniolo Courtyard, 3673 Baldwin Ave., Makawao,* ☎ *808/573–9065. No credit cards. Closed Sun. No dinner.*

$ ✕ **Pauwela Café.** Ultracasual and ultrafriendly, this spot just off Hāna Highway is worth the detour. Order a kālua-pork sandwich and a piece of coffee cake and pass the afternoon. The large breakfast burritos and homemade soups are also good. ⊠ *375 W. Kuiaha Rd., off Hāna Hwy. past Haʻikū Rd., Haʻikū,* ☎ *808/575–9242. No credit cards. No dinner.*

Hawaiian/Pacific Rim

$$–$$$ ✕ **Hāliʻimaile General Store.** What do you do with a lofty wooden build-
★ ing that used to be a camp store in the 1920s and is surrounded by a tiny town in the middle of sugarcane and pineapple fields? If you're Bev and Joe Gannon, you turn it into a legendary restaurant. The Szechuan barbecued salmon and rack of lamb Hunan style are classics. For a filling and innovative appetizer, try the sashimi napoleon: a tower of crispy wonton layered with smoked salmon. The outstanding house salad is topped with Maui onions, mandarin oranges, walnuts, and crumbled blue cheese on request. Pastry chef Teresa Gannon makes an unbelievable pineapple upside-down cake that's irresistible. The restaurant even has its own cookbook. ⊠ *900 Hāliʻimaile Rd., left at exit off Hwy. 37, 5 mi from Hāna Hwy., Hāliʻimaile,* ☎ *808/572–2666. MC, V.*

Italian

$$ ✕ **Casanova Italian Restaurant & Deli.** The pizzas, baked in a brick wood-burning oven imported from Italy, are the best on the island. This is a good Italian dinner house in an out-of-the-way location—Makawao. Casanova is also known for its daytime deli and, at night, for its extra-large dance floor and entertainment by well-known island and mainland musicians. ⊠ *1188 Makawao Ave., Makawao,* ☎ *808/572–0220. D, DC, MC, V.*

Mexican

$–$$ ✕ **Polli's.** This Mexican restaurant in the paniolo town of Makawao not only has a wide selection of such delicious taste treats as seafood enchiladas, chimichangas, quesadillas, and fajitas, but also offers to prepare any item on the menu with seasoned tofu or vegetarian taco mix instead of meat—and the meatless dishes are just as good. A special treat are the *bunuelos*—light pastries topped with cinnamon, maple syrup, and a scoop of ice cream. The intimate interior is plastered with colorful sombreros and other cantina knickknacks. ⊠ *1202 Makawao Ave., Makawao,* ☎ *808/572–7808. AE, D, DC, MC, V.*

Pan-Asian

$ ✕ **East West Café and Sushi Bar.** Everything is thoughtfully prepared and fresh, and inexpensive to boot, at this lovely spot in laid-back

Makawao. The food combines mostly Japanese preparations with Asian accents. Try the coconut-curry soup or the vegetarian noodles on the small menu. The rosemary lemonade is a clever accompaniment to the light fare. ⊠ *3682 Baldwin Ave., Makawao,* ☎ *808/572–1101. MC, V. Closed Sun. No lunch Sat.*

Seafood

$$–$$$ ✕ **Mama's Fish House.** As you enjoy the landscaped grounds and
★   ocean views at this cliff-top restaurant, check out the stone path engraved with whimsical Hawaiian geckos. But the real treat here is the fish, prepared in seven mouthwatering ways—baked in a creamy herb sauce, sautéed with macadamia nuts, or grilled with spicy wasabi butter, for example. That's why this thatched-hut restaurant with a Hawaiian nautical theme is packed every evening. The chicken, steak, and kālua pig dishes are worth trying as well. And the restaurant serves the best mai tais on the island, bar none. About 1½ mi east of Pa'ia on Hāna Highway, look for Mama's classic '40s-era Ford trucks parked on grassy knolls at both entrances. ⊠ *799 Poho Pl., Kū'au,* ☎ *808/ 579–8488. Reservations essential. AE, D, DC, MC, V.*

Steak

$$ ✕ **Makawao Steak House.** A restored 1927 house on the slopes of Haleakalā is the setting for this paniolo restaurant that serves consistently good prime rib, rack of lamb, and fresh fish. Three fireplaces, friendly service, and an intimate lounge create a cozy, welcoming atmosphere. ⊠ *3612 Baldwin Ave., Makawao,* ☎ *808/572–8711. D, DC, MC, V. No lunch.*

LODGING

Maui has the highest percentage of upscale hotel rooms and the highest average accommodation cost of any Hawaiian island. The quality level—and the opulence quotient—are way up there, making this one of the best places in the world to indulge in a first-class resort vacation. But Maui also has the state's highest concentration of condominium units; many are oceanfront and offer the ambience of a hotel suite without the cost.

The county officially sanctions relatively few B&Bs, not wanting to siphon business from the hotels. However, many alternative accommodations offer seclusion and a countryside experience, especially Upcountry and in Hāna. The majority of these are better described as guest cottages—or guest houses—that skip the breakfast part of B&B and offer instead provisions and privacy. Most are a departure from the typical resort-style accommodations associated with the island. Rates for most B&Bs range from $40 to as much as $150 per night.

For price category explanations, *see* Lodging *in* Smart Travel Tips.

West Maui

$$$$ 🏨 **Hyatt Regency Maui.** When this trendsetting property was devel-
★   oped in 1980, it set a new standard for luxury resorts: a museum-quality art collection; a seemingly endless swimming pool, with swim-through grottoes and a 130-ft water slide; fantasy landscaping (the builders used 10,000 tons of rock to fabricate the environment) with splashing waterfalls; and a collection of exotic creatures, even penguins. The Hyatt remains Kā'anapali's premier property. Several features, such as improved access for people with disabilities, an outdoor hot tub, a wedding gazebo, a seaside spa, and a beachfront bar, have kept this oasis competitive with any resort on the island. ⊠ *Kā'anapali Beach Resort, 200*

Nohea Kai Dr., Lahaina 96761, ☏ *808/661–1234 or 800/233–1234,* FAX *808/667–4499,* WEB *www.hyatt.com. 815 rooms. 4 restaurants, 6 bars, in-room safes, no-smoking floors, pool, spa, 2 18-hole golf courses, 6 tennis courts, health club, beach, library, children's programs (ages 3–12), chapel. AE, D, DC, MC, V.*

$$$$ ⊡ **Kā'anapali Ali'i.** Yes, this is a condominium, but you'd never know it; the four 11-story buildings are put together so well you still have the feeling of seclusion. Instead of tiny rooms you can choose between one- and two-bedroom apartments. Each has lovely amenities: a chaise in an alcove, a bidet, a sunken living room, a whirlpool, oak kitchen cabinets, and a separate dining room. The Kā'anapali Ali'i is maintained like a hotel, with daily maid service, an activities desk, and a 24-hour front desk. ⊠ *50 Nohea Kai Dr., Lahaina 96761,* ☏ *808/667–1400 or 800/642–6284,* FAX *808/661–1025,* WEB *www.classicresorts.com. 264 units. 2 pools, sauna, 18-hole golf course, 6 tennis courts, beach. AE, D, DC, MC, V.*

$$$$ ⊡ **Kapalua Bay Hotel.** Built in 1978 fronting what was once voted America's best beach, at lovely Kapalua Bay, this hotel has a real Maui feel to it. The exterior is understated white and natural wood, and the open lobby, filled with flowering vanda and dendrobium orchids, has a view of the ocean. The plantation-style rooms are decorated in earth tones, and all have views of Lāna'i and Moloka'i. A shopping plaza outside the main hotel entrance has some fine restaurants and boutiques. Guests receive preferred rates and tee times at three golf courses in Kapalua. ⊠ *1 Bay Dr., Kapalua 96761,* ☏ *808/669–5656 or 800/367–8000,* FAX *808/669–4694. 209 rooms. 3 restaurants, 2 pools, golf privileges, 6 tennis courts, beach. AE, DC, MC, V.*

$$$$ ⊡ **Kapalua Bay Villas.** This harmoniously designed complex of two- and three-story buildings seems to cascade down the cliffs to the sea. Privately owned and individually decorated one- and two-bedroom units may be rented through the Kapalua Bay Hotel. Condos are assigned to one of five luxury categories and regularly inspected to ensure that standards are maintained. The ocean views are great, with the island of Moloka'i in the distance and humpback whales (in season) passing close to shore. Renters enjoy a free shuttle to the hotel and guest rates for golf, tennis, and other hotel amenities. ⊠ *1 Bay Dr., Kapalua 96761,* ☏ *808/669–5656 or 800/367–8000,* FAX *808/669–4694. 125 units. Golf privileges. AE, D, DC, MC, V.*

$$$$ ⊡ **Maui Marriott.** Rooms are decorated with bright tropical colors, and nearly 90% have ocean views. Besides having access to a beachside massage tent and privileges at two 18-hole golf courses in Kā'anapali, guests can join classes for aerobics; hula; Hawaiian arts, crafts, and language; food preparation; and a number of sports. A "shipwreck" playground and an island bar are also here. The best thing here, however, is the service: the staff is genuinely friendly and helpful. ⊠ *100 Nohea Kai Dr., Lahaina 96761,* ☏ *808/667–1200 or 800/228–9290,* FAX *808/667–8300,* WEB *www.marriotthotels.com. 599 rooms, 16 suites. 4 restaurants, lobby lounge, 2 pools, 2 hot tubs, massage, golf privileges, 5 tennis courts, health club, beach, bicycles, children's programs (ages 5–12). AE, D, DC, MC, V.*

$$$$ ⊡ **Nāpili Kai Beach Club.** These lodgings on 10 beautiful beachfront acres draw a loyal following. Hawaiian-style rooms are done in seafoam green, mauve, and rattan; shoji doors open onto your lānai, with the beach and ocean right outside. The property also includes two 18-hole putting greens, four swimming pools, and an extra-large whirlpool. This is a family-friendly place, with kids' programs as well as free classes in hula and lei making. Packages that include a car, breakfast, and other extras are available if you stay five nights or longer. ⊠ *5900 Lower Honoapi'ilani Hwy., Nāpili Bay 96761,* ☏ *808/669–6271 or*

Maui Lodging

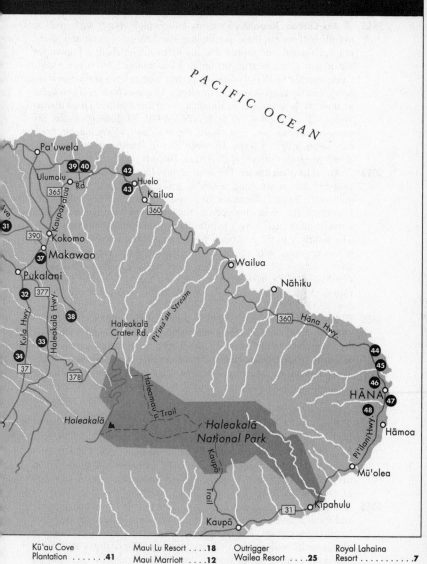

PACIFIC OCEAN

Pa'uwela
39 40
Ulumalu
42
Huelo
365 Rd. 43 Kailua
Kaupakalua
360
31
390
Kokomo
37 Makawao
Wailua
Pukalani
Nāhiku
32 377
Kula Hwy.
38
Haleakalā
Crater Rd.
360 Hāna Hwy.
33
44
34
Haleakalā Hwy.
45
37
378
46
HĀNA
47
Haleamau'u Trail
48
Haleakalā
Hāmoa
Pi'ina'au Stream
Haleakalā
National Park
Pi'ilani Hwy.
Mū'olea
Kaupō
Kipahulu
31
Kaupō

800/367–5030, FAX *808/669–5740,* WEB *www.napilikai.com. 162 rooms. Kitchenettes, 4 pools, hot tub, 2 putting greens, beach. AE, MC, V.*

$$$$ ⊞ **Ritz-Carlton, Kapalua.** Spacious, comfortable rooms with oversize
★ marble bathrooms; lānai overlooking the three-level pool; and all the grace, elegance, and service that the Ritz-Carlton chain is known for await you a this beachfront hotel. Most rooms have ocean views. Guests on the Club floors have a private lounge with complimentary snack and beverage service all day long. All guests have golf privileges at three 18-hole courses in Kapalua. ⊠ *1 Ritz-Carlton Dr., Kapalua 96761,* ☎ *808/669–6200 or 800/262–8440,* FAX *808/665–0026,* WEB *www.ritzcarlton.com. 548 rooms. 4 restaurants, lobby lounge, pool, hair salon, golf privileges, 10 tennis courts, health club, beach, children's programs (ages 5–12). AE, D, DC, MC, V.*

$$$$ ⊞ **Royal Lahaina Resort.** The lānai at this Hawaiian Hotels & Resorts property afford stunning ocean or golf-course views. What distinguishes the Royal Lahaina are the two-story cottages, each divided into four units; the bedrooms open to the trade winds on two sides. The upstairs units each have a private lānai, and downstairs units share. The walkway to the courtyard wedding gazebo is lined with stepping stones engraved with the names of past brides and grooms and their wedding dates. ⊠ *2780 Keka'a Dr., Lahaina 96761,* ☎ *808/661–3611 or 800/447–6925,* FAX *808/661–3538,* WEB *www.hawaiihotels.com. 592 rooms. 3 restaurants, 3 pools, 18-hole golf course, 11 tennis courts, beach. AE, D, DC, MC, V.*

$$$$ ⊞ **Sheraton Maui.** Set among lush gardens on Kā'anapali's best stretch of beach are the six buildings that comprise this beautiful resort. The resort sits next to 80-ft-high "Black Rock," from which divers leap in a nightly torch-lighting ritual. One of the two swimming pools looks like a natural lagoon, with rock waterways and wooden bridges. The Sheraton has family appeal—a number of rooms provide two double beds and a Murphy bed, and the hotel offers a free children's programs in the summer. Conveniences include generous room amenities and a "no-hassle" check-in that bypasses the registration desk. ⊠ *2605 Kā'anapali Pkwy., Lahaina 97671,* ☎ *808/661–0031 or 800/782–9488,* FAX *808/661–0458,* WEB *www.sheraton-maui.com. 510 rooms. 3 restaurants, lobby lounge, in-room safes, refrigerator, 2 pools, 3 tennis courts, health club, beach, children's programs (ages 5–12). AE, D, DC, MC, V.*

$$$$ ⊞ **Westin Maui.** This is a hotel for active people who like to be out and about and won't spend all their time in their rooms, which are rather small for the price. But compensations are provided—an "aquatic playground" with five heated swimming pools, privileges at two 18-hole golf courses in Kā'anapali, and the central-most position on Kā'anapali Beach. The landscaping is lush, with abundant waterfalls (15 at last count) and lagoons. A valuable Asian and Pacific art collection is displayed throughout the property. ⊠ *2365 Kā'anapali Pkwy., Lahaina 96761,* ☎ *808/667–2525 or 800/228–3000,* FAX *808/661–5831,* WEB *www.westinmaui.com. 761 rooms. 3 restaurants, lobby lounge, 5 pools, hair salon, hot tub, golf privileges, health club, beach, baby-sitting, children's programs (ages 12 and under). AE, D, DC, MC, V.*

$$$–$$$$ ⊞ **Papakea Beach Resort.** With classes on swimming, snorkeling, pineapple cutting, and more, this resort is good for people who want to stay active on their vacation. Papakea has built-in privacy because its units are spread out among 11 low-rise buildings on some 13 acres of land. You aren't really aware that you're sharing the property with 364 other units. Bamboo-lined walkways between buildings and fish-stocked ponds create a serene mood. There's a two-day minimum stay. Despite its name, there is no beach on the premises, although there are several nearby. ⊠ *3543 Honoapi'ilani Hwy., Lahaina 96761,* ☎ *808/*

669–4848 or 800/367–5637, FAX 808/669–0751, WEB *www.aston-hotels. com. 36 studios, 224 1-bedroom units, 104 2-bedroom units. 2 pools, hot tub, sauna, putting green, 4 tennis courts. AE, MC, V.*

$$$–$$$$ 🏨 **Plantation Inn.** Charm and luxury set apart this inn reminiscent of
★ a southern plantation home. Filled with Victorian and Asian furnishings, it's on a quiet street in the heart of Lahaina. Secluded lānai draped with hanging plants face a central courtyard, pool, and garden pavilion perfect for morning coffee. Each guest room or suite is decorated differently, with hardwood floors, French doors, antiques, four-poster beds, and ceiling fans. Some have kitchenettes and whirlpool baths. A generous breakfast is included in the room rate. One of Hawai'i's best French restaurants, Gerard's, adds to the allure. ✉ *174 Lahainaluna Rd., Lahaina 96761,* 🕾 *808/667–9225 or 800/433– 6815,* FAX *808/667–9293,* WEB *www.theplantationinn.com. 18 rooms. Restaurant, refrigerators, pool, hot tub. AE, MC, V.*

$$$ 🏨 **Kā'anapali Beach Hotel.** This attractive, old-fashioned hotel is full
★ of aloha and the good-natured spirit of Maui, and the employees' chorus entertains joyously most afternoons. In addition, this happy place is recognized as one of the best values on the West Side. The vintage-style Mixed Plate restaurant, known locally for its Hawaiian food, is decorated with displays honoring the many cultural traditions represented by the staff. The employees themselves contributed the artifacts. There are complimentary classes in hula, lei making, and 'ukulele playing, and guests have privileges at the two 18-hole Kā'anapali golf courses. ✉ *2525 Kā'anapali Pkwy., Lahaina 96761,* 🕾 *808/661–0011 or 800/262–8450,* FAX *808/667–5978,* WEB *www.kaanapalibeachhotel. com. 430 rooms. 2 restaurants, lobby lounge, pool, golf privileges, beach. AE, D, DC, MC, V.*

$$$ 🏨 **Mauian Hotel.** If you're looking for a quiet place to stay, this sedate hotel way out in Nāpili may be for you. The simple two-story buildings date from 1959, but the current owners have renovated the place for comfort and convenience, including fully equipped kitchens. The rooms, however, have neither televisions nor telephones. Such noisy devices are relegated to the 'Ohana Room, where a Continental breakfast is served daily. Best of all, the two-acre property opens out onto lovely Napīli Bay. ✉ *5441 Lower Honoapi'ilani Hwy., Napīli 96761,* 🕾 *808/ 669–6205 or 800/367–5034,* FAX *808/669–0129,* WEB *www.mauian.com. 44 rooms. Pool, shuffleboard, coin laundry. AE, D, MC, V.*

$$–$$$ 🏨 **Lahaina Inn.** This antique jewel is classic Lahaina—a two-story
★ wooden building that will transport you back to the turn of the 20th century. The nine small rooms and three suites shine with authentic period restoration and furnishings, including quilted bedcovers, antique lamps, and Oriental carpets—no televisions. You can sit in a wicker chair on your balcony right in the heart of town. An excellent Continental breakfast is served in the parlor. ✉ *127 Lahainaluna Rd., Lahaina 96761,* 🕾 *808/661–0577 or 800/669–3444,* FAX *808/667–9480,* WEB *www.lahainainn.com. 9 rooms, 3 suites. AE, D, MC, V.*

The South Shore

$$$$ 🏨 **Four Seasons Resort.** This is a Maui favorite, partly because of its
★ location, on one of the Valley Isle's finest beaches with all the amenities of the well-groomed Wailea Resort. Access to three 18-hole golf courses and "Wimbledon West," with 11 championship tennis courts, is included. The property itself has great appeal, with terraces, courtyards, gardens, waterfalls, and fountains. Nearly all the rooms have an ocean view and combine traditional style with tropical touches. You'll find terry robes and whole-bean coffee grinders in each room. ✉ *3900 Wailea Alanui Dr., Wailea 96753,* 🕾 *808/874–8000 or 800/334–6284,*

FAX *808/874–6449,* WEB *www.fshr.com. 380 rooms. 3 restaurants, 2 bars, pool, 2 tennis courts, golf privileges, health club, beach. AE, D, DC, MC, V.*

$$$$ ★ **Grand Wailea.** Sunny opulence is everywhere at this 40-acre resort. Elaborate water features include a 2,000-ft multilevel "canyon river-pool" with slides and grottoes. The Spa Grande cossets guests with rejuvenating offerings, from aerobics classes to exotic water-and-massage therapies. Luxury pervades the spacious ocean-view rooms, beautifully outfitted with such amenities as an overstuffed chaise longue, a comfortable writing desk, and an oversize tub and separate shower. Guests have access to three 18-hole golf courses, and tennis privileges are available. The resort can also lay claim to one of the best restaurants on Maui—Humuhumunukunukuāpuáa. ⊠ *3850 Wailea Alanui Dr., Wailea 96753,* ☏ *808/875–1234 or 800/888–6100,* FAX *808/874–2442,* WEB *www.grandwailea.com. 779 rooms. 5 restaurants, 6 bars, 3 pools, golf privileges, health club, beach, children's programs (ages 5–12), chapel. AE, D, DC, MC, V.*

$$$$ **Kamaʻole Sands.** This is a huge property for Kīhei—11 four-story buildings wrap around a grassy slope on which are clustered swimming and wading pools, a small waterfall, whirlpool baths, and barbecues. All units have kitchens, laundries, and private lānai. Managed by Castle Resorts & Hotels, this condominium property has a 24-hour front desk and an activities desk, and it is across the road from Kīhei Beach. ⊠ *2695 S. Kīhei Rd., Kīhei 96753,* ☏ *808/874–8700 or 800/367–5004,* FAX *808/879–3273,* WEB *www.castle-group.com. 11 studios; 211 1-bedroom, 83 2-bedroom, and 4 3-bedroom units. Restaurant, pool, wading pool, 4 tennis courts. AE, D, DC, MC, V.*

$$$$ **Kea Lani Hotel Suites & Villas.** A Moorish-domed, all-suite resort offers seclusion and privacy in oceanside two- and three-bedroom villas, each with its own small pool and within easy reach of attractions in Wailea and West Maui. Accommodations in the main hotel are spacious one-bedroom suites with dining lānai and marble bathrooms. Guests have access to three 18-hole golf courses, and tennis privileges are available. ⊠ *4100 Wailea Alanui Dr., Wailea 96753,* ☏ *808/875–4100 or 800/882–4100,* FAX *808/875–1200,* WEB *www.kealani.com. 413 suites, 37 villas. 3 restaurants, deli, lobby lounge, in-room VCRs, refrigerator, 3 pools, hair salon, 2 hot tubs, golf privileges, health club, beach, shops, children's programs (ages 5–12). AE, D, DC, MC, V.*

$$$$ **Maui Prince.** The attention to service, style, and presentation is apparent from the minute you walk into the delightful open-air lobby of this hotel. Rooms on three levels surround the courtyard, which is home to a Japanese garden with a bubbling stream. Each evening a small ensemble performs chamber music in the courtyard. Room decoration is understated, in tones of mauve and beige. Unfortunately, there's an earth berm between the hotel and the beach—part of the agreement the hotel had to make with the zoning commission and local residents—so an ocean view isn't possible from the first floor. ⊠ *5400 Mākena Alanui Rd., Mākena 96753,* ☏ *808/874–1111 or 800/321–6284,* FAX *808/879–8763. 290 rooms. 4 restaurants, pool, 2 18-hole golf courses, 6 tennis courts, beach. AE, DC, MC, V.*

$$$$ ★ **Outrigger Wailea Resort.** One of the most beautiful accommodations in Wailea and the oldest property on the Wailea strip, the Outrigger has an understated elegance and sophistication that is unparalleled in its price range. Rooms sit much closer to the crashing surf than current construction laws allow, and Wailea Beach is just a few steps away. The tropical lobby and interior spaces showcase a remarkable collection of Hawaiian and Pacific Rim artifacts. All of the spacious rooms have private lānai and are styled with a tropical theme. The grounds are lovely, with walks along paths accented with palm, banana, and torch ginger. There are golf privileges at three nearby courses, as well as tennis privileges at the Wailea Tennis Club. The resort also has a game bar, two hot tubs, children's programs, and a Hawaiian cultural program. The new Mandara Spa provides an array of beauty and relaxation treatments as well as massage. ✉ *3700 Wailea Alanui Dr., Wailea 96753,* ☎ *808/879–1922 or 800/922–7866,* FAX *808/874–8331,* WEB *www.outrigger.com. 516 rooms. 3 restaurants, 3 pools, 2 hot tubs, beach, children's programs (ages 5–12). AE, D, DC, MC, V.*

$$$–$$$$ 🏨 **Maui Coast Hotel.** This is an elegant seven-story hotel that you would never notice because it's set back off the street. The standard rooms are fine—very clean and modern—but the best deal is to pay a little more for one of the suites. In these you'll get an enjoyable amount of space and jet nozzles in the bathtub. And the suites adapt well to families. You can lounge by the large pool and order food and drinks from neighboring Jameson's Grill & Bar. Or walk across the street to Kama'ole Beach. There's an activities desk, too, to help you plan your time. ✉ *2259 S. Kīhei Rd., Kīhei, 96753,* ☎ *808/874–6284, 800/895–6284, or 800/426–0670,* FAX *808/875–4731,* WEB *www.westcoasthotels. com. 265 rooms, 114 suites. Restaurant, in-room safes, refrigerators, pool, dry cleaning, laundry service. AE, D, DC, MC, V.*

$$$–$$$$ 🏨 **Renaissance Wailea Beach Resort.** Most of this hotel's rooms are contained in a seven-story, T-shape building positioned on fantastic Mōkapu Beach. Tapestries and gorgeous carpets enhance the public areas. Outside, you'll find exotic gardens, waterfalls, and reflecting ponds. The VIP Mōkapu Beach Club building houses 26 luxury accommodations and has its own concierge, pool, and beach cabanas. Guest rooms are decorated in shades of cream and each has a lānai. Guests have access to the nearby golf and tennis facilities. ✉ *3550 Wailea Alanui Dr., Wailea 96753,* ☎ *808/879–4900 or 800/992–4532,* FAX *808/874–6128,* WEB *www.renaissancehotels.com. 345 rooms. 4 restaurants, lobby lounge, refrigerators, 2 pools, hot tub, basketball, health club, Ping-Pong, shuffleboard, beach, children's programs (5–12). AE, D, DC, MC, V.*

$$$–$$$$ 🏨 **Wailea Villas.** The Wailea Resort started out with three fine condominiums, named, appropriately, Wailea 'Ekahi, Wailea 'Elua, and Wailea 'Ekolu (Wailea One, Two, and Three). Since their construction, Wailea has added the Grand Champions Villas, and the adjoining Mākena Resort has built Mākena Surf and Polo Beach Club. All have beautifully landscaped grounds, large units with exceptional views, and access to five of the island's best beaches. The Wailea 'Elua Village, Polo Beach Club, and Mākena Surf are the more luxurious properties, with rates to match. The three original villas are an expansive property, with all the amenities of the fine Wailea Resort, including daily maid service and a concierge. ✉ *3750 Wailea Alanui Dr., Wailea 96753,* ☎ *808/879–1595 or 800/367–5246,* FAX *808/874–3554,* WEB *www.drhmaui.com. 9 studios; 94 1-bedroom, 157 2-bedroom, and 10 3-bedroom apartments. 6 pools. AE, MC, V.*

$$–$$$ 🏨 **Luana Kai.** Here's a prime example of the condominium-by-the-sea, perfect for setting up household for at least four days (the required minimum). There are three different room plans, suited for couples, families, or friends traveling together. Each one comes with everything you need to move in and make yourself at home—a fully stocked kitchen, dishwasher, laundry, television, and video and stereo equipment. The pool's a social place, with five gas grills, a full outdoor kitchen, and saunas for men and women. There's no beach on-site—for that, you have to go down the road a ways—but the place adjoins a grassy county park with tennis courts. ✉ *940 S. Kīhei Rd., Kīhei, 96753,* ☎ *808/ 879–1268 or 800/669–1127,* FAX *808/879–1455,* WEB *www.luanakai.com.*

113 units. Pool, sauna, putting green, 4 tennis courts, shuffleboard. AE, DC, MC, V.

$$ 🏨 **Maui Lu Resort.** This hotel, the first in Kīhei, is reminiscent of a rustic lodge. The main lobby was the summer home of the original owner, a Canadian logger. Over the years the Maui Lu has added numerous wooden buildings and cottages to its 28 acres. Of the 120 rooms, 50 are right on the beach, and some have their own private coves. The rest are across Kīhei Road on the main property. ⊠ *575 S. Kīhei Rd., Kīhei 96753,* ☎ *808/879–5881 or 800/922–7866,* 𝐅𝐀𝐗 *808/879–4627,* 𝗪𝗘𝗕 *www.aston-hotels.com. 120 rooms. Restaurant, lounge, in-room safes, refrigerators, 2 tennis courts, beach. AE, D, DC, MC, V.*

East Maui

$$$$ 🏨 **Hotel Hāna-Maui.** After a long management transition and some ups
★   and downs, this fine hotel has been restored to its former glory. One of the best places to stay in all of Hawai'i—and a departure from the usual resort-style accommodations—this small, secluded hotel in Hāna is surrounded by a 7,000-acre ranch. The original hotel buildings have white plaster walls and trellised verandas. Inside, the spacious rooms have bleach-wood floors, furniture upholstered in natural fabrics, and such welcome touches as fine art and orchids. The newer Sea Ranch Cottages, surrounding a state-of-the-art fitness center across the road, represent the best value. A shuttle carries guests to a secluded beach nearby. The restaurant on the premises, one of the few places to eat in Hāna, still needs a lot of work. ⊠ *Hāna Hwy. (Box 9), Hāna 96713,* ☎ *808/248–8211 or 800/321–4262,* 𝐅𝐀𝐗 *808/248–7264. 19 rooms, 47 cottages, 1 house. Restaurant, bar, 2 pools, massage, 2 tennis courts, exercise room, horseback riding, jogging, beach, library. AE, D, DC, MC, V.*

$$–$$$ 🏨 **Kula Lodge.** This venue isn't typically Hawaiian: the lodge resembles a chalet in the Swiss Alps, and two units even have a gas fireplace. Charming and cozy in spite of the nontropical ambience, this is a perfect spot for a romantic stay. Units are in two wooden cabins; four have lofts in addition to the ample bed space downstairs, but none have phones or TVs. On three wooded acres, the lodge has views of the valley and ocean enhanced by the surrounding forest and tropical gardens. The property has a restaurant and lounge, as well as a gift shop and a pro-tea store that will pack flowers for you to take home. ⊠ *R.R. 1, Box 475, Kula 96790,* ☎ *808/878–2517 or 800/233–1535,* 𝐅𝐀𝐗 *808/878– 2518,* 𝗪𝗘𝗕 *www.kulalodge.com. 5 units. Restaurant. AE, MC, V.*

$$ 🏨 **Heavenly Hāna Inn.** An impressive Japanese gate marks the entrance to this small upscale inn. The three suites, one a two-bedroom unit, all have TVs. Decor is spare, with Japanese overtones. The furniture was built by Hāna residents. ⊠ *Near Mile Marker 32 on Hāna Hwy. (Box 790), Hāna 96713,* ☎ *808/248–8442. 3 suites. AE, D, MC, V.*

Guest Houses and Bed-and-Breakfasts

Despite the traditional name bed-and-breakfast, many of these small-scale accommodations (both rooms and cottages) choose not to interrupt your privacy with breakfast. Instead they'll provide you with lush Upcountry or tropical surroundings that will enchant you and a kitchen that will let you do your own thing.

$$$–$$$$ 🏨 **Ekena.** This idyllic setting (Ekena means Garden of Eden in Hawaiian) is full of tropical fruit trees and exotic flowers, and it sits on a hillside near the town of Hāna with a commanding view of sea and land. There are two houses, each with a fully equipped kitchen and all necessities. Jasmine, the smaller of the two, is suited to parties of two or four. The main house, Sea Breeze, is huge (2,600 square ft), with two large master suites, but the owners restrict its occupancy to a maximum of four people. In order to ensure privacy, they also rent to only one party at a time. There's a minimum stay of three days, and children under 14 are not allowed. ⊠ *Off Hāna Hwy. (Box 728), Hāna 96713,* ☎ FAX *808/248–7047,* WEB *www.maui.net/ekena. 2 houses. No credit cards.*

$$$–$$$$ ⬜ **Huelo Point Flower Farm.** Set on a 300-ft cliff overlooking Waipo Bay, this two-acre estate is one of the most secluded inns on the island. The Gazebo Cottage is a large studio, and the 900-square-ft Carriage House sleeps four. There are two guest bedrooms in the main house, which also contains an exercise room and a fireplace. Guests are encouraged to pick fruit and flowers while strolling the grounds. ⊠ *Off Hāna Hwy., Huelo (Box 1195, Paia 96779),* ☎ *808/572–1850,* WEB *www. maui.net/huelopt. 2 rooms, 1 cottage, 1 house. No credit cards.*

$$$ ⬜ **'Ainahau.** Hidden away next to Hāna Bay, this cottage looks so-so
★ till you get inside and start looking around. The place is ingeniously and lovingly crafted and furnished with works of art. The kitchen is set up with all the details of home, including a loaded spice rack and a coffee grinder, and the cottage is equipped with cable TV and a CD player. Nature at its most benign lies around you, and the bed is both theatrical and sensuous. Hāna Settings manages this and several other getaways, provides catered meals at your order, and organizes custom Hāna weddings. ⊠ *Off Hāna Hwy. (Box 970), Hāna 96713,* ☎ *808/ 248–7849,* FAX *808/248–8267. 1 cottage. Kitchenette, in-room VCR. AE, MC, V.*

$$$ ⬜ **Hāmoa Bay House & Bungalow.** This Balinese-inspired property is
★ sensuous and secluded, a private sanctuary in a fragrant jungle. There are two buildings. The main house is 1,300 square ft and contains two bedrooms, one of them a suite set apart by a breezeway; there's a screened veranda with an ocean view and also an outdoor lava-rock shower. The 600-square-ft bungalow is a treetop perch with a giant bamboo bed and a hot tub on the veranda. Both accommodations come with complete kitchen and laundry and VCRs. Hāmoa Beach is a short walk away. ⊠ *Hāna Hwy. (Box 773), Hāna 96713,* ☎ *808/248–7884,* FAX *808/248– 7047. 1 house, 1 bungalow. In-room VCRs. No credit cards.*

$$–$$$ ⬜ **Bloom Cottage.** The name comes from the abundance of roses and other flowers that surround this well-run, classic B&B. This is life in the slow lane, with privacy and quiet and a fireplace for when the evenings are nippy. The furnishings are very Ralph Lauren with a cowhide flourish suited to this ranch-country locale 6 mi from Tedeschi Winery. The 1906 house has three rooms and is good for four to six people willing to share a single bathroom. The cottage is ideal for a couple. ⊠ *229 Kula Hwy., Kula 96790,* ☎ *808/878–1425,* FAX *661/ 393–5015. 3 rooms, 1 cottage. AE, D, MC, V.*

$$–$$$ ⬜ **Old Wailuku Inn.** This historic home, built in 1924, has been lov-
★ ingly renovated and may be the ultimate Hawaiian B&B. Each room is decorated with the theme of a Hawaiian flower, and the flower motif is worked into the heirloom Hawaiian quilt on each bed. Other features include 10-ft ceilings, floors of native hardwoods, VCRs, and (depending on the room) some delightful bathtubs. The first-floor rooms have private gardens. A hearty breakfast is included. ⊠ *2199 Kaho'okele St., Wailuku 96793,* ☎ *808/244–5897 or 800/305–4899,* WEB *www.mauiinn.com. 7 rooms. Breakfast room, in-room VCRs. AE, D, DC, MC, V.*

$$–$$$ ⬜ **Olinda Country Cottage & Inn.** The restored Tudor home and adjacent cottage are so far up Olinda Road above Makawao you'll keep thinking you must have passed it, but keep driving to reach the inn, which sits amid an 8½-acre protea farm surrounded by forest and some wonderful hiking trails. There are five accommodations in the inn: two upstairs bedrooms with private baths; the downstairs Pineapple Sweet with its French doors; an ultraromantic cottage, which looks like a dollhouse from the outside; and best of all, Hidden Cottage, with a private hot tub. It would be easy to settle in for a long winter here, but bring slippers and warm clothes—the mountain air can be chilly. ✉ *2660 Olinda Rd., Olinda 96768,* ☎ FAX *808/572–1453 or* ☎ *800/932–3435. 3 rooms, 2 cottages. No credit cards.*

$$–$$$ ★ 🏨 **Silver Cloud Guest Ranch.** Silver Cloud is in cowboy country, on the high mountainside beyond Kula and just 5 mi before ʻUlupalakua Ranch. The noble Plantation House, with six rooms, surveys pasturelands and a spellbinding panorama of islands and sea. Silence is a chief attraction in this offbeat but magnificent part of Maui. In addition to the main house, the ranch has the separate Lānai Cottage and five studios with kitchenettes (good for families) arranged like a bunkhouse in a horseshoe shape. A complete breakfast with fresh fruit and juice is served out of the Plantation House kitchen every morning. ✉ *R.R. 2, Box 201, Kula 96790,* ☎ *800/532–1111 or 808/878–6101,* FAX *808/878–2132. 11 rooms, 1 cottage. Kitchenettes (some), horseback riding. AE, D, DC, MC, V.*

$$ 🏨 **Bambula Inn.** A casual sprawling house in a quiet Lahaina residential area has two studio apartments, one attached to the house and one freestanding. No breakfast is served; this is a move-in-and-hang-out beach house. Just across the street is a small beach, and moored just offshore is a sailboat, the *Bambula*—hand-built by the owner. He likes to take his guests out for whale-watching and sunset sails, no charge. He also provides bicycles and snorkel equipment. This is a friendly, easygoing way to visit Lahaina. ✉ *518 Ilikahi St., Lahaina 96761,* ☎ *808/667–6753 or 800/544–5524,* FAX *808/667–0979,* WEB *www.bambula.com. 2 studios. Kitchenettes. D, MC, V.*

$$ 🏨 **By the Sea B&B.** If you want to stay in a B&B in Kīhei, try this pretty one. You'll be amazed at the lushness and romance that the owner has managed to create in a small lot hemmed in by apartments and commercial buildings. The private yard is a cool little Eden with a large pond and waterfall—a good place to hang out in the hammock by day or the hot tub by night. There are three self-contained apartments in the house. The honeymoon-style Palm Room on the second floor has a king bed and its own lānai. All accommodations have separate entrances and designated parking slots, and the owners provide beach equipment, fishing gear, and Continental breakfast. ✉ *20 Wailana Pl., Kīhei 96753,* ☎ *808/879–2700 or 888/879–2700,* FAX *808/879–5540. 3 rooms. Coin laundry. AE, DC, MC, V.*

$$ 🏨 **Golden Bamboo Ranch.** This secluded seven-acre estate lies in the edge-of-the-rain-forest lushness of rural Haʻikū. The owners scrupulously maintain four units—one cottage, a studio, and two suites. Each has a kitchen or kitchenette and unobstructed views across a brilliant green landscape to the sea. ✉ *422 Kaupakalua Rd., Haʻikū 96708,* ☎ *800/344–1238 or 808/572–7824,* FAX *808/572–7824,* WEB *www.goldenbamboo.com. 4 units. Kitchenettes. AE, D, DC, MC, V.*

$$ 🏨 **Halfway to Hāna House.** A private studio set in the country on Maui's lush rural north coast, this serene retreat comes with surrounding gardens and great ocean views. It's a short walk from here to natural pools and waterfalls, hiking areas, and horseback riding. The room comes with optional Continental breakfast and a well-supplied kitchenette—all the equipment you need to do your own thing. A three-night minimum stay is required. ✉ *Hāna Hwy., Box 675, Haʻikū 96708,* ☎ *808/572–1176,* FAX *808/572–3609,* WEB *www.maui.net/gailp. 1 room. No credit cards.*

$$ ⊞ **Hale Hoʻokipa Inn.** A handsome 1924 Craftsman-style house is right in the heart of Makawao town, a good home base for excursions to the crater or to Hāna. The owner has lovingly renovated the old place and furnished it with antique furniture and fine art. (She's also a certified tour guide who likes to take guests on hikes.) She has divided the house into three single rooms, each prettier than the next, and the South Wing, which sleeps four and includes the kitchen. All rooms have private bath, and Continental breakfast is served. This inn matches most people's mythical notion of grandma and grandpa's house. ⊠ *32 Pakani Pl., Makawao 96768,* ☎ *808/572–6698,* Ⅸ☒ *808/ 572–2580,* ⅧⒺⒷ *www.maui.net*/mauibnb. 3 rooms, 1 2-bedroom suite. No credit cards.

$$ ⊞ **Island View.** For that warm-sky, Upcountry-ranch feeling, head for this property on a horse farm not far from Pukalani. The owner is a master builder, and this sprawling house has obviously been a labor of love. There are bonuses for animal lovers: you'll have the company of a Dr. Dolittle–inspired assortment of animals, including Ollie, a surfing dog. Available for rental is a beautifully designed vacation "house" (one bedroom and two stories) for stays of four nights or longer. ⊠ *692E Naele Rd., Kula 96790,* ☎ *808/878–6739,* Ⅸ☒ *808/572–2265. 1 cottage. Outdoor hot tub. No credit cards.*

$$ ⊞ **Kūʻau Cove Plantation.** Here's a rare and handy location for a Maui visit—on a secluded cove midway between the town of Pāʻia and Hoʻokipa Beach Park. The home is quite handsome, dating from the late 1930s and lovingly renovated by the current owners. Furnishings emphasize wicker and rattan and have quilted floral bedcovers. In classic B&B style, the owners rent two large bedrooms in the main house, both set apart from the family living area and each with private baths and queen-size beds. There are also two private studio apartments with kitchens. Continental breakfast is served. ⊠ *2 Waʻa Pl., Kūʻau, 96779,* ☎ *808/579–8988,* Ⅸ☒ *808/579–8710,* ⅧⒺⒷ *www.maui.net*/kuaubnb. 2 rooms, 2 apartments. MC, V.

$$ ⊞ **Kula View.** This affordable home-away-from-home sits in comfortable, peaceful rural Kula. The 2,000-ft elevation makes for a pleasantly temperate climate and a panorama that takes in the West Maui mountains and the ocean on either side. Guests stay in the entire upper floor of a simple but tastefully decorated house with Laura Ashley fabrics, a breakfast nook full of wicker furnishings, a private entrance, and a deck. The hostess emphasizes hospitality, providing a welcoming "amenity basket," a very popular Continental breakfast, advice on touring, and even beach towels or warm clothes for your crater trip. This is a quiet, refreshing place to return to after a day on the road. ⊠ *140 Holopuni Rd., Kula 96790,* ☎ *808/878–6736,* ⅧⒺⒷ *www.angelfire.com/hi3/ mauibedandbreakfast/. 1 room. No credit cards.*

$–$$ ⊞ **Peace of Maui.** The small Upcountry community of Haliʻimaile, 2 mi closer to the coast than Makawao and near both Baldwin Avenue and Haleakalā Highway, is well situated for accessing the rest of the island. This small inn is a good choice for budget-minded travelers who want to be out and active all day. Six rooms in a "lodge" setting have pantries and mini-refrigerators. The kitchen and bathroom are shared. There's also a separate cottage with its own kitchen and facilities. You'll have sweeping views of the north shore and the mountains here. ⊠ *1290 Haliʻimaile Rd., Haliʻimaile 96768,* ☎ *888/475–5045 or 808/ 572–5045,* ⅧⒺⒷ *www.peaceofmaui.com. 7 rooms. No credit cards.*

$ ⊞ **Aloha Lani Inn.** This accommodation operates rather like the classic European homestay. You share a bathroom with another guest, or perhaps with the home owners, and you're welcome to the kitchen, the lānai, the laundry facilities, the phone, the snorkel gear, the kayak, and so on. It's a casual, friendly, and inexpensive way to visit the West

Side. The inn is in a quiet neighborhood within walking distance of Lahaina town. There's a two-night minimum stay. ⊠ *13 Kauaula Rd., Lahaina 96761,* ☎ *808/662–0812 or 800/572–5642,* ℻ *808/661–8045. 3 rooms. Fans, coin laundry. AE, D, MC, V.*

$ ⚏ **Makani 'Olu'olu Cottage.** These folks offer both a cottage and an 'ohana (an apartment attached to the house). The location is unusual—the heart of lush rural Ha'ikū, where the *makani* (winds) are 'olu'olu (pleasant). Both rentals are suited to one or two people, with queen beds, complete kitchens, and delightful frescoes on the walls depicting tropical scenes—original works by the multitalented landlady. The tiled 'ohana is downstairs, with its own entrance and a lānai that looks over green pastures. The cottage has decoupage shelves and an antique upright piano. ⊠ *925 Kaupakalua Rd., Ha'ikū 96708,* ☎ *808/572–8383,* ℹ️ *www.mauigateway.com. 2 rooms. No credit cards.*

NIGHTLIFE AND THE ARTS

Nightlife on Maui might be better labeled "evening life." The quiet island has little of Waikīkī's after-hours decadence. But before 10 PM there's a lot on offer, from lū'au shows and dinner cruises to concerts at "The Center." Lahaina still tries to uphold its reputation as a party town, and succeeds wildly every Halloween when thousands converge on Front Street.

Since it opened in 1994, the **Maui Arts & Cultural Center** (⊠ Above the harbor on Kahului Beach Rd., Kahului, ☎ 808/242–2787) has become the venue for more and more of the island's best live entertainment. The complex includes the 1,200-seat Castle Theater, which hosts classical, country, and world-beat concerts by touring musicians; a 4,000-seat amphitheater for large outdoor concerts; and the 350-seat McCoy Theater for plays and recitals. For information on current programs, check the **Events Box Office** (☎ 808/242–7469) or the daily newspaper, the *Maui News.*.

For nightlife of a different sort, children and astronomy buffs should try stargazing at **Tour of the Stars,** a one-hour program held nightly on the roof of the Hyatt Regency Maui in Kā'anapali. You can look through giant binoculars and a deep-space telescope. The program is run by an astronomer. A romantic program for couples, with roses and chocolate, is held on Friday and Saturday nights at 11. Check in at the hotel lobby 15 minutes prior to starting time. ⊠ *Lahaina Tower, Hyatt Regency Maui, 200 Nohea Kai Dr., Lahaina,* ☎ *808/661–1234, ext. 4727.* 🎟 *$25.* ☉ *Nightly at 8, 9, and 10; Fri. and Sat. romantic program at 11.*

Bars and Clubs

Contemporary Music

Kahale's Beach Club. A friendly, informal hangout, Kahale's offers live music (usually Hawaiian), bar drinks, burgers, fries, and artichokes every day from 10 AM till 2 in the morning. ⊠ *36 Keala Pl., Kīhei,* ☎ *808/875–7711.*

Makai Bar. Live Hawaiian and contemporary music nightly, awesome sunset views, and the best *pūpū* (appetizers) on Maui are at this comfortable spot on the Kā'anapali coast. ⊠ *Lahaina Tower, Hyatt Regency Maui, 200 Nohea Kai Dr., Lahaina,* ☎ *808/667–1200.*

Molokini Lounge. This is a pleasant bar with an ocean view, and you can even see Molokini Island before the sun goes down. Live music, often Hawaiian in theme, is performed. There's a dance floor for late-night revelry. ✉ *Lahaina Tower, Hyatt Regency Maui, 200 Nohea Kai Dr., Lahaina,* ☎ *808/667–1200.*

Jazz

Pacific'O. This highly recommended restaurant is also the most reliable place to hear live jazz on the beach. It's a mellow, pacific sort of jazz—naturally—and it plays from 9 until midnight Thursday through Saturday. Guest musicians—George Benson, for example—often sit in. ✉ *505 Front St., Lahaina,* ☎ *808/667–4341.*

Rock

Casanova Italian Restaurant & Deli. Popular Casanova claims to be the best place on the island for singles to meet. When a DJ is not spinning hits, contemporary musicians rock on with blues, country and western, rock and roll, and reggae. Past favorites have included Kool and the Gang, Los Lobos, and Taj Mahal. Expect a cover charge on nights featuring live entertainment. ✉ *1188 Makawao Ave., Makawao,* ☎ *808/572–0220.*

Cheeseburger in Paradise. This Front Street hangout is known for—what else?—big beefy cheeseburgers (not to mention a great spinach-nut burger). Locals also know it as a great place to tune in to live bands playing rock and roll, Top 40, and oldies sounds from 4:30 PM to closing. There's no dance floor, but the second-floor balcony is a good place to watch Lahaina's Front Street action. ✉ *811 Front St., Lahaina,* ☎ *808/661–4855.*

Game in the Bar. You can dance to recorded Top 40 hits in this sophisticated, high-tech disco, where laser beams zigzag high above a futuristic dance floor. The music plays from 9 to 2 on Thursday, Friday, and Saturday nights. On other nights, the room is used for private parties. Game in the Bar has pool tables and a dress code: no beach wear, jeans, or T-shirts. Expect a $10 cover charge. ✉ *Grand Wailea, 3850 Wailea Alanui Dr., Wailea,* ☎ *808/875–1234.*

Hapa's Brewhaus & Restaurant. Good food and some fine brews are on the menu here, along with sports TV, rock and funk bands, disco, hula shows, and comedy. These folks have gone all out to create a first-rate club with a large stage, roomy dance floor, state-of-the-art lighting and sound systems, and tier seating so that everyone gets a good view. Even nonsmokers will find the club comfortable: the air-conditioning system removes secondhand smoke. ✉ *Lipoa Center, 41 E. Lipoa St., Kīhei,* ☎ *808/879–9001.*

Hard Rock Cafe. Maui's version of the Hard Rock is popular with young locals as well as visitors who like their music *loud.* ✉ *Lahaina Center, 900 Front St., Lahaina,* ☎ *808/667–7400.*

Maui Brews. Live bands serve up Top 40, reggae, salsa, or some kind of rock weeknights; a DJ spins hits on weekends. This is a big hangout, with a complete bar menu of appetizers, pastas, burgers, and entrées. There are 16 kinds of draft beer, 10 specialty martinis, and a menu for kids. ✉ *Lahaina Center, 900 Front St., Lahaina,* ☎ *808/667–7794.*

Moose McGillycuddy's. The Moose offers no-cover live music on Tuesday and Thursday. Otherwise, it's recorded music, but it's played so loud you'd swear it's live. This entertaining place tends to draw a young crowd that comes to enjoy the burgers and beer, to dance, and to meet one another. Specials include a king crab dinner and, on other nights, a 22-ounce porterhouse. ✉ *844 Front St., Lahaina,* ☎ *808/667–7758.*

The Sly Mongoose. Off the beaten tourist path, The Sly Mongoose is the seediest dive bar in town, and one of the friendliest. The bartender will know your name and half your life history inside of 10 minutes, and she makes the strongest mai tai on the island. ✉ *1036 Limahana Pl., Lahaina,* ☎ *808/661–8097.*

Dinner and Sunset Cruises

***America II* Sunset Sail.** The star of this two-hour cruise is the craft it-self—a 1987 America's Cup 12-m class contender that is exceptionally smooth and steady, thanks to its renowned winged-keel design. ⊠ *Lahaina Harbor, Lahaina,* ☎ *808/667–2195.* ☜ *$30–$33.*

***Kaulana* Cocktail Cruise.** This two-hour sunset cruise (with a bit of whale-watching thrown in, in season) features a pūpū menu, open bar, and live music. ⊠ *Lahaina Harbor, Lahaina,* ☎ *808/871–1144.* ☜ *$39.*

Pride Charters. A 65-ft catamaran built specifically for Maui's waters, the *Pride of Maui* features a large cabin, a large upper sundeck for un-obstructed viewing, and a stable, comfortable ride. Breakfast, lunch, and beverages are provided. For later departures, there is an optional barbecue. ⊠ *Mā'alaea Harbor, Mā'alaea,* ☎ *808/242–0955.* ☜ *$40.*

Scotch Mist Charters. A two-hour champagne sunset sail is offered on the 25-passenger Santa Cruz 50 sloop *Scotch Mist II.* ⊠ *Lahaina Harbor, Lahaina,* ☎ *808/661–0386.* ☜ *$55.*

Windjammer Cruises. This cruise includes a prime rib and Alaskan salmon dinner and live entertainment on the 70-ft, 93-passenger *Spirit of Windjammer,* a three-masted schooner. ⊠ *283 Wili Ko Pl., Suite 1, Lahaina,* ☎ *808/661–8600.* ☜ *$69.*

Film

Maui Film Festival. In this ongoing celebration, quality films that may not show up at the local megaplex are screened weekly. Most screenings are in Maui's most luxurious movie house—Castle Theater at Maui Arts & Cultural Center. On Wednesday night the usual movies are followed by live music and poetry readings in the Candlelight Cafe. But the schedule varies, and the program is expanding. In summer the festival comes to Wailea for cinema under the stars in a program that includes music, hula, and Hawaiian storytelling. For recorded program information call ☎ 808/572–3456 or check the Web site: WEB www.mauifilmfestival.com.

Lū'au and Revues

The Feast at Lele. "Lele" is an older, more traditional name for Lahaina. This "feast" is redefining the lū'au by crossing it with fine dining is-land-style in an intimate beach setting. Both the show and the three-course gourmet meal express the spirit of a specific island culture—Hawaiian, Samoan, Tongan, or Tahitian. The wine list and liquor selections are excellent. This may be the trend of the future for would-be Polynesian royalty. ⊠ *505 Front St., Lahaina,* ☎ *808/667–5353. Reservations essential.* ☜ *$89.* ☉ *Tues., Thurs., and Sat. (more often in high season), 5:30 in winter and 6:30 in summer.*

Maui Myth & Magic Theatre. Maui's newest live theater opened in 1999 with the debut of 'Ulalena, a 75-minute musical extravaganza that is well received by audiences and Hawaiian-culture experts alike. The en-semble cast (20 singer/dancers and a 5-musician orchestra) mixes na-tive rhythms and stories with acrobatic performance and high-tech stage wizardry to give an inspiring introduction to island culture. It's movie-style seating with beer and wine for sale at the popcorn line. They also offer dinner-theater packages in conjunction with top Lahaina restau-rants. ⊠ *878 Front St., Lahaina,* ☎ *808/661–9913 or 877/688–4800. Reservations essential.* ☜ *$45.* ☉ *Tues.–Sat. 6 and 8:30.*

Nāpili Kai Beach Club Keiki Hula Show. Expect to be charmed as well as entertained when 30 children ages 6 to 17 take you on a dance tour of Hawai'i, New Zealand, Tahiti, Samoa, and other Polynesian islands. The talented youngsters make their own ti-leaf skirts and fresh-flower leis. They give the leis to the audience at the end of the show. This is a nonprofessional but delightfully engaging review, and the 80-seat ocean-front room is usually sold out. ⊠ *Nāpili Kai Beach Club, 5900 Lower Honoapi'ilani Hwy., Nāpili,* ☎ *808/669–6271.* ☎ *$40.* ۞ *Dinner Fri. at 6, show at 7:30.*

Old Lahaina Lū'au. This is the best lū'au you'll find on Maui. It's small, personal, and authentic, and is performed in an outdoor theater designed specifically for traditional Hawaiian entertainment. It feels like an old seaside village. In addition to fresh fish and grilled steak and chicken, you'll get all-you-can-eat traditional lū'au fare: kālua pig, chicken long rice, *lomilomi* salmon (massaged until tender and served with minced onions and tomatoes), *haupia* (coconut pudding), and other treats. You'll also get all you can drink. Guests sit either on tatami mats or at tables. Then there's the entertainment: a musical journey from old Hawai'i to the present with hula dancing, chanting, and singing. ⊠ *1251 Front St., Lahaina (makai of the Lahaina Cannery Mall),* ☎ *808/667–1998.* ☎ *$69.* ۞ *Nightly 5:30–8:30.*

Warren & Annabelle's. Magician Warren Gibson entices his guests into a swank nightclub setting with red carpets and a gleaming mahogany bar, then plies them with appetizers (coconut shrimp, crab cakes), desserts (rum cake, crème brûlée), and "smoking cocktails." Then he performs tableside magic while his ghostly assistant, Annabelle, tickles the ivories. The show is fun, and all the better for being not too slick. Note that this is a nightclub, so no one under 21 is allowed. ⊠ *Lahaina Center, 900 Front St.,* ☎ *808/667–6244. Reservations essential.* ☎ *$36.* ۞ *Mon.–Sat., 7 and 8:30.*

Music

Maui Philharmonic Society. The Society has presented such prestigious performers as Ballet Hispanico, the Shostakovich String Quartet, and the New Age pianist-composer Philip Glass. Performances take place in various venues around the island. ⊠ *J. Walter Cameron Center, 95 Mahalani St., Wailuku 96793,* ☎ *808/244–3771.*

Maui Symphony Orchestra. The symphony orchestra usually performs at the Maui Arts & Cultural Center, offering five seasonal concerts and a few special musical sensations as well. The regular season includes a Christmas concert, an opera gala, a classical concert, and two pops concerts outdoors. ☎ *808/244–5439.*

Theater

Baldwin Theatre Guild. Dramas, comedies, and musicals are presented by this group about eight times a year. The guild has staged such favorites as *The Glass Menagerie, Brigadoon,* and *The Miser.* Musicals are held in the 1,200-seat Community Auditorium. All other plays are presented in the Baldwin High School Mini Theatre. ⊠ *1650 Ka'ahumanu Ave., Kahului,* ☎ *808/984–5673.* ☎ *$8.*

Maui Academy of Performing Arts. For a quarter-century this group has offered fine performances as well as dance and drama classes for children and adults. It has presented such plays as *Peter Pan, Jesus Christ Superstar,* and *The Nutcracker.* MAPA has secured a new home in Wailuku at the old National Dollar Store building. At press time the group was planning to move into a new theater at 2027 Main Street by mid-2002; call ahead for location. *Main and Market Sts., Wailuku,* ☎ *808/244–8760.* ☎ *$10–$12.*

Maui Community Theatre. Now staging about six plays a year, this is the oldest dramatic group on the island, started in the early 1900s. Each July the group also holds a fund-raising variety show, which can be a

hoot. ✉ *ʻIao Theatre, 68 N. Market St., Wailuku,* ☎ *808/242–6969.*
🎭 *Musicals $10–$15, nonmusicals $8–$13.*

Seabury Hall Performance Studio. This college-preparatory school
above Makawao town offers a season of often supercharged shows in
its satisfying small theater and two dance studios. The school's formula
is to mix talented kids with seasoned adults and innovative, even off-
beat, concepts. Dance concerts are always a hit. ✉ *480 Olinda Rd., 1
mi north of Makawao crossroads,* ☎ *808/573–1257.* 🎭 *$7–$12.*

OUTDOOR ACTIVITIES AND SPORTS

Participant Sports

Biking

Maui County has designated hundreds of miles of bikeways on Maui's
roads, making biking safer and more convenient than in the past. Painted
bike lanes make it possible for a rider to travel all the way from Mākena
to Kapalua, and you'll see dozens of hardy souls pedaling under the hot
Maui sun. Some visitors rent a bike just to ride around the resort where
they're staying. Whatever your preference, you have several rental
choices, including **Island Biker** (✉ 415 Dairy Rd., Kahului, ☎ 808/877–
7744), **Maui Sports and Cycle** (✉ Long's Center, Kīhei, ☎ 808/875–8448,
South Maui Bicycles (✉ Island Surf building, Kīhei, ☎ 808/874–0068),
and **West Maui Cycles** (✉ 840 Waineʻe St., Lahaina, ☎ 808/661–9005).
Bikes rent for $10 to $20 a day. Several companies offer downhill bike
tours from the top of Haleakalā all the way to the coast.

Camping and Hiking

Let's start with the best—hiking **Haleakalā Crater** at Haleakalā National Park (✉ Haleakalā Crater Rd., Makawao, ☎ 808/572–4400).
The recommended way to explore the crater is to go in two cars and
ferry yourselves back and forth between the head of Halemauʻu Trail
and the summit. This way, you can hike from the summit down Sliding Sands Trail, cross the crater floor, investigate the Bottomless Pit
and Pele's Paint Pot, then climb out on the switchback trail (Halemauʻu).
When you emerge, the shelter of your waiting car will be very welcome.
Give yourself eight hours for the hike; wear jogging-type shoes and take
a backpack with lunch, water, and a reliable jacket for the beginning
and end of the hike. This is a demanding trip, but you will never regret or forget it.

If you want to stay longer than a day, plan on overnighting in one of
the national park's three cabins or two campgrounds. The cabins are
equipped with bunk beds, wood-burning stoves, fake logs, and kitchen
gear. To reserve a cabin you have to plan at least three months in advance and hope the lottery system is kind to you. Contact the **National
Park Service** (✉ Box 369, Makawao 96768, ☎ 808/572–9306). The
tent campsites are easy to reserve on a first-come, first-served basis. Just
make sure to stop at park headquarters to register on your way in.

Just as you enter Haleakalā National Park, **Hosmer Grove** offers an
hour-long loop trail into the "cloud forest" that will give you insight
into Hawaiʻi's fragile ecology. You can pick up a map at the trailhead.
Park rangers conduct guided hikes on a changing schedule. There are
six campsites (no permit needed), pit toilets, drinking water, and cooking shelters.

Another good hiking spot—and something totally unexpected on a tropical island—is **Polipoli Forest.** During the Great Depression the government began a program to reforest the mountain, and soon cedar,
pine, cypress, and even redwood took hold. It's cold here and foggy,

often wet or at least misty. To reach the forest, take Highway 37 all the way out to the far end of Kula. Then turn left at Highway 377. At about a half mile, turn right at Waipoli Road. Then up you go. First it's switchbacks. Then it's just plain bad—but passable. There are wonderful trails, also a small campground and a cabin that you can rent from the Division of State Parks. Write far in advance for the **cabin** (⊠ Box 1049, Wailuku 96793, ☎ 808/244–4354); for the campground, you can wait until you arrive in Wailuku and visit the **State Parks office** (⊠ 54 High St.).

ʻOheʻo Gulch is a branch of Haleakalā National Park past Hāna on the Piʻilani Highway. This is the starting point of one of the best hikes on Maui—the 2-mi trek upstream to 400-ft **Waimoku Falls.** Along the way you can take side trips and swim in the stream's basalt-lined pools. Then the trail bridges a sensational gorge and passes onto a boardwalk through a clonking, mystifying forest of giant bamboo. Down at the grassy sea cliffs, you can camp, no permit required, although you can stay only three nights. Toilets, grills, and tables are available here, but no water and no open fires.

In ʻĪao Valley, the **Hawaiʻi Nature Center** (⊠ 875 ʻĪao Valley Rd., Wailuku, 96793, ☎ 808/244–6500) leads interpretive hikes for children and their families.

Fitness & Spa Centers

Most spas and fitness centers on Maui are in hotels. If your hotel does not have a facility, ask if privileges are available at other hotels. These hotels listed offer the most comprehensive spa services. **Four Seasons Resort** (⊠ 3900 Wailea Alanui Dr., Wailea, ☎ 808/874–8000 or 800/ 334–6284). **Grand Wailea Resort & Spa** (⊠ 3850 Wailea Alanui Dr., Wailea, ☎ 808/875–1234 or 800/888–6100). **Hyatt Regency Maui** (⊠ 200 Nohea Kai Dr., Lahaina, ☎ 808/661–1234 or 800/233–1234). **Outrigger Wailea Resort** (⊠ 3700 Wailea Alanui Dr., Wailea, ☎ 808/879– 1922 or 800/922–7866). **Ritz-Carlton, Kapalua** (⊠ 1 Ritz-Carlton Dr., Kapalua, ☎ 808/669–6200 or 800/262–8440).

Outside the resorts, the most convenient and best-equipped fitness center is **24 Hour Fitness** (⊠ 150 Hāna Hwy., Kahului, ☎ 808/877– 7474); daily passes are $20. The **Maui Family YMCA** (⊠ 250 Kanaloa Ave., Kahului, ☎ 808/242–9007) offers $10 daily passes.

Golf

How do you keep your mind on the game in a place like Maui? It's very hard, because you can't ignore the view, but Maui has become one of the world's premier golf-vacation destinations. The island's major resorts all have golf courses, each of them stunning. They're all open to the public, and most lower their greens fees after 2:30 on weekday afternoons.

Elleair Golf Course. Bill Newis designed this privately owned course, which is independent of the resorts, to take advantage of its lofty location above Kīhei town. You'll get panoramic views not only out to sea but also across Haleakalā. ⊠ *1345 Piʻilani Hwy., Kīhei,* ☎ *808/ 874–0777.* 🏌 *Greens fee $75, including cart.*

Kāʻanapali Golf Courses. Two of Maui's most famous courses are here. The layout consists of the North Course, designed by Robert Trent Jones, Sr., and the South Course, laid out by Arthur Jack Snyder. ⊠ *Kāʻanapali Beach Resort, Kāʻanapali,* ☎ *808/661–3691.* 🏌 *Greens fee $130 guests, $150 nonguests, including cart.*

Kapalua Golf Club. The club has three 18-holers—the Village Course and the Bay Course, both designed by Arnold Palmer, and the Plantation Course, designed by Ben Crenshaw. Kapalua is well-known to television-sports watchers. ⊠ *300 Kapalua Dr., Kapalua,* ☎ *808/669–8044.* ☒ *Greens fee $95–$100 guests, $140–$150 nonguests, including cart; club rental $30–$40.*

Mākena Golf Course. There are two lovely 18-hole courses here, North and South, designed by Robert Trent Jones, Jr. Of all the resort courses, this one is the most remote. At one point, golfers must cross a main road, but there are so few cars that this poses no problem. ⊠ *5415 Mākena Alanui Rd., Kīhei,* ☎ *808/879–3344.* ☒ *Greens fee $90 guests, $125 nonguests, including cart.*

Sandalwood Golf Course. Sandalwood has a unique location on the slopes of the West Maui mountains just south of Wailuku, with elevated views of Haleakalā. ⊠ *2500 Honoapiʻilani Hwy., Wailuku,* ☎ *808/242–4653.* ☒ *Greens fee $75, including cart.*

Wailea Golf Club. The club has three courses: the Gold and the Blue, which were designed by Arthur Jack Snyder, and the newer Emerald, designed by Robert Trent Jones, Jr. In his design, Snyder incorporated ancient lava-rock walls to create an unusual golfing experience. ⊠ *100 Wailea Golf Club Dr., Wailea,* ☎ *808/875–5111.* ☒ *Greens fee $115 guests, $140 nonguests, including cart.*

Maui has municipal courses, where the fees are lower. Be forewarned, however, that the weather can be cool and wet, and the locations may not be convenient. The **Waiehu Municipal Golf Course** is on the northeast coast of Maui a few miles past Wailuku. ⊠ *Off Hwy. 340, West Maui,* ☎ *808/244–5934.* ☒ *Greens fee $25 weekdays, $30 weekends; cart $15.*

Hang Gliding

Armin Engert of **Hang Gliding Maui** (☎ 808/572–6557, WEB www.hang-gliding.maui.com) will take you on an instructional powered hang-gliding trip out of Hāna Airport. A 25- to 30-minute flight lesson costs $95, and a 50- to 60-minute lesson is $165. Snapshots of your flight from a wing-mounted camera cost an additional $25.

Parasailing

If you have a yen to be floating in the sky like a bird but lack the derring-do of a barnstormer, parasailing is the perfect alternative to skydiving (you gently rise several hundred feet from the ground instead of leaping out of an aircraft at 10,000 ft) or hang gliding (the safety rope holds you in your flight pattern). This is an easy and fun way to earn your wings: just strap on a harness attached to a parachute and a power boat pulls you up and over the ocean from a launching dock or from a boat's platform. To reduce interference with whales, no "thrill craft"—including parasails—are allowed in Maui waters from December 15 to April 15.

Several companies on Maui will take you for a ride that usually lasts about 10 minutes and costs $30 to $50. **Lahaina Para-Sail** (☎ 808/661–4887) lays claim to the only parasail vessel on Maui that is Coast Guard certified for 25 passengers and has bathroom facilities on board. The group will be glad to let you experience a "toe dip" or "freefall" if you request it, and the minimum weight to fly alone is 75 pounds. For safety reasons, **West Maui Para-Sail** (☎ 808/661–4060) requires that passengers weigh more than 100 pounds, or two must be strapped together in tandem.

Sporting Clays

Skillfully designed to fit inside the crater of a large cinder cone, **Papaka Sporting Clays** (⊠ 1325 S. Kīhei Rd., ☎ 808/879–5649) is an outdoor arcade dedicated to the art of shotgun shooting. The 40 stations include "Springing Teal," "High Pheasant," and "Busting Bunnies" (no real bunnies involved; the targets are clay disks). Certified instructors outfit you with a vest, earplugs, eye protection, a shotgun, and instruction. They pick you up in the Kīhei–Wailea area or at ʻUlupalakua Ranch by appointment any morning or afternoon. The cost is $95 for 75 targets. Spectators can come along for free.

Tennis

There are other facilities around the island in addition to those listed below, usually one or two courts in smaller hotels or condos. Most of them, however, are open only to their guests. The best free courts are the five at the **Lahaina Civic Center** (⊠ 1840 Honoapiʻilani Hwy., Lahaina, ☎ 808/661–4685), near Wahikuli State Park. They're available on a first-come, first-served basis.

Hyatt Regency Maui. The Hyatt has six courts, with rentals and instruction. All-day passes cost $15 for guests, $20 for nonguests. ⊠ 200 Nohea Kai Dr., Lahaina, ☎ 808/661–1234, ext. 3174.

Kapalua Tennis Garden. This complex serves the Kapalua Resort with 10 courts and a pro shop. You'll pay $10 an hour if you're a guest, $12 if you're not, and you're welcome to stay longer for free if there is no one waiting. ⊠ 100 Kapalua Dr., Kapalua, ☎ 808/669–5677.

Mākena Tennis Club. This club at the Mākena Resort, just south of Wailea, has six courts. Rates are $16 per court hour for guests, $18 for nonguests. After an hour, if there's space available, there's no charge. ⊠ 5400 Mākena Alanui Rd., Kīhei, ☎ 808/879–8777.

Maui Beach & Tennis Club. The Maui Marriott's club has five Plexipave courts, with three lighted for night play, and a pro shop. Daily rates are $10 for guests and $12 for nonguests. ⊠ 100 Nohea Kai Dr., Kāʻanapali, ☎ 808/667–1200, ext. 8689.

Royal Lahaina Tennis Ranch. In the Kāʻanapali Beach Resort on West Maui, the Royal Lahaina has 11 courts and a pro shop. Rates are a flat $10 per person per day whether you are a guest or not. ⊠ 2780 Kekaʻa Dr., ☎ 808/661–3611, ext. 2296.

Wailea Tennis Club. These are the state's finest tennis facilities, often called "Wimbledon West" because of the two grass courts. There are also 11 Plexipave courts and a pro shop. You'll pay $35 an hour per person for the hard courts. The grass courts are by well-in-advance reservation only. On weekday mornings clinics are given to help you improve your ground strokes, serve, volley, or doubles strategy. ⊠ 131 Wailea Ike Pl., Kīhei, ☎ 808/879–1958 or 800/332–1614.

Water Sports

Note that to reduce interference with whales, no "thrill craft"—specifically parasails and Jet Skis—are allowed in Maui waters from December 15 to April 15.

DEEP-SEA FISHING

If fishing is your sport, Maui is the place for it. You'll be able to throw in hook and bait for fish such as ʻahi, *aku* (skipjack tuna), barracuda, bonefish, *kawakawa* (bonito), mahimahi, Pacific blue marlin, *ono* (wahoo), and *ulua* (jack crevalle). On Maui you can fish throughout the year, and you don't need a license.

Plenty of fishing boats run out of Lahaina and Māʻalaea harbors. If you charter a boat by yourself, expect to spend in the neighborhood of $600 a day. But you can share the boat with others who are interested in fishing the same day for about $100 each. Although there are at least 10 companies running boats on a regular basis, these are the most reliable. **Finest Kind Inc.** (⊠ Lahaina Harbor, Slip 7, Box 10481, Lahaina 96767, ☎ 808/661–0338). **Hinatea Sportfishing** (⊠ Lahaina Harbor, Slip 27, Lahaina 96761, ☎ 808/667–7548). **Lucky Strike**

Charters (✉ Box 1502, Lahaina 96767, ☏ 808/661–4606). **Ocean Activities Center** (✉ 1847 S. Kīhei Rd., Suite 203A, Kīhei 96753, ☏ 808/879–4485 or 800/798–0652).

KAYAKING

The sport has been gaining popularity on the island. Kayaking off the coast of Maui can be a leisurely paddle or it can be a challenge, depending on your location, your inclination, and the weather of the day. The company to contact is **Maui Sea Kayaking** (☏ 808/572–6299, WEB www.maui.net/kayaking). They take small parties to secret spots. They like the idea of customizing their outings. For example, the guides accommodate kayakers with disabilities as well as senior kayakers, and they also offer kid-size gear. They're also into kayak surfing. And they offer a honeymoon/vow-renewal experience that could make Tarzan rekindle his appreciation for Jane.

RAFTING

These high-speed inflatable craft are nothing like the raft that Huck Finn used to drift down the Mississippi. While passengers grip straps, these rafts fly, skimming and bouncing, across the top of the sea. Because they're so maneuverable, they go where the big boats can't—secret coves, sea caves, and unvisited beaches. **Ocean Riders** (✉ 96767, Lahaina 96767, ☏ 808/661–3586), in Lahaina, takes people all the way around the island of Lāna'i. For snorkeling or gawking, the "back side" of Lāna'i is one of Hawai'i's unsung marvels.

SAILING

Because of its proximity to the smaller islands of Moloka'i, Lāna'i, Kaho'olawe, and Molokini, Maui can provide some of Hawai'i's best sailing experiences. Most sailing operations like to combine their tours with a meal, some throw in snorkeling or whale-watching, and others offer a sunset cruise.

The best and longest-running operation is the Coon family's **Trilogy Excursions** (✉ Lahaina, ☏ 808/661–4743 or 800/874–2666). They have six beautiful multihulled sailing craft, and the crews treat passengers with genuine warmth and affection. A full-day catamaran cruise to Lāna'i includes a guided van tour of the island, a barbecue lunch, beach volleyball, and a "Snorkeling 101" class, in which you can test your skills in the waters of Hulopo'e Marine Preserve. (Trilogy has exclusive commercial access.) Snorkeling gear is supplied. It also offers a Molokini snorkel cruise.

Mahana Na'ia (✉ Mā'alaea Harbor, ☏ 808/871–8636) provides good service and food on its comfortable catamaran cruise. This boat specializes in snorkel trips to Molokini. The beautiful monohull luxury yacht *Cinderella* (✉ Mā'alaea Harbor, ☏ 808/244–0009) is available for charters and for customized tours. The sleek, 65-ft cutter-rigged *World Class* (☏ 808/667–7733) offers the exhilaration of fast sailing; it picks up passengers on the sand at Kā'anapali.

Other companies offering cruises include **Maui–Moloka'i Sea Cruises** (☏ 808/242–8777), **Sail Hawai'i** (☏ 808/879–2201), *Scotch Mist Charters* (☏ 808/661–0386), and the Hyatt Regency Maui's *Kiele V* (☏ 808/661–123).

SCUBA DIVING

Maui is just as scenic underwater as it is above. In fact, some of the finest diving spots in Hawai'i lie along the Valley Isle's western and southwestern shores. If you're a certified diver, you can rent gear at any Maui dive shop simply by showing your PADI or NAUI card. Unless you're familiar with the area, however, it's probably best to hook up with a dive shop for an underwater tour.

Maui has no lodging facilities tailored to divers, but there are many dive shops that sell and rent equipment and give lessons and certification. Before signing on with any of these outfitters, however, it's a good idea to ask a few pointed questions.

Some popular outfitters include **Ed Robinson's Diving Adventures** (✉ Kīhei, ☎ 808/879–3584 or 800/635–1273), **Happy Divers** (✉ 840 Waine'e St., Suite 106, Lahaina, ☎ 808/669–0123), **Lahaina Divers** (✉ 143 Dickenson St., Lahaina, ☎ 808/667–7496), **Maui Dive Shop** (✉ Honokōwai Marketplace, ☎ 808/661–0268; ✉ 1455 S. Kīhei Rd., Kīhei, ☎ 808/879–0843), and **Pacific Dive Shop** (✉ 150 Dickenson St., Lahaina, ☎ 808/667–5331). All provide equipment with proof of certification, as well as introductory dives for those who aren't certified. Introductory boat dives generally run about $80.

Area dive sites include the following:

Honolua Bay. In West Maui, this marine preserve is alive with many varieties of coral and tame tropical fish, including large ulua, *kāhala*, barracuda, and manta rays. With depths of 20 ft to 50 ft, this is a popular spot for introductory dives. Dives are generally made only during the summer months.

Molokini Crater. At 'Alalākeiki Channel, this is a crescent-shape islet formed by the top of a volcano. This marine preserve's depth range (10 ft to 80 ft), combined with the attraction of the numerous tame fish dwelling here that can be fed by hand, makes it a popular introductory dive site.

SNORKELING

If you want a personal introduction to Maui's undersea universe, the undisputable authority is **Ann Fielding's Snorkel Maui.** A marine biologist, Fielding—formerly with University of Hawai'i, Waikīkī Aquarium, and the Bishop Museum and the author of several guides to island sealife—is the Carl Sagan of Hawai'i's reef cosmos. She'll not only show you fish, but she'll also introduce you to *individual* fish. This is a good first experience for dry-behind-the-ears types. Snorkel trips include lunch. ✉ *Box 1107, Makawao 96768,* ☎ *808/572–8437.* ✆ *$75 adults, $65 children.*

The same dive companies that take scuba aficionados on tours will take snorkelers as well. One of Maui's most popular snorkeling spots can be reached only by boat: Molokini Crater, that little bowl of land off the coast of Wailea. For about $55, you can spend a half day at Molokini, with meals provided.

Ocean Activities Center (✉ 1847 S. Kīhei Rd., Suite 203A, Kīhei, ☎ 808/879–4485) conducts a great Molokini snorkel tour.

You can find some good snorkeling spots on your own. If you need gear, **Snorkel Bob's** (✉ Nāpili Village Hotel, 5425 Lower Honoapi'ilani Hwy., Nāpili, ☎ 808/669–9603; ✉ 34 Keala Pl., Kīhei, ☎ 808/879–7449; ✉ 161 Lahainaluna Rd., Lahaina, ☎ 808/661–4421) will rent you a mask, fins, and snorkel and throw in a carrying bag, map, and snorkel tips for as little as $5 per day.

Secluded **Windmill Beach** (✉ Take Hwy. 30 3½ mi north of Kapalua; then turn onto the dirt road to the left) has a superb reef for snorkeling. A little more than 2 mi south of Windmill Beach, a dirt road leads to **Honolua Bay.** The coral formations on the right side of the bay are particularly dramatic. You'll find **Nāpili Bay,** one beach south of the Kapalua Resort, quite good for snorkeling.

Almost the entire coastline from Kā'anapali south to Olowalu offers fine snorkeling. Favorite sites include the area just out from the cemetery north of Wahikuli State Park, near the lava cone called **Black Rock,** on which Kā'anapali's Sheraton Maui Hotel is built, and the shallow coral reef south of Olowalu General Store.

The coastline from Wailea to Mākena is generally good for snorkeling. The best is found near the rocky fringes of Wailea's **Mōkapu, Ulua, Wailea,** and **Polo** beaches.

Between Polo Beach and Mākena Beach (turn right on Mākena Road just past Mākena Surf Condo) lies **Five Caves,** where you'll find a maze of underwater grottoes below offshore rocks. This spot is recommended for experienced snorkelers only, since the tides can get rough. At Mākena, the waters around the **Pu'u Ōla'i** cinder cone provide great snorkeling.

SURFING

Although on land it may not look as if there are seasons on Maui, the tides tell another story. In winter the surf is up on the northern shores of the Hawaiian Islands, and summer brings big swells to the southern side. Near-perfect winter waves on Maui can be found at **Honolua Bay,** on the northern tip of West Maui. To get there, continue 2 mi north of D. T. Fleming Park on Highway 30 and take a left onto the dirt road next to a pineapple field; a path takes you down the cliff to the beach.

Ho'okipa Beach Park (⊠ 2 mi past Pā'ia on Hwy. 36) is where the modern-day sport of surfing began on Maui. This is the easiest place to watch surfing, because there are paved parking areas and picnic pavilions in the park. A word of warning: the surfers who come here are pros, and if you're not, they may not take kindly to your getting in their way.

Pushing the envelope of big-wave surfing has reached a new level in the channel waters off Maui, where surfers get pulled out to sea and then whipped into the big waves. At Ho'okipa Beach Park, viewers with a good pair of binoculars might be able to see out past the windsurfers to view an example of tow-in surfing: Jet Ski pilots pull state-of-the-art big-wave surfers out to the 1-mi marker, where the waves can average 30 ft to 40 ft during winter swells.

You can rent surfboards and boogie boards at many surf shops. **Lightning Bolt Maui** (⊠ 55 Ka'ahumanu Ave., Kahului, ☎ 808/877–3484). **Ole Surfboards** (⊠ 277 Wili Ko Pl., Lahaina, ☎ 808/661–3459). **Second Wind** (⊠ 111 Hāna Hwy., Kahului, ☎ 808/877–7467).

WINDSURFING

It's been about two decades since Ho'okipa Bay was discovered by windsurfers, who gave this windy beach 10 mi east of Kahului an international reputation. The spot is blessed with optimal wave-sailing wind and sea conditions and, for experienced windsurfers, can offer the ultimate experience. Other locations around Maui are good for windsurfing as well—Honolua Bay, for example—but Ho'okipa is absolutely unrivaled.

Even if you're a windsurfing aficionado, chances are good you didn't bring your equipment. You can rent it—or get lessons—from these shops. Lessons range from $30 to $60 and can last anywhere from one to three hours. Equipment rental also varies—from no charge with lessons to $20 an hour. For the latest prices and special deals, it's best to call around once you've arrived. **Maui Ocean Activities** (⊠ Whalers Village, Kā'anapali, ☎ 808/667–1964). **Maui Windsurf Company** (⊠ 22 Hāna Hwy., Kahului, ☎ 808/877–4816). **Maui Windsurfari** (⊠ 425 Koloa St.,

Kahului, ☎ 808/871–7766 or 800/736–6284). **Ocean Activities Center** (✉ 1847 S. Kīhei Rd., Suite 203A, Kīhei, ☎ 808/879–4485).

Spectator Sports

Golf

Maui has a number of golf tournaments, most of which are of professional caliber and worth watching. Many are also televised nationally. One attention-getter is the **Mercedes Championships** (☎ 808/669–2440), formerly called the Lincoln-Mercury Kapalua International, held in January. This is the first official PGA tour event, held on Kapalua's Plantation Course. The Aloha Section of the Professional Golfers Association of America hosts the **GTE Hawaiian Tel Hall of Fame** (☎ 808/669–8877) championship at the Plantation Course in May and a clambake feast on the beach tops off the **Kapalua Clambake Pro-Am** (☎ 808/669–8812) in July.

At Kā'anapali the **EMC Maui Kā'anapali Classic SENIOR PGA Golf Tournament** (☎ 808/661–3691) pits veteran professionals in a battle for a $1 million purse each October.

Over in Wailea, in June, on the longest day of the year, self-proclaimed "lunatic" golfers start out at first light to play 100 holes of golf in the annual **Ka Lima O Maui** (☎ 808/875–5111), a fund-raiser for local charities. The nationally televised **Senior Skins** competition (☎ 808/875–5111) in January pits four of the most respected Senior PGA players against one another.

Outrigger-Canoe Races

Polynesians first traveled to Hawai'i by outrigger canoe, and racing the traditional craft has always been a favorite pastime in the Islands. Canoes were revered in old Hawai'i, and no voyage could begin without a blessing, ceremonial chanting, and a hula performance to ensure a safe journey. At Whalers Village in May, the two-day launch festivities for the **Ho'omana'o Challenge Outrigger Sailing Canoe World Championship** (☎ 808/661–3271) also include a torch-lighting ceremony, arts-and-crafts demonstrations, and a chance to observe how the vessels are rigged—as well as the start of the race.

Polo

Polo is popular on Maui. From April through June Haleakalā Ranch hosts "indoor" contests on a field flanked by side boards. The field is on Highway 377, 1 mi from Highway 37. During the "outdoor" polo season, mid-August to the end of October, matches are held at Olinda Field, 1 mi above Makawao on Olinda Road. There is a $3 admission charge for most games, which start at 1 PM on Sunday. The sport has two special events. One is the **Oskie Rice Memorial Tournament** on Memorial Day; the other—the **High Goal Benefit,** held on the last Sunday in October—draws challengers from Argentina, England, South Africa, New Zealand, and Australia. For information, contact Emiliano (☎ 808/572–4915).

Rodeos

With dozens of working cattle ranches throughout the Islands, many youngsters learn to ride a horse before they can drive a car. Mauians love their rodeos and put on several for students at local high schools throughout the year. Paniolos get in on the act, too, at three major annual events: the **Oskie Rice Memorial Rodeo,** usually staged the weekend after Labor Day; the **Cancer Benefit Rodeo** in April, held at an arena 3 mi east of Pā'ia; and Maui's biggest event, drawing competitors from all islands as well as the U.S. mainland, the **4th of July Rodeo,** which comes with a full-on parade and other festivities that last for days. Spectator admission fees to the competitions vary from free to $7. Cowboys are a tough bunch to tie down to a phone, but you can try calling the **Maui Roping Club** (☎ 808/572–2076) for information.

Surfing and Windsurfing

Not many places can lay claim to as many windsurfing tournaments as Maui. The Valley Isle is generally thought to be the world's preeminent windsurfing location and draws boardsailing experts from around the globe who want to compete on its waves. In March the **Hawaiian Pro Am Windsurfing** competition gets under way. In April the **Da Kine Hawaiian Pro Am** lures top windsurfers, and the **Aloha Classic World Wave Sailing Championships** takes place in October. All are held at Hoʻokipa Bay, right outside the town of Pāʻia, near Kahului. **Hookipa Surf and Sail** (☎ 808/667–5566) can provide information on windsurfing tournaments. For competitions featuring amateurs as well as professionals, check out the **Maui Race Series** (☎ 808/877–2111), six events held at Kanahā Beach in Kahului in summer when winds are the strongest and lack of big waves makes conditions excellent for the slalom (speed-racing) course. Competitors maneuver their boards close to shore, and the huge beach provides plenty of seating and viewing space. Hoʻokipa Bay's large waves are also prime territory for surfers. The **Local Motion Surfing** competition heats up the action in May, and in January the **Maui Rusty Pro,** held jointly at Honolua Bay, invites professionals to compete for a $40,000 purse.

Tennis

At the **Kapalua Jr. Vet/Sr. Tennis Championships** in May, where the minimum age is 30, players have been competing in singles and doubles events since 1979. On Labor Day, the **Wilson Kapalua Open Tennis Tournament,** Maui's grand prix of tennis, calls Hawaiʻi's hottest hitters to volley for a $12,000 purse at Kapalua's Tennis Garden and Village Tennis Center. Also at the Tennis Center, Women's International Tennis Association professionals rally with avid amateurs in a week of pro-am and pro-doubles competition during the **Kapalua Betsy Nagelsen Tennis Invitational** in December. All events are put on by the **Kapalua Tennis Club** (☎ 808/669–5677).

The Wailea Open Tennis Championship is held in spring or summer on the Plexipave courts at the **Wailea Tennis Club** (☎ 808/879–1958).

SHOPPING

Whether you head for one of the malls or opt for the boutiques hidden around the Valley Isle, one thing you should have no problem finding is clothing made in Hawaiʻi. The Hawaiian garment industry is now the state's third-largest economic sector, after tourism and agriculture.

Maui has an abundance of locally made art and crafts in a range of prices. A group that calls itself Made on Maui exists solely to promote the products of its members—items that range from pottery and paintings to Hawaiian teas and macadamia caramel corn. You can identify the group by its distinctive Haleakalā logo.

Business hours for individual shops on the island are usually 9 to 5, seven days a week. Shopping centers tend to stay open later (until 9 or 10 at least one night of the week).

Shopping Centers

Azeka Place Shopping Center. Kīhei offers this large and bustling place. Azeka I is the older half, on the makai side of the street. Azeka II, on the mauka side, has a Long's Drugs and several good lunch stops. ⊠ *1280 S. Kīhei Rd., Kīhei.*

Ka'ahumanu Center. This is Maui's largest mall and a showplace with more than 75 stores and a gorgeous glass-enclosed atrium entrance topped by an umbrella-shaded food court. Stop at Camellia Seed Shop for what the locals call "crack seed," a delicacy made from dried fruits, nuts, and sugar. Other interesting stops here include Shirokiya, a popular Japanese retailer; Maui Hands, purveyor of prints, paintings, woodwork, and jewelry by some of the island's finest artists; and such mall standards as Foot Locker, Mrs. Field's Cookies, and Kinney Shoes. ⊠ *275 Ka'ahumanu Ave., Kahului,* ☎ *808/877–3369.*

Kama'ole Shopping Center. Residents of Kīhei favor the locally owned shops at this small shopping center. ⊠ *2463 S. Kīhei Rd., Kīhei.*

Lahaina Cannery Mall. The 50 shops here are set in a building reminiscent of an old pineapple cannery. Unlike many other shopping centers in Hawai'i, the Lahaina Cannery isn't open-air, but it is air-conditioned. Recommended stops include Hawaiian Island Gems, which sells striking Hawaiian heirloom jewelry and pearls; Superwhale, with a good selection of children's tropical wear; and Kite Fantasy, one of the best kite shops on Maui. ⊠ *1221 Honoapi'ilani Hwy., Lahaina,* ☎ *808/661–5304.*

Lahaina Center. Island department store Hilo Hattie Fashion Center anchors the complex and puts on a free hula show at 2 PM every Wednesday and Friday. An additional 10,000 square ft of parking lot space here have been transformed into an ancient Hawaiian village complete with three full-size thatch huts built with 10,000 linear ft of 'ōhi'a wood from the Big Island, 20 tons of *pili* grass, and more than 4 mi of handwoven coconut *senit* (twine). Indoor entertainment is found at a four-screen cinema. The roster of shops and restaurants includes World Café and the Hard Rock Cafe for eats, and Banana Republic and McInerny for clothing. ⊠ *900 Front St., Lahaina,* ☎ *808/667–9216.*

Maui Mall. The anchor stores here are Long's Drugs and Star Market, as well as a good Japanese diner named Restaurant Matsu. The Tasaka Guri Guri Shop is an oddity. It's been around a hundred years, selling an ice cream–like confection called "guri guri" that you will find nowhere else in the world. The mall also has a whimsically designed 12-screen megaplex. ⊠ *70 Ka'ahumanu Ave., Kahului,* ☎ *808/877–7559.*

Maui Marketplace. At this 20-acre complex several outlet stores and big retailers, such as Eagle Hardware, Sports Authority, and Borders Books & Music, have made their first expansion to a Neighbor Island. The center couldn't have a more convenient location. It's at the busy intersection of Hāna Highway and Dairy Road, close to Kahului Airport. ⊠ *270 Dairy Rd., Kahului,* ☎ *808/873–0400.*

Rainbow Mall. This is one place to rub elbows with Kīhei locals out shopping. ⊠ *2439 S. Kīhei Rd., Kīhei.*

The Shops at Wailea. The Wailea resort area has an upscale mall, within walking distance of the major hotels, with such luxury boutiques as Gucci, Fendi, and Louis Vuitton, along with less expensive Gap and Banana Republic stores. There are also several galleries and restaurants. ⊠ *Between the Aston Wailea Resort and the Grand Wailea.*

Whalers Village. Chic and trendy, Whalers Village has grown into a major West Maui shopping center, with a whaling museum and more than 50 restaurants and shops. Upscale haunts include Louis Vuitton, Prada, Ferragamo, Hunting World, and Chanel Boutique. The complex also offers some interesting diversions: Hawaiian artisans display their crafts daily, hula dancers perform on an outdoor stage weeknights from 7 to 8, and a free slide show spotlighting whales and other marine life takes place at the Whale Center of the Pacific on Tuesday and Thursday at 7. ⊠ *2435 Kā'anapali Pkwy., Kā'anapali,* ☎ *808/661–4567.*

Grocery Stores

If you need groceries to take back to your condo, try the following stores, which are conveniently located and offer good selections and extended hours.

Foodland. In Kīhei town center, this is the most convenient supermarket for visitors staying in Wailea. It's open round-the-clock. ⊠ *1881 S. Kīhei Rd., Kīhei,* ☎ *808/879–9350.*

Hawaiian Moons Natural Foods. You'll find the best selection of organic produce on the island, as well as an array of Maui-made products to take home, at this health food store. ⊠ *2411 S. Kīhei Rd., Kīhei,* ☎ *808/875–4356.*

Lahaina Square Shopping Center Foodland. This Foodland serves West Maui and is open daily from 6 AM to midnight. ⊠ *840 Waineʻe St., Lahaina,* ☎ *808/661–0975.*

Safeway. Safeway has two stores on the island open 24 hours daily. The one in Lahaina serves West Maui, and the one in Kahului provides a convenient stop for visitors shopping at Kaʻahumanu Center or touring the historic sites of Central Maui before returning to Wailea lodgings. ⊠ *Lahaina Cannery Mall, 1221 Honoapiʻilani Hwy., Lahaina,* ☎ *808/667–4392;* ⊠ *170 E. Kamehameha Ave., Kahului,* ☎ *808/877–3377.*

Specialty Stores

Art

Maui has more art per square mile than any other Hawaiian island—maybe more than any other U.S. county. There are artists' guilds and co-ops and galleries galore all over the island. Art shows are held throughout the year at the Maui Arts & Cultural Center. Marine sculptors and painters showcase their work during **Celebration of Whales** at the Four Seasons Resort Wailea in January. The Lahaina Arts Society presents **Art in the Park** under the town's historic banyan tree every Friday and Saturday from 9 to 5. Moreover, the town of Lahaina hosts **Art Night** every Friday from 7 to 10. Galleries open their doors (some serve refreshments) and musicians stroll the streets.

Hot Island Glassblowing Studio & Gallery. With the glass-melting furnaces glowing bright orange and the shop loaded with mesmerizing sculptures and functional pieces, this is an exciting place to visit. The working studio, set back from Makawao's main street in "The Courtyard," is owned by a family of award-winning glassblowers. ⊠ *3620 Baldwin Ave., Makawao,* ☎ *808/572–4527.*

Hui Noʻeau Visual Arts Center. The center presents juried and nonjuried exhibits by local artists. ⊠ *2841 Baldwin Ave., Makawao,* ☎ *808/572–6560.*

Lahaina Galleries. Works of both national and international artists are displayed at the gallery's two locations in West Maui. ⊠ *728 Front St., Lahaina,* ☎ *808/667–2152;* ⊠ *Kapalua Resort, Bay Dr., Kapalua,* ☎ *808/669–0202.*

Martin Lawrence Galleries. Martin Lawrence displays the works of noted mainland artists, including Andy Warhol and Keith Haring, in a bright and friendly gallery. ⊠ *Lahaina Market Place, Front St. and Lahainaluna Rd., Lahaina,* ☎ *808/661–1788.*

Maui Crafts Guild. This is one of the most interesting galleries on Maui. Set in a two-story wooden building alongside the highway, the Guild is crammed with work by local artists. The best pieces are the pottery and sculpture. Upstairs, antique kimonos, hand-painted silks, and batik fabric are on display. ⊠ *43 Hāna Hwy., Pāʻia,* ☎ *808/579–9697.*

Maui Hands. This gallery shows work by dozens of local artists, including paniolo-theme lithographs by Sharon Shigekawa, who knows whereof she paints: she rides each year in the Kaupō Roundup. ⊠ *3620 Baldwin Ave., Makawao,* ☎ *808/572–5194;* ⊠ *Kaʻahumanu Center, 275 Kaʻahumanu Ave., Kahului,* ☎ *808/877–0368.*

Viewpoints Gallery. Viewpoints calls itself Maui's only fine-arts collective; it is a cooperative venture of about two dozen Maui painters and sculptors, representing a wide variety of styles. ⊠ *3620 Baldwin Ave., Makawao,* ☎ *808/572–5979.*

Village Gallery. This gallery, with two locations on the island, showcases the works of such popular local artists as Betty Hay Freeland, Wailehua Gray, Margaret Bedell, George Allen, Joyce Clark, Pamela Andelin, Stephen Burr, and Macario Pascual. ⊠ *120 Dickenson St., Lahaina,* ☎ *808/661–4402;* ⊠ *Ritz-Carlton, 1 Ritz-Carlton Dr., Kapalua,* ☎ *808/669–1800.*

Clothing

ISLAND WEAR

Hilo Hattie Fashion Center. Hawaiʻi's largest manufacturer of aloha shirts and muʻumuʻu also carries brightly colored blouses, skirts, and children's clothing. ⊠ *Lahaina Center, 900 Front St., Lahaina,* ☎ *808/ 661–8457.*

Liberty House. Liberty House has the kind of island wear—colorful shirts and muʻumuʻu as well as other graceful styles—worn by people who live year-round on Maui. The store has several branches on the island, including shops at the Hyatt Regency and at the Four Seasons Wailea, but the largest is the one at Kaʻahumanu Center in Kahului (☎ *808/ 877–3361).*

Reyn's. This is the place to go for high-quality aloha shirts in the subtler shades that local men favor for business attire. ⊠ *Kapalua Bay Hotel, 1 Bay Dr., Kapalua,* ☎ *808/669–5260;* ⊠ *Hyatt Regency Maui, 200 Nohea Kai Dr., Lahaina,* ☎ *808/661–0215;* ⊠ *Whalers Village, 2435 Kāʻanapali Pkwy., Kāʻanapali,* ☎ *808/661–9032.*

RESORT WEAR

Not all of Maui's casual clothing is floral. You can find island-worthy sportswear in shops all over the Valley Isle, including most of the stores that sell island wear, as well as these:

Honolua Surf Company. This chain is popular with young women for casual clothing and sportswear. ⊠ *845 Front St., Lahaina,* ☎ *808/661– 8848;* ⊠ *Whalers Village, 2435 Kāʻanapali Pkwy., Kāʻanapali,* ☎ *808/ 661–5455;* ⊠ *Lahaina Cannery Mall, 1221 Honoapiʻilani Hwy., Lahaina,* ☎ *808/661–5777;* ⊠ *2411 S. Kīhei Rd., Kīhei,* ☎ *808/874– 0999.*

SGT Leisure. You'll find resort wear by Tori Richards and other designers. Primarily, though, SGT Leisure sells its own line of informal apparel— sweatshirts, T-shirts, and accessories such as beach bags and hats—bearing their big fish logo. ⊠ *855B Front St., Lahaina,* ☎ *808/667–0661;* ⊠ *Whalers Village, 2435 Kāʻanapali Pkwy., Kāʻanapali,* ☎ *808/667–9433.*

Tropical Tantrum Outlet Store. This well-known outfitter has three retail stores on Maui, but here at the outlets you'll find a wide selection of stylish resort wear, aloha shirts, and muʻumuʻu for 50% less than at the company's retail stores. ⊠ *Azeka Place Shopping Center, 1280 S. Kīhei Rd., Kīhei,* ☎ *808/874–3835;* ⊠ *Kaʻahumanu Center, 275 Kaʻahumanu Ave., Kahului,* ☎ *808/871–8088;* ⊠ *Kamaʻole Shopping Center, 2463 S. Kīhei Rd., Kīhei,* ☎ *808/875–4433.*

Flea Market

Maui Swap Meet. This Saturday flea market is the biggest bargain on Maui, with crafts, gifts, souvenirs, fruit, flowers, jewelry, antiques, art, shells, and lots more. ⊠ *Hwy. 350, off S. Puʻunēnē Ave., Kahului.* 🎫 *50¢.* ☉ *Sat. 5:30 AM–noon.*

Food

Many visitors to Hawai'i opt to take home some of the local produce: pineapples, papayas, coconuts, or Maui onions. You can find jams and jellies—some of them "Made on Maui" products—in a wide variety of tropical flavors. Cook Kwee's Maui Cookies have gained quite a following, as have Maui Potato Chips. Both are available in most Valley Isle grocery stores. Coffee sellers now have Maui-grown and -roasted beans alongside the better-known Kona varieties.

Remember that fresh fruit must be inspected by the U.S. Department of Agriculture before it can leave the state, so it's safest to buy a box that has already passed muster.

Airport Flower & Fruit Co. Ready-to-ship pineapples, Maui onions, papayas, and fresh coconuts are available by phone. ☎ 808/243–9367 or 800/922–9352.

Take Home Maui. These folks will supply, pack, and deliver produce free to the airport or your hotel. ✉ 121 Dickenson St., Lahaina, ☎ 808/661–8067 or 800/545–6284.

Gifts

Lei Spa. In addition to being a day spa, this is a wonderful place to buy soaps, lotions, and shampoos, almost all of which are made on Maui. ✉ 505 Front St., Lahaina, ☎ 808/661–1178.

Lahaina Printsellers Ltd. Hawai'i's largest selection of original antique maps and prints pertaining to Hawai'i and the Pacific are available here. They also sell museum-quality reproductions and original oil paintings from the Pacific Artists Guild. Two smaller shops are at Whalers Village in Kā'anapali and at the Grand Wailea Resort in Wailea. ✉ Lahaina Cannery Mall, 1221 Honoapi'ilani Hwy., Lahaina, ☎ 808/667–7843.

Maui's Best. This a good stop for a wide selection of gifts from Maui and around the world. ✉ Ka'ahumanu Center, 275 Ka'ahumanu Ave., Kahului, ☎ 808/877–7959; ✉ Azeka Place Shopping Center, 1280 S. Kīhei Rd., Kīhei, ☎ 808/874–9216.

Ola's Makawao. Ola's has a delightful assortment of whimsical gifts and affordable, functional contemporary art made by artists from Hawai'i and the U.S. mainland. It is also the exclusive western-U.S. distributor for chocolates by JoMart Candies. ✉ 1156 Makawao Ave., Makawao, ☎ 808/573–1334.

Hawaiian Crafts

The arts and crafts native to Hawai'i are first on the list for many visiting shoppers. Such woods as koa and milo grow only in certain parts of the world, and because of their increasing scarcity, prices are rising. Artisans turn the woods into bowls, trays, and jewelry boxes that will last for years. Look for them in galleries and museum shops.

Hāna Coast Gallery. One of the best places to shop on the island, this 3,000-square-ft gallery houses fine art and jewelry on consignment from local artists. ✉ Hotel Hāna-Maui, Hāna Hwy., Hāna, ☎ 808/248–7332 or 800/637–0188.

Hāna Cultural Center. The center sells distinctive island quilts and other Hawaiian crafts. ✉ Ukea St., Hāna, ☎ 808/248–8622.

Kīhei Kalama Village Marketplace. This is a fun place to investigate. A shaded collection of outdoor stalls sells everything from printed and hand-painted T-shirts and sundresses to jewelry, pottery, wood carvings, fruit, and gaudily painted coconut husks—all made by local craftspeople. ✉ 1941 S. Kīhei Rd., Kīhei, ☎ 808/879–6610.

Maui Crafts Guild. Resident artists craft everything in the store—from Norfolk pine bowls to raku (Japanese lead-glazed) pottery to original sculpture. The prices are surprisingly low. ✉ 43 Hāna Hwy., Pā'ia, ☎ 808/579–9697.

Quilters Corner. Here you'll find a huge selection of Hawaiian quilts and needlepoint, as well as plenty of tropical-print fabrics, silver jewelry, and other local crafts and gift items. ⊠ *1000 Limahana Pl., Lahaina,* ☎ *808/661–0944.*

Jewelry

Haimoff & Haimoff Creations in Gold. This shop carries the original work of several jewelry designers, including the award-winning Harry Haimoff. ⊠ *Kapalua Resort,* ☎ *808/669–5213.*

Jessica's Gems. Jessica's has a good selection of Hawaiian heirloom jewelry, and its Lahaina store specializes in black pearls. ⊠ *Whalers Village, 2435 Kā'anapali Pkwy., Kā'anapali,* ☎ *808/661–4223;* ⊠ *858 Front St., Lahaina,* ☎ *808/661–9200.*

Lahaina Scrimshaw. Here you can buy brooches, rings, pendants, cuff links, tie tacks, and collector's items adorned with this intricately carved sailors' art. ⊠ *845A Front St., Lahaina,* ☎ *808/661–8820;* ⊠ *Whalers Village, 2435 Kā'anapali Pkwy., Kā'anapali,* ☎ *808/661–4034.*

Master Touch Gallery. The exterior of this shop is as rustic as all the old buildings of Makawao, so there's no way to prepare yourself for the elegance and sensuousness of the handcrafted jewelry displayed within. Owner David Sacco truly has the "master touch." ⊠ *3655 Baldwin Ave., Makawao,* ☎ *808/572–6000.*

Maui Divers. This company has been crafting gold and coral into jewelry for more than 20 years. ⊠ *640 Front St., Lahaina,* ☎ *808/661–0988.*

MAUI A TO Z

To research prices, get advice from other travelers, and book travel arrangements, visit www.fodors.com.

AIR TRAVEL

You can fly to Maui from the mainland U.S. or from Honolulu. Flight time from the West Coast to Maui is about 5 hours; from the Midwest, expect about an 8-hour flight; and coming from the East Coast will take about 10 hours, not including layovers. Maui is the most visited of the Neighbor Islands and therefore the easiest to connect to on an interisland flight. Honolulu–Kahului is one of the most heavily traveled air routes in the nation.

CARRIERS

United flies nonstop to Kahului from Los Angeles and San Francisco. American also flies into Kahului, with one stop in Honolulu, from Dallas and Chicago and nonstop from Los Angeles. Delta has through service to Maui daily from Salt Lake City, Atlanta, and Los Angeles and one nonstop daily from Los Angeles. Hawaiian Airlines has direct flights to Kahului from the U.S. West Coast.

Continental, Hawaiian, and Northwest fly from the mainland to Honolulu, where Maui-bound passengers can connect with a 40-minute interisland flight. Flights generally run about $75 one-way between Honolulu and Maui and are available from Hawaiian Airlines, Aloha Airlines, and Island Air.

➤ AIRLINES & CONTACTS: **Aloha Airlines** (☎ 808/244–9071; 800/367–5250 from the U.S. mainland). **American** (☎ 800/433–7300). **Continental** (☎ 800/525–0280). **Delta** (☎ 800/221–1212). **Hawaiian Airlines** (☎ 808/871–6132, 800/882–8811, or 800/367–5320). **Island Air** (☎ 800/652–6541). **Northwest** (☎ 800/225–2525). **TWA** (☎ 800/221–2000). **United** (☎ 800/241–6522).

AIRPORTS

Kahului Airport is efficient and remarkably easy to navigate. Its main disadvantage is its distance from the major resort destinations in West Maui. Kahului is the only airport on Maui that has direct service from the mainland.

If you're staying in West Maui, you might be better off flying into the Kapalua–West Maui Airport. The only way to get to the Kapalua–West Maui Airport is on an interisland flight from Honolulu since the short runway accommodates only small planes. Set in the midst of a pineapple field with a terrific view of the ocean far below, the little airport provides one of the most pleasant ways to arrive on the Valley Isle.

Hāna Airport isn't much more than a landing strip. Only commuter Aloha Island Air flies here, landing twice a day from Honolulu (via Moloka'i and Kahului) and departing 10 minutes later. The morning flight originates in Princeville, Kaua'i. When there is no flight, the tiny terminal usually stands eerily empty, with no gate agents, ticket takers, or other people in sight.

➤ AIRPORT INFORMATION: **Kahului Airport** (☎ 808/872–3800 or 808/872–3830). **Kapalua–West Maui Airport** (☎ 808/669–0623). **Hāna Airport** (☎ 808/248–8208).

AIRPORT TRANSFERS

It will take you about an hour, with traffic in your favor, to get from Kahului Airport to a hotel in Kapalua or Kā'anapali but only 20 to 30 minutes to go to Kīhei or Wailea. The Trans Hawaiian Airporter Shuttle runs between Kahului Airport and the West Maui hotels daily 8–4. One-way fare for adults is $13. You should call 24 hours prior to departure.

Three rental-car companies have courtesy phones inside the Kapalua–West Maui Airport terminal. Shuttles also run between the airport and the Kā'anapali and Kapalua resorts during daylight hours at regular intervals.

If you are flying into Hāna Airport and staying at the Hotel Hāna-Maui, your flight will be met. If you have reserved a rental car, the agent will usually know your arrival time and meet you. Otherwise you can call Dollar Rent A Car to pick you up.

The best way to get from the airport to your destination—and to see the island itself—is in your own rental car. Most major car-rental companies have desks or courtesy phones at each airport. They also can provide a map and directions to your hotel from the airport.

Maui has more than two dozen taxi companies, and they make frequent passes through the Kahului and Kapalua–West Maui airports. If you don't see a cab, you can call Yellow Cab of Maui or La Bella Taxi for islandwide service from the airport. Call Kīhei Taxi if you're staying in the Kīhei, Wailea, or Mākena areas. Charges from Kahului Airport to Kā'anapali run about $49; to Wailea, about $31; and to Lahaina, about $42.

➤ TAXIS & SHUTTLES: **Kīhei Taxi** (☎ 808/879–3000). **La Bella Taxi** (☎ 808/242–8011). **Trans Hawaiian Airporter Shuttle** (☎ 808/877–7308). **Yellow Cab of Maui** (☎ 808/877–7000).

BOAT & FERRY TRAVEL

Approaching the Valley Isle on the deck of a ship is an unforgettable experience. Watching the land loom ever larger conjures up the same kinds of feelings the early Polynesians probably had on their first voyage—except they didn't get the kind of lavish treatment those on board a luxury cruise ship routinely receive. You can book passage through

American Hawai'i Cruises, which offers seven-day interisland cruises departing from Honolulu on the S.S. *Constitution* and the S.S. *Independence*. Or ask about the company's seven-day cruise-resort combination packages.

➤ BOAT & FERRY INFORMATION: **American Hawai'i Cruises** (✉ 2 North Riverside Plaza, Chicago, IL 60606, ☎ 312/466–6000 or 800/765–7000).

BUS TRAVEL

Although Maui has no public transit system, a private company, Trans-Hawaiian Services, transports visitors around the West Maui and South Maui areas. One-way, round-trip, and all-day passes are available.

➤ BUS INFORMATION: **Trans-Hawaiian Services** (☎ 808/877–7308).

CAR RENTAL

During peak seasons—summer and Christmas through Easter—be sure to reserve your car well ahead of time if you haven't booked a room-car package with your hotel. Expect to pay about $35 a day—before taxes, insurance, and extras—for a compact car from one of the major companies. You can get a less-expensive deal from one of the locally owned budget companies. You'll probably have to call for a shuttle from the airport, since few of these companies have rental desks there. There is a $2 daily road tax on all rental cars in Hawai'i.

Budget, Dollar, and National have courtesy phones at the Kapalua–West Maui Airport; Hertz and Alamo are nearby. All of the above, plus Avis, have desks at or near Maui's major airport in Kahului. Roberts Tours offers car rentals through package tours. Quite a few locally owned companies rent cars on Maui, including Rent-A-Jeep, which will pick you up at Kahului Airport.

Arthur's Limousine Service offers a chauffeured superstretch Lincoln complete with bar and two TVs for $88 per hour. Arthur's fleet also includes less grandiose Lincoln Town Cars for $65 per hour with a two-hour minimum. If you want to stretch out with a company on the South Shore, call Wailea Limousine Service. Despite the name, this company also provides limousines to the Lahaina area.

➤ MAJOR AGENCIES: **Alamo** (☎ 800/327–9633). **Avis** (☎ 800/331–1212; 800/879–2847 in Canada). **Budget** (☎ 800/527–0700; 800/268–8900 in Canada). **Dollar** (☎ 800/800–4000 or 808/248–8237). **Hertz** (☎ 800/654–3131; 800/263–0600 in Canada). **National** (☎ 800/227–7368).

➤ LOCAL AGENCIES: **Arthur's Limousine Service** (☎ 808/871–5555 or 800/345–4667). **Rent-A-Jeep** (☎ 808/877–6626). **Roberts Tours** (☎ 808/523–9323). **Wailea Limousine Service** (☎ 808/875–4114; 808/661–4114 in Lahaina).

CAR TRAVEL

Maui has some 120 mi of coastline, not all of which is accessible. Less than one-quarter of its land mass is inhabited. To see the island, your best bet is a car. Most of the roads on the island have two lanes. If you're going to attempt the partially paved, patched, and bumpy road between Hāna and 'Ulupalakua, you'll be better off with a four-wheel-drive vehicle, but be forewarned: rental-car companies prohibit travel on roads they've determined might damage the car, so if you break down, you're on your own for repairs. There are two other difficult roads on Maui: one is Highway 36, or Hāna Highway, which runs 56 mi between Kahului and Hāna and includes more twists and turns than you can count. The other is an 8-mi scenic stretch of one-lane highway between Kapalua and Wailuku on the north side of the West Maui mountains.

EMERGENCIES

In an emergency, dial **911** to reach an ambulance, the police, or the fire department.

For emergency road service, there is a Honolulu-based AAA. A dispatcher will send a tow truck, but you will need to tell the driver where to take your car. Don't forget to carry your membership card with you.

For medical assistance in West Maui, call Doctors on Call. Or try a walk-in clinic at Whalers Village, West Maui Health Care Center, which was created by two doctors in 1980 to treat visitors to West Maui. It is open daily from 8 AM to 10 PM. Kīhei Clinic Medical Services is in the central part of the Valley Isle and is geared toward working with visitors in Kīhei and Wailea.

➤ DOCTORS: **Doctors on Call** (✉ Hyatt Regency Maui, Nāpili Tower, Suite 100, 200 Nohea Kai Dr., Lahaina, ☎ 808/667–7676). **Kīhei Clinic Medical Services** (✉ 2349 S. Kīhei Rd., Suite D, Kīhei, ☎ 808/879–1440). **West Maui Health Care Center** (✉ 2435 Kā'anapali Pkwy., Suite H-7, Kā'anapali, ☎ 808/667–9721).

➤ EMERGENCY SERVICES: **AAA** (☎ 800/222–4357). **Coast Guard Rescue Center** (☎ 800/552–6458).

➤ HOSPITALS: **Hāna Medical Center** (✉ Hāna Hwy., Hāna, ☎ 808/248–8294). **Kula Hospital** (✉ 204 Kula Hwy., Kula, ☎ 808/878–1221). **Maui Memorial Hospital** (✉ 221 Mahalani St., Wailuku, ☎ 808/244–9056).

LODGING

APARTMENT RENTALS

Besides the condos listed in Lodging, which operate like hotels and offer hotel-like amenities, Maui has condos you can rent through central booking agents. Most agents represent more than one condo complex (some handle single-family homes as well), so be specific about what kind of price, space, facilities, and amenities you want. The following are multiproperty agents.

➤ LOCAL AGENTS: **Ameri Resort Management, Inc.** (✉ 5500 Honoapi'ilani Rd., Kapalua 96761, ☎ 808/669–5635 or 800/786–7387). **Aston Hotels & Resorts** (✉ 2255 Kūhiō Ave., 18th fl., Honolulu 96815, ☎ 800/342–1551). **Destination Resorts** (✉ 3750 Wailea Alanui Dr., Wailea 96753, ☎ 800/367–5246). **Hawaiian Apartment Leasing Enterprises** (✉ 479 Ocean Ave., Laguna Beach, CA 92651, ☎ 714/497–4253 or 800/854–8843). **Hawai'i Condo Exchange** (✉ 1817 El Cerrito Pl., Los Angeles, CA 90068, ☎ 800/442–0404). **Hawaiian Resorts, Inc.** (✉ 1270 Ala Moana Blvd., Honolulu 96814, ☎ 800/367–7040; 800/877–7331 in Canada). **Kīhei Maui Vacations** (✉ Box 1055, Kīhei 96753, ☎ 800/542–6284). **Marc Resorts Hawai'i** (✉ 2155 Kalakaua Ave., Suite 706, Honolulu 96815, ☎ 800/535–0085). **Maui Windsurfari** (✉ 425 Koloa St., Kahului 96732, ☎ 808/871–7766 or 800/736–6284). **Vacation Locations Hawai'i** (✉ Box 1689, Kīhei, 96753, ☎ 808/874–0077 or 800/522–2757).

B&BS

The Maui Visitors Bureau refers callers to Bed & Breakfast Hawai'i. Bed and Breakfast Honolulu has statewide listings, with about 50 B&Bs on Maui. Bed & Breakfast Maui-Style has listings for about 50 B&Bs on Maui. Island Bed & Breakfast, headquartered on Kaua'i, has listings throughout the state and handles about 35 B&Bs on Maui. A directory is available for $12.95.

➤ RESERVATION SERVICES: **Bed & Breakfast Hawai'i** (☎ 808/733–1632). **Bed and Breakfast Honolulu** (☎ 808/595–7533 or 800/288–4666). **Bed & Breakfast Maui-Style** (☎ 808/879–7865). **Island Bed & Breakfast** (☎ 808/822–7771 or 800/733–1632).

MOPED TRAVEL

You can rent mopeds on the West Side at Wheels R Us for $36 a day. On the South Shore, try Wheels USA at Rainbow Mall. Rates are $25 for four hours or $31 until 4:30. Be especially careful navigating roads where there are no designated bicycle lanes. Note that helmets are optional on Maui, but eye protection is not.

➤ MOPED RENTALS: **Wheels R Us** (✉ 741 Waine'e St., Lahaina, ☎ 808/ 667–7751). **Wheels USA** (✉ 2439 S. Kīhei Rd., Kīhei, ☎ 808/875– 1221).

SHUTTLE TRAVEL

If you're staying in the right hotel or condo, there are a few shuttles that can get you around the area. The double-decker West Maui Shopping Express ferries passengers to and from Kā'anapali, Kapalua, Honokōwai, and Lahaina from 8 AM to 10 PM. The fare is $1 per person each way, and schedules are available at most hotels.

The free Kā'anapali Trolley Shuttle runs within the resort between 9 AM and 11 PM and stops automatically at all hotels and at condos when requested. All Kā'anapali hotels have copies of schedules, or you can call the Kā'anapali Operation Association.

The Wailea Shuttle and the Kapalua Shuttle run within their respective resorts and are free. Schedules are available throughout each resort.
➤ CONTACTS: **Kā'anapali Operation Association** (☎ 808/661–7370). **West Maui Shopping Express** (☎ 808/875–7841).

SIGHTSEEING TOURS
BUS & VAN TOURS

This is a big island to see in one day, so tour companies combine various sections—either Haleakalā, 'Īao Needle, and Central Maui, or West Maui and its environs—in various tour packages. Contact companies for a brochure of their current offerings. Very often hotels have tour desks to facilitate arrangements.

A tour of Haleakalā and Upcountry is usually a half-day excursion, and is offered in several versions by different companies for about $50 and up. The trip often includes stops at a protea farm and at Tedeschi Vineyards and Winery, the only place in Maui where wine is made. A Haleakalā sunrise tour starts before dawn so that visitors get to the top of the dormant volcano before the sun peeks over the horizon. Some companies throw in champagne to greet the sunrise.

A tour of Hāna is almost always done in a van, since the winding road to Hāna just doesn't provide a comfortable ride in bigger buses. Of late, Hāna has so many of these one-day tours that it seems as if there are more vans than cars on the road. Still, to many it's a more relaxing way to do the drive than behind the wheel of a car. Guides decide where you stop for photos. Tour costs run $70–$120.

Ground tour companies are usually statewide and have a whole fleet of vehicles. Some use air-conditioned buses, while others prefer smaller vans. Then you've got your minivans, your microbuses, and your minicoaches. The key is how many passengers each will hold. Be sure to ask how many stops you'll get on your tour, or you may be disappointed to find that all your sightseeing is done through a window.

Most of the tour guides have been in the business for years. Some were born in the Islands and have taken special classes to learn more about their culture and lore. They expect a tip ($1 per person at least), but they're just as cordial without one.

Polynesian Adventure Tours uses large buses with floor-to-ceiling windows. The drivers are fun and really know the island. Roberts Hawai'i Tours is one of the state's largest tour companies, and its staff can arrange tours with bilingual guides if asked ahead of time. Despite its size, Trans Hawaiian Services manages to keep its tours personal.

➤ TOUR OPERATORS: **Polynesian Adventure Tours** (⊠ 400 Hāna Hwy., Kahului 96732, ☎ 808/877–4242 or 800/622–3011). **Roberts Hawai'i Tours** (⊠ Box 247, Kahului 96732, ☎ 808/871–6226 or 800/767–7551). **Trans Hawaiian Services** (⊠ 720 Iwilei Rd., Suite 101, Honolulu 96817, ☎ 800/533–8765).

HELIOCOPTER TOURS

Helicopter flight-seeing excursions can take you over the West Maui mountains, Hāna, and Haleakalā. This is a beautiful, exciting way to see the island, and the *only* way to see some of its most dramatic areas. Tour prices usually include a videotape of your trip so you can relive the experience at home. Prices run from about $100 for a half-hour rain forest tour to $250 for a two-hour mega-experience that includes a champagne toast on landing.

It takes about 90 minutes to travel inside the volcano, then down to the village of Hāna. Some companies stop in secluded areas for refreshments. Helicopter-tour operators throughout the state come under sharp scrutiny for passenger safety and equipment maintenance. Noise levels are a concern as well; residents have become pretty vocal about regulating this kind of pollution. Don't be afraid to ask about a company's safety record, flight paths, age of equipment, and level of operator experience.

The highly recommended Blue Hawaiian Helicopters has provided aerial adventures in Hawai'i since 1985, and it has the best service and safety record. Its ASTAR helicopters are air-conditioned and have noise-blocking headsets for all passengers. Hawai'i Helicopters flies fast, twin-engine jet helicopters. Sunshine Helicopters offers a Moloka'i flight in its *Black Beauty* aircraft.

➤ TOUR OPERATORS: **Blue Hawaiian Helicopters** (⊠ Kahului Heliport, Hangar 105, Kahului 96732, ☎ 808/871–8844). **Hawai'i Helicopters** (⊠ Kahului Heliport, Hangar 106, Kahului 96732, ☎ 808/877–3900, 800/994–9099, or 800/367–7095). **Sunshine Helicopters** (⊠ Kahului Heliport, Hangar 107, Kahului 96732, ☎ 808/871–0722 or 800/544–2520).

HIKING & WALKING TOURS

Hike Maui is the oldest hiking company in the Islands, and its rainforest, mountain-ridge, crater, coastline, and archeological-snorkel hikes are led by such knowledgeable folk as ethnobotanists and marine biologists. Prices range from $75 to $125 for hikes of 5 to 10 hours, including lunch. Hike Maui supplies waterproof day packs, rain ponchos, first-aid gear, and water bottles.

The Lahaina Restoration Foundation has published a walking-tour map for interested visitors. The map will guide you to the most historic sites of Lahaina, some renovated and some not. Highlights of the walk include the Jodo Mission, the Brig *Carthaginian II*, the Baldwin Home, and the Old Court House. These are all sights you could find yourself, but the map is free and full of historical tidbits, and it makes the walk easier.

➤ TOUR OPERATORS: **Hike Maui** (⊠ Box 330969, Kahului 96733, ☎ 808/879–5270, WEB www.hikemaui.com). **Lahaina Restoration Foundation** (⊠ Baldwin Home, 696 Front St., Lahaina 96761, ☎ 808/661–3262).

HORSEBACK TOURS

Several companies on Maui offer horseback riding that's far more appealing than the typical hour-long trudge over a dull trail with 50 other horses.

Adventures on Horseback conducts five-hour outings into secluded parts of Maui. The $175 tours traverse ocean cliffs on Maui's north shore, follow the slopes of Haleakalā, and pass along streams, through rain forests, and near waterfalls, where riders can stop for a dip in a freshwater pool. Tours include breakfast, lunch, and refreshments.

Charley's Trail Rides & Pack Trips require a stout physical nature—but not a stout physique: riders must weigh under 200 pounds. Charley's overnighters go from Kaupō—a *tiny* village nearly 20 mi past Hāna—up the slopes of Haleakalā to the crater. Tours cost between $40–$160.

Pony Express Tours will take you on horseback into Haleakalā Crater. The half-day ride goes down to the crater floor for a picnic lunch. The full-day excursion covers 12 mi of terrain and visits some of the crater's unusual formations. You don't need to be an experienced rider, but the longer ride can be tough if you're unathletic. The company also offers one- and two-hour rides on Haleakalā Ranch, for between $40–$160.
➤ TOUR OPERATORS: **Adventures on Horseback** (✉ Box 1771, Makawao 96768, ☎ 808/242–7445). **Charley's Trail Rides & Pack Trips** (✉ c/o Kaupō Ranch, Kaupō 96713, ☎ 808/248–8209). **Pony Express Tours** (✉ Box 535, Kulā 96790, ☎ 808/667–2200 or 808/878–6698).

PRIVATE GUIDES

Rent-a-Local is *the* best way to see Maui—through the eyes of locals. Started by Laurie Robello, who is part Hawaiian, the company has excellent guides who will drive your car on a tour tailored to your interests. Tours cost $199 for the first two people, and $25 for each additional person.

Temptation Tours' president Dave Campbell has targeted members of the affluent older crowd (though almost anyone would enjoy these tours) who don't want to be herded onto a crowded bus. He provides exclusive tours in his plush six-passenger limovan and specializes in full-day tours to Haleakalā and Hāna, ranging from $110–$249. Dave's "Ultimate" Hāna tour includes lunch at Hotel Hāna-Maui.
➤ TOUR OPERATORS: **Rent-a-Local** (✉ 333 Dairy Rd., #102, Kahului 96732, ☎ 808/877–4042 or 800/228–6284). **Temptation Tours** (✉ 211 'Āhinahina Pl., Kula 96790, ☎ 808/877–8888.)

THEME TOURS

Once you have your bearings, you may want a tour that's a bit more specialized. For example, you might want to bike down a volcano, ride a mule, or immerse yourself in art.

A free guided tour of the Hyatt Regency Maui's art collection and gardens starts at 11 on Monday, Wednesday, and Friday. It takes you through the Hyatt's public spaces, adorned with a constantly changing multi-million-dollar collection of Asian and Pacific art. Among the treasures to be found are Chinese cloisonné, Japanese dragon pots, Thai elephant bells, Hawaiian quilts, battle shields and masks from Papua New Guinea, and such contemporary work as *The Acrobats*, a bronze sculpture by Australian artist John Robinson. If you're not fond of group tours, just pick up a copy of the hotel's "Art Guide" for a fascinating do-it-yourself experience.

Exploring the spectacular art collection housed on the grounds of the Grand Wailea is like entering an international art museum. Sculptures, artifacts, stained-glass windows, a 200,000-piece ceramic tile mosaic, paintings, and assorted works by Fernand Léger, Andy Warhol, Pablo Picasso, Fernando Botero, and noted Hawaiian artists make this excursion a must for art lovers. The tour leaves from the resort's Napua Art Gallery at 10 every Tuesday and Friday and is free for guests of the resort. Nonguests pay $6.

After instruction in safety fundamentals at Maui Downhill, you don a helmet, get on a bicycle atop Haleakalā volcano, and coast down. Lunch or breakfast is included, depending on what time you start; treks cost $95–$115.

Maui Mountain Cruisers will put you on a bicycle at the top of Haleakalā and let you coast down. Safety precautions are a top priority, so riders wear helmets. Meals are provided. Trips are $86–$99 per person; you can ride down Haleakalā in a van for $55.

The Maui Pineapple Plantation Tour takes you right into the fields in a company van. The 2½-hour, $26 trip gives you firsthand experience of the operation and its history, some incredible views of the island, and the chance to pick a fresh pineapple for yourself. Tours depart weekday mornings and afternoons from the Kapalua Logo Shop.

➤ TOUR OPERATORS: **Grand Wailea** (⌗ 3850 Wailea Alanui Dr., Wailea 96753, ☎ 808/875–1234). **Hyatt Regency Maui's art collection and gardens** (⌗ Kā'anapali Beach Resort, 200 Nokea Kai Dr., Lahaina 96761, ☎ 808/661–1234). **Maui Downhill** (⌗ 199 Dairy Rd., Kahului 96732, ☎ 808/871–2155 or 800/535–2453). **Maui Mountain Cruisers** (⌗ Box 1356, Makawao 96768, ☎ 808/871–6014). **Maui Pineapple Plantation Tour** (⌗ Kapalua Resort Activity Desk, 500 Office Rd., Kapalua 96761, ☎ 808/669–8088).

TAXIS

For short hops between hotels and restaurants, taxis can be a convenient way to go, but you'll have to call ahead. Even busy West Maui doesn't have curbside taxi service. West Maui Taxi and Yellow Cab of Maui service the entire island, but you'd be smart to consider using them just for the areas where they're located. Ali'i Cab covers West Maui, and Kīhei Taxi serves Central Maui.

➤ TAXI COMPANIES: **Ali'i Cab** (⌗ 75 Kū'ai Pl., Lahaina, ☎ 808/661–3688). **Kīhei Taxi** (⌗ Kīhei, ☎ 808/879–3000). **West Maui Taxi** (⌗ 761 Kumukahi St., Lahaina, ☎ 808/667–2605). **Yellow Cab of Maui** (⌗ Kahului Airport, ☎ 808/877–7000).

VISITOR INFORMATION

The Maui Visitors Bureau can provide you with brochures and information. Aunty Aloha's Breakfast Lū'au is a fun and tasty way to learn about exciting and often unpublicized things to do on Maui. The orientation includes live Hawaiian music, a hula show, a comical slide show, and an all-you-can-eat island-style breakfast; it runs weekdays at 8:15 AM. The cost is $14.95 for two people. Visitor Channel Seven televises visitor information 24 hours a day, including video tours, restaurant previews, and activities information.

Haleakalā Weather Forecast gives up-to-date reports on sea conditions, as well as a weather forecast for the road to Hāna and for 'Īao Valley State Park. National Weather Service/Maui Forecast covers the islands of Maui, Moloka'i, and Lāna'i.

➤ TOURIST INFORMATION: **Aunty Aloha's Breakfast Lū'au** (⌗ Kā'anapali Beach Hotel, Kā'anapali, ☎ 800/993–8338). **Haleakalā Weather Forecast** (☎ 808/871–5054). **National Weather Service/Maui Forecast** (☎ 808/877–5111). **Maui Visitors Bureau** (⌗ 1727 Wili Pā Loop, Wailuku 96793, ☎ 808/244–3530, FAX 808/244–1337, WEB www.visitmaui.com).

WHALE-WATCHING

DURING THE RIGHT TIME of year on Maui—between November and April—you can see whales breaching and blowing just offshore. The humpback whales' attraction to Maui is legendary. More than half the North Pacific's humpback population winters in Hawai'i, as they've been doing for years. At one time there were thousands of the huge mammals, but the world population has dwindled to about 1,500. In 1966 they were put on the endangered species list, which restricts boats and airplanes from getting too close.

Experts believe the humpbacks keep returning to Hawaiian waters because of the warmth. Winter is calving time for the behemoths, and the young whales, born with little blubber, probably couldn't survive in the frigid Alaskan waters. No one has ever seen a whale give birth here, but the experts studying whales off Maui know that calving is their main winter activity, since the one- and two-ton youngsters suddenly appear while the whales are in residence.

Quite a few operations run whale-watching excursions off the coast of Maui, with many boats departing from the wharves at Lahaina and Māʻalaea each day. **Pacific Whale Foundation** (✉ Kealia Beach Plaza, 101 N. Kīhei Rd., Kīhei 96753, ☎ 808/879–8811) pioneered whale-watching back in 1979 and now runs four boats, plus sea kayaks and special trips to encounter turtles and dolphins. During humpback season (Dec. 15– May 1) PWF has a marine naturalist stationed at McGregor Point Lookout (on the cliffs heading into Lahaina) and also weekdays at 12:15 on the observation deck of its Kīhei office.

Also offering whale-watching in season are **Ocean Activities Center** (✉ 1847 S. Kīhei Rd., Suite 203A, Kīhei 96753, ☎ 808/879–4485); **Island Marine** (✉ 113 Prison St., Lahaina 96761, ☎ 808/ 661–8397); and **Pride Charters** (✉ 208 Kenolio Rd., Kīhei, ☎ 808/874– 8835), whose two-hour whale-watch cruise is narrated by a naturalist from Whales Alive and Keiko (Free Willie) Foundation. Ticket prices average $20–$40, depending on the time of day and whether or not lunch is included.

3 THE BIG ISLAND OF HAWAI'I

THE VOLCANO ISLE

The Big Island is the youngest and largest island of the Hawaiian chain, and still growing: fresh lava has added black-sand beaches and has covered more than 38 square mi of land since 1983. An enviable 266 mi of coastline offer splendid multicolor beaches, but this is also an island of cool, mountainous countryside; rain forest; and coffee, orchid, and macadamia-nut plantations. In addition to fabulous resorts and world-class golf courses, adventures await in volcanic craters and blue waters, along mountainous trails, on cowboy ranches, and on the towering summit of Mauna Ke'a.

By Betty
Fullard-Leo

Updated by
Sophia
Schweitzer

NEARLY TWICE AS LARGE AS ALL THE OTHER Hawaiian Islands combined, Hawai'i (known as the Big Island to avoid confusion with the state name) is used to setting records. Perhaps most dramatically, it has the world's most active volcano: the east rift zone below Halema'uma'u on Kīlauea has been spewing lava intermittently since January 3, 1983. The island's southern tip is the southernmost point in the United States, although to the southeast, far beneath the ocean's surface, Lōihi, a sea mount bubbling lava, is slowly building another Hawaiian island, due to emerge in about 100,000 years. If you measure Mauna Ke'a from its origins 32,000 ft beneath the ocean's surface to its 13,796-ft peak, it is the tallest mountain in the world. The Keck Observatory on its summit, with one of the world's most powerful telescopes, searches the universe from the clearest place on earth for peering into the heavens.

With its diverse climate and terrain, the Big Island offers skiing (but only for experts) in winter and year-round sunshine on its southern and western shores, where the temperature averages 69°F to 84°F in July and 53°F to 75°F in January. Yet there is so much rain near Hilo, the island's major city, that its only zoo is right in the middle of a rain forest, whereas land along the Kona-Kohala Coast is generally dry, with uninhabited stretches of lava.

In earlier times, Hawai'i's kings and queens lived and played along the Kona-Kohala Coast. King Kamehameha I was born close to its northern shores, near Mo'okini Heiau, built around the end of the 5th century (a *heiau* is a stone platform that was used as a site of worship). All along the water's edge are reminders of earlier inhabitants. At Kawaihae, two heiaus—Pu'ukoholā and Mailekini—mark the site of Kamehameha's final victory in 1810 in his battle to unite the Hawaiian Islands.

Developers are becoming increasingly aware of the reverence the Hawaiian people feel for their '*āina* (land), and they attempt to preserve and restore the bits and pieces of Hawaiian history that come to light when a bulldozer rakes the land. You'll find historic markers scattered along trails and roadways, at hotel grounds, and in parks. Resorts, such as the Outrigger Waikoloa Beach, The Orchid at Mauna Lani, Kona Village, and the Aston Keauhou Beach Resort, conduct tours of petroglyph fields and historic sites. The Outrigger Waikoloa Beach at 'Anaeho'omalu Bay, the Four Seasons Resort Hualālai, and the Mauna Lani Bay Hotel and Bungalows have restored the fishponds that once supplied the tables of Hawaiian royalty.

In the calm tranquillity of the Kohala Mountains to the north, where the *paniolo* (Hawaiian cowboys) ride, or at the windswept isolation of South Point—thought to have been populated as early as AD 750—you can reflect on the lives of the early Hawaiians who crossed this land on foot. Did they bring their gods and goddesses from their ancient homeland in Tahiti and the Marquesas? Or was the goddess Pele conceived as an explanation for some violent volcanic eruption?

Five volcanoes formed the Big Island perhaps a half-million years ago: Kohala, Hualālai, Mauna Ke'a (white mountain), Mauna Loa (long mountain), and Kīlauea, which is currently active. Early Hawaiians believed that Pele lived in whichever crater was erupting. Even today, eerie stories are repeated as fact. They tell of a woman hitchhiker who dresses in red and wanders the volcano area accompanied by a small white dog. "My neighbor gave her a ride, but when he looked in the mirror she was gone!" is how one oft-repeated tale goes. As recently

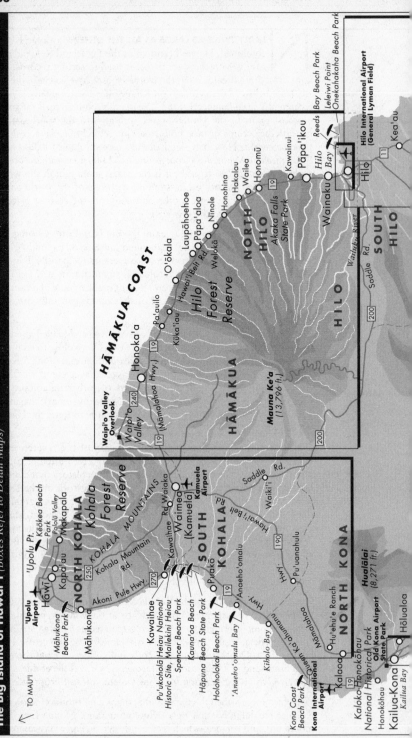

The Big Island of Hawai'i (*Boxes Refer to Detail Maps*)

TO MAUI

HĀMĀKUA COAST

Waipi'o Valley Overlook
Waipi'o Valley
Honoka'a
Pa'auilo
Kūka'iau
'O'ōkala
Laupāhoehoe
Pāpa'aloa
Ninole
Hakalau
Honohina
Honomū
Wailea
Kawainui
Pāpa'ikou
Hilo Bay
Wainaku
Hilo
Reeds Bay Beach Park
Lēleiwi Point
Onekahakaha Beach Park
Hilo International Airport (General Lyman Field)
Kea'au

19 (Māmalahoa Hwy.)
220
240
19
200
Saddle Rd.
Wailuku River
200

NORTH HILO
SOUTH HILO

Hilo Forest Reserve
Akaka Falls State Park
Wailoa River
Wekā

HĀMĀKUA
Mauna Ke'a (13,796 ft.)

Kea'au
11

NORTH KOHALA
Kohala Forest Reserve
KOHALA MOUNTAINS
Kohala Mountain Rd.

'Upolu Pt.
'Upolu Airport
Hāwī
Kapa'au
Makapala
Pololū Valley
Keōkea Beach Park
Māhukona Beach Park
Māhukona
Akoni Pule Hwy.
250
270

Waiaka
Waimea (Kamuela)
Kamuela Airport
SOUTH KOHALA
Waikoloa Rd.
Saddle Rd.
Waiki'i
Hawai'i Belt Rd.

Kawaihae
Pu'ukoholā Heiau National Historic Site, Mailekini Heiau
Spencer Beach Park
Kauna'oa Beach
Hāpuna Beach State Park
Holoholokai Beach Park
Puakō
Anaeho'omalu
'Anaeho'omalu Bay
Kībolo Bay

19
190
Pu'uanahulu

NORTH KONA
Hualālai (8,271 ft.)

Hu'ehu'e Ranch
Kona Coast Beach Park
Kona International Airport
Kalaoa
Kaloko-Honokōhau National Historical Park
Honokōhau
Old Kona Airport State Park
Kailua-Kona
Kailua Bay
Hōlualoa

Queen Ka'ahumanu Hwy.
Māmalahoa Hwy.

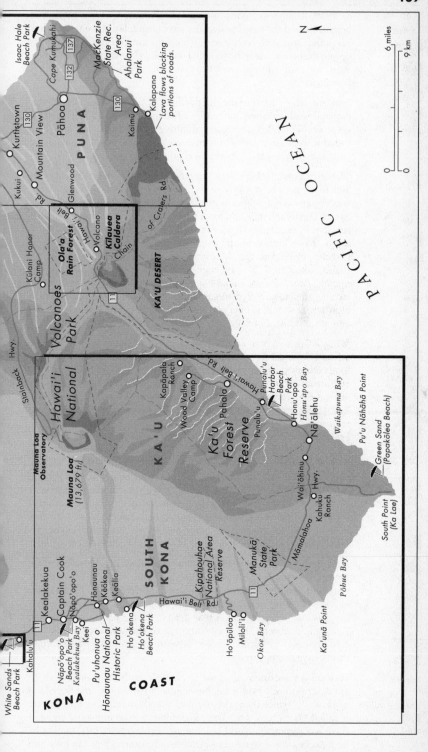

PACIFIC OCEAN

N

6 miles

9 km

PUNA

Isaac Hale Beach Park
Cape Kumukahi
137
132
MacKenzie State Rec. Area
Ahalanui Park
130
Kalapana
Lava flows blocking portions of roads.
Kaimū
Pāhoa
Kurtistown
130
Mountain View
Glenwood
Kukui
Hawaiʻi Belt Rd.
Kūlani Honor Camp
Olaʻa Rain Forest
Kīlauea Caldera
Volcano
Chain of Craters Rd.

KAʻU DESERT

Volcanoes Park

Hawaiʻi National

Stainback Hwy.

Park

Mauna Loa Observatory

Mauna Loa (13,679 ft.)

KAʻU

Kapāpala Ranch
Wood Valley Camp
Pāhala
Punaluʻu
Kaʻu Forest Reserve

Hawaiʻi Belt Rd.

Punaluʻu Harbor Beach Park
Honuʻapo
Honuʻapo Bay
Nāʻālehu
Waikapuna Bay
Puʻu Nāhāhā Point

Waiʻōhinu
Kahuku Ranch
Māmalahoa Hwy.
Green Sand (Papakōlea Beach)
South Point (Ka Lae)

SOUTH KONA

Kealakekua
Captain Cook
Nāpoʻopoʻo
Nāpoʻopoʻo Beach Park
Kealakekua Bay
Keʻei
Honaunau
Keōkea
Keālia
Puʻuhonua o Hōnaunau National Historic Park
Hoʻokena
Hoʻokena Beach Park
Hawaiʻi Belt Rd.

Kipahoehoe National Area Reserve

Manukā State Park
11

Hoʻōpūloa
Miloliʻi
Okoe Bay
Kaʻunā Point
Pōhue Bay

White Sands Beach Park
Kahaluʻu

KONA COAST

as 1959, Kīlauea exploded in a cascading fountain of fire 1,900 ft in height. Even if the past few decades have been relatively unglamorous in comparison, with lava flowing from rift zones through 'ōhi'a forests or into the ocean, nearly 200 housing units as well as the Chain of Craters Road were forced to surrender to Pele's rage. No lives, however, have been lost.

You can drive almost to the end of Chain of Craters Road, leave your car, and walk to where molten lava flows into the ocean. It's not always visible. Helicopters carry sightseers over the 2½-mi lava lake called Kupaianaha, an 800-ft cinder cone, to view steam clouds rising from the ocean as the hot lava meets the sea.

The drive along the Hāmākua Coast from Hilo, the island's county seat and the fourth-largest city in the state, to Waimea, a fast-growing wealthy cowboy town, calls attention to modern development on the island. Sugarcane stalks no longer wave in the breeze. They have been replaced by orchards of macadamia-nut trees, eucalyptus, and specialty crops (from lettuce to strawberries) raised for chefs who prepare Hawai'i regional cuisine. Macadamia nuts are big business on the Big Island, supplying 90% of the state's yield. Kona coffee; anthuriums and orchids; *pakalōlō* (marijuana—at one time said to be the state's biggest income-producing, though illegal, crop); kava, used in the pharmaceutical industry; and even vanilla and cacao are adding a new chapter to the agricultural history of the state.

While Kīlauea Volcano remains the greatest attraction to visitors, one other thing is certain: business owners in all sections of the economy have combined efforts to make the island exciting, welcoming, and fun. Significant airport expansions in the Kona area reflect their success. Several new restaurants serve the now famous Hawai'i regional cuisine. Upcountry Waimea's reconstructed Parker Ranch Shopping Center is scheduled to reopen in 2002, and the Parker Ranch hosts cowboy Friday activities—wagon tours, horseback-riding adventures, and customized hikes. Another ranch, Kahua, on the fertile slopes of the Kohala Mountains, also invites visitors to share the ranching life. In Hilo, despite the rain, the farmers' market remains the most inspiring in the state, displaying colorful produce reflecting the island's full range of climates and ethnic traditions. The Lyman Museum has been renovated with an impressive volcano-like entrance. Even remote South Point has become well worth the long drive. And for golfers, two new oceanfront courses on the west side of the island are slated for tee off in 2002.

New attractions are by and large culturally and environmentally aware. On the resort side of the island you can sail a voyaging canoe at the Orchid, learn about Hawaiian culture at ancient Pu'ukoholā Heiau, or visit the Four Seasons' Hawaiian Cultural Center, which grows coral as one of its projects. A new lū'au in Kailua-Kona, Traditions at Kahalu'u, celebrates the unique heritage of Hawaiian royalty and sacred Hawaiian grounds. New eco-adventures sprout up where former thrills have disappeared.

Hawai'i is sometimes called the Orchid Isle or the Volcano Isle (both apt descriptions, by the way), but residents always say "the Big Island of Hawai'i," since the entire chain of islands that makes up the state is called Hawai'i as well. True, nightlife is a little low-key here, and there is a rumor that good beaches are scarce, but in fact, the Big Island excites the senses and inspires the adventurer. You can hike into a crater, catch marlin weighing hundreds of pounds, discover another universe from the top of Mauna Ke'a, and outstare a shark from the safety of a submarine porthole.

Pleasures and Pastimes

Dining

In resort restaurants along the Kohala Coast, upscale eateries in Waimea, and elsewhere, cutting-edge chefs cook with the freshest local produce, fish, and herbs, creating intriguing blends of flavors that reflect the island's varied ethnic background. Events such as the Winter Wine Escape at the Westin Mauna Ke'a Beach Hotel and Cuisines of the Sun at Mauna Lani Bay Hotel draw hundreds of guests to starlit open-air dinners celebrating the bounty of the Isle's land and waters.

Fishing

A big lure for visiting fishing enthusiasts is deep-sea trolling for marlin, especially off the shores of the Big Island. Each morning an entire fleet of sportfishing boats leaves Honokōhau Harbor north of Kona in search of the elusive game fish. If the marlin aren't biting, reels are often whining with catches of local 'ahi (yellowfin tuna) and ono (wahoo).

Flora and Fauna

More than 2,000 mi away from any continental land mass, the Hawaiian Islands have developed an ecosystem unique in the world. On the Big Island, 11 distinct climatic zones across 4,038 square mi are home to hundreds of indigenous plants and birds that are today among the most endangered species on earth. Even the warm waters are unlike oceans elsewhere. More than 30% of marine mammals, such as the Hawaiian monk seal and Hawaiian spinner dolphins, are endemic. Humpback whales, which can be seen from late December to early April, and green sea turtles, visible year-round, are Big Island attractions. Fortunately, protection and preservation are now key words in Hawai'i. Hiking and water-activity guides are likely to keep their distance from the more fragile species, but they'll still give you a nature experience you'll never forget.

Golf

Many of the Big Island's courses are emerald oases in the midst of black, barren lava fields. They were designed by world-renowned architects, and on several of the courses—which range from mountainside meccas to green seaside havens—the challenges are as extraordinary as the views. Towering over them is snow-capped, 13,796-ft Mauna Ke'a, home of Poli'ahu, the Hawaiian snow goddess. Two new courses—Hokūli'a, south of Kona, and the unofficially named White Sands, on the Kohala Coast adjacent to the Orchid and Mauna Lani resorts—are projected to open in 2002. At press time, the Hokūli'a project was forced to take a break due to environmental concerns. The course at Hualālai is home to the Senior MasterCard Tournament.

Hiking

The ancient Hawaiians blazed a wide variety of trails across their archipelago, and many of these paths can still be hiked today. Part of the King's Trail at 'Anaeho'omalu, on the Big Island, winds through a field of lava rocks covered with prehistoric carvings meant to communicate stories of births, deaths, marriages, and other family events. In Hawai'i Volcanoes National Park, trails crisscross the volcanic landscape. You can choose to enter a lava tube or circle a kīpuka (verdant island surrounded by lava), home to rare Hawaiian honeycreepers. Puffs of steam warm the lava beneath your feet on the caldera hike. The serenity of remote beaches, such as the black-sand beach at Pololū in North Kohala, is only accessible to hikers. Always exercise caution: hiking in Hawai'i is not without danger, and you should not risk trails, cliffs, or areas that appear no longer in use.

Horseback Riding

With its paniolo heritage, the Big Island is a mecca for equestrians. Riders can gallop through green Upcountry pastures, ride to Kealakekua Bay to see the Captain Cook monument, saunter into Waipi'o Valley for a taste of old Hawai'i, or venture the steep descent into Pololū Valley on mules.

Lodging

Accommodations on the Big Island vary tremendously: from sunny "destination" resorts to condominiums on cool mountaintops to family-style bed-and-breakfasts in green little towns geared more toward fishing and farming than vacationing. This is the beauty of a trip to this island: you can sample that elusive thing called "the real Hawai'i" and also have time to experience the ultimate luxury vacation. But be aware that you'll need a car or a taxi if you choose to stay outside the resort areas. Also, both quality and prices vary enormously away from the resorts.

Scuba Diving

Diving on the Big Island is as good as it gets. Aquarium, in Kealakekua Bay, is a state underwater park with depths from 15 ft to more than 110 ft and is popular with experienced divers. Pine Trees, in North Kona, is an area that includes such sites as Carpenter's House, Golden Arches, and Pyramid Pinnacles—two underwater lava towers with tubes, arches, false Moorish idols, and large schools of butterfly fish. Depths run from 10 ft to 50 ft. Plane Wreck Point, off Keāhole Point, is for expert divers only. Damselfish, fantail, and filefish hover around in the shadows. Red Hill, south of Kona, encompasses six different sites of large caverns and lava tubes. Sea life in the area includes encrusting sponges, octopuses, shells, sleeping reef sharks, and abundant tropical fishes. Depths range from 10 ft to 80 ft.

Shopping

An inordinate number of talented artists seek out the solitude and beauty of the Big Island. Galleries abound in Kailua-Kona, North Kohala, Waimea, Holualoa, Volcano, Hilo, and even in such out-of-the-way burgs as Kukuihaele and Honomū, where you can purchase wonderful original artwork, fine woodwork, and other handmade crafts. Coffee drinkers will also want to bring back some Kona coffee, grown on the western slopes of the Big Island. Kona coffee has a long-standing reputation as a deluxe grind and retails for perhaps twice as much as regular brands. Be aware that blends need only contain 10% Kona coffee to bear the prestigious label. Another local product that makes a great gift are macadamia nuts. You'll find them everywhere and treated in every way—from chocolate-covered to garlic-dusted.

Skiing

Believe it or not, you can ski in Hawai'i—atop the Big Island's Mauna Ke'a volcano. It's for hardy souls only. There are no lifts, and after schussing down, you must herringbone your way back up the slope. The months of December through February are your best bets for skiing Hawaiian style; currently only one guide company is operating.

EXPLORING THE BIG ISLAND

The first secret to enjoying the Big Island to the max is: rent a car. The second: stay more than three days, or return again and again until you have seen all the facets of this fascinating place. With 266 mi of coastline made up of white-coral, black-lava, and a dusting of green-olivine beaches, and with its cliffs of lava and emerald gorges slashing into jutting mountains, the Big Island is so large and so varied that it is eas-

When you pack your MCI Calling Card, it's like packing your loved ones along too.

Your MCI Calling Card is the easy way to stay in touch when you travel. Use it to call to and from over 125 countries. Plus, every time you call, you can earn frequent flier miles. So wherever your travels take you, call home with your MCI Calling Card. It's even easy to get one. Just visit **www.mci.com/worldphone**.

EASY TO CALL WORLDWIDE

1. Just enter the WorldPhone® access number of the country you're calling from.

2. Enter or give the operator your MCI Calling Card number.

3. Enter or give the number you're calling.

Aruba ✢	800-888-8
Bahamas ✢	1-800-888-8000

Barbados ✢	1-800-888-8000
Bermuda ✢	1-800-888-8000
British Virgin Islands ✢	1-800-888-8000
Canada	1-800-888-8000
Mexico	01-800-021-8000
Puerto Rico	1-800-888-8000
United States	1-800-888-8000
U.S. Virgin Islands	1-800-888-8000

✢ Limited availability.

EARN FREQUENT FLIER MILES

SEE THE WORLD IN FULL COLOR

Fodor's Exploring Guides bring all the great sights vividly to life with hundreds of photographs, fascinating historical background, and colorful anecdotes. Detailed maps and practical information keep you headed in the right direction.

Pair a **Fodor's** Exploring Guide with your trusted Gold Guide for a complete planning package.

iest to split your stay and your sightseeing into excursions from Hilo and excursions from Kona when planning a visit.

If your schedule allows a week or 10 days on the island, you might want to spend a night in the historic town of Hilo, followed by two nights at a bed-and-breakfast near the unique Hawai'i Volcanoes National Park, and another night in Waimea before finishing up your vacation at a resort on the sunny side of the island. It's best to follow this in east coast–to–west coast order for accommodations so you won't go home with memories of Hilo's often gray skies. If you're short of time, give Hilo the once-over lightly and then see Hawai'i Volcanoes National Park on your first day, traveling the Hāmākua Coast route and making your new base in Kailua-Kona that night.

The sections below divide the island into an exploration of Hilo; a car trip from Hilo to the volcano area; a tour of the Hāmākua Coast; a walking tour of Kailua-Kona; an outing to South Kona and Ka'u; and a trip around the northwest, including Waimea and the Kohala Mountains. Later in this chapter, there's a section on the beaches you won't want to drive past.

Directions on the island are often referred to as *mauka* (toward the mountains) and *makai* (toward the ocean).

A word of caution: the Big Island is truly big, without amenities for miles on end and largely undeveloped. Each year, unmarked trails and dangerous currents claim the lives of unprepared adventurers. Swim and hike only in areas that are established and designated as safe. Take plenty of drinking water when hiking. And always let someone know where you are going.

Numbers in the text correspond to numbers in the margin and on the Hilo Vicinity, Hawai'i Volcanoes National Park and Puna, Hāmākua Coast, Kailua-Kona, South Kona and Ka'u, and Kohala District maps.

IF YOU HAVE 1 DAY

If you just have one day for the Big Island, fly directly to Hilo and rent a car or take a prearranged tour to see **Hawai'i Volcanoes National Park** ⑲. At the Kīlauea Visitor Center, watch the film on Kīlauea's eruptions, and find out about the possibility of seeing the lava flow by driving down Chain of Craters Road. Ask about area hikes, and then explore Halema'uma'u Crater, Thurston Lava Tube, fern forests, Devastation Trail, and other natural phenomena.

IF YOU HAVE 3 DAYS

With just three days on hand, it might be best to fly into Kailua-Kona and settle in a hotel, a condominium, or one of the elegant resorts on this, the sunniest side of the island.

Start in **Kailua-Kona** ㊳–㊻, learning about Big Island history by taking in Hulihe'e Palace, Moku'aikaua Church, Kamakahonu, and Kuamo'o Battlefield. Then spend the afternoon at a beach, such as 'Anaeho'omalu, Hāpuna, or Kauna'oa on the Kohala Coast. You many want to indulge yourself that first evening with *liliko'i* (passion fruit) margaritas and a leisurely dinner, but be sure to get enough rest so you can take off at high speed in the morning.

On the second day, head for Hawai'i Volcanoes National Park early so you'll have time to sightsee along the way, but keep in mind that just getting there from Kona will take more than two hours. Take Queen Ka'ahumanu Highway, turning inland to **Waimea** ㊾–㊿. Stop at the Gallery of Great Things or Cook's Discoveries to purchase exquisite Hawaiian-made crafts or continue on for a side trip to the **Waipi'o Val-**

ley Overlook ③. Zip through **Hilo** ①–⑯—unless it's a Wednesday or Saturday morning, when the farmers' market adds local color to the town. From Hilo, drive to **Hawai'i Volcanoes National Park** ⑲. Return via the same route, as the drive around South Point takes even longer.

On your third day, consider a morning snorkel cruise to Kealakekua Bay, south of Kailua-Kona. This will also give you an opportunity to see where Captain Cook was killed in 1779. As an alternative, pick up a picnic lunch and drive down to **Ka Lae** ㊾, through **South Kona and Ka'u** ㊼–㊻, to get an impression of what Hawai'i was like before developers and money changed the land. Stretch your legs hiking to windy Green Sand Beach.

If you prefer to sightsee, head north and explore the **Kohala District** ㊽–㊾, which consists of a variety of interesting stops. At Holoholokai Beach Park, at the Mauna Lani Bay Hotel and Bungalows, you'll find the Puakō Petroglyph Park. Drive on to Kawaihae and stop at the **Pu'ukoholā Heiau National Historic Site** ㊽. At Kawaihae, several restaurants and ice-cream shops guarantee a satisfactory lunch break. You'll be able to enjoy the open vistas of ocean and barren land on the way to the two sugar plantation towns, **Hāwī and Kapa'au** ㊺, where several little shops, galleries, and the Bamboo Restaurant are worth investigating. Pause in Kapa'au to snap a photo of the **King Kamehameha Statue** ㊻ and then continue directly to the **Pololū Valley** ㊼ overlook. Here, a steep trail leads to a black-sand beach with a restless surf.

IF YOU HAVE 8 DAYS

With this much time, you might consider splitting your stay into three hotels. Stay the first night in **Hilo** ①–⑯ and spend your first day exploring this old plantation town. Visit the farmers' market, shop on Kamehameha Avenue, wander through **Lyman Mission House and Museum** ⑦, and drive up to **Rainbow Falls** ⑮ and **Pe'epe'e Falls** ⑯, also known as Boiling Pots. Plant lovers will want to visit either the **Hawai'i Tropical Botanical Garden** ㉘ for its misty, rain-forest appeal or the **Nani Mau Gardens**, with its more manicured patches of tropical flowers.

Rise early on the morning of the second day to check out the **Suisan Fish Market** ④. Have breakfast and pack for your move to new accommodations around the volcano, but on the way spend much of your day on a leisurely side trip to **Pāhoa** ㉖ and Puna. Splurge on dinner at Kīlauea Lodge. Reserve your third day for a thorough exploration of **Hawai'i Volcanoes National Park** ⑲, including the drive down Chain of Craters Road at dusk to see the lava flow.

On the fourth day, move on to a hotel on the Big Island's southwestern shore. Drive back through Hilo to enjoy sightseeing—**'Akaka Falls State Park** ㉚, **Honoka'a** ㊱, **Waipi'o Valley Overlook** ㊲—along the Hāmākua Coast. Stop for lunch in the town of Parker Ranch in Upcountry **Waimea** ㊾–㊿. Make day five primarily a beach day, adding only a snorkel cruise or a little run into **Kailua-Kona** ㊳–㊽ for lunch, a visit to **Hulihe'e Palace** ㊶, and some souvenir shopping. Save the morning of the sixth day to discover North Kohala. If you're a hiker, biker, or horseback rider, you might want to book an activity that takes place in this area. For more sedate types, a tour into Waipi'o Valley is a memorable experience. After your morning adventure, the galleries and lunch spots in the little towns of **Hāwī and Kapa'au** ㊺ are alluring, and on the return drive to your hotel, history comes alive at **Mo'okini Heiau** ㊽, **Lapakahi State Historical Park** ㊾, and the **Pu'ukoholā Heiau National Historic Site** ㊽.

On the seventh day, take the high road through coffee country and head south from Kailua-Kona via the artists' colony of Hōlualoa to **Kainaliu** ㊼.

Visit the **Greenwell Site** ㊽, the headquarters and museum of the Kona Historical Society, then drive down to **Kealakekua Bay** ㊾ to contemplate the dramatic contrast between the ancient religious temple, known as **Hikiau Heiau** ㊿, and **Captain Cook Monument** �51. Even if you skip everything else, be sure to explore **Puʻuhonua O Hōnaunau** �52, and while you're in the area, check out the **St. Benedict's Painted Church** �53. Drive through the district of Kaʻu through awesome stretches of lava fields and coffee orchards. In **Ka Lae** �55, the most southern point of the United States, you'll feel the eerie isolation the first Hawaiian explorers must have experienced when they moored at this remote outpost.

The last day of your trip, the departure day, should be one of rest and relaxation—a leisurely breakfast, a brief trip to the beach, golf, or last-minute shopping.

When to Tour the Big Island

Touring the Big Island is appealing at any time of year. There are seldom traffic jams, and the weather remains basically stable year-round. It's a rare day when Kailua-Kona and the Kohala Coast are not sunny and warm; however, deluges can occur in January and February. It's difficult to predict weather in Hilo. If you are traveling in winter, you are apt to get wet on the Hāmākua side. The volcano area is always cooler because of the higher elevation, so bring a sweater or light jacket.

Hilo

Hilo is a town of both modern and rustic buildings stretching from the banks of the Wailuku River to Hilo Bay, where a few hotels rim stately Banyan Drive. Nearby, the 31-acre Liliʻuokalani Gardens, a Japanese-style park with arched bridges and waterways, was established as a safety zone after a devastating tidal wave swept away businesses and homes on May 22, 1960, killing 60 people. Residents don't worry much about a tidal wave recurring, but they haven't built anything except hotels, the park, and a golf course in that area, either.

Though the center of government and commerce for the island, Hilo is primarily a residential town. Mansions with perfectly kept yards of lush tropical foliage surround older wooden houses with rusty corrugated roofs. It's a friendly community, populated primarily by descendants of the contract laborers—Japanese, Chinese, Filipino, Puerto Rican, and Portuguese—brought in to work the sugarcane fields during the 1800s. Bring your umbrella: the rainfall averages 139 inches per year!

When the sun shines and the snow glistens on Mauna Keʻa, 25 mi in the distance, Hilo sparkles. In the rain the town takes on the look of an impressionist painting—greenery muted alongside weather-worn brown, red, and blue buildings. Several of these buildings have been spruced up to revitalize the downtown area. Often the rain blows away by noon and a colorful arch appears in the sky. One of Hilo's nicknames is the City of Rainbows.

The whole town has fewer than 1,000 hotel rooms, most of them strung along Banyan Drive. By contrast, the eight Kohala Coast resorts alone have more than 3,704 rooms combined. Nonetheless, Hilo, with a population of almost 50,000 in the entire district, is the fourth-largest city in the state and home to a branch of the University of Hawaiʻi.

A Good Drive

Begin this excursion driving southwest from the cluster of hotels along **Banyan Drive** ①, which loops around a peninsula jutting into Hilo Bay.

Lili'uokalani Gardens ②, on the right, has Japanese gardens and an arched footbridge to **Coconut Island** ③. Early risers who want to see a major local-style fish auction should head for **Suisan Fish Market** ④, at the western end of Banyan Drive, at about 7 AM. Turn right onto Kamehameha Avenue; in the park on your left is **Wailoa Center** ⑤, where you can enjoy a current art show or view the poignant history of the 1960 tsunami.

Drive across town to the Hilo Public Library on Waiānuenue Avenue, leave your car, and explore downtown Hilo on foot. In front of the library are the ponderous **Naha and Pinao stones** ⑥, which legend says King Kamehameha I was able to lift as a teenager, thus foretelling that someday he would be a powerful king. Stroll southeast along Kapi'olani Street and then turn right on Haili Street to visit the historic **Lyman Mission House and Museum** ⑦. The restored house was built in 1839 by missionaries who came from Boston to run a school for boys. Back on Haili Street, you'll come across **Haili Church** ⑧, where Protestant sermons and hymns are rendered in both Hawaiian and English. Farther down Haili Street, stop at the **Big Island Visitors Bureau** ⑨ for maps and brochures.

If you're in the mood for a quick pick-me-up, return northwest along **Keawe Street** ⑩, inspecting the plantation-style architecture along the way. By the time you reach Kalākaua Street, the benches in **Kalākaua Park** ⑪ will seem a perfect respite. A statue in the park honors the popular 19th-century king—known as the Merrie Monarch—who so much reinspired Hawaiian cultural values.

Continue makai on Kalākaua Street to visit the **Pacific Tsunami Museum** ⑫ in the former First Hawaiian Bank Building. After heading three blocks east on Kamehameha Avenue, you'll come across the **New S. Hata Building** ⑬, which houses interesting shops and restaurants; just next door, on either side of Mamo Street, the **Hilo Farmers' Market** ⑭ adds local color to the otherwise businesslike streets every Wednesday and Saturday.

You'll need your car for two popular sights a couple of miles outside of town. Drive southwest along Waiānuenue Avenue about a mile, angling to the right when the road forks, to reach **Rainbow Falls** ⑮. After a Hilo downpour, the waterfall thunders into Wailuku River gorge. Two miles or so farther up the road, also on the right, is a green sign for **Pe'epe'e Falls** ⑯, also known as Boiling Pots because of the turbulent action of the water in potholes at the base of the falls.

TIMING

Rain is inevitable in Hilo. You'll face less of a chance of getting wet, however, if you avoid the months of January, February, and March. Allow a full day to explore Hilo if you try to take in all the sights, less if you skip the Lyman Mission House and Museum and have little interest in shopping. Remember that morning hours are generally cooler for walking the streets than late afternoon, when the humidity can soar. It's definitely worth timing a visit for a Wednesday or Saturday, when the farmers' market is in full swing.

Sights to See

❶ **Banyan Drive.** The more than 50 leafy banyan trees with aerial roots dangling from the limbs were planted along here in the '30s by visiting celebrities; you'll find such names as Amelia Earhart and Franklin Delano Roosevelt on plaques on the trees. ⊠ *Begin at Hawai'i Naniloa Resort, 93 Banyan Dr..*

❾ **Big Island Visitors Bureau.** Marked by a red-and-white Hawaiian-warrior sign, the bureau is worth a visit, especially if you are just be-

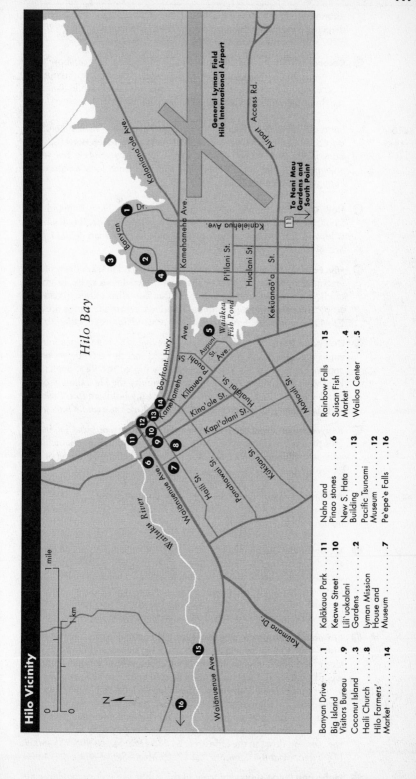

ginning your stay on the Big Island. Brochures, maps, and advice are dispensed with friendly aloha spirit. ⊠ *250 Keawe St.*, ☎ *808/961– 5797*, WEB *www.bigisland.org.* ⊙ *Weekdays 8–4:30.*

❸ Coconut Island. In ancient times a place of healing, just offshore from Lili'uokalani Gardens and across a footbridge, this small (approximately 1 acre) island draws children to play in the tidal pools while fisherfolk try their luck. ⊠ *Lili'uokalani Gardens, Banyan Dr.*

NEED A BREAK?   For a quick cup of coffee or an early and affordable breakfast before starting your day, try Queen's Court at the **Hilo Hawaiian Hotel** (⊠ 71 Banyan Dr., ☎ 808/935–9361). Take in good views of Hilo Bay while enjoying the buffet or local specialties such as French Toast made with Portuguese sweetbread.

❽ Haili Church. Originally constructed in 1859 by New England missionaries, this church was rebuilt in 1979 following a fire. Haili Church is known for its choir, which sings hymns in Hawaiian. ⊠ *211 Haili St.*, ☎ *808/935–4847.*

⑭ Hilo Farmers' Market. An abundant and colorful market draws farmers and shoppers from all over the island. Two days a week, bright orchids, anthuriums, and birds of paradise, as well as exotic vegetables, tropical fruits, and an array of baked goods, create a feast for the eyes. ⊠ *Mamo and Kamehameha Sts.* ⊙ *Wed. and Sat. 6:30 AM–2:30 PM.*

⑪ Kalākaua Park. King Kalākaua, who revived the hula dance and became the inspiration for Hilo's Merrie Monarch Festival, chose this spot to create a park. A bronze statue, sculpted in 1988, depicts the king with a taro leaf in his left hand to signify the Hawaiian peoples' bond with the land. In his right hand the king holds an *ipu,* a symbol of Hawaiian culture, chants, and hula. ⊠ *Kalākaua and Kino'ole Sts.*

⑩ Keawe Street. Buildings here have been restored to original 1920s and '30s plantation styles. While most shopping is along Kamehameha Avenue, the ambience on Keawe Street offers a nostalgic sampling of Hilo as it might have been 80 years ago.

NEED A BREAK?   A strong espresso or a creamy latte at **Bear's Coffee Shop** (⊠ 106 Keawe St., ☎ 808/935–0708) is sure to revive the tired shopper. It's a hangout for local artists as well.

❷ Lili'uokalani Gardens. This 30-acre park on either side of Banyan Drive was designed to honor Hawai'i's first Japanese immigrants. The area used to be home to business buildings until a tsunami in 1960 swept them away, taking the lives of 60 people in the process. Fish-stocked streams and half-moon bridges, pagodas, and a ceremonial teahouse make this a favorite Sunday destination for residents.

★ **❼ Lyman Mission House and Museum.** Of particular interest to history buffs, Lyman House was built in 1839 by David and Sarah Lyman, Congregationalist missionaries. It's the oldest frame building on the island. In the adjacent museum, dedicated in 1973, the Earth Heritage Gallery includes a realistic magma chamber and displays the Earth's formation and the arrival of life, with a section on Hawaiian flora and fauna. You can view unique artifacts of Hawaiian and other major ethnic groups in the Island Heritage Gallery. The gift shop sells a map of the tsunami flows in the Hilo area. ⊠ *276 Haili St.*, ☎ *808/935–5021*, WEB *www.lymanmuseum.org.* 🎟 *$7.* ⊙ *Mon.–Sat. 9–4:30.*

❻ Naha and Pinao stones. In front of the public library are two large oblong stones, the legendary Naha and Pinao stones. The Pinao stone is

HULA, THE DANCE OF HAWAI'I

LEGENDS IMMORTALIZE LAKA as the goddess of hula, portraying her as a gentle deity who journeyed from island to island, sharing the dance with all who were willing to learn. Laka's graceful movements, spiritual and layered with meaning, brought to life the history, the traditions, and the genealogy of the islanders. Ultimately taught by parents to children and by *kumu* (teachers) to students, the hula preserved without a written language the culture of these ancient peoples.

Some legends trace the origins of hula to Moloka'i, where a family named La'ila'i was said to have established the dance at Ka'ana. Eventually the youngest sister of the fifth generation of La'ila'i was given the name Laka, and she carried the dance to all the Islands in the Hawaiian chain.

Another legend credits Hi'iaka, the volcano goddess Pele's youngest sister, as having danced the first hula in the hala groves of Puna on the Big Island. Hi'iaka and possibly even Pele were thought to have learned the dance from Hōpoe, a mortal and a poet also credited as the originator of the dance.

In any case, hula thrived until the arrival of puritanical New England missionaries, who with the support of Queen Ka'ahumanu, an early Christian convert, attempted to ban the dance as an immoral activity throughout the 19th century.

Though hula may not have been publicly performed, it remained a spiritual and poetic art form, as well as a lively celebration of life presented during special celebrations in many Hawaiian homes. David Kalākaua, the popular "Merrie Monarch" who was king from 1874 to 1891, revived the hula. Dancers were called to perform at official functions. In 1906, Nathaniel Emerson wrote about hula, "Its view of life was idyllic, and it gave itself to the celebration of those mythical times when gods and goddesses moved on earth as men and women, and when men and women were as gods."

Gradually, ancient hula, called *kahiko*, was replaced with a lively, updated form of dance called 'auana (modern). Modern costumes of fresh ti-leaf or raffia skirts replaced the voluminous *pa'u* skirts made of *kapa* (cloth made of beaten bark), and the music became more melodic, as opposed to earlier chanted routines accompanied by *pahu* (drums), 'ili 'ili (rocks used as castanets), and other percussion instruments. Such tunes as "Lovely Hula Hands," "Little Grass Shack," and the "Hawaiian Wedding Song" are considered hula 'auana. Dancers might wear graceful *holomu'u* with short trains, or ti-leaf skirts with coconut bra tops.

In 1963 the Merrie Monarch Festival was established in Hilo on the Big Island and has since become the most prestigious hula competition in the state. It's staged annually the weekend after Easter, and contestants of various *halau* (hula schools) from Hawai'i and the mainland compete in the categories of Miss Aloha Hula, hula kahiko (ancient), and hula 'auana (modern). For more information, contact the **Merrie Monarch Hula Festival** (E Hawai'i Naniloa Resort, 93 Banyan Dr., Hilo 96720, P 808/935–9168).

Moloka'i stages its own Ka Hula Piko festival every May to celebrate the birth of hula. Singers, musicians, and dancers perform in a shaded glen at Papohaku Beach State Park, and nearby, islanders sell food and Hawaiian crafts. During the week preceding the festival, John Kaimikaua, the founder, and his halau present hula demonstrations, lectures, and storytelling at various Moloka'i sites.

For more information, contact the **Moloka'i Visitors Association** (⊠ Box 960, Kaunakakai 96748, ☎ 808/553–3876 or 800/800–6367).

purportedly an entrance pillar of an ancient temple built near the Wailuku River. Kamehameha I is said to have moved the 5,000-pound Naha stone when he was still in his teens. Legend decreed that he who did so would become king of all the islands. ⊠ *300 Waiānuenue Ave.*

OFF THE BEATEN PATH

NANI MAU GARDENS – About 4 mi from the center of Hilo on Highway 11, a tropical wonderland awaits. Nani Mau Gardens has several varieties of fruit trees and hundreds of varieties of ginger, orchids, anthuriums, and other tropical plants. The 20 acres include a Hawaiian cultural garden, a botanical museum, waterways, and waterfalls, as well as palm and orchid gardens. A guided tour by tram is available. The light and airy restaurant is open daily for lunch. ⊠ *421 Makalika St.,* ☎ *808/959–3500,* WEB *www.nanimau.com.* ⊡ *$10, guided tour via tram $7.* ⊙ *Daily 8:30–5.*

⓭ New S. Hata Building. Erected as a general store in 1912 by Sadanosuke Hata and his family, this historic structure now houses shops, restaurants, a bakery, and offices. During World War II the Hatas were interned and the building confiscated by the U.S. government. When the war was over, a daughter repurchased it for $100,000. A beautiful example of renaissance-revival architecture, it won an award from the state for the authenticity of its restoration. ⊠ *308 Kamehameha Ave., at Mamo St.*

NEED A BREAK?

Wander inside the New S. Hata Building and pause to enjoy a grilled Italian-style fresh-fish sandwich. Not hungry? Treat yourself to a superb espresso drink instead. Tables at **Canoes Café** (⊠ 308 Kamehameha Ave., ☎ 808/935–4070) face the large windows of the old O'Keefe bakery, which provides its famous focaccia and other breads for lunch at the café.

⓬ Pacific Tsunami Museum. A memorial to all who lost their lives in the tragedies that have struck this side of the Island, this small museum offers a poignant history of tsunamis. In a 1931 C. W. Dickey–designed building, the museum has an interactive computer center; a science room; a theater; a replica of Old Hilo Town, including its old train; a *keiki* (children's) corner; and a knowledgeable, friendly staff. In the background, a striking quilt tells a silent story. ⊠ *130 Kamehameha Ave.,* ☎ *808/935–0926,* WEB *www.tsunami.org.* ⊡ *$5.* ⊙ *Mon.–Sat. 10–4.*

⓰ Pe'epe'e Falls. The falls drop in four streams of water into a series of circular pools, and the resultant turbulent action—best seen after a good rain when the water is high—has earned them the name Boiling Pots. ⊠ *3 mi west of Hilo on Waiānuenue Ave.; keep to the right when road splits and look for a green sign.*

⓯ Rainbow Falls. After a Hilo rain, these falls thunder into Wailuku River gorge. If the sun peeks out in the morning hours, rainbows form above the mist. This quiet area surrounded by tropical vegetation is great for photos. ⊠ *Take Waiānuenue Ave. west of town 1 mi; when road forks, stay on right of Waiānuenue Ave.; look for Hawaiian-warrior sign.*

❹ Suisan Fish Market. The liveliest action in town takes place at the market's fish auction, mornings from about 7, Monday through Saturday. This is the place for local sights and sounds; it's a great place to "talk story" (chat) and listen to the almost unintelligible bidding that takes place in pidgin English. ⊠ *85 Lihiwai St. (Banyan Dr. turns left onto Lihiwai St.),* ☎ *808/935–8051.*

❺ Wailoa Center. The Wailoa Center, which is adjacent to Wailoa State Park, features changing exhibits by local artists. There's also a photographic exhibit of the 1946 and 1960 tidal waves. Just in front of the center is a 12-ft-high bronze statue of King Kamehameha I, made in Italy in the late 1980s. Check out his gold Roman sandals. ⊠ *Pi'opi'o St.,* ☎ *808/933–0416.* ☉ *Mon.–Tues. and Thurs.–Fri. 8:30– 4:30, Wed. noon–4:30.*

Hawai'i Volcanoes National Park and Puna

The most popular attraction on the Big Island, Hawai'i Volcanoes National Park is home to active Kīlauea Volcano. Even when there is no fiery display or lava flowing, you'll have plenty to see in the park, which includes the summit caldera and gently sloping northeast flank of 13,677-ft Mauna Loa volcano. With more than 150 mi of trails passing tree ferns and other tropical plants, lava tubes, cinder cones, odd mineral formations, steam vents, and the vast barren craters along Chain of Craters Road, this is the ultimate ecotour. Don't forget to take a sweater (or a jacket in winter), as temperatures can get nippy at the park's 4,000-ft elevation. Also take a flashlight if you plan to visit the shoreline lava flow around sunset.

A Good Drive

In Hilo take Highway 11, Kanoelehua Avenue, which takes you directly to the park, 30 mi to the southeast. Along the way, distinctive red-and-white Hawaiian-warrior markers designate visitor attractions. On the right of the road you'll pass **Pana'ewa Rain Forest Zoo** ⑰. Just five minutes up Stainback Highway, it's a great stop for kids—home to lively monkeys and solemn nēnē (the state bird).

About 5 mi south of Hilo on the left of Highway 11 is the marker for **Mauna Loa Macadamia Factory** ⑱. The entry road wanders through macadamia trees to a macadamia-nut processing plant with large viewing windows, a large visitor center, and a gift shop.

Follow Highway 11 through the towns of Mountain View and Glenwood to the entrance sign of **Hawai'i Volcanoes National Park** ⑲. The 359-square-mi park, established in 1916, is one of the world's most enigmatic and impressive testaments to nature's powerful beauty. Stop first at the **Kīlauea Visitor Center** to find the latest information on volcanic activity. From here, walk over to **Volcano Art Center** ⑳ to see the work of Big Island artists. Across the street from the art center is **Volcano House** ㉑, a charming lodge dating from 1941 with a huge stone fireplace. Its dining room windows edge Kīlauea and, in the center of the caldera, you'll see the steaming fire pit, called Halema'uma'u Crater. Currently the volcano is not erupting from here but from a rift zone on the flanks of Kīlauea.

You can drive the crater's circumference via the 11 mi of Crater Rim Drive. Scenic stops include the yellow, acrid-smelling sulfur banks; steam vents; and the park's Thomas A. Jaggar Museum, on the edge of Kīlauea Caldera. You'll find several easy walks along the way: Halema'uma'u Overlook (a 10-minute walk); Devastation Trail (30 minutes), and Thurston Lava Tube (20 minutes).

If you have time, drive from the center of the park down **Chain of Craters Road** ㉒—aptly named after the huge depressions. A sign midway down on the left marks a trail across the lava to **Pu'u Loa Petroglyphs** ㉓, a field of lava etchings left by early Hawaiians. It's about a 25-minute walk.

Approximately 28 mi from Kīlauea Visitor Center, on the makai side, the Waha'ula Visitor Center and the 13th-century sacrificial Waha'ula Heiau were demolished by lava in 1989 and 1997 respectively. Just be-

Hawai'i Volcanoes National Park and Puna

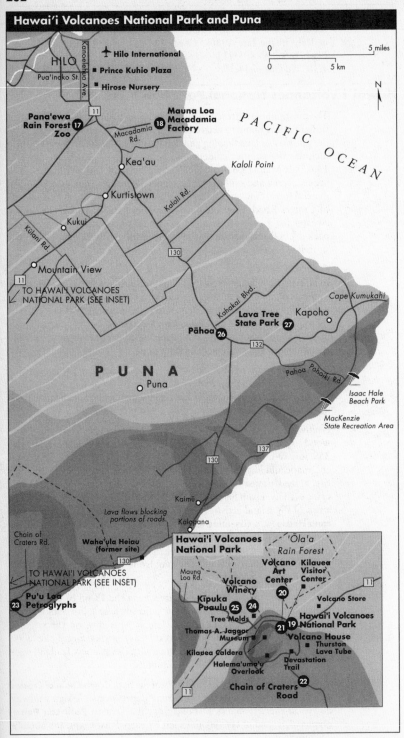

HILO

✈ Hilo International
■ Prince Kuhio Plaza
■ Hirose Nursery

Pua'inako St.

Kanoelehua Ave.

Pana'ewa Rain Forest Zoo **17**

Mauna Loa Macadamia Factory **18**

Macadamia Rd.

Kea'au

Kaloli Point

PACIFIC OCEAN

Kurtistown

Kaloli Rd.

Kukui

Kūlani Rd.

Mountain View

TO HAWAII VOLCANOES NATIONAL PARK (SEE INSET)

Cape Kumukahi

Kahakai Blvd.

Lava Tree State Park **27**

Kapoho

Pāhoa **26**

132

PUNA

Puna

Pahoa Pohoiki Rd.

Isaac Hale Beach Park

MacKenzie State Recreation Area

137

130

Kaimū

Kalapana

Lava flows blocking portions of roads.

Chain of Craters Rd.

Waha'ula Heiau (former site)

130

TO HAWAII VOLCANOES NATIONAL PARK (SEE INSET)

Pu'u Loa Petroglyphs **23**

Hawai'i Volcanoes National Park

'Ōla'a Rain Forest

Mauna Loa Rd.

Volcano Art Center

Kilauea Visitor Center

11

Volcano Winery

Volcano Store

Kīpuka Puaulu **25**

24

Hawai'i Volcanoes National Park

Tree Molds

21 **19**

Thomas A. Jaggar Museum

Volcano House

Thurston Lava Tube

Kilauea Caldera

Devastation Trail

Halema'uma'u Overlook

Chain of Craters Road **22**

11

0   5 miles

0   5 km

N

yond the area, lava has overflowed the road repeatedly since 1984. It's now closed. At road's end you may be able to walk to where lava spills intermittently into the ocean. Ask at the center before setting out. Bring drinking water and wear hiking boots. It's a long, hot trek, often over very difficult terrain, and there are no facilities.

Return via Chain of Craters Road to exit the park; turning left onto Highway 11, take the first cross road to the right toward the Volcano Golf & Country Club. Less than a mile beyond you'll find **Volcano Winery** ㉔, with a gift shop and tasting room.

Back on Highway 11 drive in a southwesterly direction to the next right and turn onto Mauna Loa Road. A sign marks Tree Molds. Each chimneylike formation was created when molten lava hardened around a tree, burning it away in the process. At the end of the road you can take a self-guided mile-long walk around **Kīpuka Puaulu** ㉕, also known as Bird Park and famous for its many native species.

Head back toward Hilo via the Old Volcano Highway, which runs parallel to Highway 11. Pause at Volcano Store for excellent bargains in cut flowers. On the road again, notice the yellow and white ginger (the aromatic flower prized for lei) and tiny, purple wild orchids that grow in profusion. Along Highway 11, several nurseries proudly sell and display bright red, pink, white, and varicolored anthuriums. The round wooden water tanks beside weathered houses indicate this area's catchment system; the city supplies water only closer to Kurtistown.

If you have extra time, take a side trip to Puna, where farmers grow everything from flowers to bananas, papayas, and pakalōlō. Tidal pools and natural springs dot this area, and there are plenty of lovely places to stop, but be aware that Puna isn't the friendliest district on the island and respect the privacy of its residents. Turn right onto Highway 130 at Kea'au and drive 11 mi to **Pāhoa** ㉖. With its wooden boardwalks, rickety old buildings, and an assortment of '60s-era characters, this tired town is reminiscent of the Wild West.

From Pāhoa, angle left onto Highway 132 and continue to **Lava Tree State Park** ㉗, where some of the cylindrical black tree molds rise 12 ft in the cool air—the only reminder of an 'ōhi'a forest taken by Mauna Loa's eruption in 1790. Eventually you'll reach the coast beyond Kapoho, a now nonexistent town where two roads cross. Turn right and follow Highway 137, along the coast, taking a break at either Isaac Hale Beach Park or MacKenzie State Recreation Area. Return to Highway 130 for the hour drive back to Hilo.

TIMING

Exploring Hawai'i Volcanoes National Park in depth could take a lifetime. Winter temperatures can dip below the cotton-shirt comfort level and misty weather prevails over clear skies and balmy afternoons, but the park is worth visiting at any time and day of the year. Open daily, this is a national park, ideal for families and therefore busier during the summer months, holidays, and weekends. Count on spending at least three-quarters of a day at the park, and keep in mind that a round trip from Kona or the resorts takes four to six hours. You may want to plan an overnight stay at one of the charming B&Bs tucked into the fern forest, particularly if you want to visit Puna as well.

It'll take you about 45 minutes to drive the distance from Hilo to the park. Allow two hours for the trip up and back down the 24 mi of the Chain of Craters Road to the Kalapana coastal district of the park, where the flowing lava hits the ocean in giant billowing clouds of steam. Add an hour or so to hike to the edge of the flow and back.

Sights to See

㉒ **Chain of Craters Road.** No food, water, or gasoline is available along this road, which descends 3,700 ft in 24 mi to the Kalapana Coast. Be sure to stock up before you head out. At road's end, you may be able to walk to where the lava flows into the ocean. ⊠ *Begins in Hawai'i Volcanoes National Park.*

★ **⑲** **Hawai'i Volcanoes National Park.** The 359-square-mi park, established in 1916, provides an unmatched volcanic experience of Earth in the making. The current eruption has been going since January 3, 1993, primarily from a vent called Pu'u O'o. It's steady and slow, appearing and disappearing from view. For updates on the flow, contact the **Kīlauea Visitor Center** (☎ 808/985–6000, WEB www.nps.gov; ☉ 7:45–5), which lies just beyond the park's entry booth. You can learn here about park wildlife and vegetation as well. If you can't see a real eruption, don't miss the hourly movie shown from 9 to 4. Hikers can obtain information about trails, ranger-escorted scenic walks, and camping permits at the center.

☾ Within the park, Halema'uma'u Crater is the steaming pit within gaping **Kīlauea Caldera.** You can hike around or into the crater. You can also drive around the crater's 11-mi circumference to **Halema'uma'u Overlook** for another view of the crater. Children may enjoy hands-on fun at the free **Thomas A. Jaggar Museum** (⊠ Crater Rim Dr., ☎ 808/985–6049; ☉ daily 8:30–5) at the edge of Kīlauea Caldera. Seismographs that measure the earth's movement will also record a child's footfall. And fascinating filmstrips document current and previous eruptions.

Nearby **Devastation Trail** was created after a 1959 eruption, when fiery lava from the smaller, adjacent **Kīlauea Iki Crater** burned the surrounding 'ōhi'a forest. The 30-minute walk on a paved path across the cinder outfall off **Crater Rim Drive** is self-guided. If you're in the park for a full day or more, you could venture on an exhilarating hike into Kīlauea Iki (*iki* means little). It takes less than a half day, but get information and maps first at the Kīlauea Visitor Center. On the 4-mi loop you'll descend 400 ft through rain forest and cross the crater floor. A 20-minute walk will take you 450 ft into **Thurston Lava Tube**, a natural tunnel about 10 ft high that formed when the cooling top and sides of a lava flow hardened and the lava inside drained away.

Yellow, acrid-smelling sulfur banks and gaping vents emitting warm steam are found throughout the cool environs of the park. Pregnant women and anyone with heart or respiratory problems should avoid both the sulfur banks and the fumes. The Park and Chain of Craters Road are open 24 hours a day, but you must obtain a backcountry hiker's permit to remain in the park area overnight. ⊠ *Hawai'i Volcanoes National Park, Highway Belt Rd. (Hwy. 11),* ☎ *808/985–6000,* WEB *www.nps.gov.* ☞ *$10 per car for 7 days.*

☾ **㉕** **Kīpuka Puaulu.** A *kīpuka* is a forested island surrounded by a sea of lava. This unique and diverse, 100-acre mesic forest is also known as Bird Park, although its real beauty lies in its rare flora. Native birds, such as the 'apapane and the 'elepaio, call from their hiding places in the thick canopy. A written guide is available at the Kīlauea Visitor Center in Hawai'i Volcanoes National Park. ⊠ *Hawai'i Volcanoes National Park, Mauna Loa Rd.*

㉗ **Lava Tree State Park.** Tree molds that rise like blackened smokestacks formed here in 1790 when a lava flow swept through the 'ōhi'a forest. Some reach as high as 12 ft. ⊠ *Hwy. 132, Puna District,* ☎ *808/974–6200.* ☞ *Free.* ☉ *Daily 30 min before sunrise–30 min after sunset.*

⑱ **Mauna Loa Macadamia Factory.** Acres of macadamia trees lead to a processing plant with viewing windows. A videotape depicts the harvesting and preparation of the nuts, and there are free samples in the roomy visitor center. Children can run off their energy on the nature trail. Feel free to bring your own picnic lunch. ⊠ *Macadamia Rd. on Hwy. 11, 5 mi south of Hilo,* ☎ *808/966–8618,* WEB *www. maunaloa.com.* ◪ *Self-guided tour free.* ◷ *Daily 8:30–5.*

㉖ **Pāhoa.** This little town has wooden boardwalks and rickety buildings reminiscent of the Wild West. The few restaurants, antiques shops, secondhand stores, tie-dye clothing boutiques, and art galleries in quaint old buildings are fun to wander through. ⊠ *Turn southeast onto Hwy. 130 at Kea'au, drive 11 mi to right turn marked Pāhoa.*

♨ ⑰ **Pana'ewa Rain Forest Zoo.** Children enjoy the monkeys and tigers in this quiet, often wet, low-key zoo, which also hosts native Hawaiian species such as the state bird—the nēnē. Trails have been paved, but take an umbrella for protection from the frequent showers. ⊠ *Stainback Hwy. off Hwy. 11,* ☎ *808/959–7224.* ◪ *Free.* ◷ *Daily 9–4.*

㉓ **Pu'u Loa Petroglyphs.** On Chain of Craters Road, just past Mile Marker 16, a sign on the left marks Pu'u Loa Petroglyphs. It's a 25-minute walk across the lava to where etchings of people, boats, and animals made by early Hawaiians are spread over a vast area of black lava. The round depressions are thought to be *piko* holes, where umbilical cords of newborns were buried. ⊠ *Hawai'i Volcanoes National Park, Chain of Craters Rd.*

⑳ **Volcano Art Center.** A celebrated art center displays the work of Big Island photographers, artists, and craftspeople. Don't miss the block prints and new color prints depicting Hawaiian legends by Dietrich Varez. The building was originally constructed to be the Volcano House in 1877, replacing a thatched-roof hut built in 1846. ⊠ *Hawai'i Volcanoes National Park, Crater Rim Dr.,* ☎ *808/967–7565.* ◷ *Daily 9–5.*

㉑ **Volcano House.** This charming old lodge, with its huge stone fireplace, 42 rooms for rent, the Ka 'Ōhelo Dining Room, and a snack bar dates from 1941. The windows in the dining room overlook Kīlauea and, in the center of the caldera, you'll see Halema'uma'u Crater. The dining room is busy with tour groups for the buffet lunch, but dinner can be a quieter experience. ⊠ *Hawai'i Volcanoes National Park, Crater Rim Dr.,* ☎ *808/967–7321.*

NEED A BREAK?
Stop by for coffee or a quick bite at the **Steam Vent Café** (⊠ Behind Volcano Store in Volcano Village, ☎ 808/985–8744). If you're looking for something substantial and need Internet access, head to the **Lava Rock Café** (⊠ Old Volcano Hwy., behind Kīlauea General Store, ☎ 808/967–8526), which serves breakfast and lunch daily and dinner Tuesday through Saturday in a breezy, pinewood-lattice setting. You'll find a variety of choices, from chicken salad to New York steak, cappuccino to wine.

㉔ **Volcano Winery.** You'll find a gift shop and tasting room at this unusual winery that creates pleasant white table wines made from symphony grapes grown nearby. Also on offer are honey wines, a red Pele Delight, Guava or Passion Chablis, and Volcano Blush. Experiments with traditional varietals such as pinot noir are under way. ⊠ *35 Pi'imauna Dr., Volcano,* ☎ *808/967–7479,* WEB *www.volcanowinery.com.* ◷ *Daily 10–5:30.*

NEED A BREAK?
Coffee and a steaming bowl of saimin at **Volcano Golf & Country Club Restaurant** (⊠ Volcano Golf & Country Club, 35 Pi'imauna Dr., Vol-

cano, ☎ 808/967–8228) can be a soul-saving meal on a cool, wet day. The restaurant, which serves breakfast and lunch, has big plate-glass windows that afford views of mist-shrouded golf greens, rare golden-blossom `ohi`a trees, and an occasional nēnē goose.

Hāmākua Coast

The Hilo–Hāmākua Heritage Coast leads past green cliffs and gorges, jungle vegetation, open emerald fields, and stunning ocean scenery along Highway 19, which runs north-northwest from Hilo. The 47-mi drive winds through little plantation towns, Pāpa`ikou, Honomū, Laupāhoe-hoe, and Honoka`a, to the end of the road at the Waipi`o Valley Over-look. The lush valley floor has maintained the ways of old Hawai`i, with taro patches, wild horses, and isolated little houses that can be reached only by hiking or by taking four-wheel-drive vehicles. You may wish to continue on to Kailua-Kona; it is a total of 95 mi via this shorter of the two coastal routes from Hilo.

A Good Drive

Seven miles north of Hilo, turn right off Highway 19 onto a 4-mi scenic drive to reach **Hawai`i Tropical Botanical Garden** ㉘, a 17-acre rain for-est preserve with a profusion of flowers beside Onomea Bay. After the scenic drive rejoins Highway 19, turn left toward **Honomū** ㉙ to travel 4 mi inland to `**Akaka Falls State Park** ㉚. An interesting wayside stop along the way, Honomū has wooden buildings that reflect a plantation past replaced by tourism-geared shops and restaurants. Head north on Highway 19 and turn left to visit the 300 acres of the still-growing **World Botanical Gardens** ㉛, with a 10-acre arboretum and a labyrinth of shrubs that your kids will love. From here you'll see stunning views of triple-tiered Umauma Falls, one of the prettiest waterfalls on the Isle.

As you continue north on Highway 19, enjoy the ride through sleepy little villages with music in their names: Honohina, Ni`nole, Pāpa`aloa. If you say every letter and pronounce *i* as "ee" and *e* as in "hey," you'll come close to the correct pronunciation. In 1946 a 56-ft tidal wave, which caused 159 deaths, crashed into this scenic coastline and washed out one of the most expensive railways ever built. **Kolekole Beach Park** ㉜, off Highway 19, has changing rooms and picnic facilities. The **Laupāhoe-hoe Train Museum** ㉝ takes you back to the time when sugar reigned along the Hāmākua Coast.

Just beyond the museum is **Laupāhoehoe Point Park** ㉞, which is good for fishing but not swimming. Farther inland, **Kalōpā State Park** ㉟ is good for hiking.

In 1995 the Honoka`a Sugar Company was the last to discontinue op-erations on this coast. Farmers are now experimenting with diversi-fied agriculture, while macadamia orchards thrive closer to **Honoka`a** ㊱, hailed as the macadamia capital of the world. Secondhand and antiques stores, with dusty dishes, fabrics, and crafts, line Honoka`a's main street.

Just before the road (Route 240) ends, 8 mi beyond Honoka`a, a sign directs you to the right to Kukuihaele, on a loop with no street name, where you'll find the Waipi`o Valley Artworks gallery. Drive on to **Waipi`o Valley Overlook** ㊲ or make arrangements at the gallery for tours to explore the 6-mi-deep valley. At the end of Route 240, the once heav-ily populated Waipi`o Valley is a tropical Eden bounded by 2,000-ft cliffs.

TIMING

If you've stopped to explore the quiet little villages with wooden board-walks and dogs dozing in backyards, or if you've spent several hours in Waipi`o Valley, night will undoubtedly be falling by the time you

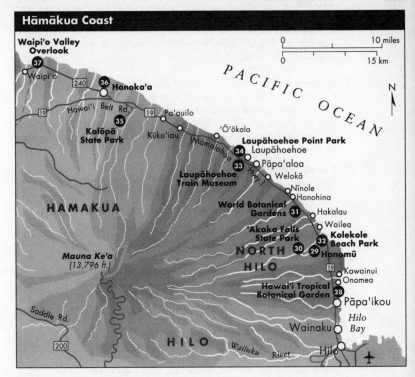

complete this journey. Don't worry: the return to Hilo via Highway 19 takes only about an hour, or you can continue on the same road to Waimea (30 minutes) and then to the Kohala Coast resorts (another 25 to 45 minutes).

Sights to See

★ ③⓪ **ʻAkaka Falls State Park.** You have to walk about 20 minutes to see the two falls, **ʻAkaka** and **Kahuna**. The easier downhill trail to your right takes you to the 400-ft Kahuna Falls first. ʻAkaka Falls drops more than 442 ft, tumbling far below into a pool drained by Kolekole Stream amid a profusion of fragrant white, yellow, and red torch ginger. ⊠ *4 mi inland off Hwy. 19, near Honomū,* ☎ *808/974–6200.* ⊡ *Free.* ⊘ *Daily 7–7.*

②⑧ **Hawaiʻi Tropical Botanical Garden.** Eight miles north of Hilo, stunning coastline views appear around each curve of the 4-mi scenic drive, lined with lush vegetation, which accesses the privately owned, nonprofit, 17-acre nature preserve beside Onomea Bay. Pathways lead past waterfalls, ponds, and more than 2,000 species of plants and flowers, including palms, bromeliads, ginger, heleconia, orchids, and ornamentals. ⊠ *27-717 Old Māmalahoa Hwy., Pāpaʻikou,* ☎ *808/964–5233,* [WEB] *www.hawaiigarden.com.* ⊡ *$15.* ⊘ *Daily 9–4.*

③⑥ **Honokaʻa.** In 1881 Australian William Purvis planted the first macadamia-nut trees in Hawaiʻi in what is now this funky, little town, occasionally still called the macadamia capital of the world. Honokaʻa is better known these days for its secondhand and antiques stores. ⊠ *Hwy. 240/Mamane St.*

NEED A BREAK? A quick stop at **Tex Drive In** (⊠ Pakalana St. and Hwy. 19, ☎ 808/775–0598) will give you a chance to taste the snack it is famous for: *malasada*, a puffy, doughy Portuguese doughnut (sans hole), deep-fried and rolled in sugar and best eaten hot. For mouthwatering pastries and a strong espresso in Honoka'a, stop in at **Mamane Street Bakery** (⊠ Mamane St., ☎ 808/775–9478), where residents from as far as Waimea and Hilo gladly shop.

㉙ Honomū. A plantation past is reflected in the wooden boardwalks and tin-roof buildings of this small, struggling town. It's fun to poke through knickknack shops such as Glass from the Past, where you'll find an assortment of old bottles. The Woodshop Gallery/Café and Ohana Gallery showcase fine local art. ⊠ *2 mi inland from Hwy. 19 en route to 'Akaka Falls State Park.*

㉟ Kalōpā State Park. At a cool 2,000-ft elevation, past the old plantation town of Pa'auilo, a lush, forested area with picnic tables and rest rooms hides an easy ¾-mi loop trail with additional paths in the adjacent 100-acre forest reserve. Small signs identify some of the plants. Cabins are available. ⊠ *12 mi north of Laupāhoehoe and 3 mi inland off Hwy. 19,* ☎ *808/974–6200.* ⚐ *Free.* ☉ *Daily 7–7 or by permit.*

㉜ Kolekole Beach Park. This beach at the mouth of the Kolekole River is not safe for inexperienced swimmers. Leave the locals surfing offshore and hike 4 mi up the river to a waterfall and pond for a chilly, refreshing dip. Facilities at the park include changing rooms, barbecue pits, and covered picnic areas. ⊠ *Off Hwy. 19,* ☎ *808/961–8311.* ⚐ *Free.* ☉ *Daily 7 AM–sunset.*

㉞ Laupāhoehoe Point Park. Come here to watch the surf pound the jagged black rocks at the base of the stunning point, but remember that this is not a safe place for swimming. Still vivid in the minds of longtime Hilo residents is the 1946 tragedy in which 20 schoolchildren and four teachers were swept to sea by a tidal wave. **Laupāhoehoe Harbor** has bathrooms, picnic tables, and stone barbecue pits. ⊠ *On northeast coastline, Hwy. 19, makai side, north of Laupāhoehoe,* ☎ *808/ 961–8311.* ⚐ *Free.* ☉ *Daily 7 AM–sunset.*

㉝ Laupāhoehoe Train Museum. Behind the stone loading platform of the once-famous Hilo Railroad, constructed around the turn of the 20th century, the former manager's house is home to a poignant display of the era when sugar was king. The railroad, one of the most expensive built in its time, was washed away by the tidal wave of 1946, destroying an important part of Hāmākua's history. ⊠ *Hwy. 19, Laupāhoehoe, mauka side,* ☎ *808/962–6300.* ⚐ *Suggested donation $2.* ☉ *Weekdays 9–4:30, weekends 10–2.*

㉟ Waipi'o Valley Overlook. Bounded by 2,000-ft cliffs, the Valley of the Kings—Waipi'o—was once a favorite retreat of Hawaiian royalty. Waterfalls drop 1,200 ft from the Kohala Mountains to the valley floor. Sheer cliffs make access difficult. The steep road from the overlook should only be attempted with a four-wheel-drive vehicle. A handful of families still cultivates taro in the pastoral valley, a few residents find refuge here, and horses roam narrow trails and rocky streams. A crescent of black sand makes it a popular spot for surfers. ⊠ *Follow Hwy. 240 8 mi northwest of Honoka'a.*

OFF THE
BEATEN PATH

WAIPI'O VALLEY – Today completely off the grid, Waipi'o was once the center of Hawaiian life, when somewhere between 4,000 and 20,000 people made it their home between the 13th and 17th centuries. In 1823, the first white visitors found 1,500 people living in this Edenlike environment amid wild fruit trees, banana patches, taro fields, and fishponds. Here, in 1780, Kamehameha I was singled out as a future ruler by reigning chiefs. In 1791 he fought Kahekili in his first naval battle at the mouth of the valley. Now, as then, waterfalls frame the landscape, but the valley has become one of the most isolated places in the state.

③ **World Botanical Gardens.** About 300 acres of former sugarcane land are slowly being transformed into a botanical center including native Hawaiian plants. In the 10-acre arboretum, which has gained full foliage, children love to wind their way through a maze of 5-ft shrubs. From within the gardens you have access to splendid views of one of the prettiest waterfalls on the isle, triple-tiered **Umauma Falls**. ✉ *Hwy. 19, from Hilo just past Mile Marker 16*, ☎ 808/963–5427, 🌐 *www.wbgi.com.* ✎ *$7.* ☉ *Mon–Sat 9–5:30.*

Kailua-Kona

The touristy seaside village of Kailua-Kona, at the base of the 8,271-ft Mt. Hualālai, has many historic sites tucked among the open-air shops and restaurants that line Aliʻi Drive, its main oceanfront street. This is where King Kamehameha I died in 1819 and where his successor, Liholiho, broke the *kapu* (taboo) system, a rigid set of laws that had provided the framework for Hawaiian government. The following year, on April 4, 1820, the first Christian missionaries from New England came ashore at Kailua-Kona.

The easiest place to park your car (a fee is charged) is at King Kamehameha's Kona Beach Hotel, but free parking is available if you enter Kailua via Palani Road, or Highway 190. Turn left onto Kuakini Highway; at a half block turn right and then immediately left into the parking lot. Walk makai on Likana Lane a half block to Aliʻi Drive.

A Good Walk

This ½-mi walk follows Aliʻi Drive south. Begin at **King Kamehameha's Kona Beach Hotel** ㊳ at the northern end of town, where artifacts and pictures of early kings are displayed in the lobby. The hotel, which borders the last residency of King Kamehameha I, **Kamakahonu** ㊴, offers free tours of a replica of the king's temple, Ahuʻena Heiau. You can also wander around the two stone platforms at the ocean's edge to view the site on your own. Next, investigate **Kailua Pier** ㊵ and the seawall where fisherfolk cast their lines in the afternoon and weavers make bowls and hats of coconut fronds. A submarine ride departs from the pier. Then take in **Huliheʻe Palace** ㊶, one of only three royal palaces in the United States, and **Mokuʻaikaua Church** ㊷, the first Christian church in the state of Hawaiʻi. Tackle a plethora of shops filled with tropical clothing, souvenir T-shirts, jewelry, and local crafts in the block-long, oceanfront **Kona Inn Shopping Village** ㊸. Much of the shopping area was converted from the old Kona Inn, a once-prestigious hotel and now a symbol of a more gracious era; Kona Inn Restaurant is still a popular gathering place for cocktails at sunset. At the southern end of Aliʻi Drive, find some shade and rest at **Hale Hālāwai Beach Park** ㊹. End your walk either a few steps to the south at **St. Michael's Church** ㊺, next to the site of the first Catholic church built in Kona in the 1840s, or continue a few blocks down to Coconut Plaza, a modern shopping square crammed with affordable ethnic restaurants and contemporary boutiques.

If you have a car, return to it now to complete your historical tour; drive to the end of Aliʻi Drive past Disappearing Sands Beach Park, the tiny blue-and-white St. Peter's Catholic Church, the ruins of a heiau, and Kahaluʻu Beach Park. There, a jagged lava lake on the edge of a bay outlines the **Kuamoʻo Battlefield and Lekeleke Burial Grounds** ㊻, where in 1819, seven months after King Kamehameha's death, Kona's last religious and bloody war marked the breakdown of the power of the Hawaiian gods.

TIMING

You can walk the whole ½-mi length of "downtown" Kailua-Kona and back again in an hour, or else spend an entire day here, taking time to browse in the shops, do the historical tours, have lunch, and breathe in the atmosphere. The drive to the Kuamo'o Battlefield and Lekeleke Burial Grounds takes less than 10 minutes. If you want to know more about Kailua's fascinating past, arrange for a guided tour by the Kona Historical Society.

Kailua-Kona enjoys year-round sunshine—except for the rare deluge. Mornings offer cooler weather, smaller crowds, and more birds singing in the banyan trees, but afternoon outings are great for cool drinks while gazing out over the ocean.

Sights to See

OFF THE BEATEN PATH

Before you start your day, have breakfast at the **Kona Ranch House** (✉ 75-5653 Olioli St., ☎ 808/329–7061). Up on the hill from King Kamehameha's Kona Beach Hotel, this pleasant plantation-style restaurant is the traditional location for Kailua-Kona residents to enjoy everything from plain oatmeal to full-on omelets, fragrant breads, and waffles topped with fruit.

ASTRONAUT ELLISON S. ONIZUKA SPACE CENTER — This informative museum 7 mi north of Kailua-Kona, at the airport, was opened in 1991 as a tribute to Hawai'i's first astronaut, who was killed in the 1986 *Challenger* disaster. The space center has computer-interactive exhibits. You can launch a miniature rocket and rendezvous with an object in space, feel the effects of gyroscopic stabilization, participate in hands-on science activities, and view educational films. ✉ Keāhole–Kona International Airport, Kailua-Kona, ☎ 808/329–3441, WEB www.onizukaspacecenter.org. 🎟 $3. ◷ Daily 8:30–4:30.

④④ Hale Hālāwai Beach Park. Benches under the trees at the ocean's edge are a perfect place to soak up the view and enjoy a calm respite from shopping in town. ✉ *Southern end of Ali'i Dr.*

★ **④① Hulihe'e Palace.** Fronted by a wrought-iron gate decorated with the royal crest, Hulihe'e Palace is one of only three royal palaces in America. The two-story residence was built of lava, coral, koa wood, and 'ōhi'a timber in 1838 by the island's governor, John Adams Kuakini, a year after he completed Moku'aikaua Church. During the 1880s it served as King David Kalākaua's summer palace. The oversize doors and koa-wood furniture bear witness to the size of some of the Hawaiian people. During weekday afternoons hula *hālau* (schools) rehearse on the grounds. ✉ *75-5718 Ali'i Dr.*, ☎ *808/329–1877.* 🎟 *$5.* ◷ *Weekdays 9–4, weekends 10–4.*

④⓪ Kailua Pier. Though most fisherfolk use Honokōhau Harbor, north of Kailua-Kona, Kailua Pier, built in 1918, is still a hub of ocean activity. Outrigger canoe teams practice and tour boats depart. Each October close to 1,500 international athletes swim 2.4 mi from the pier to begin the grueling Ironman Triathlon competition.

Along the **seawall** fisherfolk and children daily cast their lines. For youngsters, a bamboo pole and hook are easy to come by in the village, and plenty of locals are willing to give pointers. ✉ *Next to King Kamehameha's Kona Beach Hotel; the seawall is between Kailua Pier and Hulihe'e Palace on Ali'i Dr.*

③⑨ Kamakahonu. King Kamehameha I chose to spend his last years, from 1812 until his death in 1819, in this area, just outside of what is now King Kamehameha's Kona Beach Hotel, adjacent to the little beach and

Kailua-Kona

lagoon. Part of what was once a four-acre homestead complete with several houses and religious sites has been swallowed by Kailua Pier, but a replica of the temple, **Ahu'ena Heiau,** keeps history alive. Free tours start from King Kamehameha's Kona Beach Hotel. ⊠ *75-5660 Palani Rd.,* ☎ *808/329–2911.* ⊡ *Free.* ⊙ *Tours weekdays at 1:30.*

38 **King Kamehameha's Kona Beach Hotel.** Stroll through the high-ceiling lobby to view museum-quality displays of Hawaiian artifacts and mounted marlin and trophies from past Hawaiian International Billfish tournaments (from when Kailua Pier was still the weigh-in point). The 1986 winner of the tournament, a marlin that weighed in at 1,062 pounds, hangs on one wall. The 1,166-pound 1993 record setter is a floor display. ⊠ *75-5660 Palani Rd.,* ☎ *808/329–2911.*

OFF THE BEATEN PATH

KONA BREWING COMPANY & BREWPUB — A few blocks mauka of King Kamehameha's Kona Beach Hotel, Kona Brewing Company offers thirst-quenching tours and tastings. Its wheat ale, flavored with liliko'i, is a staple of the pub here, which is eclectic in its architecture, with a koa-wood bar, driftwood benches, and a historic tin roof. The pub uses local and organic produce for its pizzas. For nonbeer drinkers, an exquisite sparkling ginger ale hits the spot. ⊠ *North Kona Shopping Center, 75-5629 Kuakini Hwy.,* ☎ *808/334–2739.* ⊙ *Mon.–Thurs. 11–10, Fri.–Sat. 11–11, Sun. 4–10.*

43 **Kona Inn Shopping Village.** Much of this shopping arcade was once The Kona Inn, a hotel built in 1928 to attract a new wave of wealthy travelers. It closed in 1976. Prior to the construction of the inn, the personal heiau of King Liholiho was on this shore. Today, shops and restaurants line the boardwalk. Broad lawns with coconut trees on the ocean side are lovely for afternoon picnics. ⊠ *75-5744 Ali'i Dr.*

NEED A
BREAK? **Mrs. Barry's Kona Cookies** (⊠ 75-5744 Ali'i Dr., ☎ 808/329–6055)
serves fresh-baked cookies and muffins made with macadamia nuts and
other tropical ingredients. A refreshing lemonade is perfect for Kona's
weather. For cocktails at sunset head to the **Kona Inn Restaurant** (⊠ 75-
5744 Ali'i Dr., ☎ 808/329–4455), a traditional favorite.

46 Kuamo'o Battlefield and Lekeleke Burial Grounds. Here, in the last battle fought in Kona, in 1819, an estimated 300 Hawaiians were killed on
this vast, desolate black-lava field now filled with terraced graves. After
the death of his father, King Kamehameha I, Liholiho became king;
shortly thereafter King Liholiho ate at the table of women, thereby
breaking an ancient kapu that respected the Hawaiian gods. Chief
Kekuaokalani, vying for the throne and with radically different views
about traditions and religion, unsuccessfully challenged King Liholilho
in battle. In breaking the ancient kapu, Liholiho forced a final battle between not just him and his opponent, but more importantly between traditional and new religious beliefs in Hawaii. ⊠ *South end of Ali'i Dr.*

★ **42 Moku'aikaua Church.** The earliest Christian church on the islands was
founded here as a thatched hut by Hawai'i's first missionaries in 1820.
The present incarnation of the church was built in 1836 with black
stone from an abandoned heiau. The stone was mortared with white
coral and topped by an impressive steeple. Inside, at the back, behind
a panel of gleaming koa wood, is a model of the brig *Thaddeus.* ⊠
75-5713 Ali'i Dr., ☎ 808/329–0655.

45 St. Michael's Church. The site of the first Catholic church built in Kona,
in 1840, is marked by a small thatched structure to the left of the
present church, which dates from 1850. In front of the church a coral
grotto shrine holds 2,500 coral heads, harvested in 1940, when preservation was not yet an issue. ⊠ *75-5769 Ali'i Dr., ☎ 808/326–7771.*

NEED A
BREAK? **Island Lava Java** (⊠ 75-5799 Ali'i Dr., ☎ 808/327–2161) is a dandy
place for a cappuccino, a mocha java accompanied by a bagel, or a
scoop of Tropical Dreams ice cream.

South Kona and Ka'u

South of Kailua-Kona, Highway 11 leaves busy streets behind as it borders splendid coastline. Cradled against the slopes of Mauna Loa, lush
coffee plantations alternate with arid landscapes in the surreal empti-
ness of the most southern part of the United States. The 50-mi drive
to windswept South Point, where the first Polynesians came ashore as
early as AD 750, passes a national historic park, Pu'uhonua O Hōnaunau, the only remaining Hawaiian place of refuge, as well as a whimsically painted church. Below the highway shimmers Kealakekua Bay,
where Captain James Cook arrived in 1778, bringing radical change
to Hawai'i. Narrow, steep roads off the main highway lead to isolated
fishing towns where life unfolds far removed from modern hubris. To
the east of Highway 11, an 11,000-acre development overgrown with
ohelo berries, Ocean View Estates, testifies to the struggle it takes to
survive in this land crisscrossed by lava tubes. Mark Twain, however,
wrote some of his finest prose here, and macademia-nut farms, fine
beaches, and tiny villages offer as yet largely undiscovered beauty.

A Good Drive

From Kailua-Kona, drive south on Highway 11, also known as Hawai'i
Belt Road or Māmalahoa Highway, to historic **Kainaliu** ㊼, where several old stores once served a growing industry of farmers in the 1920s,
surviving difficult times by accepting coffee as tender. Just outside the

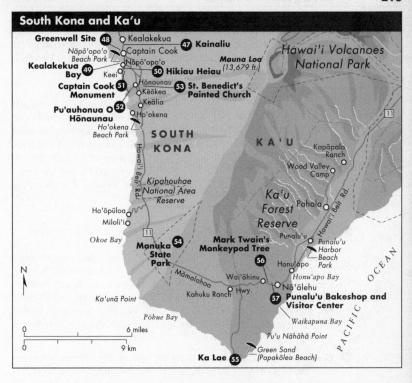

Greenwell Site ㊽ ○ Kealakekua
Captain Cook ㊼ Kainaliu
Nāpō'opo'o
Beach Park ○ Nāpō'opo'o
Kealakekua ○ Keei
Bay ㊾ ㊿ Hikiau Heiau
Captain Cook ㉛ ○ Hōnaunau
Monument ○ Kēōkea ㊼ St. Benedict's
○ Keālia Painted Church
Pu'uhonua O ㉜
Hōnaunau ○ Hp'okena
Ho'okena
Beach Park

Mauna Loa
(13,679 ft.)
Hawai'i Volcanoes
National Park

SOUTH
KONA

KA'U

Kapāpala
Ranch

Wood Valley
Camp

Ka'u
Forest
Reserve

Kipahouhae
National Area
Reserve

Ho'ōpūloa ○
Miloli'i ○

Okoe Bay

Manuka ㊻
State
Park

Mark Twain's
Monkeypod Tree

Pahala

Punalu'u ○ Punalu'u
Harbor
Honu'apo ○ Punalu'u
Beach
Park

Māmalahoa
Kahuku Ranch Hwy.
Wai'ōhinu

Honu'apo Bay

Nā'ālehu

Punalu'u Bakeshop and
Visitor Center

PACIFIC

OCEAN

Ka'unā Point

Pōhue Bay

Waikapuna Bay

Pu'u Nāhāhā Point

Ka Lae ㊵

Green Sand
(Papakōlea Beach)

N

0 _____ 6 miles
0 _____ 9 km

11

Hawai'i Belt Rd.

---

town, you'll find the **Greenwell Site** ㊽, dating to 1875, now headquarters
to the Kona Historical Society. Pick up brochures and guides here and
arrange for a tour of the D. Uchida Coffee Farm to get a glimpse of
the traditional lifestyle of Japanese coffee farming in Hawai'i.

At the junction in the town of Captain Cook, turn right and follow
the steep descent along Nāpō'opo'o Road to **Kealakekua Bay** ㊾, once
a busy Hawaiian community, but forever changed with the arrival of
Captain Cook in 1779. Park your car and walk to **Hikiau Heiau** ㊿. A
short hike over uneven ground will take you to **Captain Cook Monument** ㉛, a 27-ft-high white obelisk commemorating the explorer's
death. Dip into the calm, dolphin-friendly waves that lap onto rocky
Nāpō'opo'o Beach before taking Route 160, which hugs the coast, to
Pu'uhonua O Hōnaunau ㉜. Plan to spend some time walking around
this ancient Hawaiian sanctuary once enclosed by a 1,000-ft-long
stone wall. Visit the restored royal Hale o Keawe Heiau, built circa
1650, and wander to the tide pools south of the park. Back in your
car, head mauka on Route 160 toward Kēōkea, and turn left at Painted
Church Road to visit the whimsical **St. Benedict's Painted Church** ㊼.

Continue south on Highway 11; after about 2 mi, you'll pass the turn-
off to Ho'okena Beach Park, a busy steamer port in the 19th century.
About 12 mi farther south, at Mile Marker 88, the infamous Mauna
Loa lava flow of 1926 destroyed an entire Hawaiian fishing village.
Turn left at Mile Marker 88 for a 2-mi scenic drive along the old Māmala-
hoa Highway, then take a break at **Manuka State Park** ㊻.

Drive another 12 mi on Māmalahoa Highway to reach the windswept
South Point Road, which leads to the southernmost part of the United
States, **Ka Lae** ㊵, with its old canoe-mooring holes. You must have a
four-wheel-drive vehicle and a permit to get beyond the gate to reach
Green Sand Beach, or you can take an exhilarating 5-mi round-trip hike.

For the last leg of this drive, head east on Highway 11 to the wetter, windward towns of Wai`ōhinu and Nā`ālehu, small communities struggling in the aftermath of sugar-plantation closures. Be sure to stop first at **Mark Twain's Monkeypod Tree** ⑯ for inspiration, then at **Punalu`u Bakeshop and Visitor Center** ⑰ to buy fragrant sweetbread.

TIMING

Start your day early, as it takes two-and-a-half hours from Kona just to get to the southern end of the island. You may want to stay in one of the many cozy bed-and-breakfasts at Hawai`i Volcanoes National Park and make this a two-day excursion. Fill up on gasoline and pack some snacks as there are few amenities along the way. Chances are it'll be close to dinnertime by the time you've completed this tour, but eateries in Kona remain open late and Volcanoes National Park is only a 45-minute drive away.

Sights to See

❺❶ **Captain Cook Monument.** No one knows for sure what happened on February 14, 1779, when English explorer Captain James Cook was killed here. He chose Kealakekua Bay as a landing place in November 1778, and initiated Hawai`i's dramatic change. With new maps in hand, European sailors headed out in large numbers to trade and explore. They changed the old ways, bringing with them disease and alcohol, but also new tools, techniques, and cloth. The 27-ft-high obelisk itself wasn't erected until 1878. ✉ *Ka`awaloa, at the end of a 1-mi hiking trail off Nāpō`opo`o Beach.*

❹❽ **Greenwell Site.** Established in 1850, the homestead of Henry N. Greenwell served as cattle ranch, sheep station, post office, store complex, and family home all in one. Now, all that remains is the 1875 stone store, which is listed on the National Register of Historic Places. It is headquarters to the **Kona Historical Society** and its fascinating museum, with ranching and coffee-farming photographs and exhibits. ✉ *81-6551 Māmalahoa Hwy.,* ☎ *808/323–3222,* WEB *www.konahistorical.org.* 🎫 *By donation.* ☉ *Weekdays 9–3.*

❺⓿ **Hikiau Heiau.** The remains you see of the stone platform and walls were once an impressive state temple, a large and sacred site enclosed by stone walls, dedicated to the god Lono. When Captain Cook arrived in 1778, ceremonies in his honor were held here. ✉ *Bottom of Nāpō`opo`o Rd.*

❺❺ **Ka Lae.** Windswept Ka Lae, the southernmost point of land in the United States, has a few abandoned structures once used in the 19th and early 20th centuries to lower cattle and produce to ships anchored below the cliffs. It is thought that the first Polynesians came ashore here. Check out the old canoe-mooring holes that are carved through the rocks, possibly by settlers from Tahiti as early as AD 750. Some artifacts, thought to have been left by early voyagers who never settled here, date to AD 300. Driving down the 12-mi road, you pass Kamoa Wind Farm; turn off your engine here and listen to the eerie sound of the wind hitting the white wings of the windmills high above you. ✉ *Turn right just past Mile Marker 70 on Mamalahoa Hwy. and drive for 12 mi down South Point Rd.*

❹❼ **Kainaliu.** It doesn't seem like much, this ribbon of funky old stores, but Kainaliu hosts a wealth of traditional-Japanese family-operated shops. Browse around Heritage Stores such as Oshima's, established in 1926, and Kimura's, established in 1927, to find authentic Japanese goods beyond tourist trinkets. When times were tough, these stores survived by accepting coffee as tender. Peek into Aloha Theatre, built in 1932, where actors might be practicing a new Broadway review. ✉ *Hwy. 11, Mile Markers 112–114.*

49 **Kealakekua Bay.** Before the arrival of Captain Cook in the late 18th century, this now tranquil Historical State Park with its old steamer landing lay at the center of Hawaiian life. The rolling hills provided excellent farming, and fish were plentiful. Historians consider Kealakekua Bay as the birthing ground for the post-contact era. ⊠ *Bottom of Nāpōʻopoʻo Rd.*

54 **Manuka State Park.** This native forest offers both dry- and wetlands, spread across several lava flows. The trail follows a 2-mi loop past a pit crater and winds around ancient trees such as hau and kukui. Kids love the trees, so large you can't get your arms around them, and the trails, with their unexpected loops and turns. Rest rooms, picnic areas, and telephones are all available. ⊠ *Hwy. 11, north of Mile Marker 81,* ☏ *808/974–6200.* ☞ *Free.* ☉ *Daily 7–7.*

56 **Mark Twain's Monkeypod Tree.** Legend has it that Mark Twain, who wrote some of his work here, planted this robust, gnarled tree in 1866. In the 1950s a storm blew the tree down. New shoots have since developed into an impressive tree again. Next door is a little take-out restaurant, Mark Twain Square. ⊠ *Hwy. 11, just before Mile Marker 64.*

OFF THE BEATEN PATH — About 16 mi east of Naʻlehu, beyond Punaluʻu Beach Park, Highway 11 flashes past the little town of **Pahala.** You'll miss it if you blink. Pahala is a perfect example of a sugar-plantation town. Behind it, along a wide cane road, you enter Wood Valley, once a prosperous community, now a mere road lit by the heavy scent of night-blooming jasmine, coffee blossoms, and eucalyptus trees. Here you'll find **Wood Valley Temple** (☏ 808/928–8539), a quiet, Tibetan Buddhist retreat that welcomes guests who seek serenity and solitude.

53 **St. Benedict's Painted Church.** Whimsical, bright, and creative, the ceiling, columns, and walls of this Roman Catholic church depict Bible scenes through the paintbrush of Belgium-born priest, Father Velghe. Mass is still held every weekend. The view of Kealakekua Bay from the entrance is amazing. ⊠ *Painted Church Rd., off Hwy. 160,* ☏ *808/ 328–2227.*

57 **Punaluʻu Bakeshop and Visitor Center.** They say it's the best sweetbread—of course, it's the only sweetbread—in this area. While here, browse for rare *pohā*-berry (gooseberry) jam, look up at the old tamarind tree outside, and be sure to take some of that sweetbread home. ⊠ *Center of Naʻalehu,* ☏ *808/929–7343.* ☉ *Daily 9–5.*

52 **Puʻuhonua O Hōnaunau.** This 180-acre National Historic Park, about 20 mi south of Kailua-Kona, was, in early times, a place of refuge and healing. It was a safe haven for women in times of war as well as for kapu breakers, criminals, and prisoners of war—anyone who could get inside the 1000-ft-long wall, which was 10 ft high and 17 ft thick, was safe and could avoid punishment. **Hale-o-Keawe Heiau,** built in 1650 as the burial place of King Kamehameha I's ancestor, Keawe, has been restored. South of the park, tide pools offer another delight. Demonstrations of Hawaiian skills, games, poi pounding, canoe making, and more are scheduled occasionally. ⊠ *Rte. 160,* ☏ *808/328–2326,* WEB *www.nps.gov.* ☞ *$2.* ☉ *Weekdays 7:30 AM–11 PM, weekends 7:30 AM–8 PM.*

The Kohala District

Along the roadside of Highway 19, brightly colored bougainvillea stands out in relief against the chunky black-lava landscape that stretches as far as the eye can see. Most of the lava flows, spreading from the mountain to the sea, are from the last eruptions of Mt.

Hualālai, in 1800–01. They are interrupted only by the green oases of irrigated golf courses surrounding the glamorous luxury resorts rising along the Kona-Kohala Coast. The landscape along this long stretch of coastline changes considerably, from the cool 2,500-ft altitude of the cowboy town of Waimea to the green rolling fields that compose much of North Kohala. During the winter months, glistening humpback whales cleave the waters just offshore. On the coast you'll see ancient stone heiau and the remains of a fishing village, moving legacies of the Hawaiian people who still inhabit the area.

A Good Drive

If you're staying in Kona or at a Kohala Coast resort, begin this tour early in the morning by driving north on Queen Ka'ahumanu Highway 19 along the base of Mt. Hualālai. When you get to the split in the road 33 mi from Kailua-Kona, turn left on Highway 270 toward Kawaihae and stop at **Pu'ukoholā Heiau National Historic Site** ⑧. The park service ranger at the visitor center may tell you the history of the three heiaus, two large ones on land and a third submerged just offshore, that King Kamehameha I had his men rebuild from 1790 to 1791. You can get a good photo of the two heiaus by driving a bit farther down the road and turning into Spencer Beach Park.

Retrace your route and continue east, climbing on Highway 19 through Parker Ranch land toward Waimea. (Note: Technically, the name of the Waimea post office is Kamuela, and the name of the town is Waimea. Some say the post office is named for the son of the founder of Parker Ranch.) Where the road divides and Kohala Mountain Road (Hwy. 250) makes a sharp left, you'll find **Kamuela Museum** ⑨, home to an impressive number of Hawaiian artifacts.

Upcountry Waimea is a bustling, affluent town. There are currently about 30 places where you can find a bite to eat, and some of them are world famous. Behind the shops of High Country Traders on your right on Highway 19, **Waimea Visitor Center** ⑥⓪, in the old Lindsey House and listed on the Hawai'i Register of Historic Places, offers detailed information on the cultural and historic sites of Kohala. **Parker Ranch Visitor Center and Museum** ⑥①, on the other side of the traffic lights, chronicles the life of the family that founded the ranch in 1847. Wagon tours and horseback rides take you through the ranch paniolo-style. The **Fire House Gallery** ⑥②, which is within walking distance of the Parker Ranch Visitor Center, displays some of the island's finest artwork in unique one-person shows. To get here, walk across the Parker Ranch parking lot to the main intersection. Head to what looks like an old firehouse, a couple of buildings down, in the direction of Kailua-Kona on Highway 190.

Walk back to Parker Ranch Visitor Center and from here drive northeast on Highway 19 to pass the offices of the Keck Observatory, which has the world's largest mirrored telescope, at the top of Mauna Ke'a. Then drive by the first church on the left, but stop to peek into the cream-color **'Imiola Congregational Church** ⑥③ to view its unique koa-wood interior. Make sure to browse through Cook's Discoveries at the third traffic light for exquisite local-theme gifts.

Reverse directions and head west on Highway 19; turn right on Kohala Mountain Road (Highway 250) for a scenic ride through the mountains to Hāwī. **Kawaihae Harbor Overlook** ⑥④ affords a view of the entire coastline, including the protective breakwater, directly below. Farther on, through ironwood trees that act as windbreaks along the road, you'll see an exclusive country-home subdivision called Kohala Ranch. Here are the headquarters of Kohala Na'alapa, and just up the road, Paniolo Riding Adventures, which guides horseback riders through the countryside.

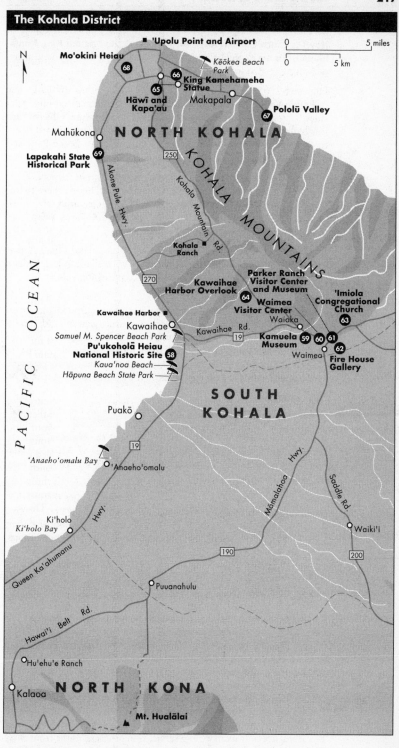

The Kohala District

'Upolu Point and Airport

Mo'okini Heiau

68

Kēōkea Beach Park

66 King Kamehameha Statue

65

Hāwī and Kapa'au

Makapala

67 Pololū Valley

N O R T H   K O H A L A

Mahūkona

69 Lapakahi State Historical Park

K O H A L A   M O U N T A I N S

250

Kohala Mountain Rd.

Akoni Pule Hwy.

Kohala Ranch

270

Kawaihae Harbor Overlook

Parker Ranch Visitor Center and Museum

64 Waimea Visitor Center

'Imiola Congregational Church

63

Kawaihae Harbor

Kawaihae Rd.

Waiaka

19

Kamuela Museum

59 60 61

62 Fire House Gallery

Waimea

Samuel M. Spencer Beach Park

Pu'ukoholā Heiau National Historic Site 58

Kaua'noa Beach

Hāpuna Beach State Park

S O U T H   K O H A L A

Puakō

19

'Anaeho'omalu Bay

'Anaeho'omalu

Māmalahoa Hwy.

Saddle Rd.

Ki'holo

Ki'holo Bay

Waiki'i

Queen Ka'ahumanu Hwy.

190

200

Puuanahulu

Hawai'i Belt Rd.

Hu'ehu'e Ranch

Kalaoa

N O R T H   K O N A

Mt. Hualālai

PACIFIC OCEAN

0   5 miles
0   5 km

Kohala Mountain Road rises and then drops gradually. After about 20 mi it rejoins Highway 270 at the old sugar-plantation village of **Hāwī** ⑥⑤. Turn right to **Kapa`au** ⑥⑤ to visit the original **King Kamehameha Statue** ⑥⑥ and browse through the many galleries and unusual gift shops nestled in restored historic buildings.

Highway 270 ends farther east at an overlook with a stunning view of **Pololū Valley** ⑥⑦. A hiking trail leads into it. Organized mule trail rides, waterfall hikes, and kayak cruises lead adventurers deeper into this hauntingly beautiful and historic area. Drive back toward Hāwī to complete the loop via Highway 270, past Kapa`a Beach Park and Māhukona Beach Park.

Turn right to remote `Upolu Point and the old `Upolu Airport. From here you'll need a four-wheel-drive vehicle or good hiking shoes to traverse a 1½-mi dirt lane to **Mo`okini Heiau** ⑥⑧, a huge, impressive work of craftsmanship built about AD 480. About 1,000 yards away from the heiau is King Kamehameha I's birthplace.

If time permits, head south on Highway 270 and make a final stop at **Lapakahi State Historical Park** ⑥⑨, where a 1-mi trail meanders through the site of once-prosperous Koai`e, an ancient fishing village.

TIMING

This is an all-day excursion covering many miles over ground that ranges from lava-covered flatlands with glorious seaside views to lush mountain pastures. If you're short on time, head either straight for Waimea to shop and dine and to visit the Parker Ranch Museum, or drive to Hāwī and Kapa`au via Highway 270 to see the dramatic history of these sugar towns. Allow a half day or more for the abbreviated trip.

Sights to See

⑥② **Fire House Gallery.** Dedicated to promoting the arts in the towns of Waimea, Hāmākua, Kohala, and Waikoloa, the Waimea Arts Council sponsors free *kaha ki`is* (one-person shows) at the Waimea Art Center, in the old fire station, the Fire House Gallery. ✉ *67-1201 Māmalahoa Hwy., near the main stoplight, Waimea,* ☎ *808/887–1052.* 🎟 *Free.* ☉ *Tues.–Thurs. and Sat. 10–2.*

⑥⑤ **Hāwī and Kapa`au.** These two old neighboring villages thrived during plantation days. There were hotels, saloons, and theaters—even a railroad. Today both towns are blossoming once again, honoring their past. Old historic buildings have been restored and are home to shops, galleries, and eateries. In Kapa`au, browse through the Hawaiian collection of **Kohala Book Shop** (✉ 54-3885 Akoni Pule Hwy., ☎ 808/ 889–6400), the largest secondhand bookstore in the state. ✉ *Kohala Mount Rd., off Hwy. 270.*

NEED A
BREAK?

It can get hot and humid in North Kohala. A great place to feel the breeze is on the lānai of the **Nanbu Courtyard** (✉ Kapa`au, ☎ 808/ 889–5546), behind the historic Old Nanbu Hotel. Open as early as 6:30 on weekdays, this friendly espresso shop serves toasted bagels, salads, and grilled sandwiches alongside home-baked macadamia-nut cookies and soft ice cream.

⑥③ **`Imiola Congregational Church.** Stop here to admire the dark koa interior and the unusual wooden calabashes hanging from the ceiling. Be careful not to walk in while a service is in progress, as the front entry of this church, which was established in 1832 and rebuilt in 1857, is behind the pulpit. ✉ *Off Hwy. 19, Waimea,* ☎ *808/885–4987.*

59 Kamuela Museum. Parker descendant Harriet Solomon and her husband, Albert, have amassed fascinating artifacts from Hawai'i and around the world in this privately owned museum. Among the Solomons' eclectic collection are Hawaiian weapons and a satiny-smooth koa table that once graced 'Iolani Palace. ⊠ *Hwys. 19 and 250, Waimea,* ☎ *808/ 885–4724.* ☐ *$5.* ☉ *Daily 8–5.*

64 Kawaihae Harbor Overlook. The overlook here provides a splended view of the coastline and Kawaihae Harbor. Of Big Island harbors, this one near the Kawaihae Shopping Center is second in size only to Hilo Harbor on the east coast. King Kamehameha I and his men launched their canoes from here when they set out to conquer the island chain. Today paddlers from all over the island gather here for races. ⊠ *Kohala Mountain Rd. (Hwy. 250).*

66 King Kamehameha Statue. This is the original of the statue in front of the Judiciary Building on King Street in Honolulu. It was cast in Florence in 1880 but lost at sea when the German ship transporting it sank near the Falkland Islands. A replica was shipped to Honolulu. Two years later an American sea captain found the original in a Port Stanley (Falkland Islands) junkyard and brought it to the Big Island. The legislature voted to erect it near Kamehameha's birthplace. Every year, on King Kamehameha Day (June 11), a magnificent abundance of leis adorns the image of Hawai'i's great king. ⊠ *Hwy. 270, Kapa'au.*

NEED A BREAK?

Jen's Kohala Café (☎ 808/889–0099), across from the King Kamehameha statue in Kapa'au, serves imaginative wraps and sandwiches all day long. Try the Greek spinach wrap—stuffed with organic baby greens, black olives, feta cheese, and pickled *pepperoncini* (small, hot chili peppers). If you're looking for something sweet, head to **Kohala Coffee Mill** (⊠ Akone Pule Hwy., ☎ 808/889–5577), an espresso café in bustling Hāwī that whips up Kona coffee, espresso drinks, and luscious iced *chai* (Indian tea). Tropical Dreams ice cream comes in such island flavors as mango and white chocolate ginger. You can also buy unique, coffee-theme gifts.

69 Lapakahi State Historical Park. A self-guided, 1-mi walking tour leads you through the ruins of the once-prosperous fishing village Koai'e, which dates as far back as the 15th century. Displays illustrate early Hawaiian fishing, salt gathering, legends, games, shelters, and crops, and a park guide is often on-site to answer questions. Since the shores off Lapakahi are now mostly a Marine Life Conservation District, and part of the site itself is considered sacred, swimming is discouraged. ⊠ *Makai side of Hwy. 270, between Kawaihae and Māhukona, North Kohala,* ☎ *808/974–6200 or 808/882–6207.* ☐ *Free.* ☉ *Daily 8–4.*

68 Mo'okini Heiau. Few people seek out this National Historic Landmark, an isolated *luakini* (sacrificial) heiau, but it is so impressive in size it may give you "chicken skin" (goose bumps), especially when you consider that it was built about AD 480. A nearby sign marks the place where Kamehameha I was born in 1758. The area is now part of the Kohala Historical Sites State Monument. ⊠ *Turn off Hwy. 270 at sign for 'Upolu Airport, near Hāwī, and hike or drive in a four-wheel-drive vehicle 1½ mi southwest,* ☎ *808/974–6200.*

★ **61 Parker Ranch Visitor Center and Museum.** The center chronicles the life of John Palmer Parker (and his descendants), who founded Parker Ranch in 1847 after befriending King Kamehameha, marrying his granddaughter, and buying two acres of land from the king for the sum of $10. Purchase your tickets here for the **Parker Ranch Historic Homes,** which are a couple of miles south of town. Mānā, the original koa-wood family residence, is open to visitors, as is Pu'ōpelu, the century-old residence of the late Richard Smart, a sixth-generation Parker who was an avid collector of Venetian glass, antiques, and oils by classic artists. Fridays, Hawaiian craft and music demonstrations take place at the historic homes. A ride with Parker Ranch Wagon Tours allows you a comfortable, albeit old-fashioned, visit of the pastures. Also available are horseback rides and walking tours. ⊠ *Parker Ranch Shopping Center, Hwy. 19, Waimea,* ☎ *808/885–7655,* WEB *www. parkerranch.com.* 🎟 *Museum $6, homes $8.50.* ☉ *Museum daily 9–5, homes daily 10–5.*

| NEED A BREAK? | At the **Little Juice Shack** in the Parker Ranch Shopping Center (⊠ Hwy. 19, ☎ 808/885–1686), you can treat yourself to fresh juices made with carrots, beets, or watermelon, to name a few. Add a shot of wheatgrass juice from the crop grown in the windows. Sample an organic spinach salad or six-grain turkey sandwich, or, on a cold day, try the thick and spicy five-pepper chowder. |

⑰ Pololū Valley. You'll want to have cameras ready for this view of rugged coastline pounded by relentless surf and ribboned by silver waterfalls. A trail leads into a valley that in ancient days was heavily populated. The valleys beyond provide water for the Kohala Ditch, the ingenious project that used to bring water to the sugar plantation. The former ditch trails have become inaccessible and dangerous. A kayak cruise, a mule ride, and a ditch-trail hike reveal more of this dramatic part of Kohala history. ⊠ *End of Hwy. 270.*

★ ㊳ Pu'ukoholā Heiau National Historic Site. In 1790 a prophet told King Kamehameha I to build **Pu'ukoholā Heiau** and dedicate it to the war god Kūkā'ilimoku by sacrificing his principal Big Island rival, Keoua Kuahu'ula. By doing so the king would achieve his goal of conquering the Hawaiian Islands. The sacrifice was made, and the prophecy was fulfilled in 1810. Weather permitting (the trail is closed on windy days), you can take a short walk over arid landscape from the visitor center to Pu'ukoholā Heiau and then cross the road to the smaller **Mailekini Heiau,** constructed about 1550. Entry into the temples is not permitted. The center offers brochures, exhibits, and audiovisual and interpretive talks, and organizes Hawaiian arts-and-crafts programs on a regular basis. ⊠ *Hwy. 270, Kawaihae,* ☎ *808/882–7218,* WEB *www.nps.gov.* 🎟 *Free.* ☉ *Daily 7:30–4.*

㊿ Waimea Visitor Center. The old Lindsey House—a restored ranch cabin built in 1909 and now listed on the Hawai'i Register of Historic Places—serves as a visitor center. Part of the Waimea Preservation Association, it offers detailed information on Kohala's many historic and cultural sites. ⊠ *65-1291 Kawaihae Rd., behind High Country Traders, Waimea,* ☎ *808/885–6707,* WEB *www.northhawaii.net.* ☉ *Mon.–Sat. 9:30–4:30.*

| NEED A BREAK? | If you're in the mood for a mug of steaming caffe latte with a hot croissant, stop by the **Waimea Coffee Company** (⊠ Parker Square, off Kawaihae Rd., ☎ 808/885–4472), where you'll also find a nice selection of gourmet gifts. At **Aioli's** (⊠ 'Opelo Plaza, Hwy. 19 and 'Opelo Rd., ☎ 808/885–6325) you can pick up delightful ready-to-go box lunches or opt for a custom-made sandwich. Tuesday through Saturday evening, bistro-style dinners are served from 5 to 8. Friendly **Tako Taco Taqueria** (⊠ Kawaihae Rd., next to Parker Sq., ☎ 808/887–1717) serves superb fresh, organic Mexican fare. You can get it to go or eat it in the small, boldly painted eatery. |

BEACHES

Don't believe it if anyone tells you the Big Island lacks beaches. It actually has 80 or more, and new ones appear—and disappear—regularly. In 1989 a new black-sand beach, Kamoamoa, formed when molten lava shattered as it hit cold ocean waters. Kamoamoa was the largest of the black-sand beaches, more than ½ mi long and 25 yards wide, until it was closed by new lava flows in 1992. Some beaches are just a little hard to get to—several are hidden behind elaborate hotels or down unmarked roads.

Note that many beaches have dangerous undertows—rip currents and pounding shore breaks may cause serious risk anywhere, at any time. The surf tends to get rough in winter. To be safe, swim only when you see other visitors swimming in the area. Local surfers are not an indication that the area is safe. Few public beaches have lifeguards.

That said, the most beautiful, swimmable white-sand beaches stretch along the Kohala coastline. And they are truly spectacular. Beaches below are listed in a counterclockwise direction around the island, starting from the northern tip. For overnight permits, necessary at all parks, contact the Department of Land and Natural Resources for state parks and the Department of Parks and Recreation for county parks.

Kēōkea Beach Park. Driving back from the end of Highway 270 at the Pololū overlook to the north, you'll see a curvy road angle off to the right. Follow it for a mile, past the cemetery with the weathered old stones, and you'll come upon the green lawns and large picnic pavilion of Kēōkea Beach Park. The black-boulder beach is suited for fishing in the calm summer months, but heavy surf makes this a hazardous swimming beach. Picnic tables, rest rooms, showers, drinking water, electricity, and a campsite make this a popular weekend destination for local folks. ⊠ *Off Hwy. 270, near Pololū overlook,* ☎ *808/961–8311.*

Māhukona Beach Park. Next to the abandoned Port of Māhukona, in the Kohala District, where sugar was once shipped by rail to be loaded on boats, Māhukona Beach's old docks and buildings are a treat for photographers. Divers and snorkelers can view both marine life and remnants of shipping machinery in the clear water. Water activities are often off-limits, however, due to heavy surf. This is a pleasant picnicking spot, with rest rooms, showers, and a camping area, but no sandy beach. ⊠ *Off Hwy. 270, Māhukona,* ☎ *808/961–8311.*

Spencer Beach Park. This spot is popular with local families because of its reef-protected, gently sloping white-sand beach, and it's safe for swimming year-round. Close to large shade trees are cooking and camping facilities, showers, abandoned tennis courts, and a large covered pavilion with electrical outlets. You can walk from here to the Puʻukoholā and Mailekini heiaus. ⊠ *Entry road off Hwy. 270, uphill from Kawaihae Harbor,* ☎ *808/961–8311.*

★ **Kaunaʻoa Beach at Westin Mauna Keʻa Beach Hotel.** It's a toss-up whether this or neighboring Hāpuna is the most beautiful beach on the island. Kaunaʻoa unfolds like a white crescent, and it slopes very gradually. It's a great place for snorkeling. In winter, however, the powerful waves can be dangerous. Amenities are hotel-owned. Public parking places are limited, and it's first-come, first-served. ⊠ *Entry through gate to Mauna Keʻa Beach Resort, off Hwy. 19.*

★ **Hāpuna Beach State Park.** This beach, part of a 61-acre park, forms a ½-mi crescent of glistening sand guarded by rocky points at either end. The surf can be hazardous in winter, but in summer the gradual slope of the beach can stretch as wide as 200 ft into a perfectly blue ocean—ideal for swimming, snorkeling, and body surfing. State cabins are available, and there is a convenient snack bar. Lifeguards are not always on duty, so take care. ☒ *Between Mauna Ke'a Beach and Mauna Lani resorts, off Hwy. 19,* ☎ *808/974–6200.*

Holoholokai Beach Park. A rocky beach of black-lava formations and white-coral clinkers is fine for surfers and snorkelers, and a small grassy area is available to sunbathers. Bathrooms, picnic tables, and barbecue grills are nicely maintained. Just before the beach park, you can explore historic Puakō Petroglyph Park: Malama Trail meanders 7⁄10 mi through brush and kiawe trees to an area of lava covered with the ancient etchings of Hawaiian figures and animals. ☒ *Off Hwy. 19 at Mauna Lani Bay Hotel and Bungalows.*

'Anaeho'omalu Beach, at Outrigger Waikoloa Resort. This expansive beach on the west coast, also known as A-Bay, is perfect for swimming, windsurfing, snorkeling, and diving. Some equipment is for rent at the north end. Be sure to wander around the ancient fishponds and petroglyph fields. ☒ *Follow Waikoloa Beach Dr. to Royal Waikoloan Resort, then signs to park and beach right-of-way to south.*

Ki'holo Bay. The unmarked road across a vast lava field requires a 20-minute hike, so take plenty of water. Private homes are built along the oceanfront. The huge, spring-fed Luahinewai Pond anchors the south end of the bay, and the three black-pebble beaches are fine for swimming in calm weather. At the northern end, Wainānāli'i Pond (a 5-acre lagoon) is a feeding site for green sea turtles. The two ponds are off-limits to swimmers. Kamehameha I had a well-stocked fishpond here that was destroyed by lava in 1859. You'll find good swimming here but no facilities. ☒ *Hwy. 19, Mile Marker 81.*

Kona Coast Beach Park. In a primitive setting, this sandy white beach nestles in a bay area with gentle surf. It has a limited number of picnic tables shaded by coconut trees fed by bubbling fresh-water springs, but no drinking water. Portable toilets are the only additional facilities. ☒ *Sign about 1 mi north of Keāhole–Kona International Airport, off Hwy. 19, marks rough 1½-mi road to beach,* ☎ *808/974–6200.*

Kaloko–Honokōhau National Historical Park. Part of a new 1160-acre park, two beaches, rich in archeology and good for swimming, are down the road from Honokōhau Harbor. 'Alula is a slip of white sand, a short walk over lava to the left of the harbor entrance. Honokōhau Beach, a ¾-mi stretch with ruins of ancient fishponds, is north of the harbor. At the north end of the beach, a historic trail leads mauka across the lava to a freshwater pool. A Hawaiian settlement up until the 19th century, the park is rapidly being developed as a cultural and historical site. For information about the park visit its headquarters, a 5- to 10-minute drive away. ☒ *Off Hwy. 19, at Honokōhau Harbor, or via park access between Mile Markers 96 and 97; Park Headquarters, Kaloko New Industrial Park, 73-4786 Kanalani St., #14,* ☎ *808/329–6881,* WEB *www.nps.gov.* ☽ *Park road gate from 8 AM–3:30 PM.*

Old Kona Airport Park. The unused runway—great for jogging or running—is still visible above this beach at Kailua Park, which has picnic tables, showers, bathroom facilities, tennis courts, and palm trees strung out along the shore. The beach has a sheltered, sandy inlet with tidal pools for children, but for adults it's better for snorkeling than it is for swimming. An offshore surfing break known as Old Airport is popular with Kona surfers. ☒ *North end of Kuakini Hwy., Kona,* ☎ *808/327–4958 or 808/974–6200.*

White Sands, Magic Sands, or Disappearing Sands Beach Park. Now you see it, now you don't. Overnight, winter waves wash away this small white-sand beach on Ali'i Drive just south of Kailua-Kona. In summer you'll know you've found it when you see the body- and board surfers. Rest rooms, showers, a lifeguard tower, and a coconut grove create a favorite and convenient summer hangout, but this isn't a great beach for swimming. ⊠ *4½ mi south of Kailua-Kona on Ali'i Dr.,* ☎ *808/961–8311.*

Kahalu'u Beach Park. This spot was a favorite of King Kalākaua, whose summer cottage is on the grounds of the Aston Keauhou Beach Resort next door. Kahalu'u is popular with commoners, too, and on weekends there are just too many people. On the other hand, this is one of the best snorkeling places. A strong riptide during high surf pulls swimmers away from shore. Facilities include a pavilion, rest rooms, showers, a lifeguard tower, and limited parking. A narrow path takes you directly to the Resort's Beach Bar & Grill, which serves sandwiches and plate lunches. ⊠ *5½ mi south of Kailua-Kona on Ali'i Dr.,* ☎ *808/961–8311.*

Ho'okena Beach Park. You'll feel like an adventurer when you come upon Ho'okena, at the northern end of Kauhakō Bay. When Mark Twain visited, 2,500 people populated the busy seaport village. You can still find gas lampposts dating from the early 1900s. This dark-gray coral-and-lava-sand beach offers good swimming, snorkeling, and bodysurfing. Rest rooms, showers, and picnic tables are available at the park. The access road is narrow and bumpy. ⊠ *2-mi drive down road bordered by ruins of stone wall off Hwy. 11, 23 mi south of Kailua-Kona,* ☎ *808/961–8311.*

Nāpō'opo'o Beach Park. The best way to enjoy this marine preserve is to take a snorkel, scuba, or glass-bottom boat tour from Keauhou Bay. A 27-ft white obelisk indicates where Captain James Cook was killed in 1779. While this six-acre beach park has a picnic pavilion, the beach consists of rocks, making access into the water difficult. ⊠ *Kealakekua Bay.*

Green Sand (Mahana) Beach. You need good hiking shoes, or a permit and a four-wheel-drive vehicle to get to this truly green crescent, one of the most unusual and prettiest beaches on the island. The beach lies at the base of Pu'u o Mahana, a cinder cone formed during an early eruption of Mauna Loa; the greenish tint is caused by an accumulation of olivine that forms in volcanic eruptions. Swimming is dangerous in this windy, remote area, and there are no facilities. Still, in calm water close to the shore, the aquamarine surf feels great and you find yourself in a surreal grass plain landscape. Follow the trail 2 to 3 mi along the shoreline. Or obtain a four-wheel-drive permit from **Hawaiian Homelands** (⊠ 160 Baker Ave., Hilo 96720, ☎ 808/974–4250). They'll give you a key to the gate for a $25 deposit. ⊠ *2½ mi northeast of South Point, off Hwy. 11,* ☎ *808/974–4250.*

Punalu'u Beach Park. The endangered Hawaiian green sea turtle nests in the black sand of this beautiful and easily accessible beach. Fishponds are just inland. At the northern end of the beach near the boat ramp lie the ruins of a heiau and a flat sacrificial stone. This used to be a sugar and army port until the tidal wave of 1946 destroyed the buildings. Offshore rip currents are extremely dangerous, though you'll see a few local surfers riding the waves. There are rest rooms across the road. Inland is a memorial to Henry Opukaha'ia. In 1809, when he was 17, Opukaha'ia swam out to a fur-trading ship in the harbor and asked to sail as a cabin boy. When he reached New England, he entered the Foreign Mission School in Connecticut, but he died of typhoid fever in 1818. His dream of bringing Christianity to the Islands inspired the American Board of Missionaries in 1820 to send the first Protestant missionaries to Hawai'i. ⊠ *Hwy. 11, 27 mi south of Volcanoes National Park,* ☎ *808/961–8311.*

Ahalanui Park. This three-acre beach park with a ½-acre pond heated by a volcanic steam opened in 1993 to replace earlier beach parks that were lost to lava flows. The pond here is good for swimming, but the nearby ocean is rough. Drinking water and a few tables are available for picnicking, and there are portable rest rooms. ✉ *Kapoho coast, southeast of Pāhoa, 2½ mi south of junction of Hwys. 132 and 137, Puna District,* ☏ *808/961–8311.*

MacKenzie State Recreation Area. This 13-acre park shaded by ironwoods is good for picnicking. You can't swim here, but there are rest rooms. ✉ *Off Hwy. 137, 2 mi south of junction with Hwy. 132, Puna District,* ☏ *808/961–8311.*

Isaac Hale Beach Park. Oceanfront park facilities include rest rooms and picnic areas. It's a good place for an afternoon nap but is dangerous for swimming. ✉ *Off Hwy. 137, north of junction with Hwy. 132, Puna District,* ☏ *808/961–8311.*

Onekahakaha Beach Park. A protected, white-sand beach makes this a favorite for Hilo families with small children. Lifeguards are on duty year-round. The park has picnic pavilions, rest rooms, and showers. ✉ *Follow Kalaniana'ole Ave. east 3 mi south of Hilo,* ☏ *808/961–8311.*

Leleiwi Beach Park and Richardson Ocean Park. Near Hilo, along Hilo's Keaukaha shoreline laced with bays, inlets, lagoons, and pretty parks, these two beaches are adjacent to each other. The grassy area is ideal for picnics. The beaches are rocky and dangerous for swimming, though you can dip your feet in the shallow areas. ✉ *2349 Kalaniana'ole Ave.; follow Kalaniana'ole Ave. east along the water about 4 mi south of Hilo,* ☏ *808/961–8311.*

Reeds Bay Beach Park. Rest rooms, showers, drinking water, calm and safe swimming, and proximity to downtown Hilo are the enticements of this cove. Cold freshwater springs seep from the bottom of a nearby pond and rise in the saltwater. ✉ *Banyan Dr. and Kalaniana'ole Ave., Hilo,* ☏ *808/961–8311.*

DINING

Choosing a place to eat in the western part of the Big Island is difficult, as there are many good, established restaurants and a wide variety of ethnic eateries. All along Ali'i Drive in Kailua-Kona, sunny little restaurants and cafés with indoor-outdoor seating serve numerous cuisines as well as regular American/Hawai'i regional menus. Hotels along the Kohala Coast invest in top chefs and, between that and the opulent settings, diners are rarely disappointed. Upcountry Waimea—just a 40-minute drive inland from the resorts—also has an array of restaurants. While Hilo's dining scene may seem less exciting, restaurants are often inexpensive family places where good, substantial food makes up for lack of atmosphere. For price category explanations, *see* Dining *in* Smart Travel Tips.

Hilo

American/Casual

$$ ✗ **Harrington's.** A popular and reliable steak and seafood restaurant right on Reeds Bay, Harrington's has a dining lānai that extends over the water. The fresh mahimahi meunière, served with browned butter, lemon, and parsley, and the Slavic steak, thinly sliced and slathered with garlic butter, are two popular dishes. Daily specials might include lobster-stuffed 'ahi and chicken Florentine. ✉ *135 Kalaniana'ole Ave.,* ☏ *808/961–4966. MC, V. No lunch weekends.*

$–$$ ✗ **Fiasco's.** Fiasco's is famous for its margarita specials and 27 varieties of domestic and imported beer. You can't go wrong at this inexpensive restaurant close to movie theaters and Hilo's largest shopping mall: fajitas, chicken wings, and an all-you-can-eat soup-and-salad bar. There is live entertainment Thursday, Friday, and Saturday nights. ✉ *200 Kanoelehua Ave.,* ☏ *808/935–7666. AE, D, MC, V.*

$–$$ ✕ **Seaside.** This family-home eatery is casual and can get noisy at times. It's also one of the best fish restaurants around. Most of the fish served are raised in the 10-acre pond or are caught in Hawaiian-style fish traps when they swim in from the ocean via a connecting waterway. Fried *āholehole* (young Hawaiian flagtail) is a signature dish, as is mullet steamed in ti leaves. Both the patio and the dining room afford great water views. Beer, wine, and sake are available. ⊠ *1790 Kalaniana'ole Ave.,* ☏ *808/935–8825. MC, V. Closed Mon. No lunch.*

$–$$ ✕ **Uncle Billy's Restaurant.** The decor is pure Hawaiian kitsch—right out of 1930s Hollywood—but the thatched roofs, tinkling capiz-shell wind chimes, and Tahitian-print curtains add to the fun, as does a free nightly hula show. Choose from mahimahi meunière, teriyaki chicken, and other local specialties. ⊠ *Hilo Bay Hotel, 87 Banyan Dr.,* ☏ *808/935–0861. AE, D, DC, MC, V. No lunch.*

$ ✕ **Ken's House of Pancakes.** For years this 24-hour coffee shop between the airport and the Banyan Drive hotels has been a gathering place for Hilo residents. Ken's serves good pancakes and omelets. They're cheap, too. This is a fun, inexpensive diner, with close to 180 items on the menu, all served around the clock; a paniolo prime-rib night; and a "Golden Oldies" Sunday. ⊠ *1730 Kamehameha Ave.,* ☏ *808/935–8711. Reservations not accepted. AE, D, DC, MC, V.*

Chinese

$–$$$ ✕ **Ting Hao.** This Mandarin restaurant on the edge of Hilo Bay emphasizes fresh island fish with offerings that change daily. Entrées include spicy Szechuan and Hunan dishes and scrumptious specialties from Taiwan and Beijing. The special slow-roasted Peking duck, wrapped in a Mandarin pastry layer and served with plum sauce, must be ordered a day in advance. ⊠ *Hawai'i Naniloa Resort, 93 Banyan Dr.,* ☏ *808/935–8888. AE, D, DC, MC, V. Closed Tues.*

Hawaiian

$ ✕ **Kuhio Grille.** There is no ambience to speak of, and your water is served in unbreakable plastic, but if you're searching for local fare— that eclectic and undefinable fusion of ethnic cuisines—Kuhio Grille is a must. Sam Araki serves a one-pound *laulau* (ti-leaf steamed dish), made with Waipi'o Valley–grown taro leaves and pork, alongside "loco" plate lunches and grilled meats. It's a cafeteria-like place at the edge of Hilo's largest shopping mall, and is open 24 hours on weekends. ⊠ *Prince Kūhiō Shopping Plaza, 111 E. Puainako St., at Hwy. 11,* ☏ *808/959–2336. MC, V.*

Italian

$$ ✕ **Pescatore.** An intimate old-world atmosphere with dark wood and plush red chairs is the setting for traditional dishes such as veal with sage and prosciutto, and a classic cioppino. It's right in downtown Hilo and is recommended for families. In addition to lunch and dinner daily, the restaurant serves breakfast on weekends. ⊠ *235 Keawe St., at Haili St.,* ☏ *808/969–9090. AE, D, MC, V.*

Japanese

$$ ✕ **Ocean Sushi Deli.** Fresh seafood dishes and superb sushi rolls will make you quickly forget the mediocre ambience of Formica tables and neon lights. Authentic and affordable, most sushi rolls are just $4.50 each, and there are dozens from which to choose. 'Ahi *poke* (seasoned raw tuna), fried limpets, and chewy *taco* (octopus) salad are favorites with the local crowd, but there are also more familiar, equally delectable dishes such as sake-steamed scallops. The place is popular and almost always crowded. ⊠ *239 Keawe St.,* ☏ *808/961–6625. AE, MC, V.*

Big Island Dining

$ ✕ **Honu's Nest.** This tiny restaurant (just four tables and a window bar) overlooking Hilo Bay is a local favorite. A Japanese menu with a contemporary local twist includes luscious and spicy curries, tempura, and homemade ginger and teriyaki sauces. Each *donburi* (bowl of rice topped with your menu choice) or *teishaku* (plate with rice on the side) comes with fragrant miso soup. The staff is friendly, the ceramic bowls are exquisite, and the prices are hard to beat. Try to avoid Hilo's lunch rush hour. ⊠ *270 Kamehameha Ave.,* ☎ *808/935–9321. Reservations not accepted. No credit cards. Closed Sun. No dinner.*

Thai

$ ✕ **Royal Siam.** More than 50 Thai dishes appear on the menu of this well-established restaurant in the heart of the old downtown district. Many vegetarian choices are available. Try one of the five fresh curries or tangy stir-fried garlic shrimp with coconut milk and wild mushrooms. ⊠ *70 Mamo St.,* ☎ *808/961–6100. AE, D, DC, MC, V. Closed Sun.*

Volcano

Contemporary

$$–$$$ ✕ **Kīlauea Lodge.** Chef Albert Jeyte combines contemporary trends with traditional cooking styles from his native Germany, France, and America. Built in 1938 as a scouting retreat, the restaurant still has the original stone "Friendship Fireplace" embedded with coins from around the world. The roaring fire, koa tables, and warm lighting create a cozy, intimate lodge ambience. Entrées come with a delicious soup du jour, salad, and freshly baked three-grain bread. The signature dessert, a Grand Marnier custard, is sensational. ⊠ *Old Volcano Hwy., Volcano Village,* ☎ *808/967–7366. AE, MC, V. No lunch.*

$–$$ ✕ **Surt's.** Chef Surt Thammountha's fusion cuisine combines Asian fire with European traditions. In a modern setting of glass tables with Fiesta ware and bold stemware, guests may enjoy such specialties as escargot on mushroom caps in creamy champagne sauce, lobster ravioli, and blackened `ahi with a Mediterranean tomato sauce. A nice wine list adds to unexpectedly fine dining on top of a volcano. A second location, Surt's By the Bay, serves lunch and dinner in downtown Hilo. ⊠ *Old Volcano Hwy., Volcano Village,* ☎ *808/967–8511;* ⊠ *60 Keawe St., Suite 103, Hilo,* ☎ *808/969–9601. AE, D, DC, MC, V.*

Continental

$$–$$$ ✕ **Ka `Ōhelo Dining Room.** Perched right at the edge of Kīlauea Crater in a mountain-lodge setting, this restaurant serves up breakfast and luncheon buffets primarily for tour groups during the day. But at night it's quiet. The setting, at the rim of a volcano, is the thing, but you won't go wrong with the fresh catch of the day or the prime rib. ⊠ *Volcano House, Hawai`i Volcanoes National Park,* ☎ *808/967–7321. AE, D, DC, MC, V.*

Kailua-Kona and South Kona

American/Casual

$$–$$$$ ✕ **Chart House at Waterfront Row.** Many come to this casual chain restaurant, which overlooks the ocean from the shopping and dining complex on Ali`i Drive, for drinks and appetizers. The extensive menu is reliable and seldom changes. Dinners include a good selection of fresh local fish. A cool gray, teal, and peach interior, and prints of old Hawaiian maps on the tables complement the artwork displayed. ⊠ *75-5770 Ali`i Dr., Kailua-Kona,* ☎ *808/329–2451. AE, DC, MC, V. No lunch.*

$$-$$$$ ✕ **Jameson's by the Sea.** Sit outside next to the ocean or just inside the picture windows for glorious sunset views over Magic Sands Beach. When the water is calm this is a most romantic place. You can choose between three or four island fish specials daily, including Cajun-style preparations. Sautéed scallops with lemon butter and capers and Jameson's special creamy clam chowder are popular as well. ✉ 77-6452 Ali'i Dr., Kailua-Kona, ☎ 808/329–3195. AE, D, DC, MC, V. No lunch weekends.

$-$$$ ✕ **Kona Inn Restaurant.** This open-air restaurant, which faces a wide lawn with the ocean beyond, has been a longtime favorite for cocktails at sunset. Fresh fish—'ahi and mahimahi—and chicken entrées are consistently delectable. Burgers at lunch are generously sized and reasonably priced, and the steak fries are just right. ✉ 75-5744 Ali'i Dr., Kailua-Kona, ☎ 808/329–4455. AE, MC, V.

$$ ✕ **Kona Beach Restaurant at King Kamehameha's Kona Beach Hotel.** The buffet-style meals at this Kailua-Kona hotel are themed and great for families: Monday it's Hawaiian, Friday and Saturday prime rib and seafood. Tables overlook a torchlit lawn. Beyond is the beach, with outrigger canoes and a thatched house built on a restored heiau. A Sunday champagne brunch is served from 9 to 1. ✉ 75-5660 Palani Rd., Kailua-Kona, ☎ 808/329–2911. AE, D, DC, MC, V.

$ ✕ **Bubba Gump Shrimp Company.** For all you shrimp lovers and Forrest Gump fans, the Big Island sports its own spin-off restaurant, right at the ocean's edge. This was once an old-timers' restaurant but is now chaotic and attracts a rambunctious, young crowd. There's a lot of shrimp—for breakfast, lunch, and dinner every day—and you attract the attention of your waiter with a sign that says: RUN FORREST RUN. ✉ 75-5776 Ali'i Dr., Kailua-Kona, ☎ 808/331–8442. AE, D, DC, MC, V.

$ ✕ **Ocean View Inn.** To those on a tight budget, this local hangout facing the pier at Kailua Bay has been a lifesaver for breakfast, lunch, and dinner since the 1920s. Chinese and American food are on the plate-lunch menu, and you can get Hawaiian specialties à la carte. Although there is no atmosphere to speak of, the servings are ample. ✉ 75-5683 Ali'i Dr., Kailua-Kona, ☎ 808/329–9998. No credit cards. Closed Mon.

Contemporary/Hawaiian

$$-$$$ ✕ **Huggo's.** Open windows extend out over the rocks at the ocean's edge, and at times you can almost touch the manta rays drawn to the spotlights at night. Relax with a Kīlauea cocktail for two, or feast on fresh local seafood. For lighter fare, try an exquisite dinner-size salad with fresh bread. This popular spot also offers nightly live entertainment and can get crowded. Huggo On the Rocks, next door, serves tropical drinks. ✉ 75-5828 Kahakai Rd., off Ali'i Dr., Kailua-Kona, ☎ 808/329–1493. D, DC, MC, V.

$$ ✕ **Palm Café.** An open-air, elegant restaurant with sophisticated track lights and beautiful red, white, and black decor overlooks the ocean and is within walking distance of downtown Kailua-Kona. Among its fresh, Pacific Rim dishes are such entrées as 'ahi filet in ginger and soy sauce, and daily fresh fish prepared three different ways. Appetizers made with local produce include Manuka farms' spinach salad with Hawai'i's famous pipi kaula (beef). ✉ 75-5805 Ali'i Dr., Kailua-Kona, ☎ 808/329–8200. AE, D, DC, MC, V. Closed Mon.

$$ ✕ **Sam Choy's Restaurant.** In the Kaloko Industrial Park near Keāhole–Kona International Airport, Sam's attracts workers in the surrounding area for hearty, local-style breakfasts and lunches—saimin, stew omelets, and Hawaiian burritos. The restaurant has no liquor license, but Tuesday through Saturday nights, customers bring their own wine and settle in for some hearty Hawai'i regional cuisine. The inexpensive menu almost always includes fresh fish, Chinese honey duck, and macadamia-nut-crusted chicken breast. ✉ *73-5576 Kauhola St., Bay 1, Koloko Industrial Park, Kailua-Kona,* ☎ *808/326–1545. D, MC, V. BYOB.*

$–$$ ✕ **Ke'ei Café.** It may not look like much, this small restaurant housed in a former seafood market, but you can expect delicious dinners with Brazilian, Asian, and European flavors and fresh ingredients provided by local farmers. Try the Thai red curry or wok-seared 'ahi accompanied by a selection from the extensive wine list. This is the only place south of Kailua-Kona for a fine meal. At press time Ke'ei Café was planning to build a larger restaurant closer to the town of Kainaliu. ✉ *Hwy. 11, south of Mile Marker 106, Hōnaunau,* ☎ *808/328–8451. Reservations essential. No credit cards. Closed Sun.–Mon.*

Continental

$–$$ ✕ **Tropics at Royal Kona Resort.** At dusk, when the sun outlines the boats bobbing offshore, you'll have a lovely, peaceful view at this open-air dining room overlooking Kailua Bay and within walking distance of central Kailua-Kona. The restaurant serves daily breakfast buffets and is open four nights a week for à la carte dinners, but the place is known for its ample seafood and prime-rib buffets on Tuesday, Friday, and Saturday nights, a good-value feast for big eaters. The hotel hosts lū'au four times a week. ✉ *75-5852 Ali'i Dr., Kailua-Kona,* ☎ *808/329–3111. AE, D, DC, MC, V.*

Eclectic

$$–$$$ ✕ **Edward's at Kanaloa.** This local favorite has delicious Mediterranean food with North African and Middle Eastern overtones, and dinner prices are within reason. The Moroccan-spiced Tagine chicken comes atop saffron couscous. The Aegean salmon and shrimp are served with roasted-red-pepper sauce. Luscious desserts vary daily but always include a praline chocolate-mousse cake. ✉ *Kanaloa at Kona, 78-261 Manukai St., Kailua-Kona,* ☎ *808/322–1434 or 808/322–9625. AE, DC, MC, V.*

$–$$ ✕ **Oodles of Noodles and Paradise Spice Café.** Renowned chef Amy Ferguson-Ota combines Southwestern flavors with Hawai'i regional cuisine and a touch of French. The lunch and dinner menu features noodles of all types, in all shapes, from all ethnic backgrounds—be it as delicate spring rolls or as a crisp garnish to an exquisite salad. Breakfasts include classic French toast and other conventional items. Hawaiian native woods like mango, 'ohi'a, and koa complement vivid blue, green, and yellow walls. ✉ *Crossroads Shopping Center, 75-1129 Henry St., Kailua-Kona,* ☎ *808/329–9222. AE, D, DC, MC, V.*

French

$$–$$$ ✕ **La Bourgogne.** A genial husband-and-wife team owns this relaxing, country-style restaurant with dark-wood walls and private, romantic booths. The traditional-French menu features classics such as beef filet with a cabernet sauvignon sauce, escargot, rack of lamb with roasted garlic and rosemary, and a less-traditional venison with a pomegranate glaze. ✉ *Kuakini Plaza S. on Hwy. 11, 77-6400 Nālani, Kailua-Kona,* ☎ *808/329–6711. Reservations essential. AE, D, DC, MC, V. No smoking. Closed Sun. and Mon. No lunch.*

Greek

$–$$ ✕ **Cassandra's Greek Taverna.** The blue and white colors of the Greek flag decorate Cassandra's, complementing the many authentic selections. Greek salads, a gyro plate of sliced beef with roast potatoes, *dolmades* (grape leaves stuffed with meat and rice), moussaka, and a variety of souvlaki (lamb, beef, chicken) keep dinners interesting, but the restaurant's main attractions are the occasional belly dancer Saturday night and Far East live soloist music on Friday. ✉ *75-5719 W. Ali'i Dr., Kailua-Kona,* ☎ *808/334–1066. AE, D, DC, MC, V. No lunch Sun.*

Indonesian

$–$$ ✕ **Sibu.** In the heart of Kailua-Kona and hidden by large potted plants inside a tiny shopping mall, this small Indonesian restaurant is a favorite with locals. Try shrimp flavored with delicate lemongrass, coconut milk, and fragrant Indonesian spices or a hearty vegetable *satay* (grilled, marinated cubes of meat) with lush cherry tomatoes grilled over an open flame. ✉ 75-5695 Ali'i Dr., Kailua-Kona, ☎ 808/329–1112. *No credit cards.*

Italian

$$–$$$ ✕ **Michaelangelo's.** This pasta restaurant on the second level of Waterfront Row offers great oceanside dining, and the menu appeals to early bird hungry families. Pastas, with such toppings as lobster and garlic, or scallops in creamy macadamia-nut sauce, come with homemade focaccia. The place rocks after 10 with a live DJ. ✉ *Waterfront Row, Kailua-Kona,* ☎ 808/329–4436. *D, DC, MC, V.*

Japanese

$–$$ ✕ **Teshima's.** Local businesspeople show up at Teshima's whenever they're in the mood for reliable Big Island Japanese-American cooking. Service is so-so, but residents come for the sashimi, beef *hekka* (beef and vegetables cooked together in an iron pot), and puffy shrimp tempura. You might also want to try a *teishoku* (tray) of assorted Japanese delicacies. The restaurant is 15 minutes south of Kailua-Kona. ✉ *Māmalahoa Hwy., Honalo,* ☎ 808/322–9140. *No credit cards.*

Thai

$–$$ ✕ **Thai Rin Restaurant.** The friendly owner, the quiet atmosphere, and the affordable prices make this an attractive spot for lunch or dinner. The restaurant, within walking distance of downtown Kailua-Kona, is modest, but the food is authentic and adequate. Thai spring rolls, green-papaya salad, crab stir-fry, and Thai garlic shrimp or squid are favorites. ✉ 75-5799 Ali'i Dr., Kailua-Kona, ☎ 808/329–2929. *AE, D, DC, MC, V.*

Kohala Coast

American/Casual

$$$–$$$$ ✕ **The Grill at The Orchid at Mauna Lani.** With an award-winning
★ wine list and a superb menu, this stellar restaurant has earned a top-notch reputation. Rich koa-wood paneling and a piano with a small dance floor give it an old-world ambience. Entrées expand on the cuisine of high-end steak houses, with robust dishes such as a 23-ounce porterhouse with asparagus and roasted Waimea-tomato salsa. Open-air seating is available, and the service is impeccable. ✉ *The Orchid at Mauna Lani, 1 N. Kanikū Dr., Kohala Coast,* ☎ 808/885–2000. *Reservations essential. AE, D, DC, MC, V.*

$$–$$$ ✕ **Big Island Steak House.** The walls here are adorned with Hawaiian kitsch dating from the '30s, '40s, and '50s—'ukuleles, steamer trunks, a zany grass-skirted gorilla, and the like. As the name implies, the place serves steak—large portions in different styles, straight from the grill and without much fanfare. On the menu are also seafood dishes, such as coconut shrimp, and vegetarian pastas. ✉ *King's Shops, Waikoloa Resort, Waikoloa Beach Dr., Waikoloa,* ☎ 808/886–8805. *AE, D, MC, V. No lunch.*

$–$$ ✕ **Harbor Grill.** The view of Matson storage containers on the docks of Kawaihae Harbor may not seem too exciting, yet this popular little restaurant is always packed. Try the great crab cakes, or order local fish any way you want. Monday night is lobster night. You may have to wait for one of the lānai tables, or you can dine inside in a funky area full of beachcombing treasures. ✉ *Kawaihae Harbor, Hwy. 270, Kawaihae,* ☎ 808/882–1368. *V.*

$–$$ ✕ **Palm Terrace at the Hilton Waikoloa Village.** This open-air restaurant sits next to a cascading waterfall and a pond with gliding swans. It's open for American-style breakfast, with such dishes as fresh fruit and smoked salmon, and offers affordable buffet dinners that may include seafood, prime rib, or barbecue. ⊠ *425 Waikoloa Beach Dr., Waimea,* ☎ *808/886–1234. AE, D, DC, MC, V. No lunch.*

Cajun/Creole

$$–$$$ ✕ **Roussel's.** Here's a touch of New Orleans cuisine smack in the middle of a golf course. The entrées that have made Roussel's popular include shrimp Creole, gumbo, and blackened prime rib. The restaurant bows to golfers' demands as well, with burgers, club sandwiches, and chicken wings available during much of the day. The big white-frame windows that open to the trade winds add plantation-style richness to the experience. ⊠ *68-1792 Melia St., Waikoloa Village Golf Club, Waikoloa,* ☎ *808/883–9644. AE, DC, MC, V. No dinner Sun.–Mon.*

Chinese

$$–$$$ ✕ **Kirin.** This Chinese restaurant in Hilton Waikoloa Village serves authentic Cantonese fare in a classic setting that includes rare Chinese artifacts and several 1000-year-old Chinese furnishings. More than a hundred exotic dishes appear on the menu, many with ingredient combinations you may not be used to, but which prove to be delicious. How about prawns with honey-glazed walnuts and a citrus dressing or a whole open-flame-roasted Peking duck? ⊠ *425 Waikoloa Beach Dr., Waimea,* ☎ *808/886–1288. AE, D, DC, MC, V.*

$–$$$ ✕ **Grand Palace Chinese Restaurant.** A reasonable alternative in a land of high-price hotel dining, this successful and friendly Chinese restaurant is open for lunch and dinner. An extensive menu offers Chinese items from most regions, including such standards as egg foo young, wonton soup, chicken with snow peas, and beef with broccoli. More adventurous are sautéed local seafood, lobster, and sizzling shrimp with garlic sauce. Etched-glass panels add a nice touch to the decor. ⊠ *King's Shops, Waikoloa Resort, Waikoloa Beach Dr., Waikoloa,* ☎ *808/886–6668. AE, DC, MC, V.*

Contemporary/Hawaiian

$$$$ ✕ **Hale Samoa at Kona Village Resort.** Slightly formal, superbly ro-
★   mantic, this Kona Village restaurant has a magical atmosphere, especially in the glow of sunset. In a Samoan setting with tapa screens and candles, you can feast on prix-fixe dinners that change daily. Specialties may include papaya and coconut bisque, duck stuffed with andouille sausage on a mango-and-orange coulis, or wok-charred prime strip loin. Reservations can be made only on the day you want to dine, and they are essential. The entry road to Kona Village is 6 mi out on Highway 19 from Kailua. Resort wear is the norm here at dinner. ⊠ *Queen Ka'ahumanu Hwy., Kohala Coast,* ☎ *808/325–5555. Reservations essential. AE, DC, MC, V. Closed Wed., Fri., and 1 wk in Dec. No lunch*

$$$–$$$$ ✕ **Coast Grille at the Westin Hāpuna Beach Prince Hotel.** This spacious,
★   high-ceiling seafood restaurant has a lānai overlooking the ocean. Oyster lovers should head straight to the oyster bar. When available, the must-try fish here is the delicate farm-raised *moi,* a fish that in ancient times was enjoyed only by chiefs. Otherwise, savor such specialties as grilled rare 'ahi steak Napoleon with foie gras, or rack of lamb with a peppercorn crust. Save room for the white chocolate ginger parfait with macadamia praline mousse. ⊠ *Westin Hāpuna Beach Prince Hotel, 62-100 Kauna'oa Dr., Waimea,* ☎ *808/880–1111. AE, D, DC, MC, V.*

$$$–$$$$ ✕ **Kamuela Provision Company at the Hilton Waikoloa Village.** You'll have a spectacular view of the Kohala-Kona coastline as you sample flavorful Pacific fusion selections such as a bouillabaisse with nori *cros-*

tini (toasted bread) and red-curry aioli, or brochette of beef tenderloin. Tables along the lānai open to sea breezes. It's a great place to sip cocktails. Thursday through Saturday, a pianist provides dance music in the lounge in the evening. The Wine Bar, a new addition to the restaurant, has more than 40 labels available by the glass and hosts monthly wine events. ⊠ *425 Waikoloa Beach Dr., Waimea,* ☎ *808/886–1234. AE, D, DC, MC, V.*

$$$–$$$$ ✕ **Pahu i'a at Four Seasons Resort Hualālai.** The English translation ★ for the word *pahu i'a* is "aquarium." For sure, the 9-by-4-ft centerpiece in the entrance casts a dreamy light through this exquisite restaurant, which is closer to the ocean than any other. Outdoor deck seating is romantic even at breakfast. Meals are imaginative and beautifully presented. Choose sophisticated entrées such as grilled marinated veal sirloin in a red wine *jus;* or Keāhole lobster on a bed of warm spinach, topped with a mushroom salad with a shoyu and citrus reduction. Warm chocolate soufflé is the most popular dessert. ⊠ *Four Seasons Resort Hualālai, 100 Ka'ūpūlehu Dr., Ka'ūpūlehu/Kona,* ☎ *808/325–8000. No lunch. AE, D, DC, MC, V.*

$$–$$$$ ✕ **The Batik at Westin Mauna Ke'a Beach Hotel.** For the hotel's ele- ★ gant signature restaurant—with its glass-enclosed, split-level waterfront dining room—executive chef Thomas Woods combines French-Mediterranean elements with Asian influences to create dazzling dishes such as roasted breast of pheasant with mushrooms, artichokes, and foie gras. Romantic dinner music complements the evening. ⊠ *62-100 Mauna Ke'a Beach Dr., Waimea,* ☎ *808/882–7222. AE, D, DC, MC, V. Closed Tues. and Sat.*

$$–$$$$ ✕ **CanoeHouse at the Mauna Lani Bay Hotel and Bungalows.** This open- ★ air beachfront restaurant, surrounded by fishponds and with its signature shining koa canoe, is widely hailed as one of Hawai'i's best. Its cuisine is Pacific Rim the way it used to be: a matching of pure Asian and Western flavors with imaginative entrées such as grilled lemon-pepper scallops with wild mushrooms and Chinese-mustard soy sauce, and a unique steak-and-lobster combination that includes Kona-raised lobster, roasted shiitake mushrooms, jasmine rice, and liliko'i butter. Finish your meal with a velvety crème brûlée. ⊠ *68-1400 Mauna Lani Dr., Kohala Coast,* ☎ *808/885–6622. AE, D, DC, MC, V.*

$$–$$$ ✕ **Gallery Restaurant at Mauna Lani Bay Hotel and Bungalows.** Bordering the Francis H. I'i Brown Golf Course, the open-air Gallery has a comfortable clubhouse atmosphere with an impressive koa bar. Fresh island ingredients find their way into appealing dishes, including five different preparations for local fish. Try it grilled with roasted fennel and Waimea yellow tomatoes or blackened with a passion fruit beurre blanc. ⊠ *68-1400 Mauna Lani Dr., Kohala Coast,* ☎ *808/885–7777. AE, D, DC, MC, V. No dinner Sun.–Mon.*

$$–$$$ ✕ **Hawai'i Calls at Outrigger Waikoloa Beach.** With its retro art, Hawai'i Calls offers a nostalgic taste of the past, from the '20s to the '50s, when surfer Duke Kahanamoku was king. The menu, however, is contemporary and fresh, with specialties such as steamed moi stuffed with shrimp and water chestnuts and served with a Cantonese green-onion and black-bean sauce. Next door, the Clipper Lounge serves romantic drinks. ⊠ *69-275 Waikoloa Beach Dr., Waikoloa,* ☎ *808/ 886–6789. AE, D, DC, MC, V.*

$$–$$$ ✕ **The Pavilion at Westin Mauna Ke'a Beach Hotel.** Relax on the lānai overlooking the white sands of Kauna'oa Beach in this family-oriented restaurant that serves traditional fare such as pastas and grilled items as well as sophisticated regional-style seafood. There's also an elaborate breakfast buffet that includes everything from carrot juice and bagels with smoked salmon to miso soup. At night, below in the lapping waves, you'll see manta rays swim underneath torch lights.

⊠ *62-100 Mauna Ke'a Beach Dr., Waimea,* ☎ *808/882–7222. AE, D, DC, MC, V.*

\$\$–\$\$\$ ✕ **Roy's Restaurant at Waikoloa.** At Roy's Restaurant, there's an
★ enormous selection of appetizers that you can order as starters or
make a complete meal of: if you decide not to select an individual wood-
oven pizza (hard choice!), try *pūpū* (hors d'oeuvre) such as blackened
'ahi with a hot soy-mustard butter sauce, sweet onion tart, or baby back
ribs. There's an extensive wine list to go with the innovative fare of
Roy Yamaguchi, one of the inventors of Hawai'i regional cuisine.
Window tables overlook a golf-course lake. Be forewarned that the place
tends to get noisy. ⊠ *King's Shops, Waikoloa Resort, Waikoloa Beach
Dr., Waikoloa,* ☎ *808/886–4321. AE, D, DC, MC, V.*

\$\$ ✕ **Bamboo Restaurant.** It's out of the way, the food is quite wonderful, and the service has a country flair. Creative entrées feature fresh
island fish prepared several ways; Thai-style fish, for example, combines lemongrass, kaffir lime leaves, and coconut milk for an exquisite
flavor. The restaurant is proud of its passion fruit margaritas and refreshing passion fruit iced tea. The decor is inviting and artistic, com-
bining such elements as bamboo finishes, bold artwork, and an old
unfinished wooden floor. Friday and Saturday nights local musicians
entertain. ⊠ *Old Takata Store, Hwy. 270, Hāwī,* ☎ *808/889–5555.
DC, MC, V. Closed Mon. No dinner Sun.*

Eclectic

\$\$ ✕ **Orchid Court at The Orchid at Mauna Lani.** Seafood fettuccine, salads and sandwiches, chilled vegetable wraps, and fresh fish that may
be wok-seared or served with ginger butter suit the light, fresh ambience of this casual, family-oriented restaurant bordering the resort's
native gardens. This is also a great place to start the day with a fine
breakfast. ⊠ *1 N. Kanikū Dr., Kohala Coast,* ☎ *808/885–2000. AE,
D, DC, MC, V. No lunch.*

Italian

\$\$–\$\$\$ ✕ **Donatoni's at the Hilton Waikoloa Village.** Antipasti and scrumptious
dishes with the subtle sauces of northern Italy are served in this romantic restaurant. From *orecchiette* (little disk-shape pasta) with goat cheese,
fresh tomatoes, and herbs, to old-world osso buco with risotto, this intimate place sets out to please. Reminiscent of an Italian villa and overlooking a lagoon, Donatoni's has tables on various levels and a wide lānai.
Be sure to look over the extensive Italian wine and champagne list, and
treat yourself to an authentic tiramisu for dessert. ⊠ *425 Waikoloa Beach
Dr., Waimea,* ☎ *808/886–1234. AE, D, DC, MC, V. No lunch.*

\$\$ ✕ **Café Pesto.** Popular, and crowded at lunchtime, this boldly decorated harborside restaurant has earned a reputation for its innovative
pizzas and other Mediterranean dishes prepared with Pacific Rim flair
and island ingredients. Sample a pizza with chili-grilled shrimp, shiitake mushrooms, and cilantro crème fraîche; garlic shrimp; or the popular risotto made with Kona lobster and sweet Thai chilies. A second
location is in Hilo right across from the bay. ⊠ *Kawaihae Shopping
Center, Kawaihae,* ☎ *808/882–1071;* ⊠ *New S. Hata Bldg., 308
Kamehameha Ave., Hilo,* ☎ *808/969–6640. AE, D, DC, MC, V.*

Japanese

\$\$–\$\$\$\$ ✕ **Imari at the Hilton Waikoloa Village.** This elegant Japanese restau-
★ rant, complete with waterfalls and a teahouse, serves sukiyaki and tempura aimed to please mainland tastes. Beyond the display of Imari
porcelain at the entrance, you'll find *teppan yaki,* (beef or shrimp
cooked table-side), *shabu shabu* (thin slices of beef cooked in broth)
prepared at your table, and an outstanding sushi bar. Impeccable service by kimono-clad waitresses adds to the quiet, refined ambience. ⊠

425 Waikoloa Beach Dr., Waimea, ☎ *808/886–1234. AE, D, DC, MC, V. No lunch.*

$$$ ✕ **Hakone at Westin Hāpuna Beach Prince Hotel.** It's hard not to start
★ whispering in this tranquil and graceful restaurant, open only at night,
where exquisite Japanese sukiyaki and a superb sampler buffet com-
pete with an elaborate sushi bar. You can also opt for entrées such as
assorted tempura or Hakone's signature dish, broiled swordfish with
an Asian cream sauce. A beautiful selection of sake is guaranteed to
enliven your meal. ✉ *Westin Hāpuna Beach Prince Hotel, 62-100
Kauna'oa Dr., Waimea,* ☎ *808/880–1111. AE, D, DC, MC, V. Closed
Sun.–Tues. No lunch.*

Mexican

$–$$ ✕ **Tres Hombres Beach Grill.** This casual, inexpensive Californian-
Mexican restaurant serves burgers, sandwiches, and chilies *rellenos*
(mildly roasted and stuffed with cheese) at lunch. Dinner items include
bean-and-rice combinations, fresh fish, salads, and steaks. A "fit for
life" menu features low-fat entrées. A separate bar is known for its Mexican beer and tequila selection. ✉ *Kawaihae Shopping Center, Kawaihae,* ☎ *808/882–1031;* ✉ *Ali'i Dr. and Wālua Rd., Kailua-Kona,* ☎
808/329–2173. MC, V.

Waimea

American/Casual

$$–$$$ ✕ **Koa House Grill.** In the heart of cowboy country, this family restau-
rant has developed into a busy lunch stop for Waimea's business
crowd. Its down-to-earth dinners vary between bold, all-American
flavors like garlic mashed potatoes and Asian accents such as passion
fruit and ginger. Shrimp scampi is a favorite, and there are also large
steaks and pastas on the menu. A full salad bar features fresh Waimea
greens. Large windows open out onto the Keck Observatory headquarters
and offer a glimpse of the mountains. ✉ *Waimea Shopping Center, 65-
1144 Māmalahoa Hwy.,* ☎ *808/885–2088. AE, D, MC, V.*

$$ ✕ **Parker Ranch Grill.** With cowhides serving as wallpaper and riding
boots as doorknobs, this popular restaurant makes no mistake about
its paniolo identity and Parker Ranch heritage. In front of a blazing hearth
fire, the koa tables, set with hand towels instead of napkins, are a per-
fect setting for "Kamuela pride" beef entrées. A separate bar area of-
fers a variety of pūpū. At press time the Grill was closed due to extensive
reconstruction at the Parker Ranch Shopping Center; the restaurant was
scheduled to reopen by December 2001. ✉ *Parker Ranch Shopping Cen-
ter, 67-1185 Māmalahoa Hwy.,* ☎ *808/887–2624. AE, D, MC, V.*

Contemporary

$$–$$$ ✕ **Merriman's.** This is the signature restaurant of Peter Merriman, one
★ of the pioneers of Hawai'i regional cuisine. Don't miss the opportu-
nity to sample his imaginative and impeccable dishes using local pro-
duce. Merriman's is the home of the original wok-charred 'ahi, usually
served with exquisite buttery Wainaku corn. If you prefer meat, try the
Kahuā Ranch lamb, raised to the restaurant's specifications, or opt for
the prime "Kansas City Cut" steak, grilled to order and served with
pinot noir garlic butter. The extensive wine list includes 22 selections
poured by the glass, and the staff is refreshingly knowledgeable. ✉ *'Opelo
Plaza, Hwy. 19 and 'Opelo Rd.,* ☎ *808/885–6822. Reservations es-
sential. AE, MC, V.*

$$ ✕ **Daniel Thiebaut.** The historic Chock In Store, built in 1900, is open
again: underneath its 11-ft-high ceilings, seven separate dining areas
that once functioned as retail spaces and living quarters now showcase collectibles such as porcelain and original bar stools, as well as a

long redwood community dining table, once the store's countertop. Sig Zane fabrics add warmth to the decor. Chef Thiebaut's French style is enhanced by an Asian touch. Start with a signature appetizer—sweet-corn crab cake with a lemongrass, coconut, and lobster sauce—and save room for theme desserts such as six different strawberry variations when in season. ⊠ *65-1259 Kawaihae Rd.,* ☎ *808/887–2200. AE, D, DC, MC, V.*

Continental

$–$$ ✕ **Edelweiss.** Faithful local diners and visitors alike flock to this relaxed, family-oriented restaurant with rustic redwood furnishings. The chef's rack of lamb is always excellent. A varied menu includes 15 to 20 daily specials (such as a sausage platter and fresh seafood), many rich and with a German flavor. ⊠ *Hwy. 19, entering Waimea,* ☎ *808/885–6800. MC, V. Closed Sun.–Mon. and Sept.*

LODGING

You'll almost always be able to find a room on the Big Island, but you might not get your first choice if you wait until the last minute. Make reservations six months to a year in advance if you're visiting during the winter season, December 15 through April 15. The week after Easter Sunday, when the Merrie Monarch Festival is in full swing, all of Hilo's rooms are taken. Kailua-Kona bursts at the seams in mid-October during the Ironman World Triathlon Championship. (Even tougher than trying to find a room at these times is trying to find a rental car.)

Hotel and car package deals are often available in all price categories; a reputable travel agent should be able to furnish up-to-date information. Some of the older hotels do not have air-conditioning, but they will almost always have fans. All rooms have a TV and phone unless otherwise indicated.

If you choose a bed-and-breakfast, inn, or an out-of-the-way hotel, explain your expectations fully and ask plenty of questions before booking. Be clear about your travel and location needs. Some places require stays of two or three days. Many B&Bs close to Hawai'i Volcanoes National Park are not the best locations for beach and sun worshipers: rain forests come with the price of humid conditions. When booking, ask about car-rental arrangements, as many B&B networks can offer discounted rates. For price category explanations, *see* Lodging *in* Smart Travel Tips.

Hilo

$$$ 🏨 **Shipman House Bed & Breakfast Inn.** Situated on 5½ acres of lush ★ grounds on Reed's Island, and possibly Hilo's most-photographed mansion, the Shipman House is on the national and state registers of historic places. The 100-year-old turreted "castle" has three gracious B&B rooms in the house and two separate cottage units. The house is furnished with antique koa and period pieces, some dating from the days when Queen Lili'uokalani came to tea. On Tuesday night guests are invited to watch the ancient dances of an authentic hula school. If you want to play music yourself, a concert grand piano is available. ⊠ *131 Ka'iulani St., 96720,* ☎ *808/934–8002 or 800/627–8447,* ℻ *808/934–8002,* 🌐 *www.hilo-hawaii.com. 3 rooms, 2 cottage units. Fans, refrigerators, library. AE, MC, V. CP.*

$$–$$$ 🏨 **Hawai'i Naniloa Resort.** Ask for a room with an ocean or bay view when you book a room at this hotel situated on the edge of Hilo Bay. With its glass walls overlooking a manicured lawn and cliffs, the hotel expresses the modest, older elegance of Hilo's past. Rooms are decorated in shades of green and coral. The premium rooms on the ninth floor are especially nice, as is the more expensive premium suite. The spa specializes in Hawaiian treatments. An executive golf course, the Naniloa Country Club, is across Banyan Drive. Several shops are on lobby level. ✉ *93 Banyan Dr., 96720,* ☎ *808/969–3333; 800/367–5360 from the mainland; 800/442–5845 interisland,* FAX *808/969–6622,* WEB *www.naniloa.com. 280 rooms, 15 suites. 2 restaurants, bar, refrigerators, health club, dance club. AE, DC, MC, V.*

$$–$$$ 🏨 **Hilo Hawaiian Hotel.** With large bay-front rooms offering spectacular views of Mauna Keʻa and Coconut Island, this is one of the most pleasant lodgings on Hilo Bay. Streetside rooms overlook the golf course. Most accommodations have private lānai, and kitchenettes are available in the one-bedroom suites. Views of the bay are showcased in the Queen's Court dining room, and the Waiʻoli Lounge has entertainment Friday and Saturday. ✉ *71 Banyan Dr., 96720,* ☎ *808/935–9361; 800/367–5004 from the mainland; 800/272–5275 interisland,* FAX *808/961–9642,* WEB *www.castleresorts.com. 286 rooms, 6 suites. Restaurant, bar, refrigerators, pool, meeting room. AE, D, DC, MC, V.*

$$–$$$ 🏨 **Hilo Seaside Hotel.** The most pleasant rooms here have private lānai and overlook the koi-filled lagoon or are situated around the pool. Lots of foliage along the walkways and friendly personnel create a Hawaiian ambience. This is a peaceful place, except when planes take off and land, as the hotel is near the airport's flight path. Some units have kitchenettes and all have air-conditioning. ✉ *126 Banyan Way, 96720,* ☎ *808/935–0821 or 800/367–7000,* FAX *808/969–9195,* WEB *www.sand-seaside.com. 136 rooms. Restaurant, pool. AE, D, DC, MC, V.*

$$ 🏨 **Hale Kai Bjornen Bed & Breakfast.** On a bluff above Hilo Bay, just 2 mi from downtown Hilo, this 5,400-square-ft modern home has four impeccable rooms and a private loft that is ideal for families—all with grand ocean views and within earshot of lapping waves. All units have private baths and patios, with access to a pool and a hot tub; fresh flowers and bedspreads from Portugal add a warm, European touch. The Norwegian-Hawaiian hosts, Evonne and Paul Bjornen, serve a delightful breakfast—macadamia-nut waffles, Portuguese sausage, fruits, breads, and special egg dishes—on an outdoor deck or in the kitchen's bay-window dining area. ✉ *111 Honoliʻi Pali St., 96720,* ☎ *808/935–6330,* FAX *808/935–8439,* WEB *www.interpac.net/halekai. 4 rooms, 1 suite. Fans, pool, hot tub, laundry service. No credit cards.*

$$ 🏨 **Hilo Bay Hotel, Uncle Billy's.** Don't expect more than a casual, inexpensive place to stay at this friendly, easygoing hotel—a popular stopover for Neighbor Islanders who enjoy proprietor Uncle Billy Kimo's Hawaiian hospitality. A nightly hula show and entertainment during dinner are part of the fun. ✉ *87 Banyan Dr., 96720,* ☎ *808/935–0861; 800/367–5102 from the mainland; 800/442–5841 interisland,* FAX *808/935–7903,* WEB *www.unclebilly.com. 120 rooms. Restaurant, bar, kitchenettes, refrigerators, pool, meeting room. AE, D, DC, MC, V.*

$$ 🏨 **The Inn at Kulaniapia.** With an awesome view of Hilo Bay 4 mi below, as well as access to a magnificent 120-ft waterfall that tumbles into a 300-ft-wide swimming pond, the inn is an oasis of beauty and tranquility. Trails meander to the river, and the activities of both Hilo and Volcano are only a 15-minute drive away over sugarcane roads. Hosts Jane and Len Sutton added Asian accents, koa, and eucalyptus wood floors to the inn. A small generator must run two hours every day (it's a bit noisy). Buffet-style breakfasts are served, and you can cook an informal dinner on the barbecue. ✉ *Box 11338, 96721,* ☎ *808/966–6373 or 888/838–6373,* WEB *www.waterfall.net. 4 rooms. MC, V.*

$–$$ 🏨 **Dolphin Bay Hotel.** All units have kitchens in this clean, modest hotel in a verdant two-acre Hawaiian garden setting four blocks from Hilo Bay. Coffee and fresh fruit are offered daily, and the staff is helpful and

238

Big Island Lodging

welcoming. The rooms do not have phones, but a pay phone is in the lobby. Guests of the hotel, which is in a residential area called Pu'ue'o, return repeatedly, and it's ideal for families who seek a friendly home base. ✉ 333 'Iliahi St., 96720, ☎ 808/935–1466, FAX 808/935–1523, WEB www.dolphinbayhilo.com. 13 rooms, 4 1-bedroom units, 1 2-bedroom unit. Kitchenettes. MC, V.

$ ☷ **Arnott's Lodge.** Owner Doug Arnott has created an ever-expanding budget lodge minutes away from the airport for backpackers, bicyclists, and other active visitors. You can choose from tenting, dormitory-style bunk beds, and semiprivate or private accommodations. Four rooms in a renovated adjacent house have private, tiled bathrooms. Some rooms can be linked to create a family unit. The lodge provides a shared kitchen and a separate gazebo with video facilities. The setting is lush, oceanside wilderness. A young international clientele takes advantage of guided hikes and barbecues provided by the lodge. ✉ 98 'Apapane Rd., 96720, ☎ 808/969–7097, FAX 808/961–9638, WEB www.arnottslodge.com. 12 semiprivate units, 6 private units, 36 bunks. Camping, coin laundry, travel services, airport shuttle. AE, D, DC, MC, V.

$ ☷ **Wild Ginger Inn Bed & Breakfast.** This 24-room inn is reminiscent of '40s Hawai'i plantation-style accommodations. Funky and wildly pink with turquoise trim, the old, wooden building has simple rooms that appeal mostly to a younger crowd. Most rooms have double and twin beds. A big lawn and a jungle garden run along a stream bank. A complimentary buffet breakfast is served on the lānai lobby. There are no phones in the rooms, but pay phones are available. ✉ 100 Pu'u'eo St., 96720, ☎ 808/935–5556 or 800/882–1887, FAX 808/969–1225, WEB www.wildgingerinn.com. 24 rooms. Refrigerators, coin laundry. D, MC, V. CP.

Puna

$–$$$$ ☷ **Kalani Oceanside Eco-Resort.** An unusual tropical getaway, Kalani is an out-of-the-way retreat with healthful cuisine, nearby thermal springs, and a variety of programs on Hawaiian culture, healing, gay relationships, Watsu-therapy (water shiatsu) training, and ecology. Accommodations include campsites, shared rooms with shared bath, cottage units, lodge rooms with private or shared bath, and private, luxurious tree-house units. Bathing suits are optional both on the nearby beach and in the evenings at the resort's Olympic-size pool. ✉ Hwy. 137, Pahoa-Beach Rd., Pahoa 96778, ☎ 808/965–7828 or 800/800–6886, WEB www.kalani.com. 24 rooms, 9 cottages, 4 tree-house units, 3 guest houses. Fans, pool, hot tub, sauna, tennis court, camping, laundry service. AE, D, DC, MC, V.

Volcano/South Point

$$–$$$$ ☷ **Carson's Volcano Cottages.** You can choose the privacy of a romantic hideaway with a full kitchen and a hot tub in the midst of hapu ferns; a deluxe oceanfront cottage down at Kapoho, an hour away; or the intimate rooms and cottages on the property itself. Each unit has its own theme decor and comes with maid service; some units have television. Elaborate breakfasts in the main house's cozy dining room include home-baked breads and such dishes as spinach quiche and poi doughnuts. ✉ Box 503, Volcano 96785, ☎ 808/967–7683 or 800/845–5282, FAX 808/967–8094, WEB www.carsonscottage.com. 5 rooms, 6 cottages. Dining room. AE, D, MC, V.

$–$$$$ ☷ **Chalet Kīlauea Collection.** The Collection comprises five inns and lodges and six vacation houses in and around Volcano Village; the theme rooms, suites, and vacation homes range from basic to extravagant. Best-known is the Inn at Volcano—a "boutique resort." The two-story TreeHouse Suite, with wraparound windows, marble wet bar, and fireplace, gives one the impression of floating on the tops of tree ferns. Afternoon tea is served before a fireplace. A candlelit breakfast under a glittering chandelier adds a touch of elegance. ✉ *Wright Rd., Volcano Village 96785,* ☎ *808/967–7786 or 800/937–7786,* FAX *808/ 967–8660,* WEB *www.volcano-hawaii.com. 11 rooms, 9 suites, 6 houses. AE, D, DC, MC, V.*

$$$ ☒ **Hydrangea Cottage & Mountain House.** On a landscaped jungle estate about a mile away from Hawai'i Volcanoes National Park, the Cottage is a private retreat with a wraparound covered deck and floor-to-ceiling windows looking out over giant tree ferns—home to rare Hawaiian birds. The Mountain House has three bedrooms, each with its own bath. Antique furnishings add to the quiet atmosphere. Both units have a kitchen as well as fixings for you to prepare breakfast. This protected hideaway must be booked via Hawai'i's Best Bed & Breakfasts. ✉ *Reservations: Box 563, Kamuela 96743,* ☎ *808/885– 4550 or 800/262–9912,* FAX *808/885–0559,* WEB *www.bestbnb.com. 1 3-bedroom house, 1 cottage. No credit cards.*

$$$ ☒ **Kīlauea Lodge.** A mile from the Hawai'i Volcanoes National Park
★ entrance, this country inn is possibly the most elegant place to stay in the area. The original building dates from the 1930s, and rooms have their own wood-burning fireplaces. Rich quilts and photographs reflect a Hawaiian theme, but the antiques are distinctly European. There are two separate cottages—one of which is Tutu's Place, a 1929 remodeled two-bedroom cottage off the main property—as well a deluxe honeymoon suite. The restaurant, run by chef-owner Albert Jeyte, has earned a reputation for excellent food. The gift shop sells Jeyte's most popular sauces. Breakfast is included in the price of the room. ✉ *Old Volcano Hwy., about 1 mi northeast of Volcano Store, Volcano Village 96785,* ☎ *808/967–7366,* FAX *808/967–7367,* WEB *www. kilauealodge.com. 11 rooms, 2 cottages. Restaurant, dining room, hot tub. MC, V.*

$$–$$$ ☒ **Hale Ohia Cottages.** Built in 1931 as a vacation home for the
★ Dillingham family, this charming estate has a Japanese hot tub surrounded by ancient trees and glorious gardens. Antique furnishings and unique collectibles, fireplaces, and antique stained glass create a romantic ambience for restful, cozy hours spent close to Hawai'i Volcanoes National Park. The luxurious Ihilani cottage is an octagonal hideaway with a private garden. A luxury unit, prosaically named "Number 44" but poetic as can be with skylights and a see-through fireplace, has a bedroom that incorporates an old watertank. ✉ *Hale Ohia Rd. off Hwy. 11, Volcano Village 96785,* ☎ *808/967–7986 or 800/455–3803,* FAX *808/967–8610,* WEB *www.haleohia.com. 4 suites, 4 cottages. Refrigerators, hot tub. D, DC, MC, V. CP.*

$$–$$$ ☒ **Sunterra Resorts at Sea Mountain.** Avid golfers and seekers of seclusion will appreciate these modest condominiums, bordered by the ocean and fairways and a 25-minute drive away from Hawai'i Volcanoes National Park. The property is adjacent to the black-sand Punalu'u Beach Park, home of the green sea turtle preserve. Condominium units are not plush but have a country feel, rattan furnishings, complete kitchens, lānai, and cleaning services. Higher rates apply for one-night stays. ✉ *95-789 Ninole Loop Rd. (turn off Hwy. 11 at Punalu'u), Punalu'u 96777,* ☎ *808/928–6200 or 800/344–7675,* FAX *808/928–8075,* WEB *www.sunterra.com. 17 1-bedroom units, 6 2-bedroom units, 5 studios. Kitchenettes, pool, 18-hole golf course, 4 tennis courts. MC, V.*

$$–$$$ ☒ **Volcano House.** The charm of the Volcano House is its location at the edge of Kīlauea Caldera, so plan on paying a bit extra to book one of the rooms with a crater view. The clean and comfortable rooms in the main building have period koa furniture. Dinner at the Ka 'Ōhelo Dining Room can stir romance, as can a drink in front of an 'ōhi'a-

wood fire in the lobby's stone fireplace. ✉ *Crater Rim Dr., Box 53, Hawai'i Volcanoes National Park 96718,* ☎ *808/967–7321,* ℻ *808/ 967–8429. 42 rooms. Restaurant. AE, D, DC, MC, V.*

$–$$$ 🏨 **My Island Bed & Breakfast Inn.** Gordon, Joann, and daughter Ki'i Morse opened their historic century-old home and seven-acre botanical estate to visitors in 1985. The house is the oldest in Volcano, built in 1886 by the Lyman missionary family. Three rooms, sharing two baths, are available in the main house. Scattered around the area are five guest houses and another three rooms in private garden apartments. You won't start the day hungry after a deluxe all-you-can-eat breakfast. ✉ *19-3896 Old Volcano Hwy., Volcano Village (Box 100, Volcano 96785),* ☎ *808/967–7216 or 808/967–7110,* ℻ *808/967–7719,* 🌐 *www.myislandinnhawaii.com. 6 rooms, 3 with bath; 5 guest houses. No credit cards.*

$–$$$ 🏨 **Volcano Inn.** Nestled among tree ferns within a rain forest, Volcano Inn offers a choice of private cedar cottages with enormous picture windows, or rooms in the main building, which is a 15-minute walk from the center of Volcano Village. Either way, the owners provide a breakfast every morning that includes fresh eggs and whole-grain breads. Guests of the main-building rooms must share a pay phone. ✉ *19-3820 Old Volcano Hwy., Volcano Village (Box 490, Volcano 96785),* ☎ *808/967– 7293 or 800/997–2292,* ℻ *808/985–7349,* 🌐 *www.volcanoinn.com. 5 rooms, 5 cottages. Refrigerators. AE, D, DC, MC, V.*

$ 🏨 **Shirakawa Motel.** In the remote Ka'ū District, midway between Kona and Hilo near Nā'ālehu, the southernmost town in the United States, this bare and basic motel has been run by the same family since 1921. Families can get connecting units with cooking facilities, though there are places to eat nearby in town. A large one-bedroom unit has a full kitchen. ✉ *95-6040 Māmalahoa Hwy. 11, Wai'ōhinu (Box 467, Nā'ālehu 96772),* ☎ *808/929–7462. 12 rooms. No credit cards.*

Upcountry Kona District

$$$ 🏨 **Hōlualoa Inn.** Six spacious rooms are available in this cedar home situated on a 40-acre estate with glorious coastal views. The inn is in Upcountry Kona amid coffee bushes and fruit orchards, 4 mi above Kailua Bay, and the artists' town of Hōlualoa is steps away. Each room has an island theme. The premium Balinese suite has wraparound windows with stunning views. A lavish breakfast includes estate-grown coffee as well as homemade breads and macadamia-nut butter. Rooftop gazebos inspire quiet, relaxing moments, and for stargazers there's a telescope. ✉ *76-5932 Māmalahoa Hwy. (Box 222), Hōlualoa 96725,* ☎ *808/324–1121 or 800/392–1812,* ℻ *808/322– 2472,* 🌐 *www.konaweb.com/HINN. 6 rooms. Pool, hot tub, billiards. AE, D, DC, MC, V.*

$$–$$$ 🏨 **Hale Maluhia Country Inn B&B.** Family antiques, full use of a modern tiled kitchen, an inviting family and living room, and a Japanese slate Jacuzzi hot tub are among the comforts guests enjoy at this friendly plantation estate, right off a winding coffee road and surrounded by macadamia and mango trees. Breakfast, including make-your-own omelets, is served on the lānai. There's a tiny waterfall and koi pond, with hideaway garden seats scattered around the property. A spacious, romantic cottage is also available. ✉ *76-770 Hualalai Rd., Kailua-Kona 96740,* ☎ *808/329–5773 or 800/559–6627,* ℻ *808/326–5487,* 🌐 *www.hawaii-inns.com. 4 rooms, 1 cottage. Hot tub. AE, D, MC, V.*

Kailua-Kona and South Kona

$$$$ 🏨 **Aston Kona by the Sea.** Complete modern kitchens, tile lānai, and washers and dryers can be found in every suite of this comfortable oceanfront condo complex. An open-air lobby and a helpful reception desk add to the friendly atmosphere. Despite being near the bustling town of Kailua-Kona, the place is quiet and relaxing. The nearest sandy beach is 2 mi away, but the pool is next to the ocean. ⊠ *75-6106 Ali'i Dr., Kailua-Kona 96740,* ☎ *808/327–2300 or 800/922–7866,* ℻ *808/ 327–2333,* WEB *www.aston-hotels.com. 37 1-bedroom units, 41 2-bedroom units. Pool, hot tub. AE, D, DC, MC, V.*

$$$$ **🏨 Horizon Guest House.** About 30 mi south of Kona, at an elevation
★ of 1,100 ft on 40 acres overlooking the Kona Coast, this private luxury retreat offers tranquility, comfort, sweeping views, and a state-of-the-art solar-heated pool. Hawaiian quilts, collectibles, and antiques give personality and warmth to the four spacious suites, all with private lānai. Host Clem Classen's generous breakfast starts your day. The estate borders the native forests of the 15,000-acre McCandles Ranch, home to the endangered Hawaiian crow. Children under the age of 14 are not permitted, and smoking is not allowed on the property. ⊠ *Box 268, Honaunau 96726,* ☎ *808/328–2540 or 888/328–8301,* ℻ *808/ 328–8707,* WEB *www.horizonguesthouse.com. 4 suites. Refrigerators, pool, hot tub, library. MC, V.*

$$$$ **🏨 Kanaloa at Kona.** The 13-acre grounds provide a verdant setting
★ for this low-rise condominium complex bordering the Keauhou-Kona Country Club. Large one-, two-, and three-bedroom apartments have koa-wood cabinetwork and washer-dryers; oceanfront villas have private hot tubs. Edward's at Kanaloa Restaurant serves excellent Mediterranean cuisine in a romantically tropical atmosphere. ⊠ *78-261 Manukai St., Kailua-Kona 96740,* ☎ *808/322–9625, 808/322–2272, or 800/688–7444,* ℻ *808/322–3818,* WEB *www.outrigger.com. 79 units. Restaurant, kitchenettes, 3 pools, 2 tennis courts. AE, D, DC, MC, V.*

$$$–$$$$ **🏨 Aston Keauhou Beach Resort.** This newly renovated oceanfront
★ hotel, just 5 mi south of Kailua-Kona, gets kudos for its central location and for the unique history and preservation of its 10-acre grounds, which include an ancient heiau, a sacred fishpond, and a replica of the summer home of King David Kalākaua. Sage-green rooms overlook the ocean, Hualālai Mountain, and Keauhou's historic fishing grounds. Consider a nightcap at the Verandah bar, just feet away from lapping waves. The hotel's lū'au, led by Nani Lim, is an authentic interpretation of the area's royal past. The hotel is adjacent to Kahalu'u, one of the Big Island's best snorkeling beaches, and the rooms on that side may get noisy. ⊠ *78-6740 Ali'i Dr., Kailua-Kona 96740,* ☎ *808/322– 3441 or 800/922–7866,* ℻ *808/322–3117,* WEB *www.aston-hotels.com. 311 rooms, 6 suites. Restaurant, bar, pool, 6 tennis courts, health club, beach, meeting room. AE, D, DC, MC, V.*

$$$–$$$$ **🏨 Kailua Plantation House B&B.** At the ocean's edge just outside Kailua-Kona, this majestic two-story house was built in 1990 as a B&B, with four rooms upstairs (two overlooking the ocean) and one oceanfront suite downstairs. Rooms with private lānai are done in a unique range of styles and named to reflect their decor—Pilialoha (Friendship Room) or Ali'i Wikolia (Queen Victoria Room), for example. An extensive display of local art is displayed along the second-story stairwell. Delicious breakfasts may include avocado omelets and island-style pancakes. ⊠ *75-5948 Ali'i Dr., Kailua-Kona 96740,* ☎ *808/329– 3727 or 888/357–4262,* ℻ *808/326–7323,* WEB *www.kphbnb.com. 5 rooms. AE, MC, V.*

$$$–$$$$ **🏨 Royal Kona Resort.** Of the major hotels, the spacious Royal Kona Resort is nearest to Kailua on the south side of town and right across from shops and restaurants. It has a distinctive profile and extends into a bay, giving the impression that it sits on the water. There is a private lagoon with a sandy beach. The resort may not be as luxurious as those on the Kohala Coast, but with a new phone system and in-room data ports, it is certainly adequate for busy travelers. Rooms are decorated

in aqua and sea-foam color schemes. ✉ 75-5852 Ali'i Dr., Kailua-Kona 96740, ☎ 808/329–3111 or 800/919–8333, FAX 808/329–9532, WEB www.royalkona.com. 452 rooms, 8 suites. Restaurant, bar, in-room data ports, in-room safes, refrigerators, pool, 4 tennis courts, spa, beach, meeting room. AE, D, DC, MC, V.

$$–$$$$ ▥ **Kona Bali Kai.** These older, family-style condominium units midway between Kailua-Kona and Keauhou Country Club are less than 2 mi from White Sands Beach and all have kitchen-dining areas. Only the mountainside ones have air-conditioning. Ask for a place makai rather than mauka of the road. ✉ 76-6246 Ali'i Dr., Kailua-Kona 96740, ☎ 808/329–9381 or 800/535–0085, FAX 808/326–6056, WEB www.marcresorts.com. 14 rooms, 62 condominiums (13 studios, 25 1-bedroom, 24 2-bedroom). Pool, hot tub, coin laundry. AE, D, DC, MC, V.

$$$ ▥ **Hale Kona Kai.** This small, three-story vacation condominium on the ocean's edge, next door to the Royal Kona Resort, requires a three-day minimum stay. These privately owned units are all furnished differently. The corner units with wraparound lānai have the best views. The Hale Kona Kai is within walking distance of restaurants and shops. ✉ 75-5870 Kahakai Rd., Kailua-Kona 96740, ☎ 808/329–2155 or 800/421–3696, FAX 808/329–2155. 22 units. Pool. AE, MC, V.

$$$ ▥ **King Kamehameha's Kona Beach Hotel.** Rooms are not particularly special here (fifth- and sixth-floor oceanfront rooms are best), but this is the only central Kailua-Kona hotel with a white-sand beach. Right next to Kailua Pier, this is the most conveniently located of the major hotels. Free tours explore the grounds and Ahu'ena Heiau, which King Kamehameha I had reconstructed in the early 1800s. The hotel serves an ample champagne brunch every Sunday and hosts beachfront Polynesian dinner shows. ✉ 75-5660 Palani Rd., Kailua-Kona 96740, ☎ 808/329–2911 or 800/367–6060, FAX 808/329–4602, WEB www.konabeachhotel.com. 450 rooms, 5 suites. 2 restaurants, 2 bars, pool, sauna, 4 tennis courts, beach. AE, D, DC, MC, V.

$$–$$$ ▥ **Kona Seaside Hotel.** What you get here is location. This hotel, a combination of the old Hukilau Hotel and the adjoining Kona Seaside, is right across the street from Kailua Bay. Rooms nearest the main street are built around a pool. The small rooms have tiny bathrooms and showers but are adequate. ✉ 75-5646 Palani Rd., Kailua-Kona 96740, ☎ 808/329–2455 or 800/560–5558, FAX 808/329–6157, WEB www.sand-seaside.com. 223 rooms, 1 suite. Restaurant, bar, 2 pools, meeting room. AE, D, DC, MC, V.

$$ ▥ **Kona Bay Hotel, Uncle Billy's.** These two- and four-story motel-type units are right in the center of town, across the street from the ocean. The atmosphere is friendly and casual, with relaxed open-air dining around the pool. Some rooms have kitchenettes. The place is owned and managed by the same local family that owns the Hilo Bay Hotel, Uncle Billy's. ✉ 75-5739 Ali'i Dr., Kailua-Kona 96740, ☎ 808/329–1393 or 800/367–5102, FAX 808/329–9210, WEB www.unclebilly.com. 146 rooms. Restaurant, bar, pool. AE, D, DC, MC, V.

$$ ▥ **Kona Magic Sands.** Located near Magic Sands Beach, this condo complex is great for swimmers and sunbathers in summer (the sand washes away in winter). Units vary because they are individually owned, but all are oceanfront. All units have kitchens, some have enclosed lānai, and some come with air-conditioning. ✉ 77-6452 Ali'i Dr., Kailua-Kona 96740, ☎ 808/329–9393 or 800/553–5035, FAX 808/326–4137, WEB www.konahawaii.com. 37 rooms. Restaurant, bar, kitchenettes, pool. MC, V.

$ ▥ **Kona Tiki Hotel.** The best thing about this three-story walk-up budget hotel, about a mile south of Kailua-Kona, is that all the units have lānai right next to the ocean. The rooms are modest but pleasantly decorated nonetheless. Guests can sunbathe by the seaside pool, where a buffet breakfast is also served. There are no in-room TVs or phones. ✉ *75-5968 Ali'i Dr., Kailua-Kona 96745,* ☎ *808/329–1425,* FAX *808/327–9402,* WEB *www.konatikihotel.com. 15 rooms. Fans, refrigerators, pool. No credit cards. CP.*

$ 🏨 **Manago Hotel.** You'll get a great ocean view high above the Kona Coast in the newer wing of this family-run three-story hotel, the oldest operating hotel in the area. In remembrance of his grandparents, who built the main hotel in 1917, the proprietor has maintained one Japanese-style room with tatami mats and a *furo* (deep bathtub). The other rooms are nothing special, and none have phones, but the Manago has an authentic old Hawai'i ambience, especially in the bar and local-style restaurant. ✉ *81-6155 Māmalahoa Hwy. (Box 145), Captain Cook 96704,* ☎ *808/323–2642,* FAX *808/323–3451,* WEB *www.managohotel.com. 64 rooms, 42 with bath. Restaurant. D, MC, V.*

Kohala Coast and Waikoloa

$$$$ 🏨 **Aston the Shores at Waikoloa.** These red-tile-roof villas are set amid landscaped lagoons and waterfalls at the edge of the championship Waikoloa Village Golf Course. The spacious villas and condo units— ground floor and upper floor are available separately—are privately owned, so all furnishings are different. Sliding glass doors open onto large lānai. Units have washer-dryers and come with maid service. ✉ *69-1035 Keana Pl., Waikoloa 96738,* ☎ *808/886–5001 or 800/922–7866,* FAX *808/886–8414,* WEB *www.aston-hotels.com. 75 1- and 2-bedroom units, 1 3-bedroom villa. Kitchenettes, pool, hot tub, 2 tennis courts. AE, D, DC, MC, V.*

$$$$ 🏨 **Four Seasons Resort Hualālai.** Four clusters of bungalows house six
★ or eight luxurious rooms each in this romantic oceanfront hotel—consistently rated among the best in the country—at historic Ka'ūpūlehu. Natural china-matte slate floors, Hawaiian artwork, warm earth and cool white tones, and large two-sink bathrooms with glass-door showers create a peaceful haven. Ground-level rooms have outdoor garden showers. Natural ponds—attracting rare native birds—dot the property. The educational Hawaiian Cultural Center honors the grounds' spiritual heritage, and the Sports Club and Spa offers guests top-rate health and fitness options. The resort's golf course annually hosts the Senior PGA Tournament of Champions. The Kids for All Seasons program provides complementary child-care service, and a teen program includes a state-of-the-art game room. ✉ *100 Ka'ūpūlehu Dr., Ka'ūpūlehu/Kona (Box 1269, Kailua-Kona 96745),* ☎ *808/325–8000 or 800/332–3442,* FAX *808/325–8100,* WEB *www.fourseasons.com. 243 rooms, 31 suites. 3 restaurants, 5 pools, 18-hole golf course, 8 tennis courts, beach, children's programs (ages 5–11), concierge, meeting rooms, airport shuttle. AE, DC, MC, V.*

$$$$ 🏨 **Hilton Waikoloa Village.** This 62-acre property on a rocky stretch
★ of coast is elaborately landscaped, with shaded pathways passing by items from a multimillion-dollar Pacific Island art collection and connecting three tower buildings. Shuttle trams and boats will take you to your destination if you don't want to walk. The pool has a 175-ft water slide, a meandering river that connects smaller pools, and a man-made sand beach bordering a four-acre lagoon. You can have an encounter with the resort's dolphins through a special lottery, or practice your swing at one of two golf courses or your putt on an 18-hole putting course. The Kohala Spa has some of the finest fitness facilities on the island. The resort has several restaurants, including one at a boat-landing pavilion. ✉ *425 Waikoloa Beach Dr., Waikoloa 96738,* ☎ *808/886–1234 or 800/445–8667,* FAX *808/886–2901,* WEB *www.hiltonwaikoloavillage.com. 1,240 rooms, 57 suites. 9 restaurants, 7 bars,*

3 pools, 2 18-hole golf courses, 8 tennis courts, beach, children's programs (ages 5–12). AE, D, DC, MC, V.

$$$$ 🏨 **Islands at Mauna Lani.** Surrounded by saltwater ponds, streams, and waterfalls are two- and three-bedroom condominium town homes. Each air-conditioned unit has a private drive with two-car garage. Both the dining room downstairs and the second floor open onto private lānai with views of luxurious gardens. Guests have access to the beach club at Mauna Lani Bay Hotel and Bungalows as well as the tennis courts and fitness facilities at the nearby racquet club. There are several dining options throughout the Mauna Lani Bay Hotel and Bungalows Resort. ✉ *Classic Resorts, 68-1310 Mauna Lani Dr., Kohala Coast 96743,* ☎ *808/885–5022 or 800/642–6284,* 🅵🅰🆇 *808/885–5015,* 🆆🅴🅱 *www. maunalani-point.com. 15 2-bedroom units, 1 3-bedroom unit. Pool, hot tub, 2 18-hole golf courses, 6 tennis courts, beach. AE, DC, MC, V.*

$$$$ 🏨 **Kona Village Resort.** Without phones, TVs, or radios it is easy to
★   feel you are part of an extended Polynesian *ohana* (family), with your own thatched-roof *hale* (house) near the resort's sandy beach. Built on the grounds of an ancient Hawaiian village, the modern bungalows reflect the styles of Polynesian cultures—Tahitian, Hawaiian, or Samoan, for example. The extra-large rooms are cooled by ceiling fans; some have hot tubs. Rates include meals, an authentic Polynesian Friday night lū'au, history and petroglyph tours, tennis, sports activities, and rides in the resort's glass-bottom boat. Children's programs are offered, except in the months of May and September. ✉ *Queen Ka'ahumanu Hwy., Kailua-Kona 96745,* ☎ *808/325–5555 or 800/367–5290,* 🅵🅰🆇 *808/ 325–5124,* 🆆🅴🅱 *www.konavillage.com. 125 bungalows. 2 restaurants, 3 bars, 2 pools, hot tub, 3 tennis courts, health club, beach, boating, children's programs (ages 6–17), meeting room, airport shuttle. AE, DC, MC, V. FAP.*

$$$$ 🏨 **Mauna Lani Bay Hotel and Bungalows.** Almost all the spacious rooms
★   in this modern hotel have ocean views, and all have a large lānai. Comfortable furnishings grace rooms with natural fabrics and teak. The resort is known for its two spectacular golf courses. Pacific Rim cuisine is served at the oceanfront CanoeHouse. Lighter eaters can graze on appetizers in the Honu Bar or any of the other four eateries. The annual Cuisines of the Sun celebration in July brings celebrity guest chefs together for a top-notch food-and-wine extravaganza. ✉ *68-1400 Mauna Lani Dr., Kohala Coast 96743,* ☎ *808/885–6622 or 800/367– 2323,* 🅵🅰🆇 *808/885–6183,* 🆆🅴🅱 *www.maunalani.com. 335 rooms, 10 suites, 5 bungalows. 6 restaurants, 5 bars, in-room safes, in-room VCRs, refrigerators, pool, 2 18-hole golf courses, 16 tennis courts, children's programs (ages 5–12). AE, D, DC, MC, V.*

$$$$ 🏨 **Mauna Lani Point Condominiums.** Elegant and spacious two-story suites are set off by themselves on one of the world's most beautiful oceanside golf courses. It's just a few steps away from the Mauna Lani Bay Hotel and Bungalows, where guests may use the golf and tennis facilities. The privately owned units, individually decorated according to the owners' tastes, come with washer-dryers and maid service. ✉ *68-1310 Mauna Lani Dr., Kohala Coast 96743,* ☎ *808/885–5022 or 800/642–6284,* 🅵🅰🆇 *808/885–5015,* 🆆🅴🅱 *www.classicresorts.com. 24 1-bedroom units, 37 2-bedroom units, 1 3-bedroom unit. Kitchenettes, pool, hot tub, sauna. AE, DC, MC, V.*

$$$$ 🏨 **The Orchid at Mauna Lani.** Situated around botanical gardens and
★   waterfall ponds, this elegant, romantic hotel stretches along 32 beachfront acres. Rooms are refined, with European luxury; marble bathrooms and fluffy robes are only part of the pampering. The Orchid's signature restaurant, The Grill, features a terrific wine list presented by a knowledgeable sommelier. The Spa without Walls blends ancient wisdom with modern fitness facilities and treatments—outdoors if

you wish. There's a protected swimming lagoon, and, for those who wish to explore Polynesian navigational skills, the resort offers 2½-hour voyages aboard an authentic double-hulled sailing canoe. ⊠ *1 N. Kanikū Dr., Kohala Coast 96743,* ☎ *808/885–2000 or 800/845–9905,* FAX *808/885–5778,* WEB *www.orchid-maunalani.com. 538 rooms, 54 suites. 3 restaurants, 4 bars, pool, sauna, spa, 2 18-hole golf courses, 10 tennis courts, health club, beach, snorkeling, boating, children's programs (ages 5–12). AE, D, DC, MC, V.*

$$$$ 🏨 **Outrigger Waikoloa Beach.** On the site of ancient royal fishponds, historic trails, and petroglyph fields, this 15-acre resort honors the unique Hawaiian history of the grounds. Rooms have Hawaiian art and bamboo-type furnishings and private lānai with views of the ocean or of immaculate gardens. Oversize cabana rooms overlook the lagoon and nearby ocean. Good, affordable dining is available at the Hawai'i Calls Restaurant. The resort has a spa, Hawaiian Rainforest Salon & Spa, and lies next to the white-sand beach of 'Anaeho'omalu Bay. ⊠ *69-275 Waikoloa Beach Dr., Waikoloa 96738,* ☎ *808/886–6789 or 800/922–5533,* FAX *808/886–7852,* WEB *www.outrigger.com. 524 rooms, 21 suites. Restaurant, 2 bars, pool, 2 hot tubs, sauna, spa, 2 18-hole golf courses, 6 tennis courts, health club, beach, children's programs (ages 5–12), coin laundry, meeting rooms. AE, D, DC, MC, V.*

$$$$ 🏨 **Westin Hāpuna Beach Prince Hotel.** This Kohala Coast luxury hotel
★ fronts white-sand Hāpuna, one of the best beaches in the United States. The hotel is a glitzy beauty with floors of slate tile. All rooms have at least some ocean view and all have spacious, marble bathrooms and private lānai. Meandering pathways lead to restaurants, beach facilities, and a spectacular golf course. The showpiece of the hotel is the 8,000-square-ft, four-bedroom Hāpuna Suite with its own swimming pool and 24-hour butler service. A hiking trail connects Westin Hāpuna with its partner, Westin Mauna Ke'a, but a frequent shuttle makes the commute painless. A year-round Keiki Camp looks after your children, and a new Star Gazing Program, four nights a week, shows off Hawaii's clear, star-studded skies. ⊠ *62-100 Kauna'oa Dr., Kamuela 96743,* ☎ *808/880–1111 or 800/882–6060,* FAX *808/880–3112,* WEB *www. hapunabeachprincehotel.com. 314 rooms, 36 suites. 5 restaurants, 2 bars, pool, beauty salon, hot tub, spa, 18-hole golf course, 13 tennis courts, health club, meeting room. AE, D, DC, MC, V.*

$$$$ 🏨 **Westin Mauna Ke'a Beach Hotel.** This world-class oceanfront re-
★ sort hotel was developed by Laurence S. Rockefeller in 1965 and borders one of the islands' finest white-sand beaches. Rare works of art, such as a 7th-century Buddha statue, enhance walkways and open spaces. The rooms have a natural look with beige tiles and carpets complemented by pastel colors. They all feature original artwork and antiques. The fitness center has cardiovascular machines and free weights. Shuttles operate between the Westin Mauna Ke'a and the adjacent Westin Hāpuna Beach Prince Hotel, allowing guests to use the facilities at both stellar hotels. Wine and food lovers might want to plan a stay during the annual Winter Wine Escape in November. ⊠ *62-100 Mauna Ke'a Beach Dr., Kohala Coast 96743,* ☎ *808/882–7222 or 800/882–6060,* FAX *808/880–3112,* WEB *www.maunakeabeachhotel.com. 300 rooms, 10 suites. 5 restaurants, in-room safes, pool, hair salon, 2 18-hole golf courses, 13 tennis courts, health club, beach. AE, D, DC, MC, V.*

$$$–$$$$ 🏨 **Waikoloa Villas at Waikoloa Village.** This is about the only moderately priced Waikoloa-area accommodation, but it's 6 mi inland. It borders the fairways of Waikoloa Village Golf Club. The wide-open spaces of cowboy country attract golfers and the horsey set. Individually owned condominium units are all decorated differently, but all are tasteful and have ceiling fans and washer-dryers. Two-night minimum stays are required. ⊠ *68-3840 Lua Kua St. (Box 38-5134),*

Waikoloa 96738, ☎ *808/883–9144 or 800/535–0085,* FAX *808/883–8740,* WEB *www.marcresorts.com. 3 1-bedroom units, 8 2-bedroom units, 2 3-bedroom units. 2 pools, 18-hole golf course, 2 tennis courts, horseback riding. AE, MC, V.*

$–$$$ 🏠 **Kohala Guest House.** Set amid citrus trees and tropical foliage, at the end of the road in North Kohala, these comfortable rooms offer a taste of what it's like to live in a rural Hawaiian area that's still close enough to the bustling activity of the towns Hāwi and Kapa'au. The units are just 30 minutes away from white-sand beaches. Gracious hostess Nani Svendsen welcomes you with a tropical flower arrangement, and fruit when in season. ⊠ *Box 172, Kapa'au 96755,* ☎ *808/889–5606,* FAX *808/889–5572,* WEB *home1.gte.net/svendsen. 1 cottage, 3 houses (for families or rented as separate room units). No credit cards.*

Waimea/Hāmākua Coast

$$–$$$$ 🏠 **Jacaranda Inn.** Built in 1897, this sprawling, historic estate was once home to the Parker Ranch manager; it has been completely restored in raspberry, violet, and lavender colors, with lots of koa wood and Upcountry Victorian elements. The eight suites and cottage, each with different decorative themes, are booked under two separate plans. Plan A includes daily maid service, full breakfasts, and a bottle of wine; Plan B is simpler, with Continental breakfast and less service. The cottage sleeps up to six and has a hot tub. Six suites have a whirlpool tub. The Jacaranda is close to Waimea shops as well as to beaches. ⊠ *65-1444 Kawaihae Rd., Kamuela 96743,* ☎ *808/885–8813,* FAX *808/885–6096,* WEB *www.jacarandainn.com. 8 suites, 1 cottage. Recreation room. MC, V. BP or CP.*

$$$ 🏠 **Waimea Gardens Cottage.** These two charming streamside country cottages have kitchens stocked with your choice of breakfast items. French doors, antique furnishings, window boxes spilling over with flowers, and a fireplace create a romantic ambience. It's 8 mi from the island's beaches, on the sunny side of Waimea, and you can awake on cool, Upcountry mornings to collect your own eggs from the quiet flock of miniature hens outside. ⊠ *Reservations: Hawai'i's Best Bed and Breakfasts, Box 563, Kamuela 96743,* ☎ *808/885–4550 or 800/262–9912,* FAX *808/885–0559,* WEB *www.bestbnb.com. 2 cottages. No credit cards. CP.*

$$ 🏠 **Waimea Country Lodge.** In cool Upcountry surroundings, this lodge has rooms that look out onto green pastures. Modern furnishings and Hawaiian quilt bedspreads make this an adequate and friendly place. Six of the rooms have their own kitchenette. ⊠ *65-1210 Lindsey Rd., Waimea (Box 2559, Kamuela 96743),* ☎ *808/885–4100,* FAX *808/885–6711. 21 rooms. Kitchenettes. AE, D, DC, MC, V. CP.*

$–$$ 🏠 **Kamuela Inn.** Every room in this modest inn, just twenty minutes from the island beaches, is attractively designed. A penthouse suite sleeps six and has a sunset lānai and full kitchen; several rooms have kitchenettes. Continental breakfast is served on the breakfast lānai. The inn has a peaceful country setting, an art gallery, and is close to the center of Waimea. Not all rooms have phones. ⊠ *65-1300 Kawaihae Rd. (Box 1994), Kamuela 96743,* ☎ *808/885–4243 or 800/555–8968,* FAX *808/885–8857,* WEB *www.hawaii-bnb.com. 20 rooms, 11 suites. AE, D, DC, MC, V.*

$ 🏠 **Hotel Honoka'a Club.** This basic, bargain, no-smoking hotel is 45 minutes from Hilo and close to Waipi'o Valley. Rustic rooms range from lower-level dormitory-style hostel units with shared bathrooms to upper-story rooms with private bath, queen-size beds, and a complimentary Continental breakfast. Collectors may enjoy poking through the secondhand stores in the country town of Honoka'a, which also has several reasonably priced restaurants. ⊠ *45-3480 Māmane St. (Box*

247), *Honoka'a 96727,* ☎ *808/775–0678 or 800/808–0678,* WEB *home1.gte.net/honokaac/. 13 rooms, 5 hostel rooms. MC, V.*

NIGHTLIFE AND THE ARTS

Clubs and Cabarets

If you're the sort of person who doesn't come alive until after dark, you're going to be pretty lonely on the Big Island. Blame it on the plantation heritage. People did their cane-raising in the morning.

Breakwater. This disco at the Hawai'i Naniloa Resort in Hilo competes with the crashing surf on Thursday, Friday, and Saturday nights starting at 10 PM. ⊠ *93 Banyan Dr., Hilo,* ☎ *808/969–3333.*

Fiasco's. Most Friday and Saturday nights you'll find margarita specials, a huge selection of beers, and bands (blues, rock, and soul) at this lively restaurant. Call to find out about players and times. ⊠ *200 Kanoelehua Ave., Hilo,* ☎ *808/935–7666.*

Honu Bar. Thursday through Saturday you'll find easy-listening jazz at this elegant spot in the Mauna Lani Bay Hotel and Bungalows on the Kohala Coast. A dance floor, appetizers, imported cigars, and fine cognacs make this a popular, upscale gathering spot. ⊠ *68-1400 Mauna Lani Dr., Kohala Coast,* ☎ *808/885–6622.*

Huggo's. Jazz, country, and even rock bands perform at this popular restaurant, so call ahead of time to find out what's on. On Tuesdays it's open microphone to popular tunes. ⊠ *75-5828 Kahakai Rd., Ali'i Dr., Kailua-Kona,* ☎ *808/329–1493.*

Lulu's. A young crowd gyrates until 1:30 AM Thursday through Saturday to hot dance music selected by a professional DJ. ⊠ *75-5819 Ali'i Dr., Kailua-Kona,* ☎ *808/331–2633.*

Michaelangelo's. On the second level of the Waterfront Row complex, this Italian restaurant starts rocking after 10 every night with a live DJ. ⊠ *Waterfront Row, Kailua-Kona,* ☎ *808/329–4436.*

Film

Hilo

Kress Cinemas (⊠ 174 Kamehameha Ave., ☎ 808/961–3456) often screens selected art films. After decades of being closed, the historic **Palace Theatre** (⊠ 38 Haile St., ☎ 808/934–7010), built in 1925, now shows film-festival movies and other artistic work. Films are shown regularly at the state-of-the-art **Prince Kuhio Stadium Cinemas** (⊠ Prince Kūhiō Plaza, 111 E. Puainako St., ☎ 808/959–4595). **Waiākea Theaters 1, 2, and 3** (⊠ Waiākea Kai Shopping Plaza, 88 Kanoelehua Ave., ☎ 808/935–9747) sells good-value tickets.

Kailua-Kona

Keauhou Theatres (⊠ Keauhou Shopping Center, 78-6831 Ali'i Dr., ☎ 808/324–7200) is a splendid seven-theater complex.**Kona Marketplace Cinemas** (⊠ Kona Marketplace, across from Kona Inn Shopping Village, 75-5725 Ali'i Dr., ☎ 808/329–4488) shows new releases right in the historic village. The 10-screen **Makalapua Stadium Cinemas** (⊠ Makalapua Ave., next to Big Kmart, ☎ 808/327–0444) has stadium seating and digital surround sound.

Around the Island

Honoka'a Peoples Theaters (⊠ Manane St., Honoka'a, ☎ 808/775–0000) shows movies on weekends. **Kahei Theater** (⊠ Hwy. 270, Hāwī, ☎ 808/889–6831) screens first-run movies Friday, Saturday, and Sunday evenings. **Na'alehu Theater** (⊠ Hawai'i Belt Rd., Hwy. 11, Na'alehu, ☎ 808/929–9133) often shows movies Friday, Saturday, and Sunday nights.

Hula

For hula lovers, the biggest show of the year and the largest event of its kind in the world is the annual **Merrie Monarch Festival** (⊠ Hawai'i Naniloa Resort, 93 Banyan Dr., Hilo 96720, ☎ 808/935–9168). Honoring the legacy of King David Kalākaua, Hawai'i's last king, the festival is staged in Hilo at the spacious Edith Kanaka'ole Stadium during the first week following Easter Sunday. Hula hālau compete in various classes of ancient and modern dance styles. You need to reserve accommodations and tickets up to a year in advance.

Lū'au and Polynesian Revues

Kailua-Kona

Aston Keauhou Beach Resort. "Traditions at Kahalu'u" is the name of this authentic event directed by well-known Hawaiian teacher Nani Lim and her troupe. Lim keeps entertainment narrowly focused on Hawaiian history with a "chicken-skin" (goose bumps–giving) reenactment of the royal days. The Hawaiian buffet is lavish and complete. ⊠ 78-6740 Ali'i Dr., ☎ 808/322–3441. 🍽 $70. ⊙ Thurs. at 5:30.

King Kamehameha's Kona Beach Hotel's Island Breeze Lū'au. Witness the arrival of the Royal Court by canoe and have pictures taken at this beachfront event that includes a 22-course buffet, an open bar, and a show. ⊠ 75-5660 Palani Rd., ☎ 808/326–4969 or 808/329–2911. 🍽 $54. ⊙ Tues.–Thurs. and Sun. at 5:30.

Royal Kona Resort. This resort lights lū'au torches for a full Polynesian show and a Hawaiian-style buffet four times a week in an oceanfront setting. ⊠ 75-5852 Ali'i Dr., ☎ 808/329–3111, ext. 4. 🍽 $55 includes beer and wine. ⊙ Mon., Wed., Fri., and Sat. at 5:30.

Kohala Coast and Waikoloa

Hilton Waikoloa Village. The Hilton seats 400 people outdoors at the Kamehameha Court, where the acclaimed Polynesian group Tihati performs a lively show. A buffet dinner provides samplings of Hawaiian food, as well as fish, beef, and chicken to appeal to all tastes. The price includes one tropical drink. ⊠ 425 Waikoloa Beach Dr., Waikoloa, ☎ 808/886–1234. 🍽 $62. ⊙ Fri. at 5:45.

Kona Village Resort. In its utter isolation, the lū'au here is one of the most authentic and traditional in the Islands. As in other lū'au, activities include the steaming of a whole pig in the *imu* (ground oven). Mainland taste buds might reject some items, such as raw *'opihi* (a limpet, considered a chewy delicacy in Hawai'i), but there is plenty to appeal to the less adventurous. A Polynesian show on a stage over a lagoon is magical. ⊠ 6 mi north of Keāhole–Kona International Airport, off Queen Ka'ahumanu Hwy., Kailua-Kona, ☎ 808/325–5555. 🍽 $74. ⊙ Fri. from 5; walking tour 5:30, imu ceremony 6:30, dinner at 7, show at 8.

Outrigger Waikoloa Beach. The Outrigger offers a great-value Sunday- and Wednesday-night lū'au at the Lū'au Grounds, where entertainment includes a Samoan fire dance as well as songs and dances of various Pacific cultures. Traditional Hawaiian dishes are served alongside more familiar fare. ⊠ 69-275 Waikoloa Beach Dr., Waikoloa, ☎ 808/886–6789. 🍽 $60 includes open bar. ⊙ Wed. and Sun. at 5:30.

Westin Mauna Ke'a Beach Hotel. Every Tuesday chefs come together here to create a traditional Hawaiian *pa'ina* (dinner feast), which includes the classic *kālua* (roasted in an underground oven) pig. On the gracious North Pointe Lū'au Grounds of the Mauna Ke'a Hotel, guests sample the best of Hawaiian cuisine while listening to the enchanting songs of Nani Lim and her spellbinding hula hālau. ⊠ 62-100 Mauna Ke'a Beach Dr., Kohala Coast, ☎ 808/882–7222. 🍽 $70. ⊙ Tues. at 5:30.

Sunset Cruises

Captain Beans' Polynesian Dinner Cruise. This is the ever-popular standby in sunset dinner cruises. You can't miss it—as the sun sets in Kailua, look out over the water and you'll see a big gaudy boat with distinctive orange sails. This cruise is corny, and dinner is nothing great, but it's an experience, with unlimited drinks and a Hawaiian show. This is for adults only. ✉ *Kailua Pier, Kailua-Kona,* ☎ *808/329–2955.* 🎫 *$57, including dinner, entertainment, and open bar.* ☉ *Sails Sat.–Mon. and Wed.–Thurs. at 5:15–7:15 PM, Tues. and Fri at 7–9 PM.*

🐚 **Hawai'i Ocean Adventures.** The *Pacific Passion* is a 40-ft-long single-hull boat that will take you from Honokōhau Harbor to dolphin-rich waters while the sun sets in the distance. Appetizers and beverages are part of the three-hour cruise. No alcohol is served, but you may bring your own if you wish. The captain and crew are eager to share local legends and knowledge about the area. ✉ *Honokōhau Harbor, Slip J-38, Kailua-Kona,* ☎ *808/325–0766,* WEB *www.hawaiioceanadventures.com.* 🎫 *$53.* ☉ *Tues. and Thurs. 5–8 PM.*

Theater

Aloha Performing Arts Center. Local talent stages musicals and Broadway plays at this center near Kailua-Kona. ✉ *Aloha Theatre Café, Hwy. 11, Kainaliu,* ☎ *808/322–9924.*

Hilo Community Players. This group stages plays on an occasional basis. ✉ *141 Kalākaua Ave., Hilo,* ☎ *808/935–9155.*

Kahilu Theater Foundation. For legitimate theater, the little town of Waimea is your best bet. The Kahilu Theater Foundation hosts internationally acclaimed performances on a regular basis. ✉ *Parker Ranch Center, Hwys. 19 and 190, Waimea,* ☎ *808/885–6868.*

Waimea Community Theatre. Local talent performs in musicals and plays at the Parker School Theater. ✉ *Uilani Plaza, Waimea,* ☎ *808/885–5818.*

OUTDOOR ACTIVITIES AND SPORTS

Participant Sports

The Big Island attracts active people. Whether you like to run, ride, bicycle, hike, sail, or even ski, there is so much to explore. Two Upcountry ranches conduct unique horseback-riding and hiking tours through cowboy land. A new family boat has taken to Honokōhau Harbor, and more water activities than ever before can be found in the calmer seas of the Kailua-Kona area. An increased number of eco-adventures around Volcano and in the Kona areas focus on the island's wondrous ecosystem.

Many Big Island activities are best done with guided tours, but don't worry: groups are usually small.

Brochures that designate self-guided trails for mountain biking, driving, and walking tours are available at Hawai'i Visitor Bureau outlets.

Biking

With its hills and dirt roads, the Big Island is a biker's haven. A few companies offer daily or weeklong trips. Although you should be fairly fit for these extended bicycling tours, how far you ride is up to you: the support van that carries gear will also stop to pick up tired riders. Helmets are a must, and bicycle shorts add greatly to personal comfort on long trips.

Backroads Bicycle Touring. This company has been pushing pedaling in Hawai'i since 1985. It conducts six-day biking trips on the southern part of the island, with a day of hiking in Hawai'i Volcanoes National Park and snorkeling and kayaking off Kona shores. Lodgings alternate between luxury resorts and old Hawaiian inns. The $2,300 fee includes meals and accommodations, but bicycle and airfare are extra. ⊠ *801 Cedar St., Berkeley, CA 94710-1800,* ☎ *510/527–1555 or 800/462–2848,* WEB *www.backroads.com.*

Bicycle Adventures, Inc. Six- and eight-day tours of the Big Island accommodate both easygoing bikers and hard-core enthusiasts. You'll enjoy beach time, snorkeling, hiking excursions, comfortable accommodations, and fine dining in addition to visits to Kīlauea Volcano and Pu'uhonua O Hōnaunau. The cost of $1,730 to $2,066 does not include bicycle rental. ⊠ *Box 11219, Olympia, WA 98508,* ☎ *360/786–0989 or 800/443–6060,* WEB *www.bicycleadventures.com.*

C&S Outfitters. These folks in Waimea offers guided tours, have a wealth of knowledge about the island's biking trails, and rent a range of bikes. They have a shop for accessories and repair needs, plus they rent kayaks, other beach equipment, and camping gear. ⊠ *64-1066 Mamalahoa Hwy. (Box 2338), Kamuela 96743,* ☎ *808/885–5005.*

Mauna Ke'a Mountain Bikes, Inc. Daily tours in the Hāmākua rain forest area, on the slopes of Mauna Ke'a, and downhill in Kohala, as well as bike rentals are offered by this company. Tour prices range from $65 to $130. ⊠ *Box 44672, Kamuela 96743,* ☎ *808/883–0130 or 888/ 682–8687,* WEB *www.bikehawaii.com.*

BIKE RENTAL

If you want to strike out on your own, consider renting a bicycle in Kailua-Kona at **B&L Bike and Sports** (⊠ 75-5699 Kopiko Pl., ☎ 808/ 329–3309), **Dave's Bike & Triathlon Shop** (⊠ 75-5669 Ali'i Dr., ☎ 808/ 329–4522), **Hawaiian Pedals** (⊠ Kona Inn Shopping Village, 75-5744 Ali'i Dr., ☎ 808/329–2294), or **HP BikeWorks.** (⊠ 74-5599 Luhia St., Suite F-3, ☎ 808/326–2453). **Red Sail Sports** (⊠ 425 Waikoloa Beach Dr., ☎ 808/886–2876), on the Kohala Coast, rents mountain bikes by the hour, for hotel guests only, at the Hilton Waikoloa Village.

Fitness and Spa Centers

Several health clubs around the island offer inexpensive day passes for your routine workout; they have showers and lockers. With 10 spas encircling the island, you can find rejuvenation easily. Five of the major hotels have spa facilities that may be used by nonguests.

Aston Keauhou Beach Resort. At the Kalona Spa you can opt for spa treatments and an oceanside or garden massage, or use a fitness room that overlooks the bay. ⊠ *78-6740 Ali'i Dr., Kailua-Kona,* ☎ *808/322–3441.*

Club. High-tech fitness facilities are available here for a daily rate of $10. ⊠ *75-5699 Kopiko Rd., Kailua-Kona,* ☎ *808/326–2582.*

Four Seasons Resort Hualālai. This may well be the most beautiful spa on the island, but you have to be a guest of the hotel to indulge in the top-rate health and fitness options. ⊠ *100 Ka'ūpūlehu Dr., Ka'ūpūlehu/Kona,* ☎ *808/325–8000.*

Hawai'i Naniloa Resort. Nonguests can use the spa and fitness center for $15. ⊠ *93 Banyan Dr., Hilo,* ☎ *808/969–3333.*

Hilton Waikoloa Village. The hotel is home to the well-known and spacious Kohala Spa ($30 daily), where you can even find a healthy smoothie at the Spa Café. ⊠ *425 Waikoloa Beach Dr., Waimea,* ☎ *808/886–1234.*

Kona Village Resort. Kona Village remains true to its secluded, romantic, and luxurious isolation with a health club open to resort guests only. ⊠ *Queen Ka'ahumanu Hwy., Kailua-Kona,* ☎ *808/325–5124.*

Mauna Lani Bay Hotel and Bungalows. Nonguests are welcome for massages and oceanside healing treatments. ✉ *68-1400 Mauna Lani Dr., Kohala Coast,* ☎ *808/885–6622.*

The Orchid at Mauna Lani. The Spa Without Walls program offers luxurious treatments indoors and outdoors. Ancient Hawaiian techniques, fragrant herbal wraps, and floral milk baths are just a sampling of what's available. A spa pass for the gym and hot tub is $16. ✉ *1 N. Kanikū Dr., Kohala Coast,* ☎ *808/885–2000.*

Outrigger Waikoloa Beach. The Hawaiian Rainforest Spa and Salon here features traditional Hawaiian healing arts as well as the latest spa therapies and aromatherapy facials. A $20 day pass lets you use the workout room and the sauna. ✉ *69-275 Waikoloa Beach Dr., Waikoloa,* ☎ *808/886–6789.*

Pacific Coast Fitness. This fitness center in Upcountry Waimea offers daily classes and has state-of-the-art equipment; the fee is $8 daily. ✉ *65-1298A Kawaihae Rd., Waimea,* ☎ *808/885–6270.*

Spencer Health and Fitness Center. Exercise addicts can try this $10-a-day health club in Hilo. ✉ *197 Keawe St., Hilo,* ☎ *808/969–1511.*

Westin Hāpuna Beach Prince Hotel. The hotel provides daily $15 passes for its fitness room and offers herbal treatments and massages, including an invigorating Hawaiian sea salt cleansing. ✉ *62-100 Kauna'oa Dr., Waimea,* ☎ *808/880–1111.*

Westin Mauna Ke'a Beach Hotel. A state-of-the-art fitness center for guests only is in the hotel's private beachfront building. ✉ *62-100 Mauna Ke'a Beach Dr., Kohala Coast,* ☎ *808/882–7222.*

Golf

If there is one thing the Big Island is known for, it's the beautiful golf courses. Like green oases they quicken the black, arid landscape of lava rock fields. Five of the Big Island's golf courses—two at the Westin Mauna Ke'a Beach Hotel, two at the Mauna Lani Hotel, and the course at the Four Seasons Resort Hualālai—are repeatedly chosen by golfing magazines as the best, the most spectacular, and the favorite. At press time, two new courses—Hokūli'a, south of Kona, and White Sands, on the Kohala Coast and adjacent to the Orchid and Mauna Lani resorts—were planning to open in 2002, though the Hokūli'a project was forced to take a break due to environmental concerns.

Ali'i Country Club. Known as the Mountain Course, the 18 holes here offer awesome views of the Kona Coast. The pros try to avoid the lava and play the high side. ✉ *78-7000 Ali'i Dr., Kailua-Kona,* ☎ *808/322–2595.* 🏌 *Greens fee $120, twilight $85.*

Big Island Country Club. At a 2,500-ft elevation, this course has a dramatic layout and stunning views. Formerly a private-membership course, this is now open to the public. ✉ *71-1420 Māmalahoa Hwy., Kailua-Kona,* ☎ *808/325–5044.* 🏌 *Greens fee $69, twilight $59.*

Discovery Harbor Golf Course. At this course, designed by Robert Trent Jones, Sr., and located on the southern end of the island, you can play 18 holes, par 72. It can get windy here, but the cost is hard to beat. ✉ *Kamaoa Rd., take South Point Rd. off Hwy. 11,* ☎ *808/929–7353.* 🏌 *Greens fee $28; cart included.*

Francis H. I'i Brown Golf Course at the Mauna Lani Hotel. This demanding and stunningly beautiful course was redesigned in 1991 by Nelson Wright Haworth and is now two 18-hole courses (North and South). The men's tee at the 15th hole of the South Course is famous among golfers because they must carry their tee shot over a stretch of open ocean to reach the green. ✉ *68-1400 Mauna Lani Dr., Kohala Coast,* ☎ *808/885–6655.* 🏌 *Greens fee for either course, for nonguests, $185, twilight $65; cart included.*

Hāmākua Country Club. At this friendly nine-hole course, designed in 1925, greens fees are deposited into a drop box on an honor system. ⊠ *41 mi north of Hilo on ocean side of Hwy. 19, Honoka'a,* ☎ *808/ 775–7244.* ☞ *Greens fee $15; no carts available.*

Hāpuna Golf Course. Landscaped with indigenous plants, trees, and grasses, this course at the Westin Hāpuna Beach Prince Hotel aims to be environmentally sensitive. It's also one of the best, a challenging par-72 course designed by Arnold Palmer and Ed Seay in 1992. Both the 1st and 18th holes are within easy walking distance of Westin Mauna Ke'a Beach Hotel. ⊠ *62-100 Kauna'oa Dr., Waimea,* ☎ *808/880–3000.* ☞ *Greens fee for nonguests $185, twilight $95; cart included.*

Hilo Municipal Golf Course. On the east side of the island is this 18-hole, flat, course with four sets of tees. It's near the airport. Bring both water and an umbrella. ⊠ *340 Haihai St., Hilo,* ☎ *808/959–7711.* ☞ *Greens fee nonresidents, weekdays $20, weekends $25; cart $14.50.*

Hualālai Golf Course. This Jack Nicklaus–designed course is a masterpiece. Players can see the ocean from every hole. Play here is a treat reserved for Four Seasons Resort Hualālai guests and resort residents, so the course is seldom crowded. ⊠ *100 Ka'ūpūlehu Dr., Ka'ūpūlehu/Kona,* ☎ *808/325–8480.* ☞ *Greens fees $160.*

Kona Country Club. The Ocean Course at this Kailua-Kona club offers an 18-hole adventure with panoramic views. ⊠ *78-7000 Ali'i Dr., Kailua-Kona,* ☎ *808/322–2595.* ☞ *Greens fee $120, twilight $85; cart included.*

Mākālei Hawai'i Country Club. On the cool slopes of Hualālai Mountain, the course climbs from 1,800 to 2,800 ft and is home to peacocks, wild turkeys, and pheasants that wander across the bent-grass greens. ⊠ *72-3890 Hawai'i Belt Rd., Kailua-Kona,* ☎ *808/325–6625.* ☞ *Greens fee $110, twilight $50; cart included.*

Mauna Ke'a Beach Resort Golf Course. This extremely challenging championship par-72, 18-hole course receives award after award from golf magazines. It was designed by Robert Trent Jones, Sr. ⊠ *62-100 Mauna Ke'a Beach Dr., Kohala Coast,* ☎ *808/882–5400.* ☞ *Greens fee $185, twilight $95; cart included.*

Naniloa Country Club Golf Course. The Naniloa is a nine-hole course convenient to Hilo's major hotels. For one fee you may take the course twice. ⊠ *120 Banyan Dr., Hilo,* ☎ *808/935–3000.* ☞ *Greens fee $40; cart $7.*

Sea Mountain Golf Course. This course is above the shores of a black-sand beach about 30 mi south of Volcano Village. The 18-hole, par-72 course stretches from the Pacific Coast up the slopes of Mauna Loa. ⊠ *Hwy. 11, Ninole Loop Rd., Punalu'u,* ☎ *808/928–6222.* ☞ *Greens fee $45; cart included.*

Volcano Golf & Country Club. This 18-hole, par-72 course perches on the rim of Kīlauea Volcano, an elevation of 4,000 ft. It is comfortably cool, and on clear days you'll have glamorous views. It was originally built in 1922. Four ponds have been added since, but only one has water. ⊠ *Hawai'i Volcanoes National Park,* ☎ *808/967–7331.* ☞ *Greens fee $63; cart included.*

Waikoloa Beach Golf Course. Designed by Robert Trent Jones, Jr., in 1981, this course sprawls over historical grounds at the two Waikoloa resorts. An 18-hole, par-70 course with three sets of tees, it wends through lava formations and has beautiful ocean views. ⊠ *Waikoloa Beach Dr., Waikoloa,* ☎ *808/886–6060.* ☞ *Greens fee for nonguests $185 for 18 holes, $100 for 9 holes; cart included.*

Waikoloa King's Golf Course. This par-72 Tom Weiskopf/Jay Morrish–designed 18-hole course has four large lakes and four sets of tees and is adjacent to the Hilton Waikoloa Village. ⊠ *600 Waikoloa Beach Dr., Waikoloa,* ☎ *808/886–7888.* ☞ *Greens fee for nonguests $185 for 18 holes; $100 for 9 holes; cart included.*

Waikoloa Village Golf Club. You'll have beautiful views at this 1,000-ft elevation. The club is 6 mi up from the resorts and is the second of the two Waikoloa courses designed by Robert Trent Jones, Jr. ✉ 68-1792 Melia St., Waikoloa Village, ☎ 808/883–9621. ⛳ Greens fee $80, twilight $50; cart included.

Waimea Country Club. Wedged inside a eucalyptus forest is this 18-hole, bent-grass greens, par-72 course that opened in 1994. It lies in the cool, misty highlands on the Hilo side of Waimea and often gets rainy in the afternoons. ✉ 47-5220 Māmalahoa Hwy., Waimea, ☎ 808/885–8053. ⛳ Greens fee $85, twilight $50; cart included (call for reduced rates for golfers who want to walk).

Hiking and Camping

For the fit adventurer, hiking is a great way to explore the Big Island's natural beauty. Trails crisscross the slopes of Mauna Keʻa and plunge into Kīlauea Iki Crater. If you're eager to learn as you hike through pristine wilderness, you may want to book a guided nature trek with experienced naturalists and bird-watchers.

To explore the wilderness of Hawaiʻi Volcanoes National Park, consider staying at the inexpensive **Nāmakani Paio Cabins,** at a 4,000-ft elevation. These are managed by Volcano House, a concession of the National Park Service. Each cabin has a double bed, two bunk beds, and electric lights. Guests should bring extra blankets, as it gets cold in these basic units. Each cabin has a grill outside, but you must bring your own firewood. ✉ Volcano House, Box 53, Hawaiʻi Volcanoes National Park, 96718, ☎ 808/967–7321, ℻ 808/967–8429. ⛳ Single or double $40; a $32 refundable deposit allows guests to pick up bedding and keys (for cabins and separate bath facilities) at Volcano House.

A challenging, little-known trek leads to the top of 13,677-ft **Mauna Loa.** It's 20 mi one-way, with overnight stops at two cabins, one at 10,000 ft and the other at the summit. You should count on spending three to four days on this hike, which is possibly the hardest in the Hawaiian Islands, with arctic conditions. You must obtain a permit before setting out at the visitor center in Hawaiʻi Volcanoes National Park. Here you can also get permits for two other backcountry hikes—along the coast or across the East Rift Zone. ✉ Hawaiʻi Volcanoes National Park, Volcano 96785, ☎ 808/985–6000, Ⱳⱸⰱ www.nps.gov.

For information about the Big Island's state parks, including Hāpuna Beach and Kalopa Park, contact the **Department of Land and Natural Resources, State Parks Division** (✉ 75 Aupuni St., Hilo 96720, ☎ 808/974–6200).

For general hiking information, topographic and other maps, as well as up-to-date hiking guides, contact **Hawaiʻi Geographic Society** (✉ Box 1698, Honolulu 96806, ☎ 800/538–3950).

For information on camping at county parks, including Spencer Beach Park, contact the **Department of Parks and Recreation** (✉ 25 Aupuni St., Hilo 96720, ☎ 808/961–8311, Ⱳⱸⰱ www.hawaii-county.com).

Horseback Riding

In addition to the companies listed below, the Mauna Keʻa Beach Hotel maintains stables in Upcountry Waimea. Most other hotels offer transportation to commercial stables. Ask at your hotel activities desk.

King's Trail Rides OʻKona, Inc. Riders take a four-and-a-half-hour excursion to Captain Cook monument in Kealakekua Bay. The trip includes snorkeling and lunch for $95. Custom rides can also be arranged. ✉ Hwy. 11, Mile Marker 111, Kealakekua, ☎ 808/323–2388, Ⱳⱸⰱ www.konacowboy.com.

Kohala Na'alapa. Here, adjacent to the white fence of Kohala Ranch, riders of all levels are invited to take open-pasture rides on historic Kahua Ranch. Forested areas alternate with splendid panoramic views. Excursions range from $55 to $75. ⊠ *Kohala Mountain Rd., Hwy. 250,* ☎ *808/889–0022.*

Paniolo Riding Adventures. Trail rides for beginners to buckaroos pass through lush Kohala ranch land. You'll never be nose-to-tail on these rides. Two-and-a-half-hour rides are $85. A four-hour Paniolo Picnic Adventure (bring your own lunch) is $125, and custom rides are available. ⊠ *Kohala Mountain Rd., Hwy. 250,* ☎ *808/889–5354,* WEB *www.panioloadventures.com.*

Waipi'o Na'alapa Trail Rides. Twice-daily rides through the Waipi'o Valley are offered for $75. The departure point is at Waipi'o Valley Artworks in Kukuihaele, past Honoka'a, where a four-wheel-drive vehicle takes riders to the horses. ⊠ *Waipi'o Valley Artworks, Off Hwy. 240, Kukuihaele,* ☎ *808/775–0419 for information about trail rides; 808/775–0958 for Artworks.*

Waipi'o Ridge Stables. Two different rides around the rim of Waipi'o are offered, one for $75 and one for $145. Riders meet at Waipi'o Valley Artworks in Kukuihaele and are shuttled by four-wheel-drive vehicles to the horses. ⊠ *Waipi'o Valley Artworks, Off Hwy. 240, Kukuihaele,* ☎ *808/775–1007 for information about trail rides; 808/ 775–0958 for Artworks,* WEB *www.topofwaipio.com.*

Skiing

Skiing on Mauna Ke'a is for experienced skiers only. Currently the ski area has no lodge or lifts.

Ski Guides Hawai'i. Christopher Langan of Mauna Ke'a Ski Corporation is the only outfit licensed to furnish transportation, guide services, and ski equipment on Mauna Ke'a. Snow can fall from Thanksgiving through June, but the most likely months are February and March. For an eight-hour day trip for up to six people, Langan charges $250 per person, including refreshments and lunch, equipment, guide service, transportation from Waimea, and four-wheel-drive shuttle back up the mountain after each ski run. ⊠ *Box 1954, Kamuela 96743,* ☎ *808/885–4188 in ski season; 808/884–5131 off-season,* WEB *www.skihawaii.com.*

Tennis

School and park courts are free and open to anyone who wishes to play, though students have first priority during school hours at high school courts. Contact the **Department of Parks and Recreation** (⊠ 25 Aupuni St., Hilo 96720, ☎ 808/961–8311, WEB www.hawaii-county.com) for a full list of all public Big Island tennis courts.

The eight courts (three lighted for night play) at **Hilo Tennis Stadium** (⊠ Pi'ilani and Kalanikoa Sts., Hilo, ☎ 808/961–8720) require a small fee. There are four free, lighted courts at **Lincoln Park** (⊠ Kino'ole and Ponahawai Sts., Hilo. In Hilo you will find courts at the **University of Hawai'i–Hilo** (⊠ 200 Kawili St., Hilo, ☎ 808/974–7520). **Waiākea Racket Club** (⊠ 400 Hualani St., Hilo, ☎ 808/961–5499) is open to the public for a reasonable fee.

You can play for free at the **Kailua Playground** (⊠ 75-5794 Kuakini Hwy., Kailua-Kona), where the wait may be long. Tennis courts are available at the **Old Kona Airport** (⊠ North end of Kuakini Hwy., Kailua-Kona). Nonguests can play for a fee on the four courts at the **Royal Kona Resort,** at the **Aston Keauhou Beach Resort,** and at the **King Kamehameha's Kona Beach Hotel.**

There are two free, lighted courts at **Waimea Park** (⊠ Hwy. 19, Waimea). Courts at **Sunterra Resorts at Sea Mountain** are open at an hourly charge.

Outrigger Waikoloa Beach, Hilton Waikoloa Village, and **The Orchid at Mauna Lani** have superb courts you can book as a nonguest. **Mauna Ke'a Beach Hotel** maintains 13 courts in a beautiful 12-acre oceanside tennis park. The pro shop carries the most complete line of tennis wear on the Kohala Coast.

Water Sports

DEEP-SEA FISHING

Along the Kona Coast you'll find some of the world's most exciting "blue water" fishing. Although July, August, and September are peak months, with a number of tournaments, charter fishing goes on year-round. You don't have to compete to experience the thrill of landing a big Pacific blue marlin or other game fish. More than 50 charter boats, averaging 26 to 58 ft, are available for hire, most of them out of **Honokōhau Harbor,** just north of Kailua. Prices for a full day of fishing range from $150 for shared charters to $900 for private trips. Half-day charters are also available in the $70 to $550 range. Tackle, bait, and ice are furnished, but you'll have to bring your own lunch. Most boats do not allow you to keep your entire catch, although if you ask, many captains will send you home with a few fish fillets.

Make arrangements for deep-sea fishing at your hotel activities desk or stop by at the **Charter Desk** (⊠ Kailua-Kona, ☎ 808/329–5735) at Honokōhau Harbor; you can pick up a lunch-to-go for the trip at the **Fish Dock Deli & Store** (☎ 808/329–8389) next door.

With its varied fleet, the **Charter Locker** (☎ 808/326–2553, WEB www.aerialsportfishingkona.com) has been in business since 1964. **Charter Services Hawai'i** (☎ 808/334–1881 or 800/567–5650, WEB www.konazone.com) represents 12 boats ranging from 33 to 46 ft. **Kona Activities Center** (☎ 808/329–3171 or 800/367–5288) provides bookings and information for several charter companies. Book charters directly or get information about tournaments at **Kona Charter Skippers Association** (☎ 808/329–3600 or 800/762–7546, WEB www.konabiggamefishing.com). **Notorious Sport Fishing** (☎ 808/325–7558 or 888/584–5662, WEB www.interpac.net/-jackc) favors small groups of up to six people. For the true fishing enthusiast, **Reel Action Light-Tackle Sportfishing** (☎ 808/325–6811) runs an open-center console boat and offers light-tackle fishing, including fly-fishing.

The biggest of the fishing competitions is the five-day **Hawaiian International Billfish Tournament** held annually in August since 1959. It attracts teams from around the world. The tournament weighs not just the "Big Blue," but also the boats' cleanliness, crew, and equipment. Tournament results can serve as a helpful guide in choosing which boat to charter. In addition, be sure to describe your expectations when you book your charter so the booking agent can match you with a captain and a boat you will like.

Big fish are weighed in daily at **Honokōhau Harbor's Fuel Dock.** Try to be there in the afternoon between 4 and 5 to watch the weigh-in of the day's catch. It might just be another "grander" (more than 1,000 pounds).

KAYAKING

Kayaks provide an excellent means of observing Hawai'i's diverse marine life and serene shores. Thirty percent of marine mammals are unique to the Big Island, and coral reefs are endangered; as a result, many bays are protected marine preserves. When you venture out, be sure to respect Hawai'i's waters. A reputable kayak shop can point out friendly locations, as currents can be dangerous.

Hawai'i Ocean Adventures (Honokōhau Harbor, Slip J-38, Kailua-Kona, ☎ 808/325–0766, WEB www.hawaiioceanadventures.com) conducts snorkeling and kayaking expeditions, often in dolphin-rich waters, from its vessel Pacific Passion. Adventure fees start at $53.

Kona Boy's Kayaks (✉ 79-7539 Hawai'i Belt Rd., south of Mile Marker 113, Kealakekua, ☎ 808/328–1234, WEB www.oceanecotours.com) provides kayak sales and rentals, complete with gear and coolers, as well as guided tours. A tandem kayak costs $45 for the day. Tours run between $79 and $125.

PARASAILING, SAILING, AND WINDSURFING

Parasailers sit in a harness attached to a parachute that lifts off from the boat deck and sails aloft. Passengers can choose to glide 7 or 10 minutes at 400- or 800-ft heights. Call **UFO Parasail** (✉ Across the street from Kailua Pier, Kailua-Kona, ☎ 808/325–5836, WEB www.ufoparasailing.com) to make arrangements for parasailing. Costs range from $47 to $57.

Ralph Blancato and Kalia Potter of **Maile Charters** (✉ Kawaihae Harbor, Kawaihae, ☎ 808/326–5174 or 800/726–7245, WEB www.adventuresailing.com) offer unique around-the-Islands sailing adventures that range from half-day to five-day journeys. Island cuisine meals, itineraries, and activities are custom-designed. Private cabins and hot showers keep you comfortable. Fees start at $575 for six passengers for a half day.

One of the best windsurfing locations on the Big Island is at 'Anaeho'omalu Bay, on the beach in front of **Outrigger Waikoloa Beach.** Call Ocean Sports at the Royal Waikoloan Resort (☎ 808/886–6666) to obtain information.

SCUBA DIVING

Two-tank dives should cost from $80 to $125, depending on whether or not you're certified and whether you're diving from a boat or from the shore. Many dive outfits have underwater cameras for rent. Instruction with PADI, SDI, or TDI certification in three to five days is $250 to $550. The Kona Coast has calm waters for diving, and dive operators are helpful about suggesting dive sites as far south as Pu'uhonua O Hōnaunau. Some companies also teach surfing, and most rent out dive equipment, snorkel gear, and other water toys. A few organize otherworldly manta ray dives at night or whale-watching cruises in season.

A reputable scuba charter to consider in Kailua-Kona is **Big Island Divers** (✉ 75-5467 Kaiwi St., Kailua-Kona, ☎ 808/329–6068, WEB www.bigislanddivers.com). **Body Glove Cruises** (✉ Kailua Pier, Kailua-Kona, ☎ 808/326–7122 or 800/551–8911, WEB www.bodyglovehawaii.com) has a 55-ft catamaran that sets off from the Kailua Pier daily for a 4½-hour dive and snorkel cruise, which includes breakfast and a buffet lunch. Children are welcome. **Kohala Divers Ltd.** (✉ Kawaihae Shopping Center, downstairs, Kawaihae, ☎ 808/882–7774, WEB www.kohaladivers.com) offers a complete package of diving services. **Kona Coast Divers** (✉ 74-5614 Palani Rd., Kailua-Kona, ☎ 808/329–8802, WEB www.konacoastdivers.com) is a reputable, friendly outfit that has been around a long time. **Ocean Eco Tours** (✉ 79-7539 Hawai'i Belt Rd., south of Mile Marker 113, Kealakekua, ☎ 808/324–7873, WEB www.oceanecotours.com) is an eco-friendly, full-service outfit eager to share a wealth of knowledge. At ʻAnaehoʻomalu Bay at the Outrigger Waikoloa Beach on the Kohala Coast, **Red Sail Sports** (✉ 425 Waikoloa Beach Dr., ☎ 808/886–2876) organizes scuba dives from the 38-ft Lani Kai. **Sandwich Isle Divers** (✉ 75-5729 I Aliʻi Dr., Kailua-Kona, ☎ 808/329–9188, WEB www.sandwichisledivers.com) is centrally located and well-established.

SNORKELING AND SURFING

Colorful tropical fish frequent the lava outcroppings along many Big Island shorelines, so it's easy to arrange a do-it-yourself snorkeling tour by renting masks and snorkels from any of the many diving outfits in Kona or at the resorts. If you are island-hopping and want to drop off your equipment on Oʻahu, Maui, or Kauaʻi, consider **Snorkel Bob's** (✉ Aliʻi Dr. next to the Royal Kona Resort, Kailua-Kona, ☎ 808/329–0770), where prices start at $9 a week for a simple set.

Many snorkel cruises are available. Shop for prices, ask about the size of the boat, and make sure you know what is included and how much the extras, such as underwater cameras, cost.

Among the Big Island's wet-and-wild offerings is the **Captain Zodiac Raft Expedition** (✉ Honokōhau Harbor, Kailua-Kona, ☎ 808/329–3199, WEB www.captainzodiac.com) along the Kona Coast. The exciting four-hour trip on this inflatable raft explores gaping lava-tube caves, searches for dolphins and turtles, and drifts through Kealakekua Bay for snorkeling. The cost is $69.

At Keauhou Bay **Fair Wind and Orca Raft Adventure** (✉ Keauhou Bay, Kailua-Kona, ☎ 808/322–2788, WEB www.fair-wind.com) conducts 4½-hour morning and 3½-hour afternoon excursions. Fair Wind is a 60-ft double-decker catamaran, which supplies snorkel gear, a 15-ft water slide, a dive tower, estate coffee, and even prescription lenses. Morning sails include a barbecue lunch. The *Orca*, a 28-ft inflatable raft, cleaves the waves in a high-thrill, fast-pace ride not for the weak at heart. It also makes time for snorkeling and gentler floating opportunities. Morning sails cost $85 on the *Fair Wind* and $69 on the *Orca*; afternoon trips are $50 for both vessels.

Spectator Sports

Golf

Ample opportunities for celebrity spotting exist at golf tournaments, held at resort golf courses in the Kohala area. The biggest and best is the **MasterCard Championship** (☎ 800/417–2770), a Senior PGA Tour event hosted by Four Seasons Resort Hualālai, in January.

Polo

Mauna Keʻa Polo Club. Matches sponsored by the club are scheduled every Sunday October through mid-December. ✉ Waikiʻi Ranch, off Saddle Rd., 6½ mi from Māmalahoa Hwy., ☎ 808/322–3880. ⊞ $3.

Tennis

The world's best players compete in January in the **USTA Challenger** (✉ Kohala Coast, ☎ 518/274–4615, WEB www.tesports.com) on the courts of Hilton Waikoloa Village. The resort hosts various other tournaments throughout the year.

Triathlon

The highly popular **Ironman Triathlon** (☎ 808/329–0063, WEB www.ironmanlive.com), with its $325,000-purse race, is limited to 1,500 competitors, who swim 2.4-mi, bicycle 112 mi, and run a 26.2-mi marathon. Entrants must qualify through other international competitions. The annual grueling event begins with the ocean swim from Kailua Pier at

7 AM on a Saturday in October. Close to 7,000 volunteers along Ali'i Drive, Queen Ka'ahumanu Highway, and the turnaround in Hāwī provide encouragement and much-needed water to the world's top athletes.

SHOPPING

Residents like to complain that there isn't much to shop for on the Big Island, but unless you're searching for career clothes or high-tech computer toys, you'll find plenty to deplete your pocketbook. Kailua-Kona has a range of souvenirs from far-flung corners of the globe. Resorts along the Kohala coast have high-quality, exclusive clothing, art, and accessories. Galleries and boutiques, many with the work of award-winning local artists, fill historic buildings in Waimea and North Kohala.

In general, stores and shopping centers on the Big Island open at 9 or 10 AM and close by 6 PM. Hilo's Prince Kūhiō Shopping Plaza stays open until 9 weekdays. In Kona, most shops in shopping plazas that are geared toward tourists remain open till 9 PM. Big outlets such as KTA (a supermarket in Kona Coast Shopping Center) or Wal-Mart on Henry Street are open until midnight.

Shopping Centers

In Hilo the most comprehensive mall, similar to mainland malls, is **Prince Kūhiō Shopping Plaza** (⊠ 111 E. Puainako St., at Hwy. 11). Here you'll find Liberty House for fashion, Safeway for food, and Longs Drugs for just about everything else. The older **Hilo Shopping Center** (⊠ 70 Kekuanaoa St., at Kīlauea Ave.) has several air-conditioned shops and restaurants, great cookies at Lanky's Bakery, and plenty of free parking. Hilo's **Waiakea Center** (⊠ Makaala, across Prince Kuhio Shopping Plaza, Hwy. 11) is home to Borders Books & Music, Island Naturals, and Wal-Mart.

Shopping in Kailua-Kona has begun to go the way of mainland cities with Wal-Mart, a huge Safeway, and Borders Books & Music at **Crossroads Shopping Center** (⊠ 75-1000 Henry St.). **Keauhou Shopping Center** (⊠ 78-6831 Ali'i Dr., Kailua-Kona) is home to a variety of stores and boutiques and a post office where you can drop off postcards. An abundance of small shopping malls along Ali'i Drive in Kailua-Kona tend to blend into one another. Virtually all of them offer merchandise to appeal to visitors.

On the makai side of Ali'i Drive, extending an entire block, is **Kona Inn Shopping Village** (⊠ 75-5744 Ali'i Dr., Kailua-Kona, ☎ 808/329–6573), crammed with boutiques selling bright pareos (beach wraps) and knickknacks as well as coffee shops and restaurants. Here **Island Salsa** (☎ 808/329–9279) has great tropical toppers and gift T-shirts, and **Honolua Surf Company** (☎ 808/329–1001) is filled with cool beachwear.

Coconut Plaza (⊠ 75-5795–75-5825 Ali'i Dr., Kailua-Kona), just south of Kona Inn Shopping Village, hides coffee shops, boutiques, ethnic restaurants, and an exquisite gallery in its meandering labyrinth of airy buildings.

In Kailua-Kona, head north on **Palani Road** from Kailua Pier toward the intersection with Highway 19; **Kopiko Plaza** and **Lanihau Center**, on your right, house Longs Drug, gift stores, sandwich shops, and a budget-friendly Sack 'n Save Foods. On your left, you'll find **North Kona Center** and **Kona Coast Shopping Center.**

Just north of Kona, off Highway 19, islanders find bargains at Big Kmart (⊠ Makalapua Ave.) in the **Makalapua Center.** Of more interest might be the large Liberty House, a statewide chain store with nice selections in apparel, bedding, lingerie, and gifts.

King's Shops (⊠ 250 Waikoloa Beach Dr., Waikoloa, ☎ 808/886–8811) houses Under the Koa Tree, with its upscale gift items by artisans, Crazy Shirts, and Malia for quality clothing. Stop by at Kona Wine Market for fine wines.

The harborside **Kawaihae Center** (⊠ Hwy. 270, Kawaihae) houses restaurants, a dive shop, a bathing suit store, and art galleries, including the new Green Flash.

In Waimea, browse around boutiques in **Parker Square** (⊠ Kawaihae Rd., Waimea ☎ 808/885–7178) and in the adjacent **High Country Traders**, where you may find hand-stitched Hawaiian quilts. **Waimea Center** (⊠ Hwy. 19, Waimea) is home to a good health food store; an unusual, San Francisco–style gift shop, Without Boundaries; and much more.

Parker Ranch Shopping Center (Hwy. 19, Waimea) was closed for reconstruction at press time, but will reopen some time in 2002. The Juice Shack; Parker Ranch Visitor Center; and a few stores in the back, including Reyn's, an authentic aloha-shirt apparel shop, are valiantly keeping their doors open for now.

Specialty Stores

Books and Maps

Basically Books (⊠ 160 Kamehameha Ave., Hilo, ☎ 808/961–0144 or 800/903–6277) stocks one of Hawai'i's largest selections of maps and charts, including USGS, topographical, and raised relief maps. It also has Hawaiiana books with great choices for children. **Book Ends** (⊠ 590 Kailua Rd., Kailua-Kona, ☎ 808/261–1996) is an independent bookstore. **Kohala Book Shop** (⊠ 54-3885 Akoni Pule Hwy., Kapa'au, ☎ 808/889–6400) in the historic Nanbu Hotel is the largest used bookstore in the state, with one of the most complete Hawaiian and Pacific collections in the nation and rare first editions. **Middle Earth Bookshoppe** (⊠ 75-5719 Ali'i Dr., Kailua-Kona, ☎ 808/329–2123) is an independent bookstore with superb maps and an esoteric collection of literary works.

Candies and Chocolates

There's nothing like a gift of macadamia nuts dipped in chocolate or truffles filled with guava, ginger, or passion fruit. Two large facilities make a gourmet adventure out of gift shopping. The chocolate factory **Big Island Candies** (⊠ 585 Hinano St., Hilo, ☎ 808/935–8890) lets you tour and taste before you buy. **Kailua Candy Company** (⊠ 74-5563 Kaiwi St., Kailua-Kona, ☎ 808/329–2522) makes chocolate using locally grown cacao beans. Of course, tasting is part of the fun. Through a glass wall you can watch the chocolate artists at work.

Hawaiian Art and Crafts

You'll find exquisite ceramics, Japanese tea sets, and affordable bamboo ware at **Ets'ko** (⊠ 35 Waiānuenue Ave., Hilo, ☎ 808/961–3778). Step into **Dragon Mama** (⊠ 266 Kamehameha Ave., Hilo, ☎ 808/934–9081) to find authentic Japanese fabrics, futons, and antiques. Hilo's **Most Irresistible Shop** (⊠ 256 Kamehameha Ave., ☎ 808/935–9644; Prince Kuhio Plaza, 111 E. Puainako St., at Hwy. 11, ☎ 808/959–6515) lives up to its name with unique gifts from the Pacific. Be it ginger soap or girls' Sanrio wear, there is something for everyone.

On your way to Hawai'i Volcanoes National Park, be sure to visit the workshop of **Dan DeLuz's Woods, Inc.** (⊠ Hwy. 11, Mile Marker 12, Mountain View, ☎ 808/968–6607; ⊠ 64-1013 Māmalahoa Hwy., Waimea, ☎ 808/885–5856), where master bowl-turner Dan DeLuz creates works of art from 50 types of exotic wood grown on the Big Island.

In Hawai'i Volcanoes National Park, **Volcano Art Center** (☎ 808/967–7565) remains a favorite with everyone. The Art Center represents more Hawai'i island artists than any other gallery and carries a selection of fine art prints and oils as well.

If you're driving around the Big Island via the South Point route, stop at **Wood Works** (✉ Māmalahoa Hwy., next to Manago Hotel, ☎ 808/323–2247) next to the Manago Hotel in Captain Cook for rocking chairs, wooden pens, boxes, clocks, and frames, almost all made of koa wood. It's closed Wednesday and Sunday.

If you're driving north from Hilo, take time to browse through the remote **Waipi'o Valley Artworks** gallery (✉ Off Hwy. 240, Kukuihaele, ☎ 808/775–0958). You'll find finely crafted wooden bowls, paintings by local artists, and jewelry and accessories. You can also make arrangements here for tours into and around Waipi'o Valley.

Waimea is home to many art and craft shops. At Parker Square in **Gallery of Great Things** (✉ Kawaihae Rd., ☎ 808/885–7706), you might fall in love with the Ni'ihau shell leis ($300–$5,000) they occasionally have. More affordable perhaps are koa mirrors and other high-quality artifacts from all around the Pacific basin. **Cook's Discoveries** (✉ 64-1066 Māmalahoa Hwy., Waimea, ☎ 808/885–3633), in a red-roof, ranch-green building, is one of the best places in the state to shop for high-end Hawaiian gifts. Patti Cook, the owner, is a treasure of Hawaiiana knowledge. **Mauna Ke'a Galleries** (✉ 65-1298 Kawaihae Rd., Waimea, ☎ 808/887–2244) specializes in rare vintage collectibles, including hula dolls, prints, and koa furniture.

Remote North Kohala is home to dozens of artists and hosts a remarkable number of galleries in its old restored plantation buildings along the main street (Akoni Pule Highway) through Hāwī and Kapa'au. Start toward the Pololū end and visit **Rankin Gallery** (☎ 808/889–6849) in the old Wo On Store, next to the Chinese temple. At **Ackerman Gallery** (☎ 808/889–5971), painter Gary Ackerman; his wife, Yesan; and their daughter, Camille, have a fine and varied collection of gifts for sale in two locations near the King Kamehameha statue. Be sure to stop at the Old Nanbu Hotel, a historic building constructed in 1898, which was rescued from demolition in 1999. Here, working in the front window of his store, **Elements** (☎ 808/889–0760), John Flynn creates exquisite, delicate jewelry such as silver maile lei and gold waterfalls. The shop also showcases carefully chosen gift items, including unusual ceramics. **Nanbu Gallery** (☎ 808/889–0997) features the paintings of owner Patrick Sweeney and other island artists. Inside the Bamboo Restaurant in Hāwī, **Kohala Koa Gallery** (☎ 808/889–0055) seduces visitors with koa-wood pieces such as rocking chairs and writing desks. It also has a wealth of gift items such as boxes, jewelry, and Hawaiian wrapping paper.

Just upcountry of Kailua-Kona is the little coffee town of Hōlualoa, where several galleries crowd the narrow street. Most shops here close at 4 or 5 PM and are closed all day Sunday and Monday. The **Kona Arts center** (✉ Māmalahoa Hwy., Hōlualoa) has drawn an entire community of artists and is open to curious drop-in visitors. Men can pick up an authentic lau hala hat for some top-level sun protection at **Kimura's Lauhala Shop** (✉ Māmalahoa Hwy., Hōlualoa, ☎ 808/324–0053). **Hōlualoa Gallery** (✉ Māmalahoa Hwy., Hōlualoa, ☎ 808/322–8484) has stunning *raku* (Japanese lead-glazed pottery).

Geared toward cruise-ship passengers with little time, **Made on the Big Island** (✉ King Kamehameha's Kona Beach Hotel, 75-5660 Palani Rd., at Kailua Pier, Kailua-Kona, ☎ 808/326–4949) is one-stop shopping for traditional Big Island gifts. You'll find quite a few treasures here, such as koa boxes and bonsai trees that may be exported. At **Rift Zone** (✉ Coconut Plaza, 75-5801 Ali'i Dr., Kailua-Kona, ☎ 808/331–1100), owned by ceramist Robert Joiner and his wife, Kathy, you'll find ceramics but also exquisite jewelry, bowls, ornaments, and hand-blown glass. For hula instruments, intricate feather headbands, and other original art head to **Alapaki's Hawaiian Gifts** (✉ Keauhou Shopping Village, 78-6831 Ali'i Dr., Kailua-Kona, ☎ 808/322–2007).

Vintage and Resort Wear

Hotel shops generally offer the most attractive and original resort wear but prices run higher than elsewhere.

For rare vintage clothing and authentic antique jewelry, browse through the selection at **Flamingo's** (✉ Kona Inn Shopping Village, 75-5744 Ali'i Dr., Kailua-Kona, ☎ 808/329–4122).

In **Keauhou Shopping Center** (✉ 76-6831 Ali'i Dr.) in Kailua-Kona, stop in at Borderlines (☎ 808/322–5003) for colorful women's apparel. **Under the Sun** (☎ 808/322–3316) next door, sells bathing suits, including separates and tan-throughs.

Upcountry in the one-street town of Kainaliu, **Paradise Found** (✉ Māmalahoa Hwy. 11, ☎ 808/322–2111) has contemporary silk and rayon clothing. If you'd like to take home some of Hawai'i's splashy material, try **Kimura's Fabrics** (✉ Māmalahoa Hwy. 11, Kainaliu, ☎ 808/322–3771).

At **Adasa** (✉ 3 Opelo Plaza, Waimea, ☎ 808/887–0997) designer Donna Lore carries high-end couture, her own designs, and matching accessories. Custom design is also possible.

In North Kohala, in the historic 1932 Toyama Building, **As Hāwī Turns** (✉ Akoni Pule Hwy., Hāwi, ☎ 808/889–5023) adds a sophisticated touch to breezy resort wear, pareos, and hand-painted silk clothing. There are vintage and secondhand treasures, crafts, and gifts as well.

The well-known **Sig Zane Designs** (✉ 122 Kamehameha Ave., Hilo, ☎ 808/935–7077) sells distinctive island wearables with bold colors and motifs. **Hilo Hattie** (✉ Prince Kuhio Plaza, 111 E. Puainako St., Hilo, ☎ 808/961–3077; ✉ Kopiko Plaza., Kailua-Kona, ☎ 808/329–7200) matches his-and-her aloha wear and carries a huge selection of casual clothes, slippers, jewelry, and souvenirs. Call for free transportation from selected hotels.

Tropical Flowers and Produce

You can buy tropical blooms at **Akatsuka Orchid Gardens** (✉ Hwy. 11, Volcano, ☎ 808/967–8234) and have them shipped home. The nursery is in Volcano, a 10-minute drive from Hawai'i Volcanoes National Park.

At **Ali'i Gardens Market Place** (✉ Ali'i Dr., 1½ mi south of Kona Inn Shopping Village, Kailua-Kona, ☎ 808/334–1381) individual entrepreneurs sell everything from tropical flowers to Kona coffee, baskets, souvenirs, and crafts. It's more of a flea market than a farmer's market.

In addition to selling and shipping miniature brassaia lava plantings and other bonsai plants, **Fuku-Bonsai Cultural Center** (✉ Ola'a Rd., Kurtistown, ☎ 808/982–9880), which is on the way to Volcano, has free educational exhibits of different ethnic styles of pruning.

At **Hilo Farmers' Market** (✉ Kamehameha Ave. and Mamo St., Hilo) farmers sell a profusion of tropical flowers, high-quality produce, and gourmet macadamia nuts. This colorful, open-air market—the most popular in the state—takes place on Wednesday and Saturday from 6:30 AM to 2:30 PM.

The low-key **Kona Inn Farmers' Market** (⊠ 75-7544 Ali`i Dr., Kona Inn Shopping Village Parking Lot, Kailua-Kona) is filled with colorful tropical flowers and locally grown produce, including macadamia nuts and coffee. It takes place Wednesday and Saturday from 7 am until 3 pm.

The old stone **Volcano Store** (⊠ Old Volcano Hwy., Volcano Village, ☎ 808/967–7210), near Hawai`i Volcanoes National Park, has excellent bargains in cut flowers and will ship them for you as well.

THE BIG ISLAND A TO Z

To research prices, get advice from other travelers, and book travel arrangements, visit www.fodors.com.

AIR TRAVEL
Several domestic and international airlines serve the Big Island's two airports from the mainland as well as from the other islands. Charters around the Islands are available from Keāhole–Kona International Airport, through Big Island Air, in nine-passenger aircraft at hourly rates starting at $770.

CARRIERS

Both national and local airlines offer daily flights to several cities on the mainland. Connections of airlines listed are direct, but keep in mind that you can fly anywhere as long as you're willing to transfer on Oahu or Maui. Hawaiian Airlines, for example, now services San Diego, San Francisco, Portland, Las Vegas, and Seattle from Honolulu.

United offers daily direct flights from San Francisco and Los Angeles to Keāhole–Kona International Airport. Hawaiian Airlines has one flight direct daily from Los Angeles. Aloha Airlines now has daily trips connecting Oakland and Las Vegas with the Islands. Canada 3000 offers a direct flight into Kona from Vancouver.

Between the Neighbor Islands, Aloha and Hawaiian airlines offer frequent jet flights, which take about 45 minutes from Honolulu to Hilo International Airport and 34 minutes from Honolulu to Kona. Fares are approximately $100. Maui-based Pacific Wings offers daily service between Waimea and Honolulu and Waimea and Maui. Flights depart once a day, and seating is limited.

Aloha Airline's sister commuter carrier Island Air provides flights to Hawai`i's resort and smaller community destinations.
➤ Airlines & Contacts: **Aloha Airlines** (☎ 800/367–5250 or 808/935–5771). **Big Island Air** (☎ 808/329–4868 or 800/303–8868). **Canada 3000** (☎ 877/658–3000 or 808/327–9485). **Hawaiian Airlines** (☎ 800/882–8811). **Island Air** (☎ 808/329–8183 or 800/652–6541). **Pacific Wings** (☎ 888/575–4546 or 808/873–0897). **United** (☎ 800/241–6522).

AIRPORTS
The Big Island has two main airports: Keāhole–Kona International Airport, near Kailua-Kona, and Hilo International Airport. Visitors whose accommodations are on the west side of the island normally fly into Kona. If you're staying on the eastern side, in Hilo or near Volcano, fly into Hilo. Midway between Hilo and Kailua-Kona, a small airstrip is used primarily by residents of Waimea. In North Kohala a deserted airstrip, Upolo Point, services small, private planes only.

➤ AIRPORT INFORMATION: **Keāhole–Kona International Airport** (☎ 808/329–2484; 808/329–3423 for visitor information). **Hilo International Airport** (General Lyman Field; ☎ 808/934–5801; 808/934–5840 for visitor information). **Waimea-Kohala Airport** (☎ 808/885–4520).

AIRPORT TRANSFERS

Keāhole–Kona International Airport is about 7 mi (a 10-minute drive) from Kailua-Kona. The Keauhou resort area stretches another 6 mi to the south beyond Kailua. Visitors staying at the upscale resorts along the Kona-Kohala Coast should allow 30 to 45 minute to reach their hotels by car.

Hilo International Airport is just 2 mi, or a five-minute drive, from Hilo's Banyan Drive hotels. If you have chosen a B&B closer to Hawai'i Volcanoes National Park, plan on a 40-minute drive from Hilo International Airport.

If you have booked out-of-the-way accommodations near Waimea, you might want to fly into Waimea-Kohala Airport, but be sure to arrange your rental car in advance, as few car-rental companies service that airport.

Limousine service with a chauffeur who will act as your personal guide is $75–$90 an hour, with a two-hour minimum. A few have all the extras—TV, bar, and narrated tours, plus Japanese-speaking guides.

Only one company, Roberts Hawai'i Minibus, offers group minibus services from the airports in both Kailua-Kona and Hilo. You'll need to make arrangements well in advance.

There is no regularly scheduled shuttle service from either main airport, although private service is offered by the Kohala Coast resorts to the north of Keāhole–Kona International Airport. The rates for this service vary depending on the distance, but are less than a taxi. Check-in is at the Kohala Coast Resort Association counters at the Aloha and Hawaiian airlines arrival areas. SpeediShuttle arranges shared rides from Keāhole–Kona International Airport and is less expensive than a taxi, but you must call ahead of time.

Guests staying in Kailua or at the Keauhou resort area to the south of the airport should check with their individual hotels upon booking to see if shuttle service is available.

Taxis are generally on hand for plane arrivals at both major airports. Taxis from Hilo International Airport to Hilo charge about $9 for the 2-mi ride to the Banyan Drive hotels. A number of taxis service Keāhole–Kona International Airport. Several offer guided tours. Fares start at about $20 for transport to King Kamehameha's Kona Beach Hotel.

➤ TAXIS & SHUTTLES: **A-1 Bob's Taxi** in Hilo (☎ 808/959–4800). **Aloha Taxi** in Kona (☎ 808/325–5448). **Hilo Harry's Taxi** in Hilo (☎ 808/935–7091). **Luana Limousine** in Kona (☎ 808/326–5466). **Marina Taxi** in Kona (☎ 808/329–2481). **Paradise Taxi** in Kona (☎ 808/329–1234). **Roberts Hawai'i Minibus** (☎ 808/329–1688 in Kona; 808/966–5483 in Hilo; or 800/831–5541). **SpeediShuttle** in Kona (☎ 808/329–5433).

BOAT & FERRY TRAVEL

Three cruise lines sail their luxury vessels among the Islands, visiting Kailua-Kona and Hilo on the Big Island. Point of departure and of final return is Honolulu. Costs for seven- or eight-day cruises range from $1,390 to $4,290, depending on your choice of cabin and time of year.

➤ BOAT & FERRY INFORMATION: **American Hawai'i Cruises:** *S.S. Independence* (☏ 800/513–5022, WEB www.cruisehawaii.com). **Norwegian Cruise Lines:** *Superstar Leo* (☏ 800/327–7030, WEB www.ncl.com). **United States Lines:** *M.S. Patriot* (☏ 877/330–6871, WEB www.unitedstateslines.com).

BUS TRAVEL

Hele-On Bus operates Monday through Saturday between Hilo and Kailua-Kona, at $5.25 each way. An additional $1 is charged for luggage and backpacks that do not fit under the seat. The bus departs from Lanihau Center on Palani Road in Kailua-Kona at 6:45 AM, arriving in Hilo at 9:45 AM. It leaves from the Mo'oheau Bus Terminal, between Kamehameha Avenue and Bayfront Highway in Hilo, at 1:30 PM and arrives in Kailua-Kona at 4:30 PM.

The Hele-On also operates in the Hilo and Kailua-Kona town areas themselves for 75¢ and up; exact fare is required.

Within Keauhou, a shuttle runs from hotels and condos to Keauhou Shopping Center and the Kona Country Club golf course.

Roberts Hawai'i links the Waikoloa resort area with Kailua-Kona with shuttle buses from 7 AM to 7 PM. Ask for a schedule at your hotel. Reservations are required.

➤ BUS INFORMATION: **Hele-On Bus** (☏ 808/961–8744). **Hele-On Keauhou Shuttle** (☏ 808/322–3500). **Roberts Hawai'i** (☏ 808/329–1688).

CAR RENTAL

If you pick up an auto at either airport and drop it off at the other, be aware that it could cost you as much as $75 extra. To get the best rate on a rental car, book it in conjunction with an interisland Hawaiian or Aloha airlines flight, or ask your travel agent to check out room-and-car packages. Drivers must be 25 years or older.

Most agencies make you sign an agreement that you won't drive on Saddle Road between Hilo and Waimea, but if you're thinking about stargazing, you'll probably want to take the road up to Mauna Ke'a for the clearest views. Only Harper Rentals lets you drive on Saddle Road in its four-wheel-drive vehicles. Driving on Saddle Road can be dangerous, and there are no gas stations or emergency phones. You might consider a four-wheel-drive vehicle from any agency to reach other rugged shoreline sites.

Two companies on the island rent RVs. Island RV gives you a ready-to-go vacation that includes a complete itinerary, equipment rentals, and customized care; Harper Rentals just gets you the RV as is. Linens are available at both outfits.

➤ MAJOR AGENCIES: **Alamo** (☏ 800/327–9633). **Avis** (☏ 800/321–3712). **Budget** (☏ 800/527–0700). **Dollar** (☏ 800/800–4000). **Hertz** (☏ 800/654–3011). **National** (☏ 800/227–7368). **Thrifty** (☏ 800/367–2277).

➤ Local Agencies: **Island RV** (☏ 808/334–0464 or 800/406–4555, WEB www.islandrv.com). **Harper Truck and Car Rentals** (☏ 808/969–1478 or 800/852–9993).

CAR TRAVEL

An automobile is necessary to see the sights of the Big Island in any reasonable amount of time. Even if you're solely interested in relaxing at your self-contained megaresort, you may still want to rent a car, simply to travel to Kailua-Kona or to the restaurants in Waimea.

Though there are about eight car-rental companies from which to choose, cars can be scarce during holiday weekends, special events, and peak seasons—from mid-December through mid-March. It is best to book well in advance.

EMERGENCIES

Dial **911** in an emergency to reach the police, fire department, or an ambulance. Call one of the hospitals listed for a doctor or dentist close to you. The Volcano Update Hotline provides 24-hr recorded information.

➤ EMERGENCY SERVICES: **Police** (☎ 808/935–3311). **Poison Control Center** (☎ 800/362–3585). **Volcano updates** (☎ 808/985–6000).

➤ HOSPITALS: **Hilo Medical Center** (✉ 1190 Waiānuenue Ave., Hilo, ☎ 808/974–4700). **Kona Community Hospital** (✉ Hwy. 11 at Hau Kapila St., Kealakekua, ☎ 808/322–9311). **North Hawai'i Community Hospital** (✉ 67-1125 Māmalahoa Hwy., Waimea, ☎ 808/885–4444).

MOTORCYCLE TRAVEL

Scooters and motorcycles can be rented in Kailua-Kona across from King Kamehameha's Kona Beach Hotel. Some words of warning: Big Island roads often have narrow shoulders, and the drafts from oversize tour buses swooping by can double the excitement of a simple Sunday ride. Helmets are advised but not mandatory in Hawai'i.

➤ MOTORCYCLE RENTAL: **DJ's Rentals** (☎ 808/329–1700 or 800/993–4647).

LODGING

B & Bs

Members of the Big Island–based Hawai'i Island Bed and Breakfast Association are listed with phone numbers and rates in a comprehensive on-line brochure from the Hawai'i Island Bed and Breakfast umbrella organization. Or you can go with several network booking agencies that try to meet your needs on an individual basis.

➤ RESERVATION SERVICES: **Bed & Breakfast Honolulu (Statewide)** (☎ 800/288–4666, FAX 808/595–2030, WEB www.hawaiibnb.com). **Go Native Hawai'i** (☎ 800/662–8483, WEB www.gonativehi.com). **Hawai'i Island B & B Association** (WEB www.stayhawaii.com). **Hawai'i's Best Bed and Breakfasts** (☎ 808/885–4550 or 800/262–9912, FAX 808/885–0559, WEB www.bestbnb.com).

TAXIS

Several companies advertise guided tours by taxi, but it is an expensive way to travel, with a trip around the island totaling about $350.

SIGHTSEEING TOURS

AIRPLANE & HELICOPTER TOURS

Gazing at a waterfall that drops a couple of thousand feet into multiple pools is absolutely breathtaking. You can also fly above the lava lake on Kīlauea, then follow the flow to the ocean, where clouds of steam billow into the air. (The lava flow has been changing locations and sometimes goes underground, so ask exactly what you'll see when you book your flight.) For a fee, some tour companies will record your flight as a souvenir if you wish. You can go in small planes that carry three to nine passengers or shining helicopters. Expect to pay anywhere from $140 for 45-minute flights to $300-plus for two hours, and make reservations in advance. Departure points are from resort helipads or from the airports.

Big Island Air and Island Hoppers Hawai'i offer plane tours. Island Hoppers Hawai'i leaves from Hilo for 50-minute flights, and from Kailua-Kona for 2 and 2½-hour flights. Blue Hawaiian Helicopters, Hawai'i Helicopters, Sunshine Helicopters, and Vocano Helicopters all offer helicopter tours leaving from one of the two major airports or a private landing pad.

➤ TOUR OPERATORS: **Big Island Air** (✉ Keāhole–Kona International Airport, ☎ 808/329–4868 or 800/303–8868). **Blue Hawaiian Helicopters** (✉ Hilo International Airport or Waikoloa Helipad, ☎ 808/961–5600 or 800/745–2583, WEB www.bluehawaiian.com). **Hawai'i Helicopters** (✉ Hilo and Keāhole–Kona International Airports, ☎ 800/994–9099, WEB www.hawaii-helicopters.com). **Island Hoppers Hawai'i** (✉ Hilo and Keāhole–Kona International Airports, ☎ 808/969–2000 or 800/538–7590, WEB www.fly-hawaii.com). **Sunshine Helicopters** (✉ Helipad at the Hāpuna Beach Prince Hotel, ☎ 808/882–1223 or 800/622–3144, WEB www.sunshinehelicopters.com). **Volcano Helicopters** (✉ Hilo International Airport, ☎ 808/961–3355).

ALL-TERRAIN-VEHICLE AND HUMMER TOURS

A different way to experience the Big Island's rugged coastline and wild ranch lands is through an off-road adventure. At higher elevations, weather can be nippy and rainy, but views can be awesome. You can ride in your own all-terrain vehicle or share a Hummer. Protective gear is provided. Tours are priced around $100.

➤ TOUR OPERATORS: **ATV Outfitters Hawai'i** (✉ Old Sakamoto Store, Hwy. 270, Kapa'au, ☎ 808/889–6000, WEB www.outfittershawaii.com). **HMV Tours** (✉ Hwy. 250, Hawi, ☎ 808/889–6922 or 877/449–6922, WEB www.hmvtours.com). **Kahua Ranch ATV Rides** (✉ Hwy 250, 10 mi north of Waimea, ☎ 808/882–7954, WEB www.kahuaranch.com).

BOAT TOURS

A voyage on a traditional double-hulled sailing canoe is available through Hahalua Lele along the Kohala shores near The Orchid at Mauna Lani. You'll get a good sense of the ancient art of navigation. The crew spices up the tour with Hawaiian history and legends. Expect to pay $100.

Unique among the abundance of water adventures is the *Atlantis IV* submarine tour from Kailua Pier, across from King Kamehameha's Kona Beach Hotel in Kona; it feels more like an amusement-park ride than the real thing. A large glass dome in the bow and 13 viewing ports on the sides allow clear views of the watery world. Children must be at least 3 ft tall. Fees for adults are around $85.

➤ TOUR OPERATORS: **Atlantis IV Submarine** (☎ 808/329–6626 or 800/548–6262, WEB www.atlantisadventures.com). **Hahalua Lele** (☎ 808/885–2000, ext. 7524).

BUS TOURS

Roberts Hawai'i conducts a Hilo–Volcano–Kalapana tour out of Hilo, and an 11-hour circle-island tour from Kailua-Kona. Costs range from $45 to $55.

➤ TOUR OPERATOR: **Roberts Hawai'i** (☎ 808/329–1688 in Kona; 808/966–5483 in Hilo; or 800/831–5541, WEB www.roberts-hawaii.com).

COFFEE-FARM TOURS

Coffee farms around the South Kona and Upcountry Kona coffee belt area from Hōlualoa to Hōnaunau generally welcome visitors. You'll observe the whole process, from green beans to package. Often, macadamia nuts are for sale, and the brew, of course, is always ready. Some tours are self-guided, and most are free. The exception is the Kona Coffee Living History Farm (known as the D. Uchida Farm), unique in its heritage of coffee pioneers. The site, which has been preserved and restored by the Kona Historical Society and won a National Trust Preservation award in 2000, includes a 1913 farm house surrounded by coffee trees, a Japanese bath house, Kuriba (coffee processing mill), and Hoshidana (traditional drying platform). Tours of the farm are available by reservation only and cost $20.

➤ TOUR OPERATORS: **Bay View Farms** (✉ ½ mi past St. Benedict's Painted Church, Painted Church Rd., Hōnaunau, ☎ 808/328–9658). **Greenwell Farms** (✉ 81-6581 Māmalahoa Hwy., Kealakekua, ☎ 808/ 323–2862). **Holualoa-Kona Coffee Company** (✉ 77-6261 Old Māmalahoa Hwy., Hwy. 180, Hōlualoa, ☎ 808/322–9937 or 800/334–0348). **Kona Coffee Living History Farm** (known as the D. Uchida Farm; ✉ Kona Historical Society, 81-6551 Māmalahoa Hwy., Kealakekua, ☎ 808/323–2006). **Royal Kona Coffee Museum and Coffee Mill** (✉ 83-5427 Māmalahoa Hwy., next to the tree house in Hōnaunau, ☎ 808/ 328–2511).

GARDEN TOURS

Several botanical gardens across the island welcome you to meander along the trails and study the diversity of the local flora. Often overlooked is the Amy B. H. Greenwell Ethnobotanical Garden, with its wealth of Hawaiian cultural traditions. It is home to 250 plants, including food and fiber crops, on 12 acres, that were typical in an early Hawaiian *ahupua'a*, a pie-shape land division that ran from the mountains to the sea. Call to find out about guided tours and visiting hours.

➤ TOUR OPERATOR: **Amy B. H. Greenwell Ethnobotanical Garden** (✉ 82-6188 Māalahoa Hwy., Captain Cook, ☎ 808/323–3318, WEB www.bishopmuseum.org/greenwell/).

MAUNA KE'A ASTRONOMY TOURS

The clearest place in the world for viewing the heavens is reputedly the summit of 13,796-ft Mauna Ke'a. The trick is getting there. It takes Saddle Road and a four-wheel-drive vehicle to reach the top; freezing temperatures and arctic conditions are common at the summit, and the air is thin. Be sure to take along warm parkas.

If you're driving to the summit on your own, stop in first at the Onizuka Center for International Astronomy Visitor Information Station, at a 9,300-ft elevation. Technically it can be reached in a standard automobile. To reach this station from Hilo, which is about 34 mi away, take Highway 200, Saddle Road, and turn right at Mile Marker 28 onto Summit Access Road. The observatory patio here is the best amateur observation site on earth, with five telescopes and a knowledgeable staff, so you might not need to go farther. The station offers stargazing programs (for gazers of all ages) Thursday–Sunday at 6 PM as well as daytime programs with exhibitions and videos. From the visitor station, for those 16 and older, an escorted summit tour of four-wheel-drive vehicles makes free trips to the Mauna Ke'a observatories on weekends. Departure is at 1 PM, and reservations are not required. You must be in good health and not pregnant.

As an easier alternative, book a tour with a reliable company. Tour operators usually provide parkas, as well as telescopes, snacks, and meals when appropriate. They pick you up at convenient locations, including the resorts. Excursion fees range from about $100 to $150.

➤ CONTACTS: **Arnott's Lodge & Hiking Adventures** from Hilo (☎ 808/ 969–7097, WEB www.arnottslodge.com). **Hawai'i Forest & Trail** (from Kailua-Kona and the Kohala Coast resorts; ☎ 808/331–8505 or 800/ 464–1993, WEB www.hawaii-forest.com). **Hawaiian Eyes Land Tours** (from resorts on Kohala Coast; ☎ 808/937–2530). **Onizuka Center for International Astronomy Visitor Information Station.** (✉ Summit Access Rd., ☎ 808/961–2180). **Paradise Safaris** (from Kailua-Kona, King's Shops, and Waimea; ☎ 808/322–2366 or 888/322–2366, WEB www.maunakea.com).

RANCH TOURS

Two ranches that have shaped Big Island history have opened their lands to guided visitor activities. The 8000-plus acres of Kahua Ranch—known for its lamb, beef, and hydroponic vegetables—hold legendary stories about King Kamehameha. The owners provide horseback riding, ATV adventures, mountain biking, and hiking. There is even a guest house. Because this is private land, you must call ahead for fees and directions.

A covered wagon pulled by a pair of draft horses leads you through a portion of the 225,000-acre Parker Ranch. If you are a reasonably experienced horseback rider, you can also participate in a two-hour trek that includes a cattle drive. Hiking tours are available as well.
➤ TOUR OPERATORS: **Hawai'i Forest & Trail's Kahua Cloud Forest Adventure** (☎ 808/331–8505 or 800/464–1993, WEB www.hawaii-forest. com). **Hawaiian Walkways' Parker Ranch Hikes** (Waimea Office Center, Bldg. 2, Suite 1, Waimea, ☎ 808/775–0372 or 800/457–7759, WEB www.hawaiianwalkways.com). **Kahua Ranch Tours** (✉ Kahua Ranch, Hwy. 250, ☎ 808/882–7954 or 808/882–4646, WEB www.kahuaranch. com). **Parker Ranch Wagon Tours and Rides.** (✉ Parker Ranch Visitor Center, Hwy. 19, Waimea, ☎ 808/885–7655, WEB www.parkerranch. com).

VALLEY TOURS

Although you certainly can hike down into the Waipi'o and Pololū valleys that frame the Kohala Mountains, more fun might be to hoof it with a mule or horseback tour. Or consider a guided tour around the rim by a four-wheel-drive vehicle. You'll be treated to breathtaking views along historic trails, and experienced guides are happy to recount the ancient history of this land. Costs range from $25 to $95.
➤ FOUR-WHEEL, WAGON, SHUTTLE TOURS: **Waipi'o Rim Backroad Adventures** (☎ 808/775–1122). **Waipi'o Valley Shuttle** (☎ 808/775–7121). **Waipi'o Valley Wagon Tours.** (☎ 808/775–9518).
➤ HORSEBACK TOURS: **Waipi'o (Na'alapa) Stables** (☎ 808/775–1007). **Waipi'o on Horseback** (☎ 808/775–7291).
➤ MULE TOURS: **Hawai'i Forest and Trail** (☎ 808/331–8505 or 800/464–1993, WEB www.hawaii-forest.com).

WALKING & HIKING TOURS

Maps and brochures for self-guided walking tours in historic areas or parks are often available on-site or at locations listed below. In Kailua-Kona, interpretive guides from the Kona Historical Society conduct various guided tours for a small fee.

As for nature hikes, to get to some of the best trails and places, it's worth going with a skilled guide. Costs range from $75 to $150, and hikes include picnic meals and gear such as binoculars, ponchos, and walking sticks. The outfits mentioned here also offer customized adventure tours. Hawai'i Earth Guides Eco-Adventures specializes in custom adventures and hikes; adventure spas of three or seven days are also available. Expert naturalist guides from Hawai'i Forest and Trail take you to 500-ft Kalopa Falls in North Kohala, on bird-watching expeditions, and through normally inaccessible areas of Hawai'i Volcanoes National Park and Hawaiian rain forests. Hawaiian Walkways conducts several tours—waterfall hikes, flora and fauna explorations, and jaunts through Hawai'i Volcanoes National Park, as well as custom-designed trips.
➤ HISTORIC TOURS: **Big Island Visitors Bureau** (✉ 250 Keawe St., ☎ 808/961–5797 or 808/886–1655). **Kona Historical Society** (✉ 81-6551 Māmalahoa Hwy., Kealakekua, ☎ 808/323–2005, WEB www. konahistorical.org).

➤ NATURE HIKES: **Hawai'i Earth Guides Eco-Adventures** (☎ 800/949–3483 or 808/329–7116, WEB www.eco-adventure.com). **Hawai'i Forest and Trail** (☎ 808/331–8505 or 800/464–1993, WEB www.hawaii-forest. com). **Hawaiian Walkways** (☎ 808/775–0372 or 800/457–7759, WEB www.hawaiianwalkways.com).

WHALE-WATCHING TOURS

Most Hawaiian whale-watching cruises focus on the migratory humpbacks that are seen here only from December through April, but Captain Dan McSweeney's offers three-hour trips year-round to find six other species of whales that rarely stray far from the Kona Coast. The cost is $56. You can also try one of the many snorkeling, sailing, and kayaking companies.

➤ TOUR OPERATOR: **Captain Dan McSweeney's Year-Round Whale Watching Adventures** (⊠ Honokōhau Harbor, Kailua-Kona, ☎ 808/322–0028 or 888/942–5376, www.ilovewhales.com).

WATER-SPORTS TOURS

You can sail, cruise the ocean, fish, and snorkel to your heart's content on the Big Island, but two unique water tours stand apart from the others. One is a $75 kayak adventure down the pitch-black, eerie tunnels of the 22½-mi Kohala Ditch—irrigation ditches, built in 1905 by Japanese workers. You'll emerge now and then to pristine rain forests. "Flumin the ditch" in an inner tube used to be a dangerous and exciting pastime for sugar plantation children. The other tour, provided by Hawaiian Adventure Tours, is a land-and-water package that combines hiking, swimming, snorkeling, and kayaking in eight- or ten-day adventures on two or three Islands.

➤ TOURS AND OPERATORS: **Flumin' Da Ditch** (⊠ 55-519 Hāwī Rd., Hwy. 250, Hāwī, ☎ 808/889–6922, WEB www.flumindaditch.com). **Hawaiian Adventure Tours** (⊠ Kapa'au, ☎ 808/889–0227 or 800/659–3544, WEB www.hawaiianadventuretours.com).

VISITOR INFORMATION

Information and brochures are dispensed at the Big Island Visitors Bureau (BIVB) booths at Big Island airports and at the offices in Hilo and King's Shops. If you rent a car, be sure to get a "Drive Guide." These handy booklets have all the maps you'll probably need to navigate the island. Several state, county, and resort organizations and Web sites for visitors are invaluable.

Visit the bookstores below for detailed street maps, and call the weather hotline for daily reports.

➤ BOOKSTORES: **Basically Books** (⊠ 160 Kamehameha Ave., Hilo, ☎ 808/961–0144). **Borders Books & Music** (⊠ 75-1000 Henry St., Kailua-Kona, ☎ 808/331–1668; ⊠ 301 Maka'ala, Hilo, ☎ 808/933–1410). **Middle Earth Bookshoppe** (⊠ 75-5719 Ali'i Dr., Kailua-Kona, ☎ 808/329–2123).

➤ TOURIST INFORMATION: **Big Island Visitors Bureau** (⊠ 250 Keawe St., Hilo, ☎ 808/961–5797, FAX 808/961–2126; 250 Waikoloa Beach Dr., B12, King's Shops, Waikoloa, 96738, ☎ 808/886–1655, WEB www. bigisland.org). **Destination Hilo** (⊠ 400 Hualani Bldg., Hilo 96720, ☎ 808/935–5294). **Destination Kona Coast** (⊠ Box 2850, Kailua-Kona 96745, ☎ 808/325–5794). **Hawai'i Visitors and Convention Bureau** (WEB www.gohawaii.com). **Kona–Kohala Resort Association.** (⊠ 69-275 Waikoloa Beach Dr., Waikoloa 96743, ☎ 808/886–4915 or 800/318–3637, WEB www.kkra.org). **Weather** (☎ 808/961–5582).

4 KAUA'I

THE GARDEN ISLE

Greenest and most tropical of all, Kaua'i is the only Hawaiian island with sizable rivers. Polynesians first chose to settle here on the banks of the bubbling Wailua, on the east coast. The lushness of the misty, magical north shore is a startling contrast to the west coast's Waimea Canyon—the "Grand Canyon of the Pacific"—with its rich, vivid coloration of copper, rust, and gold.

NICKNAMED THE GARDEN ISLE, Kauaʻi is Eden epitomized. In the mountains of Kōkeʻe, lush swamps ring with the songs of rare birds, and the heady aroma of ginger blossoms sweetens the cool rain forests of Hāʻena. Time and nature carved the elegant spires along the remote northwestern shore known as the Nā Pali (cliffs) Coast as seven coursing rivers gave life to the valleys where ancient Hawaiians once dwelled. Today visitors can explore this Pacific paradise by land, sea, and air—hiking along the Kalalau Trail, kayaking up the Hanalei River, or hovering in a helicopter high above 5,148-ft Waiʻaleʻale, the wettest spot on earth.

By Betty
Fullard-Leo

Though devastating hurricanes are rare in Hawaiʻi, in September 1992 Hurricane ʻIniki swept right across the island and caused hundreds of millions of dollars' worth of damage. The people of Kauaʻi were quick to rebuild and revitalize their communities, and today Kauaʻi looks better than ever thanks to extensive renovations and improvements.

The Garden Isle is a laid-back, restful retreat—an island of unmatched physical beauty that easily rewards those who love the great outdoors. You can take a boat trip up Nā Pali Coast to snorkel in azure waters; ride a horse-drawn coach around a plantation-era sugar estate; or play golf on the world-class greens of Princeville Resort, where a majestic mountain peak, nicknamed Bali Hai, rises just beyond the fairways. Then again, you might just want to saddle up and go horseback riding into Waimea Canyon and see why these steep ridges and ravines are often called the "Grand Canyon of the Pacific."

One road runs almost all the way around the island but dead-ends on either side of a 15-mi stretch of the rugged Nā Pali Coast. Driving from one end to the other takes you past lustrous green stands of sugarcane, which are gradually being replaced with coffee and macadamia-nut orchards. Dating from 1836, when Hawaiʻi's first sugar mill was built in Kōloa, sugar was a key economic force on the island until the early 1990s. Patches of taro are found around Hanalei Valley. This longtime staple of the Hawaiian diet is grown for its root (to make poi, a puddinglike accompaniment for fish and meat) as well as its leaves (used to wrap and cook food). Traveling around the island, you'll see such movie settings as the Hulēʻia River, where Indiana Jones made his daring escape at the beginning of *Raiders of the Lost Ark*. Other locations on the island were used in filming *Honeymoon in Vegas, Jurassic Park,* and *Six Days, Seven Nights.*

Kauaʻi, the fourth-largest island in the Hawaiian chain, has its capital in Līhuʻe, a town whose government buildings resemble a small New England village. Līhuʻe is the island's commercial center, yet its collection of businesses—a pair of banks, a library, a school, a museum, some family-run restaurants, and hotels—is small enough to keep the pace unhurried.

On the south coast the sunny beaches and clear skies around Poʻipū have spawned a crop of classy condos and resort hotels. The area has also come into its own as a golf destination, and several fine restaurants have found a home here as well. Head west, beneath the slopes of the Hoary Head Mountains, to encounter such storybook plantation villages as Hanapēpē, Kalāheo, and Waimea—where Captain James Cook first landed back in 1778. Beyond Waimea lies Polihale Beach, an idyllic stretch of golden sand sprawled beneath the cool highlands of Kōkeʻe State Park.

From the southwestern part of Kaua'i you can see the island of Ni'ihau 17 mi off the coast. Until 1987 no uninvited guests were allowed to visit this family-owned island. Most people who live in Hawai'i still consider Ni'ihau off-limits, but its mysteries can now be breached by helicopter—three-hour Kaua'i-based tours touch down beside a Ni'ihau beach or crater for curious explorers.

North of Līhu'e the climate turns cooler and wetter, and everything sparkles in luxuriant shades of green. In Wailua and Kapa'a several resort complexes huddle along a picturesque shoreline called the Royal Coconut Coast for its abundant array of palms. As you head farther north to Anahola, Kīlauea, Princeville, and Hanalei, vines and flowers flourish. At the end of the road, in Hā'ena, you'll encounter a misty otherworldliness conjuring up the legends of the ancients.

More myths are attached to the natural landscape of Kaua'i than to any other Hawaiian island. A favorite among locals is the legend of the Menehune, a community of diminutive yet industrious workers said to have lived on Kaua'i before the Polynesians. Few people actually saw the Menehune because they worked in privacy at night—practicing, it seems, their impressive stoneworking skills. There are bridges, walls, fishponds, and other solid constructions attributed to the engineering skill of these mysterious mythical stonemasons.

Kaua'i is the oldest of the Hawaiian Islands, and its 550 square mi are rich in natural history and the resonance of past cultures. A sense of relaxation and unaffected natural beauty calmly welcomes all who step off the plane at the Līhu'e Airport and wraps them in a lei of traditional Hawaiian hospitality. The people in the tourism and hospitality industry here work hard to keep visitors and guests satisfied, and the aloha spirit reigns everywhere. In fact, many feel that Kaua'i's people are the friendliest in all the Islands and that this splendid jewel of an island harbors all that nature allows from a tropical paradise.

Pleasures and Pastimes

Beaches

As the oldest of the Hawaiian Islands, Kaua'i has had more time to develop—and perfect—its beaches. The Garden Isle is embraced by stretches of magnificent ivory sands, many with breathtaking mountain backdrops. Po'ipū, on the south shore, has the sandiest, most consistently sunny beaches for water lovers. Here is some of the island's best swimming, snorkeling, and bodysurfing, in waters that are generally safe year-round. You do need to look out for occasional patches of coral, which can leave a nasty cut on your foot.

The north shore is a different story altogether. Although some of Kaua'i's most scenic beaches are here, they are treacherous in winter. In summer, however, they are safe for swimming.

The beaches that front the hotels and condominiums along the eastern shore are conducive to seaside strolling but less favorable for swimming. The strong surf and rip currents of the winter months are unpredictable, and it's often windy. If you want beaches with plenty of wide open spaces, drive to the west coast beyond Waimea. This is where many locals go to fish and swim, and you'll catch the best sunsets from this vantage point. Waimea has a black-sand beach where sunsets are dramatic, while the Kekaha and Barking Sands beaches are a dazzling white-sand continuation of the beach that starts beneath the cliffs at Polihale.

Beaches along the northwest shore are inaccessible except to those who hike the rugged Nā Pali trail from the opposite end of the road at Hā'ena

HAWAIIAN MYTHS AND LEGENDS

THE BEST-KNOWN DEITY in Hawaiian lore is Pele, the volcano goddess. Although visitors are warned not to remove lava rocks from Pele's domain without her permission, some do and find themselves dogged by bad luck until they return the stolen items. The Hawai`i Volcanoes National Park Service often receives packages containing chunks of lava along with letters describing years of misfortune.

Tales of Pele's fiery temper are legion. She battled Poli`ahu, ruler of snowcapped Mauna Ke`a on the Big Island, in a fit of jealousy over the snow goddess's extraordinary beauty. She picked fights with her peace-loving sister, Hi`iaka, turning the younger goddess's friends into pillars of stone. And her recurring lava-flinging spats with suitor Kamapua`a, a demigod who could change his appearance at will, finally drove him into the sea, where he turned into a fish to escape from her wrath.

But Pele can be kind if the mood suits her. It is said that before every major eruption, she appears in human form as a wrinkled old woman walking along isolated back roads. Those who offer her a ride home return home to find a river of boiling magma abruptly halted inches from their property or diverted around their houses. Those who pass her by find their homes devastated by molten lava. Many hula *hālau* (schools) still make pilgrimages to the rim of Kīlauea—Pele's home on the Big Island—where they honor the fickle goddess with prayers, chants, and offerings of gin and flower leis.

A less volatile but equally intriguing figure in Hawaiian lore is Māui, a demigod who is credited with pulling the Hawaiian Islands up from the bottom of the sea with a magic fishhook, pushing the sky away from the treetops because it had flattened all the leaves, and—his most prestigious feat—lassoing the sun as it came up over the top of Haleakalā and demanding that it move more slowly across the sky in summer so that Māui's mother would have longer daylight hours to dry her *kapa* (cloth made from bark).

In addition to battling the elements and each other, gods were thought to have intervened in the daily lives of early Hawaiians. Storms that destroyed homes and crops, a fisherman's poor catch, or a loss in battle were blamed on the wrath of angry gods. And according to legend, an industrious race of diminutive people called *menehune* built aqueducts, fishponds, and other constructs requiring advanced engineering knowledge unavailable to early Hawaiians. Living in remote hills and valleys, these secretive workers toiled only in darkness and completed complex projects in a single night. Their handiwork can still be seen on all the Islands.

Also at night, during certain lunar periods, a traveler might inadvertently come across the Night Marchers—armies of dead warriors, chiefs, and ancestral spirits whose feet never touch the ground as they tread the ancient highways, chanting and beating their drums, and pausing only to claim the spirits of their brethren who died that night. It was believed that such an encounter would mean certain death unless a relative among the marchers pleaded for the victim's life.

The moral? Leave the lava rocks as they are and pick up any elderly hitchhikers you might come across. Straightforward enough. And hightail it in the other direction if you hear mysterious chanting or drum beating.

or who book a boat tour along the north shore. Some tour operators offer a hiker-camper drop-off service from May through September, transporting passengers one way so they can enjoy a secluded beach, then hike back on their own.

Dining

The sugar plantations of 19th-century Kaua'i brought together a universe of cultures as workers from other countries sought new jobs in Hawai'i. With them came an international array of foods, reflected in the cuisines found today on Kaua'i. You can choose from among Hawai'i regional restaurants or those preparing Chinese, Japanese, Thai, Mexican, Italian, and French specialties, mixed with a heavy dose of traditional Hawaiian food, available in just about any town on the island. When it's time for a snack, look for the carryout wagons that are often parked at major beaches. They serve local foods, such as the "plate lunch"—two scoops of rice served with such entrées as teriyaki beef or chicken, veal cutlet, or luncheon meat. Another standard component is a mound of either macaroni salad or potato salad, with a few token greens thrown in for show. The "mixed plate" is a plate lunch with two or sometimes three entrée selections.

Lodging

Part of the appeal of the Garden Isle is its range of hotel properties—from swanky and pricey resorts to rustic mountaintop cabins to barebones lodgings whose main appeal is a rock-bottom price. Sunshine seekers often head south to the shores of Po'ipū, where three- and four-story condos line the coast and the gentle surf is ideal for swimming. Po'ipū has more condos than hotels, with prices in the moderate to expensive range, although several oceanfront cottages are in demand with budget travelers. Guests interested in the history of the islands often stay on the east coast near the Wailua River, home to Kaua'i's first inhabitants. Many of the hotels here place an emphasis on the legends and lore of the area. The beaches are so-so for swimming but nice for sunbathing. Farther north are the swanky hotels and condominiums of Princeville Resort. You can't go wrong here, because just about any accommodation offers views of the bay or the chiseled mountain peaks of Hanalei. Golfers find the courses here a paradise. Bed-and-breakfasts are an attractive option if you're looking for a more settled-in and residential experience. There's a range of private homes scattered around the island. A good booking service can help you locate one.

Outdoor Activities and Sports

GOLF

Princeville Resort's stunning Robert Trent Jones, Jr.–designed Prince Course is rated the second most difficult course in Hawai'i. The resort's (and Jones's) neighboring Makai Course is also beautiful, with the so-called Zen bunker (a boulder in the middle of a huge sand trap) and an eighth hole played across an ocean chasm. Jack Nicklaus's Kiele course has many greens positioned diagonally to the fairway. Nicklaus's adjacent Lagoons course is less dramatic and wider. As you play the four closing holes of Jones's Po'ipū Bay course you will hear the crashing surf on your left. Endangered wildlife, such as the nēnē goose, monk seal, and sea turtle, can often be spotted—the geese in ponds on the back nine, and the seals and turtles on the beach or in the water below. Kiahuna Plantation, Jones's fourth design on Kaua'i, is a challenging inland course that winds over streams, through woods, and past lava formations.

HIKING

Best known for the challenging north shore Kalalau Trail, Kaua'i is also a mecca for hikers. Trails at Kōke'e State Park range from easy to difficult and overlook the green ramparts of the Nā Pali coastline or showcase views of the painted wonders of Waimea Canyon. Easy excursions through Keāhua Forestry Arboretum, Limahuli Garden, and other tropical gardens appeal to all ages.

HORSEBACK RIDING

Kaua'i offers possibly the broadest selection of equestrian outings of all the Islands. You can saddle up to ride along the rim of Waimea Canyon, to a secluded waterfall, along the edge of a moonlit beach, or through the greenest of mountain pastures.

WATER SPORTS

Safe yet exciting water adventures are possible through a vast number of companies. Kayaks can be rented for do-it-yourself or guided excursions. This is the only island where you have the choice of kayaking on rivers, ancient fishponds, or in the ocean. Fishing, scuba, and snorkel guides are quick to locate the spots where the biggest and most colorful array of fish hang out, and surfing and windsurfing instructors can help you soar like a tropical bird across the cresting waves.

There are three great dive sites on Kaua'i. Cannon's Reef, on the north shore, drops quickly from the shoreline, forming a long ledge permeated with lava tubes. Plate coral is found here, and turtles are a common sight. You may come across white tip sharks sleeping in caverns or patrolling the ledge. Depths range from 30 ft to 60 ft, and you can only dive here in summer. General Store, at Kukui'ula, is the site of a 19th-century shipwreck. The horseshoe-shape ledge and two caverns teem with schools of lemon butterfly fish that follow divers around. There are also green moray eels and black coral at this site, which runs to depths of 65 ft to 80 ft. Sheraton Caverns, off Po'ipū, are formed by three immense, parallel lava tubes. There is a lobster nursery in one cavern, sea turtles swim in all three, and the occasional white tip shark cruises by. Depths range from 35 ft to 60 ft.

EXPLORING KAUA'I

The main road tracing the island's perimeter takes you past a variety of easily explored landscapes and attractions. There are magical mountains, cascading waterfalls, verdant fern grottoes, mist-shrouded caves, and a lighthouse designated a National Historic Landmark. All around the island are beautiful overlooks where you can stop to take a breath and soak up the fragrant beauty.

Directions on the island are often referred to as *mauka* (toward the mountains) and *makai* (toward the ocean).

Great Itineraries

With Līhu'e as your point of departure, it's easy to explore the island by traveling to sights along its eastern and northern coasts, then visiting attractions around Līhu'e itself, and finally striking out toward the southern and western coasts. Each of these routes can easily fill a day of sightseeing. Allow one day for the north and east sections of the island and another day for sights to the south and west. To fully enjoy the sunning, surfing, hiking, golfing, and other activities and adventures on Kaua'i, plan on spending at least five or six days.

Numbers in the text correspond to numbers in the margin and on the Kaua'i map.

IF YOU HAVE 2 DAYS

In two full days you can barely scratch the surface of Kaua'i's idyllic beauty. Plan to stay along the southeast shoreline, anywhere from

NI'IHAU *Lehua Island*

Lehua Landing
Ki'i Landing

Pu'uwai
Ki'eki'e
Nonopapa

Kamalino

N

0   2 miles
0   2 km

Waikapala'e and
Waikanaloa Wet Caves

Hā'ena State Park

Limahuli
Garden
12 Hā'ena
Beach

Ke'e Beach
State Park 14

11

Maniniholo
Dry Cave

13

Hanakāpī'ai Beach

NĀ PALI COAST

Kalalau Trail

36 ■ Pu'u O Kila Lookout

Kōke'e
Lodge Kalalau Lookout

55

Kōke'e

*Kōke'e
State Park*

Polihale
State Park

*Nā Pali-Kona
Forest Reserve*

W A I M E A

Kōke'e Rd.

35

Waimea
Canyon

Waimea Canyon Dr.

Menehune
Ditch

32

Kekaha Beach Park

Kekaha

34 33 Waimea

West Kaua'i
Visitor and
Technology Center

31 Ft. Elisabeth

Kaulakahi Channel

Hanapēpē Valley
and Canyon Lookout 28

50

Hanapēpē 29

Port
Allen

27

Salt Pond
Beach Park

30

Burn's
Field

Ka
Vis
an

N

0   5 miles
0   5 km

← TO
NI'IHAU

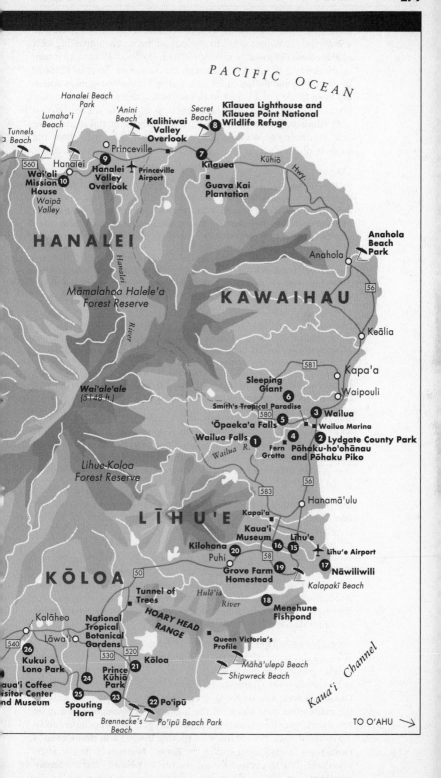

PACIFIC OCEAN

Tunnels
a Beach

Lumaha'i
Beach

Hanalei Beach
Park

'Anini
Beach

Kalihiwai
Valley
Overlook

Secret
Beach

Kīlauea Lighthouse and
Kīlauea Point National
Wildlife Refuge

8

560

Hanalei

Wai'oli
Mission
House

10

Waipā
Valley

9

Princeville

Hanalei
Valley
Overlook

Princeville
Airport

7

Kīlauea

Guava Kai
Plantation

Kūhiō Hwy.

HANALEI

Hanalei
River

Māmalahoa Halele'a
Forest Reserve

KAWAIHAU

Anahola

Anahola
Beach
Park

56

Keālia

581

Kapa'a

Wai'ale'ale
(5148 ft.)

Sleeping
Giant

6

Smith's Tropical Paradise

'Ōpaeka'a Falls

5

Waipouli

580

3 Wailua

Lihue-Koloa
Forest Reserve

Wailua Falls

1

Fern
Grotto

4

Wailua R.

Wailua Marina

2 Lydgate County Park

Pōhaku-ho'ohānau
and Pōhaku Piko

56

583

Hanamā'ulu

LĪHU'E

Kapai'a

Kaua'i
Museum

Kilohana

20

Puhi

50

Grove Farm
Homestead

16

58

15

Līhu'e

Līhu'e Airport

17

Nāwiliwili

KŌLOA

Tunnel of
Trees

Hulē'ia
River

19

Kalapakī Beach

18

Menehune
Fishpond

Kalāheo

Lāwa'i

National
Tropical
Botanical
Gardens

HOARY HEAD
RANGE

Queen Victoria's
Profile

540

26

Kukui o
Lono Park

aua'i Coffee
isitor Center
nd Museum

530

520

21

Kōloa

Māhā'ulepū Beach

Shipwreck Beach

Kaua'i Channel

24

25

Spouting
Horn

Prince
Kūhiō
Park

23

22 Po'ipū

Brennecke's
Beach

Po'ipū Beach Park

TO O'AHU →

Po'ipū to Kapa'a, and then spend one day exploring in either direction. Beginning your trek in **Līhu'e** ⑮, drive around the harbor at **Nāwili- wili** ⑰, then head up the hill to the lookout for an encompassing view of **Menehune Fishpond** ⑱, connecting with Highway 50 until a left turn on Highway 520 takes you through the Tunnel of Trees to **Kōloa** ㉑ for shopping and **Po'ipū** ㉒ for sightseeing. Follow the signs to **Spout- ing Horn** ㉕ for a quick look at this natural waterspout and then con- tinue on through Po'ipū for a beach break at Brennecke's. Visit the ruins of **Ft. Elisabeth** ㉛ for a glimpse of Russia's influence on this island. Then proceed directly to **Waimea Canyon** ㉟ to revel in colorful vistas and fresh, cool air. It's a 36-mi return to Līhu'e.

On your second day, make your goal the end of the road at Hā'ena, 40 mi northwest of Līhu'e. On the way, stretch your legs at the **Kīlauea Lighthouse and Kīlauea Point National Wildlife Refuge** ⑧. Check out the orchard and have some juice at Guava Kai Plantation. Stop briefly at the **Maniniholo Dry Cave** ⑪ and at **Waikapala'e and Waikanaloa Wet Caves** ⑬ before turning around and heading to Hanalei for lunch. Spend the afternoon at the beach before heading back.

IF YOU HAVE 4 DAYS

Four days will allow you to cover the same ground as you would in two days, but you'll have more leisure time to enjoy beach and shop- ping breaks. Spend the first day exploring **Līhu'e** ⑮ more thoroughly. Get a feeling for Kaua'i's history at the **Kaua'i Museum** ⑯ and then drive south to **Kōloa** ㉑ for some leisurely shopping. Have lunch and soak up some rays on the beach in **Po'ipū** ㉒ before calling it a day.

A drive directly to Kōke'e on the second day will allow time for longer hikes and perhaps a stop at a west-side beach as well as a trek around the ruins of **Ft. Elisabeth** ㉛ on the return leg.

The third day should be devoted to an exploration of Kaua'i's north shore. Take in **Kīlauea Lighthouse and Kīlauea Point National Wildlife Refuge** ⑧, examine **Maniniholo Dry Cave** ⑪ and **Waikapala'e and Waikanaloa Wet Caves** ⑬, and amble through **Limahuli Garden** ⑫. Then stop in Hanalei for lunch before stretching out at **Ke'e Beach State Park** ⑭ in the afternoon sun.

On your fourth day stick close to Kapa'a. In the morning, make the **Fern Grotto** your destination, either going aboard one of the Wailua river boats or renting a kayak and asking directions before paddling off on the river. On your return, pick up a plate lunch or a few picnic supplies. Then drive up Mā'alo Road to see the **Pōhaku-ho'ohānau and Pōhaku Piko** ④ (royal birthing stones) and **'Ōpaeka'a Falls** ⑤. If you follow the road nearly to its end, you'll come upon the Keāhua Forestry Arboretum, where picnic tables and a freshwater pool offer a sooth- ing respite. Finish up at Kapa'a for some last-minute shopping at the Coconut Marketplace.

IF YOU HAVE 6 DAYS

With six days you might want to split your vacation nights into two hotels, spending the first two nights on the south side and the last three at Princeville on the north shore. On the first day, explore the **Waimea Canyon** ㉟ area, also stopping at **Ft. Elisabeth** ㉛ and perhaps walking the main street (one block off the highway) of **Hanapēpē** ㉙, a quiet town with an extraordinary number of art galleries. Spend the morn- ing of the second day in **Līhu'e** ⑮, touring **Grove Farm Homestead** ⑲ (with prior reservations) and/or the **Kaua'i Museum** ⑯. In the after- noon take time to explore the main street of **Kōloa** ㉑ and see **Spout- ing Horn** ㉕ in Po'ipū. Then relax during the late afternoon at the beach.

Pack and get away early on the third day so you can take in the **Fern Grotto,** the **Pōhaku-ho'ohānau and Pōhaku Piko** ④, and **'Ōpaeka'a Falls** ⑤, with a little time for having lunch or shopping in Kapa'a on your way to your new north-shore location.

On the fourth day you might simply want to revel in the beauty of your new surroundings: play golf, visit the spa, paddle a kayak up Hanalei River, or soak in the sun at the pool. For hikers, the fifth day could involve a long hike along the Kalalau Trail to Hanakāpī'ai Beach and inland to the falls; if you prefer a less-strenuous stroll, investigate the grounds at **Limahuli Garden** ⑫, a peaceful retreat with archeological sites and plants identified by signage. In any case, this fifth day is the time to drive to the end of the road at Hā'ena, visiting **Maniniholo Dry Cave** ⑪ and **Waikapala'e and Waikanaloa Wet Caves** ⑬ along the way and lunching at one of the casual little restaurants in Hanalei.

Reserve your sixth and final day to accomplish activities and see sights you missed along the northeast shore. You might discover Secret Beach (officially called Kauapea Beach), which is just to the left of **Kīlauea Lighthouse and Kīlauea Point National Wildlife Refuge** ⑧; shop at Kong Lung Center in Ki'lauea; seek out a farmers' market; or explore a side road to 'Anini Beach. Of course, if you've had enough sightseeing, this last day could be a repeat of day four—a day to relax and to dream about repeating day four endlessly.

When to Tour Kaua'i

Kaua'i is beautiful in every season; however, if it's hot beach weather you prefer, you might schedule your visit from June through October, when rainfall is at its lightest. The northern coast of Kaua'i generally receives more rainfall than the rest of the island, particularly during the December to February span. To avoid family crowds, time a visit for pre- and postschool months, May or October, for example, when the weather is generally fine and plenty of rooms are available.

The Heavenly Northeast

Traveling north from Līhu'e, you'll encounter green pastureland, lush valleys, and untamed tropical wilderness. An area rich in history and legend, it was one of the first communities of the Polynesians who settled here more than 1,000 years ago. As the road turns west, tracing the island's north shore, you'll time-travel through historic plantation towns and the definitely here-and-now resort of Princeville, winding up in the mist-shrouded primeval wilds around Ke'e Beach and Nā Pali Coast State Park.

A Good Drive

Head north out of Līhu'e on Highway 56, the main artery that traces the eastern and northern coasts of Kaua'i and forms the main artery for a tour of the region. For an early scenic side trip turn left on Mā'alo Road (Highway 583) at the bottom of the hill in Kapai'a. Then drive 4 mi to **Wailua Falls** ①, one of the Aloha State's most beautiful cascades. Backtrack to Highway 56 and continue north toward Wailua. A short drive makai at Kaua'i Resort will take you to a former "city of refuge," **Lydgate County Park** ②. Today the park's community-built Kamalani Playground offers a present-day refuge to parents with active kids in the car.

On the mauka side of Highway 56, follow the sign directing you to Wailua Marina, where cruise boats depart for the Fern Grotto. Continue north on Highway 56 to the historic town of **Wailua** ③, the island's early capital. Past the mouth of the Wailua, turn left off Highway 56 onto Kuamo'o Road (Highway 580). Just beyond Wailua River State

Park on your left is one of seven revered *heiau* (stone platforms that were the site of worship) and the royal birthing stones, **Pōhaku-ho'ohānau and Pōhaku Piko** ④. Farther up Kuamo'o Road, you'll reach the most intact of the stone temples, Poli'ahu, complete with storyboards. On clear days you can see Wai'ale'ale, the misty peak that is the source of the Wailua River. Across the road are the spectacular **'Ōpaeka'a Falls** ⑤. For a look at this beautiful cascade, return to Kuamo'o Road and drive 1 mi to the lookout on the right.

Adventurers can follow Kuamo'o Road another 7 or 8 mi to its end in Keāhua Forestry Arboretum for a picnic amid aromatic yellow ginger. A huge, shady mango tree on a riverbank in the arboretum comes equipped with a dangling rope, so take your bathing suit, because the spirit of Tarzan is sure to surface when you see the inviting pool below.

Head back to Highway 56 and drive north toward the historic village of Waipouli, now famous for its Coconut Marketplace, a low-rise shopping complex with storefronts that open invitingly onto a large central mall. On your left you'll pass a mountain ridge resembling a mythical **Sleeping Giant** ⑥. It's thought to be the body of a sleeping warrior. Follow the meandering highway along the eastern coast to Kapa'a, Kaua'i's largest town and home to quaint shops and eateries.

To the north you'll pass Keālia and the turnoff to Anahola Beach Park. Seven mi farther is **Kīlauea** ⑦, another former plantation town worth a brief stop if only to check out Kong Lung, a one-of-a-kind boutique filled with Hawaiiana and other fine treasures, or to buy pastries or a loaf of fresh-baked bread from Kīlauea Bakery and Pizza. Turn right on Kolo Road when you see the post office, next to which is Christ Memorial Episcopal Church. Take the first left off Kolo Road, onto Kīlauea Road, and follow it to the end, where you'll find **Kīlauea Lighthouse and Kīlauea Point National Wildlife Refuge** ⑧.

Return through Kilauea and continue west until you reach Mile Marker 25 on Highway 56. You'll be at Kalihi Wai Valley Overlook, a splendid point for photographing the valley and the glimmering waterfall across the road. As you drive farther along you'll pass Princeville Airport (on the mauka side of the road) before you reach **Hanalei Valley Overlook** ⑨, across the street from the Princeville Shopping Center. From here you can look out across vast acres of taro fields in the valley below. The road descends and switches back to cross a rustic, arched one-lane bridge dating from 1912, then switches back again into the town of Hanalei, home to the 19th-century **Wai'oli Mission House** ⑩.

West of Hanalei the highway (now labeled 560 on street signs) winds its way between the mountains and the sea and crosses a series of old one-lane bridges. As the road rises and curves left, look for the marker to Lumaha'i Beach, where some scenes in *South Pacific* were filmed amid a spectacular setting of majestic cliffs, black lava rocks, and hala trees.

Continuing west, just past Mile Marker 8, you'll see a right turn through a grove of trees. This takes you to Tunnels Beach. A little farther, on the mauka side, is **Maniniholo Dry Cave** ⑪. Just across the way is Hā'ena State Park. A few miles farther, also on the mauka side, is a national tropical botanical garden, **Limahuli Garden** ⑫, with its ancient taro *loi* (terraces), stone walls, and well-marked, peaceful paths. Less than ½ mi up the highway, a five-minute walk uphill takes you to **Waika-pala'e and Waikanaloa Wet Caves** ⑬. When you reach the end of Highway 560 in Hā'ena, you'll be at the Kalalau trailhead near **Ke'e Beach State Park** ⑭. Here, where an ancient stone hula platform is still intact, Laka, Hawaiian goddess of the hula, did most of her dancing. You might still be able to catch her spirit here . . . then come away with a sway in your hips!

TIMING

Without stopping, you can drive the 40 mi from Līhu'e to Hā'ena in less than 90 minutes. You'll probably want to allow a full day, however, including meal breaks, to stop and explore at least some of the sights along the way, take a short hike around Hā'ena's caves, and pause for some photos. The northeast is green year-round, but profusions of unusual wildflowers are a sure sign of spring.

Sights to See

Fern Grotto. A 3-mi boat ride up the Wailua River culminates at a yawning lava tube covered with enormous fishtail ferns. You can rent a kayak, hire a boat and captain, or take one of the popular boat tours to this site, which is only approachable via the river.

OFF THE BEATEN PATH

GUAVA KAI PLANTATION – Try a free sample of juice and jelly at the visitor center. Then stretch your legs with a nature walk through a 480-acre guava orchard with displays of medicinal plants beside a heart-shape fishpond. The nearest sight is Kīlauea. ⊠ *Hwy. 56, 34 mi north of Līhu'e; turn mauka onto Kuawa Rd. off Hwy. 56, near turnoff to Kīlauea, and follow signs.* ☎ *808/828–6121.* ☞ *Free.* ☺ *Daily 9–5.*

⑨ Hanalei Valley Overlook. From this panoramic overlook you can see more than a half mi of taro, plus the 900 acres that compose a National Wildlife Refuge for endangered waterfowl. In the 1850s Robert Wyllie attempted to establish a coffee plantation here. After that failed the Chinese farmed rice in the valley until the early 1900s. Now the valley floor is a patchwork of taro, a staple of the traditional Hawaiian diet. One of the state's red-caped Hawaiian-warrior site markers identifies this spot. ⊠ *Hwy. 56, Princeville.*

★ ⑭ Ke'e Beach State Park. You can view the spectacular Nā Pali coastline from this idyllic beach. This is also where you'll find the start of the difficult 11-mi **Kalalau Trail.** Another path leads from the beach to an open, grassy meadow with a stone altar called **Lohi'au's Hula Platform.** Treat this beautiful site with reverence, for it is full of historical and spiritual *mana* (power). It's said that Laka, goddess of the hula, did most of her dancing on this very spot. Today's hula practitioners sometimes leave offerings here for her. ⊠ *Western end of Hwy. 560, Hā'ena.*

⑦ Kīlauea. This former plantation town is known today for its aquacultural successes, especially with prawns. It has also distinguished itself as the guava capital of the world. One of Kīlauea's most notable buildings, **Christ Memorial Episcopal Church** (⊠ Kolo St.), dates from 1941. The church is constructed of native lava rock, and its stained-glass windows came from England. Also worth visiting is the **Kong Lung Center** (⊠ 2490 Keneke St.), which houses the unique Kong Lung Co. boutique and Kīlauea Bakery and Pizza, known for its pizza and bread sticks. ⊠ *Hwy. 56, 25 mi north of Līhu'e.*

★ ⑧ Kīlauea Lighthouse and Kīlauea Point National Wildlife Refuge. A beacon for passing air and sea traffic since it was built in 1913, the lighthouse, a National Historic Landmark, still has the largest clamshell lens of any lighthouse in the world, but it has laid aside its traffic responsibilities. The Kīlauea Wildlife Refuge surrounds the lighthouse and is home to eight species of seabirds, some of them endangered. Two-hour guided hikes are conducted through the refuge Monday through Thursday; reserve ahead. ⊠ *Kīlauea Lighthouse Rd., Kīlauea,* ☎ *808/828–0168 or 808/828–1413,* WEB *www.kilauea-point.com.* ☞ *$3.* ☺ *Daily 10–4.*

NEED A
BREAK?
Banana Joe's Tropical Fruit Farm (✉ 5-2719 Kūhiō Hwy., Kīlauea,
☎ 808/828–1092) occupies a rustic yellow shelter with a distinctly
Polynesian look to it on the mauka side of Highway 56, just past the
turnoff to Kīlauea. Sample the Kaua'i-grown fruit here (fresh, dried, or
in smoothies and salads). It's the perfect tropical energy booster.
Banana Joe's also sells fresh corn and other vegetables in season.

★ ⑫ **Limahuli Garden.** This lovely, natural spot is one of five gardens and
three preserves known as the National Tropical Botanical Garden.
Limahuli's sometimes steep ¾-mi trail passes ancient taro loi, labeled
plants and trees, and mountain streams. Picnicking is not allowed
here, and reservations are required for guided tours. ✉ *Hwy. 560, Hā'ena,*
☎ *808/826–1053,* WEB *www.ntbg.org.* ✄ *Self-guided tour $10, guided
tour $15.* ☉ *Tues.–Fri. and Sun. 9:30–4.*

🖑 ❷ **Lydgate County Park.** The park, named for the Reverand J. M. Lydgate,
founder of the Līhu'e English Union Church, houses a children's playground and the remains of a heiau. In pre–Captain Cook days, the area
was a city of refuge for Hawaiians who had violated one of the religious *kapu* (taboos). If they made their way to this beachfront haven,
they could escape banishment or death by remaining until their families arranged for their forgiveness. ✉ *Near the mouth of Wailua River,
turn makai off Hwy. 56 onto Lehu Dr. and left onto Nalu Rd.* ✄ *Free.*
☉ *Daily.*

⑪ **Maniniholo Dry Cave.** An eerie grotto said to have been dug by a
Menehune chief searching for an evil spirit, this cave was a site of ancient worship. Walk 75 yards into it—if you dare—but don't be
spooked; one or another Hawaiian goddess removed the traces of evil
that lurked here long ago, most likely Laka and her hula followers.
Across the highway from Maniniholo Dry Cave is **Hā'ena State Park,**
a fine beach for swimming when there's no current. The well-protected
Tunnels Beach adjoins Hā'ena State Park. A lunch wagon stands ready
to feed hungry surfers and sightseers. ✉ *Hwy. 560, Hā'ena.*

OFF THE
BEATEN PATH
NĀ PALI COAST AND STATE PARK – This is Kaua'i's ultimate adventure
hike, so even if you plan only to complete the first 2 mi of the hike from
Ke'e Beach to Hanakāpī'i, start early, wear rugged shoes, and carry a
picnic lunch and plenty of drinking water. The Kalalau Trail dips and
rises along the misty, fluted oceanside cliffs, leaving you breathless—
and not just from the climbing. A white-sand beach at the head of
Hanakāpī'i Valley is a fine stopping point for day hikers. Those in good
shape may want to follow an unmaintained trail an additional 2 mi to
the waterfall and freshwater pool at the back of the valley. A campsite
exists at Hanakāpī'ai, but the waiting list for permits is long.

Serious backpackers can complete an 11-mi trek—if they can make the
initial 800-ft climb out of the valley. The hike crosses streams that bisect
a series of valleys, and then passes waterfalls and wild fruit trees until
4 mi later you reach another campsite at Hanakoa Valley. Hanakoa
Falls, ⅓ mi inland, provides a refreshing cool shower. Campsites are on
old Hawaiian agricultural terraces that still have coffee trees, planted in
the 1800s, growing on them.

The last 5 mi of the trail culminates at Kalalau Valley and Beach.
Nearby, after the final stream crossing, a red-dirt trail leads uphill to
an old heiau. A nearby campsite can be crowded in fine weather,
when many adventurers seek out Kalalau's legendary beauty.

Backpackers headed to Kalalau must obtain permits from the Department of Land and Natural Resources and are limited to five nights in the

Nā Pali State Park. Hiking the trail during the rainy winter season should not be attempted as flash floods are a danger. Tour boats no longer take passengers along the Nā Pali shore from Hanalei on the north side of the island, but in the summer months, when the ocean is calm, boats run from Port Allen on the west coast, and kayakers can take a guided tour or explore the coastline in their own rental kayaks.

★ ❺ **'Ōpaeka'a Falls.** A dramatic waterfall plunges hundreds of feet to the pools below. 'Ōpaeka'a means "rolling shrimp," which refers to the little creatures that are said to have been so abundant at one time that they could be seen tumbling in the falls to the pool below. ⊠ *Hwy. 580 (Kuamo'o Rd.), Wailua.*

❹ **Pōhaku-ho'ohānau and Pōhaku Piko.** These two rocks make Wailua one of the most sacred sites in all Hawai'i, as it was here that all the royal births of Kaua'i took place. An expectant royal mother supported her back against the birthing stone Pōhaku-ho'ohānau. After the newborn's umbilical cord fell off, it was wrapped in *kapa* (cloth made from bark) and deposited in the crevices of the Pōhaku Piko for safekeeping. Just up the road is Poli'ahu Heiau, where storyboards tell about the heiau, the Wailua River area, and its former inhabitants. ⊠ *Hwy. 580 (Kuamo'o Rd.), Wailua.*

❻ **Sleeping Giant.** Puni, a mythical giant, is said to be represented in this formation on Mount Nounou. Sleeping face up, his back outlining the mountain ridge, he has dozed here undisturbed since hungry villagers fed him stones after he ate all their taro and fish. ⊠ *Hwy. 56, about 1 mi north of Wailua River.*

☪ **Smith's Tropical Paradise.** Right next to Wailua Marina on the east side of the island, Smith's Tropical Paradise is 30 acres of family fun, with orchards, jungle paths, exotic foliage, tropical birds, ethnic village settings, and tranquil lagoons. A lū'au banquet and live show are offered Monday, Wednesday, and Friday from 5 to 9, and there is free shuttle service from Wailua. Reservations are essential for the lū'au, shuttle, and show. ⊠ *174 Wailua Rd., Kapa'a,* ☎ *808/821–6895.* ⊡ *$5, lū'au and show $54.* ⊙ *Daily 8:30–4.*

OFF THE BEATEN PATH	**SUNSHINE MARKETS –** If you want to rub elbows with the locals and get an eyeful of homegrown produce and flowers, head for one of these County of Kaua'i–sponsored outdoor markets, held once a week at five locations around the island, including sessions in Kapa'a and Kīlauea. Hours and locations change frequently. Call County of Kaua'i (☎ 808/241–6303, ⓌⒺⒷ www.kauaigov.org) for a current schedule.

⓭ **Waikapala'e and Waikanaloa Wet Caves.** Said to have been dug by Pele, goddess of fire, these watering holes used to be clear, clean, and great for swimming. Now stagnant, they're nevertheless a photogenic example of the many haunting natural landmarks of Kaua'i's north shore. Waikanaloa is visible right beside the highway. Across the road from a small parking area, a five-minute uphill walk leads to Waikapala'e. ⊠ *Western end of Hwy. 560, Hā'ena.*

❸ **Wailua.** Kaua'i's first communities were built along the Wailua River. Among Wailua's historic treasures, tucked away along the riverbanks, are remnants of important heiau. The town itself was the island's early capital. Its name means "two waters" in Hawaiian. ⊠ *Hwy. 56, 7 mi north of Līhu'e.*

NEED A BREAK?	Every be-bopper who remembers the '50s fondly will love **Beezers** (⊠ 1380 Kūhiō Hwy., Kapa'a, ☎ 808/822–4411), just a few miles

north of Wailua. Its jukebox plays tunes you can sing to, the walls are decked with pictures of Marilyn and Elvis, and the counter has red leatherette stools. Malts, root-beer floats, and a Mustang Sally (chocolate brownie topped with ice cream and smothered in hot fudge, whipped cream, and nuts) make this a great haven on hot days.

❾ Wailua Falls. You may recognize this impressive cascade from the opening sequences of the *Fantasy Island* television series. Kaua'i has plenty of picturesque waterfalls, but this one surpasses most. ⊠ *End of Hwy. 583 (Ma'alo Rd.), 4 mi west of Hwy. 56.*

❿ Wai'oli Mission House. This 1837 mission was once the home of missionary teachers Lucy and Abner Wilcox. Its prim and proper koa-wood furnishings are straight out of missionary Hawai'i, and its tidy architecture feels as if it belongs back in New England. Half-hour guided tours are available. ⊠ *Kūhiō Hwy., Hanalei,* ☎ *808/245–3202.* 💲 *Donations accepted.* ☉ *Tues., Thurs., and Sat. 9–3.*

NEED A
BREAK?

Bubba's (⊠ Hanalei Center, Hanalei, ☎ 808/826–7839) is where you can find the Slopper (open-face burger with chili) or a Hubba Bubba (burger, hot dog, chili, and rice). Burgers range in size from ⅙ pound to the three-patty Big Bubba, and there are chicken burgers, fish burgers, corn dogs, and fish-and-chips, too. Orders, filled quickly and with just the irreverent humor you'd expect at a place called Bubba's, may be eaten at the four picnic tables on the lawn right out front.

Līhu'e and Southward

As you follow the main road south from Līhu'e the air seems to become gradually warmer and drier. This is one way to tell you're nearing the region called Po'ipū, named after the south-shore resort town that is its unofficial center. The sun shines steadily on the populated, friendly beaches here. A string of condominiums and hotels lines the coastline, and an impressive variety of water sports is available.

A Good Drive

Begin in **Līhu'e** ⑮, the commercial and political center of Kaua'i, and visit the **Kaua'i Museum** ⑯, where displays and an exciting aerial movie provide an overview of this tropical isle. Head south on Rice Street, the town's main road, until it dead-ends; then turn right onto Wa'apā Road, which takes you to **Nāwiliwili** ⑰, Kaua'i's major port. From Wa'apā Road, turn right onto Hulemalu Road and follow the Hulē'ia River to view **Menehune Fishpond** ⑱.

Return to Nāwiliwili, take a left on Nāwiliwili Road (Highway 58), and look on your right for **Grove Farm Homestead** ⑲. This 80-acre plantation estate and living museum affords a wonderful look at 19th-century agricultural life on the island. At the intersection of Nāwiliwili Road and Highway 50, turn left and head west on Highway 50. Two miles farther on your right you'll find the entrance to **Kilohana** ⑳, another attraction with shops and galleries that will enrich your experience of earlier plantation days.

Continuing west on Highway 50, you'll pass the majestic slopes of the Hoary Head Mountains. On the top of the range to your right is a formation called Queen Victoria's Profile, indicated by a Hawaiian-warrior marker. When you get to the intersection of Highways 50 and 520, you have reached Kōloa Gap, a natural pass between Mt. Wai'ale'ale on your right and the Hoary Heads on your left. Turn left onto Highway 520 (Maluhia Road), also known as the Tunnel of Trees because of the eucalyptus trees that border the road to form a canopy overhead.

Highway 520 takes you to **Kōloa** ㉑, site of Kauai'i's first sugar mill, dating from 1835. Kōloa's main street is lined with old buildings that have been preserved to house shops, art galleries, and restaurants. Head south on Highway 520, which here is also called Po'ipū Road. At the fork stay to the left.

From here turn right onto Honowili Road, which takes you through the heart of sunny **Po'ipū** ㉒, the major resort area of Kaua'i's south shore. On the makai side of the road are Po'ipū Beach Park and Brennecke's Beach, prime spots for sunbathers and bodysurfers. Return to Po'ipū Road and follow it past the stunning Hyatt Regency Kaua'i, which fronts Shipwreck Beach. The road abruptly turns to dirt, but 3 mi farther awaits beautiful Māhā'ulepū Beach. To reach it, follow the road to the T intersection, turn right, stop at the gates to sign in (this is private property), and park at the end of the dirt road to walk to the beach. Explorers willing to search can find an interesting cave site at the far end of this beach if they hike inland beside a little stream.

When you head back on Po'ipū Road, instead of turning to Kōloa go left onto Lāwa'i Road just after you cross the bridge over Waikomo Stream. You'll soon come to **Prince Kūhiō Park** ㉓, honoring the birthplace of one of Hawai'i's most beloved members of Congress. Beyond the park is the visitor center for the **National Tropical Botanical Gardens** ㉔, a botanical research center and showcase for a multitude of rare and endangered plant species. At the end of this beachfront road is **Spouting Horn** ㉕, a waterspout that shoots up out of an ancient lava tube. Its rising plume signals your drive's end.

TIMING

From Līhu'e to Po'ipū it's only 14 mi, but since there is plenty to see, you can easily devote a day or two to this itinerary. If you have only a half day, try to make it an afternoon, so you can watch the sunset from Brennecke's Beach. The bodysurfers on this legendary beach are something to see, especially if it's summer—big-wave season.

Sights to See

❶⑨ **Grove Farm Homestead.** One of Kaua'i's oldest plantation estates, founded in 1864, today offers a look at 19th-century life on Kaua'i. On the 80 acres composing this living museum are the original family home filled with turn-of-the-20th-century memorabilia, workers' quarters, and elaborate gardens of tropical flowers and tall palm trees. Tours, which are limited to six people, may not be appropriate for young children, as they last two hours. Reservations are essential. ⊠ *Hwy. 58, ½ mi south of Nāwiliwili Rd., Līhu'e,* ☎ *808/245–3202.* ☞ *$5 donation.* ☉ *Tour Mon. and Wed.–Thurs. at 10 and 1.*

❶⑥ **Kaua'i Museum.** A permanent display, "The Story of Kaua'i," provides an overview of the Garden Isle and traces its mythology and its geological and cultural history. It's highlighted by a 30-minute aerial movie. The island of Ni'ihau is also represented in the museum. Works by local artists are on display in the Mezzanine Gallery, and the gift shop offers a good selection of books and crafts by local artists. ⊠ *4428 Rice St., Līhu'e,* ☎ *808/245–6931.* ☞ *$5.* ☉ *Weekdays 9–4, Sat. 10–4.*

★ ⑳ **Kilohana.** Dating from 1935, this is the site of the old Wilcox sugar plantation, which has been transformed into a 35-acre visitor attraction. The estate is a beautiful showpiece from plantation days, with agricultural exhibits, local arts and crafts, horse-and-carriage rides, specialty shops, and a garden courtyard restaurant called Gaylord's, which is pleasant for breakfast or Sunday brunch. ⊠ *3-2087 Kaumuali'i Hwy. (Hwy. 50), Līhu'e,* ☎ *808/245–5608.* ☞ *Free.* ☉ *Mon.–Sat. 9:30–9:30, Sun. 9:30–5.*

㉑ Kōloa. Kaua'i's first sugar mill began operating here in 1835. You can see the remains of its old stone smokestack on the right side of the road. A sculpture depicting the various ethnic groups that made their mark on the sugar industry on Kaua'i sits on a small green nearby. The main street of Kōloa is lined with old buildings that have been preserved to house expensive boutiques, an old general store, and a selection of restaurants. Placards outside each building describe its original tenants and tell about life in the old mill town. ⊠ *Hwy. 520.*

NEED A BREAK? An open-air establishment called **Pizzetta** (⊠ 5408 Old Kōloa Rd., Kōloa, ☎ 808/742–8881) concocts the best *mai tai* cocktail (rum with orange and lime juice) on the island. A rustic wood-panel room at the back, with an open deck, makes up the bar area. Sit by one of the huge open windows and watch the world go by. When you're ready for dinner, order a pizza or choose a freshly made fettuccine.

★ ⑮ Līhu'e. The commercial and political center of Kaua'i County, which includes the islands of Kaua'i and Ni'ihau, Līhu'e is the home of the island's major airport and harbor. Its main thoroughfare, Rice Street, offers a short, pleasant stroll from the War Memorial and Convention Hall (Rice and Hardy streets), past government offices, to the Līhu'e Shopping Center (Rice Street and Highway 50). ⊠ *Hwys. 56 and 50.*

NEED A BREAK? If you're looking for a down-home Kaua'i-style meal or a filling snack, stop by **Hamura Saimin** (⊠ 2956 Kress St., Līhu'e, ☎ 808/245–3271), a ramshackle diner with booths and counter seating. Each day the Hiraoka family serves about 1,000 orders of saimin, a steaming bowl of broth and noodles with varying garnishes. This little landmark also turns out tasty chicken and beef grilled on barbecue sticks, as well as *liliko'i* (passion fruit) chiffon pie.

⑱ Menehune Fishpond. Secretive little workers are said to have built these intricate walls, 4 ft thick and 5 ft high, for a princess and prince. Today the walls of this ancient aquaculture structure, also known as *'alekoko*, still contain placid waters where mullet thrive and kayakers enjoy blissful serenity. ⊠ *Hulemalu Rd., Niumalu.*

㉔ National Tropical Botanical Gardens. A good example of a tropical green thumb can be found at this 252-acre scientific research center (McBryde Gardens) and 100-acre estate property (Allerton Gardens) for botany and horticulture. The visitor center showcases 2,600 different plant species, some of them rare and endangered Hawaiian varieties. There's a gift shop, too. The grounds are open only for visitors with reservations for the guided 2½-hour walking tour. ⊠ *Meet at the visitor center across from Spouting Horn parking lot, Lāwa'i Rd., Po'ipū,* ☎ 808/ 332–2623. ☞ $30. ☉ *Tours Tues.–Sat. at 9, 10, 1, and 2.*

⑰ Nāwiliwili. At Kaua'i's major port a host of fishing and recreational boats come and go, and tour boats offer snorkeling and sightseeing adventures along the coast. This is a port of call for container ships, U.S. Navy vessels, and the American Hawai'i Cruise line. Nearby there's protected swimming and sunbathing at **Kalapakī Beach**. ⊠ *Makai end of Wa'apā Rd., Līhu'e.*

㉒ Po'ipū. The major resort town of the south shore remains irrepressibly sunny despite the shadowy hulk of an empty hotel looming eerily on the beach. Although the Stouffer Waiohai resort has not reopened since Hurricane 'Iniki blew through in 1992, the Sheraton Kaua'i Resort and a half dozen condominiums, including Kiahuna Plantation, rim the beach's golden sands. Boogie-boarders, swimmers, and families enjoy the good-time atmosphere. ⊠ *Hwy. 520.*

㉓ **Prince Kūhiō Park.** The park behind the Prince Kūhiō Condominium honors the birthplace of one of Hawai'i's most beloved congressional representatives, Prince Jonah Kūhiō Kalaniana'ole, a man who might have become Hawai'i's king if Queen Lili'uokalani had not been overthrown in 1893. ✉ *Lāwa'i Rd., Po'ipū.*

★ ㉕ **Spouting Horn.** Kaua'i's natural wonders never cease. This one is a waterspout that shoots up like Old Faithful out of an ancient lava tube. Follow the paved walkways around this area, because the rocks are slippery and people have been known to fall in. Vendors sell inexpensive souvenirs and costume jewelry here, but you'll also find one of the best selections of rare and treasured Ni'ihau shell necklaces. When purchasing a Ni'ihau shell lei, ask for a certificate of authenticity and an address in case you need to reorder or repair your purchase at a later date. ✉ *Lāwa'i Bay, Lāwa'i Rd., Po'ipū.*

The Western Route and Kōke'e

Heading west along Kaua'i's south shore, you'll pass through one former plantation town after the next, each with its own story to tell: Hanapēpē, whose salt ponds have been harvested since ancient times; Ft. Elisabeth, from which an enterprising Russian tried to take over the island in the early 1800s; and Waimea, home of the Menehune Ditch, supposedly built by the legendary race of little people.

From Waimea you can drive up along the rim of magnificent Waimea Canyon to reach the crisp, cool climate of Kōke'e, which ranges from 3,200 to 4,200 ft above sea level. Here you'll discover another facet of this ancient island: sequoia forests and swamplands are home to remarkable indigenous birds and plants. A mountain lodge welcomes guests with old-style warmth and hospitality.

From the Burns Field airstrip here on the western side of the island, helicopter tours depart for the "Forbidden Isle" of Ni'ihau. Snorkeling excursions can be planned from Port Allen harbor. By land, sea, or air, this part of Kaua'i is worth exploring.

A Good Drive

The west side of the island offers a look at the sleepiest—as well as the most dramatic—sections of Kaua'i. Begin this tour by heading west on Highway 50 out of Līhu'e. The first town you come to is tiny Lāwa'i, which once housed the Kaua'i Pineapple Cannery. In its wake, Lāwa'i has emerged as a significant producer of tropical fruits and plants. The next town along Highway 50 is Kalāheo. Turn left on Pāpālina Road to make the climb to **Kukui o Lono Park** ㉖, where you can bliss out on Japanese gardens and spectacular scenic vistas.

Beyond Kalāheo, a left turn onto Highway 540 will take you to the **Kaua'i Coffee Visitor Center and Museum** ㉗, where two restored camp houses contain a minimuseum. Highway 540 loops back to 50. Heading in either direction back to Highway 50 will take you past acres of shiny-leaf coffee trees, but if you travel the loop, you'll miss the **Hanapēpē Valley and Canyon Lookout** ㉘. This dramatic divide holds a place in Hawaiian history as the site of Kaua'i's last battle in 1824.

Hanapēpē ㉙, the "Biggest Little Town on Kaua'i," lies just west of the lookout. At the fork turn right to drive down Hanapēpē's dusty main street, or angle left and follow Highway 50 past the town. Then turn makai on Lele Road to reach **Salt Pond Beach Park** ㉚. Early Hawaiians harvested salt here. Nearby is Burns Field, Kaua'i's first airfield and the departure point for flightseeing adventures and helicopter trips to Ni'ihau. It's a taste of a more primitive Hawai'i. Just around the bend and across the bay from the airstrip is Port Allen Harbor, the shipping center for the west side of the island and home base for snorkeling excursions.

Head west again on Highway 50 and look on the makai side of the road for the Hawaiian-warrior marker to **Ft. Elisabeth** ㉛. The ruins of this stone fort are testament to a time when Imperial Russia had designs on conquering the Islands. Cross the Waimea River Bridge and take your first right on Menehune Road, which leads you 2½ mi up Waimea Valley to **Menehune Ditch** ㉜, a stone aqueduct carved with the mysterious markings of an earlier era. As you enter **Waimea** ㉝ you might spot the statue commemorating Captain Cook's arrival here in 1778. The remains of a missionary church built here in 1846 should hold your interest as well. On the right, **West Kaua'i Visitor and Technology Center** ㉞ houses attractive photo displays and computers that download information on Kaua'i—simply touch the screen indicating your field of interest.

Highway 50 meanders through the sugar town of Kekaha. Eventually it passes the Pacific Missile Range Facility. Take the right fork after you pass the missile range and you can follow Highway 50 to where it ends near Polihale State Park. The park is accessible only by a dirt road through sugarcane fields. During or after heavy rain, you might want to skip it. When the road is passable, though, it's worth a visit to this immense stretch of glistening golden sand fringed by dramatic mountains.

You have two choices for visiting **Waimea Canyon** ㉟, the "Grand Canyon of the Pacific." The main route, Kōke'e Road (Highway 550), makes a steep climb from Kekaha. The other, more scenic option is Waimea Canyon Drive, which you pick up near the western edge of Waimea, by the church. It's narrow but well paved and climbs quickly for immediate views of the town and ocean below. A few miles up, the roads converge and continue the steep ascent; spectacular bird's-eye views out over the canyon encompass you. Be sure to stop at the Pu'u-ka-Pele and Pu'u-hinahina lookouts for the most appealing vistas. As the road rises to 4,000 ft it passes through Kōke'e State Park, with its cozy Kōke'e Lodge. The road out of the park leads past the NASA Tracking Station.

Waimea Canyon Drive ends 4 mi above the park at the **Kalalau Lookout** ㊱. This is the beginning of a beautiful hiking trail that passes Pu'u-o-Kila Lookout. Be sure to bring a jacket for the cool weather here.

TIMING

The 36-mi drive from Līhu'e to Waimea Canyon takes about 90 minutes with no stops for botanical gardens, beaches, or quaint little towns. If you want to spend a half day or more hiking in the canyon, you might save south-shore sightseeing for another day. Save at least a half day for your air adventure over to Ni'ihau. In winter be prepared for chilly temperatures in the heights above the canyon, especially in the early morning.

Sights to See

★ ㉛ **Ft. Elisabeth.** The ruins of this stone fort, built in 1816 by an agent of the Imperial Russian government named Anton Scheffer, are reminders of the days when Scheffer tried to conquer the island for his homeland. King Kaumuali'i eventually chased the foreigner off the island. The crumbling walls of the fort, at the ocean's edge, are cleared of brush intermittently and cover about an acre. ✉ *Hwy. 50, Waimea.*

㉙ **Hanapēpē.** This quiet farming town on the south coast supplies Kaua'i with much of its produce and all the islands with Lappert's ice cream.

Hanapēpē Road had a featured role (as an Australian town) in the television miniseries *The Thorn Birds*. Today shops sell koa wood and other crafts. Talented artist James Hoyle has his art gallery here. **Burns Field**, Kaua'i's first airfield and now the base of operations for several helicopter companies, is nearby. Just to the east is **Port Allen** harbor, still the shipping center for the west side of Kaua'i and headquarters of the McBryde Company, which has replaced its cane fields with coffee trees. If you want further proof that Hanapēpē was once a power center, check out **'Ele'ele Shopping Center** on Lele Road. It was the first "modern" shopping center built on Kaua'i. ⊠ *Hwy. 50.*

NEED A BREAK? You can sit at the spiffy black-and-white bar for a quick espresso or relax at one of a dozen tables while you dine on vegetarian food with French-Italian flair. You'll find garden burgers, Caesar salads, soup, croissants, and calzones at **Hanapēpē Café and Espresso** (⊠ 3830 Hanapēpē Rd., Hanapēpē, ☏ 808/335–5011). There's a vegetarian breakfast and lunch menu Tuesday through Saturday, with coffee and pastries served until 3. Dinner, with live music by local guitarists, is served Friday from 6 to 9, but reservations are hard to come by.

28 Hanapēpē Valley and Canyon Lookout. This dramatic divide once housed a thriving Hawaiian community, and some remains of its taro patches still exist. Hanapēpē is a historic canyon: it's the site of Kaua'i's last battle, led in 1824 by Humehume, son of the island's King Kaumuali'i. ⊠ *Hwy. 50.*

★ **36 Kalalau Lookout.** Near the end of the road high above Waimea Canyon, Kalalau Lookout marks the head of a challenging hiking trail that also passes **Pu'u-o-Kila Lookout**. On a clear day at either spot you can gaze right down into the gaping valley at sawtooth ridges and waterfalls. But stick around for a few minutes if clouds are obscuring the view. Winds are strong up here and just might blow away the clouds so you can snap a photo. If you turn your back to the valley and look to the northwest, you might pick out the shining sands of Kalalau Beach, gleaming like a tiny golden thread against the vast blue Pacific. ⊠ *Waimea Canyon Dr., 4 mi north of Kōke'e State Park.*

27 Kaua'i Coffee Visitor Center and Museum. Two restored camp houses, dating from the days when sugar was the main agricultural crop in the islands, house a museum, visitor center, and gift shop. About 3,400 acres of McBryde sugar land have become Hawai'i's largest coffee plantation. Visitors can walk among the trees, view old grinders and roasters and a video to learn how coffee is processed, and sample the various estate roasts. ⊠ *870 Halawili Rd., off Hwy. 50, west of Kalāheo*, ☏ *808/335–0813.* ☑ *Free.* ☉ *Daily 9–5.*

26 Kukui o Lono Park. Translated as "light of the god Lono," Kukui o Lono has serene Japanese gardens and a display of significant Hawaiian stones—an anchor stone and salt pan—collected by Walter McBryde, the sugar-plantation heir who founded the estate in the 1900s. Spectacular panoramic views make this one of Kaua'i's most scenic park areas and an ideal picnic spot. There's also a golf course spread across a nine-acre expanse. ⊠ *Pāpālina Rd., Kalāheō.* ☑ *Free.* ☉ *Daily 6–6.*

NEED A BREAK? Ten kinds of hot dogs, burgers made with such fresh fish as mahimahi, and a big condiment bar make **Mustard's Last Stand** (⊠ Corner of Hwy. 50 and Old Kōloa Rd., Lāwa'i, ☏ 808/332–7245) an appropriate, if not essential, stop while you're touring. After you eat, the kids can be photographed riding a curling fiberglass wave while you shop for deals in the adjacent Old Hawaiian Trading Company.

㉜ Menehune Ditch. Archeologists claim that this aqueduct was built before the first Hawaiians lived on Kaua'i, and it is therefore attributed to the industrious hands of the legendary, tiny Menehune. The way the flanged and fitted cut-stone bricks are stacked and assembled indicates a knowledge of construction that is foreign to Hawai'i, and the ditch is inscribed with mysterious markings. Until someone comes up with a better suggestion, the Menehune retain the credit for this engineering feat. ⊠ *Menehune Rd., Waimea Valley.*

㉚ Salt Pond Beach Park. Hawaiians harvested salt for almost 200 years here. They let the sun evaporate the seawater in mud-lined drying beds, then gathered the salt left behind. This is a safe area for swimming. ⊠ *Lele Rd., Hanapēpē.*

㉝ Waimea. This is the town that first welcomed Captain James Cook to the Sandwich Islands in 1778. An easy-to-miss monument on the mauka side of the road commemorates his landfall, as does a statue near the entry to town. Waimea was also the place where Kaua'i's King Kaumuali'i ceded his island to the unifying efforts of King Kamehameha. Waimea played host to the first missionaries on the island, and you can still see what's left of their old **Waimea Christian Hawaiian and Foreign Church** on Mākeke Road. Constructed in 1846, the church was made of huge timbers brought down from the mountains 8 mi away, as well as limestone blocks from a nearby quarry. The church suffered severe damage from Hurricane 'Iniki, but the beautiful stonework of its front and side walls is worth a photo. ⊠ *Hwy. 50.*

★ ㉟ Waimea Canyon. Created by an ancient fault in the earth's crust, the canyon has been eroding over the centuries due to weather, wind, and the water of its rivers and streams. The "Grand Canyon of the Pacific" is 3,600 ft deep, 2 mi wide, and 10 mi long. Its deep reds, greens, and browns are ever changing in the light. Be sure to allow time to soak up the views from **Pu'u-ka-Pele** and **Pu'u-hinahina** lookouts.

Kōke'e State Park, at the north end of Waimea Canyon, is 4,000 ft above sea level. Here the air is cool and crisp, and the vegetation turns to evergreens and ferns. This 4,345-acre wilderness park is full of wild fruit, heady flowers, and colorful rare birds that make their home in these forests. A 45-mi network of hiking trails takes you to some of Kaua'i's most remote places. Before you set off, ask about trail conditions. ⊠ *Hwy. 550 (contact Koke'e Natural History Museum, below, or Division of State Parks, Box 1671, 96766),* ☎ *808/335–9975.*

Kōke'e Natural History Museum in the park holds displays of plants, native birds, and other wildlife, as well as a weather exhibit that describes the formation of hurricanes. ⊠ *Koke'e State Park,* ☎ *808/335–9975.* ▣ *Donation suggested.* ⊙ *Daily 10–4.*

NEED A BREAK?	Treat yourself to a cup of coffee or a sandwich at **Kōke'e Lodge** (⊠ 3600 Kōke'e Rd., Mile Marker 15, Kōke'e State Park, ☎ 808/335–6061), a comfortably rustic mountaintop inn. With temperatures almost always nippy outside, this is a warm retreat for breakfast or lunch from 9 to 3:30. Peruse the gift shop for T-shirts, postcards, or Kōke'e memorabilia.

㉞ West Kaua'i Visitor and Technology Center. Computers with touch screens bring to life the island's history and attractions at this state-of-the-art visitor center. ⊠ *9565 Kaumualī Hwy. (Hwy. 50), Waimea,* ☎ *808/338–1332,* ᵂᴱᴮ *www.kauaivisitorscenter.com.* ▣ *Free.* ⊙ *Daily 9–5.*

BEACHES

The waters that hug the island are clean, clear, and inviting, but be careful to go in only where it's safe. All beaches on Kaua'i are free and open to the public, and none have a phone number. For information about beaches around the island, call the **County Department of Parks and Recreation** (☎ 808/241–6670) and the **Department of Land and Natural Resources** (☎ 808/274–3446).

The list of beaches below starts from the western end of Highway 50 and goes counterclockwise around the island to the end of the road on the north shore.

Polihale Beach Park. Flanked by impressive sea cliffs, this magnificent beach stretches from the town of Kekaha to end miles away within 140-acre Polihale State Park. The beach is beautiful for sunbathing, beach-combing, and surf-casting, but the rip currents are often too rough for swimming, and there are no lifeguards. Locals dune-buggy here on weekends. ⊠ *Drive to end of Hwy. 50 and turn left at Hawaiian-warrior marker onto dirt road, which leads several mi through sugarcane fields; turn left at small national park sign.*

Kekaha Beach Park. Stretching for miles along the south shore, this strip of sand brings to mind the long beaches of southern California. Dune-buggying is popular here. If you don't like the noise, stay away. There are no lifeguards, rest rooms, or showers. ⊠ *Hwy. 50 west of Kekaha.*

Salt Pond Beach Park. A protected bay here is particularly safe for swimmers, so this is a real family spot. There are picnic tables under covered pavilions, showers, rest rooms, lifeguards, and a large grassy lawn. Camping is allowed. ⊠ *Follow Lele Rd., on makai side off Hwy. 50 in Hanapēpē.*

Po'ipū Beach Park. A prime bodysurfing and sunbathing spot, Po'ipū Beach has clean white sand. It's a fun place for a picnic or a barbecue under the palm trees. There are lifeguards, showers, rest rooms, and a take-out deli across the street. A stroll on the beach takes you past a half dozen condominiums to the Sheraton Kaua'i Resort, which has an inviting cocktail lounge overlooking the beach—a cool respite from the hot sun. ⊠ *Po'ipū Rd. on south shore, opposite Ho'ōne and Pane Rds.*

Brennecke's Beach. A steady stream of small- to medium-size waves makes this a bodysurfer's heaven. Waves are bigger here in summer than in winter. Showers, rest rooms, and lifeguards are on hand, and there are several food stands nearby. ⊠ *Po'ipū Rd. on south shore.*

Keoneloa, or Shipwreck Beach. Nicknamed Shipwreck Beach for an old wooden boat that wrecked on the 2-mi stretch of sand fronting the Hyatt Regency, this beach is popular with surf casters who fish from Makawehi Point on the east side of the beach. Sea turtles and monk seals like the coves, but strong rip currents and shore break can make swimming dangerous for human water lovers, and there are no lifeguards. Showers, rest rooms, and a walkway can be found along the dunes. ⊠ *Turn into Hyatt Regency Po'ipū Resort, drive along the east side of the hotel, and turn right.*

Kalapakī Beach. This sheltered bay is ideal for swimming, surfing, and windsurfing in the small waves. It fronts the Kaua'i Marriott Resort and Beach Club. Rest rooms, lifeguards, showers, and food and drink are nearby. ⊠ *Nāwiliwili off Wapa'a Rd., which runs from Līhu'e.*

Lydgate County Park. Depending on the wind, this is a good spot for family picnicking and swimming (there are lifeguards here), with a swimming area protected by a rock wall and a covered pavilion. Any time of year it's a nice place for beachcombing and reflecting on the days when this was a Hawaiian city of refuge. Rest rooms and showers are available, and there's a large playground for kids. ⊠ *Before mouth of Wailua River turn makai off Hwy. 56 onto Lehu Dr. and left onto Nalu Rd.*

Anahola Beach Park. This quiet length of sand edged by a grassy park on the east shore offers calm waters for swimming and snorkeling. The Makalena Mountains are your backdrop here. There are rest rooms and showers but no lifeguards. ⊠ *After Mile Marker 13 on Hwy. 56, turn makai on Anahola Rd.*

★ **'Anini Beach County Park.** Safest of the north-shore beaches, this 3-mi stretch of golden sand lies beside a reef-protected blue lagoon, making it ideal for beginning windsurfers, snorkelers, and swimmers. A beachside park, polo field, campground, public rest rooms, showers, grills, and picnic tables keep families happy year-round. There are no lifeguards here. ⊠ *Turn makai off Hwy. 56 onto Kalihi Wai Rd. on Hanalei side of Kalihi Wai Bridge; road angles left along beach onto 'Anini Rd.*

Hanalei Beach Park. With views of the Nā Pali Coast and tree-shaded picnic tables, this is beach-bum heaven. But swimming here can be treacherous. Stay near the old pier, where the water is a bit calmer. There are rest rooms, showers, and lifeguards. ⊠ *In Hanalei turn makai at Aku Rd. and right at dead end.*

Lumaha'i Beach. Known for its striking natural beauty, Lumaha'i is flanked by high mountains and lava rocks. In the movie *South Pacific,* this is where Mitzi Gaynor sang "I'm Gonna Wash That Man Right Outta My Hair." Swimming is good only in summer. There are no lifeguards, showers, or rest rooms. ⊠ *On winding section of Hwy. 56 west of Hanalei between Mile Markers 4 and 5. Park on makai side of road and walk down a steep path to the beach.*

★ **Tunnels Beach.** Kaua'i's best-protected, big, deep lagoon for swimming and snorkeling is rimmed by a beach shaded with ironwood trees. There are no lifeguards, showers, or rest rooms. ⊠ *½ mi past Mile Marker 8 on Hwy. 56. Turn makai onto dirt road that runs through grove of trees. If parking lot is full, continue ½ mi to Hā'ena Beach Park and walk back.*

Hā'ena Beach Park. This beach on Maniniholo Bay is good for swimming when the surf is down, which means summertime. There are rest rooms, showers, camping facilities, picnic tables, and food wagons, but no lifeguards. ⊠ *On north shore near end of Hwy. 56 across from lava-tube sea caves.*

★ **Ke'e Beach.** In summer this is a fine swimming beach, with a reef just made for snorkeling. In winter, big waves wash away the sand, so stay out of the water and enjoy the views of the Nā Pali Coast. This is where the Kalalau Trail begins. Changing facilities are available, as are showers and rest rooms, but there are no lifeguards. ⊠ *Northern end of Hwy. 56, 7 mi west of Hanalei.*

Hanakāpī'ai Beach. It's a 2-mi hike to this crescent of beach, which changes length and width throughout the year as fierce winter waves rob the shoreline of sand and summer's calm returns it. Be very careful swimming here in summer, and don't even think of going in during the winter swells. Hike an additional 2 mi inland beside the adjacent stream and you'll find Hanakāpī'ai Falls, which splashes into a freshwater pool perfect for shutterbugs or a cool dip. ⊠ *Mi 2 of Kalalau Trail, which begins near Ke'e Beach, at northern end of Hwy. 56.*

DINING

In addition to preparing all kinds of ethnic dishes, a growing contingent of independent restaurateurs experiment with Hawai'i regional cuisine, using the best produce grown on native soil. On Kaua'i there is an especially heavy emphasis on local fruits. Thanks to the abundance of fish in the waters surrounding Kaua'i, the catch of the day is always well worth trying.

Restaurants are open daily unless otherwise noted. Reservations are rarely required on Kaua'i, but it's never a mistake to avoid disappointment and call ahead. For an explanation of price categories, *see* Dining *in* Smart Travel Tips.

The East Coast

American

$–$$ ✕ **Eggbert's.** If you're big on breakfasts, try indoor or outdoor dining at Eggbert's, in the Coconut Marketplace. It's a great spot for omelets, banana pancakes, and eggs Benedict, all of which are served until 3 PM. You can even create your own Benedicts, adding mushrooms, spinach, or other meats and veggies as you please. Such kid-size meals as Pigs in a Blanket keep down the cost of family outings here. ⊠ *Coconut Marketplace, 4-484 Kūhiō Hwy., Kapa'a,* ☎ *808/822–3787. MC, V.*

Contemporary

$$ ✕ **A Pacific Cafe.** With its East-meets-West atmosphere and cutting-
★ edge cuisine, chef Jean-Marie Josselin's restaurant has won high acclaim and numerous awards. He combines a love of Asian cooking with a commitment to fresh, homegrown ingredients. The menu changes daily. In true nouvelle fashion Josselin might present grilled moonfish with black-olive polenta, sun-dried tomatoes, pancetta, and shiitake mushrooms, or lamb with a red wine–mint glaze and garlic mashed potatoes. The macadamia-nut torte comes topped with toasted coconut, and the crème brûlée, a huge portion served in a pastry shell, is deliciously creamy. ⊠ *Kaua'i Village Shopping Center, 4-831 Kūhiō Hwy., Kapa'a,* ☎ *808/822–0013. AE, D, DC, MC, V. No lunch.*

$–$$ ✕ **Caffé Coco.** A riot of tropical foliage surrounds this little restored plantation cottage and hangs from an overhead arbor in an outdoor dining area. The café, an attached black-light art gallery, and an artful shop called Bambulei make this a fun stop for any meal. Tasty dishes made from island products range from coco-custard French toast at breakfast to pot-sticker appetizers, 'ahi (yellowfin tuna) nori wraps, and Greek salads. "Fresh from the Garden" jams, salsas, and condiments are available to sample or take home. ⊠ *4-369 Kūhiō Hwy., Wailua,* ☎ *808/822–7990. MC, V. Closed Mon.*

Eclectic

$ ✕ **Wailua Family Restaurant.** You can't miss this place: it's lit up like a Christmas tree with 25,000 lights hanging from the ceiling. You can order a 22-ounce prime rib and other entrées from the menu, but buffets are the most reasonable at under $10 for either lunch or dinner. Kids can order Mickey Mouse–shape pancakes for breakfast, and the dinner buffet is stocked with something for everyone: soba noodles, poi, taco salads, and *lomilomi* salmon (massaged until tender and served with minced onions and tomatoes). A seafood bar is featured at dinner, but best of all, the kids will love creating their own cake with toppings at the dessert bar. ⊠ *4-361 Kūhiō Hwy., Kapa'a,* ☎ *808/822–3325. MC, V.*

Japanese

$$ ✕ **Lemongrass Grill, Seafood and Sushi Bar.** Clean-looking pine paneling lines the walls, bar stools are made of rustic natural *kiawe* (mesquite-type wood) branches, and comfortable rattan chairs pull up to polished wood tables at this charmingly renovated plantation house. At the sushi bar you can order Caterpillar sushi made with shrimp, Dragon sushi made with butterfish or the popular California rolls

296

Kaua'i Dining

0   5 miles

0   5 km

N

Hā'ena State Park

Hanakāpī'ai Beach

NĀ PALI COAST

Kalalau Trail

Kalalau Lookout

55   Kōke'e State Park

Polihale State Park

WAIMEA

Kōke'e Rd.

Waimea Canyon Dr.

Waimea Canyon

50

55

Menehune Ditch

Kekaha Beach Park

Kekaha

1   2   Waimea

Fort Elisabeth

Kaulakahi Channel

50

3

Hanapēpē   Port Allen

Salt Pond Beach Park

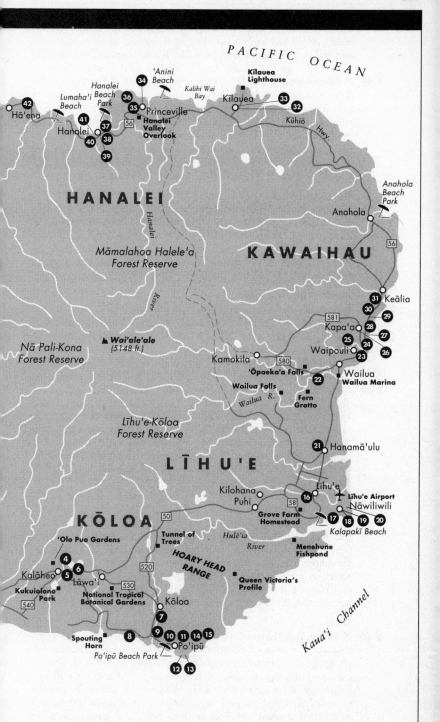

PACIFIC OCEAN

 Hā'ena

42

Lumaha'i
Beach

Hanalei
Beach
Park

'Anini
Beach

Kalihi Wai
Bay

Kīlauea
Lighthouse

34

36

35

Princeville

Kīlauea

Kīlauea

33

32

Kūhiō

Hwy.

41

37

40

38

39

Hanalei

56

Hanalei Valley
Overlook

HANALEI

Hanalei
River

Anahola

Anahola
Beach
Park

KAWAIHAU

56

Māmalahoa Halele'a
Forest Reserve

Nā Pali-Kona
Forest Reserve

▲ Wai'ale'ale
(5148 ft.)

Kamokila

580

'Ōpaeka'a Falls

Wailua Falls

Wailua R.

Fern
Grotto

Keālia

31

30

29

581

Kapa'a

28

27

25

24

26

Waipouli

23

Wailua

Wailua Marina

22

Līhu'e-Kōloa
Forest Reserve

LĪHU'E

21

Hanamā'ulu

Kilohana

Puhi

Grove Farm
Homestead

58

Līhu'e

16

Līhu'e Airport

Nāwiliwili

17

18

19

20

Kalapakī Beach

KŌLOA

50

'Olo Pua Gardens

Tunnel of
Trees

Hule'ia
River

Menehune
Fishpond

4

6

Kalāheo

5

Lāwa'i

530

Queen Victoria's
Profile

HOARY HEAD
RANGE

520

Kukuiolono
Park

540

National Tropical
Botanical Gardens

Kōloa

7

Spouting
Horn

8

9

10

11

14

15

Po'ipū

12

13

Po'ipū Beach Park

Kaua'i Channel

with crab and avocado. A window into the kitchen lets you watch the chefs prepare your 'ahi *lumpia* (spring roll), hoisin-barbecued chicken breast, or braised lamb shank. Seating is outside, upstairs, at a sushi bar, and in a separate room. ⊠ *4-885 Kūhiō Hwy., Kapa'a,* ☎ *808/ 821–2888 or 808/822–2288. AE, D, DC, MC, V. No breakfast or lunch.*

$–$$ ✕ **Restaurant Kintaro.** This pretty restaurant with sliding shoji-screen doors and Asian prints on the walls serves complete sukiyaki dinners in an iron pot and tempura combinations that use fresh local fish. *Teppan* (grilled) dinners include tender hibachi shrimp sautéed in lemon butter and served with bean sprouts and steamed rice. Dinners come with chilled buckwheat noodles, miso soup, rice, Japanese pickles, and tea. A sushi bar is also on hand. ⊠ *4-370 Kūhiō Hwy., Kapa'a,* ☎ *808/ 822–3341. AE, D, DC, MC, V. Closed Sun. No lunch.*

Natural Foods

$ ✕ **Papaya's.** Courtyard dining is the draw at this well-stocked natural foods market, which is also a restaurant under the whale tower at Kaua'i Village. Sit beneath a pretty blue umbrella and enjoy grilled fish, a vegetarian burger, pasta with pesto, or Thai and Mexican fare. Takeout is also available. ⊠ *Kaua'i Village Shopping Center, 4-831 Kuhio Hwy., Kapa'a,* ☎ *808/823–0190. AE, D, MC, V. Closed Sun.*

Steak and Seafood

$$–$$$ ✕ **Kapa'a Fish & Chowder House.** The gray-and-blue color scheme of this open-air restaurant is punctuated by thick hanging ferns and nautical memorabilia. More than a dozen daily fish selections are served sautéed with a variety of sauces. Ask for a table in the Edenlike Orchid Room. ⊠ *4-1639 Kūhiō Hwy., Kapa'a,* ☎ *808/822–7488. AE, D, DC, MC, V.*

$–$$ ✕ **Bull Shed.** The A-frame design of this popular restaurant imparts a distinctly rustic feel, but the interior is brightened by light-color walls and unobstructed ocean views. Although it is known especially for prime rib, teriyaki sirloin, and fresh fish, the Alaskan king crab and homemade desserts are also good. Entrées come with salad from a rather basic salad bar and bread, but in true local style, plates are light on vegetables. ⊠ *796 Kūhiō Hwy., Kapa'a,* ☎ *808/822–3791. AE, D, DC, MC, V. No lunch.*

$–$$ ✕ **Wailua Marina Restaurant.** Dockside views of boats chugging along the Wailua River make this an ideal stop before or after a trip to the Fern Grotto. An open-air dining lānai is perched right on the water, next to shores where ancient Hawaiian communities once stood. For the large number of people it serves, the restaurant has a surprisingly thoughtful menu. Baked stuffed chicken is cooked in plum sauce and served with a lobster salad, and there's a good choice of steak, stuffed pork chops, and fresh seafood dishes. ⊠ *Wailua River State Park, Wailua Rd., Wailua,* ☎ *808/822–4311. AE, DC, MC, V. Closed Mon.*

Thai

$–$$ ✕ **Mema, Thai Chinese Cuisine.** Such menu items as broccoli with oyster sauce and cashew chicken reveal their Chinese origins, but the emphasis in this attractive restaurant is on Thai dishes. A host of curries—red, green, yellow, and house—made with coconut milk and kaffir lime leaves runs from mild to mayhem in spiciness. You have a choice of chicken, beef, pork, or shrimp with several side dishes, such as stir-fried eggplant with fresh basil. Orchids, torch ginger, and Asian memorabilia highlight a pretty-in-peach interior. ⊠ *Wailua Shopping Plaza, 4-361 Kūhiō Hwy., Kapa'a,* ☎ *808/823–0899. AE, D, DC, MC, V. No lunch weekends.*

The North Coast

American/Casual

$–$$ ✕ **Hanalei Gourmet.** A casual north-shore atmosphere has made this a popular hangout. There are bar and table seating and big open windows. The TV over the bar is usually tuned to sports and music programs, but the clientele is generally too busy eating and talking to watch. Breakfasts include lox and bagels with cream cheese, and croissant sandwiches with bacon and scrambled eggs. Lunch and dinner menus feature hot sandwiches, burgers, salads, soups, fresh catch, big *pūpū* (appetizer) platters, and picnic items to go. There's live music of one sort or another every night. ✉ *5-5161 Kūhiō Hwy., across from Ching Young Center, Hanalei,* ☎ *808/826–2524. D, DC, MC, V.*

$–$$ ✕ **Old Hanalei Coffee Company.** In a restored 1920s home, this green-and-white breakfast emporium provides a wake-up call with its specialty coffees, waffles, and egg dishes. Pastries include aloha bars made with chocolate chips and macadamia nuts. Visits here can be habit-forming and relatively inexpensive. Relax on the pretty white porch, sip your cappuccino, and watch the Hanalei scene drift by. ✉ *5-5183 Kūhiō Hwy., across from Ching Young Center, Hanalei,* ☎ *808/826–6717. D, MC, V. No lunch or dinner.*

Contemporary

$$–$$$ ✕ **Cafe Hanalei and Terrace.** Indoor and outdoor tables take full ad-
★ vantage of glorious views of Hanalei Bay and the peak popularly known as Bali Hai. The Sunday brunch and daily breakfast buffet are feasts of made-to-order omelets, crêpes, and fresh fruit, but the vanilla Belgian waffles and smoked peppered salmon with bagels, cream cheese, and capers are equally delicious. Lunch selections include Japanese specialties in addition to lobster bisque, cobb salad, and super sandwiches. For dinner try steamed 'ōpakapaka (snapper) with ginger, cilantro, and mushrooms, or sample Friday night's seafood buffet. ✉ *Princeville Hotel, Princeville Resort, 5520 Ka Haku Rd., Princeville,* ☎ *808/826–9644. Reservations essential. AE, D, DC, MC, V.*

$$ ✕ **Postcards Cafe.** In what was once an old house in the rice fields, this "Old Hawai'i" restaurant is decorated with vintage photos and postcards to capture the mood of an earlier era, but the food is deliciously up-to-date. Smoothies and salads made with organic fruits and vegetables, vegan dishes, Thai coconut curry, and taro fritters highlight a varied menu that emphasizes local seafood. Desserts, often made with macadamia nuts and in-season fruits, have an island flavor. Brunch is great, but service can be slow. ✉ *5-5075A Kūhiō Hwy., Hanalei,* ☎ *808/826–1191. AE, MC, V. No lunch.*

$$ ✕ **Surf's on the Beach.** Kaua'i's northernmost restaurant is spacious and gracious, with in-your-face views of breaking surf just beyond the Mexican-tile floors. French-Asian influences are found in entrées such as moonfish with crab butter sauce and grilled *shutome*-steak (swordfish) sandwich with lemongrass. There's also a nice lobster ravioli, and you can finish your meal with a light liliko'i-mango tiramisu. The attached Lava Vent deli provides fresh take-out sandwiches; bring some along if you're planning to picnic on a hike to Hanakāpī'ai Beach at the end of the road. ✉ *5-7132 Kūhiō Hwy., Hanalei,* ☎ *808/826–0060. AE, D, MC, V.*

$–$$ ✕ **Bamboo Bamboo.** Individual pizzas from the wood-burning oven come with an imaginative 'ahi sashimi with wasabi and cream cheese topping. Smoked mahimahi salad, seafood pasta with marinara sauce, and filet mignon with potatoes au gratin and Kaua'i asparagus are choices to fit any appetite. Ask to sit on the roofed deck, where you can relax even when the rain falls on surrounding ginger, banana, and plumeria plants. Bamboo Bamboo has indoor and garden-patio dining, an exhibition kitchen, and a good wine selection. ⊠ *Hanalei Center, 5-5161 Kūhiō Hwy., Hanalei,* ☎ *808/826–1177. AE, MC, V.*

$–$$ ✕ **Lighthouse Bistro.** This out-of-the-way restaurant has a comfortable plantation look with windows that open wide to the outdoors, terra-cotta floors, bamboo chairs, and Hawaiian artwork on the walls that's for sale. Some entrées have an Italian flair, such as seafood linguine or tortellini. Others, such as stuffed shrimp in phyllo and chicken *satay* (chicken grilled on skewers) with Thai peanut sauce, are more Pacific Rim. ⊠ *2484 Kaneke St., at Lighthouse Rd., Kīlauea,* ☎ *808/828–0480. MC, V.*

$–$$ ✕ **Zelos Beach House.** Call the menu eclectic—what else could you say about its American-Italian-Thai-Creole leanings? The decor, however, is strictly South Pacific at this "beach-blanket bingo goes to the South Seas" kind of place. A bamboo bar, *lau hala* (pandanus leaf) mats on the walls, a kayak overhead, and Tahitian-print bar stools add to the fun—and the food is good. Burgers and burritos are served on an open-air deck. For dinner, large salads, fresh fish, pasta, steak, and chicken pesto tortellini fill the bill. ⊠ *5-5156 Kūhiō Hwy., Hanalei,* ☎ *808/826–9700. MC, V.*

Italian

$$–$$$ ✕ **La Cascata.** Terra-cotta floors, hand-painted murals, and trompe l'oeil paintings give La Cascata an Italian-villa flair, and picture windows offer dazzling views of Hanalei Bay. The menu emphasizes light sauces; plenty of pastas; plus fresh seafood, beef, and lamb. Savor smoked Hawaiian marlin with fresh asparagus and caviar or sample sautéed shrimp, lobster, clams, and scallops on pasta with a spicy tomato-fennel sauce. Top it off with an airy tiramisu or the day's sorbet selection. ⊠ *Princeville Hotel, Princeville Resort, 5520 Ka Haku Rd., Princeville,* ☎ *808/826–9644. Reservations essential. AE, D, DC, MC, V. No lunch.*

Mexican

$–$$ ✕ **Roadrunner Bakery and Café.** Casual with a capital "C," the Roadrunner has a counter where you can order fresh-baked taro rolls or bread in addition to breakfast pastries and espresso coffee. Vegetarian selections are available at lunch and dinner. The *huevos rancheros* have eggs, tomatillo sauce, beans, cheese, salsa, guacamole, rice, and tortillas. Burritos are huge. The filling for the Black Dog is pork, grilled taro, and black beans. Mexican scenes painted on the walls, hanging plants, and ceiling fans give the place a let-it-all-hang-out atmosphere. ⊠ *2430 Oka St., Kīlauea,* ☎ *808/828–8226. MC, V.*

Steak and Seafood

$$–$$$ ✕ **Bali Hai.** Views of the bay are as memorable as the cuisine at this open-air, tropical restaurant that is richly appointed with natural wood. A specialty is Kaua'i onion soup topped with melted provolone cheese and croutons. For entrées you can choose from a wide variety of preparations for three types of fresh seafood served nightly. Lamb, filet mignon, and vegetarian dishes are also on the menu. For breakfast there are poi pancakes, fried taro, eggs, and griddle fare. In the adjacent Happy Talk Lounge there's nightly entertainment. ⊠ *Hanalei Bay Resort, 5380 Honoiki Rd., Princeville,* ☎ *808/826–6522. AE, D, DC, MC, V.*

$$–$$$ ✕ **Chuck's Steak House.** A *paniolo* (Hawaiian cowboy) feeling permeates this split-level eatery, where saddles and blankets hang from the open-beam ceiling. Barbecued pork ribs, lobster, chicken, and Alaskan king crab are all good, but fresh island seafood and Black Angus beef are what Chuck's is known for. Can't make up your mind? They can put steak alongside almost any other entrée on a combination platter. The salad bar comes with all entrées. Save room for dessert—Chuck's special mud pie is a winner. ⊠ *Princeville Shopping Center, 5-4280 Kūhiō Hwy., Princeville,* ☎ *808/826–6211. AE, D, DC, MC, V. No lunch weekends.*

Līhu'e and Vicinity

American/Casual

$$ ✕ **JJ's Broiler.** Easy to find, with dining on an open deck overlooking Kalapakī Bay, this is a nautically natty place to stop for lunch or dinner. The Caesar salad could use a little spicing up, but thick and crispy French fries, potato skins, burgers, and pastrami-and-Swiss club sandwiches are reliable favorites for lunch. Dinners, with the likes of herbed seafood linguine and coconut shrimp, are fancier and come with a salad bar rolled to your table. The house specialty is Slavonic steak, a broiled sliced tenderloin dipped in a buttery wine sauce. There's a shuttle bus from the harbor to take you here—a nice touch for those arriving by sea. ⊠ *Anchor Cove, Nāwiliwili,* ☎ *808/246–4422. D, MC, V.*

$$ ✕ **Whalers Brew Pub.** The view of the ocean and Kalapakī Bay is breathtaking whether you sit inside or outside under umbrella-shaded tables. Some diners like to sit at high "chronie bars" while they chomp on beer-battered fish-and-chips or a 20-ounce whale of a burger. Others choose regular tables and healthier family fare: Whaler's salad bar, island-style barbecued ribs with cole slaw, or mahimahi sandwiches with French fries. Eight handcrafted ales brewed in the gleaming tanks near the entry are on offer. Seating for 300 includes separate areas for private parties. A 400-gallon aquarium adds an airy ambience. ⊠ *3132 Ninini Point St., Lihu'e,* ☎ *808/245–2000. AE, D, DC, MC, V.*

Eclectic

$$–$$$ ✕ **Kukui's Poolside Restaurant and Bar.** An imaginative marriage of Asian, Hawaiian, Mexican, and Continental tastes characterizes the menu at this comfortable restaurant. Open-air tables face the hotel's sprawling pool—a perfect spot to enjoy a lunch or an afternoon snack of *kālua* (roasted) pork quesadillas or Thai-chicken pizza. A more formal atmosphere prevails at dinnertime, when the menu reflects fresh island flavors. Try lemon-rosemary chicken or *char-siu* (marinated and barbecued) pork loin with crispy noodles. At breakfast the temptations are twofold: a buffet or a full à la carte menu. ⊠ *Kaua'i Marriott Hotel Resort & Beach Club, 3610 Rice St., Līhu'e,* ☎ *808/246–5171. AE, D, DC, MC, V.*

$ ✕ **Dani's Restaurant.** Kaua'i residents frequent this big and bare local eatery near the Līhu'e Fire Station. Owners Tsutao and Harriet Morioka have created a friendly come-as-you-are ambience for breakfast or lunch. Dani's is a good place to try lū'au food without commercial lū'au prices. You can order Hawaiian-style *laulau* (pork wrapped in ti leaves and steamed) or kālua pig and rice. Other island-style dishes include Japanese-prepared *tonkatsu* (pork cutlet) and teriyaki beef, and there's an all-American New York steak. ⊠ *4201 Rice St., Līhu'e,* ☎ *808/245–4991. No credit cards. Closed Sun. No dinner.*

Italian

$–$$ ✕ **Café Portofino.** Dining here affords a panorama of mountain, sea, and sky across from Kalapakī Bay; get a table out on the lānai for the best views. The northern-Italian cuisine includes such fresh pasta dishes as fettuccine in tomato, mushroom, garlic, and herb sauce. Specials might be rabbit with white wine and herbs, or sweetbreads in a cream sauce on a bed of linguine. Italian gelato is made fresh daily, and there's nightly entertainment. ⊠ *Pacific Ocean Plaza, 3501 Rice St., Nāwiliwili,* ☎ *808/245–2121. AE, D, DC, MC, V. No lunch weekends.*

Japanese

$–$$ ✕ **Hanamā'ulu Restaurant, Tea House, Sushi Bar and Robatayaki.** The first dining room with adjacent bar that you enter in this old brown building is unexciting, but make reservations and ask for seating in one of the traditional Japanese rooms around the garden complete with carp in a peaceful pond. Chinese plate lunches with soup, salad, fried chicken, chop suey, crisp wontons, and spare ribs are the best deal, but traditional Japanese fare such as sashimi; sushi; *teishoku* (set meal) platters with miso soup, tempura shrimp, fish, and vegetables; chicken *katsu* (cutlet); and *robatayaki* (grilled seafood and meat) are the main attractions. ✉ *1-4291 Kūhiō (Hwy. 56), Hanamā'ulu,* ☎ *808/245–2511 or 808/245–3225. MC, V. Closed Mon.*

Seafood

$$–$$$ ✕ **Duke's Canoe Club.** This popular club is a feast of beautiful native woods, greenery, and Duke Kahanamoku memorabilia, enhanced by the sound of a waterfall running alongside the staircase that leads from the upstairs dining room to the beachside Barefoot Bar. Prime rib, seafood coconut curry, and smoked marlin are available, but the best order here is the fresh catch of the day—prepared as you like it, from broiled plain to firecracker Thai-chili-glazed. Hula pie (Oreo-cookie crust with ice cream) is the star of the dessert menu—with strolling musicians as an accompaniment. A bar menu and lunch are available. ✉ *Kalapakī Beach, Līhu'e,* ☎ *808/246–9599. AE, D, DC, MC, V.*

The South and West Coasts

American

$–$$ ✕ **Camp House Grill.** A simple plantation-style camp house on the road to Waimea Canyon has been transformed into a quaint little restaurant with creaky wooden floors. The food is equally down-home, with hamburgers, cheeseburgers, chicken, pork ribs, and fresh fish aimed to please families. Barbecued specialties include chicken and ribs, and huge sandwiches are served at lunchtime. Home-style breakfasts are available, and pies are baked fresh daily. As you enter Kalāheo heading west, look for the blue building on the right. There are also two other locations: 1-3959 Kaumuali'i Hwy. (Highway 50) in Hanapēpē (☎ 808/335–5656), and Kaua'i Village on the Kūhiō Hwy. in Kapa'a (☎ 808/822–2442). ✉ *Kaumuali'i Hwy. (Hwy. 50), Kalāheo,* ☎ *808/ 332–9755. MC, V.*

Contemporary

$$–$$$ ✕ **Shells Restaurant.** You'll hear the surf as you dine here on the lānai or inside the high-ceilinged restaurant. Big shell chandeliers salvaged after Hurricane 'Iniki light the dining room, and the airy, tropical room has rattan furnishings that make it easy to relax. Menu highlights include crab cakes, rack of lamb with herb and hoisin crust, and fresh fish prepared three ways and served with angel-hair pasta and prawns. A great tropical topper is Hanna Banana, a macadamia-nut ice cream concoction with rum sauce; there's also a selection of desserts from the buffet. The adjacent Point lounge affords an ocean view and has indoor and outdoor seating for predinner cocktails at sunset. ✉ *Sheraton Kaua'i Resort, 2440 Ho'onani Rd., Po'ipū Beach, Kōloa,* ☎ *808/ 742–1661. AE, D, DC, MC, V. No lunch.*

$$ ✕ **The Beach House.** The Beach House may have the best ocean view
★ of any restaurant on the south shore. It's equally possible to get swept away by the cuisine here, with chef Linda Yamada in charge. The menu changes more often than the work of local artists on the walls, but you might find Kaua'i-asparagus salad and Local Boy paella, fire-roasted 'ahi, or lemongrass-and-kaffir-lime-leaf-crusted scallops on the menu.

A coconut-butter *mochi* (doughy Japanese rice cake) sundae is the sweetest finale. ☒ *5022 Lawai Rd., Kōloa,* ☎ *808/742–1424. AE, D, DC, MC, V. No lunch.*

$–$$ ✕ **Plantation House Café.** The wooden floors, green shutters, and white decks of this friendly family restaurant resemble those of early plantation homes. Sit-down meals and takeout are offered for lunch and dinner, and they also serve espresso and bakery goods at breakfast. You can order eight kinds of pizza, including Hawaiian, which is served with fresh pineapple. There's something on the menu to suit anyone's taste—from barbecued half chicken to rock shrimp with fettucine and white clam sauce to desserts of coconut macadamia-nut bread pudding—and everything is delicious. Wine and beer are served. ☒ *Po'ipū Shopping Village, 2360 Kiahuna Plantation Dr., Po'ipū Beach,* ☎ *808/742–7373. AE, D, DC, MC, V.*

$–$$ ✕ **Tomkats Grille.** This casual drop-in eatery keeps kids happy during lunch or early dinner hours with tropical ponds, a little waterfall, and a section of the menu geared to young tastes. Adults might pass up the PB&J for chicken marinara, barbecued pork ribs, a burger, or a Reuben accompanied by a glass of wine or a choice of 35 ales, stouts, ports, and lagers. Plenty of Tomkats' Nibblers—buffalo wings, stuffed mushrooms, jalapeño poppers—enliven happy hour from 4 to 6. ☒ *5402 Kōloa Rd., Kōloa,* ☎ *808/742–8887. DC, MC, V.*

$–$$ ✕ **Waimea Brewing Company.** This Kaua'i brew pub fits the laid-back ambience of Waimea Plantation Cottages, where it is housed in a spacious, airy room with hardwood floors surrounded by open-air decks. Entrées served in two sizes and at reasonable prices attract locals and visitors on their way to Waimea Canyon. The chef turns out smoked-chicken quesadillas, grilled portobellos, hamburgers, kalbi beef short ribs, and fresh fish. Dine indoors amid rattan furnishings or at a bar decorated with petroglyphs and colored with Kaua'i red dirt. It's a good place to pick up a picnic basket on the way to the canyon, or stop on the way back for a Wai'ale'ale Golden Ale or Alakai Stout and a little live music on weekends. ☒ *9400 Kaumuali'i Hwy., Waimea,* ☎ *808/338–9733. MC, V.*

Eclectic

$$–$$$ ✕ **Roy's Po'ipū Bar & Grill.** Hawai'i's culinary superstar Roy Yamaguchi
★ opened his sleek Kaua'i restaurant in 1994, and it quickly became a mecca for fans of his Euro-Asian Pacific cuisine. Who but Roy would turn smoked duck into *gyoza* (Japanese dumplings) and serve the appetizer with star-fruit passion sauce, or team fresh seared 'ōpakapaka with orange shrimp butter and Chinese black bean sauce? There are 15 to 20 or more specials nightly. Dark-chocolate soufflé and volcanic puffed pastry are regulars on the dessert menu. ☒ *Po'ipū Shopping Village, 2360 Kiahuna Plantation Dr., Po'ipū Beach,* ☎ *808/742–5000. AE, D, DC, MC, V. No lunch.*

$–$$ ✕ **Green Garden.** Hanging and standing plants throughout characterize this aptly named family-run restaurant, a favorite dining spot for Kaua'i residents and visitors since 1948. The Green Garden is very low-key, and the servers treat you like longtime friends. The food is no-frills local fare. Come here for the atmosphere first and the meals second. Dinner includes some 30 items of local, Asian, and American influence. The seafood special is breaded mahimahi fillet, scallops, oysters, and deep-fried shrimp. The homemade desserts are the best part of a meal here, particularly the liliko'i chiffon pie. ☒ *Hwy. 50, Hanapēpē,* ☎ *808/335–5422. AE, MC, V. Closed Tues.*

Italian

$$ ✕ **Casa di Amici.** Casa di Amici means "house of friends," and with rattan furnishings under ceiling fans inside and deck seating with sweeping ocean views outside, it feels like the kama'aina home the building once was. The menu is broader than Italian-Mediterranean, including French, Thai, Japanese, and Vietnamese touches, but you'll find traditional antipasti, *zuppe* (soup), pasta, *insalata* (salads), and *pietanza maggiore* (main courses). Order your favorite pasta with your choice of sauce, or savor the house scampi. Black tiger prawns are served with lobster thermidor ravioli, and sautéed duck breast is enhanced with a Jamaican-spiced raspberry-hoisin demi-glace. A pianist plays dinner music on the weekends. ⊠ *2301 Nalo Rd., Po'ipū,* ☎ *808/742–1555. AE, D, DC, MC, V. No lunch.*

$$ ✕ **Dondero's at the Hyatt Regency Kaua'i.** Inlaid marble floors, ornate green tile work, and ivy and Italianate murals make it difficult to choose between indoor and outdoor dining in this elegant restaurant. Porcini-mushroom crêpes with Parmesan sauce, a perfectly seasoned Caesar salad, and *spiedini* (skewered lobster, scallops, and shrimp suspended over tender gnocchi pillows) might have sprung from an artist's palate. Chocolate hazelnut torte and sinfully rich crème brûlée are decadent indulgences to close the meal. ⊠ *Hyatt Regency Kaua'i Resort and Spa, 1571 Po'ipū Rd., Po'ipū Beach,* ☎ *808/742–1234. AE, D, DC, MC, V. No lunch.*

$$ ✕ **Plantation Gardens.** Once the residence of a plantation manager, this historic structure now serves Italian food in a Polynesian atmosphere—a mix you'll find only in Aloha Land. Gardens with torchlit paths, rich wood interiors, and veranda dining will spark romance. Fresh herbs come from the manager's garden, and the island fish might have been caught only hours before reaching your table. Flavors are outstanding in such dishes as marinated grilled eggplant filled with goat cheese and sun-dried tomatoes; pizza with portobello mushrooms, pancetta, and fontina cheese baked in the wood-burning oven; or the meltingly tender osso buco served with saffron risotto. ⊠ *2253 Po'ipū Rd., Kiahuna Plantation, Kōloa,* ☎ *808/742–2216. AE, DC, MC, V. No lunch.*

$–$$ ✕ **Pomodoro.** Pink linens, rattan chairs, and two walls of windows brighten this intimate, family-run restaurant. Begin with prosciutto and melon, and then proceed directly to the lasagna, a favorite of the chefs, who are two Italian-born brothers. Other menu highlights include eggplant or veal parmigiana and scampi in a garlic, caper, and white wine sauce. Freshly baked garlic bread and seasonal vegetables come with each meal. ⊠ *Upstairs at Rainbow Plaza, Kaumuali'i Hwy. (Hwy. 50), Kalāheo,* ☎ *808/332–5945. MC, V. No lunch.*

Steak and Seafood

$$–$$$ ✕ **House of Seafood.** Tropical vines wrap themselves around the handsome exposed beams of this restaurant overlooking the Po'ipū Resort tennis courts. Under this establishment's soaring ceilings try island seafood, from 'ahi to *weke* (goatfish). Preparations for 10 types of fish vary nightly. A variety of shellfish is also available, including lobster. Caesar salad is made fresh at your table, and all entrées come with fresh vegetables, almond rice pilaf, and freshly baked rolls. Delicious kiwi crêpes flambées and bananas Foster garner raves for dessert. ⊠ *Po'ipū Kai Resort, 1941 Po'ipū Rd., Po'ipū,* ☎ *808/742–6433. AE, D, DC, MC, V. No lunch.*

$$–$$$ ✕ **Tidepools.** The Hyatt Regency Kaua'i has three superb restaurants, but this one delivers the most tropical atmosphere. Dine in one of the grass-thatched huts that float on a koi-filled pond, and enjoy views of the romantic torchlit grounds and starry Po'ipū skies. A major advocate of Hawai'i regional cuisine, which utilizes Kaua'i-grown products, the chef prepares fish with a variety of local flavors. Specialties include macadamia-crusted fish, prime rib, and filet mignon. ⊠ *Hyatt Regency Kaua'i Resort and Spa, 1571 Po'ipū Rd., Po'ipū Beach,* ☎ *808/742–1234, ext 4260. AE, D, DC, MC, V. No lunch.*

$$ ✕ **Brennecke's Beach Broiler.** This place, right across from Po'ipū Beach Park, has been around for years, and happily so. Large open windows look out onto palm trees and the ocean, and pretty window boxes filled with petunias further brighten the scene. The restaurant specializes in kiawe-wood broiled foods—New York steak covered with mushrooms and beef ribs smothered in barbecue sauce. Brennecke's also serves fresh mussels, Hawaiian spiny lobster, and deluxe burgers. The well-stocked all-you-can-eat salad bar with bread and chowder is a good deal. ⊠ *Ho'one Rd., Po'ipū,* ☎ *808/742–7588. AE, D, DC, MC, V.*

$$ ✕ **Kalāheo Steak House.** It's the huge cut of prime rib, the tender top sirloin, the Cornish game hen in spicy herb and citrus marinade, and the succulent Alaskan king crab legs that make locals seek out this restaurant. Dinners are served with salad, rolls, and a choice of rice or baked potato. Rum cake, baked fresh daily, comes with Lappert's ice cream (made at a factory just up the road). Wines range from $8 to $25 a bottle. Children up to 11 can order from a separate low-priced menu. Ceiling fans stir the air through open wooden louvers in the dark wood-paneled interior of this old building. ⊠ *4444 Papalina Rd., Kalāheo,* ☎ *808/332–9780. D, MC, V. No lunch.*

$$ ✕ **Keoki's Paradise.** Seafood stars at this Po'ipū favorite, styled to resemble a dockside boathouse. Though it sits in a corner of the inland Po'ipū Shopping Village, tinkling streams, lush foliage, and thatched roofs over the bar create an outdoor Polynesian atmosphere. Even the appetizers have an ocean flavor—from sashimi to fisherman's chowder. There is a sampling of beef, chicken, and pork-rib entrées for committed carnivores, but the day's fresh catch is what brings patrons to Keoki's. Choose from a half-dozen preparation styles and sauces, and save room for the hula pie. ⊠ *Po'ipū Shopping Village, 2360 Kiahuna Plantation Dr., Po'ipū Beach,* ☎ *808/742–7534. AE, D, DC, MC, V.*

$$ ✕ **Wrangler's Steakhouse.** Wrangler's seems right out of the Wild West, with wooden floors and tables, denim-upholstered seating, and saddles and a stagecoach on display. Steak—sizzling and prepared with either garlic, capers, peppers, or teriyaki—can be ordered in a he-man 16-ounce size, but if meat is not your thing, opt for the fresh catch, scampi, or at lunch one of the Mexican entrées. Local folks love the kaukau tin lunch: soup, rice, beef teriyaki, and shrimp tempura served in a three-tiered tin lunch pail (the kind that sugar plantation workers once carried). A gift shop features local crafts (and sometimes a craftsperson); a deck out back allows open-air dining; and the adjoining Pacific Pizza and Deli, with some of the most imaginative pizzas around, is part of the same family-run complex. ⊠ *98-52 Kaumuali'i Hwy., Waimea,* ☎ *808/338–1218. AE, MC, V. Closed Sun.*

LODGING

Whether you choose to stay at a plush Po'ipū resort or condo, where you can bask all day in the sun; at the posh Princeville Resort, where you can enjoy world-class golfing; or at a Coconut Coast guest house, where you can take advantage of an abundance of nearby shops and restaurants, make advance reservations. Peak months are February and August. When booking your accommodations, ask about such extras as tennis, golf, honeymoon, and room-and-car packages. For explanations of price categories, *see* Lodging *in* Smart Travel Tips.

306

Kaua'i Lodging

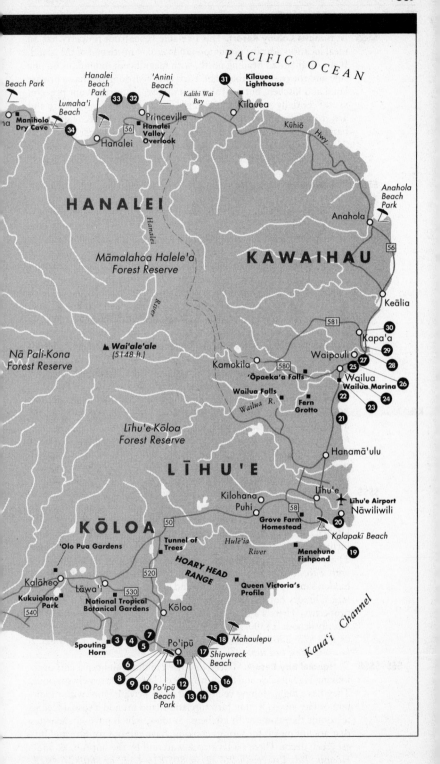

PACIFIC OCEAN

Beach Park

Hanalei
Beach
Park

'Anini
Beach

Kīlauea
Lighthouse

Kalihi Wai
Bay

31

Kīlauea

Lumaha'i
Beach

33 32

Kīlauea

Maniholo
Dry Cave

Princeville

34

Hanalei
Valley
Overlook

56

Kūhiō
Hwy.

Hanalei

HANALEI

Anahola
Beach
Park

Anahola

Hanalei

River

KAWAIHAU

56

Māmalahoa Hale'a
Forest Reserve

Keālia

Nā Pali-Kona
Forest Reserve

▲ Wai'ale'ale
(5148 ft.)

581

30

Kapa'a

Waipouli

27   29

Kamokila

580

25

28

'Ōpaeka'a Falls

Wailua

Wailua Marina

26

Wailua Falls

Fern
Grotto

22

24

Wailua R.

23

Līhu'e-Kōloa
Forest Reserve

21

LĪHU'E

Hanamā'ulu

Kilohana

Līhu'e

Līhu'e Airport

Puhi

Nāwiliwili

KŌLOA

Grove Farm
Homestead

58

20

'Olo Pua Gardens

50

Kilohana
Puhi

Kalapakī Beach

Tunnel of
Trees

Hule'ia

River

Menehune
Fishpond

19

Kalāheo

HOARY HEAD
RANGE

Lāwa'i

520

Queen Victoria's
Profile

Kukuiolono
Park

530

National Tropical
Botanical Gardens

Kōloa

540

7

Mahaulepu

3   4

18

Spouting
Horn

5

Po'ipū

17

Shipwreck
Beach

11

6

8

12

Po'ipū
Beach
Park

15   16

9   10

13   14

Kaua'i Channel

The East and North Coasts

$$$$ 🏨 Hanalei Colony Resort. This five-acre beachfront property has an ideal location near the mysterious and verdant north end of the island. It sits on the road heading north, with magnificent mountains on one side and the ocean on the other. Each two-bedroom unit has a private lānai and kitchen, but no TVs or phones will interrupt your peaceful visit. Free daily workshops teach guests about Hawaiian culture and art, from stringing lei to weaving lau hala mats. A barbecue gazebo is handy when you don't want to dine in the restaurant next door. ⊠ 5-7130 Kūhiō Hwy. (Box 206), Hā'ena 96714, ☎ 808/826–6235 or 800/628–3004, FAX 808/826–9893, WEB www.hcr.com. 52 suites. Kitchenettes, pool, hot tub, coin laundry. AE, MC, V.

$$$$ 🏨 Princeville Hotel. As you walk through the enormous, grand lobby,
★   you can't miss the sweeping views across Hanalei Bay and the majestic backdrop of Bali Hai's mountain peaks. It's as if you've truly arrived in the Land of the Lotus Eaters. Almost all guest rooms take advantage of this jaw-dropping vista. All have marble bathrooms, gold-plated fixtures, handsome appointments, and a bathroom feature called a privacy window, which can be opaque or, with a flip of a switch, clear so you can see the view outside while in the shower. A drink at sunset at the Living Room, the lobby bar, is an event, complete with a traditional Hawaiian ceremony. There's often entertainment, such as a jazz trio, here in the evening. There are two top-ranked 18-hole golf courses, one of which was voted one of the 10 best in the country in 1998 by *Golf Digest.* An exercise room is in the hotel, and a health club can be reached by shuttle. The pool area, with several hot tubs and a swim-up bar, is stunning. The hotel has a convenient check-in procedure: the valet parking attendant has your room key, and the bellhop who delivers your bags checks you in. ⊠ 5520 Ka Haku Rd. (Box 3069), Princeville 96722, ☎ 808/826–9644 or 800/826–4400, FAX 808/826–1166, WEB www.princeville.com. 201 rooms, 51 suites. 3 restaurants, 2 bars, minibars, room service, pool, massage, 2 18-hole golf courses, 8 tennis courts, exercise room, health club, beach, children's programs (ages 5–12), dry cleaning, laundry service, concierge, business services, meeting room, travel services. AE, D, DC, MC, V.

$$$$ 🏨 Secret Beach Hideaway. You could start a romance or write the great American novel—anything seems possible at the five sumptuous, very private retreats here. Three one-bedroom, one-bath cottages with kitchens and indoor-outdoor garden showers have marble and granite touches. Picture windows in the living rooms of each cottage frame 11 acres of landscaped grounds—one with a natural waterfall, the other with a freshwater stream—that slope to Secret Beach; few find these hidden sands, a haven for families and privacy-seekers. The two other larger, luxury houses, which attract Hollywood types, are on separate properties. There's a onetime cleaning fee of $125, and a refundable security deposit is $500. ⊠ 2884 Kauapea Rd. (Box 781), Kīlauea 96754, ☎ 808/828–2862 or 970/925–7445, FAX 971/925–1662. 3 cottages, 2 houses. Fans, hot tub.

$$$–$$$$ 🏨 Hanalei Bay Resort. Sixteen low-rise buildings sit atop a cliff overlooking Hanalei Bay and the north shore. Units are extremely spacious. They have high, sloping ceilings and large private lānai with mountain or bay views. Rattan furniture and island art add a casual feeling to rooms that come with kitchens. Studios, which have kitchenettes that are not meant for serious cooking, have rattan furniture and forest green decor. There's a lava-rock waterfall by the hot tub. ⊠ 5380 Honoiki Rd., Princeville 96722, ☎ 808/826–6522 or 800/827–4427, FAX 808/826–6680, WEB www.hanaleibayresort.com. 161 rooms, 75 *suites. Restaurant, lobby lounge, kitchenettes, pool, hot tub, 18-hole golf course, 4 tennis courts, coin laundry. AE, D, DC, MC, V.*

$$$–$$$$ ▦ **Holiday Inn SunSpree Resort.** This hotel has ocean views, but it's a short walk via Lydgate Park to the beach. Kids love the playground at the park, and the beach has a protected area so it's safe for youngsters. A bubbling waterfall and exotic flowers enhance the lobby, and rooms have dark-green carpets, pastel colors, rattan furnishings, and large windows. A complimentary children's program and such adult activities as shuffleboard, tennis, and beach volleyball are part of the package. ✉ *3-5920 Kūhiō Hwy., Kapa'a 96746,* ☎ *808/246–6976 or 800/465–4329,* FAX *808/823–6666,* WEB *www.basshotels.com. 188 rooms, 2 suites, 26 cabana suites. Restaurant, deli, lobby lounge, 2 pools, hot tub, 2 tennis courts, exercise room, shuffleboard, volleyball, children's programs (ages 4–12). AE, D, DC, MC, V.*

$$$–$$$$ ▦ **Kaua'i Coast Resort.** Eight miles north of Līhu'e Airport and set along an uncrowded stretch of Waipouli Beach, this condominium resort is well situated for east- and north-shore sightseeing. It's also a five-minute drive from the Wailua Municipal Golf Course and within walking distance of the Coconut Marketplace. The three-building, three-story resort consists of one- and two-bedroom condos and some time-share units. They are decorated in rich sage, persimmon, and golds following the theme of "My Old Hawaiian Home." A pool with a waterfall is visible from the spacious lānai of many rooms. ✉ *4-484 Kūhiō Hwy., Kapa'a 96746,* ☎ *808/822–3441 or 800/922–7866,* FAX *808/822–0843,* WEB *www.kauaicoasthawaii.com. 108 1- and 2-bedroom condos and time-shares, 6 hotel rooms. Restaurant, lobby lounge, refrigerators, 2 pools, hot tub, tennis court. AE, D, DC, MC, V.*

$$$–$$$$ ▦ **Kaua'i Coconut Beach Resort.** On 11 acres of beachfront property midway between north- and south-shore attractions and within walking distance of three major shopping centers, this full-service resort's location can't be beat. Its nightly lū'au is considered the most authentic by many, and free hula and torch-lighting shows at sunset perpetuate aloha spirit. Rooms have pale green walls, peach accents, and floral bedspreads. ✉ *Kūhiō Hwy. (Box 830), Kapa'a 96746,* ☎ *808/822–3455 or 800/222–5642,* FAX *808/822–1830,* WEB *www.hawaiihotels.com. 309 rooms, 2 suites. Restaurant, lobby lounge, air-conditioning, refrigerators, room service, pool, hot tub, 3 tennis courts, jogging, shuffleboard, meeting room. AE, D, DC, MC, V.*

$$$–$$$$ ▦ **Outrigger Lae Nani.** Ruling Hawaiian chiefs once returned from ocean voyages to this spot, now host to condominiums comfortable enough for minor royalty. An oceanside heiau and hotel-sponsored Hawaiiana programs, with a booklet for self-guided historical tours, are nice extras. Units are all decorated differently, with full kitchens and expansive lānai. Your view of landscaped grounds is interrupted only by a large pool before ending at a sandy ocean beach. A barbecue and picnic area is on-site as well. ✉ *410 Papaloa Rd., Kapa'a 96746,* ☎ *808/822–4938 or 800/688–7444,* FAX *808/822–1022,* WEB *www.outrigger.com. 84 condominiums (60 rentals). Picnic area, kitchenettes, pool, tennis court, beach. AE, D, DC, MC, V.*

$$$ ▦ **Aston Islander on the Beach.** The eight three-story buildings of this pleasant six-acre beachfront property have a low-key Hawai'i plantation look. Rooms have showers but not tubs; dark carpeting is brightened by open-air lānai and lovely green lawns outside. A free-form pool is right next to a golden-sand beach, and you can take the lounge chairs to the ocean's edge. Shops, restaurants, and a cinema are at the adjacent Coconut Marketplace. ✉ *484 Kūhiō Hwy., Kapa'a 96746,* ☎ *808/822–7417 or 800/847–2786,* FAX *808/822–1947. 194 rooms, 2 suites. Restaurant, bar, pool, hot tub, tennis court, volleyball, coin laundry, meeting room. AE, D, DC, MC, V.*

$$$ 🏨 **Plantation Hale Resort.** These attractive units, across from the beach and near Coconut Marketplace, have kitchens, garden lānai, and a homey feel. Rooms are clean and pretty, with rose carpets, white rattan furnishings, and pastel colors. You couldn't ask for a more convenient location for dining, shopping, and sightseeing on either end of the island. Request a unit on the makai side, away from Kūhiō Highway. ⊠ *484 Kūhiō Hwy., Kapa'a 96746,* ☎ *808/822–4941 or 800/775–4253,* FAX *808/822–5599,* WEB *www.plantation-hale.com. 160 condominiums (143 rentals). Air-conditioning, in-room safes, kitchenettes, 3 pools, hot tub, putting green. AE, D, DC, MC, V.*

$$–$$$ 🏨 **Kaua'i Sands.** The green-and-blue decor of the rooms may seem outdated, but with the ocean right outside and your need to get wet and tan primary . . . who cares about colors? Wide lawns to the beach look inviting for playing or unwinding, and for shade you'll find a restaurant and lounge up close to sunswept seas and ocean vistas. Units in the two two-story buildings are air-conditioned; those with kitchenettes cost a few extra dollars. For money-saving beachfront accommodations this establishment might serve you well. ⊠ *420 Papaloa Rd., Kapa'a 96746,* ☎ *808/822–4951 or 800/367–7000,* FAX *808/922–0052,* WEB *www.sand-seaside.com. 198 rooms, 2 suites. Restaurant, lobby lounge, kitchenettes, 2 pools. AE, D, DC, MC, V.*

$$ 🏨 **Kapa'a Sands.** With only 20 condominiums, the Kapa'a Sands is an intimate gem. Located seaside on the eastern coast, it's on the site of an old Japanese Shinto temple—an old rock etched with kanji is a remnant of its presence. Small rooms are equipped with ceiling fans, appropriate for beachside bungalows, and have full kitchens, all with dishwashers and garbage disposals. Ask for an oceanfront room to get an open-air lānai. The landscaping around the eight two-story buildings includes meandering pathways lined with palms, gingers, and other tropical flora. ⊠ *380 Papaloa Rd., Kapa'a 96746,* ☎ *808/822– 4901 or 800/222–4901,* FAX *808/822–1556,* WEB *www.kapaasands.com. 20 condominiums. Fans, in-room VCRs, pool. MC, V.*

$–$$ 🏨 **Hotel Coral Reef.** This older, well-maintained hotel is right on the sand's edge, although the swimming in front of the hotel is not as good as at the public beaches nearby. Colorful bedspreads liven up the bare-minimum furnishings. Upper units have carpeting. Ground-level rooms are done in terrazzo tile with patios that lead directly to the beach, where there are barbecue grills. Oceanfront accommodations have private lānai and refrigerators. Continental breakfast is served. The property is ideally situated, near shopping, dining, and sightseeing, and the rates are attractive. ⊠ *1516 Kūhiō Hwy., Kapa'a 96746,* ☎ *808/822–4481 or 800/843–4659,* FAX *808/822–7705,* WEB *www.hotelcoralreef.com. 24 rooms, 2 suites. Beach, coin laundry. MC, V.*

Līhu'e and Vicinity

$$$$ 🏨 **Kaua'i Marriott Resort & Beach Club.** Public areas here impart a sense
★ of grandeur, carried out by an elaborate tropical garden, luxuriant plantings, and waterfalls right off the lobby, plus there's a huge, cinematic pool worthy of Xanadu. Poolside dining makes use of this two-tier, templelike extravaganza. The hotel nestles in the 800-acre, independently owned Kaua'i Lagoons Resort. There's a lovely beach and lagoon to rest beside as well. ⊠ *3610 Rice St., Kalapakī Beach, Līhu'e 96766,* ☎ *808/245–5050 or 800/220–2925,* FAX *808/245–5049,* WEB *www. marriotthotels.com. 356 rooms, 11 suites, 232 time-share units. 2 restaurants, lobby lounge, minibars, room service, pool, outdoor hot tubs, spa, 2 18-hole golf courses, 7 tennis courts, health club, beach, children's programs (ages 5–12). AE, D, DC, MC, V.*

$$$$ 🏨 **Radisson Kaua'i Beach Hotel.** Designed with sensitivity to the history of the nearby Wailua River area, this low-rise, horseshoe-shape hotel surrounds a pool complex designed with rock-sculpted slopes, waterfalls, tropical flowers, and a cave resembling the Fern Grotto. Each night at sunset, staff members in native dress light 100 tiki torches around the pools. Guest rooms are attractive in rich tones with maroon accents and dark wood, and lānai have views of mountains, gardens, or the sea. ⊠ *4331 Kaua'i Beach Dr., Līhu'e 96766,* ☎ *808/245–1955 or 800/688–7444,* FAX *808/246–9085,* WEB *www.radissonkauai.com. 341 rooms, 8 suites. 2 restaurants, lobby lounge, room service, 4 pools, hot tub, 18-hole golf course, 4 tennis courts, health club. AE, D, DC, MC, V.*

$$ 🏨 **Garden Island Inn.** This handy three-story inn, across the road from Kalapakī Beach and Anchor Cove shopping center, is a bargain. The facilities and fantasy of the elegant Kaua'i Marriott are just down the beach. Orchid suites on the top floor and tropical rooms on the second have lānai and glimpses of the ocean. Budget rooms are on the ground floor. Rooms have linoleum tile and queen or two twin beds. Innkeepers Steve and Susan Layne loan boogie boards and snorkeling and golf equipment and give away fruit from their trees. ⊠ *3445 Wilcox Rd., Kalapakī Bay 96766,* ☎ *808/245–7227 or 800/648–0154,* FAX *808/245–7603,* WEB *www.gardenislandinn.com. 21 rooms, 2 suites. Air-conditioning, fans, kitchenettes. AE, DC, MC, V.*

The South Coast

$$$$ 🏨 **Embassy Vacation Resort Po'ipū Point.** Kaua'i's most luxurious
★ condominium complex combines hotel services with such condo-style amenities as kitchens, washers and dryers, and a barbecue area. Large suites have plush carpeting, European-style cabinetry, and granite kitchen countertops. The 22-acre grounds include lily ponds, reflecting pools, and a swimming pool surrounded by sand. Complimentary Continental breakfast and evening cocktail reception are hosted in the club room. ⊠ *1613 Pe'e Rd., Kōloa 96756,* ☎ *808/742–1888 or 800/426–3350,* FAX *808/742–1924,* WEB *www.embassykauai.com. 210 1- and 2-bedroom suites. Bar, kitchenettes, pool, hot tubs, health club, concierge. AE, D, DC, MC, V.*

$$$$ 🏨 **Gloria's Spouting Horn Bed & Breakfast.** The most elegant ocean-
★ front bed-and-breakfast on Kaua'i, this cedar home was built by owners Gloria and Bob Merkle specifically to house guests. Breakfast, snacks, and a chilled beverage are available in the comfortable common room with its soaring A-frame ceiling and ocean-immediate deck. Waves dash the black rocks below, while just above the ocean's edge a sand beach invites sunbathers. All three bedrooms have four-poster beds with romantic canopies and Hawaiian quilts, oceanside lānai, and bathrooms with deep soaking tubs and separate showers. ⊠ *4464 Lawai Rd., Po'ipū,* ☎ *808/742–6995,* WEB *www.gloriasbedandbreakfast.com. 3 rooms. Refrigerators, in-room VCRs, pool. No credit cards.*

$$$$ 🏨 **Hyatt Regency Kaua'i Resort and Spa.** This superbly designed, dra-
★ matically handsome, classic Hawaiian low-rise hotel has airy courtyards and gardens. Rooms, two-thirds with ocean views, further the plantation theme with bamboo and wicker furnishings and island art. Five acres of meandering fresh- and saltwater swimming lagoons are beautifully set amid landscaped grounds. The Anara Spa and Fitness Center, with a food bar, lap pool, hot tub, and massage rooms, covers 25,000 square ft. ⊠ *1571 Po'ipū Rd., Kōloa 96756,* ☎ *808/742–1234 or 800/233–1234,* FAX *808/742–6265,* WEB *www.hyatt.com. 60 rooms, 37 suites. 5 restaurants, 2 bars, 3 lobby lounges, minibars, room service, 3 pools (1 saltwater), spa, 18-hole golf course, 4 tennis courts, health club, beach, nightclub. AE, D, DC, MC, V.*

$$$$ 🏨 **Outrigger Kiahuna Plantation.** The expansive lawns of this 35-acre oceanfront resort hold 42 plantation-style, low-rise buildings. The

one- and two-bedroom units have pastel color schemes and rattan furnishings. The administrative office and an excellent Italian restaurant, Piatti, are in a lovely sugar-plantation manor house dating from the early 1900s. Lily ponds and Hawaiian gardens with plant labels enhance the setting. ⊠ *2253 Po'ipū Rd., Kōloa 96756,* ☎ *808/742–6411 or 800/688–7444,* FAX *808/742–1698,* WEB *www.outrigger.com. 333 1- and 2-bedroom condominium units. Restaurant, kitchenettes, pool, 18-hole golf course, 6 tennis courts. AE, DC, MC, V.*

$$$$ 🏨 **Po'ipū Kapili.** Ultraspacious one- and two-bedroom units, minutes from Po'ipū restaurants, enjoy garden and across-the-street ocean views combined with privacy. Architects managed to give a plantation look to the two-story, white-frame exteriors and double-pitched roofs, which complement the tropical landscaping. Decorator-designed interiors include full kitchens and entertainment centers. You can mingle at a weekly morning coffee hour held beside the ocean-view pool. There is an herb garden, and an on-site library is stocked with videos and books. ⊠ *2221 Kapili Rd., Kōloa 96756,* ☎ *808/742–6449 or 800/ 443–7714,* FAX *808/742–9162,* WEB *www.poipukapili.com. 60 condominiums. In-room VCRs, pool, 2 tennis courts, library. MC, V.*

$$$$ 🏨 **Po'ipū Shores.** These three low-rise buildings, with a pool in front of the middle one, sit right on a rocky point above pounding surf—a perfect spot for whale- or turtle-watching. Weddings are staged on a little lawn beside the ocean. A sandy swimming beach is a 10-minute walk away. Units are all decorated differently by individual owners. Two share a sundeck, the rest have lānai, but all have great windows and many of them have bedrooms on the ocean side. Kitchens have microwaves and washer and dryers. In addition, there are two barbecue areas on the property. ⊠ *1775 Pe'e Rd., Kōloa 96756,* ☎ *808/742– 7700 or 800/367–5004,* FAX *808/742–9720,* WEB *www.castle-group.com. 39 condominium suites. Fans, kitchenettes, pool. AE, MC, V.*

$$$$ 🏨 **Sheraton Kaua'i Resort.** The lobby opens onto a central courtyard surrounded by shops and an area under a banyan tree where Hawaiian artisans stage demonstrations. Four-story guest wings are right on the beach or in a garden cluster. Beachfront rooms in muted sand and eggshell colors are highlighted with tapa dividers, and garden rooms have a brighter palette. A wedding gazebo has an ocean backdrop. There's a children's pool, and children's programs are free in summer. ⊠ *2440 Ho'onani Rd., Po'ipū Beach, Kōloa 96756,* ☎ *808/742–1661 or 888/847–0208,* FAX *808/742–9777,* WEB *www.sheraton.com. 399 rooms, 14 suites. 4 restaurants, bar, room service, 2 pools, massage, 3 tennis courts, exercise room, beach, water slide, children's programs (ages 5–12), meeting room. AE, D, DC, MC, V.*

$$$$ 🏨 **Whalers Cove.** All 38 two-bedroom condos in two low-rise buildings face the water and share a swimming pool, which is almost near enough to the surf to cast out a fishing line. The rocky beach is good for snorkeling, but a short drive or brisk walk will get you to a sandy stretch. A handsome koa-bedecked reception area offers full services for the plush units. The grandest bathrooms have whirlpool tubs on raised platforms, separate showers, and twin sinks. Two barbecue areas, big picture windows, spacious living rooms, lānai, and modern kitchens with washer-dryers make this a place to leave home for. ⊠ *2640 Pu'uholo Rd., Kōloa 96756,* ☎ *808/742–7571 or 800/225– 2683,* FAX *808/742–1185,* WEB *www.whalers-cove.com. 38 2-bedroom condominiums. Kitchenettes, fans, pool, hot tub. AE, MC, V.*

$$$–$$$$ 🏨 **Makahuena at Po'ipū.** Extra-large, tastefully decorated suites with white tile and sand-color carpets are housed in two- and three-story white wooden buildings surrounded by well-kept lawns. Suites have kitchens and washer-dryers. There's a barbecue area on the property. Situated close to the center of Po'ipū on a rocky point over the ocean, the Makahuena is near Shipwreck and Poʻipū beaches. ⊠ *1661 Peʻe Rd., Poʻipū 96756,* ☎ *808/742–2482 or 800/367–5004,* FAX *808/742–2379,* WEB *www.castleresorts.com. 79 2- and 3-bedroom suites. Pool, hot tub, tennis court. AE, MC, V.*

$$$–$$$$ ▦ **Suite Paradise Poʻipū Kaī.** Luxuriously appointed apartments, many with cathedral ceilings and all with big windows overlooking spreading lawns, give this property the feeling of a spacious, quiet retreat inside and out. Big furnished lānai have views to the ocean and across the 110-acre landscaped grounds. Some units are two-level, some have sleeping lofts, and all are furnished with modern kitchens. There are barbecue facilities as well. The House of Seafood restaurant is on the property. A two-night minimum stay is required. ⊠ *1941 Poʻipū Rd., Kōloa 96756,* ☎ *808/742–6464 or 800/367–8020,* FAX *808/742–9121,* WEB *www.suite-paradise.com. 130 1- and 2-bedroom condominiums. Restaurant, fans, in-room safes, in-room VCRs, 6 pools, hot tub, 9 tennis courts. AE, D, DC, MC, V.*

$$$ ▦ **Garden Isle Cottages.** The theme of each of these reasonably priced, spacious oceanside accommodations is Hawaiian, and tropical flower gardens surround the cottages for an exotic touch. It's a five-minute walk to the restaurants of nearby Poʻipū. Five of seven units have kitchens with microwaves, ceiling fans, and washers and dryers, so request this when you reserve if it's important to you. Units do not have telephones. There's also a barbecue area. ⊠ *2666 Puʻuholo Rd., Kōloa 96756,* ☎ *808/742–6717 or 800/742–6711,* WEB *www.oceancottages. com. 7 cottages. Fans. No credit cards.*

$$$ ▦ **Kūhiō Shores.** Every unit in this four-story waterfront condo has an ocean view, with large windows and spacious lānai to help you enjoy it whenever you can tear yourself away from the surfing and snorkeling activity right outside. Accommodations are large—a sure sign that individual owners enjoy vacationing here themselves—with tropical-tone rattan furniture and kitchens. ⊠ *5050 Lāwaʻi Beach Rd., Kōloa 96756,* ☎ *808/742–7555, 808/742–1391, or 800/367–8022,* FAX *808/ 742–1559,* WEB *www.r7r.com. 75 1- and 2-bedroom condominium suites. Restaurant, kitchenettes, beach, coin laundry. MC, V.*

$$–$$$ ▦ **Poʻipū Plantation.** Pretty one-acre grounds planted with plumeria, ti, and other tropical foliage surround three two-story cottage-style buildings. Upper-level units have ample decks with ocean views. All units have hardwood floors and vaulted ceilings, and are decorated in light, airy shades of white and pale pink. A full breakfast is served, and the hosts provide beach towels, mats, some children's toys, and free local phone calls. ⊠ *1792 Peʻe Rd., Kōloa 96756,* ☎ *808/742–6757 or 800/ 634–0263,* FAX *808/742–8681,* WEB *www.poipubeach.com. 3 B&B rooms, 9 1- and 2-bedroom cottages. Air-conditioning, fans, in-room VCRs, kitchenettes, hot tub, coin laundry. D, MC, V.*

$$–$$$ ▦ **Sunset Kahili.** Views from the lānai at this five-story ocean-edge building take in great ocean sunsets, and you can catch a glimpse of the spray from Spouting Horn. The hotel is situated on a bluff and built around a circular swimming pool. Privately owned apartments are individually furnished in an island motif. Narrow kitchens are equipped with everything right down to hot pads, and include microwaves and washers and dryers. There's a barbecue area on the grounds. ⊠ *1763 Peʻe Rd., Poʻipū 96756,* ☎ *808/742–7434 or 800/827–6478,* FAX *808/742–6058,* WEB *www.sunsetkahili.com. 24 condominium units. Fans, in-room VCRs, kitchenettes, pool. AE, D, DC, MC, V.*

$$ ▦ **Kauaʻi Cove Cottages.** Three modern cottages sit side by side at the mouth of Waikomo Stream beside an ocean cove that offers super snorkeling. The studios, each with complete kitchen, have an airy tropical decor under cathedral ceilings. Private patios on the ocean side have their own gas grills. There is a $25 cleaning fee for stays of less

than three nights. VCRs are available upon request. ⊠ *2672 Pu'uholo Rd., Po'ipū 96756,* ☎ *808/742–2562 or 800/624–9945,* WEB *www. kauaicove.com. 3 cottages. Kitchenettes, snorkeling. D, MC, V.*

$–$$　🏠 **Kōloa Landing Cottages.** Guests are treated like family here by the helpful owners. Kōloa Landing has five cottages, including a studio that's about a 5-minute walk from a swimming beach. Accommodations sleep two to eight. Open-beam ceilings, fans, and light-color decor keep the interiors cool. Book well in advance for these in-demand, comfortably spacious, but not overly fancy accommodations with kitchens and phones. Barbecue grills are available as well. ⊠ *2704-B Ho'onani Rd., Kōloa 96756,* ☎ *808/742–1470 or 800/779–8773. 5 cottages, 2 rooms. Fans, kitchenettes, coin laundry. No credit cards.*

The West Side

$$$　🏠 **Waimea Plantation Cottages.** Tucked into a coconut grove, these reconstructed sugar-plantation cottages, near the stunning Waimea Canyon and many beautiful beaches, make for a laid-back vacation experience. The one- to five-bedroom cottages are unpretentious to the point of being a bit rough around the edges, but they're spacious and all have porches. Wooden floors, ceiling fans, rattan furniture, and claw-foot bathtubs are mixed with modern kitchens and cable TVs. Barbecue grills, hammocks, porch swings, a gift shop, and museum are on the property. Cottages are steps away from a black-sand beach with equally murky water. ⊠ *9400 Kaumuali'i Hwy. (Box 367), Waimea 96796,* ☎ *808/338–1625 or 800/992–4632,* FAX *808/338–2338,* WEB *www.waimea-plantation.com. 48 cottages. Restaurant, bar, fans, pool, horseshoes, beach. AE, D, DC, MC, V.*

$　🏠 **Kōke'e Lodge.** Outdoors-oriented visitors appreciate Kaua'i's mountain wilderness at this lodge that's a little different from the usual beach-front property one expects on a tropical isle. Twelve rustic cabins have wood-burning stoves (wood is a few dollars extra) to ward off any chill from the mountain air. The Lodge restaurant serves a light breakfast and lunch between the hours of 9 and 3:30 daily. Many residents head for Kōke'e for the weekend, so make your reservations in advance. Advance payment is required. Credit cards are accepted for bookings 10 days in advance. Otherwise, personal checks are preferred. ⊠ *3600 Kōke'e Rd., Mile Marker 15, Kekaha (Box 819, Waimea 96796),* ☎ *808/335–6061. 12 cabins. Restaurant. D, DC, MC, V.*

NIGHTLIFE AND THE ARTS

People on Kaua'i take great pride in their culture and enjoy sharing their unique traditions with those who come to call. As a result, on the Garden Isle you will find more traditional Hawaiiana and less razzmatazz and glitz than on neighboring O'ahu.

Most of the island's dinner and lū'au shows take place within a hotel or resort; major credit cards are accepted. Hotel lounges and restaurant bars offer live music with no cover charge.

Check the local newspaper, the *Garden Island Times,* for listings of weekly happenings. Free publications such as *Kaua'i Gold, This Week on Kaua'i,* and *Kaua'i Magazine* also list entertainment events. You can pick them up at the Hawai'i Visitors Bureau and at Līhu'e Airport.

Bars and Clubs

For the most part, discos never fit into the serenity of Kaua'i, and the bar scene is extremely limited. The major resorts generally host their own live entertainment and happy hours. The drinking age in Hawai'i is 21, and if you look younger than that, you may be asked to show some identification. All bars and clubs that serve alcohol must close at 2 AM, except for those with a cabaret license, which allows them to close at 4 AM.

The following establishments present dance music on a regular basis.

Duke's Barefoot Bar. Contemporary Hawaiian music is performed in the beachside bar on Thursday and Friday, and upstairs a traditional Hawaiian trio plays nightly for diners. ⊠ *Kalapakī Beach, Līhu'e,* ☎ *808/246–9599.* ☉ *Barefoot Bar Thurs. 4–6, Fri. 9–11.*

Hanalei Gourmet. The sleepy north shore comes alive each evening in this small, convivial setting. The emphasis here is on local jazz, rock, and folk music. ⊠ *5-5161 Kūhiō Hwy., Hanalei Center, Hanalei,* ☎ *808/826–2524.* ☉ *Mon.–Sat. 8–10:30, Sun. 4–9.*

Tropics. A sports bar on the weekends, this funky hangout presents live island-style music several nights a week. ⊠ *4-1330 Kūhiō Hwy., at Kauwila St., Kapa'a,* ☎ *808/822–7330.* ☉ *Mon. and Wed.–Sat. 8–11.*

Whalers Brew Pub. In Līhu'e, you can dance to live music (usually reggae or contemporary Hawaiian) on most Friday and Saturday nights in peak season. ⊠ *3132 Ninini Point St., Līhu'e,* ☎ *808/245–2000.* ☉ *Fri. and Sat. from 7 pm in peak season.*

Lū'au

Drums of Paradise Lū'au. More than just music and dance, this hotel lū'au features displays of Hawaiian artwork, as well as a traditional and contemporary menu to suit all tastes and the dances of Polynesia. ⊠ *Hyatt Regency Kaua'i Resort and Spa, 1571 Po'ipū Rd., Po'ipū Beach,* ☎ *808/742–1234.* ☒ *$62.50.* ☉ *Thurs. and Sun. 5:45–9.*

Kaua'i Coconut Beach Resort Lū'au. The music, dance, and food of Polynesia come together at this hotel-based lū'au, regarded by many as the island's best. It takes place in a lovely setting of flaming tiki torches. ⊠ *Coconut Plantation, Kūhiō Hwy., Kapa'a,* ☎ *808/822–3455, ext. 651.* ☒ *$55.* ☉ *Nightly 6–9.*

Pa'ina o Hanalei. The blowing of the conch calls guests to the beach at Hanalei Bay for a Hawaiian feast and "A Show of Splendor by the Sea" with local entertainers. ⊠ *Princeville Hotel, Princeville Resort, 5520 Ka Haku Rd.,* ☎ *808/826–9644.* ☒ *$59.50.* ☉ *Mon., Wed., and Thurs. 5:50 –9.*

Reflections of Paradise. Set at a historic estate-turned-shopping center, this lū'au, catered by Gaylords restaurant, captures the feeling of an old-time family party. Sip mai tais before sampling the buffet line, then relax for a vibrant Polynesian review. ⊠ *3-2087 Kaumuali'i St., Līhu'e,* ☎ *808/821–6895.* ☒ *$52.* ☉ *Mon., Wed., and Fri. 6:30.*

Smith's Tropical Paradise Lū'au. Amid 30 acres of tropical flora and fauna, this lū'au begins with the traditional blowing of the conch shell and *imu* (underground oven) ceremony, followed by cocktails, an island feast, and an international show in the Lagoon Amphitheater. ⊠ *174 Wailua Rd., Kapa'a,* ☎ *808/821–6895.* ☒ *$52.* ☉ *Mon., Wed., and Fri. 5–9:15.*

Tahiti Nui Lū'au. This venerable institution is a welcome change from the standard commercial lū'au. It's smaller (about 40 guests) and put on by a family that really knows how to party. The all-you-can-eat buffet includes kālua pig that has been slow-roasted in an imu, and the show features plenty of dancing, music, and laughs. ⊠ *Kūhiō Hwy., Hanalei,* ☎ *808/826–6277.* ☒ *$40.* ☉ *Wed. 6.*

Music

Very little classical arts activity takes place on laid-back Kaua'i.

Kaua'i Community College Performing Arts Center (✉ 3-1901 Kaumuali'i Hwy., Līhu'e, ☎ 808/245–8311) provides a venue for Hawaiian music and dance as well as visiting performers. Call to find out what's on the bill. The **Kaua'i Concert Association** (☎ 808/245–7464) offers a seasonal program at the Arts Center. The **Līhu'e Public Library** (✉ 4344 Hardy St., Līhu'e, ☎ 808/241–3222) sometimes plays host to storytelling, musical presentations, and arts-and-crafts events.

Theater

The **Kaua'i Community Players** (✉ Līhu'e Parish Hall, 4340 Nāwiliwili Rd., Līhu'e, ☎ 808/245–7700) is a talented local group that presents a variety of plays throughout the year. The **Kaua'i International Theatre** (✉ Kaua'i Village Shopping Center, 4831 Kūhiō Hwy., Kapa'a, ☎ 808/821–1588) presents six shows per season plus other entertainment in a 62-seat, air-conditioned theater.

OUTDOOR ACTIVITIES AND SPORTS

Participant Sports

Biking

Kaua'i Adventure Trek. This 4½-hour bike, hike, and beach adventure follows an old cane road through Grove Farm Plantation, stops for a tour of the island's first sugar mill, then heads for Māhā'ulepū Beach where a picnic lunch is served. Trips are geared to novice and intermediate-level bikers; this is one of the few bike companies to furnish electric bikes for riders who prefer to take the easy way. Vans carry bikers back to Kilohana Plantation, now home to upscale shops and Gaylord's restaurant. ✉ 3-2087 Kaumuali'i Hwy., Līhu'e 96766, ☎ 808/245–3440 or 808/635–8735, WEB www.kauaiadventuretrek.com.

Kaua'i Coasters. You can coast for five hours starting at dawn from the Waimea Canyon Rim. It's a scenic 12 mi—all downhill—with a Continental breakfast included. ✉ Box 3038, Līhu'e 96766, ☎ 808/639–2412.

Outfitters Kaua'i. Ride right out the door to tour Po'ipū on a rented bike or get information on how to do a self-guided tour of Kōke'e State Park and Waimea Canyon. The company also leads coasting tours (under the name Bicycle Downhill, Canyon to Coast) from Waimea Canyon to the island's west-side beaches. ✉ 2827-A Po'ipū Rd., Po'ipū 96756, ☎ 808/742–9667.

Pedal 'n' Paddle. This company rents bicycles for $20 a day. Hourly and weekly rates are also available. ✉ Ching Young Village, Hanalei, ☎ 808/826–9069, WEB www.pedalnpaddle.com.

MOUNTAIN BIKING

Triathletes need to train to conquer the 12-mi Power Line Trail, which begins in the mountains above Wailua in Keāhua Arboretum—you'll see the poles heading across the mountains—and ends mauka of Princeville Resort. You're sure to be covered in red clay mud from head to toe by the time you're halfway into the ride, but you'll have views of Wai'ale'ale that are usually seen only from the air. Be sure your mountain bike is in top condition, take plenty of water and energy bars, and let someone know when and where you are going. If you rent a mountain bike, explain what you've got in mind and heed any advice offered by the experts.

Fitness and Spa Centers

Anara Spa at the Hyatt Regency Kaua'i. Nonguests are welcome to use the spa facilities at this resort in the Po'ipū. For $25 per day you'll have use of the weight room, lap pool, steam room, sauna, and hot tub in the deluxe 25,000-square-ft facility. Spa cuisine is available from 7 to 2 at Kupono Café next door. ⊠ *Hyatt Regency Kaua'i Resort and Spa, 1571 Po'ipū Rd., Po'ipū,* ☎ *808/742–1234.*

Kaua'i Athletic Club. This centrally located facility offers a $12.50 day pass that grants you access to saunas, racquetball, aerobics classes, swimming, cardio-fitness instruction, and a hot tub. ⊠ *4370 Kukui Grove, Līhu'e,* ☎ *808/245–5381.*

Princeville Health Club & Spa. You'll find state-of-the-art equipment here in a workout room surrounded by inspiring views of mountains, sea, and sky; a day pass is $15. A variety of facials and body and massage treatments are available for total relaxation. ⊠ *53-900 Kūhiō Hwy., Princeville,* ☎ *808/826–5030.*

Golf

Kaua'i Lagoons Golf Club. Two Jack Nicklaus–designed par-72 courses adjoin the Kaua'i Marriott Resort and Beach Club. The championship Kiele course challenges golfers of all levels. The links-style Mokihana course promises a satisfying round for everyone. Forty acres of tropical lagoons provide breathtaking views. ⊠ *3351 Ho'olaulea Way, Līhu'e,* ☎ *808/241–6000.* ☒ *Greens fee Kiele $170, Mokihana $120; shared cart and same-day use of practice facility included.*

Kiahuna Plantation Golf Club. On the southern part of the island is this Robert Trent Jones, Jr.–designed 18-hole course. There are equipment rentals, a pro shop, a restaurant, and a bar. ⊠ *2545 Kiahuna Plantation Dr., Kōloa,* ☎ *808/742–9595.* ☒ *Greens fee nonresidents $75, midday and twilight discounts; shared cart included.*

Kukui-o-lono Golf Course. You can play nine holes or a full round here in a peaceful wooded hilltop setting with spectacular views of Kaua'i's eastern shore. ⊠ *854 Pu'u Rd., Kalāheo,* ☎ *808/332–9151.* ☒ *Greens fee $7; cart $6 for 9 holes, club rental $6.*

Po'ipū Bay Resort Golf Course. This 18-hole links-style course has been the site of the PGA Grand Slam for many years. It's next to the Hyatt Regency Kaua'i. ⊠ *2250 'Ainakō St., Po'ipu*

Princeville Resort Makai Course. Kaua'i's best-known golf facility, the Makai Course was designed by Robert Trent Jones, Jr., and includes a pro shop, driving range, practice area, lessons, club rental and storage, and snack bar. This course has been the setting for the LPGA Women's Kemper Open, including the Helene Curtis Pro-Am. ⊠ *Hwy. 56, Princeville,* ☎ *808/826–3580.* ☒ *Greens fee $100 guests, $120 nonguests; shared cart included.*

Princeville Resort Prince Course. This 18-hole, Robert Trent Jones, Jr.–designed course has spectacular ocean and mountain views and is also rated Kaua'i's toughest course. A restaurant and bar are open for breakfast and lunch. ⊠ *Off Hwy. 56, Princeville,* ☎ *808/826–5000.* ☒ *Greens fee $125 guests, $175 nonguests; cart included.*

Puakea Farm Golf Course. Kaua'i's newest course, opened in 1997, is a 10-hole beauty, and made *Sports Illustrated's* list of the top 10 nine-hole courses in the country. ⊠ *4315 Kalepa St., Līhu'e,* ☎ *808/245–8756.* ☒ *Greens fee $45 for 10 holes, $65 for 20 holes; cart included.*

Wailua Municipal Golf Course. This municipal course sits next to the Wailua River and beach and has a pro shop, driving range, and restaurant. Its 18 holes have hosted national tournaments. ⊠ *3-5351 Kūhiō Hwy., Wailua,* ☎ *808/241–6666.* ☒ *Greens fee $25 weekdays, $35 weekends; carts $14.*

Hiking and Camping

Before planning any hike or camping trip on Kaua'i, contact the **Department of Land and Natural Resources** (⊠ State Parks Division, 3060 'Eiwa St., Room 306, Līhu'e 96766, ☎ 808/274–3446) for information on which campsites and trails are open and their condition. For your safety, wear sturdy shoes, bring plenty of water, never hike alone, stay on the trail, and avoid hiking when it's wet and slippery. All hiking trails on Kaua'i are free.

Kaua'i's prize hiking venue is the **Kalalau Trail,** which begins at the western end of Highway 56 and proceeds 11 mi to Kalalau Beach. With hairpin turns, sometimes very muddy conditions, and constant ups and downs, this hike is a true test of endurance and can't be tackled round-trip in one day. For a good taste of it, hike just the first 2 mi to Hanakāpī'ai Beach. For the best trail and weather conditions, hike Kalalau between May and September.

If you plan to hike beyond Hanakāpī'i to Kalalau (☞ Heavenly Northeast *in* Exploring Kaua'i), a camping permit must be obtained from the Department of Land and Natural Resources. Permits must also be obtained to camp at Miloli'i, Koke'e, and Polihale. Permits, which are issued for five nights maximum, are free and can be requested up to a year in advance. These state campsites assess a charge of $10 for those along the Kalalau trail, $5 for other locations.

Kōke'e State Park. The park is a glorious 45-mi network of hiking trails of varying difficulty, all worth the walk. Its acres of native forests, home to many species of birds, are a wonder to behold. The Kukui Trail takes hikers right down the side of Waimea Canyon. Awa'awapuhi Trail leads 4 mi down to a spectacular overlook into the canyons of the north shore. Pleasant, shaded campsites can be reserved through the Parks Department. All hikers should register at Kōke'e Park headquarters, which offers trail maps and information. ⊠ *Kōke'e Rd., 20 mi north of Hwy. 50, Kekaha,* ☎ *808/335–9975.*

Polihale Beach Park. Tent camping is permitted at this westernmost beach in the United States. Three sets of numbered campsites have rest rooms, outdoor showers, picnic tables, and grills. Swimming can be dangerous when the waves are rough. ⊠ *Follow Hwy. 50 to its end on the western shore of Kaua'i,* ☎ *808/274–3446.*

Waimea Canyon State Park. Five tent campsites are hidden along the floor of Waimea Canyon near the Waimea River. You'll find the Kukui Trailhead for hiking in along Waimea Canyon Road. You may want to hike beyond the first campsite to Lonomea Camp, about 6 mi in, where you'll find pit toilets, roofed shelters, and a picnic table. Near Hipalau Camp are two waterfall-fed pools worth hiking to even if you don't camp at the site. ⊠ *Drive 7½ mi north on Waimea Canyon Rd., then hike approximate 6 mi on the Kukui Trail,* ☎ *808/274–3433.*

Horseback Riding

Kaua'i's scenic mountain pastures and shorelines can be explored on escorted rides along panoramic oceanside cliffs and beaches.

CJM Country Stables. This company in Po'ipū charges $65 to $90 for three guided rides: a two-hour ranch ride with ocean scenery, a three-hour hidden-valley beach breakfast ride, and a 3½-hour swim and picnic ride. ☎ *808/742–6096.*

Esprit de Corps. In Kapa'a, Esprit de Corps offers private lessons, pony parties for children, and half-day horse camps, as well as trail rides that range from three-hour jaunts for $99 to eight-hour excursions for $350 that include lunch. Group trail rides require some experience as they allow trotting and cantering. Weddings on horseback can be arranged, and private custom rides for less experienced riders are available. ☎ *808/822–4688.*

Princeville Ranch Stables. Guided horseback tours from this very professional operation take riders into the less-explored reaches of the island. A 90-minute country ride is $55 per person. A scenic three-hour bluff ride is $100 and includes a snack. A four-hour waterfall picnic ride is $110, including lunch. ☎ *808/826–6777.*

Silver Falls Ranch. At this Kīlauea ranch you can take an individual excursion or private lesson, or join a two-hour Hawaiian Discovery ride with refreshments ($78) or a three-hour Silver Falls ride ($105) that includes picnicking by a waterfall and a swim in a secluded freshwater pool. ☎ *808/828–6718.*

Tennis

Kaua'i has 20 lighted public tennis courts and more than 70 private courts at the hotels.

Hanalei Bay Resort (⊠ 5380 Honoiki Rd., Princeville, ☎ 808/826–6522) has eight courts. Guests play free; nonguests pay $6 per hour.

Hyatt Regency Kaua'i (⊠ 1571 Po'ipū Rd., Po'ipū Beach, ☎ 808/742–1234) has four courts, a pro shop, and a tennis pro. The cost is $20 per hour.

Kaua'i Coconut Beach Resort (⊠ Kūhiō Hwy., Kapa'a, ☎ 808/822–3455) offers three courts. Guests play free; nonguests pay $7.

Princeville Tennis Center (⊠ 4080 Lei-o-papa Rd., Princeville, ☎ 808/826–9823) has six courts. The cost is $12 for 90 minutes or as long as the courts are not in demand.

The Tennis Club at the Kaua'i Lagoons (⊠ 3351 Ho'olaulea Way, Līhu'e, ☎ 808/241–6000) has the island's only tennis stadium and seven courts for mere mortals. Two hours of court time cost $20. Private lessons, lessons for two, and a daily clinic are available.

Water Sports

FISHING

For freshwater fishing, head for the bass- and trout-filled streams near Kōke'e and Waimea Canyon. A 7-day visitor license for $10 or a 30-day license for freshwater fishing for $20, must be obtained from the **Department of Land and Natural Resources** (⊠ 3060 'Eiwa St., Līhu'e 96766, ☎ 808/274–3446).

No matter which company you choose for ocean fishing, plan to spend $120 to $150 for a three-quarter day of charter fishing on a shared basis, $85 to $100 for a half day on a shared basis, $600 to $750 for an exclusive three-quarter day, and $450 to $550 for an exclusive half day.

'Anini Fishing Charters (⊠ Box 594, Kīlauea 96754, ☎ 808/828–1285 or 808/639–8415) has a 33-ft sport cruiser, *Sea Breeze V,* that skipper Bob Kutkowski completed himself for sport or bottom-fishing charters.

Sportfishing Kaua'i (⊠ Box 1195, Kōloa 96756, ☎ 808/639–0013) runs 33-ft and 38-ft six-passenger custom sportfishers.

True Blue (⊠ Box 1722, Kalapakī Beach, Līhu'e 96766, ☎ 808/246–6333) offers charters on a roomy 55-ft Delta certified to carry 32, and a Rainbow Runner sailboat that carries 28, but fishing trips are limited to 10 anglers.

KAYAKING

Aloha Canoes and Kayaks. Guided excursions in double-hulled Hawaiian-owned and -operated canoes give novices a chance to try their hand at paddling, while an experienced steersman makes sure you reach your intended destination. The guide takes canoers up a jungle river to a mountain pool on three- and three-and-a-half-hour adventures.

✉ *3366 Wa'apa Rd., Līhu'e 96766,* ☎ *808/246–6804 or 877/473–5446,* WEB *www.hawaiikayaks.com.* ⛵ *$70, with lunch $82.*

Island Adventures. Twice a day guides take paddlers up Hulei'a River in the heart of a National Wildlife Refuge. After a snack, the two-and-a-half-hour excursions ends with a hike and van transportation back to civilization. ✉ *Box 3370, Līhu'e 96766,* ☎ *808/245–9662 or 808/639–9333.* ⛵ *$52.*

Kayak Kaua'i. In addition to renting kayaks to individuals, this outfit also offers half- and full-day guided kayak tours along the Nā Pali Coast and up the Hanalei and Wailua rivers with snorkeling included in the Hanalei excursion. ✉ *Box 508, Hanalei 96714,* ☎ *808/826–9844 or 800/437–3507.* ⛵ *$50–$160.*

Outfitters Kaua'i. This company offers guided kayak excursions for novices as well as longer Nā Pali Coast and jungle-stream paddles. Experienced paddlers can rent a kayak, grab a plastic-coated map, and discover a romantic waterfall on their own. ✉ *2827-A Po'ipū Rd., Po'ipū 96756,* ☎ *808/742–9667 or 888/742–9887.* ⛵ *Guided tour $72–$84, kayak rentals $35–$45.*

Paradise Outdoor Adventures. Paradise provides topographical maps, motorboat and kayak rentals, and guided excursions. A half-day guided Wailua Jungle-River Safari includes a hike to a waterfall and lunch for $85. ✉ *1-561 Kūhiō Hwy., Kapa'a 96746,* ☎ *808/822–1112 or 877/422–6287.* ⛵ *2-person kayak $50 per day.*

Wailua River Kayak Adventures. Rent a kayak that holds two adults and two small children, bring your own picnic lunch, and follow the map on your own adventure. You can also book a guided tour to Wailua's Secret Falls. This is the most convenient place to get a kayak for use on the river. ✉ *411 Kaholalele St., Kūhiō Hwy., Kapa'a 96746,* ☎ *808/822–5795 or 808/639–6332.* ⛵ *Guided tour $75, kayak rentals $25–$50.*

SCUBA DIVING

Dive Kaua'i Scuba Center. This shop offers an introductory half-day scuba excursion for $98. Two-tank shore dives for certified divers cost $98, a refresher course is $83, and a five-day PADI (scuba-diving certification) course is $395. A boat dive with two tanks costs $115, including equipment. ✉ *976 Kūhiō Hwy., No. C, Kapa'a 96746,* ☎ *808/822–0452 or 800/828–3483.*

Ocean Odyssey. Ocean Odyssey will arrange lessons, shore dives, night dives, and even underwater videotaping for you. Packages range from a simple one-tank shore dive starting at $65 for certified divers to three- to five-day PADI certification courses. ✉ *Box 869, 'Ele'ele 96705,* ☎ *808/245–8681.*

Seasport Divers. This full-service PADI, NAUI, and SSI training facility has a full range of dive options, from beginner lessons and introductory dives to private charters. It also offers equipment rental and repair service. ✉ *2827 Po'ipū Rd., Kōloa 96756,* ☎ *808/742–9303 or 800/685–5889.*

SNORKELING

The following experts operate entertaining and well-run snorkeling cruises. Several companies depart from the north shore for snorkeling trips along the scenic Nā Pali Coast. Schedules vary with the weather. Call in advance for details.

Blue Water Sailing (☎ *808/828–1142*) ferries snorkelers to south-shore sites on a 12-passenger, 42-ft luxury Pearson sailing yacht, the *Lady Leanne II*. A fun excursion for all ages and with the only mono-hull sailing charter on Kaua'i, this four-hour snorkeling voyage includes gear, instruction, swimming, fishing, a gourmet picnic lunch, snacks, and beverages. In winter you might catch glimpses of whales. Trips leave from Port Allen mid-September through mid-May and from other ports during the rest of the year. The cost is $115. A two-hour sunset sail that carries 15 is $60. A 42-ft power boat, *Blue Water Express,* also cruises Kaua'i's waters from Port Allen.

Captain Andy's Sailing Adventures (☎ 808/335–6833) takes up to 49 passengers on its 55-ft catamaran *Spirit of Kaua'i;* cruises depart from Port Allen and Kukui'ula Harbor in Po'ipū. The rate for the four-hour morning snorkel-picnic tour is $85, including gear and lunch. Whale-watching excursions are run during the winter months. Seasonal Nā Pali Coast tours are offered that include Continental breakfast, lunch, snorkeling gear, and instruction for $109.

Catamaran Kahanu (☎ 808/335–3577) offers a four-and-a-half-hour Nā Pali Coast cruise on a 36-ft power catamaran. The trip includes snorkeling, whale- or dolphin-watching, lunch, and a bit of Hawaiian history and culture presented by the Hawaiian owners-operators. The price is $105 for adults.

Hanalei Sea Tours (☎ 808/826–7254 or 800/733–7997) runs marine-ecology whale-watching tours during the winter and year-round snorkeling tours on Power Cats and rigid-hull inflatable rafts. Narrated sightseeing trips range from $60 to $130 and take from two hours to a full day. Longer cruises include snorkeling gear, Continental breakfast, lunch, and cold drinks.

Hanalei Watersports (☎ 808/826–7509) provides scuba and surfing lessons in addition to guided kayak and snorkel tours. Accommodating guides can craft a full day's land-and-sea adventure to suit your every whim. There's also an idyllic $85 sunset cruise from the Princeville Resort aboard a Hawaiian outrigger canoe equipped with a traditional sail and a paddling canoe. Prices run the gamut.

HoloHolo Charters (☎ 808/335–0815 or 800/848–6130) has a deluxe snorkel cruise that takes in the Nā Pali Coast and also anchors near the private island of Ni'ihau. Continental breakfast and a deluxe lunch buffet are served on the 61-ft power catamaran during the seven-hour excursion. Wine, beer, soda, and juice are included in the $156 fee. Three other shorter (and less expensive) excursions are offered on the 48-ft sailing catamaran *Leila* and the 61-ft high-speed power cat *HoloHolo.*

Nā Pali EcoAdventures (☎ 808/826–6804 or 800/659–6804) takes groups on five-hour snorkeling and snack excursions, four-hour sightseeing trips along the north shore, and two-hour winter whale-watch cruises in power catamarans that hold 26 or 35 people. Rates are $60 and up.

SURFING AND WINDSURFING

'Anini Beach Windsurfing (⊠ 'Anini Beach, ☎ 808/826–9463) stands ready to help you get started as a windsurfer. An introductory group lesson and certification lesson include equipment; each of three one-hour sessions is $75. Private lessons are available, and sailboard rentals are $25 per hour or $65 per day.

At **Margo Oberg Surfing Lessons** (⊠ Nukumoi Surf Shop, Po'ipū Beach, next to Brennecke's Beach Broiler, ☎ 808/742–8019) seven-time world surfing champion Margo Oberg furnishes surfboards, and she and her staff give dry-land and wave instruction to beginning surfers. Lessons are $50 for one-and-a-half hours.

SHOPPING

Kaua'i may not have the myriad shopping alternatives of its cosmopolitan neighbor, O'ahu, but what it does have is character. Along with a few major shopping malls, Kaua'i has some of the most delightful mom-and-pop shops and family-run boutiques imaginable.

Kaua'i also offers one-of-a-kind options for souvenirs. For instance, the famous shell jewelry from nearby Ni'ihau is sometimes sold on Kaua'i for less than it is on other islands. The Garden Isle is also known for its regular outdoor markets where you can find bargain prices on various souvenirs and produce and get a chance to mingle with island residents.

Kaua'i's major shopping centers are open daily from 9 or 10 to 5, although some stay open until 9. Stores are basically clustered around the major resort areas and Līhu'e.

Department Stores

Mainland-style department stores reached Kaua'i years ago, carrying an all-inclusive selection of moderately priced merchandise. **Big Kmart** (⊠ Kukui Grove Center, 3-2600 Kaumuali'i Hwy., Līhu'e, ☎ 808/245–7742) has groceries and just about anything you could want for your trip, from film to flip-flops. **Sears** (⊠ Kukui Grove Center, 3-2600 Kaumuali'i Hwy., Līhu'e, ☎ 808/246–8301) carries merchandise for the home plus a nice line of casual clothes. **Wal-Mart** (⊠ 3-3300 Kūhiō Hwy., Līhu'e, ☎ 808/246–1599) has some Hawaiian-print tropical-style clothing.

Shopping Centers

Ching Young Village. In the heart of Hanalei, Ching Young draws people to its Village Variety Store with cheap prices on beach towels, macadamia nuts, film and processing, wet suits—you name it. There's also a well-stocked Hanalei Natural Foods store; a few steps away is Evolve Love Artists Gallery, where you can find work by local artisans. ⊠ *Kūhiō Hwy., Hanalei.*

Coconut Marketplace. This is part of a larger complex of resort hotels and restaurants; more than 70 shops sell everything from snacks and slippers to scrimshaw. ⊠ *4-484 Kūhiō Hwy., Kapa'a.*

'Ele'ele Shopping Center. Kaua'i's west side has a scattering of stores, including those at this no-frills shopping center where several tour-boat companies have offices. It's a good place to rub elbows with local folk or to grab a quick bite to eat at the casual Grinds restaurant. ⊠ *Hwy. 50 near Hanapēpē.*

Hanalei Center. The old Hanalei School, a building listed on the Historic Register, has been refurbished and rented out to boutiques and restaurants. After you dig through '40s and '50s vintage clothing and memorabilia in the Yellow Fish Trading Company or search for that unusual gift at Sand People, you can grab a shave ice (the Hawaiian version of a snow cone) and relax on the front deck or lawn or go Italian for lunch at a charming courtyard restaurant called Café Luna. ⊠ *5-5161 Kūhiō Hwy., Hanalei,* ☎ 808/826–7677.

Kaua'i Village Shopping Center. In this Kapa'a shopping village the buildings are built in the style of 19th-century plantation towns. ABC Discount Store sells sundries, Safeway sells groceries and alcoholic beverages, Wyland Gallery sells island art, and Kaua'i One-Hour Photo provides speedy film processing. Lovers of Hawaiian culture should check out Kaua'i Heritage Center, which sponsors cultural workshops and dance and displays authentic crafts that are also for sale. ⊠ *4-831 Kūhiō Hwy., Po'ipū Beach.*

Kilohana Plantation. A unique collection of plantation-style shops and galleries is housed on both levels of the main house as well as in quaint guest cottages. Here you'll find an emphasis on the handcrafted goods of the islands; for example, the Artisans Room, in the plantation's guest bedroom, sells paintings by Rosalie Rupp Prussing, carvings by Russ

Graff, and collages by Cece Rodriguez, as well as limited-edition prints, ceramics, and glass. The Hawaiian Collection Room, in the restored cloak room, focuses on unusual crafts, with Ni'ihau shell leis and scrimshaw. ⊠ *3-2087 Kaumuali'i Hwy., 1 mi west of Līhu'e.*

Kinipopo Shopping Village. On Kūhiō Highway in Kapa'a, across from Wailua Family Restaurant, is this tropical-garden setting for casual shopping. Here you'll find the Goldsmith's Gallery, which sells handcrafted Hawaiian-style gold jewelry, and Tin Can Mailman bookstore, filled with old collectible and new Hawaiian books and paper ephemera. You can also rent water skis and beach paraphernalia here at Kaua'i Water Ski & Surf Co. ⊠ *4-356 Kūhiō Hwy., Kapa'a.*

Kong Lung Center. The center houses Kong Lung Co., a gift shop filled with special treasures from around the world, and around its grassy courtyard are a couple of shops, including Island Soap and Candle Works and Plantation Pottery, where you can view the production process. Kīlauea Bakery, also in the courtyard, is legendary for pizza and bread sticks. ⊠ *2490 Keneke St., Kīlauea.*

Kukui Grove Center. This is Kaua'i's largest assemblage of shops. Besides the island's major department stores, it offers a Longs Drugs for personal needs and Star Market for groceries. You'll find island-inspired garb at Hawaiian Islands Creations, Kaua'i-made gifts at Kaua'i Products Store, and athletic footwear at Foot Locker. ⊠ *3-2600 Kaumuali'i Hwy. on Hwy. 50, just west of Līhu'e.*

Old Kōloa Road. The main street of Old Kōloa isn't really a shopping center, but it concentrates several boutiques and eateries in one handy location. Favorites are Kōloa Ice House and Deli, which sells shave-ice fantasies laced with tropical syrups; Kōloa Fish Market, for a take-out taste of *poke* (chopped and pickled raw fish) or sashimi; and Progressive Expressions, which offers surfing and windsurfing accessories, swimwear, and beachwear.

Po'ipū Shopping Village. Catering mainly to guests in nearby hotels and condos, the two dozen shops here sell resort wear, gifts, souvenirs, sundries, jewelry, and art, and there are a half dozen restaurants as well. The upscale Black Pearl Kaua'i and Hale Manu, with "gifts for the spirited," are particularly appealing. ⊠ *2360 Kiahuna Plantation Dr., Po'ipū Beach.*

Princeville Shopping Center. This is an upscale little gathering of such trendy shops as Kaua'i Kite and Hobby Shop, Pretty Woman, and JM's Jewels. If you're vacationing in a nearby condo and want to shop for dinner, you'll also find a Foodland, where you can pick up not only dinner but a bottle of wine to sip at sunset. ⊠ *5-4280 Kūhiō Hwy., Princeville.*

Waimea Canyon Plaza. The little town of Kekaha is proud of its tidy complex of shops selling local foods, souvenirs, and gifts. ⊠ *Kōke'e Rd. at Hwy. 50, Kekaha.*

Waipouli Town Center. On the east coast of the island in Kapa'a you'll find a modest collection of 10 shops where you can buy a T-shirt at Waipouli Variety and then grab a good-value plate lunch or other local food at Waipouli Restaurant. ⊠ *4-901 Kūhiō Hwy., Kapa'a.*

Specialty Stores

Books

Borders Books & Music. A healthy section of books focused on Hawai'i are are offered, plus plenty of magazines for beach reading. ⊠ *Kukui Grove Shopping Center, 4303 Nāwiliwili Rd., Līhu'e,* ☎ *808/246–0862.*

Kaua'i Museum. The gift shop at the museum sells some fascinating books, maps, and prints. ⊠ *4428 Rice St., Līhu'e,* ☎ *808/245–6931.*

Clothing

Crazy Shirts. This chain has a wide variety of shirts, from classy to crazy designs. It's a good place for active wear. ⊠ *Po'ipū Shopping Village, 2360 Kiahuna Plantation Dr., Po'ipū Beach,* ☎ *808/742–9000;* ⊠ *Anchor Cove, 3416 Rice St., Līhu'e,* ☎ *808/245–7073;* ⊠ *Kaua'i Village Shopping Center, 4-831 Kūhiō Hwy., Kapa'a,* ☎ *808/823–6761;* ⊠ *5356 Kōloa Rd., Kōloa,* ☎ *808/742–7161.*

Liberty House. You can purchase high-quality designer labels as well as nice resort wear at this island chain. ⊠ *Kukui Grove Center, 3-2600 Kaumuali'i Hwy., Līhu'e,* ☎ *808/245–7751.*

M. Miura Store. M. Miura carries a great assortment of clothes for the outdoor fanatic, including tank tops, visors, swimwear, and Kaua'i-style T-shirts. ⊠ *4-1419 Kūhiō Hwy., Kapa'a,* ☎ *808/822–4401.*

Paradise Sportswear. This is the retail outlet of the folks who invented Kaua'i's popular "red dirt" shirts, which are dyed and printed with the characteristic local soil. Do let the salesperson tell you the charming story behind these shirts. Sizes from infants up to 5X are available. ⊠ *4350 Waialo Rd., Port Allen,* ☎ *808/335–5670.*

ISLAND WEAR

Hilo Hattie Fashion Factory. This is the big name in inexpensive aloha wear for tourists throughout the Islands. You can visit the factory, a mile from Līhu'e Airport, to pick up cool, comfortable aloha shirts and mu'umu'u in bright floral prints, as well as other souvenirs. ⊠ *3252 Kūhiō Hwy., Līhu'e,* ☎ *808/245–3404.*

Tropical Shirts. Come here for the beautiful clothing embroidered by local artists. There is also a selection of the island's unique "red dirt" T-shirts. ⊠ *Po'ipū Shopping Village, 2360 Kiahuna Plantation Dr., Po'ipū Beach,* ☎ *808/742–6691.*

Flowers

Kaua'i Tropicals. You can have this company ship heliconia, anthuriums, ginger, and other tropicals directly from the flower farm in 5-ft boxes. ⊠ *3870 Waha Rd., Kalāheo 96741,* ☎ *808/332–9071 or 800/303–4385.*

Food

You may not be able to resist Kaua'i's own yummy specialties while on the island. The **Kaua'i Products Council** (⊠ Box 3660, Līhu'e 96788, ☎ 808/823–8714) will tell you the best places to find Kaua'i Kookies, taro chips, Kaua'i boiled peanuts, salad dressings, and jams and jellies made from locally grown fruit, as well as nonfood items handcrafted on the island.

Kaua'i now produces more coffee than any other island in the state, and the local product, somewhat milder than the Big Island's better-known Kona coffee, makes a worthy souvenir. Coffee can be purchased at the source, **Kaua'i Coffee Visitor Center and Museum** (⊠ 870 Halawili Rd., off Hwy. 50, west of Kalāheo, ☎ 808/335–0813 or 800/545–8605).

Near Līhu'e you can buy fresh pineapple, sugarcane, ginger, coconuts, local jams, jellies, and honey, plus Kaua'i-grown papayas, bananas, and mangos in season—all at **Kaua'i Fruit and Flower Company** (⊠ 3-4684 Kūhiō Hwy., ☎ 808/245–1814). Special gift packs are available, inspected and certified for shipment out of the state.

Don't forget to try a big scoop of **Lappert's Ice Cream** (⊠ 1-3555 Kaumuali'i Hwy., Hanapēpē, ☎ 808/335–6121; ⊠ Coconut Marketplace, 4-484 Kūhiō Hwy., Kapa'a, ☎ 808/822–0744; ⊠ 5242 Kōloa Rd., Kōloa, ☎ 808/742–1272; ⊠ Princeville Shopping Center, 5-4280 Kūhiō Hwy., Princeville, ☎ 808/826–7393), created by Walter Lappert in Hanapēpē in 1983 and now a favorite all over Hawai'i. The

Lappert shops also sell locally produced gourmet coffees, which are easier to ship home than the ice cream.

Some of the best prices on Hawai'i's famous macadamia nuts are available at **Star Market** (⊠ Kukui Grove Center, 3-2600 Kaumuali'i Hwy., Līhu'e, ☎ 808/245–7777).

Gifts

Hilo Hattie Fashion Factory. This is the place where you can buy all the hats, baskets, inexpensive shell jewelry, rubber slippers, golf towels, and other trinkets you need to carry home to friends and family. The location is perfect for a last-minute stop en route to Līhu'e Airport. ⊠ *3252 Kūhiō Hwy., Līhu'e,* ☎ *808/245–3404.*

Kong Lung Co. This elegant gift shop, sometimes called the Gump's of Kaua'i, combines clothing, glassware, books, and artwork. It is housed in a beautiful 1892 stone structure on the way to the lighthouse in out-of-the-way Kīlauea. Thriftier souls might find the "gently used and new fashions" upstairs at Reinventions to their liking. ⊠ *2490 Keneke St., Kīlauea,* ☎ *808/828–1822.*

Lee Sands' Eelskin. Eelskin is popular on the Islands, and you can buy it wholesale here at this spot in the Hawaiian Trading Post. It's an unusual store, with other skin lines such as sea snake, chicken feet, and frog. A lizard card case is available for about $12. ⊠ *Hwy. 50 at Kōloa Rd., Lāwa'i,* ☎ *808/332–7404.*

Village Variety Store. How about a fun beach towel for the folks back home? That's just one of the gifts you can find here, along with shell leis, Kaua'i T-shirts, macadamia nuts, and other great souvenirs at low prices. ⊠ *Ching Young Village, Kūhiō Hwy., Hanalei,* ☎ *808/826–6077.*

Hawaiian Arts and Crafts

Art Shop. This intimate gallery in Līhu'e sells original oils, photos, and sculptures. ⊠ *3196 'Akahi St., Līhu'e,* ☎ *808/245–3810.*

Kahn Galleries. You can purchase the works of many local artists—including seascapes by George Sumner and Roy Tabora—at this gallery's locations. ⊠ *Coconut Marketplace, 4-484 Kūhiō Hwy., Kapa'a,* ☎ *808/822–3636;* ⊠ *Kilohana Plantation, 3-2087 Kaumuali'i Hwy., Līhu'e,* ☎ *808/246–4454;* ⊠ *Kaua'i Village Shopping Center, 4-831 Kūhiō Hwy., Kapa'a,* ☎ *808/822–4277;* ⊠ *Old Koloa Town,* ☎ *808/742–2277;* ⊠ *Hanalei Center, 5-5161 Kūhiō Hwy., Hanalei,* ☎ *808/826–6677.*

Kapaia Stitchery. Featured here are quilting and other fabric arts, plus kits for trying your own hand at various crafts; the kits are great gifts for crafters. ⊠ *Kūhiō Hwy. in a red building ½ mi north of Līhu'e,* ☎ *808/245–2281.*

Kaua'i Heritage Center. Authentic reproductions of old (and new) Hawaiian crafts by Kaua'i artisans are displayed here. Sales of feather hatbands, nose flutes, *konane* game boards and playing pieces (konane is a Hawaiian game similar to checkers), calabashes, and woven lau hala hats and pocketbooks help to support the center's cultural workshops and programs, which sometimes take place in the courtyard by the clock tower. ⊠ *Kaua'i Village, 4-831 Kūhiō Hwy., No. 838, Kapa'a,* ☎ *808/821–2070.*

Kaua'i Products Store. Every seed lei, every finely crafted koa-wood box, every pair of tropical-flower earrings in this boutique is handcrafted on Kaua'i. ⊠ *Kukui Grove Center, 3-2600 Kaumuali'i Hwy., Līhu'e,* ☎ *808/246–6753.*

Wyland Galleries. This gallery showcases the work of Wyland, a famed artist of marine life. You can buy his original works, lithographs, prints, and sculptures, plus pieces by other island artists. Wyland is known for his massive wall murals, and you can see an example of his work on Kūhiō Highway, on the side of a building fronting Kaua'i Village. ⊠ *Kaua'i Village, 4-831 Kūhiō Hwy., Kapa'a,* ☎ *808/822–9855; Po'ipū Shopping Village, 2360 Kiahuna Plantation Dr., Po'ipū Beach,* ☎ *808/742–6030.*

Ye Olde Ship Store & Port of Kaua'i. Scrimshaw-decorated pocket and army knives, boxes, and other gift items are available at this store in the Coconut Marketplace. The shop carries the work of nearly 40 scrimshaw artists and sponsors an annual contest celebrating the art form. ⊠ *Coconut Marketplace, 4-484 Kūhiō Hwy., Kapa'a,* ☎ *808/ 822–1401.*

Jewelry

Jim Saylor Jewelers. A good selection of gems from around the world is showcased here with black pearls, diamonds, and unique settings. Jim Saylor has been designing these pretty keepsakes for more than 20 years on Kaua'i. ⊠ *1318 Kūhiō Hwy., Kapa'a,* ☎ *808/822–3591.*

Kaua'i Gold. A wonderful selection of rare Ni'ihau shell leis ranging from $20 to $200 and up is available here. Take time to ask about these remarkable necklaces before you buy; you'll appreciate the craftsmanship, understand the sometimes high prices, and learn to care for and preserve their fragile beauty. The store also has a selection of 14-karat gold jewelry. ⊠ *Coconut Marketplace, 4-484 Kūhiō Hwy., Kapa'a,* ☎ *808/822–9361.*

Remember Kaua'i. Pick up a memento of your trip in the form of jewelry, Ni'ihau shell necklaces, or other gift items here. They also run a booth at Po'ipū Spouting Horn. ⊠ *Radisson Kaua'i Beach Hotel, 4331 Kaua'i Beach Dr., Līhu'e,* ☎ *808/639–9622.*

KAUA'I A TO Z

To research prices, get advice from other travelers, and book travel arrangements, visit www.fodors.com.

AIR TRAVEL

Several short daily flights can take you from Honolulu to Kaua'i, and there is limited service from Los Angeles and San Francisco.

CARRIERS

Two main carriers offer daily round-trip flights from Honolulu International Airport to Līhu'e Airport. The rates go up and down depending on which airline is trying to outdo the other, ranging from about $70 to $125 one-way. It's a 30- to 40-minute flight. Aloha Airlines offers more than 20 round-trip flights a day between Honolulu and Līhu'e. Hawaiian Airlines has 14 round-trip flights. United Airlines has a daily direct flight from Los Angeles and San Francisco to Līhu'e Airport.

➤ AIRLINES & CONTACTS: **Aloha Airlines** (☎ 808/245–3691 or 800/ 367–5250). **Hawaiian Airlines** (☎ 808/838–1555 or 800/367–5320). **United Airlines** (☎ 800/241–6522).

AIRPORTS

The Līhu'e Airport is 3 mi east of the town of Līhu'e and handles most of the air traffic in and out of Kaua'i. Once you arrive, if you have any immediate questions, stop by the Līhu'e Airport Visitor Information Center, outside each baggage-claim area.

North of Līhu'e is Princeville Airport, a tiny strip in the middle of rolling ranch lands and sugarcane fields today used primarily by private planes. Princeville Airport is just a five-minute drive from the Princeville development area, which is home to condos and a luxurious accommodation called the Princeville Hotel. The airport is also about a 10-minute drive from the shops and accommodations of sleepy Hanalei.

➤ AIRPORT INFORMATION: **Līhu`e Airport** (☎ 808/246–1400; 808/246–1440 for Visitor Information Center). **Princeville Airport** (☎ 808/826–3040).

AIRPORT TRANSFERS

Līhu`e Airport is a mere five-minute drive from the town of Līhu`e. If you're staying in Wailua or Kapa`a, your driving time from Līhu`e is 15 minutes, and to Princeville and Hanalei it takes about 45 minutes. If you're staying in Hanalei, flying into Princeville Airport can save you some driving time.

To the south, it's a 30-minute drive from Līhu`e to Po`ipū, the major resort area. To Waimea it takes one hour, and if you choose the rustic accommodations in the hills of Kōke`e, allow a good hour and a half of driving time from Līhu`e.

Check with your hotel or condo to see if it offers free shuttle service from the airport.

Car-rental companies have offices at both airports. They'll also provide you with driving directions to your hotel or condo.

For luxurious transportation between the airport and your accommodations, contact Custom Limousine Service. Rates are $73.50 per hour, with a two-hour minimum. North Shore Limousine can pick you up at Princeville Airport.

Taxi fares around the island are $2 at the meter drop plus $2 per mile. That means a taxicab from Līhu`e Airport to Līhu`e town runs about $6 and to Po`ipū about $32, excluding tip. Akiko's Taxi offers its services from the east side of the island. Po`ipū Taxi will take you to Līhue` and Po`ipū. Scotty Taxi provides quick service around the airport and Līhu`e. From the Princeville Airport to Hanalei, you'll pay about $14 when you ride with the North Shore Cab Company, which serves only the northeast portion of the island.

➤ TAXIS & SHUTTLES: **Akiko's Taxi** (☎ 808/822–7588). **Custom Limousine Service** (☎ 808/246–6318). **North Shore Cab Company** (☎ 808/826–6189). **North Shore Limousine** (☎ 808/826–6189). **Po`ipū Taxi** (☎ 808/639–2042 or 808/639–2044). **Scotty Taxi** (☎ 808/245–7888).

BIKE TRAVEL

A two-wheeler is an exciting way to cruise around the Garden Isle. Kaua`i's country roads are generally uncrowded, so you can ride along at your own pace and enjoy the views. This is a safe island to explore by bicycle, as long as you exercise caution on the busier thoroughfares. Guests can rent bikes from the activities desks of certain hotels around the island. Check with your concierge or front desk.

BUS TRAVEL

Excursion buses take visitors to such attractions as the Fern Grotto, Waimea Canyon, Spouting Horn, Ft. Elisabeth, `Ōpaeka`a Falls, and Menehune Fishpond.

CAR RENTAL

Unless you plan to do all of your sightseeing as part of guided van tours, you will want a rental car on Kaua`i. The vast beauty of the island begs to be explored, and its attractions are sprinkled from one end to the other. Reserve your vehicle in advance, especially during the peak seasons of summer, the Christmas holidays, and February.

Right across from the baggage-claim area at Līhu`e Airport you'll find several rental-car firms, as well as vans that will shuttle you to offices nearby. Rental companies also have desks at Princeville Airport. Several lesser-known and local companies offer slightly lower rates. Daily prices for a car from the major-name companies begin at $30, unless you rate a discount through AAA, AARP, or by other means. A fly-drive deal can sometimes reduce that cost, and many hotels and even some condos offer packages that include rental cars. There is a $3 daily surcharge on all rentals.

Several companies operate reservation desks at the major hotels on the island. Booking a rental car at a hotel desk on the spur of the moment is generally more expensive than reserving it from the airport in advance.

Alamo, Avis, Budget, Dollar, Hertz, and National have offices at the Līhu'e Airport. Alamo also has offices at the Princeville Airport and at the Hyatt Regency Po'ipu. Hertz maintains an office at the Kaua'i Marriott Resort.

You can get some good deals on a car if you book with one of Kaua'i's budget or used-car rental companies. These include the reliable West-side Enterprises, which rents cars and jeeps. It keeps its vehicles in good shape and offers free delivery and pickup of your car at your hotel or condo in Po'ipū.

➤ AGENCIES: **Alamo** (☎ 800/462–5266). **Avis** (☎ 800/831–8000; 808/ 742–1627 at the Hyatt Regency). **Budget** (☎ 800/527–0700). **Dollar** (☎ 800/342–7398; 800/800–4000 from outside HI). **Hertz** (☎ 800/ 654–3011). **National** (☎ 800/227–7368). **Westside Enterprises** (☎ 808/332–8644).

CAR TRAVEL

Although Kaua'i is relatively small, its sights reach from one end of the island to the other. You can walk to the stores and restaurants in your resort area, but the important attractions of the island are generally not within walking distance of each other. As a result, you'll probably want to rent a car, unless you plan to do all your sightseeing with tour companies.

It's easy to get around on Kaua'i, for it has one major road that almost encircles the island. Your rental-car company will supply you with a map with enlargements of each area of the island. The traffic on Kaua'i is pretty light most of the time, except in the Līhu'e and Kapa'a areas during rush hour (6:30 to 8:30 AM and 3:30 to 5:30 PM). Major attractions are indicated by a Hawaiian-warrior marker on the side of the road.

Although Kaua'i looks like paradise, it has its fair share of crime. Lock your car wherever you park it. Don't leave valuables in the car, and pay attention to parking signs, particularly in Līhu'e.

One doesn't see many limousines cruising the country roads of Kaua'i, but if the idea intrigues you, contact Custom Limousine Service. Among its options are airport service, touring, wedding packages, lei greetings, and complete ground handling. North Shore Limousine specializes in service in the Hanalei and Princeville areas.

CRUISE TRAVEL

A romantic way to visit Kaua'i for a short time is to book passage on an interisland cruise ship. The massive white "love boat," the S.S. *Independence,* homeported on Maui, and the M.S. *Patriot,* based in Honolulu, depart each Saturday night and stop at the other four main Hawaiian islands. At each port of call you may get off the ship for sightseeing and shore excursions. At Kaua'i, the ships dock at Nāwiliwili on the southeast coast. Optional extension packages allow you to add a hotel stay before or after the cruise in the port of your choice. American Hawai'i Cruises has been presenting these successful seven-day excursions for years.

> Cruise Information: **American Hawai'i Cruises** (⊠ Robin St. Wharf, 1380 Port of New Orleans Pl., New Orleans, LA 70130-1890, ☎ 800/765–7000).

EMERGENCIES

For police, ambulance, or fire department in case of any emergency, dial **911.**

The Kaua'i Medical Clinic (KMC) has a staff with 32 different specialties, so it can handle all medical problems. It has lab and X-ray facilities, physical therapy, optometry, and emergency rooms. The main clinic is in Līhu'e. Other KMC clinics are in Kīlauea, Kukui Grove, 'Ele'ele, Kōloa, and Kapa'a.

Except for Long's Drugs, which often stays open until 9, most pharmacies close about 5 PM on Kaua'i. The Kaua'i Medical Clinic has a well-stocked pharmacy at its main clinic.

> Doctors: **Kaua'i Medical Clinic** (⊠ 3420-B Kūhiō Hwy., Līhu'e, ☎ 808/245–1500; 808/245–2471 for pharmacy, ☎ 808/245–1831 for 24-hr on-call physicians; ⊠ North Shore Clinic, Kīlauea, ☎ 808/828–1418; ⊠ Kukui Grove, ☎ 808/246–0051; ⊠ 'Ele'ele, ☎ 808/335–0499; ⊠ Kōloa, ☎ 808/742–1621; ⊠ Kapa'a, ☎ 808/822–3431).

> Hospitals: **Kaua'i Veterans Memorial Hospital** (⊠ 4643 Waimea Canyon Dr., Waimea, ☎ 808/338–9431). **Wilcox Memorial Hospital** (⊠ 3420 Kūhiō Hwy., Līhu'e, ☎ 808/245–1100).

> Pharmacies: **Long's Drugs** (⊠ Kukui Grove Center, Hwy. 50, Līhu'e, ☎ 808/245–8871). **Shoreview Pharmacy** (⊠ 4-1177 Kūhiō Hwy., Suite 113, Kapa'a, ☎ 808/822–1447). **Westside Pharmacy** (⊠ 1-3845 Kaumuali'i Hwy., Hanapēpē, ☎ 808/335–5342).

LODGING

B&BS

Two bed-and-breakfast reservation services are based in Kaua'i. Bed and Breakfast Kaua'i has been in operation in Princeville for many years. Bed and Breakfast Hawai'i can help you find the right home away from home to suit your needs.

Island wide reservations services, such as Hawaiian Islands Bed and Breakfasts and Vacation Rentals, book bed-and-breakfast rooms and cottages on all Hawaiian islands. All Islands Bed and Breakfast is a longtime professional service on O'ahu. Bed and Breakfast Honolulu advertises homestays and studios and helps with rental cars.

> Reservation Services: **All Islands Bed and Breakfast** (⊠ 463 'Iliwahī Loop, Kailua 96734, ☎ 808/263–2342 or 800/542–0344, FAX 808/263–0308, WEB home.hawaii.rr.com/allislands). **Bed and Breakfast Hawai'i** (⊠ Box 449, Kapa'a 96746, ☎ 808/822–7771 or 800/733–1632, FAX 808/822–2723, WEB www.bandb-hawaii.com). **Bed and Breakfast Honolulu** (⊠ 3242 Kā'ohinani Dr., Honolulu 96817, ☎ 808/595–7533 or 800/288–4666, FAX 808/595–2030, WEB www.hawaiibnb.com). **Bed and Breakfast Kaua'i** (⊠ 105 Melia St., Kapa'a 96746, ☎ 808/822–1177 or 800/822–1176, FAX 808/822–5757, WEB www.bnb-kauai.com). **Hawaiian Islands Bed and Breakfasts and Vacation Rentals** (⊠ 1277 Mokulua Dr., Kailua 96734, ☎ 808/261–7895 or 800/258–7895, FAX 808/262–2181, WEB www.lanikaibb.com).

SIGHTSEEING TOURS

There are three major methods for getting a good guided look at the Garden Isle: by land, by sea, and by air. You can book these tours through the travel desk of your hotel or call directly.

The companies that take you on guided ground tours of Kaua'i use big air-conditioned buses and stretch limousines as well as smaller vans.

The latter seem to fit in more with the countrified atmosphere of Kaua'i. When you make your reservations, ask what kind of vehicle you'll be riding in and which tours let you get off and look around. The guides are friendly and generally know their island inside out. It's customary to tip them $2 or more per person for their efforts.

If you're interested in a north-shore sea excursion, be forewarned that big winter waves often cause trips to be canceled, so call first to find out if the company you're interested in is operating.

BOAT TOURS

Hawai'i's forests and marshes are home to rare and exceptional flora and fauna that often go unseen. In addition to kayak rentals and half-day tours for intrepid explorers that traverse mountains, rivers, and ocean, Kayak Kaua'i also offers a Discovery Tour of Kaua'i for $1,350 (including accommodations, transportation, and meals): a seven-day paddling and hiking adventure with six nights spent in out-of-the-way inns and cottages.

Cruise boats depart Wailua Marina at the mouth of the Wailua River for the Fern Grotto. Round-trip excursions, on 150-passenger flat-bottom riverboats, take an hour and a half, including time to walk around the grotto and environs. During the boat ride, guitar and 'ukulele players regale you with Hawaiian melodies and tell the history of the river. The 3-mi upriver trip culminates at a yawning lava tube that is covered with enormous fishtail ferns. Two companies offer several trips daily to Fern Grotto. Wai'ale'ale Boat Tours offers a Fern Grotto tour for $15. Smith's Motor Boat Service's $15 tour gets passengers involved in singing and learning hula motions while on board.

Blue Water Sailing offers a two-hour sunset cruise in the turquoise waters of the southern shore on 12-passenger, 42-ft luxury Pearson sailing yachts, which leave from Port Allen. Juice, sodas, and snacks are included in the $60 cost. A half-day snorkel sail is $115, including a deli lunch.

Captain Andy's Sailing Adventures' 55-ft catamaran *Spirit of Kaua'i* takes passengers on a two-hour sunset sail along the south shore. Hors d'oeuvres and beverages are included in the $50 cost. Captain Andy also offers a four-hour snorkeling excursion with snacks for $85 and a five-hour Nā Pali Coast cruise from Port Allen with breakfast and lunch for $109.

Liko Kaua'i Cruises tour the northern coastline in a 49-ft powered catamaran while captains share Hawaiian history and legends. Boats depart for 5-hour tours, with time for snorkeling, from Kīkīaola Harbor in Waimea.

Nā Pali Explorer departs at 7:30 AM from Port Allen to tour the Nā Pali Coast (weather permitting) in a 49-ft adventure craft with an onboard toilet and shade canopy. During the winter months, whale-watching can get up close and personal, as the boat gets you down close to the water. Scenic 2½-hour cruises include a snack; longer snorkel trips include Continental breakfast and a picnic lunch, snorkel gear, and a Hawaiian cultural specialist to answer questions. Rates range from $65 to $118, and charters are available.

➤ TOUR OPERATORS: **Blue Water Sailing** (✉ Box 1318, Hanalei 96714, ☎ 808/828–1142). **Captain Andy's Sailing Adventures** (✉ Box 1291, Kōloa 96756, ☎ 808/335–6833). **Kayak Kaua'i** (✉ Box 508, Hanalei 96714, ☎ 808/826–9844 or 800/437–3507). **Liko Kaua'i Cruises** (✉ Box 18, Waimea 96796, ☎ 808/338–0333 or 888/732–5456). **Nā Pali Explorer** (✉ 9935 Kaumuali'i Hwy., Waimea 96796, ☎ 808/338–9999 or 877/335–9909). **Smith's Motor Boat Service** (✉ 174

Wailua Rd., Kapa'a 96746, ☎ 808/821–6892). **Wai'ale'ale Boat Tours** (✉ 6455 Makana Rd., Kapa'a 96746, ☎ 808/822–4908).

FOUR-WHEEL-DRIVE AND ALL-TERRAIN-VEHICLE TOURS

You'll get *way* off the beaten track on Aloha Kaua'i Tours' four-wheel-drive van excursion into Kōke'a, along the rugged side of Waimea Canyon, and through a mountain tunnel to the top of Kilohana Crater. Also offered is a half-day backroads tour and a "SeaFun" snorkeling tour. Prices range from $50 to $90.

You must be 16 or older to operate your own ATV, but Kaua'i ATV Tours can still be a family adventure, as younger kids bounce along on a jeep to the same destinations. The $90 three-hour jaunt takes you through a private sugar plantation with fabulous vistas and a historic cane-haul tunnel. The $130 four-and-a-half-hour tour visits two secluded waterfalls and includes lunch. On the longer excursion, you'll hike through a bamboo forest, swing on a rope, and plunge into a brisk fresh-water pool at the base of the falls.
➤ TOUR OPERATORS: **Aloha Kaua'i Tours** (✉ 1702 Kaleukana St., Līhu'e 96766, ☎ 808/245–4888 or 800/452–1113). **Kaua'i ATV** (✉ 3412 Weliweli Rd., Kōloa 96756, ☎ 808/742–2734 or 877/707–7088).

HELICOPTER TOURS

Kaua'i from the air is mind-boggling. In an hour you can see waterfalls, craters, and places that are inaccessible even by hiking trails. Expect to pay $125 or more per person for the longest, most comprehensive tours, but call around for itineraries. A shorter, less-expensive flight might suit your needs. Don't be afraid to ask about the pilot's experience and safety record. The companies use top-of-the-line equipment, and the operators listed below have reliable flight experience.

Around-the-island, photographer's-delight tours are aboard four- and six-passenger Bali Hai Helicopters from Port Allen Airport on Kaua'i's west side. Hawai'i Helicopters flies out of Princeville on the north shore and offers three tours ranging from 30 to 60 minutes. Island Helicopters flies out of Līhu'e Airport for 55-minute tours over stunning valleys and waterfalls. Ask about special discounts sometimes available with coupons from free visitors' pamphlets. South Sea Tour Co. has a choice of tours available from Līhu'e. Will Squyres Helicopter Tours offers group rates and charters from Līhu'e Airport.
➤ TOUR OPERATORS: **Bali Hai Helicopters** (☎ 808/335–3166 or 800/325–8687). **Hawai'i Helicopters** (☎ 808/826–6591 or 800/994–9099). **Island Helicopters** (☎ 808/245–8588 or 800/829–5999). **South Sea Tour Co.** (☎ 808/245–2222 or 800/367–2914). **Will Squyres Helicopter Tours** (☎ 808/245–8881 or 888/245–4354).

NI'IHAU TOUR

Once Ni'ihau was called the Forbidden Isle. Now it takes only 12 minutes to fly from Kaua'i to an island that few outsiders have set foot on since Elizabeth Sinclair bought it from King Kamehameha V in 1864. This 72-square-mi island just 17 mi from Kaua'i is now run by the Robinson family, who raise cattle and sheep on the barren, arid land. The Robinsons continue to preserve Ni'ihau as a refuge of primitive Hawai'i. Island residents speak Hawaiian and do not use electricity, plumbing, or telephones. They get around on bikes and horses. Bruce Robinson initiated Ni'ihau Helicopters in 1987 in order to supplement the cost of medical evacuation via helicopter for emergency situations for residents. Tours avoid the western coastline, especially the village of Pu'uwai, where the island's 200 residents live. Flights depart from and return to Kaua'i's Burns Field, near Hanapēpē, and are conducted in an Agusta 109 twin-engine, seven-passenger, single-pilot helicopter. Depending on the weather a stop may be made near the sunken crater of Lehua, or on a cliff overlooking the beach coves of Keanahaki Bay. It's the perfect tour for those with a yen to explore untrammeled territory. There is a four-passenger minimum for each flight, and reservations are essential. Ground transportation is not available. Lunch or snack is included. The three-and-a-half-hour tour is $250 per person.

➤ TOUR OPERATOR: **Ni'ihau Tours** (✉ Ni'ihau Helicopters, Box 370, Makaweli 96769, ☎ 808/335–3500 or 877/441–3500).

ORIENTATION TOURS

The Round-the-Island Tour, sometimes called the Wailua River/Waimea Canyon Tour, gives a good overview of the island, because you get to see all the sights, including Ft. Elisabeth, 'Ōpaeka'a Falls, and Mene-hune Fishpond. Guests are transported in air-conditioned 17-passen-ger minivans. The trip includes a boat ride up the Wailua River to Fern Grotto, and then a drive around the island to scenic views above Waimea Canyon. The tour stops at a casual restaurant for lunch (not included in tour price). Companies offering Round-the-Island ground tours include Polynesian Adventure Tours and Roberts Hawai'i Tours.

The Best of Kaua'i whirlwind day-long tour, sponsored by the North Shore Cab Company, for $139 per person, focuses on the highlights of the east and north shores. It includes a visit to Kilohana, a refurbished planta-tion mansion in Līhu'e, followed by a boat ride to the Fern Grotto. Later, you take a tour of Kīlauea Lighthouse and end with a helicopter tour out of Līhu'e Airport. Ground transportation is in 15-passenger, air-con-ditioned vans. North Shore Cab will pick you up at Līhu'e Airport or at your hotel if it's on the north or east side of the island.

Kaua'i Island Tours takes you around Kaua'i in 11-, 21-, 45-, and 57-passenger vans and 4-passenger Lincoln Town Cars.

Trans Hawaiian Services offers English- and Japanese-language tours of Waimea Caynon and Hanalei.

➤ TOUR OPERATORS: **Best of Kaua'i Tour** (✉ Box 757, Hanalei 96714, ☎ 808/826–6189). **Kaua'i Island Tours** (✉ Box 1645, Līhu'e 96766, ☎ 808/245–4777 or 800/733–4777). **Polynesian Adventure Tours** (✉ 3113-B Oihana St., Līhu'e 96766, ☎ 808/246–0122 or 800/622–3011). **Roberts Hawai'i Tours** (✉ Box 3389, Līhu'e 96766, ☎ 808/245–9558 or 888/472–4729). **Trans Hawaiian Services** (✉ 1770 Haleukana St., Puhi 96766, ☎ 808/245–5108 or 800/533–8765).

THEME TOURS

Gay and Robinson Sugar Mill Tours take you first into the heart of a cane field, where you learn about the history and the cultivation of sugar in Hawai'i, then concludes with a hard-hat tour in one of the few re-maining working sugar mills in the Islands. The roar of the giant gears, crushing machines, and centrifuges would strike joy in the heart of any "Tim the Toolman" type. Tours are available weekdays from 8:45 to 12:45 for $30.

Hawai'i Movie Tours' comfortable minibuses with big television screens carry 14 passengers from the southeast end of the island to the north shore to see movie locations filmed in *Jurassic Park, Raiders of the Lost Ark, South Pacific, Blue Hawaii, Gilligan's Island,* and more. One stop is for a picnic lunch at 'Anini Beach. A deluxe tour, for $295, includes helicopter viewing, a boat trip to the Fern Grotto, lunch, and a lū'au. The standard tour is $89.

➤ TOUR OPERATORS: **Gay and Robinson Sugar Mill Tours** (✉ 423 Kaua-makani Ave., Kaumakani 96747, ☎ 808/335–2824). **Hawai'i Movie Tours** (✉ 356 Kūhi'o Hwy., Kapa'a 96746, ☎ 808/822–1192 or 800/628–8432, WEB www.hawaiimovietour.com).

WALKING TOURS

History buffs curious about Kapa'a's sugarcane-, pineapple-, and rice-growing past and the World War II years will enjoy Kapa'a History Tours' 90-minute laid-back stroll from Kawamura Store in the heart of Kapa'a town. This insider's look led by locals covers the story of Kapa'a's Japanese stone lantern before pausing for refreshments. Tours take place on Tuesday, Thursday, and Saturday at 10 AM and cost $10.

To see a lifestyle that is rapidly vanishing, take the unique, volunteer-led Plantation Lifestyles Walking Tour through the residential housing of a real mill camp. In the shadow of the old sugar mill, the dirt lanes of the 70-year-old camp are shaded by fruit trees and tropical gardens, and sometimes elderly residents come out to say aloha. Reservations are needed for the $10 1½- to 2-hour tours that begin at 9 AM every Tuesday, Thursday, and Saturday at Waimea Plantation Cottages.
➤ TOUR OPERATORS: **Kapa'a History Tour** (✉ 4-1540 Kūhi'o Hwy., Kapa'a 96746, ☎ 808/821–1778 or 808/245–3373). **Plantation Lifestyles Walking Tour** (✉ Box 1178, Waimea 96796, ☎ 808/335–2824).

TAXIS

A cab will take you all around the island, but you'll pay dearly for the service. The cost for each mile is $2, after a $2 meter drop, so from Līhu'e to Po'ipū the price is $32; from Līhu'e to Princeville, $60, excluding tip. Your best bet is to call a cab for short distances only (to a restaurant, for instance). A 5-mi cab ride will run you about $12 plus tip. The drivers are often from Kaua'i, which means they'll give you information about the island.

Akiko's Taxi operates from Kapa'a. City Cab is a reliable taxi company using Līhu'e as a home base. Based in Princeville, the North Shore Cab Company provides complete ground handling services for the north and east sections of the island.
➤ TAXI COMPANIES: **Akiko's Taxi** (☎ 808/822–7588). **City Cab** (☎ 808/245–3227). **North Shore Cab Company** (☎ 808/826–6189).

VISITOR INFORMATION

The Hawai'i Visitors and Convention Bureau is easy to find on Rice Street, Līhu'e's main thoroughfare, right near the Kaua'i Museum. The bureau has a good selection of brochures and other visitor's literature, including such free weekly visitor's magazines as *Spotlight Kaua'i* and *This Week on Kaua'i,* and the quarterly *Menu* magazine.

Po'ipū Resort Association is the central source of information about the south shore. You can make on-line reservations through the organization's Web site, and maps and brochures are sent on request.
Activity centers, such as Pahiō Activities and the Chopper Shop, will help visitors book tours, arrange sporting excursions, rent cars, reserve rooms in hotels and condos, and even plan weddings.
➤ TOURIST INFORMATION: **Chopper Shop** (✉ Po'ipū Shopping Village, 2360 Kiahuna Plantation Dr., Po'ipū Beach, ☎ 808/742–1263). **Hawai'i Visitors and Convention Bureau** (✉ 4334 Rice St., Suite 101, Līhu'e 96766, ☎ 808/245–3971 or 800/262–1400, FAX 808/246–9235, WEB www.kauaivisitorsbureau.org). **Pahiō Activities** (✉ 4331 Kaua'i Beach Dr., Līhu'e, ☎ 808/246–0111). **Po'ipū Resort Association** (✉ Box 730, Kōloa 96756, ☎ 808/742–7444 or 888/744–0888, FAX 808/742–7887, WEB www.poipu-beach.org).

5 MOLOKA'I

THE FRIENDLY ISLE

Something about this island makes it stand
out from its neighbors. You can see it in
the way the sun hits the water of ancient
fishponds or hear it as the waves break
on Pāpōhaku Beach. There's a mysterious
sensuality here that springs from the island's
history and inspires its present.

By Marty
Wentzel

Updated by
Betty
Fullard-Leo

NICKNAMES FOR MOLOKA'I have come and gone. In ancient times it was called "Moloka'i of the Potent Prayers" for its powerful *kahuna* (priests) who worshiped in solitude. During the late 1800s it was dubbed the "Forbidden Isle" because Hawai'i's lepers were banished here to a remote peninsula on the northern shore called Kalaupapa. Only in the last few decades has it worn the nickname "Friendly Isle."

Today those who visit the Friendly Isle's shores quickly become aware of its down-to-earth charm. As its neighboring islands become crowded with high-rise hotels, Moloka'i greets its guests modestly with a handful of basic accommodations and unusual sightseeing alternatives.

The Friendly Isle seduces visitors to explore its enveloping tropical outdoors. You can ride a mule or hike a switchback trail down a steep mountain to Kalaupapa, the historic colony once reserved for sufferers of Hansen's disease (leprosy). Tours of the settlement begin at the base of towering sea cliffs. To the east, a horse-drawn wagon tour takes you to Hawai'i's largest *heiau* (a stone platform that was used as a site of worship) and through enormous mango and coconut groves. In the island's highest reaches, atop Mt. Kamakou, you can explore the Kamakou Preserve, a 2,774-acre refuge for endangered birds, plants, and wildlife. Moloka'i also appeals to visitors who enjoy adventure at a personal pace. Plenty of opportunities are available for snorkeling, swimming, hiking, and sunbathing, but there are fewer facilities for organized sports such as fishing, horseback riding, tennis, and golf.

A major plus of the Friendly Isle is that it is uncluttered. You can drive your rental car down any road and take your time looking around without fear of someone honking at you to maintain the speed limit. Sometimes yours is the only car on the road. There are no buildings higher than three stories, no elevators, no traffic jams, and no stoplights. The fanciest hotel is a 22-room lodge in tiny Maunaloa town.

Moloka'i has miles and miles of undeveloped countryside, such as the picturesque farmlands of Moloka'i Ranch (the island's largest local landholder) and the acres of abandoned pineapple fields. Pineapples—seemingly synonymous with Hawai'i in the popular imagination—were once big business for the Dole and Del Monte companies, but the crop's significance to the island's economy has sharply diminished in the face of foreign competition.

At night from beaches on the western shore, you can see the twinkling lights of O'ahu 25 mi across the channel. In spirit, however, Moloka'i is much, much farther away from its highly developed neighbor. With its slow pace and simple beauty, Moloka'i drowses in another era, and, if its 6,861 proud people have their way, it's likely to stay that way.

Pleasures and Pastimes

Dining

The choice of restaurants on Moloka'i is limited. During a week's stay, you might easily hit all the dining spots worth a visit, then return to your favorites for a second round. The dining scene is fun, nevertheless, because it is a microcosm of Hawai'i's diverse cultures. You'll find locally grown vegetarian foods, spicy Filipino cuisine, and Hawaiian-style fish—such as 'ahi or aku (types of tuna), mullet, and moonfish, grilled, sautéed, or sliced and mixed with seaweed and eaten raw as *poke* (marinated raw fish)—all on Ala Malama Street in Kaunakakai, with pizza, pasta, and ribs only a block away. What's more, the price is right. Most eateries fall into our least expensive category ($). For something a bit fancier (but casual just the same), try dinner at the Lodge at Moloka'i Ranch.

Festivals and Seasonal Events

The island has several events around which you might want to plan a trip. The year kicks off with the Ka Moloka'i Makahiki Festival in January, a day when Islanders and visitors get together to compete in ancient Hawaiian games. Translated, Moloka'i Ka Hula Piko means a "Celebration of the Birth of Hula on Moloka'i." The annual daylong event in May brings performances by some of the state's best hula troupes, musicians, singers, lecturers, and storytellers. It's all in tribute to Kā'ana, on the slopes of Maunaloa Mountain, which is reputed to be the birthplace of the hula. The Moloka'i-to-O'ahu Canoe Race is the world's major long-course outrigger canoeing event. It begins near the harbor of Haleolono. After paddling across the rough Kaiwi Channel, participants finish at Ft. DeRussy Beach in Waikīkī. The event takes place each September (women) and October (men). Thanksgiving Day weekend, the Moloka'i Ranch Rodeo draws cowpokes for contests ranging from bull riding to barrel racing.

Lodging

Moloka'i appeals less to travelers who like impeccable furnishings and swanky amenities than to those who appreciate genuine Hawaiian hospitality in down-home surroundings. Hotel and condominium properties range from adequate to funky. The island's only major resort, Kaluako'i Hotel and Golf Club, was closed at press time, awaiting purchase by new owners. Kaunakakai's accommodations lend themselves to visitors on a tight budget and to those who want a central location. There is also a handful of bed-and-breakfasts, as well as the luxury Camps at Moloka'i Ranch, where you can stay in a bungalow-size tent, complete with a queen-size bed and a private bathroom.

Your interest in sports might influence your lodging choice. The Camps at Moloka'i Ranch is the place for people who want to be active: horseback riding, mountain biking, snorkeling, kayaking, and other activities are in close proximity, and guests are given priority when it comes to availability. For those interested in spa treatments and additional comforts, the Lodge at Moloka'i Ranch in Maunaloa is the island's newest and most luxurious accommodation. Ke Nani Kai and Wavecrest have tennis courts available only to guests.

Outdoor Activities and Sports

Moloka'i's unspoiled beauty, sunny skies, and fragrant winds constantly beckon outdoors lovers. Moloka'i's leading adventure, by far, is a mule ride down a narrow 1,664-ft cliff over a 3-mi, 26-switchback trail to Kalaupapa National Historical Park. You can also take a guided trek through Kamakou Preserve, a Hawai'i Nature Conservancy for endangered plants and birds, but arrangements must be made in advance. Kayakers and hikers can head out on their own or try a guided excursion. At Kaunakakai Wharf you can arrange for a fishing charter, a sailing-snorkeling-scuba outing, or a whale-watching cruise. Divers should try Mokuho'oniki Island, at the east end of the island. It was once a military bombing target, and artifacts from World War II are scattered throughout its many pinnacles and drop-offs. The area is home to barracuda and gray reef sharks. Black coral is also found here. Depths range from 30 ft to 100 ft.

EXPLORING MOLOKA'I

Moloka'i is long and shaped like a slipper, with the "heel" facing west and the "toe" pointing to the east. The imaginary dividing line is the town of Kaunakakai, which is right in the center of the island's southern shore. West, Central, and East Moloka'i are used as natural divisions in this chapter.

You'll have the most fun if you explore at your own pace in a rental car. Most of the highlights are natural landmarks—waterfalls, valleys, overlooks, and the like—and it's nice to get out and wander around an area at your leisure without worrying that you'll miss the tour bus.

Directions on Moloka'i are often referred to as *mauka* (toward the mountains) and *makai* (toward the ocean).

Great Itineraries

Moloka'i is small enough that you can drive it end to end in a single day. There are no traffic jams to hold you up—unless you get behind a horseback rider or a couple of friendly locals who have stopped their vehicles in the middle of the road to chat. The essence of Moloka'i is the "hang loose" attitude, so to experience the island properly, pace yourself—focus on visiting just a few sights per day.

Numbers in the text correspond to numbers in the margin and on the Moloka'i map.

IF YOU HAVE 1 DAY

Book a **Moloka'i Mule Ride** ④ and a tour of **Kalaupapa** ⑥ prior to leaving home. Fly into Ho'olehua Airport and drive to Ka La'e, where the steep, 26-switchback trail begins. The tour of the former leper colony, where some 43 people live with the now manageable illness currently known as Hansen's disease, is the most emotionally moving experience on Moloka'i, and if you ask nicely, you might be able to convince your driver to stop at **Pālā'au State Park** ⑤ for a photo of the Phallic Rock before you head back to the airport in the afternoon. For less-adventurous souls, flights directly to Kalaupapa can be arranged, thereby eliminating the grueling mule ride.

IF YOU HAVE 2 DAYS

Maunaloa ③ on West Moloka'i makes a good starting point, particularly because many visitors stay in the area. Spend a little time poking through the jumble of treasures at the Plantation Gallery and the adjacent Big Wind Kite Factory, then explore town. Stop for lunch at the Village Grill. On Moloka'i, one of the first orders of business for any vacation ought to be to relax, so by afternoon you'll want to head for the nearest beach. This could be Kaluako'i Hotel and Golf Club's own Kawākiu Beach or, if you prefer privacy, **Pāpōhaku Beach** ②, a few miles southwest of the hotel. Reserve the second day for the **Moloka'i Mule Ride** ④ and a tour of **Kalaupapa** ⑥, taking in **Pālā'au State Park** ⑤ and the Phallic Rock afterward. If you've got the stamina after the ride, stop by **Coffees of Hawai'i** ⑧, **R. W. Meyer Sugar Mill and Moloka'i Museum** ⑦, and **Purdy's Macadamia Nut Farm** ⑨. If not, pause for some island-style corned beef hash or a burger with the locals at the Kamuela's Cookhouse before heading back to your resort.

IF YOU HAVE 4 DAYS

Follow the itinerary above for your first two days, and then visit **Kaunakakai** ⑫ on your third day to pick up souvenirs, sample ethnic foods, and stop at the Kanemitsu Bakery, a local institution, for the ingredients for a picnic later in the day. Check out **Kaunakakai Wharf** ⑬; you might rent a kayak to take along, or set out on a fishing or scuba excursion from here. Otherwise, continue on a leisurely drive to Moloka'i's east end. Along the way, you'll find such sightseeing points as **Kaloko'eli Fishpond** ⑭, St. Joseph's church near **Kamalō** ⑮, and 'Ili'ili'ōpae Heiau, turning around for the return drive when you reach

Hālawa Valley ⑱. Your final day should be reserved for your own pleasures—perhaps a morning game of golf, an easy hike, a return to the beach, or an easy drive to see anything you might have missed.

When to Tour Moloka'i

Moloka'i's weather is good year-round, and you'll seldom encounter crowds. At any time of year the west end of the island is relatively dry and free of rain—hence its arid landscape. The island gets an influx of visitors during special events and festivals, but for a real taste of old Hawai'i you might want to visit during these weekends anyway. Just be sure you make reservations for accommodations and a rental car well in advance if you schedule a trip during the Moloka'i Ka Hula Piko in May or during any major holiday.

West Moloka'i

Much drier than the east, the western region of the island is largely made up of Moloka'i Ranch, a 53,000-acre tract. Its rolling pastures and farmlands are presided over by Maunaloa, a sleepy little plantation town with a dormant volcano of the same name. West Moloka'i has another claim to fame: Pāpōhaku, the island's best beach.

A Good Drive

This driving tour focuses on two of Moloka'i's areas of "civilization." If you're approaching the west end from Kaunakakai on Highway 460 (also called the Kamehameha V Highway), turn right down Kaluako'i Road and right again at the sign for **Kaluako'i Hotel and Golf Club** ①. Park in one of the many small public lots in front of the resort and then stroll the grounds. Stop on the hillside above the beach for gorgeous ocean views, particularly at sunset.

Back behind the wheel, turn right out of Kaluako'i Hotel and Golf Club and follow Kaluako'i Road 2 mi to the west until it dead-ends. This shoreline drive takes you past a number of lovely beach parks, including **Pāpōhaku Beach** ②, the largest white-sand beach on the island. To find a place to get out and stroll in the sand, look for a big sign for the beach on the makai side of the road.

Turn around and follow Kaluako'i Road back past the resort entrance, and continue uphill to its intersection with Highway 460. Turn right and drive 2 mi on Highway 460 (Maunaloa Highway) to **Maunaloa** ③, a former plantation town with a colorful past, a charming present, and controversial plans for the future. In 1997, the island's first cinema was opened by Moloka'i Ranch in Maunaloa, and in 1998 the first fast-food restaurant—a KFC—started serving. A 22-room lodge complete with spa facilities was completed in August of 1999, and for those interested in country living at its best, Moloka'i Ranch has subdivided house lots and opened model homes in Maunaloa. All these changes are in the name of employment and economic opportunity.

TIMING

If you follow this excursion at a leisurely Moloka'i pace, it will take you the better part of a day, particularly if your accommodations are not on the west end of the island. A walk around Kaluako'i Hotel and Golf Club can take an hour or more.

Another hour can fly by at Pāpōhaku Beach as you dig your toes in its sands and picnic (that KFC in Maunaloa could come in handy) on its shady grassy area. Avoid sitting or walking on the beach between 11 and 1, when the sun is at its peak. Allow one hour for exploring Maunaloa's main street to shop for souvenirs and chat with local shop own-

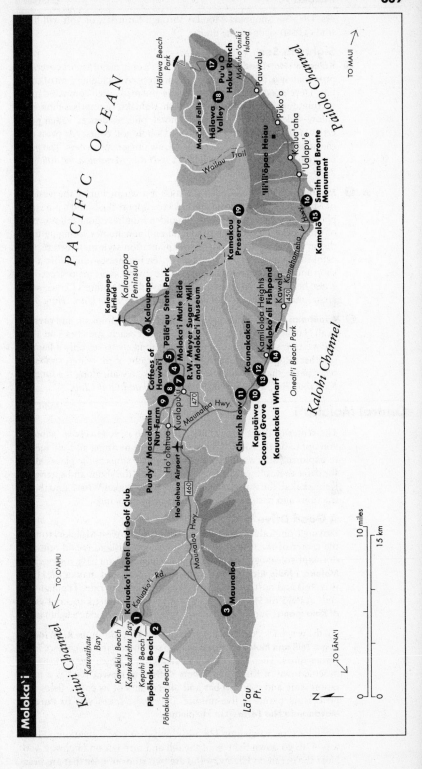

ers. Do your shopping Monday through Saturday, or you will likely find CLOSED signs on the doors.

Sights to See

❶ Kaluako'i Hotel and Golf Club. Moloka'i's only major resort covers approximately 6,700 acres of beachfront property, including 5 mi of coastline. Developed in 1968, it looks tame and manicured compared to the surrounding wilds of Moloka'i Ranch. Kaluako'i comprises three bungalow-style condominiums and a hotel, plus residences, ranch properties, a 10-acre beach park, and an 18-hole golf course. At press time the hotel and golf course were closed, awaiting new owners. The property remains open, however. ⊠ *Kaluako'i Rd., Maunaloa,* ☎ *808/552–2555 or 888/552–2550.*

★ ❸ Maunaloa. This blink-and-you'll-miss-it town anchoring the west end of Moloka'i was established in 1923 to support the island's pineapple plantation. Although the fields of golden fruit have gone fallow, many of the workers' dwellings still stand and new homes springing up at the far end of town evoke an earlier plantation-style architecture. Colorful local characters run the half-dozen businesses (including a kite shop and a classic old market) along the town's short main street. This is also headquarters for Moloka'i Ranch, with its Outfitters Center, rodeo arena, and luxury lodge. ⊠ *Western end of Maunaloa Hwy. (Hwy. 460).*

❷ Pāpōhaku Beach. The most splendid beach on Moloka'i, and perhaps in all Hawai'i, Pāpōhaku, the island's biggest beach, stretches 3 mi along the western shore. On busier days you're likely to see only a handful of other people. If the waves are up, stay out of the water; sunbathe, relax in the shade of its grassy area, or take a walk along the sand. ⊠ *Kaluako'i Rd., 2 mi from Kaluako'i Hotel and Golf Club.*

Central Moloka'i

The center of the island is where the action is, relatively speaking. If you opt to do the Moloka'i Mule Ride in the morning and still feel up to exploring afterward, you can make quick stops at the places along the drive that follows. Central Moloka'i has the shops and eateries of Kaunakakai, the water sports based at Kaunakakai Wharf, and the attractions and natural beauty of the central highlands.

A Good Drive

Driving from Kaluako'i Hotel and Golf Club in West Moloka'i toward the center of the island, you can see how the island is laid out: two dormant volcanoes connected by a vast plain. If you have reserved the **Moloka'i Mule Ride** ④, go directly to Kala'e. Head mauka on Highway 460 and north on Highway 470 to reach the ride. The highway ends at **Pālā'au State Park** ⑤, where you can admire knockout views of **Kalaupapa** ⑥ and the Kalaupapa Peninsula. Bring along a light jacket.

On the way back down the hill on Highway 470, stop at the **R. W. Meyer Sugar Mill and Moloka'i Museum** ⑦ to see photos and machinery from earlier times. Then turn right on Farrington Highway to visit the minuscule town of Kualapu'u, where **Coffees of Hawai'i** ⑧ has a plantation store and espresso bar and offers tours of its coffee fields and processing plant. A five-minute drive west takes you to **Purdy's Macadamia Nut Farm** ⑨ in Ho'olehua.

Head back on Farrington Highway, and then take a right onto Highway 470; go down the rest of the hill and turn left on Highway 460. Near the ocean on Highway 460 are two stops of note that are practically right across the road from each other: **Kapuāiwa Coconut Grove** ⑩ and **Church Row** ⑪. Follow Highway 460 east to reach **Kau-**

nakakai ⑫, Moloka'i's "big city." If you love the ocean, you'll want to locate **Kaunakakai Wharf** ⑬, home base for deep-sea fishing excursions and other aqua adventures.

TIMING

Allow at least a day to explore this part of the island. If you save the Moloka'i Mule Ride for another day, there's no need to rush. Otherwise many shops in Kaunakakai may be closed by the time you get there. If you like big breakfasts, reserve an hour for Kamuela's Cookhouse. During your tour of the highlands, take an hour to visit the sugar museum and another hour or more for the macadamia-nut farm and plantation store. Enjoy these activities Monday through Saturday, since they're closed on Sunday. Once you hit Kaunakakai, indulge yourself: take an hour or two to stroll around town and "talk story" (chat) with the locals. Be sure to save a half hour for snacks at the Kanemitsu Bakery, a local institution.

Sights to See

⑪ **Church Row.** Standing cheek by jowl along the highway are several houses of worship with primarily native Hawaiian congregations. Notice the unadorned, boxlike style of architecture so familiar to missionary homes. ⊠ *Mauka side of Hwy. 460, 5½ mi southwest of airport.*

⑧ **Coffees of Hawai'i.** Tour 500 acres of shiny-leaf coffee trees in a mule-drawn wagon, and then move indoors for an illuminating tour of the coffee processing plant. ⊠ *Farrington Hwy., off Hwy. 470, Kualapu'u,* ☎ 808/567–9241, WEB *www.coffeehawaii.com.* ⊠ *$14.* ☉ *Tours Mon.– Sat., 10–1.*

NEED A BREAK?

In a green plantation-style country store with a big front lānai and fields of coffee trees is **Coffees of Hawai'i Espresso Bar and Gift Shop** (⊠ Farrington Hwy., Kualapu'u, ☎ 808/567–9023), where you can sample the three coffee varieties grown on 450 acres of central Moloka'i land. Try an ice-cream laced Mocha Momma, or *liliko'i* (passion fruit) cheesecake, and wash it down with an espresso or cappuccino.

⑥ **Kalaupapa.** Kalaupapa is the name of a peninsula, a town, and a park. Views of the peninsula from Kalaupapa Lookout in Pālā'au State Park are a standout. Founded in the 1860s and now a National Historical Park, the town of Kalaupapa was once a community of about 1,000 victims of Hansen's disease (leprosy) who were banished from other parts of Hawai'i. A Belgian man named Joseph de Veuster, ordained in Hawai'i in 1864 and known as Father Damien, committed himself to the care of the afflicted until he died here of the same disease in 1889. At press time there were 43 patients still living in Kalaupapa—now by choice, as the disease is controlled by drugs and patients are no longer carriers. Visitors will most likely not see any patients other than perhaps the tour guide, who might be a bit disfigured, with missing fingers or something unusual about the face. The history of the community is fascinating and heart wrenching. The settlement is accessible via the ☞ **Moloka'i Mule Ride** in Kualapu'u or by **Damien Tours** (☎ 808/ 567–6171). Note that no one under the age of 16 is allowed to visit Kalaupapa, and everyone—even those who walk down—must be part of a tour. ⊠ *North end of Hwy. 470.*

⑩ **Kapuāiwa Coconut Grove.** At first glance this looks like a sea of coconut trees. Close-up you'll see that the tall, stately palms are planted in long, elegant rows leading down to the sea. This is one of the last surviving royal groves planted by Prince Lot, who ruled Hawai'i as King Kamehameha V from 1863 until his death in 1872. ⊠ *Makai side of Hwy. 460, 5½ mi south of airport.*

★ ⑫ **Kaunakakai.** Moloka'i's commercial hub is a quiet center—not as much commercial commotion as the other links in this island chain. What Kaunakakai does have is personality: it looks like an Old West movie set. Along its one-block main drag is a cultural grab bag of restaurants and shops. People are friendly and willing to supply directions, and no one dresses in anything fancier than a mu'umu'u or aloha shirt. More often, the preferred dress is shorts and a tank top. ⊠ *Hwy. 460, about 3 blocks north of Kaunakakai Wharf.*

NEED A
BREAK?
Stop by **Kanemitsu Bakery and Restaurant** (⊠ 79 Ala Malama St., ☎ 808/553–5855) for a taste of its *lavosh,* a Kanemitsu specialty of flatbread flavored with sesame, Maui onion, Parmesan cheese, or jalapeño. Or try the round Moloka'i bread—a sweet, pan-style white loaf that makes excellent French or cinnamon toast. There is also an assortment of rolls, buns, doughnuts, pies, and cakes. You can sit right at the counter and have a diner-style breakfast or lunch. Kanemitsu is closed Tuesday.

⑬ **Kaunakakai Wharf.** The docks, once bustling with watercraft exporting pineapples, now ship out potatoes, tomatoes, baby corn, herbs, and other produce. The wharf is also the starting point for various excursions, including deep-sea fishing, sailing, snorkeling, whale-watching, and scuba diving. ⊠ *Hwy. 450 and Ala Malama St.; drive makai on Kaunakakai Pl., which dead-ends at the wharf.*

★ ❹ **Moloka'i Mule Ride.** To reach the town of ☞ Kalaupapa, do it on the back of a sure-footed, stubborn steed. Mount a friendly mule and wind your way along a 3-mi, 26-switchback trail built in 1886 as a supply route to the settlement below. Once in Kalaupapa, you'll get a guided tour of the town and a picnic lunch. No one under the age of 16 is allowed to visit Kalaupapa, and everyone—even those who walk down—must be part of a tour. The trail is very steep, down some of the highest sea cliffs in the world. It's narrow and has no rails, so if it's muddy, the ride is cancelled. Only those in good shape should attempt the ride, as two hours each way on a mule can take its toll. The entire tour takes seven hours. You can also arrange to hike instead of taking a mule down to Kalaupa; hikers need to start walking by 8 to coordinate with the guided tour of the facility. It's wise to make reservations for the tour before arrival, as mules are limited. ⊠ *100 Kala'e Hwy. (Hwy. 470), Kualapu'u,* ☎ *808/567–6088,* WEB *www.muleride.com.* ⊡ *$150, including picnic lunch, Damien Tour, and completion certificate.* ☉ *Tour Mon.–Sat. 8–3:30.*

★ ❺ **Pālā'au State Park.** One of the island's few formal recreation areas, this cool retreat commands 233 acres at a 1,000-ft elevation. A short path through a heady pine forest leads to **Kalaupapa Lookout,** a magnificent overlook with views of the town of Kalaupapa and the 1,664-ft-high sea cliffs protecting it. Informative plaques have facts about leprosy, Father Damien, and the colony itself. The park is also the site of **Phallic Rock,** known as Kauleonānāhoa to the ancient Hawaiians. It is said that if women sit by this large rock formation they will become more fertile. The park, open daily, is well maintained, with camping facilities, washrooms, and picnic tables. ⊠ *Take Hwy. 460 west from Kaunakakai and then head mauka on Hwy. 470, which ends at the park.* ⊡ *Free.*

❾ **Purdy's Macadamia Nut Farm.** Moloka'i's only working macadamia-nut farm is open for tours. A family business on Hawaiian homestead land in Ho'olehua, it takes up 1½ acres with a flourishing grove of some 50 trees more than 70 years old. Taste a fresh, delicious nut right out of its shell. Then try the farm's fresh macadamia-blossom honey. Look for Purdy's sign behind Moloka'i High School. ⊠ *Lihipali Ave., Ho'ole-hua,* ☎ *808/567–6601.* 🎟 *Free.* ⊙ *Weekdays 9:30–3:30, Sat. 10–2.*

❼ R. W. Meyer Sugar Mill and Moloka'i Museum. Built in 1877, this old mill has been reconstructed to signify Moloka'i's agricultural history. The old equipment is still in working order, including a mule-driven cane crusher, redwood evaporating pans, some copper clarifiers, and a steam engine. A museum with changing exhibits on the island's early history and a gift shop are on the premises, as well. The facility also serves as the campus for Elderhostel programs. ⊠ *Hwy. 470, Kala'e, 2 mi southwest of Pālā'au State Park,* ☎ *808/567–6436.* 🎟 *$2.50.* ⊙ *Mon.–Sat. 10–2.*

East Moloka'i

On the beautifully undeveloped eastern end of Moloka'i, you'll find ancient fishponds, a magnificent coastline, splendid ocean views, and a gaping valley that's been inhabited for centuries. The east is flanked by Mt. Kamakou, at 4,961 ft the island's highest point, and home to the Nature Conservancy's Kamakou Preserve. There are miles of rain forests burgeoning with tropical fruit, misty valleys with waterfalls, and ancient lava cliffs jutting out from the sea.

A Good Drive

The road from Kaunakakai east on Highway 450 is 30 mi long, and much of it runs next to the ocean. The farther east you drive, the wilder the coastline, changing from white sandy beaches to rocky shores. Be forewarned that the road, which hugs the shore as it twists and turns, is fraught with bumps and potholes. However, there are several bays beside which you can stop and take a breather. Keep your eyes open for mile markers along the side of the road. At times, they'll be your only references for locating the sights of the east side.

Six miles east of Kaunakakai, look offshore to see **Kaloko'eli Fishpond** ⑭, surrounded by the most picturesque of Moloka'i's historic rock walls. After another 5 mi you reach the natural harbor of **Kamalō** ⑮, followed a mile later by the easy-to-miss **Smith and Bronte Monument** ⑯, dedicated to a pair of transpacific pilots. At Mile Marker 15, a hidden trail leads to the enormous 'Ili'ili'ōpae Heiau. Close to Mile Marker 20 the road climbs and winds through **Pu'u O Hoku Ranch** ⑰, a vast Upcountry expanse with sparkling ocean panoramas.

The road east dead-ends at **Hālawa Valley** ⑱, a lush destination beckoning you to explore its inner reaches on foot. Please don't. Although there is a gorgeous 3-mi trail to the back of the valley, landowners here are known to chase away unsuspecting hikers. You're better off heading for the luscious, tropical **Kamakou Preserve** ⑲. Hiking tours can be arranged in advance.

TIMING

Give yourself a full day for this meandering drive, especially if you want to break it up with a picnic at one of the beach parks. From Kaunakakai, you can complete the tour in a half day. If you're going to tour the Kamakou Preserve, allow a full day. The sights on the east end of the island are natural, so opening hours don't apply. You might want to save this excursion for a weekend and visit the shops and attractions of East and Central Moloka'i during the week, when they're open.

Sights to See

⑱ Hālawa Valley. As far back as AD 650 a busy community lived in this valley, the oldest recorded habitation on Moloka'i. Hawaiians grew fruit and taro and fished here until 1946, when a fierce tidal wave struck. Now much of the valley is overrun with lush vegetation, though you can still see the remains of house platforms and garden walls. At the base of the road into Hālawa Valley is the beginning of a 3-mi trail that leads back to Moa'ula Falls, a 250-ft cascade. Exploring the trail is not recommended unless you are with an authorized guide, as the valley landowners are not hiker-friendly. ⊠ *Eastern end of Hwy. 450.*

OFF THE BEATEN PATH

'ILI'ILI'ŌPAE HEIAU – Human sacrifices once took place at this impressive, hard-to-find heiau, listed on the National Register of Historic Places. As long as a football field, it is a well-preserved example of Hawai'i's ancient outdoor shrines. This revered site is said to hold great power to this day. Please act with respect by speaking in a soft voice. The sacrifices were introduced by Tahitian immigrants who came between AD 1090 and 1240, but the heiau could have existed before then—as early as AD 650, the time of the first island habitation. The old religion, which included human sacrifice, was no longer practiced as of 1819. Don't wander off the designated trail. The whole area is private property. The owners don't object to people simply visiting the heiau, but permission should be requested by phoning 808/558–8380. ⊠ *15 mi east of Kaunakakai and ½ mi inland of Hwy. 450; park on the side of road, look for Wailau Trail sign, and walk about 10 min mauka until you see sign on left for heiau.*

★ ⑭ **Kaloko'eli Fishpond.** With its narrow rock walls connecting two points of the shore, Kaloko'eli is typical of the numerous fishponds that define southern Moloka'i. Many of them were built around the 13th century. This early type of aquaculture, unique to Hawai'i, exemplifies the ingenuity of precontact Hawaiians. Fishpond walls were built of lava rocks or coral or both. You can see the tops of the dark circular stone walls a foot or two above the surface of the water all along the coast. Usually they were built on fringing reefs. One or more openings were left in the wall, where gates with grills (wooden slats side by side) called *makaha* were installed. These gates could be opened and closed. They allowed seawater and tiny fish to enter the enclosed pond, kept larger predators out, and allowed water to circulate so the pond didn't get stagnant. The ponds were stocked with fish too big to escape through the slats, but tiny fish that entered and were not eaten by bigger ones often grew too big to get out. When fish were needed, they were harvested by net. At one time there were 62 fishponds around Molokai's coast. ⊠ *Hwy. 450 about 6 mi east of Kaunakakai.*

★ ⑲ **Kamakou Preserve.** Tucked away on the slopes of Mt. Kamakou, Moloka'i's highest peak, is a Hawai'i Nature Conservancy property affording a safe haven for endangered birds and plants. With its 2,774 lush acres, the preserve is a dazzling wonderland full of wet *'ohi'a* (hardwood trees of the myrtle family, with red blossoms called lehua flowers) forests, rare bogs, and native trees and wildlife. Guided hikes can be arranged in advance. Hikers meet at Ho'olehua Airport at 8:30 and return by 4. About 12 hikes, limited to eight people, are held each year on Saturday. Reservations in writing are required well in advance. You can visit the park without the tour, but you need a four-wheel-drive vehicle, and the Nature Conservancy requests that you sign in first and get directions at the following address. ⊠ *The Nature Conservancy, 23 Pueo Pl. (Box 220), Kualapu'u 96757,* ☎ *808/553–5236,* WEB *www.tnc-hawaii.org.* ⊡ *Free; donation suggested for guided hike, $10 members, $25 nonmembers (includes one-year membership).*

⑮ **Kamalō.** A natural harbor used by small cargo ships during the 19th century, this is also the site of St. Joseph's, a tiny white church built by Father Damien in the 1880s. ⊠ *Hwy. 450 about 11 mi east of Kaunakakai, on makai side.*

⑰ Puʻu O Hoku Ranch. A 14,000-acre private spread in the highlands of East Molokaʻi, Puʻu O Hoku was developed in the '30s by wealthy industrialist Paul Fagan. Highway 450 cuts right through this rural gem with its green pastures and grazing horses and cattle. As you drive along enjoy the splendid views of Maui and Lānaʻi. The small island off the coast is **Mokuhoʻoniki,** where the military practiced bombing techniques during World War II. ⊠ *Hwy. 450 about 20 mi east of Kaunakakai.* WEB *www.puuohoku.com*

⑯ Smith and Bronte Monument. This humble site tucked away in a grove of trees and bushes is dedicated to Ernest Smith and Emory Bronte, Americans who crash-landed here in 1927. They were the first civilians to complete a transpacific flight from California, a noteworthy feat even if it did have a bumpy ending. They ran out of fuel over Molokaʻi and ended up in a grove of kiawe trees, both wings having been sheared off the airplane and the fuselage broken in two. Amazingly, the aviators walked away with only scratches from the trees. ⊠ *Hwy. 450, 12 mi east of Kaunakakai, makai side.*

NEED A BREAK?

The best place to grab a snack or stock up on picnic supplies is the **Neighborhood Store ʻN Counter** (⊠ Hwy. 450, 16 mi east of Kaunakakai, Pukoʻo, ☏ 808/558–8498). It's the last store on your drive heading east from Kaunakakai on Highway 450.

BEACHES

Molokaʻi has numerous beaches, many of them quite remote and undisturbed, so don't be surprised if you're the only person sunbathing for miles. The largest and most beautiful beaches are along the west coast, but steer clear of their high winter waves. Beaches fronting the Kaunakakai hotels and condominiums are narrow and less appealing, yet the shallow waters are almost always calm for wading. At the extreme east end of the island is the beach fronting Hālawa Valley, a nice place to relax after the long drive it takes to get there. All of the beaches are free and open to the public. None have telephones. To find out more about them, contact the **Department of Parks, Land and Natural Resources** (⊠ Box 153, Kaunakakai 96746, ☏ 808/ 567–6083).

West Molokaʻi

Kawākiu Beach. One of the best swimming beaches on Molokaʻi, Kawākiu is part of the Kaluakoʻi Hotel and Golf Club. It has also been set aside as a beach park in honor of its archeological sites, including house platforms and structures from an ancient Hawaiian settlement. Outdoor showers are available at the resort, but there are no lifeguards. ⊠ *Kaluakoʻi Rd., northern end of bay in front of Kaluakoʻi Hotel and Golf Club.*

Kapukahehu Bay. Locals like to surf just out from this bay in a break called Dixie's or Dixie Maru. The sandy protected cove is usually completely deserted during the weekdays but can fill up when the surf is up. There are no facilities. ⊠ *Drive about 3½ mi beyond Pāpōhaku Beach to end of Kaluakoʻi Rd. on northwest end of island; beach access sign on makai side of road points to parking lot.*

Kepuhi Beach. Ideal for strolling, sunbathing, and watching the sunset, this white-sand beach stretches about ½ mi in front of Kaluakoʻi Hotel and Golf Club. However, it is fairly windy here all year long, which makes the swimming somewhat dangerous during high tide. There are outdoor showers at the resort but no lifeguards. ⊠ *Kaluako'i Hotel and Golf Club, Kaluako'i Rd.*

★ **Pāpōhaku Beach.** Perhaps the most sensational beach in Hawai'i, Pāpōhaku is a 3-mi-long strip of white sand, the longest of its kind on the island. It's also quite wide, so you can sunbathe at a comfortable distance from your neighbor. Some places are too rocky for swimming; look carefully before entering the water and go in only when the waves are small (generally in summer). Between the parking lot and the beach are outdoor showers, picnicking facilities, and a rest room. There are no lifeguards. ⊠ *Kaluako'i Rd.; 2 mi beyond Kaluako'i Hotel and Golf Club, look for sign on makai side of road.*

Central Moloka'i

Oneali'i Beach Park. From this spot there are smashing views of Maui and Lāna'i across the Pailolo Channel. It's also the only decent beach park on the island's south-central shore. A narrow and long beach, Oneali'i has adequate swimming in calm waters year-round, along with rest rooms, outdoor showers, and tree-shaded picnic tables. There are no lifeguards. ⊠ *Hwy. 450, east of Hotel Moloka'i.*

East Moloka'i

Hālawa Beach Park. The long drive to Hālawa Valley is worth it, in part because it culminates in this pretty, curving beach flanked by cliffs. Swimming is safe only during the summer. Watch out for the hazardous currents and high surf in winter. A small pavilion with grassy areas on either side is popular with locals for family picnics. An outdoor shower is available, but there aren't any lifeguards. ⊠ *Drive east on Hwy. 450 until it dead-ends at beach.*

DINING

Moloka'i is not the dining hub of the islands. Still, with low prices and a host of local specialties to try, most diners are happy and enjoy the laid-back island atmosphere. Restaurants listed are open daily unless otherwise noted. For an explanation of price categories, *see* Dining *in* Smart Travel Tips.

West Moloka'i

$$ ✕ **Maunaloa Room.** Bar none, the Maunaloa Room serves the finest
★ (and priciest) haute cuisine on the island. The chef describes his menu as "Moloka'i regional" and buys as many ingredients as possible locally. This is one of the few places you can order such fancy appetizers as a Moloka'i *'opihi* (a crunchy limpet), *lumpia* (egg roll) stuffed with *kālua* (roasted in an underground oven) duck, or coconut-crusted shrimp. Entrées follow a steak-and-seafood theme, with the catch of the day prepared in Mediterranean, Asian, or local (with alae salt, a pale-orange salt found in Moloka'i and Kaua'i) styles. An open-air deck affords views of the ocean 3 mi off. Inside, the decor follows a ranch theme with wooden tables and wagon-wheel chandeliers with electric candles. ⊠ *Lodge at Moloka'i Ranch, 8 Maunaloa Hwy., Maunaloa,* ☎ *808/660–2725. AE, MC, V.*

$$ ✕ **The Village Grill.** Diners might arrive on horseback, Harley, or Honda rent-a-car to the Village Grill, but they're all bound to get a real taste of local favorites—prime rib, New York steak, pizza—flavored with locally grown herbs. Half the fun is cooking your own on a stone grill, brought to the table so your meal is guaranteed hot. Try a Cow Pie for dessert, a mound of vanilla, macadamia-nut, and coffee ice cream in a graham-cracker crust with three sweet sauces. The restaurant sports a historic bar that once graced O'ahu's Pearl City Tav-

ern. ⊠ *Mauka side of Maunaloa Hwy., Maunaloa,* ☏ *808/552–0012. AE, DC, MC, V. No lunch weekends.*

Central Moloka'i

$–$$ ✕ **Oceanfront Dining Room (Hotel Moloka'i Restaurant).** An earlier Hawai'i seems palpable as you sit at open-air, candlelit tables and gaze across outrigger canoes to the ocean a few feet away. It's a toss-up whether to order Moloka'i coconut shrimp deep-fried in a tempura batter, or the broiled baby-back ribs smothered in barbecue sauce. Friday and Saturday nights' combination of prime rib specials and island entertainers makes this a popular local gathering place. ⊠ *Makai side of Kamehameha V Hwy., Kaunakakai,* ☏ *808/553–5347. AE, D, DC, MC, V.*

$ ✕ **Kamuela's Cookhouse.** A cozy, casual little family-owned restaurant is the only eatery in rural Kualapu'u, so you'll rub elbows with locals and tourists alike during breakfast and lunch. A breakfast of homemade corned beef hash or a humongous meal called The Works—with buttermilk pancakes, eggs, and home fries—will keep you fueled all day. For lunch, burgers and club and Monte Cristo sandwiches are lighter fare than plates of chicken and pork *katsu* (breaded cutlets) and other entrées served with rice. Paintings of hula dancers and island scenes highlight the green-and-white decor. An old wagon marks the front of the diner, which looks like a little plantation house, across the street from the Kualapu'u Market. ⊠ *Farrington Hwy., 1 block west of Hwy. 470, Kulapūu,* ☏ *808/567–9655. No credit cards.. Closed Mon.*

$ ✕ **Moloka'i Drive Inn.** Open since 1960, this simple eatery in the heart of Kaunakakai is Moloka'i's answer to McDonald's. You'll find the usual take-out staples—hot dogs, fries, and sundaes. But locals come here for the food they grew up on, such as saimin (noodle soup), shave ice (snow cone with flavored syrup), and the beloved *loco moco* (rice topped with a hamburger and fried egg and covered in gravy). ⊠ *857 Ala Malama St., Kaunakakai,* ☏ *808/553–5655. No credit cards.*

$ ✕ **Moloka'i Pizza Cafe.** This cheerful order-at-the-counter restaurant is a popular gathering spot for visitors and locals. Pizza, sandwiches, salads, pasta, soft-serve ice cream, homemade pies, and fresh fish are simply prepared and tasty. ⊠ *Kaunakakai Pl. on Wharf Rd., Kaunakakai,* ☏ *808/553–3288. Reservations not accepted. No credit cards.*

$ ✕ **Outpost Natural Foods.** Vegetarian cuisine has made its way to Kaunakakai in the form of this unpretentious natural foods store and carryout, just off Ala Malama Street. It stocks good salads as well as vegetarian burritos, tempeh burgers, and a daily hot-entrée special such as curried vegetables. The fruit smoothies are delicious, and the produce is fresh. ⊠ *70 Makaena St., Kaunakakai,* ☏ *808/553–3377. Reservations not accepted. No credit cards. Closed Sat.*

$ ✕ **Oviedo's.** Kaunakakai may seem lacking in ways, but it does have two authentic Filipino diners. Oviedo's, where the waitresses treat you like family, is the better of the two. It specializes in *adobos* (stews) with traditional Filipino spices and sauces. Try the tripe, pork, or beef adobo for a real taste of tradition. You can eat in or take out. ⊠ *145 Ala Malama St., Kaunakakai,* ☏ *808/553–5014. Reservations not accepted. No credit cards.*

$ ✕ **Sundown Deli.** This clean little rose-color deli serves primarily freshly made take-out food. Sandwiches can be ordered on a half-dozen types of bread, and the Portuguese bean soup and chowders are rich and filling. Specials, which might include the likes of vegetarian quiche, change daily. The chiffonlike liliko'i pie is great with an espresso. Vitamins and local-theme T-shirts are also available. ⊠ *145 Ala Malama Ave., Kaunakakai,* ☏ *808/553–3713. Reservations not accepted. AE, MC, V. Closed Sun. No dinner.*

LODGING

Several of the lodging establishments listed in this chapter arrange outdoor excursions and have sports facilities that aren't accessible to nonguests and are hard to find elsewhere. Check each review to find the accommodation that best suits your needs. Some properties also offer free shuttle transportation from the airport—ask when you book your room. For an explanation of price categories, *see* Lodging *in* Smart Travel Tips.

West Moloka'i

$$$$ ⚐ **The Camps at Moloka'i Ranch.** Comfortable camping is the name
★ of the game at these one- and two-unit tents managed by Moloka'i Ranch. Canvas and yurt tents are grouped in distinct locations. Individuals and families are booked into Kaupoa Beach Camp, which is right beside the beach. Upcountry near Maunaloa and the rodeo arena—with views of Cook pines, grassy pasturelands, and the ocean—is Paniolo Camp. Kolo Cliffs Camp is on a bluff overlooking the ocean a short distance from the beach. Paniolo and Kolo are usually reserved for groups. Mounted on wooden platforms, tents have solar-powered running water and lights and self-composting flush toilets. A full buffet breakfast is included in the rate; lunch and dinner, served family-style in an open-air pavilion, cost extra. Box lunches are also available, and individual ice chests are restocked with soft drinks daily. Extensive outdoor activities, including snorkeling, kayaking, and clay shooting, are available with discounted rates to guests. In addition, a ropes course includes cooperative activities that build trust and communication among guests. A 980-ft "zipline" over a ravine is one of many elements that challenge participants. Shuttle transport to and from the airport and between the Molokai Ranch camps and Maunaloa town requires a small fee, but eliminates the need for a rental car. ⊠ *Maunaloa Hwy. (Box 259), Maunaloa 96770,* ☎ *808/552–2791 or 877/726–4656,* 𝖥𝖠𝖷 *808/534–1606,* 𝖶𝖤𝖡 *www.molokai-ranch.com. 100 tents. Hiking, horseback riding, snorkeling, boating, mountain bikes. AE, MC, V.*

$$$$ ⚏ **The Lodge at Moloka'i Ranch.** Moloka'i's newest and plushest ac-
★ commodation is this plantation-style lodge with wraparound lānai. Each of the 22 suites has its own name and decor, as well as a private lānai. Some rooms have skylights for stargazing at night. Ranching memorabilia reminiscent of the 1930s and '40s and artwork by local artists decorate guest room walls. An impressive stone fireplace in the central great room and a games room make socializing pleasant during cool Moloka'i evenings, and pathways and a greenhouse make the grounds worth exploring during the day. Spa facilities here exude a tranquil, country feeling with massage rooms, juice bar, and separate sauna facilities for men and women. Guests can reserve Moloka'i Ranch activities (horseback rides, fishing, mountain biking, etc.). ⊠ *Maunaloa Hwy. (Box 259), Maunaloa 96770,* ☎ *808/660–2722 or 877/726–4656,* 𝖥𝖠𝖷 *808/534–1606,* 𝖶𝖤𝖡 *www.molokai-ranch.com. 22 suites. Restaurant, bar, air-conditioning, pool, sauna, spa, recreation room. AE, MC, V.*

$$$ ⚏ **Ke Nani Kai.** This well-managed condominium complex is set back from the water. Views are of the gardens and golf course, but the beach is a mere five-minute walk away. Furnished lānai have flower-laden trellises, and the spacious interiors are decorated with tropical rattans and pastels. Each unit has a washer-dryer and a fully equipped kitchen. ⊠ *Kaluako'i Rd. (Box 289), Ke Nani Kai Resort, Maunaloa 96770,* ☎ *808/552–2761 or 800/535–0085,* 𝖥𝖠𝖷 *808/552–0045,* 𝖶𝖤𝖡 *www.marcresorts.com. 120 condominiums (27 rentals). Kitchenettes, pool, 18-hole golf course, 2 tennis courts. AE, D, DC, MC, V.*

$$–$$$ ✦   **Paniolo Hale.** Perched high on a ledge overlooking the beach, Paniolo Hale is one of Moloka'i's best condominium properties. Some units have spectacular ocean views. Guests can choose from among studios and one- or two-bedroom units, all with screened lānai and kitchens; some have hot tubs for an additional charge. Kitchens are well equipped, and the rooms are tidy and simple. Adjacent to the Kaluako'i Golf Course and a stone's throw from the Kaluako'i Hotel and Golf Club, the property is some nights a playground for wild turkeys and deer. ✉ *Lio Pl. (Box 190), Maunaloa 96770,* ☎ *808/552–2731 or 800/367–2984,* ℻ *808/552–2288,* WEB *www.paniolohaleresort.com. 77 condominiums (22 rentals). Kitchenettes, pool, golf privileges, paddle tennis. AE, MC, V.*

$$ **Kaluako'i Villas.** Studios and one-bedroom ocean-view suites are decorated in blue and mauve, with island-style art, rattan furnishings, and private lānai. Units are spread out in 21 two-story buildings covering 29 acres. Guests can take advantage of Kaluako'i Hotel and Golf Club's many activities, though there are no signing privileges. ✉ *1131 Kaluako'i Rd. (Box 200), Maunaloa 96770,* ☎ *808/552–2721 or 800/367–5004,* ℻ *808/552–2201,* WEB *www.castleresorts.com. 36 rooms, 11 suites, 2 1-bedroom cottages. In-room VCRs, kitchenettes, pool, 18-hole golf course, shops. AE, MC, V.*

Central Moloka'i

$$$ **Moloka'i Shores.** Every room in this oceanfront, three-story property has a view of the water. Guests can stay in either one-bedroom, one-bath units or two-bedroom, two-bath units. All have furnished lānai, which look out on four acres of tropical gardens. In addition, picnic tables and barbecue areas are available. ✉ *Kamehameha Hwy., No. 450 (Box 1037), Kaunakakai 96748,* ☎ *808/553–5954 or 800/535–0085,* ℻ *800/633–5085. 100 units (30 1-bedroom rentals, 2 2-bedroom rentals). Kitchenettes, pool, shuffleboard. AE, D, MC, V.*

$$–$$$ **Hotel Moloka'i.** Though this hotel is right on the beach, the pool on premises is a better alternative for swimming. Furnishings are tropical, with basket swings on the lānai, white rattan accents in the rooms, and wood beams on the ceiling. The hotel often offers overnight deals in conjunction with airlines and rental-car companies. Ask about this when you make your reservation. The Oceanfront Dining Room serves breakfast, lunch, dinner, and libations. ✉ *Kamehameha V Hwy. (Box 1020), Kaunakakai 96748,* ☎ *808/553–5347 or 800/367–5004,* ℻ *808/553–5047,* WEB *www.hotelmolokai.com. 45 rooms. Restaurant, fans, pool. AE, D, DC, MC, V.*

$ **A Hawaiian Getaway.** If you want to learn about Moloka'i's history and culture, consider staying here: gracious hosts Lawrence and Catherine Aki have an extensive library and also conduct cultural hikes. The two rooms are small and simply decorated, and guests use the same entrance, bathroom, and living room as the proprietors. Both rooms have double beds, and one has a television and VCR. Laundry facilities are available. You're within walking distance of Kaunakakai. ✉ *270 Kaiwi St., Kaunakakai 96748,* ☎ *808/553–9803 or 800/274–9303. 2 rooms with shared bath. Library. No credit cards.*

East Moloka'i

$$$ **Dunbar Beachfront Cottages.** Two two-bedroom, two-bath cottages, each with its own secluded beach, are right on the ocean about a quarter mile apart. It's a good spot for swimming and snorkeling and great for whale-watching during the winter months. Covered lānai have panoramic vistas of Maui, Lana'i, and Kaho'olawe across the ocean. These spotlessly clean, serene cottages with complete kitchens are hard to leave at the end of a three-night minimum stay. ⊠ *HC01, Box 901, Kauanakakai 96748,* ☎ *808/558–8153 or 800/673–0520,* FAX *808/558– 8153,* WEB *www.molokai-beachfront-cottages.com. 2 cottages. Kitchenettes, fans, in-room VCRs, beach. No credit cards.*

$$–$$$ ⊞ **Hale Kawaikapu.** A cottage and a house, both fully furnished, are available for weekly or longer rentals on a 10-acre oceanfront site. The house sleeps six and has a large lānai with a queen-size sofa bed and large dining-room table. The two bedrooms have Polynesian decor. The cottage, which has grass mats on the floor, sleeps four with two sofa beds in a downstairs living area and a queen bed in an upstairs loft cooled by a ceiling fan. ⊠ *East of Kaunakakai on Kamehameha V Hwy. (Reservations: 532 'Elepaio St., Honolulu 96816),* ☎ *808/521–9364. 1 house, 1 cottage. Fans. No credit cards.*

$$–$$$ ⊞ **Kamalo Plantation Cottage and Moanui Beach House.** At these tropical paradises 15 and 25 minutes east of Kaunakakai, guests can stay in either of two cottages. Each Polynesian-style cottage has a fully equipped kitchen, living room, dining room, and deck. One cottage is set right beside a good snorkeling beach and has great views from its huge deck. The other is surrounded by lush foliage. Home-grown fruit and fresh-baked bread are provided at breakfast. ⊠ *10½ mi and 20 mi east of Kaunakakai off Hwy. 450 (HC 1, Box 300), Kaunakakai 96748,* ☎ FAX *808/558–8236,* WEB *www.molokai.com/kamalo. 2 cottages. Kitchenettes. No credit cards.*

$$–$$$ ⊞ **Pu'u O Hoku Ranch.** At the east end of Moloka'i, near Mile Marker 25, are three ocean-view accommodations on 14,000 isolated acres of pastures and forestland. The draws here are the views and the peaceful surroundings. One Country Cottage has two bedrooms, basic wicker furnishings, and lau hala matting on the floors. The airy four-bedroom cottage has a small deck and a somewhat Balinese ambience. The lodge, which has 11 rooms opening off a main hallway and seven bathrooms, is similarly decorated. Groups can book the full lodge for $900 nightly. A pool and horseback riding are available on the property. ⊠ *Hwy. 450 (Box 1889, Kaunakakai 96748),* ☎ *808/558–8109,* FAX *808/558–8100,* WEB *www.puuohoku.com. 1 2-bedroom cottage, 1 4-bedroom cottage, 11 rooms in lodge. No credit cards.*

$$ ⊞ **Honomuni House.** A tropical garden setting, complete with waterfalls and a freshwater stream, awaits you 17 mi east of Kaunakakai on Highway 450. Inside there's an equipped kitchen, one bedroom, one bath, and a large living-dining room. ⊠ *Hwy. 450 (HC 1, Box 700, Kaunakakai 96748),* ☎ *808/558–8383. 1 house. Kitchenette. No credit cards.*

$–$$ ⊞ **Wavecrest.** An oceanfront, south-shore condominium 13 mi east of Kaunakakai, this property is suited to travelers who want to explore the east side of the island. Individually decorated one- and two-bedroom condominiums have full kitchens. Each has a furnished lānai, some with views of Maui and Lāna'i. Be sure to ask for an updated unit when you make your reservation. The shallow water here is bad for swimming but good for fishing. ⊠ *Hwy. 450 near Mile Marker 13 (Friendly Isle Realty, 75 Ala Malama, Kaunakakai 96748),* ☎ *808/553–3666 or 800/600–4158,* FAX *808/553–3867,* WEB *www.molokairealty.com. 126 1- and 2-bedroom condominiums (10 rentals). Kitchenettes, pool, 2 tennis courts, shuffleboard. V.*

NIGHTLIFE AND THE ARTS

Moloka'i doesn't have much of a nightlife in the traditional sense. Locals enjoy simply sitting around with friends and family, sipping a few cold ones, strumming 'ukulele and guitars, singing old songs, and talking story. Still, opportunities are available to kick up your heels for a festive night out. Go into Kaunakakai, pick up a copy of the weekly *Moloka'i Dispatch*—available along Ala Malama Street at Misaki's Inc., Friendly Market Center, or Moloka'i Wines 'n' Spirits—and see if there's a church supper or square dance taking place where you can mingle.

Bars and Clubs

Moloka'i Brewing Company. When it opened late in 2000, this modern minibrewery in the center of Kaunakakai became one of Molokai's few after-dark hangouts. Besides rubbing elbows with Islanders in the evening, the Brewing Company is a good place for a casual breakfast, lunch, or dinner. ⊠ *Malama St., Kaunakakai,* ☎ *808/553–5187.*

Film

Maunaloa Town Cinemas. Folks from all around Moloka'i come here nightly for current blockbusters. ⊠ *Maunaloa Hwy., Maunaloa,* ☎ *808/ 552–2707.*

OUTDOOR ACTIVITIES AND SPORTS

Fitness and Spa Centers

The Spa Venture is Moloka'i's one true spa facility. With natural-wood decor lending a rustic feeling to locker rooms and other facilities, the spa fits right in with the low-key, ranchlike atmosphere of its surroundings. Massages, saunas, and fitness equipment are available. ⊠ *The Lodge at Moloka'i Ranch, Maunaloa Hwy., Maunaloa,* ☎ *808/ 660–2710.* ▨ *Free admittance for Lodge guests, fee for nonguests.*

Golf

Compared with the more commercialized Neighbor Islands, Moloka'i has a relatively mellow golf scene. The **Ironwood Hills Golf Club** in Upcountry Kala'e is a public nine-hole course. This was pastureland until the Del Monte Corporation turned it into a golf course for plantation workers in 1928. The course was redesigned in 1990. It gets windy in the afternoons, so it's a good idea to call for a morning tee time. ⊠ *Turn off Hwy. 460 onto 470 and go north uphill 3½ mi; the dirt road to the golf course is on the left side; Kualapu'u,* ☎ *808/567–6000.* ▨ *Greens fee $14; cart $14.*

The **Kaluako'i Golf Course** at the Kaluako'i Hotel and Golf Club, formerly the best golf option on the island, was closed at press time, awaiting new owners. Call ahead to see if it has reopened. The 18-hole, 6,564-yard course was designed by Ted Robinson and includes five holes next to the beach. ⊠ *Kaluako'i Hotel and Golf Club, Kaluako'i Rd., 3½ mi from intersection with Hwy. 460,* ☎ *808/552–2739.*

Hiking

You can make a day of hiking to Kalaupapa and back along the 3-mi, 26-switchback trail that is also used for the Moloka'i Mule Ride. The trail is well maintained by the National Park Service. You will need a permit to hike the trail, as well as a confirmed reservation with **Damien Tours** (☎ 808/567–6171) to tour Kalaupapa. For further information contact the **National Park Service** (⊠ Box 2222, Kalaupapa 96742, ☎ 808/567–6802).

Hālawa Falls Cultural Hike is a guided trek through private property on the east end of Moloka'i in the lush and lovely Hālawa Valley. Along the way the guide points out a heiau, old rock walls, house sites, and native fruit trees. At Moa'ula Falls you can swim in the pool and eat food you have brought yourself. Hikers meet at 8:30, begin hiking by 9:45, and return by 2. Hikes take place daily, and reservations are required. ⊠ *Meet at Neighborhood Store, beyond Mile Marker 15 on Hwy. 450,* ☎ *808/553–4355 after 5.* ▨ *$25.*

At **Historical Hikes of West Moloka'i,** Lawrence and Catherine Aki of A Hawaiian Getaway guide six hikes ranging from two to six hours that focus on Moloka'i's cultural past. One hike treks to an ancient adze quarry; another follows the remains of an ancient paved trail. Other hikes investigate the remains of an early fishing village at Kaupoa Bay, and explore high sea cliffs where Hawaiian chiefs played games during the makahiki season. Lunch is provided on intermediate and advanced hikes. ⊠ *Meet at Moloka'i Ranch Outfitters Center, Maunaloa Hwy., Maunaloa,* ☎ *808/552–2797, 808/553–9803, or 800/274– 9303,* WEB *www.molokai-aloha.com/hikes.* ⊡ *$45–$125.*

Horseback Riding

Moloka'i Horse and Wagon Ride is a 1½-hour ride that takes in a heiau, a mountain lookout to search for whales in the ocean below, a mango grove, and a beach. Trips take six riders and start at 10. Call to make arrangements. ⊠ *15 mi east of Kaunakakai off Hwy. 450, Kaunakakai,* ☎ *808/558–8380.* ⊡ *$50.*

Water Sports

FISHING

Based at Kaunakakai Wharf, the four-passenger, 31-ft cruiser **Alyce C.** (☎ 808/558–8377) runs excellent sportfishing excursions. Shared cost is about $200 a day, $150 a half day. On an exclusive basis, the cost is approximately $400 for a full day, $350 for a three-quarter day, and $300 for a half day.

Also departing from Kaunakakai Wharf, **Fun Hogs Hawai'i** (☎ 808/ 567–6789) runs the 27-ft *Ahi* for half-day ($350), six-hour ($400), and full-day ($450) sportfishing. Full-day bottom fishing trips with all equipment furnished are $500. Fly-fishing excursions are also available (bring your own rods for fly-fishing).

SAILING

The 42-ft Cascade sloop *Satan's Doll* is your craft with **Moloka'i Charters** (☎ 808/553–5852). The company arranges two-hour sails for $40 per person. Half-day sailing trips cost $50 per person, including soft drinks and snacks. A minimum of four people is required, but shared charters can be arranged.

SNORKELING AND SCUBA DIVING

Bill Kapuni's Snorkel & Dive (☎ 808/553–9867 or 877/553–9867) leaves Kaunakakai Wharf daily for two-hour snorkeling excursions. Whale-watching cruises in season, underwater massages, and diving certification can all be arranged. Prices vary with the length of dive and number of people involved.

You can book a snorkeling excursion or, in season, a whale-watching cruise for $65 per person with **Fun Hogs Hawai'i** (⊠ Box 424, Ho'ole-hua 96729, ☎ 808/567–6789). Fun Hogs' boat *Ahi* also conducts custom-designed cruises. During the calmer summer months, 8- to 10-hour north-shore sightseeing trips are offered.

Moloka'i Charters (⊠ Box 1207, Kaunakakai 96748, ☎ 808/553–5852) takes people via sailboat on full-day snorkeling excursions to the island of Lāna'i for $90 per person. Soft drinks and a picnic lunch are included.

Jim Brocker, owner of **Moloka'i Fish and Dive** (⊠ 61 Ala Malama St., ☎ 808/553–5926), in Kaunakakai, can fill you in on how to find the best snorkel sites and can rent you the gear.

SHOPPING

Moloka'i has two major commercial drags: Maunaloa Road in Maunaloa and Ala Malama Street in Kaunakakai. Happily, there are no department stores or shopping malls, and the fanciest clothes you'll find are pretty mu'umu'u and colorful aloha shirts. But now that you've gone totally "native," could you ask for anything more?

Each tiny hamlet has emporiums with flair and diversity; the best bargains are locally made artwork and jewelry.

Most stores in Kaunakakai are open Monday through Saturday between 9 and 6. In Maunaloa most shops close by 4 in the afternoon and all day Sunday. Call ahead to confirm hours.

West Moloka'i

A handful of family-run businesses line the main drag of Maunaloa, a rural plantation town. Shop proprietors always extend the aloha spirit to visitors.

Arts and Crafts

Plantation Gallery (⊠ 120 Maunaloa Hwy., Maunaloa, ☏ 808/552–2364) is Maunaloa's best arts-and-crafts emporium, crammed with everything from clothes to sculpture to musical instruments.

Clothing

A Touch of Moloka'i (⊠ Kaluako'i Hotel and Golf Club, Kaluako'i Rd., Maunaloa, ☏ 808/552–0133) sells resort wear with tropical prints.

Grocery Store

Victuals and travel essentials are available at the **Maunaloa General Store** (200 Maunaloa Hwy., Maunaloa, ☏ 808/552–2346). Open Monday through Saturday from 8 until 6, it's convenient for guests staying at the nearby condos of Kaluako'i Hotel and Golf Club, who shop here for meat, produce, dry goods, and the fixings for their holiday libations.

Kites

The **Big Wind Kite Factory** (⊠ 120 Maunaloa Hwy. Maunaloa, ☏ 808/552–2364), a fixture of the Maunaloa community, has custom-made, appliquéd kites you can fly or display. Designs range from hula girls to tropical fish. Also in stock is a wide variety of kite kits, paper kites, minikites, and wind socks. Ask to go on the factory tour, and then take a free kite-flying lesson.

Central Moloka'i

You can walk from one end of Kaunakakai's main street (Ala Malama) to the other in about five minutes—unless you like to browse, of course. Ho'olehua has just one must-shop stop, the Plantation Store, next to Coffees of Hawai'i.

Clothing

Casual, knockabout island wear is available at the **Imports Gift Shop** (⊠ 82 Ala Malama St., Kaunakakai, ☏ 808/553–5734), across from Kanemitsu Bakery. **Moloka'i Island Creations** (⊠ 62 Ala Malama St., Kaunakakai, ☏ 808/553–5926) carries exclusive swimwear, beach cover-ups, sun hats, and tank tops. **Moloka'i Surf** (⊠ 130 Kamehameha Hwy., Kaunakakai, ☏ 808/553–5093) is known for its wide selection of Moloka'i T-shirts, swimwear, and sports clothing.

Grocery Stores

Friendly Market Center (⊠ 93 Ala Malama St., Kaunakakai, ☏ 808/553–5595) is the best-stocked supermarket on the island. Its slogan—

"Your family store on Moloka'i"—is truly credible: hats, T-shirts, and sun-and-surf essentials keep company with fresh produce, meat, groceries, liquor, and sundries. The store is open weekdays from 8:30 to 8:30 and Saturday from 8:30 to 6:30.

Misaki's Inc. (⊠ 78 Ala Malama St., Kaunakakai, ☎ 808/553–5505) is a grocery with authentic island allure. It has been in business since 1922. Pick up housewares and beverages here, as well as your food staples, Monday through Saturday from 8:30 to 8:30 and Sunday from 9 until noon.

Don't let the name **Moloka'i Wines 'n' Spirits** (⊠ 77 Ala Malalma St., Kaunakakai, ☎ 808/553–5009) fool you. Along with a surprisingly good selection of fine wines and liquors, the store also carries gourmet cheeses and snacks. It's open Sunday through Thursday from 9 AM until 10 PM, Friday and Saturday until 10:30 PM.

Island Goods
The Plantation Store (⊠ Kualapu'u Base Yard, Farrington Hwy., ☎ 808/567–9023), open daily from 10 until 3, is the only shop of interest in Kualapu'u. Once inside, you'll find the most complete range of Moloka'i-made products on the island, particularly 100% Moloka'i coffee. In the market for seed bracelets, or perhaps some jewelry made from coconut shells and wiliwili seeds? This is your place. You'll also find local artwork, homemade jellies and jams, island soaps, pen-and-ink drawings of Moloka'i landscapes, and handcrafted pottery.

Jewelry
Along with casual clothing, the **Imports Gift Shop** (⊠ 82 Ala Malama St., Kauanakai, ☎ 808/553–5734) has a decent collection of 14-karat-gold chains, rings, earrings, and bracelets, plus a jumble of Hawaiian quilt pillows, books, and postcards. It also carries Hawaiian heirloom jewelry, unique replicas of popular Victorian pieces. These stunning gold pieces are made to order with your Hawaiian name inscribed on them. **Moloka'i Island Creations** (⊠ 62 Ala Malama St., Kaunakakai, ☎ 808/553–5926) carries its own unique line of jewelry, including sea opal, coral, and sterling silver, as well as other gifts and resort wear.

Sporting Goods
Moloka'i Bicycle (⊠ 80 Mohala St., Kaunakakai, ☎ 808/553–3931) rents and sells mountain and road bikes as well as jogging strollers, kids trailers, helmets, and racks. It supplies maps and information on biking and hiking, and will drop off and pick up equipment for a fee nearly anywhere on the island.

Make **Moloka'i Fish and Dive** (⊠ 61 Ala Malama St., Kaunakakai, ☎ 808/553–5926) the main source for your sporting needs, from snorkeling rentals to free and friendly advice. Owner Jim Brocker knows the island inside out and can recommend the best spots for fishing and diving. Ask to see his original-design Moloka'i T-shirts and the best books about Moloka'i.

MOLOKA'I A TO Z

To research prices, get advice from other travelers, and book travel arrangements, visit www.fodors.com.

AIR TRAVEL
If you're flying in from the mainland United States, you must first make a stop in Honolulu. From there, it's a 25-minute trip to the Friendly Isle.

CARRIERS

Hawaiian Airlines flies its DC-9 jet aircraft daily between O'ahu and Moloka'i. A round-trip ticket can cost up to $200 per person. Island Air provides daily flights between Molokai and O'ahu or Maui on its 18-passenger deHaviland Dash-8 Twin Otters. Pacific Wings flies an eight-passenger Cessna three times daily between O'ahu and Moloka'i.

Pacific Wings also flies from Honolulu to Ho'olehua Airport for $180 round-trip; from Honolulu to the airstrip in Kalaupapa costs $186 round-trip, and you must first have a land-tour confirmation for Kalaupapa. Your arrival should coincide with one of the authorized ground tours of the area. Otherwise you'll be asked to leave.

➤ AIRLINES & CONTACTS: **Hawaiian Airlines** (☎ 800/367–5320). **Island Air** (☎ 800/323–3345). **Pacific Wings** (☎ 808/873–0877 or 888/575–4546).

AIRPORTS

Moloka'i's transportation hub is Ho'olehua Airport, a tiny airstrip 8 mi west of Kaunakakai and about 15 mi east of Kaluako'i Hotel and Golf Club.

An even smaller airstrip serves the little community of Kalaupapa on the north shore.

➤ AIRPORT INFORMATION: **Airstrip** (☎ 808/567–6331). **Ho'olehua Airport** (☎ 808/567–6140).

AIRPORT TRANSFERS

From Ho'olehua Airport, it takes about 10 minutes to reach Kaunakakai and 25 minutes to reach the condominiums of Kaluako'i Hotel and Golf Club by car. Since there's no rush hour on the Friendly Isle, traffic won't be a problem. There is no bus service.

From the Ho'olehua Airport, it's easy to find your way on the island's roads. Turn right on the main road, Highway 460 (also called Maunaloa Highway), to reach Kaluako'i Hotel and Golf Club and left if you're staying in Kaunakakai. Budget and Dollar are the two car-rental companies with offices at Ho'olehua Airport, and Island Kine Rent-a-Car offers airport pickup.

Shuttle service for two passengers costs about $18 from Ho'olehua Airport to Kaunakakai and about $18 to Kaluako'i Hotel and Golf Club. For shuttle service via a car or a van, call Moloka'i Off-Road Tours and Taxi. Kukui Tours and Limousines has drivers available seven days a week, from 8 to 5.

➤ TAXIS & SHUTTLES: **Kukui Tours and Limousines** (☎ 808/553–8022). **Moloka'i Off-Road Tours and Taxi** (☎ 808/553–3369).

CAR RENTAL

Budget maintains a convenient counter that's hard to miss as soon as you enter the baggage claim area at the airport. Dollar also has offices at Ho'olehua Airport, and your rental car can be picked up in the parking lot. Expect to pay between $30 and $50 per day for a standard compact and from $36 to $55 for a midsize car. Rates are seasonal and may run higher during the peak winter months. It's best to make rental arrangements in advance. If you're flying on Island Air or Hawaiian Airlines, see whether fly-drive package deals are available—you might luck out on a less-expensive rate.

Locally owned Island Kine Rent-a-Car offers airport pickup and sticks to one rate year-round for vehicles in a broad spectrum from two- and four-wheel drives to 15-passenger vans.

➤ MAJOR AGENCIES: **Budget** (☎ 800/527–7000). **Dollar** (☎ 800/367–7006).

➤ LOCAL AGENCIES: **Island Kine Rent-a-Car** (☎ 808/553–5242).

CAR TRAVEL

If you want to explore Moloka'i from one end to the other, it's best to rent a car. With just a few main roads to choose from, it's a snap to drive here. You'll find gas stations in Kaunakakai and Maunaloa. When you park your car, be sure to lock it. Thefts aren't unknown. Drivers must wear seat belts or risk a $42 fine. Children under three must ride in a federally approved child passenger restraint device, easily leased at the rental agency. Ask your rental agent for a free *Moloka'i Drive Guide*.

EMERGENCIES

Round-the-clock medical attention is available at Moloka'i General Hospital.

➤ EMERGENCY SERVICES: **Ambulance and general emergencies** (☎ 911). **Coast Guard** (☎ 808/244–5256). **Fire** (☎ 808/553–5601 in Kaunakakai; 808/567–6525 in at Ho'olehua). **Police** (☎ 808/553–5355).

➤ HOSPITALS: **Moloka'i General Hospital** (✉ 280A Puali St., Kaunakakai, ☎ 808/553–5331).

SIGHTSEEING TOURS

ADVENTURE TOURS

Walter Naki is a friendly, knowledgeable guide who custom-designs Moloka'i Action Adventures tours to Moloka'i's outdoors attractions. One of his most popular excursions is a north-shore cruise aboard a 21-ft Boston Whaler. He is also a competent guide for year-round fishing trips. Prices vary.

➤ TOUR OPERATOR: **Moloka'i Action Adventures** (☎ 808/558–8184).

BIKE TOURS

Moloka'i Bicycle's guides have the exclusive right to take mountain bikers to Pu'u O Hoku Ranch. You might ride along an eastern ridge rimming Hālawa Valley to four waterfalls and a remote pool for swimming, or pedal on sea cliffs to a secluded beach. Daily tours for a minimum of two people cost $45 per person for a half day, and $65 for a full day, including lunch.

➤ TOUR OPERATOR: **Moloka'i Bicycle** (☎ 808/553–3931).

KALAUPAPA TOURS

Damien Tours of this former leper colony are operated by longtime residents of Kalaupapa who are well versed in its history. The four-hour van tour begins and ends at Kalaupapa Airport if you arrive by air, or at the foot of the 3-mi trail if you hike down the mountain. Tours depart at 10:15 Monday–Saturday and cost $30. No one under 16 is allowed. Bring your own lunch and water.

➤ TOUR OPERATOR: **Damien Tours** (☎ 808/567–6171).

MO'OMOMI DUNES

The Nature Conservancy conducts about 12 tours annually of Mo'omomi Dunes, a fine example of a pristine coastal ecosystem on West Moloka'i. The educational walks are for those interested in geology, archeological sites, rare plants, snails, and Hawai'i's extinct bird species. Tours are on Saturday and must be booked months in advance. The suggested donation is $10 for members, and $25 for nonmembers.

➤ TOUR OPERATOR: **The Nature Conservancy** (✉ 23 Pueo Pl. [Box 220], Kualapu'u 96757, ☎ 808/553–5236).

Visit Hālawa Valley, Kalaupapa Lookout, Maunaloa town, and other points of interest in the comfort of an air-conditioned van. Pat and Alex Pua'a are your personal guides. They'll even help you mail a coconut back home. Tours cost $50, begin at 9, and end at 2:30.

➤ TOUR OPERATOR: **Moloka'i Off-Road Tours and Taxi** (☎ 808/553–3369 or 808/552–2218).

Island residents Junior and Nani Rawlins take folks on a scenic and informative amble in a horse-drawn wagon. First stop is 'Ili'ili'ōpae Heiau, the largest outdoor shrine in Hawai'i. Next, tour the largest mango grove in the world before hitting the beach for coconut husking, barbecuing, and fishing. Call for arrangements and directions. Tours cost $50, include lunch, and are available daily.

➤ TOUR OPERATOR: **Moloka'i Wagon Ride** (☎ 808/558–8132 or 808/558–8380.

SHUTTLE TRAVEL

Kukui Tours and Limousines offers half-day and full-day tours to various points of interest on the island in seven-passenger vehicles. Moloka'i Off-Road Tours and Taxi provides personalized service to any point on the island.

➤ CONTACTS: **Kukui Tours and Limousines** (☎ 808/553–8022). **Moloka'i Off-Road Tours and Taxi** (☎ 808/553–3369).

VISITOR INFORMATION

You can pick up free brochures and tourist information in kiosks and stands at the airport in Ho'olehua or at the Moloka'i Visitors Association at 10 Kamehameha V Highway in Kaunakakai. Car-rental agencies distribute the free *Moloka'i Drive Guide* along with maps and other up-to-date information.

Moloka'i Visitors Association is centrally located in Kaunakakai, so you may want to drop by for any travel information once you are on the island. Maui Visitors Bureau offers advice on accommodations and tours and provides other visitor information.

➤ TOURIST INFORMATION: **Maui Visitors Bureau** (✉ Box 580, Wailuku, Maui 96793, ☎ 808/244–3530, WEB www.visitmaui.com). **Moloka'i Visitors Association** (✉ Box 960, Kaunakakai 96748, ☎ 808/553–3876 or 800/800–6367, WEB molokai-hawaii.com).

6   LĀNAʻI

A visit to Lānaʻi can be either simple or elegant. You can spend your days covered in red dust from off-road adventures or in your best whites, rubbing elbows with sophisticated travelers. No matter what your style, solitude is always easily found on this remote island— though you may happen upon the occasional deer on a hillside, glimpse dolphins playing in Mānele Bay, or encounter spirits lingering in the ancient fishing village of Kaunolū.

By Marty
Wentzel

Updated by
Sophia
Schweitzer

ALTHOUGH, TODAY, LĀNAʻI is an island that welcomes visitors with its rustic charm, it hasn't always been so amiable. The earliest Polynesians believed it to be haunted by evil ghosts who gobbled up unsuspecting souls. In 1836, a pair of missionaries named Dwight Baldwin and William Richards came and went after failing to convert the locals to Christianity. In 1854, a group of Mormons tried to create the City of Joseph here, but they were forced to abandon their mission after a drought in 1857.

One of Lānaʻi's more successful visitors was a man named Jim Dole (1877–1958). In 1922, Dole bought the island for $1.1 million and began to grow pineapples on it. He built Lānaʻi City on the flatlands, where the crater floor is flanked by volcanic slopes. Then he planned the harbor at Kaumālapaʻu, from which his pineapples would be shipped. Four years later, as he watched the first harvest sail away to Honolulu, the enterprising businessman could safely say that Dole Plantation was a success.

For decades, Lānaʻi was known as the Pineapple Island, with hundreds of acres filled with the golden fruit. But in the late 1980s pineapples ceased to be profitable because of global competition. The solution? Dole built two new hotels and developed a tourism industry that is starting to thrive.

The island's only population center, Lānaʻi City, is an old plantation town with a few family-run shops and diner-style eateries as well as an art center and gallery. Tall Cook pines shade streets filled with tiny houses with colorful facades, tin roofs, and tidy gardens. Many of the town's 2,800 residents are descendants of plantation workers who came to the island in the 1920s from Korea, China, Japan, and the Philippines.

Lānaʻi City is smack in the middle of the island and all around it are natural wonders: to the northwest lies the Garden of the Gods, where rocks and boulders are scattered across a crimson landscape as if some divine being had placed them there as a sculpture garden. Adjacent is a trail leading through the Kānepuʻu Preserve, a dryland forest with some 48 native species, including the endangered Hawaiʻian gardenia. On the southern tip, the waters at Hulopoʻe Beach are so clear that within a minute of snorkeling you can see turquoise and jade fish. After hiking or driving to the summit of Lānaʻihale, a 3,370-ft-high windswept perch in the eastern reaches, you'll find a splendid view of nearly every Hawaiian island.

Though Castle & Cooke, Inc. (formerly Dole Foods) still owns 98% of this 141-square-mi island, the pineapple fields have given way to sophisticated resorts and championship golf courses. Despite these additions, Lānaʻi remains remote and intimate, earning its new nickname of "Hawaiʻi's Most Secluded Island."

Pleasures and Pastimes

Dining

Lānaʻi has developed its own version of Hawaiʻi regional cuisine. The upscale menus at the Lodge at Kōʻele and Mānele Bay Hotel draw on the bounty provided by local hunters and fisherfolk—everything from Mānele ʻahi (yellowfin tuna) to Lānaʻi venison. Lānaʻi City's simple but eclectic fare ranges from sandwiches and pizza to Louisiana ribs and tempeh vegetarian burgers.

Golf

Lānaʻi has two championship golf courses. The pine-covered fields of The Experience at Kōʻele stretch across rolling hills punctuated by lakes, streams, and waterfalls. At The Challenge at Mānele, the Pacific Ocean makes a daunting water hazard: dolphins and whales have been known to distract even the most serious golfer.

Hiking and Biking

Only 30 mi of Lāna'i's roads are paved. But red-dirt roads and trails, ideal for hiking and mountain biking, will take you to abandoned villages with historic *heiau* (stone altars), isolated beaches, and forest preserves. Follow a self-guided walk through Hawai'i's largest native dryland forest or explore the Munro Trail over Lāna'ihale with views of plunging canyons and all of Hawai'i Nei.

Lodging

Though Lāna'i has few properties, it does have a range of price options. The Lodge at Kō'ele and Mānele Bay Hotel are luxury resorts, which their rates reflect. If you're on a budget, seek out a bed-and-breakfast or consider the Hotel Lāna'i. House rentals give you a taste of life on the island but are usually pricey.

Snorkeling and Scuba Diving

When you have a dive site like Cathedrals—with pinnacle formations and mysterious caverns—it's no wonder that snorkeling and scuba-diving buffs consider exploring the waters off Lāna'i akin to having a religious experience. For the best underwater viewing, try Hulopo'e Beach, a Marine Conservation Area, or go on an excursion with Trilogy or Lāna'i Ecoadventure Centre.

EXPLORING LĀNA'I

Most of Lāna'i's sights are out of the way—rent a four-wheel-drive vehicle, ask your hotel's concierge for a road map, make sure you have a full tank, and bring a snack. Admission is free to all sights mentioned.

In the Islands, the directions *mauka* (toward the mountains) and *makai* (toward the ocean) are often used. The main road in Lāna'i, Highway 440, is also called Kaumālapa'u Highway or Mānele Road.

Great Itineraries

Lāna'i is small enough to explore in a couple of days of leisurely travel.

Numbers in the text correspond to numbers in the margin and on the Lāna'i map.

IF YOU HAVE 1 DAY

If you can only tear yourself away from your lounge chair long enough to squeeze in one day of exploring, rent a four-wheel-drive vehicle and get to know the back roads, where the landscape's power and beauty are immutable. If you're staying at the Lodge at Kō'ele or Hotel Lāna'i, allow time to see the **Garden of the Gods** ⑦ and the **Kānepu'u Preserve** ⑥ in the morning. After lunch in **Lāna'i City** ⑩, drive down to **Lu'ahiwa Petroglyphs** ② and **Kaunolū** ③, followed by a late-afternoon swim at **Hulopo'e Beach.** Guests of the Mānele Bay Hotel should reverse the itinerary.

IF YOU HAVE 3 DAYS

On the first day, follow the above itinerary. On the second day, take an adventurous tour of the undeveloped north and east shores. Pack a picnic lunch and start the day with a drive to **Shipwreck Beach** ⑨ for a morning walk and some sunbathing. Then drive along the bumpy coastal road to **Keōmuku** ⑪, **Kahe'a Heiau** ⑫, **Naha** ⑬, and **Lōpā Beach.** Retrace your route, ending the day's adventures with drinks at your hotel's lounge. Start your third day with a cool morning hike up

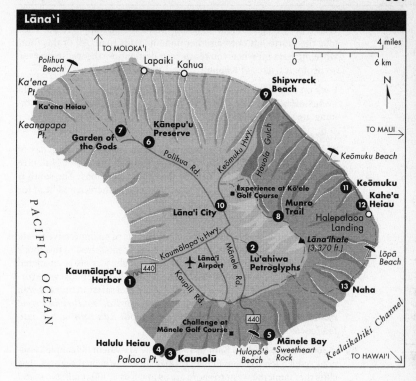

Lāna'i

the **Munro Trail** to Lāna'ihale. An afternoon swim or spa treatment at your hotel will help to soothe sore muscles.

IF YOU HAVE 5 DAYS
Follow the three-day itinerary and then dedicate the fourth day to the sport of your choice, be it golf on the championship courses, tennis at the Mānele Bay Hotel or the Lodge at Kō'ele, horseback riding from The Stables at Kō'ele, or sporting clays in the highlands. On the fifth day, take a half-day fishing trip or snorkeling–scuba diving expedition. In the afternoon, stroll around Lāna'i City and pick up some souvenirs while you "talk story" (chat) with the locals.

When to Tour Lāna'i

Lāna'i is generally warm and clear, though winter weather is cooler and less predictable. It's sunniest at sea level, while up-country, in Lāna'i City, the nights and mornings can be chilly and the fog can settle in on the tops of the pine trees.

South and West Lāna'i

Pineapples once blanketed the Pālāwai Basin, the flat area south of Lāna'i City. Today it's used primarily for agriculture and grazing and holds historic and natural treasures. You will need a four-wheel-drive vehicle to explore this rugged area.

A Good Drive

From Lāna'i City, drive south on Highway 440 a few blocks until you reach a major intersection. Go straight, following the highway west to **Kaumālapa'u Harbor** ①, the island's main seaport. Backtrack to the intersection, turn right, and take Highway 440 south. After about a mile you'll see a dirt road on your left leading to the **Lu'ahiwa Petroglyphs** ② and its ancient rock carvings.

Return to Highway 440 and drive another 2 mi south until the road veers left. Here, go straight on bumpy and unpaved Kaupili Road. Then take the fourth left onto another unnamed dirt road. All of this four-wheeling pays off when you reach your destination: the well-preserved archeological sites of **Kaunolū** ③ and **Halulu Heiau** ④.

Back on Highway 440, drive down the long, steep hill. At the bottom awaits **Mānele Bay** ⑤. The road ends at the island's only true swimming area, Hulopo'e Beach.

TIMING

Although it's a small area, south and west Lāna'i deserve a full day of exploration. If you like water sports, spend half the day at Hulopo'e Beach and use the rest for visiting the other attractions. The south is almost always sunny, clear, and warm, so wear sunscreen and head for shade at midday.

Sights to See

❹ **Halulu Heiau.** The carefully excavated remains of an impressive heiau, which was actively used by Lāna'i's earliest residents, attest to this spot's sacred history. As late as 1810, this hilltop sight was also considered a place of refuge, where those who had broken *kapu* (taboos) were forgiven, and where women and children could find safety in times of war. ⊠ *From Lāna'i City, follow Hwy. 440 (Mānele Rd.) south; when road makes sharp left, continue straight on Kaupili Rd.; turn makai onto the fourth dirt road.*

❶ **Kaumālapa'u Harbor.** Built in 1926 by the Hawaiian Pineapple Company, which later became Dole, this is Lāna'i's principal seaport. The cliffs that flank the western shore are as much as 1,000 ft tall. No water activities are allowed here, but if you're in the area on Thursday, you'll witness the arrival of the barge, upon whose weekly deliveries the island depends. ⊠ *From Lāna'i City, follow Hwy. 440 (Kaumālapa'u Hwy.) west as far as it goes; turn left and drive about 7 mi makai.*

❸ **Kaunolū.** Set atop the island's highest cliffs, Kaunolū was a prosperous fishing village in precontact times. This important archeological site includes terraces, stone floors, and platforms where 86 houses and 35 shelters once stood. The impressive 90-ft drop to the ocean is called **Kahekili's Leap.** Warriors would make the death-defying jump into the mere 12 ft of water below to show their courage to Hawai'i's King Kamehameha I, who used the island as his summer hideaway. ⊠ *From Lāna'i City follow Hwy. 440 (Mānele Rd.) south; when road makes sharp left, continue straight on Kaupili Rd. through pineapple fields; turn makai onto fourth dirt road.*

❷ **Lu'ahiwa Petroglyphs.** On a steep slope overlooking the Pālāwai Basin are 34 boulders with carvings. Drawn in a mixture of ancient and historic styles dating to the late 1700s and early 1800s, the simple stick-figure illustrations depict life on Lāna'i. Some of the stones are believed to possess the spiritual power of rain gods. ⊠ *From Lāna'i City, follow Hwy. 440 (Mānele Rd.) south 1 mi to an unmarked dirt road that leads left through pineapple fields; at end of that road, walk up unmarked trail to petroglyphs.*

❺ **Mānele Bay.** The site of a Hawaiian village dating from AD 900, Mānele Bay is flanked by lava cliffs that are hundreds of feet high. Though a Marine Life Conservation District, it's the island's only public boat harbor, and was the location of most post-contact shipping until Kaumālapa'u Harbor was built in 1926. The ferry to and from Maui also pulls in here.

Just offshore you can catch a glimpse of **Pu'upehe**. Often called Sweetheart Rock, the isolated 50-ft-high islet carries a sad Hawaiian legend. The rock is named after Pehe, a woman so beautiful that her husband, afraid that others would steal her away, kept her hidden in a sea cave. One day, while Pehe was alone, the surf surged into the cave and she drowned. With the help of the gods, her grief-stricken husband buried her offshore on the summit of this rock, and then jumped to his own death. ⊠ *From Lāna'i City, follow Hwy. 440 (Mānele Rd.) south to bottom of hill and look for harbor on your left.*

North and East Lāna'i

The north and east sections contain Lāna'i City, but the rest of the area is wild and untouched, with a ghost town and deserted heiau being the only other traces of civilization. The best way to explore the area's distinctive beauty is by four-wheel-drive vehicle, since most attractions are only accessible by rugged dirt roads.

A Good Drive

From Lāna'i City, take Keōmuku Highway north. Turn left on the road between The Stables at Kō'ele and its tennis courts. This leads you to a dirt road, which cuts through hay fields for a couple of miles. At the crossroad, turn right onto Polihua Road, which heads north through the dryland forest of **Kānepu'u Preserve** ⑥ and, 1½ mi beyond, to the **Garden of the Gods** ⑦.

Return to Keōmuku Highway, turn left, and drive toward the top of the hill. Make a right onto the only major dirt road in sight, and you're on your way to the **Munro Trail** ⑧, a 9-mi route that runs over the top of Lāna'ihale, the mountain that rises above Lāna'i City.

After enjoying the views from the trail, head back to Keōmuku Highway, and follow its long descent to **Shipwreck Beach** ⑨, an 8-mi expanse of sand. Here, stretch your legs and look for glass balls (used as flotation devices for fishing nets) and other washed-up treasures.

Return to **Lāna'i City** ⑩ for an afternoon drink and some browsing in its gift stores. Or if you feel adventurous, head southeast. At the end of the paved road (Keōmuku Highway, which dead-ends at Shipwreck Beach), turn right and follow the very bumpy dirt road. Five miles later you will see dozens of tall coconut trees and a historic church. This is the site of **Keōmuku** ⑪, where 2,000 people once lived. A mile and a half farther down the road, you can see the ruins of a temple called **Kahe'a Heiau** ⑫. The road ends 3 mi later at the remnants of an old Hawaiian fishpond at **Naha** ⑬ and the often-deserted Lōpā Beach.

TIMING
Give yourself a day to tour the island's northern and eastern reaches. You can visit all the sights any day of the year, but keep your eye on the sky. It's more apt to rain in the highlands than in Lāna'i City. If you're a hiker, you'll want a day just to enjoy the journey up to Lāna'ihale. A walk along Shipwreck Beach makes a nice morning outing. Since most of the driving is on bumpy roads, it takes more time to reach such places as the Garden of the Gods and Keōmuku than it does actually to experience them. But getting there is half the fun.

Sights to See

★ ❼ **Garden of the Gods.** This preternatural plateau is scattered with boulders of different sizes, shapes, and colors, the products of a million years of wind erosion. Its lunar appearance changes colors from rich red to brown as the sun sets. Magnificent views of the Pacific Ocean, Moloka'i, and, on clear days, O'ahu, provide the perfect backdrop for photographs. Stand quietly and you might also spot deer. ☒ *From the Stables at Kō'ele, follow dirt road through hay fields 2 mi; turn right at crossroads and head through ironwood forest 1½ mi.*

⑫ Kahe'a Heiau. At what was once a central place of worship for the people of Lāna'i, you must look hard through the overgrowth to see the remaining stone platforms and walls or the old wharf used by the Maunalei Sugar Company to ship cane. Some say that the company failed here because attempted construction of a railroad disturbed the sacred stones: the gods became angry, turned the drinking water salty, and the population of the surrounding Keōmuku Village was devastated by illness. ☒ *6½ mi southeast from where Keōmuku Hwy. dead-ends at Shipwreck Beach, on dirt road running along north shore.*

❻ Kānepu'u Preserve. The 590 acres of this native dryland forest are under the stewardship of the Nature Conservancy of Hawai'i. Kānepu'u contains the largest remnant of this extremely rare forest type. More than 45 native species of plants, including the endangered Hawaiian gardenia, grow in the shade of such rare trees as Hawaiian sandalwood, olive, and ebony. A short self-guided loop trail, with eight signs illustrated by local artist Wendell Kaho'ohalahala, reveals this ecosystem's beauty and the challenges it faces. ☒ *Polihua Rd., 6 mi north of Lāna'i City,* ☎ *808/537–4508,* WEB *www.tnc-hawaii.org/.* ◷ *9–4.*

⑪ Keōmuku. During the late 19th century, this busy Lāna'i community of some 900 residents served as the headquarters of the Maunalei Sugar Company. After the company failed, the land was used for ranching, but by 1954 the area had been abandoned. Its church, Malamalama, is the oldest on the island, and was restored by volunteers. There's an eerie beauty about Keōmuku, with its crumbling, weed-choked stone walls and homes. ☒ *5 mi along unpaved road southeast of Shipwreck Beach.*

⑩ Lāna'i City. This tidy plantation town was built in 1924 by Jim Dole. It reflects his wish to create a model plantation village: a simple grid of roads lined with tall Cook pines and all the basic services a person might need. Visit the **Lāna'i Arts & Culture Center** (☒ 339 7th Ave.) to get a glimpse of this island's creative abundance.

★ ❽ Munro Trail. This 9-mi path winds along a pine-covered ridge and through rain forest. It was named after George Munro, manager of the Lāna'i Ranch Co., who began a reforestation program in the 1950s to provide a much-needed watershed. Be careful: this isn't an easy hike, and the roads get very muddy. The trail climbs **Lāna'ihale**, which means "House of Lāna'i." At 3,370 ft, it's the island's highest point; on clear days you'll be treated to a panorama of canyons, valleys, and almost all of the Hawai'ian Islands. Trade winds can be strong at the summit, so bring a jacket. ☒ *From Lodge at Kō'ele head north on Keōmuku Hwy. for 1¼ mi, then turn right onto tree-lined dirt road; trailhead is ½ mi past cemetery on right.*

⑬ Naha. An ancient rock-walled fishpond—visible at low tide—lies here, where the sandy shorelines end and the cliffs begin their rise along the island's south, west, and north shores. The beach is a frequent resource for local fisherfolk, but the treacherous tides make this a dangerous place for swimming. ☒ *East side of Lāna'i, at end of dirt road that runs from end of Keōmuku Hwy. along eastern shore.*

★ ❾ Shipwreck Beach. Beachcombers come for shells and washed-up treasures; photographers for great shots of Moloka'i, just across the Kalohi Channel; and walkers for the broad, 8-mi-long stretch of sand. Kaiolohia, as it's also called, is not, however, for swimmers. The tanker that's rusting offshore is a clue that these aren't friendly waters. ☒ *End of Keōmuku Hwy. heading north.*

BEACHES

Though all of Lāna'i's beaches provide peaceful strolls, sunbathing, and, of course, sunsets, only Hulopo'e Beach is safe for swimming. To reach most of the beaches, listed clockwise from the south, you will need a four-wheel-drive vehicle; note that it is illegal to go four-wheeling on the beaches themselves.

Hulopo'e Beach. Hulopo'e is one of the best beaches in all of Hawai'i. The sparkling crescent of this Marine Life Conservation District beckons with perennially clear waters that are safe for swimming, great snorkeling reefs, tide pools, and views of spinner dolphins at play. Shady trees and grassy expanses are perfect for picnics, and there are showers, rest rooms, and changing facilities. It's a five-minute walk from the Mānele Bay Hotel. ☒ *From Lāna'i City follow Hwy. 440 (Mānele Rd.) south to bottom of hill; road dead-ends at beach's parking lot.*

Polihua Beach. Due to its more obscure location and frequent high winds, this beach is often deserted, except for the turtles that nest here. Because of strong currents, swimming is dangerous, but its long strand of white sand and glorious views of Moloka'i are memorable. ☒ *Northwest shore, 11 mi from Lāna'i City, past Garden of the Gods.*

Shipwreck Beach. Shipwreck is an 8-mi stretch of sand on the 9-mi wide Kalohi Channel between Lāna'i and Moloka'i. The beach has no lifeguards, no changing rooms, and no outdoor showers. ☒ *North shore, 10 mi north of Lāna'i City at end of Keōmuku Hwy.*

DINING

Although Lāna'i's restaurant choices are limited, the menus are wideranging. If you dine at the Lodge at Kō'ele or Mānele Bay Hotel, you'll be treated to top-notch cuisine served in upscale surroundings. Lāna'i City's restaurants are unpretentious with simple fare and nondescript service. A lesser known alternative is the clubhouse at the Challenge golf course, which stays open till 9 PM several nights every week. For price categories, *see* Dining *in* Smart Travel Tips.

South and West Lāna'i

$$$ ✗ **'Ihilani.** The Mānele Bay Hotel's dining room shimmers with crys-
★   tal, exquisite china, and silver. Moonlight filters through the glass ceiling of its open-air terrace. Executive chef Edwin Goto uses fresh island ingredients to create a cuisine he calls "Mediterranean gourmet." The menu changes with the seasons but may include such dishes as grilled filet mignon with seared foie gras or roasted pheasant breast with a Madeira truffle sauce. You can opt for a five-course food-and-wine pairing menu. ☒ *Mānele Bay Hotel,* ☎ *808/565–7700. Reservations essential. AE, DC, MC, V. No lunch.*

North and East Lāna'i

$$$ ✗ **Formal Dining Room.** Reflecting the elegant country atmosphere of
★   the Lodge at Kō'ele, this romantic octagonal restaurant offers intimate tables close to a roaring fireplace. The walls are hand-stenciled by local artists. The changing menu is an expansion of Hawaiian regional cuisine that includes specialties such as roasted Lāna'i venison loin and Hawaiian *moi,* a fish that in ancient times was savored only by chiefs. The wine list has selections from small wineries. ☒ *Lodge at Kō'ele,*

☎ *808/565–7300. Reservations essential. Jacket required. AE, DC, MC, V. No lunch.*

\$\$–\$\$\$ ✕ **Henry Clay's Rotisserie.** Don't overlook this popular spot at the Hotel Lāna'i. Louisiana-style ribs, Cajun-style shrimp, gumbo, and seafood jalapeño over fettuccine add up to what Chef Henry Clay Richardson calls "American country," but he brings it back home with island venison, seafood, island produce. A fireplace and paintings by local artists add to the country ambience. ⊠ *Hotel Lāna'i, 828 Lāna'i Ave., Lāna'i City,* ☎ *808/565–7211. MC, V.*

\$ ✕ **Blue Ginger Café.** This small, no-frills eatery may look run-down with its bare floor and plastic tablecloths, but the menu is diverse, and the wonderful owner, Georgia Abilay, has turned this place into one of the town's most popular hangouts. At breakfast, try a three-egg omelet with rice or fresh pastries, which are available each morning. Lunchtime selections range from mainland staples such as burgers, chef's salad, and pizza, to Hawaiian staples such as saimin. Try the stir-fry fish or Mexican fare for dinner. ⊠ *409 7th Ave., Lāna'i City,* ☎ *808/565–6363. No credit cards.*

\$ ✕ **Pele's Other Garden.** Mark and Barbara Zigmond's dynamic little eatery is a deli, juice bar, and bistro all in one, and adds a healthy twist to the Lāna'i City dining scene with mile-high sandwiches, vegetarian dishes, and fresh-baked breads. The signature Italian grinder is a great reward after an arduous hike. You can also order tantalizing picnic lunches served in a convenient cooler bag. Recently, the tiny spot expanded both its space and hours and now turns into a tablecloth-dining experience at night with a selection of pasta dishes. ⊠ *811 Houston St., Lāna'i City,* ☎ *808/565–9628 or 888/764–3354. AE, DC, MC, V.*

LODGING

For years the island's only accommodation was the no-fuss Hotel Lāna'i in Lāna'i City. Today, you can choose among classy resorts, pleasant bed-and-breakfasts, and a few rental houses. For an explanation of price categories, *see* Lodging *in* Smart Travel Tips.

South and West Lāna'i

\$\$\$\$ ☷ **Mānele Bay Hotel.** This property has spectacular views of Lāna'i's
★ dramatic coastline and beyond. Courtyard gardens, arcades, breezeways, and bridges connect guest-room buildings with the main entrance. The architecture and decor combine both Mediterranean and traditional Hawaiian elements. Asian art, as well as work by local artists, fills the common areas. The crescent of Hulopo'e Bay is just minutes away. ⊠ *Box 310, Lāna'i City 96763,* ☎ *808/565–7700 or 800/321–4666,* 𝔽𝔸𝕏 *808/565–3868,* 𝕎𝔼𝔹 *www.lanai-resorts.com. 222 rooms, 28 suites. 4 restaurants, bar, minibars, room service, pool, spa, 18-hole golf course, 6 tennis courts, archery, health club, library, children's programs. AE, DC, MC, V.*

North and East Lāna'i

\$\$\$\$ ☷ **Captain's Retreat.** Within walking distance of town, this two-story cedar private home is the ultimate group getaway, with 3,000 square ft, four bedrooms (including one master suite with private bath and patio), a redwood deck, an outside shower, and a roomy kitchen. Single-room bookings aren't available here, but if the rate is split between friends or a family (the house accommodates 10 comfortably), this turns out to be a reasonably priced alternative. ⊠ *Okamoto Realty, 730 Lāna'i Ave., Lāna'i City 96763,* ☎ *808/565–7519 or 888/565–6106,* 𝕎𝔼𝔹 *www.lanairental.com. 1 4-bedroom unit. MC, V.*

$$$$ ⊞ **Jasmine Garden, Pink House, and Lāna'i Avenue Plantation House.**
Michael and Susan Hunter, who run the Dreams Come True B&B, rent
out three houses—and four-wheel-drive vehicles. Jasmine Garden is in
the older section of Lāna'i City and has three bedrooms with skylights
(one king size, two queen size), three marble baths (one with whirlpool), and a well-equipped granite kitchen. The four-bedroom Lāna'i
Avenue Plantation House, near the center of Lāna'i City, also has marble baths and a granite kitchen, as well as wooden floors and a large
deck with mountain views. The Pink House, surrounded by papaya,
banana, and eucalyptus trees, has two queen-size bedrooms and a
deck. It's a five-minute walk to the center of Lāna'i City. Weekly and
monthly rates are available for all properties. ⊠ *Jasmine St. at 13th*
Ave., Lāna'i City 96763, ☎ *808/565–6961 or 800/566–6961,* 🅵🅰🆇 *808/*
565–7056, 🆆🅴🅱 *www.10kvacationrentals.com. 2 4-bedroom units, 1 2-*
bedroom unit. Car rental. AE, D, MC, V.

$$$$ ⊞ **Lodge at Kō'ele.** On 21 acres in the highlands at the edge of Lāna'i
★ City, this grand country estate feels like a luxurious mountain retreat.
Secluded by old pines, 1½ mi of paths meander through theme gardens,
along a pond, and past an orchid greenhouse. Inside, beamed ceilings,
stone fireplaces, a music room, a tea room, and the magnificent Great
Hall (where afternoon tea with scones and clotted cream is served) create an Old World ambience. The porch offers views of spectacular sunsets. The Lodge can be a romantic getaway, but it's great for *keiki*
(children) as well. Children's programs focus on the island's cultural
and environmental heritage, and include becoming a *paniolo* (Hawaiian cowboy), building a volcano, discovering petroglyphs, and more.
⊠ *Box 310, Lāna'i City 96763,* ☎ *808/565–7300 or 800/321–4666,*
🅵🅰🆇 *808/565–3868,* 🆆🅴🅱 *www.lanai-resorts.com. 88 rooms, 14 suites. 2*
restaurants, bar, lobby lounge, minibars, room service, pool, 18-hole
golf course, 3 tennis courts, archery, croquet, health club, horseback
riding, children's programs. AE, DC, MC, V.

$$–$$$ ⊞ **Hotel Lāna'i.** Built in 1923 to house visiting plantation executives,
this 11-room inn was once the only accommodation on the island. The
old front porch with its big wicker chairs is a perfect spot to read the
paper and enjoy a drink. The rooms, with country quilts and original
plantation-era pictures, make you feel like you're staying in someone's
home. A Continental breakfast with fresh-baked breads is included in
the rate. ⊠ *828 Lāna'i Ave., Lāna'i City 96763,* ☎ *808/565–7211 or*
800/795–7211, 🅵🅰🆇 *808/565–6450,* 🆆🅴🅱 *www.onlanai.com. 11 rooms.*
Restaurant. AE, MC, V.

$$ ⊞ **Blue Ginger Vacation Rental.** Georgia Abilay, of Blue Ginger Café
fame, owns this two-bedroom vacation home in a newer neighborhood
of Lāna'i City. Grounds have tropical plants and roses, and room
decor is modern. One of the bedrooms has a double bed, the other has
two twin beds, and the living room's overstuffed couch converts to a
bed. Breakfast can be arranged courtesy of the café. ⊠ *421 Lama St.,*
Lāna'i City 96763, ☎ *808/565–6363 or 808/565–6666. 1 two-bed-*
room unit. No credit cards.

$$ ⊞ **Dreams Come True.** Michael and Susan Hunter's bed-and-breakfast
in the heart of Lāna'i City has canopy beds, antique furnishings, and
memorabilia from their many years in Asia and on Lāna'i. Fresh fruit
from their own trees enhances the generous breakfast. Susan is a trained
massage therapist and provides in-house massage for $50 an hour. Ve-
hicle rental is also available. ⊠ *547 12th St., Lāna'i City 96763,* ☎ *808/*
565–6961 or 800/566–6961, 🅵🅰🆇 *808/565–7056,* 🆆🅴🅱 *www.go-native.*
com/inns. 3 rooms. Massage, car rental. AE, D, MC, V.

NIGHTLIFE AND THE ARTS

The 153-seat **Lāna'i Theater and Playhouse** (☎ 808/565–7500), a '30s landmark, presents first-run movies. The cozy cocktail lounge at the **Lodge at Kō'ele** (✉ Lāna'i City, ☎ 808/565–7300) stays open until 11 PM. The lodge also features music in its Great Hall every evening from 7 to 10. The classy lounge at the **Mānele Bay Hotel** (✉ Lāna'i City, ☎ 808/565–7700), Hale Aheahe (House of Gentle Breezes), offers entertainment every evening. Lāna'i's **Visiting Artist Program** (☎ 800/321–4666) brings authors and musicians to the island for free, informal presentations. Past visitors have included jazz guitarist Howard Alden and film critics Andrew Sarris and Molly Haskell. These events take place at either the Lodge at Kō'ele or the Mānele Bay Hotel.

OUTDOOR ACTIVITIES AND SPORTS

Participant Sports

Camping

Destination Lāna'i (☎ 808/565–7600 or 800/947–4774) can help you locate no-frills camp sites. **Lāna'i Company** (☎ 808/565–3978) operates one great, little camp ground at Hulopo'e Beach with clean rest rooms, fire pits, and showers. You must obtain a permit. **Lāna'i Ecoadventure Centre** (☎ 808/565–7373) in town rents out camping gear and provides a wealth of inside tips.

Fitness and Spa Centers

The Fitness Center at the Lodge at Kō'ele. The center is small, but it provides state-of-the-art equipment. Yoga classes are scheduled throughout the week, and, in conjunction with The Spa at Mānele, specialty treatments and massages are available. *Lodge at Kō'ele,* ☎ *808/565–7300.*
The Spa at Mānele. Treat yourself to signature treatments such as the Ali'i Banana Coconut Scrub and the Hehi Lani-Royal Foot Treatment. Massages start at $95 for 50 minutes. A fitness center with cardiovascular equipment, free weights, whirlpools, and a steam room is also on-site. ✉ *Mānele Bay Hotel, Lāna'i City,* ☎ *808/565–7700.*

Golf

Cavendish Golf Course. This nine-hole course in the pines is free, but a donation for upkeep is requested. Call the Lodge at Kō'ele concierge (☎ 808/565–7300) for information and directions. Bring your own clubs.
Challenge at Mānele. This world-class 18-hole course was designed by Jack Nicklaus. The clubhouse serves lunch as well as light dinners until 9 PM Thursday through Monday. ✉ *Mānele Bay Hotel,* ☎ *808/565–2222.* 🏌 *Greens fee $135 for guests of the Lodge at Kō'ele or Mānele Bay Hotel, $185 nonguests; cart included.*
Experience at Kō'ele. The Lodge at Kō'ele has an 18-hole championship course designed by Greg Norman. There's also an 18-hole executive putting course, free to guests but not accessible to nonguests. The clubhouse serves lunch. ✉ *Lodge at Kō'ele,* ☎ *808/565–4653.* 🏌 *Greens fee $135 guests, $185 nonguests; cart included.*

Hiking

Lāna'i is a hiker's paradise with trails—some with whimsical names such as Eucalyptus Ladder, Old Cowboy Trail, and Ancient Graveyard—snaking through dryland forest, over rugged grasslands and along splendid shores. Make sure to get a good map.

Koloiki Ridge is a wide, easy trail of about 2 ½ mi behind the Lodge at Kō'ele that overlooks the island's north side.

Lāna'i Fisherman Trail takes about an hour, and follows the oceanside perimeter of Mānele Bay Hotel, along cliffs bordering the golf course. **The Munro Trail,** a strenuous 9-mi trek that takes about eight hours, is the island's most popular hike. There is an elevation gain of 1,400 ft, leading you to the lookout at Lāna'i's highest point, Lāna'ihale. **Shipwreck Beach** offers a light adventure for beachcombers with its remote 8-mi trail.

Horseback Riding

The Stables at Kō'ele (☎ 808/565–4424) take you through scenic high-country trails. They have a corral full of well-groomed horses for riders of all ages and skill levels. Trail rides start at $40 for one hour, $65 for two hours. You can also arrange lessons, private rides, or customized day-long rides with lunch.

Mountain Biking

Lāna'i Ecoadventure Centre (☎ 808/565–7373). John and Kris, the friendly couple here, rent 21-speed mountain bikes for $29 per day. They also offer half-day ($69) and full-day ($119) tours.

The **Lodge at Kō'ele** (☎ 808/565–7300) rents mountain bikes to guests of the lodge and of the Mānele Bay Hotel for $8 per hour or $40 per day.

Sporting Clays

Lāna'i Pine Sporting Clays and Archery Range. The rustic, 14-station sporting clays course is in a pine-wood valley overlooking the sea. A single shooter can complete the course in an hour. Cost is $135 for 100 targets and $75 for 50 targets. Beginners can start with an introductory, 25-target lesson for $65. Each October, celebrities—Arnold Schwarzenegger and Tom Selleck have been among them—host the cash-winning Open Play Target Shoot. You have to arrange to play the course through your hotel. The Archery Range has 12 stations with straw bales and 15- or 35-yard ranges. Private and group lessons are offered, with an introduction starting at $45. Experienced archers can use the range for $35 an hour. Equipment is included. ⊠ *Off Keōmuku Hwy.,* ☎ *808/559–4600.*

Water Sports

DEEP-SEA FISHING

Spinning Dolphin Fishing Charters (☎ 808/565–6613) handles both heavy and light tackle fishing on its 28-ft diesel-powered Omega sport fisher. Half-day ($400) and full-day ($800) charters out of Mānele Bay are private, with a six-person maximum. Bring your own lunch. Juice and ice are provided.

SNORKELING AND SCUBA DIVING

Hulopo'e Beach is one of Hawai'i's most outstanding snorkeling destinations. Several companies offer snorkeling tours and the hotels can rent equipment as well.

Some say scuba diving doesn't get better than off the shores of Lāna'i. The dive site **Cathedrals,** off the south shore, gets its name from the spacious caverns created by numerous pinnacles that rise from depths of 60 ft to just below the water's surface. In these beautiful chambers lurk spotted moray eels, lobster, and ghost shrimp. **Sergeant Major Reef,** on the south shore, is made up of three parallel lava ridges, a cave, and an archway, with rippled sand valleys between the ridges. Depths range from 15 to 50 ft.

Lāna'i Ecoadventure Centre (☎ 808/565–7373) offers unique kayak and snorkel adventures in remote locations, often excellent whale-watching spots. The four- to five-hour morning excursions cost around $69.

You can also take introductory scuba-diving courses, one- and two-tank dives, and certification courses.

Spinning Dolphin Fishing Charters (☎ 808/565–6613) offers private snorkel and sightseeing tours. When the whales are here (December through April), three-hour whale-watching tours are available.

Trilogy Oceansports Lāna'i (☎ 808/667–7721 or 888/628–4800, WEB www.sailtrilogy.com) offers a daily four-hour morning snorkel sail on a 51-ft catamaran with lessons, equipment, and meals included. They charter two-tank dives on their catamarans for experienced divers for $160—ask about the availability of introductory dives. You can also book a blue water dolphin watch, whale-watching sails, and a sunset cruise. It's best to book trips through your hotel concierge.

SHOPPING

Except for the boutiques at the Lodge at Kō'ele and Mānele Bay Hotel which are handy for stocking up on suntan lotion, aspirin, books, and other vacation necessities, Lāna'i City is the island's only place to shop. Its main streets, 7th and 8th, have shops straight out of the '20s: general stores with personal, congenial service. Business hours are generally Monday through Saturday 9–noon and 1:30–5.

General Stores

International Food and Clothing Center. You may not find everything the name implies, but this old-fashioned emporium does stock items for your everyday needs, from hardware to beer, wine, and spirits. ⊠ 833 'Ilima Ave. Lāna'i City, ☎ 808/565–6433.

Lāna'i City Service. In addition to being a gas station and car-rental operation, this outfit sells fast food, sundries, T-shirts, and island crafts in the **Plantation Store** and in **Nani's Corner.** ⊠ 1036 Lāna'i Ave. Lāna'i City, ☎ 808/565–7227.

Pine Isle Market. You can get everything from cosmetics to canned vegetables here at one of Lāna'i City's two supermarkets. It's a great place to buy fresh fish. ⊠ 356 8th Ave., Lāna'i City, ☎ 808/565–6488.

Richard's Shopping Center. Richard Tamashiro founded this store in 1946, and the Tamashiro clan continues to run the place. Along with groceries, the store has a fun selection of Lāna'i T-shirts. ⊠ 434 8th Ave. Lāna'i City, ☎ 808/565–6047.

Clothing

Local Gentry. This tiny, classy store has clothing for every need, from beach wear and casual summer dresses to evening resort wear, shoes, and hats. ⊠ 363 7th St. Lāna'i City, ☎ 808/565–9130.

Crafts

Akamai Trading. Akamai Trading sells such Lāna'i crafts as pine-tree bowls and flower-dyed gourds alongside island posters, T-shirts, and tropical jellies and jams. It's also the only place in town that serves cappuccino and espresso. ⊠ 408 8th Ave., ☎ 808/565–6587.

Gifts With Aloha. Hand-painted clothing and casual resort wear is sold alongside the work of local artists including ceramic ware, raku (Japanese-style lead-glazed pottery), fine hand-blown glass, and watercolor prints. ⊠ 811-B Houston St., ☎ 808/565–6589.

Lāna'i Arts and Culture Center. The home of the Lāna'i Art Program, which offers art classes, has a gift shop that sells unique Lāna'i handicrafts, from painted silk scarves to beaded jewelry. ⊠ 339 7th Ave., ☎ 808/565–7503.

LĀNA'I A TO Z

To research prices, get advice from other travelers, and book travel arrangements, visit www.fodors.com.

AIR TRAVEL

To reach Lāna'i from the mainland United States, you must first stop at O'ahu's Honolulu International Airport or at Maui's Kahului Airport. From either airport it takes about a half hour to fly to Lāna'i. Round-trip tickets for this leg of the trip start at $150.

CARRIERS

Hawaiian Airlines offers two round-trip flights daily on DC-9 jets. Island Air offers 12 flights daily on 18-passenger Dash-6s and 37-seat Dash-8s.

➤ AIRLINES & CONTACTS: **Hawaiian Airlines** (☎ 800/882–8811). **Island Air** (☎ 808/484–2222 or 800/323–3345).

AIRPORTS

The small Lāna'i Airport is in the southwest area of the island. There's a federal agricultural inspection station so that guests departing to the mainland can check luggage directly.

➤ AIRPORT INFORMATION: **Lāna'i Airport** (☎ 808/565–6757).

AIRPORT TRANSFERS

Lāna'i Airport is a 10-minute drive from Lāna'i City. If you're staying at the Hotel Lāna'i, the Lodge at Kō'ele, or the Mānele Bay Hotel, you'll be met by a shuttle. If you're staying elsewhere in Lāna'i City, make arrangements with your hosts ahead of time. There are no public buses or taxis on the island. If you want to travel in style, splurge on a private limousine, $42 to the Lodge at Kō'ele or $81 to Mānele Bay Hotel.

➤ TAXIS & SHUTTLES: **Rabaca's Limousine Service** (☎ 808/565–6670).

BOAT & FERRY TRAVEL

Ferries cross the channel five times daily, departing from Lahaina on Maui and Mānele Bay Harbor on Lāna'i. The crossing takes 45 minutes and costs $25 each way.

➤ BOAT & FERRY INFORMATION: **Expeditions** (☎ 808/661–3756 or 800/695–2624).

CAR RENTAL

Renting a car is essential if you plan to do a lot of exploring. Compact cars are available, but most of Lāna'i's sights require a four-wheel-drive vehicle. Make your reservations way in advance of your trip, because Lāna'i's fleet of vehicles is limited. Fees for Jeep Wranglers run around $130 a day and compact cars are about $60. Four-wheel-drive Cherokees are also available for about $145 per day. Lāna'i City Service, a subsidiary of Dollar Rent A Car, is open daily 7–7. Lāna'i Ecoadventure Centre offers 4x4 Suburbans for $79 to $99; weekly rentals are also available. You can also rent four-wheel-drive vehicles from Michael and Susan Hunter, proprietors of the Dreams Come True bed-and-breakfast and Jasmine Garden vacation rentals.

➤ LOCAL AGENCIES: **Lāna'i City Service.** (⊠ Lāna'i Ave. at 11th St., ☎ 808/565–7227 or 800/533–7808). **Lāna'i Ecoadventure Centre** (⊠ 8th Ave., next to the police station, ☎ 808/565–7373).

CAR TRAVEL

There is only 30 mi of paved road and secondary roads aren't marked. From Lāma'i City, the streets extend outward as paved roads with two-way traffic. Keōmuku Highway runs north to Shipwreck Beach, and

Highway 440, also known as Mānele Road or Kaumālapaʻu Highway, runs south down to Mānele Bay and Hulopoʻe Beach and west to Kaumālapaʻu Harbor. The rest of your driving takes place on bumpy, muddy roads best navigated by a four-wheel-drive vehicle.

The island doesn't have traffic lights, and you'll never find yourself in a traffic jam. However, as some attractions don't have signs, it's easy to get lost; before heading out on your explorations, ask at your hotel desk for a road and site map, and ask for confirmation that you're headed in the right direction. The only gas station on the island is in Lānaʻi City, at Lānaʻi City Service.

EMERGENCIES

The Lānaʻi Community Hospital is the island's health-care center. It has 24-hour ambulance service and a pharmacy.

➤ CONTACTS: **Lānaʻi Community Hospital** (✉ 628 7th St., ☎ 808/565–6411).

➤ EMERGENCY NUMBERS: **Police, fire, ambulance** (☎ 911).

SIGHTSEEING TOURS

Lānaʻi Ecoadventure Centre's popular 4x4 Adventure Trek takes you to the island's most scenic places, stopping where and when you want. Guides "talk story" about local history and the unique plants and animals. They even provide binoculars, snorkeling gear, snacks, and drinks. Expect to pay around $70. Coastal bike tours and off-road mountain bike treks— beginner through intermediate—also start at around $70.

Rabaca's Limousine Service offers four-wheel-drive tours.

➤ CONTACTS: **Lānaʻi Ecoadventure Centre** (✉ 8th Ave., next to the police station, ☎ 808/565–7737 or 808/565–7373, WEB www. adventurelanai.com). **Rabaca's Limousine Service** (☎ 808/565–6670).

VISITOR INFORMATION

Destination Lānaʻi, the island's visitors bureau, is your best bet for general information and maps. Feel free to stop in, but be aware that opening hours are erratic. The Maui Visitors Bureau has some information on the island as well as Maui.

➤ TOURIST INFORMATION: **Destination Lānaʻi** (✉ 730 Lānaʻi Ave., Suite 102, Lānaʻi City 96763, ☎ 808/565–7600, WEB www.aloha.net/ádlanai/). **Maui Visitors Bureau** (☎ 808/244–3530, WEB www.visitmaui.com).

7 BACKGROUND AND ESSENTIALS

Portraits of Hawai`i

Books and Videos

Chronology

Smart Travel Tips A to Z

Hawaiian Vocabulary

Menu Guide

Map of Hawaiian Islands

THESE VOLCANIC ISLES

Dawn at the crater on horseback. It's cold at 10,023 ft above the warm Pacific—maybe 45°F. The horses' breath condenses into a smoky cloud, and the riders cling to their saddles. It's eerily quiet except for the creak of straining leather and the crunch of volcanic cinders underfoot, sounds that are absurdly magnified in the vast empty space that yawns below.

This is Haleakalā, the "house of the sun." It's the crown of east Maui and the largest dormant volcano crater in the world. Every year thousands of visitors shake themselves awake at three in the morning to board vans that take them from their comfortable hotels and up the world's most steeply ascending auto route to the summit of Haleakalā National Park. Sunrise is extraordinary here. Colors from the palest pink to the most fiery red slowly spread across the lip of the summit. Mark Twain called it "the sublimest spectacle" he had ever witnessed.

But sunrise is only the beginning. The park encompasses 28,665 acres, and the valley itself is 21 mi in circumference and 19 square mi in area. At its deepest, it measures 3,000 ft from the summit. The two towers of Manhattan's World Trade Center could be placed one atop the other and still not reach the top. While Haleakalā is dormant, the vast, wondrous valley here isn't a single crater created by some devastating explosion. Misnamed by the first European explorers, Haleakalā's huge depression is actually a caldera, formed by the collapsing of the main cone. What you see today is the result of eons of wind and rain wearing down what was once a small crater at the original summit peak. The small hills within the valley are volcanic cinder cones, each the site of an eruption.

More than anything, entering Haleakalā is like descending to the moon. Trails for hiking and horseback riding crisscross the crater for some 32 mi. The way is strewn with volcanic rubble, crater cones, frozen lava flows, vents, and lava tubes. The colors you see on your descent are muted yet dramatic—black, yellow, russet, orange, lavender, brown, and gray, even a pinkish-blue. It seems as if nothing could live here, but in fact this is an ecosystem that sustains, among other, more humble life forms, the surefooted mountain goat, the rare nēnē goose (no webbing between its toes, the better to negotiate this rugged terrain with), and the strange and delicate silversword. The silversword, a spiny, metallic-leaf plant, once grew abundantly on Haleakalā's slopes. Today it survives in small numbers at Haleakalā and at high elevations on the Big Island of Hawai'i. The plants live up to 20 years, bloom only once, scatter their seeds, and die.

The valley's starkness is overwhelming. Even shadows cast in the thin mountain air are flinty and spare. It's easy to understand why in the early days of the U.S. space program moon-bound astronauts trained here.

It is also not difficult to see this place as a bubbling, sulfurous cauldron, a direct connection not to the heavens but to the core of the earth. Haleakalā's last—and probably final—eruption occurred in 1790, a few years after a Frenchman named Jean-François de Galaup, Comte de La Pérouse, became the first European to set foot on Maui. The rocky area on the southwest side of east Maui known as La Pérouse Bay is the result of that flow. That fiery outburst was only one of many in Hawai'i over the millennia, just as Maui and its now-cold crater are just one facet of the volcanic variety of the Aloha State.

Large and small, awake or sleeping, volcanoes are Hawai'i's history and its heritage. Behind their beauty is the story of the flames that created this ethereal island chain. The tale began some 25 million years ago, yet it is still unfinished. The islands in the Hawaiian archipelago are actually the upper bodies of immense mountains rising from the bottom of the sea. Formed by molten rock known as magma, the islands were slowly pushed up from the earth's volatile mantle, forced through cracks in the thin crust of the ocean floor. The first ancient eruptions cooled and formed pools on the Pacific bottom. Then, as magma spilled from the vents over millions of years, the pools became ridges and grew into crests. The latter built upon themselves over the eons, until finally they towered above the surface of the sea.

As the islands cooled in the Pacific waters, the lava slopes slowly bloomed, over centuries, with colorful flora. With ample rain and abundant sunshine, seeds, spores, and eggs of living creatures were carried by the winds and currents to these isolated volcanic isles more than 2,000 mi from the closest major landmass, and were nourished into a paradise of greenery.

This type of volcano, with its slowly formed, gently sloping sides, is known as a shield volcano, and each of the Hawaiian isles is composed of them. As long as the underwater vents spew the lifeblood lava out from the earth's core and into the heart of the mountain, a shield volcano will continue to grow.

The Hawaiian Islands rest on an area called the Pacific Plate, a vast shelf of land making its way slowly to the northwest by about 2 to 3 inches per year. The result is that contact between the submarine vents and the volcanoes' conduits for magma is gradually disrupted. Surface eruptions slow down and finally stop altogether, and these volcanoes ultimately become extinct.

That, at least, is one explanation. Another—centuries older and still revered in Hawaiian art and song—centers upon Pele, the beautiful and tempestuous daughter of Haumea, the Earth Mother, and Wakea, the Sky Father. Pele is the Hawaiian goddess of fire, the maker of mountains, melter of rocks, eater of forests, and burner of land—both creator and destroyer. Legend has it that Pele came to the Islands long ago to flee from her cruel older sister, Na Maka o Kahai, goddess of the sea. Pele ran first to the small island of Ni'ihau, making a crater home there with her digging stick. But Na Maka found her and destroyed her hideaway, so Pele again had to flee. On Kaua'i she delved deeper, but Na Maka chased her from that home as well. Pele ran on—from O'ahu to Moloka'i, Lana'i to Kaho'olawe, Molokini to Maui— but always and ever Na Maka pursued her.

Pele came at last to Halema'uma'u, the vast firepit crater of Ki'lauea, and there, on the Big Island, she dug deepest of all. There she is said to remain, all-powerful, quick to rage, and often unpredictable; the mountain is her impenetrable fortress and domain— a safe refuge, at least for a time, from Na Maka o Kahai.

Interestingly, the chronology of the old tales of Pele's flight from isle to isle closely matches the reckonings of modern volcanologists regarding the ages of the various craters. Today, the Big Island's Ki'lauea and Mauna Loa retain the closest links with the earth's superheated core and are active and volatile, though three other volcanoes that shaped the island are not. The remaining Hawaiian volcanoes have been carried beyond their magma supply by the movement of the Pacific Plate. Those farthest to the northwest in the island chain are completely extinct. Those at the southeasterly end of the island chain— Haleakalā, Mauna Ke'a, and Hualālai—are dormant and slipping away, so that the implacable process of volcanic death has begun. As erosion continues, the islands will someday melt back into the sea.

The largest island of the archipelago, the Big Island of Hawai'i rises some 13,796 ft above sea level at the sum-

Portraits

mit of Mauna Ke'a. Mauna Loa is nearly as high at 13,667 ft. Geologists believe it required more than 3 million years of steady volcanic activity to raise these peaks up above the waters of the Pacific. From their bases on the ocean floor, these shield volcanoes are the largest mountain masses on the planet.

Mauna Loa's little sister, Ki'lauea, at about 4,077 ft, is the most active volcano in the world. Between the two volcanoes, they have covered nearly 200,000 acres of land with their red-hot lava flows over the past 200 years or so. In the process, they have ravished trees, fields, meadows, villages, and more than a few unlucky humans. For generations, Ki'lauea, in a continually eruptive state, has pushed molten lava up from the earth's magma at 1,800°F and more. But as active as she and Mauna Loa are, their eruptions are comparatively safe and gentle, producing continuous small flows rather than large bursts of fire and ash. The exceptions were two explosive displays during recorded history—one in 1790, the other in 1924. During these eruptions, Pele came close to destroying the Big Island's largest city, Hilo. She also gave residents another scare as recently as 1985.

It is around these major volcanoes that the island's Hawai'i Volcanoes National Park was created. A sprawling natural preserve, the park attracts visitors from around the world for the unparalleled opportunity to view, up close and in person, the visual wonders of Pele's kingdom of fire. Geology experts and volcanologists have been coming for a century or more to study and to improve methods for predicting the times and sites of eruptions.

Thomas Augustus Jaggar, preeminent volcanologist and student of Ki'lauea, built his home on stilts wedged into cracks in the volcanic rock of the crater rim. Harvard-trained and universally respected, he was the driving force behind the establishment of the Hawaiian Volcano Observatory at Ki'lauea in 1912. When he couldn't raise research funds from donations, public and private, he raised pigs to keep the scientific work going. After Jaggar's death, his wife scattered his ashes over the great fiery abyss.

The park is on the Big Island's southeastern flank, about 30 minutes out of Hilo on the aptly named Volcano Highway. Wear sturdy walking shoes and carry a warm sweater. It can be a long hike across the lava flats to see Pele in action, and at 4,000 ft above sea level, temperatures can be brisk, however hot the volcanic activity. So much can be seen at close range along the road circling the crater that Ki'lauea has been dubbed the "drive-in volcano."

At the park's visitor center sits a large display case. It contains dozens of lava-rock "souvenirs"—removed from Pele's grasp and then returned, accompanied by letters of apology. They are sent back by visitors who say they regret having broken the *kapu* (taboo) against removing even the smallest grain of native volcanic rock from Hawai'i. A typical letter might say: "I never thought Pele would miss just one little rock, but she did, and now I've wrecked two cars . . . I lost my job, my health is poor, and I know it's because I took this stone." The letters can be humorous, or poignant and remorseful, requesting Pele's forgiveness.

It is surprisingly safe at the crater's lip. Unlike Japan's Mount Fuji or Washington State's Mount Saint Helens, Hawai'i's shield volcanoes spew their lava downhill, along the sides of the mountain. Still, the clouds of sulfur gas and fumes produced during volcanic eruptions are noxious and heady and can make breathing unpleasant, if not difficult. It has been pointed out that the chemistry of volcanoes—sulfur, hydrogen, oxygen, carbon dioxide—closely resembles the chemistry of the egg.

It's an 11-mi drive around the Ki'lauea crater via the Crater Rim Road, and the trip takes about an hour. But it's better to walk a bit. There are at least eight major trails in the park, ranging from short 15-minute strolls to the three-day, 18-mi (one way) Mauna Loa Trail. An easy, comfortable walk is Sulfur Banks, with its many steaming vents creating halos of clouds around the rim of Ki'lauea. The route passes through a forest of sandalwood, flowers, and ferns.

Just ahead is the main attraction: the center of Pele's power, Halema'uma'u. This yawning pit of flame and burning rock measures some 3,000 ft wide and is a breathtaking sight. When Pele is in full fury, visitors come in droves, on foot and by helicopter, to see her crimson expulsions coloring the dark earth and smoky sky. Ki'lauea's most recent violent activity has occurred at mountainside vents instead of at the summit crater. Known as rift zones, they are lateral conduits that often open in shield volcanoes.

Ki'lauea has two rift zones, one extending from the summit crater toward the southwest, through Kau, the other to the east-northeast through Puna, past Cape Kumakahi, into the sea. In the last two decades, repeated eruptions in the east rift zone have blocked off 12 mi of coastal road—some under more than 300 ft of rock—and have covered a total of 10,000 acres with lava. Where the flows entered the ocean, roughly 200 acres have been added to the Big Island.

Farther along the Crater Rim Road (about 4 mi from the visitor center) is the Thurston Lava Tube, an example of a strangely beautiful volcanic phenomenon common on the Islands. Lava tubes form when lava flows rapidly downhill. The sides and top of this river of molten rock cool, while the fluid center flows on. Most formations are short and shallow, but some measure 30 to 50 ft high and hundreds of yards long. Lava tubes were often used to store remains of the ancient Hawaiian royalty—the ali'i. The Thurston Lava Tube sits in a beautiful prehistoric fern forest called Fern Jungle.

Throughout the park, new lava formations are continually being created. These volcanic deposits exhibit the different types of lava produced by Hawai'i's volcanoes: 'a'ā, the dark, rough lava that solidifies as cinders of rock; and the more common pāhoehoe, the smooth, satiny lava that forms the vast plains of black rock in ropy swirls known as lava flats, which in some areas go on for miles. Other terms that help identify what may be seen in the park include caldera, which are the open, bowl-like lips of a volcano summit; ejecta, the cinders and ash that float through the air around an eruption; and olivine, the semiprecious chrysolite (greenish in color) found in volcanic ash.

But this volcanic landscape isn't all fire and flash, cinders, and devastation. Hawai'i Volcanoes National Park is also the home of some of the most beautiful of the state's black-sand beaches; forest glens full of lacy butterflies and colorful birds such as the dainty flycatcher, called the 'elepaio; and exquisite grottoes sparked with bright wild orchid sprays and crashing waterfalls. Even as the lava cools, still bearing a golden, glassy skin, lush, green native ferns—ama'uma'u, kupukupu, and 'ōkupukupu—spring up in the midst of Pele's fallout, as if defying her destructiveness or simply confirming the fact that after fire she brings life.

Some 12 centuries ago, in fact, Pele brought humans to her verdant islands: the fiery explosions that lit Ki'lauea and Mauna Loa probably guided the first explorers to Pele's side from the Marquesas Islands, some 2,400 mi away across the trackless, treacherous ocean.

Once settled, they worshiped her from a distance. Great numbers of religious heiau (outdoor stone platforms) dot the landscapes near the many older and extinct craters scattered throughout Hawai'i, demonstrating the reverence the native islanders have always held for Pele and her creations. But the ruins of only two heiau are to be found near the very active crater at Halema'uma'u. There, at the center of the capricious Pele's power, native Hawaiians caution one even today to "step lightly, for you are on holy ground."

In future ages, when mighty Ki'lauea is no more, this area will still be a volcanic isle. Beneath the blue Pacific waters, fiery magma flows and new mountains form and grow. Off the Big Island of Hawai'i a new island is forming. Still ½ mi below the water's surface, it won't be making an appearance any time soon, but already has a name. Just below the surface, Loihi waits.

— Gary Diedrichs

THE ALOHA SHIRT: A COLORFUL SWATCH OF ISLAND HISTORY

Elvis Presley had an entire wardrobe of them in the '60s films *Blue Hawaii* and *Paradise, Hawaiian Style*. During the '50s, entertainer Arthur Godfrey and bandleader Harry Owens often sported them on television shows. John Wayne loved to lounge around in them. Mick Jagger felt compelled to buy one on a visit to Hawai'i in the 1970s. Dustin Hoffman, Steven Spielberg, and Bill Cosby avidly collect them.

From gaudy to grand, from tawdry to tasteful, aloha shirts are Hawai'i's gift to the world of fashion. It has been more than 50 years since those riotously colored garments made their first appearance as immediately recognizable symbols of the Islands.

The roots of the aloha shirt go back to the early 1930s, when Hawai'i's garment industry was just beginning to develop its own unique style. Although locally made clothes did exist, they were almost exclusively for plantation workers and were constructed of durable palaka or plain cotton material.

Out of this came the first stirrings of fashion: Beachboys and schoolchildren started having sport shirts made from colorful Japanese kimono fabric. The favored type of cloth was the kind used for children's kimonos— bright pink and orange floral prints for girls; masculine motifs in browns and blues for boys. In Japan, such flamboyant patterns were considered unsuitable for adult clothing, but in the Islands such rules didn't apply, and

it seemed the flashier the shirt, the better—for either sex. Thus, the aloha shirt was born.

It was easy and inexpensive in those days to have garments tailored to order; the next step was moving to mass production and marketing. In June 1935, Honolulu's best-known tailoring establishment, Musa-Shiya, advertised the availability of "Aloha shirts—well tailored, beautiful designs and radiant colors. Ready-made or made to order . . . 95¢ and up." This is the first known printed use of the term that would soon refer to an entire industry. By the following year, several local manufacturers had begun full-scale production of "aloha wear." One of them, Ellery Chun of King-Smith, registered as local trademarks the terms "Aloha Sportswear" and "Aloha Shirt" in 1936 and 1937, respectively.

These early entrepreneurs were the first to create uniquely Hawaiian designs for fabric as well—splashy patterns that would forever symbolize the Islands. A 1939 *Honolulu Advertiser* story described them as a "delightful confusion (of) tropical fish and palm trees, Diamond Head and the Aloha Tower, surfboards and leis, ukuleles and Waikīkī beach scenes."

The aloha wear of the late 1930s was intended for—and mostly worn by— tourists, and interestingly, a great deal of it was exported to the mainland and even Europe and Australia. By the end of the decade, for example, only 5% of the output of one local firm, the Kamehameha Garment Company, was sold in Hawai'i.

World War II brought this trend to a halt, and during the postwar period, aloha wear really came into its own in Hawai'i itself. A strong push to support local industry gradually nudged island garb into the workplace, and kama'āina began to wear the clothing that previously had been seen as attire for visitors.

In 1947, for example, male employees of the City and County of Honolulu were first allowed to wear aloha shirts "in plain shades" during the summer months. Later that year, the first observance of Aloha Week started the tradition of "bankers and bellhops . . . mix(ing) colorfully in multihued and tapa-designed Aloha shirts every day," as a local newspaper's Sunday magazine supplement noted in 1948. By the 1960s, "Aloha Friday," set aside specifically for the wearing of aloha attire, had become a tradition. In the following decade, the suit and tie practically disappeared as work attire in Hawai'i, even for executives.

Most of the Hawaiian-theme fabric used in manufacturing aloha wear was designed in the Islands, then printed on the mainland or in Japan. The glowingly vibrant rayons of the late '40s and early '50s (a period now seen as aloha wear's heyday) were at first printed on the East Coast, but manufacturers there usually required such large orders, local firms eventually found it impossible to continue using them. By 1964, 90% of Hawaiian fabric was being manufactured in Japan—a situation that still exists today.

Fashion trends usually move in cycles, and aloha wear is no exception. By the 1960s, the "chop suey print" with its "tired clichés of Diamond Head, Aloha Tower, outrigger canoes (and) stereotyped leis" was seen as corny and garish, according to an article published in the *Honolulu Star-Bulletin.* But it was just that outdated aspect that began to appeal to the younger crowd, who began searching out old-fashioned aloha shirts at the Salvation Army and Goodwill thrift stores. These shirts were dubbed "silkies," a name by which they're still known, even though most of them were actually made of rayon.

Before long, what had been 50¢ shirts began escalating in price, and a customer who had balked at paying $5 for a shirt that someone had already worn soon found the same item selling for $10—and more. By the late 1970s, aloha-wear designers were copying the prints of yesteryear for their new creations.

The days of bargain silkies are now gone. The few choice aloha shirts from decades past that still remain are offered today by specialized dealers for hundreds of dollars apiece, causing many to look back with chagrin to the time when such treasures were foolishly worn to the beach until they fell apart. The best examples of vintage aloha shirts are now rightly seen as art objects, worthy of preservation for the lovely depictions they offer of Hawai'i's colorful and unique scene.

— DeSoto Brown

"The Aloha Shirt: A Colorful Swatch of Island History" first appeared in ALOHA magazine. Reprinted with permission of Davick Publications.

WHAT TO READ AND WATCH BEFORE YOU GO

Books

If you like your history in novel form you'll enjoy James A. Michener's *Hawaii* for its overall perspective; it's also available on audiocassette. Captain James Cook's *A Voyage to the Pacific Ocean*, one of the first guidebooks to the Islands, contains many valid insights; *Shoal of Time*, by Gavan Daws, chronicles Hawaiian history from Cook's time to the 1960s. History also comes to life in the pages of *Travels in Hawaii*, by Robert Louis Stevenson; *History Makers of Hawaii*, by A. Grove Day, is a biographical dictionary of people who shaped the territory from past to present. To gain familiarity with the gods and goddesses who have also had a hand in this land's development, read *Hawaiian Mythology* by Martha Beckwith. *Hawai'i's Story by Hawai'i's Queen*, the tale of the overthrow of the Hawaiian monarchy in Queen Lili'uokalani's own words, is poignant and thought-provoking. For a glimpse of military history, *Pearl Harbor: Fact and Reference Book* by Terrance McCombs, is a collection of both well-known facts and lesser-known trivia. For a truly Hawaiian perspective, *Voices of Wisdom: Hawaiian Elders Speak* by M. J. Harden shares interviews with some of Hawai'i's most respected elders, Hawai'i's traditional keepers of knowledge and wisdom.

A whole new genre of Hawaiian writing offers insights into island lifestyles through the use of pidgin prose and local settings. Paul Wood's essays, collected in *Four Wheels, Five Corners: Facts of Life in Upcountry Maui*, are quirky tales of life on a rock in the middle of the Pacific. Recent novels that capture the South Seas texture include *Shark's Dialogue*, by Kiana Davenport; this book weaves together multiethnic stories, legends, and ancient beliefs to create a mystical air.

Wild Meat and the Bully Burgers, by Lois Ann Yamanaka, a tale of growing up on the Big Island, is told in an authentic native voice. Writers Paul Theroux, Barbara Kingsolver, and Maxine Hong Kingston are among those who share stories about the Islands in *Hawaii: True Stories of the Island Spirit,* a collection edited by Rick and Marcie Carroll.

Those interested in the outdoors may want to pick up *A Guide to Tropical and Semitropical Flora,* by Loraine Kuck and Richard Tongg. The *Handbook of Hawaiian Fishes,* by W. A. Gosline and Vernon Brock, is great for snorkelers. *Hawaii's Birds,* put out by the Hawai'i Audubon Society, is perfect for bird-watchers. *Hawaiian Hiking Trails,* by Craig Chisholm, is just the guide for day hikers and backpackers. Find your perfect place in the sand with *Hawaii's Best Beaches* by John R. K. Clark, a guide to the 50th state's 50 best beaches. *Surfing: The Ultimate Pleasure,* by Leonard Lueras, covers everything about the sport, from its early history to the music and films of its later subculture.

Preparing your palate for an upcoming visit, or have you returned from the Islands in love with haute Hawaiian cuisine? *The New Cuisine of Hawaii,* by Janice Wald Henderson, is beautifully designed and features recipes from the 12 chefs credited with defining Hawai'i regional cuisine. One of these pioneers, celebrity chef Roy Yamaguchi, has opened a veritable empire of restaurants across the Islands. His cookbook *Roy's Feasts from Hawaii* provides an in-depth taste of the Islands in addition to some gorgeous photography and background. Rachel Laudan's *The Foods of Paradise* describes local foods and their histories in addition to providing recipes. *Hawaiian Country Tables* by Kaui Philpotts spotlights vintage Island recipes and dishes and gives readers an unusual entrée into Hawai'i's history.

For swaying musicologists, there's *Hula Is Life, The Story of Maiki Aiu and Hālau Hulo o Maiki,* by Rita Aryioshi; it's the definitive book on hula's origins and development. Hawaiian music lovers might take note of the ideas presented in *Strains of Change: Impact of Tourism on Hawaiian Music* by Elizabeth Tatar. *Hawaiian Traditions in Hawaii,* by Joan Clarke, is an illustrated book detailing ethnic celebrations in the Islands. Robert Shaw traces the history of the Islands through the tradition of quilting in his artful book *Hawaiian Quilt Masterpieces.* Instead of just taking home a lei, learn how to make one: *Hawaiian Lei Making,* by Laurie Shimizu Ide, offers a photographic guide and reference tool for making floral leis. Albert J.Schütz's souvenir-worthy paperback, *All About Hawaiian,* is a good introduction to the authentic language of the Islands and recent efforts to preserve it. **Hawai'i Magazine** (✉ 3 Burroughs Rd., Irvine, CA 92618, ☎ 949/855–8822; subscription $15 for six issues) is an attractive bimonthly magazine devoted to the 50th state.

Videos

To view Hawai'i on video before your arrival, take a look at *Forever Hawaii,* a video portrait of Hawai'i's six major islands.

The video *Hawaii on Foot,* with Robert Smith, gives hikers a peek at some of the best trails on O'ahu, Maui, the Big Island, and Kaua'i. It is available from **H.O.A. Publications** (✉ 102-16 Kaui Pl., Kula 96796, ☎ 808/678–2664). For lovers of dance, hula comes alive in the *1999 Merrie Monarch Festival Highlights.* This hula festival, held each spring on the Big Island, is Hawai'i's most prestigious competition. The video is available from WEB www.BooklinesHawaii. com, or by phone by calling ☎ 800/ 828–4852.

Movie buffs enjoy *Made in Paradise: Hollywood's Films of Hawaii and the South Seas,* by Luis Reyes. It points out movie locations and pokes gentle fun at some of the misinformation popularized by Tinseltown's version of Island life. Guided tours of Kaua'i locations used in filming are provided by **Hawai'i Movie Tours** (☎ 800/628–8432). Its tours are highly recommended.

Most people automatically think of Elvis when the words "Hawai'i" and "movie" are mentioned in the same sentence. Elvis Presley's Hawaiian-filmed movies are *Girls! Girls! Girls!* (1962), *Paradise, Hawaiian Style* (1966), and *Blue Hawaii* (1962), which showcases O'ahu's picturesque Hanauma Bay and Kaua'i's Coco Palms Resort, the site of Elvis's celluloid wedding.

Films such as Shirley Temple's *Curly Top* (1935); *Waikiki Wedding* (1937), with Bing Crosby; and *Gidget Goes Hawaiian* (1962) feature Hawai'i's beaches, palm trees, and hula dancers. The Islands' winter waves have taken center stage in a legion of hang-ten films of which only *North Shore* (1987) is on video.

Military-theme movies filmed in Hawai'i include *Mister Roberts* (1955), starring Henry Fonda, Jack Lemmon, and James Cagney; and *Lt. Robin Crusoe, USN* (1966), with Dick Van Dyke. Some serious military films, often dealing with World War II, with Hawaiian locales frequently posing as the South Pacific, include *Between Heaven and Hell* (1956), starring Robert Wagner; *The Enemy Below* (1957), with Robert Mitchum; and John Wayne's *Donovan's Reef* (1963). *Tora! Tora! Tora!* (1971) recreated the December 7, 1941, bombing of Pearl Harbor. For *Flight of the Intruder*(1991), director John Milius turned taro farms at the base of Kaua'i's Mount Wai'ale'le into the rice paddies of Southeast Asia.

Hawai'i has repeatedly doubled for other places. Kaua'i's remote valleys and waterfalls and O'ahu's Kualoa Ranch portrayed a Costa Rican dinosaur preserve in Steven Spielberg's *Jurassic Park* (1993). The opening beach scene of that movie's sequel, *The Lost World* (1997), was also filmed on Kaua'i. Spielberg was no stranger to Kaua'i, though, having filmed Harrison Ford's escape via seaplane from Kaua'i's Menehune Fishpond in *Raiders of the Lost Ark* (1981). The fluted cliffs and gorges of Kaua'i's rugged Nā Pali Coast play the misunderstood beast's island home in *King Kong* (1976), and a jungle dweller of another sort, in *George of the Jungle* (1997), frolicked on Kaua'i. Harrison Ford returned to the island for 10 weeks during the filming of *Six Days, Seven Nights* (1998), a romantic adventure set in French Polynesia.

Mitzi Gaynor washed that man right out of her hair on Kaua'i's Lumaha'i Beach in *South Pacific* (1958). And the tempestuous love scene between Burt Lancaster and Deborah Kerr in *From Here to Eternity* (1954) took place on O'ahu's Halona Cove beach.

The film version of James A. Michener's story *Hawaii* (1967) chronicles the lives of the Islands' missionary families. *Picture Bride* (1995) tells the story of a young Japanese girl who arrives on the Islands to face harsh realities as the wife of a sugar-plantation laborer she has only seen in a photograph. And in *Race the Sun* (1996), a group of Big Island high school students build a solar-powered car and go on to win an international competition.

Other movies with Hawai'i settings include *Black Widow* (1987), in which journalist Debra Winger travels to the Big Island's lava fields to prevent a murder; *Honeymoon in Vegas* (1992); *Under the Hula Moon* (1995); and *A Very Brady Sequel* (1997).

HAWAI'I AT A GLANCE

ca. AD 500 The first human beings to set foot on Hawaiian shores are Polynesians, who travel 2,400 mi in 60- to 80-ft canoes to the islands they name Havaiki after their legendary homeland. Researchers today believe they were originally from Southeast Asia and that they discovered the South Pacific Islands of Tahiti and the Marquesas before ending up in Hawai'i.

ca. 1758 Kamehameha, the Hawaiian chief who unified the Islands, is born.

1778 In January, Captain James Cook, commander of the H.M.S.*Resolution* and the consort vessel H.M.S.*Discovery,* lands on the island of Kaua'i. He names the archipelago the Sandwich Islands after his patron, the Earl of Sandwich. In November, he returns to the Islands for the winter, anchoring at Kealakekua Bay on the Big Island.

1779 In February, Cook is killed in a battle with Hawai'i's indigenous people at Kealakekua.

1785 The isolation of the Islands ends as British, American, French, and Russian fur traders and New England whalers come to Hawai'i. Tales spread of thousands of acres of sugarcane growing wild, and farmers come in droves from the United States and Europe.

1790 Kamehameha begins his rise to power with a series of bloody battles.

1791 Kamehameha builds Pu'ukoholā Heiau (temple) on the Big Island and dedicates it by sacrificing a rival chief, Keoua Kuahu'ula, whom he has killed.

1795 Using Western arms, Kamehameha wins a decisive confrontation on O'ahu. Except for Kaua'i, which he tries to invade in 1796 and 1804, this completes his military conquest of the Islands.

1810 The chief of Kaua'i acknowledges Kamehameha's rule, giving him suzerainty over Kaua'i and Ni'ihau. Kamehameha becomes known as King Kamehameha I, and he rules the unified Kingdom of Hawai'i with an iron hand.

1819 Kamehameha I dies, and his oldest son, Liholiho, rules briefly as Kamehameha II, with Ka'ahumanu, Kamehameha I's favorite wife, as co-executive. Ka'ahumanu persuades the new king to abandon old religious *kapu* (taboos), including those that forbade women to eat with men or to hold positions of power. The first whaling ships land at Lahaina on Maui.

1820 By the time the first missionaries arrive from Boston, Hawai'i's social order is beginning to break down. First, Ka'ahumanu and then Kamehameha II defy kapu without attracting divine retribution. Hawaiians, disillusioned with their own gods, are receptive to the ideas of Christianity. The influx of Western visitors also introduces to Hawai'i Western diseases, liquor, and what some view as moral decay.

1824 King Kamehameha II and his favorite wife die of measles during a visit to England. Honolulu missionaries give both royals a Christian burial outside Kawaiaha'o Church, inspiring many Hawaiians to convert to the Protestant faith. The king's younger brother, Kau'ikea'ōuli, becomes King Kamehameha III, a wise and gentle sovereign who reigns for 30 years with Ka'ahumanu as regent.

1832 Ka'ahumanu is baptized and dies a few months later.

1840 The Wilkes Expedition, sponsored by the U.S. Coast and Geodetic Survey, pinpoints Pearl Harbor as a potential naval base.

1845 Kamehameha III and the legislature move Hawai'i's seat of government from Lahaina, on Maui, to Honolulu, on O'ahu.

1849 Kamehameha III turns Hawai'i into a constitutional monarchy, and the United States, France, and Great Britain recognize Hawai'i as an independent country.

1850 The Great Mahele, a land commission, reapportions the land to the crown, the government, chiefs, and commoners, introducing for the first time the Western principle of private ownership. Commoners are now able to buy and sell land, but this great division becomes the great dispossession. By the end of the 19th century, white men own four acres for every one owned by a native Hawaiian. Some of the commission's distributions continue to be disputed to this day.

1852 As Western diseases depopulate the Islands, a labor shortage occurs in the sugarcane fields. For the next nine decades, a steady stream of foreign labor pours into Hawai'i, beginning with the Chinese. The Japanese begin arriving in 1868, followed by Filipinos, Koreans, Portuguese, and Puerto Ricans.

1872 Kamehameha V, the last descendent of the king who unified the Islands, dies without heirs. A power struggle ensues between the adherents of David Kalākaua and William Lunalilo.

1873 Lunalilo is elected Hawai'i's sixth king in January. The bachelor rules only 13 months before dying of tuberculosis.

1874 Kalākaua vies for the throne with the Dowager Queen Emma, the half-Caucasian widow of Kamehameha IV. Kalākaua is elected by the Hawai'i Legislature, against protests by supporters of Queen Emma. American and British marines are called in to restore order, and Kalākaua begins his reign as the "Merrie Monarch."

1875 The United States and Hawai'i sign a treaty of reciprocity, assuring Hawai'i a duty-free market for sugar in the United States.

1882 King Kalākaua builds 'Iolani Palace, an Italian renaissance–style structure, on the site of the previous royal palace.

1887 The reciprocity treaty of 1875 is renewed, giving the United States exclusive use of Pearl Harbor as a coaling station. Coincidentally, successful importation of Japanese laborers begins in earnest (after a false start in 1868).

1891 King Kalākaua dies and is succeeded by his sister, Queen Lili'uokalani, the last Hawaiian monarch.

1893 After a brief two-year reign, Lili'uokalani is removed from the throne by American business interests led by Lorrin A. Thurston (grandson of the missionary and newspaper founder Asa Thurston). Lili'uokalani is imprisoned in 'Iolani Palace for nearly eight months.

1894 The provisional government converts Hawai'i into a republic and proclaims Sanford Dole president.

1898 With the outbreak of the Spanish-American War, president William McKinley recognizes Hawai'i's strategic importance in the Pacific and moves to secure the Islands for the United States. On August 12, Hawai'i is officially annexed by a joint resolution of Congress.

1901 Sanford Dole is appointed first governor of the territory of Hawai'i. The first major tourist hotel, the Moana (now called the Sheraton Moana Surfrider), is built on Waikīkī Beach.

1903 James Dole, a cousin of Sanford Dole, produces nearly 2,000 cases of pineapple, marking the beginning of Hawai'i's pineapple industry. Pineapple eventually surpasses sugarcane as Hawai'i's number-one crop.

1907 Fort Shafter Base on O'ahu, headquarters for the U.S. Army, becomes the first permanent military post in the Islands.

1908 Dredging of the channel at Pearl Harbor begins.

1919 Pearl Harbor is formally dedicated by the U.S. Navy. Representing the Territory of Hawai'i in the U.S. House of Representatives, Prince Jonah Kūhiō Kalaniana'ole—the adopted son of Kapi'olani, the wife of Kalākaua, and with his brother one of the designated heirs to the throne of the childless Lili'uokalani—introduces the first bill proposing statehood for Hawai'i.

1927 Army lieutenants Lester Maitland and Albert Hegenberger make the first successful nonstop flight from the mainland to the Islands. Hawai'i begins to increase efforts to promote tourism, the industry that eventually dominates development of the Islands. The Matson Navigation Company builds the Royal Hawaiian Hotel as a destination for its cruise ships.

1929 Hawai'i's commercial interisland air service begins.

1936 Pan American World Airways introduces regular commercial passenger flights to Hawai'i from the mainland.

1941 At Pearl Harbor the U.S. Pacific Fleet is bombed by the Japanese, forcing U.S. entry into World War II. Nearly 4,000 men are killed in the surprise attack.

1942 James Jones, with thousands of others, trains at Schofield Barracks on O'ahu. He later writes about his experience in *From Here to Eternity*.

1959 Congress passes legislation granting Hawai'i statehood. In special elections the new state sends to the U.S. House of Representatives its first American of Japanese ancestry, Daniel Inouye, and to the U.S. Senate its first American of Chinese ancestry, Hiram Fong. Later in the year, the first Boeing 707 jets make the flight from San Francisco in a record five hours. By year's end 243,216 tourists visit Hawai'i, and tourism becomes Hawai'i's major industry.

1986 Hawai'i elects its first native Hawaiian governor, John Waihe'e.

1992 Hurricane 'Iniki, the most devastating hurricane to hit Hawai'i, tears through Kaua'i on September 11. The island's people, infrastructure, gardens, and tourism industry have happily all since recovered.

1993 After native Hawaiians commemorate the 100th anniversary of the overthrow of Queen Lili'uokalani with a call for sovereignty, Congress issues an apology to the Hawaiian people for the annexation of the Islands.

1997 After 34 years of planning, construction, and endless litigation, O'ahu's H-3 "Trans-Koolau" freeway linking Pearl Harbor to the Windward side of O'ahu finally opens. Opposition to the highway centered on the route through the Hālawa and Haiku valleys, areas of historical and religious significance to native Hawaiians. The price tag for this scenic roadway with a million-dollar view? More than 1 billion in state and federal tax dollars.

1998 The U.S.S. *Missouri* comes to her final resting place in Pearl Harbor. The battleship, on whose decks the Japanese signed their surrender agreement in World War II, is now a floating museum, permanently docked at Ford Island.

2001 Kīlauea Volcano on the Big Island of Hawai'i reached the 19th year of its current eruptive phase and the longest phase of such activity in recorded volcanic history.

ESSENTIAL INFORMATION

AIR TRAVEL

Hawai'i is a major destination link for flights traveling to and from the U.S. mainland, Asia, Australia, New Zealand, and the South Pacific. Many of the major airline carriers serving Honolulu fly direct to the islands of Maui, Kaua'i, and the Big Island, allowing visitors to bypass connecting flights out of Honolulu. For the more spontaneous traveler, island-hopping is easy, with flights departing Honolulu every 20 to 30 minutes daily until mid-evening. International travelers also have options. O'ahu and the Big Island are gateways from foreign destinations into the United States. Entering into the Islands via the Big Island's Keāhole-Kona International airport can save international visitors a considerable amount of time spent clearing U.S. Customs, which during peak arrival times at Honolulu International Airport can be considerable.

BOOKING

When you book **look for nonstop flights** and **remember that "direct" flights stop at least once.** Try to avoid connecting flights, which require a change of plane. For more booking tips and to check prices and make on-line flight reservations, log on to www.fodors.com.

CARRIERS

From the U.S. mainland, American and Delta serve Honolulu and Maui. Continental flies into Honolulu and Kaua'i. Northwest flies into Honolulu. From the West Coast of the United States, United flies to Honolulu, Maui, the Big Island, and Kaua'i.

Hawaiian Airlines connects the U.S. mainland to Honolulu, Kaua'i, Maui, and the Big Island, and provides interisland flights. Aloha Airlines connects from Oakland, California, to Maui and Honolulu, and also provides interisland service. Island Air and Pacific Wings provide interisland service.

➤ MAJOR AIRLINES: **American** (☎ 800/433–7300). **Continental** (☎ 800/525–0280). **Delta** (☎ 800/221–1212). **Northwest** (☎ 800/225–2525). **United** (☎ 800/241–6522).

➤ SMALLER AIRLINES: **Aloha Airlines** (☎ 800/367–5250). **Hawaiian Airlines** (☎ 800/367–5320).

➤ DIRECT FLIGHTS FROM THE U.K.: **Air New Zealand** (☎ 0181/741–2299). **American** (☎ 0345/789–789). **Continental** (☎ 0800/776–464). **Delta** (☎ 0800/414–767). **United** (☎ 0800/888–555). **Trailfinders** (✉ 42–50 Earls Court Rd., Kensington, London, W8 6FT, ☎ 020/7937–5400) can arrange bargain flights.

➤ INTERISLAND FLIGHTS: **Aloha Airlines** (☎ 800/367–5250). **Hawaiian Airlines** (☎ 800/367–5320). **Island Air** (☎ 800/323–3345). **Pacific Wings** (☎ 888/575–4546).

CHECK-IN & BOARDING

Assuming that not everyone with a ticket will show up, airlines routinely overbook planes. When everyone does, airlines ask for volunteers to give up their seats. In return, these volunteers usually get a certificate for a free flight and are rebooked on the next flight out. If there are not enough volunteers, the airline must choose who will be denied boarding. The first to get bumped are passengers who checked in late and those flying on discounted tickets, so **get to the gate and check in as early as possible,** especially during peak periods.

Always **bring a government-issued photo I.D. to the airport;** a passport is best. You may be asked to show it before you are allowed to check in.

Plan to **arrive at the airport 45 to 60 minutes before departure for interisland flights, 60 to 90 minutes for domestic flights, and at least 2 hours prior to departure for travel to international destinations.** Although the Neighbor Island airports are smaller and more casual than Honolulu International, during peak times they can also be quite busy. Allot extra travel time to all airports during morning and afternoon rush-hour traffic periods. Prior to check-in, all luggage being taken out of Hawai'i must pass agricultural inspection. Fruit, plants, and processed foods that have been labeled and packed for export (including pineapples, papaya, coconuts, flowers, and macadamia nuts) are permitted. Fresh fruit and other agricultural items, including seed leis, are not, and will be confiscated.

CUTTING COSTS

The least expensive airfares to Hawai'i must usually be purchased in advance and are nonrefundable. It's smart to **call a number of airlines, and when you are quoted a good price, book it on the spot**—the same fare may not be available the next day. Always **check different routings** and look into using different airports. Travel agents, especially low-fare specialists (☞ Discounts & Deals), are helpful. **Check local and community newspapers** when you're in the Islands for deals and coupons on interisland flights.

Consolidators are another good source. They buy tickets for scheduled international flights at reduced rates from the airlines, then sell them at prices that beat the best fare available directly from the airlines, usually without restrictions. Sometimes you can even get your money back if you need to return the ticket. Carefully read the fine print detailing penalties for changes and cancellations, and **confirm your consolidator reservation with the airline.**

In Hawai'i, both **Aloha Airlines** and **Hawaiian Airlines** offer travelers multi-island air passes that allow unlimited interisland travel during a specific time period at a reduced rate.

➤ CONSOLIDATORS: **Cheap Tickets** (☎ 800/377–1000). **Discount Airline Ticket Service** (☎ 800/576–1600). **Unitravel** (☎ 800/325–2222). **Up & Away Travel** (☎ 212/889–2345). **World Travel Network** (☎ 800/409–6753).

➤ DISCOUNT PASSES: **Aloha Airlines** (☎ 800/367–5250). **Hawaiian Airlines** (☎ 800/367–5320).

ENJOYING THE FLIGHT

For more legroom, **request an emergency-aisle seat.** Don't sit in the row in front of the emergency aisle or in front of a bulkhead, where seats may not recline. If you have dietary concerns, **ask for special meals when booking.** These can be vegetarian, low-cholesterol, or kosher, for example. On long flights, try to maintain a normal routine, to help fight jet lag. At night, **get some sleep.** By day, **eat light meals, drink water** (not alcohol), and **move around the cabin** to stretch your legs. For additional jet-lag tips consult *Fodor's FYI: Travel Fit & Healthy* (available at bookstores everywhere).

FLYING TIMES

Flying time is about 10 hours from New York, 8 hours from Chicago, 5 hours from Los Angeles, and 15 hours from London, not including layovers.

HOW TO COMPLAIN

If your baggage goes astray or your flight goes awry, complain right away. Most carriers require that you **file a claim immediately.**

➤ AIRLINE COMPLAINTS: U.S. Department of Transportation **Aviation Consumer Protection Division** (✉ C-75, Room 4107, Washington, DC 20590, ☎ 202/366–2220, ⊞ www.dot.gov/airconsumer). **Federal Aviation Administration Consumer Hotline** (☎ 800/322–7873).

AIRPORTS

Hawai'i's major airport is Honolulu International, on O'ahu, 20 minutes (9 mi) west of Waikīkī. To travel interisland from Honolulu, visitors depart from either the interisland terminal or the commuter-airline terminal, located in two separate structures adjacent to the main overseas terminal building. A free bus service, the Wiki Wiki Shuttle, operates between terminals.

Maui has two major airports: Kahului Airport, which handles major airlines and interisland flights, and Kapalua-West Maui Airport, served by Aloha Airlines and Pacific Wings. If you're staying in West Maui and you're flying in from another island, you can avoid an hour's drive from the Kahului Airport by flying into Kapalua–West Maui Airport. The tiny town of Hāna in East Maui also has an airstrip, served by commuter planes from Honolulu. Flying here is a great option if you want to avoid the long drive to Hāna from one of the other airports.

Those flying to the Big Island of Hawai'i regularly land at one of two fields. Keāhole-Kona International Airport, on the west side, best serves Kailua-Kona, Keauhou, and the Kohala Coast. Hilo International Airport is more appropriate for those going to the east side. Waimea-Kohala Airport, called Kamuela Airport by residents, is used primarily for commuting among the Islands.

On Kaua'i, visitors fly into Līhu'e Airport, on the east side of the island.

Moloka'i's Ho'olehua Airport is small and centrally located, as is Lāna'i Airport on that island. Both rural airports handle a limited number of flights per day. Visitors coming from the mainland to these islands must first stop in O'ahu and change to an interisland flight.

➤ AIRPORT INFORMATION: O'ahu: **Honolulu International Airport** (☎ 808/836–6413 or 808/836–6411). Maui: **Kahului Airport** (☎ 808/872–3800 or 808/872–3830), **Kapalua–West MauiAirport** (☎ 808/669–0623), **Hāna Airport** (☎ 808/248–8208). The Big Island: **Keāhole-Kona International Airport** (☎ 808/329–2484 or 808/329–3423), **Hilo International Airport** (☎ 808/934–5801), **Waimea-Kohala Airport** (☎ 808/887–8126). Kaua'i: **Līhu'e Airport** (☎ 808/246–1400). Moloka'i:**Ho'olehua Airport** (☎ 808/567–6140). Lāna'i: **Lāna'i Airport** (☎ 808/565–6757).

BIKE TRAVEL

Hawai'i's natural beauty, breathtaking coastal routes, and year-round fair weather make it attractive to explore by bike. However, on many roads, bicycle lanes are limited or nonexistent, and **cyclists must contend with heavy traffic on the more populated islands.** Biking on O'ahu may require some skillful maneuvering; bike routes on the Neighbor Islands include the challenge of the Big Island's 225-mi circle-island route, cycling downhill at Maui's Haleakalā crater, exploring the lush routes of tropical Kaua'i, and mastering off-road mountain biking on Lāna'i and Moloka'i. Visitors can rent bikes for some solo cruising, join local cycling clubs for their weekly rides, or hit the road with outfitters for tours that go beyond the well-traveled paths.

➤ BIKE MAPS: **Big Island Mountain Bike Association** (☎ 808/961–4452). **The Division of Forestry and Wildlife, Kaua'i**(☎ 808/274–3433). **Honolulu City and County Bike Coordinator** (☎ 808/527–5044).

➤ BIKE RENTALS: **Blue Sky Rentals** (O'ahu, ☎ 808/947–0101). **Dave's Triathlon Shop** (Big Island, ☎ 808/329–4522). **Kaua'i Cycle and Tour** (Kaua'i, ☎ 808/821–2115). **West Maui Cycles** (Maui, ☎ 808/661–9005).

BIKES IN FLIGHT

Most airlines accommodate bikes as luggage, provided they are dismantled and boxed. Airlines sell bike boxes, which are often free at bike shops, for about $5 (it's at least $100 for bike bags). International travelers can sometimes substitute a bike for a piece of checked luggage at no charge; otherwise, the cost is about $100. Domestic and Canadian airlines charge $25–$50.

BOAT & FERRY TRAVEL

Ferry travel in the Islands is limited to daily service between Lahaina, Maui, and Manele Bay, Lāna'i. The 9-mi crossing costs $50 round-trip and takes about 45 minutes or so, depending on ocean conditions (which can make this trip a rough one). Reservations are essential.

➤ BOAT & FERRY INFORMATION: **Excursions/Lāna'i Passenger Ferry** (☎ 808/661–3756).

BUS TRAVEL

Getting around by bus is an option on O'ahu, but on Neighbor Islands services are limited and car rental is recommended. O'ahu's transportation system, known just as "TheBus," is one of the island's best bargains. Fares per ride are $1.50, and with more than 68 bus routes you can even do a O'ahu circle-island tour.

The Big Island's county bus, called "The Hele-On" Bus, travels a Kailua-Kona–to–Hilo route once daily except Sunday. There are limited routes to other areas. On the island of Kaua'i, the "Kaua'i Bus" travels two main routes, one going north to Hanelei from Līhu'e and one going south from Līhu'e to Kōloa and Po'ipū. Routes don't come close to many of the island's resorts or best-known attractions, but do wind through residential towns. Maui has no public bus service, but a private commercial company, Trans-Hawaiian Services, does have regular bus routes within various resort areas and to popular attractions. Check with your hotel desk upon arrival for schedules. Neighbor Island public transportation does not run on Sunday.

➤ BUS INFORMATION: **"TheBus"** on O'ahu (☎ 808/848–5555 or 808/296–1818, then press 8287). **"Hele-On" Bus** on the Big Island (☎ 808/961–8744). **Kaua'i Bus** on Kaua'i (☎ 808/241–6410). **Trans-Hawaiian Services** on Maui (☎ 808/877–7308).

BUSINESS HOURS

Even people in paradise have to work. Local business hours are generally 8 to 5 weekdays. Banks are usually open Monday through Thursday 8:30 to 3 and until 6 on Friday. Some banks have Saturday morning hours. Twenty-four-hour money access is available through ATM machines, which are plentiful.

Many self-serve gas stations stay open around-the-clock, withfull-service stations usually open from around 7 AM until 9 PM. U.S. post offices are open from 8:30 AM to 4:30 PM weekdays, 8:30 to noon on Saturday. On O'ahu, the Ala Moana post office branch is the only branch, other than the main Honolulu International Airport facility, that stays open until 4 PM on Saturday.

MUSEUMS & SIGHTS

Most museums generally open their doors between 9 AM and 10 AM and stay open until 5 PM Tuesday through Saturday. Many museums operate with afternoon hours only on Sunday and close on Monday. Visitor attractions hours vary throughout the state, but most are open daily with the exception of major holidays such as Christmas. **Check local newspapers upon arrival for attraction hours and schedules if visiting over holiday periods.** The local dailies carry a listing of "What's Open/What's Not" for those time periods.

SHOPS

Stores in resort areas sometimes open as early as 8, with shopping-center opening hours varying from 9:30 to 10 on weekdays and Saturday, a bit later on Sunday. Bigger malls stay open until 9 weekdays and Saturday and close at 5 on Sunday. Boutiques in resort areas may stay open as late as 11.

CAMERAS & PHOTOGRAPHY

Today's underwater "disposable" cameras can provide terrific photos for those once-in-a-lifetime underwater experiences. Film developing is available on all Islands. Many hotel/resort sundry stores offer the service, and larger department stores, such as Long's Drugs, have one-hour service for regular film developing and overnight service for panoramic film.

The *Kodak Guide to Shooting Great Travel Pictures* (available at bookstores everywhere) is loaded with tips.

➤ PHOTO HELP: **Kodak Information Center** (☎ 800/242–2424).

EQUIPMENT PRECAUTIONS

Don't pack film and equipment in checked luggage, where it is much more susceptible to damage. X-ray machines used to view checked luggage are becoming much more powerful and therefore are much more likely to ruin your film. Always **keep film and tape out of the sun.** Carry an extra supply of batteries, and **be prepared to turn on your camera or camcorder** to prove to security personnel that the device is real. Always **ask for hand inspection of film,** which becomes clouded after repeated exposure to airport X-ray machines, and **keep videotapes away from metal detectors.**

CAR RENTAL

You can rent anything from a $26-a-day econobox to a $1,100-a-day Ferrari. It's wise to **make reservations in advance,** especially if visiting during peak seasons or for a major convention or sporting event. This is especially true on the Neighbor Islands, where rental fleets are smaller and cars can sell out quickly.

Rates in Honolulu begin at $38 a day ($164 a week) for an economy car with air-conditioning, automatic transmission, and unlimited mileage. Rates on Maui begin at $32 a day ($144 a week) for the same. This does not include tax, insurance, and a $2-per-day road tax.

➤ MAJOR AGENCIES: **Alamo** (☎ 800/327–9633; 020/8759–6200 in the U.K.). **Avis** (☎ 800/331–1212; 800/879–2847 in Canada; 02/9353–9000 in Australia; 09/525–1982 in New Zealand; 0870/606–0100 in the U.K.). **Budget** (☎ 800/527–0700; 0144/227–6266 in the U.K., through affiliate Europcar). **Dollar** (☎ 800/800–4000; 0124/622–0111 in the U.K., where it is known as Sixt Kenning; 02/9223–1444 in Australia). **Hertz** (☎ 800/654–3131; 800/263–0600 in Canada; 020/8897–2072 in the U.K.; 02/9669–2444 in Australia; 09/256–8690 in New Zealand). **National Car Rental** (☎ 800/227–7368; 0845/722–2525 in the U.K., where it is known as National Europe).

CUTTING COSTS

For a better rental deal, **check out local and national promotions as well as discounts offered through frequent-flyer programs, automobile clubs, or business or military affiliations.** Many rental companies in Hawai'i also offer coupons for discounts at various attractions that could save you money later on in your trip. To get the best deal, **book through a travel agent**

who will shop around, or check out car-rental Web sites for special offers. Also **price local car-rental companies,** although the service and maintenance may not be as good as those of a major player. Remember to ask about required deposits, cancellation penalties, and drop-off charges if you're planning to pick up the car in one city and leave it in another. If you're traveling during a holiday period, make sure that a confirmed reservation guarantees you a car.

➤ LOCAL AGENCIES: **AA Aloha Cars-R-US** (☎ 800/655–7989). **JN Car and Truck Rentals** (☎ 808/831–2724) on O'ahu. **Thrifty Car Rental** (☎ 808/831–2277, WEB www.thrifty.com) on O'ahu, Kaua'i, the Big Island, and Maui. **VIP Car Rentals** (☎ 808/922–4605) on O'ahu.

INSURANCE

When driving a rented car you are generally responsible for any damage to or loss of the vehicle as well as for any property damage or personal injury that you may cause. Before you rent, see what coverage your personal auto-insurance policy and credit cards provide.

For about $15 to $20 per day, rental companies sell protection, known as a collision- or loss-damage waiver (CDW or LDW), that eliminates your liability for damage to the car. In most states you don't need a CDW if you have personal auto insurance or other liability insurance. However, **make sure you have enough coverage to pay for the car.** If you do not have auto insurance or an umbrella policy that covers damage to third parties, purchasing liability insurance and a CDW or LDW is highly recommended.

REQUIREMENTS & RESTRICTIONS

In Hawai'i you must be 21 years of age to rent a car and you must have a valid driver's license and a major credit card. Those under 25 will pay a daily surcharge of $15.

You'll pay extra for child seats (about $3 a day), which are compulsory for children under five, and for additional drivers (about $2 per day). Non-U.S. residents need a reservation voucher (for prepaid reservations that were made in the traveler's home country), a passport, a driver's license, and a travel policy that covers each driver, when picking up a car.

In Hawai'i your unexpired mainland driver's license is valid for up to 90 days.

SURCHARGES

Before you pick up a car in one city and leave it in another, **ask about drop-off charges or one-way service fees,** which can be substantial. Note, too, that some rental agencies charge extra if you return the car before the time specified in your contract. To avoid a hefty refueling fee, **fill the tank just before you turn in the car,** but be aware that gas stations near the rental outlet may overcharge.

CAR TRAVEL

Technically, the Big Island of Hawai'i is the only island you can completely circle by car, but each island offers plenty of sightseeing from its miles of roadways. O'ahu can be circled except for the roadless west-shore area around Ka'ena Point. Elsewhere, major highways follow the shoreline and traverse the island at two points. Rush-hour traffic (6:30 to 8:30 AM and 3:30 to 6 PM) can be frustrating around Honolulu and the outlying areas, as many thoroughfares allow no left turns due to contra-flow lanes. Parking along many streets is curtailed during these times, and towing is strictly practiced. **Read curbside parking signs** before leaving your vehicle, even at a meter.

GASOLINE

Regardless of today's fluctuating gas prices, you can pretty much count on having to pay about 20% more at the pump for gasoline in the Islands than on the U.S. mainland.

ROAD CONDITIONS

It's difficult to get lost in most of Hawai'i. Roads and streets, although they may challenge the visitor's tongue, are well marked. **Keep an eye open for the Hawai'i Visitors and Convention Bureau's red-caped warrior signs,** which mark major visitor attractions and scenic spots. Ask for a map at the car-rental counter. Free visitor publications containing good-quality road maps can be found on all Islands, too.

Kaua'i has a well-maintained highway running south from Līhu'e to Barking Sands Beach; a spur at Waimea takes you along Waimea Canyon to Kōke'e State Park. A northern route also winds its way from Līhu'e to end at Hā'ena, the beginning of the rugged and roadless Nā Pali Coast. Maui also has its share of impenetrable areas, although four-wheel-drive vehicles rarely run into problems on the island. Saddle roads run between the east and west landmasses composing Maui. Other highways follow the western coasts of East and West Maui. Although Moloka'i and Lāna'i have fewer roadways, car rental is still worthwhile and will allow plenty of interesting sightseeing. **Opt for a four-wheel-drive vehicle** if dirt-road exploration holds any appeal.

RULES OF THE ROAD

Be sure to **buckle up.** Hawai'i has a strictly enforced seat-belt law for front-seat passengers. Children under 4 must be in a car seat (available from car-rental agencies). Children 18 and under, riding in the backseat, are also required by state law to use seat belts. The highway speed limit is usually 55 mph. In-town traffic moves from 25 to 40 mph. Jaywalking is very common, so be particularly watchful for pedestrians, especially in congested areas such as Waikīkī. Unauthorized use of a parking space reserved for persons with disabilities can net you a $150 fine.

Asking for directions will almost always produce a helpful explanation from the locals, but you should be prepared for an island term or two. Instead of using compass directions, remember that Hawai'i residents refer to places as being either *mauka* (toward the mountains) or *makai* (toward the ocean) from one another. Other directions depend on your location: in Honolulu, for example, people say to "go Diamond Head," which means toward that famous landmark, or to "go *'ewa,*" meaning in the opposite direction. A shop on the mauka–Diamond Head corner of a street is on the mountain side of the street on the corner closest to Diamond Head. It all makes perfect sense once you get the lay of the land.

CHILDREN IN HAWAI'I

Sunny beaches and many family-oriented cultural sites, activities, and attractions make Hawai'i a very *keiki* (child) friendly place. Here kids can swim with a dolphin, surf with a boogie board, visit an active volcano, or ride a sugarcane train. Parents should **use caution on beaches and during water sports.** Even waters that appear calm can harbor powerful rip currents. And remember that the sun's rays are in operation full-force year-round here. Sunblock for children is essential. If you are renting a car, don't forget to **arrange for a car seat** when you reserve. For general advice about traveling with children, consult *Fodor's FYI: Travel with Your Baby* (available in bookstores everywhere).

Most major resort chains in Hawai'i offer children's activity programs for kids ages 5 to 12. These kid clubs provide opportunities to learn about local culture, make friends with children from around the world, and to experience age-appropriate activities while giving moms and dads a "time-out." Upon arrival, **check out the daily local newspapers for children's events.** The *Honolulu Advertiser's* "TGIF" section each Friday includes a section on keiki activities with a local flavor.

FLYING

If your children are two or older, **ask about children's airfares.** As a general rule, infants under two not occupying a seat fly at greatly reduced fares or even for free.

Experts agree that it's a good idea to use safety seats aloft for children weighing less than 40 pounds. Airlines set their own policies: U.S. carriers usually require that the child be ticketed, even if he or she is young enough to ride free, since the seats must be strapped into regular seats. Do **check your airline's policy about using safety seats during takeoff and landing.** And since safety seats are not allowed everywhere in the plane, get your seat assignments early.

When reserving, **request children's meals or a freestanding bassinet** if you need them. But note that bulk-head seats, where you must sit to use the bassinet, may lack an overhead bin or storage space on the floor.

LODGING

Families can't go wrong choosing resort locations that are part of larger hotel chains such as Hilton, Sheraton, and Outrigger. Many of these resorts are located on the best beaches on each island, have an array of activities created for kids, and are centrally located. Outrigger's "Ohana" brand hotels are off the beachfront, but provide great value at good prices. Many condominium resorts now also offer children's activities and amenities during holiday periods. Most hotels allow children under a certain age to stay in their parents' room at no extra charge, but others charge for them as extra adults. Be sure to **find out the cutoff age for children's discounts. Also check for special seasonal programs, such as "kids eat free" promotions.**

➤ Best Choices: **Aston Hotels** (☎ 800/443–5550, WEB www.aston-hotels.com). **Four Seasons Resorts** (☎ 800/819–5053, WEB www.fourseasons.com). **Hilton Hawaii** (☎ 800/445–8667, WEB www.hilton.com/hawaii). **Hyatt Hawaii** (☎ 800/554–9288, WEB www.hyatt.com). **Lanai Resorts** (☎ 800/321–4666, WEB www.luxurycollection.com). **Moloka'i Ranch** ☎ (800/254–8871, WEB www.molokai-ranch.com). **Outrigger Hotels** (☎ 800/922–5533, WEB www.outrigger.com). **Sheraton Resorts** (☎ 800/325–3535, WEB www.sheratonhawaii.com).

SIGHTS & ATTRACTIONS

Top picks for children run the gamut from the natural attractions that kids can enjoy for free to some fairly expensive amusements. On O'ahu, kid favorites include hiking Diamond Head, snorkeling Hanauma Bay, learning about marine life at Sea Life Park, playing ancient Hawaiian games at Waimea Valley Adventures Park, and touring through South Pacific cultures at the Polynesian Cultural Center. On Maui, kid favorites include the Sugarcane Train that runs between Lahaina and Kā'anapali, snorkeling at Molokini Island, and whale-watching after a visit to the Maui Ocean Center. Visiting Hawai'i Volcanoes National Park, touring the Mauna Loa Macadamia Factory near Hilo, swimming with dolphins at the Hilton Waikoloa, and horseback riding at Parker Ranch are fun things to do on the Big Island.

Kaua'i is where kids go to explore film locations such as Peter Pan's Never-Never Land and Jurassic Park. They can learn to water-ski on the Wailua River, visit Kōke'e National Park, or just spend the day swimming Po'ipū's sunny south shores. Lāna'i and Moloka'i are great islands for adventurous kids. At Moloka'i Ranch, families can sleep in "tentalows" and tackle the rope-challenge course for excitement. On Lāna'i, four-wheel-drive off-road adventure tours take families to destinations such as Shipwreck Beach and Manele Bay, where the dolphins sometimes come to play. Places that are especially appealing to children are indicated by a rubber-duckie icon (☺) in the margin.

COMPUTERS ON THE ROAD

New hotels and resorts, or those that have been recently renovated, often have in-room computer dataports. Many hotels that cater to the business traveler also have business centers with full computer setups that allow even the leisure traveler to check e-mail while away from home. At Internet cafés throughout the Islands you can get a steaming cup of Kona coffee while checking your e-mail or surfing the Web for an hourly fee. If you don't want to travel with your laptop computer but want to have access to your e-mail while on the road, **open an account with a Web-based e-mail system such as Hotmail that gives you access to your mail through any Internet connection.**

CONSUMER PROTECTION

Whenever shopping or buying travel services in Hawai'i, **pay with a major credit card,** if possible, so you can cancel payment or get reimbursed if there's a problem. If you're doing business with a particular company for the first time, **contact your local Better Business Bureau and the attorney general's offices** in your state and (for U.S. businesses) the company's

home state as well. Have any complaints been filed? Finally, if you're buying a package or tour, always **consider travel insurance** that includes default coverage (☞ Insurance).

➤ BBBs: **Council of Better Business Bureaus** (✉ 4200 Wilson Blvd., Suite 800, Arlington, VA 22203, ☎ 703/276–0100, FAX 703/525–8277, WEB www.bbb.org).

CRUISE TRAVEL

When Pan Am's amphibious *Hawai'i Clipper* touched down on Pearl Harbor's waters in 1936, it marked the beginning of the end of regular passenger-ship travel to the Islands. From that point on, the predominant means of transporting visitors would be by air, not by sea. Today, however, cruising to Hawai'i is making a comeback.

No regularly scheduled American ships steam between the mainland and Hawai'i. Although foreign-owned vessels often ply the Pacific, the Jones Act of 1896 prohibits them from carrying passengers between two U.S. ports unless the ships first stop at an intervening foreign port or carry the passengers to a foreign destination. What that means is that you must book with one of the major lines passing through Honolulu.

Cruises within the Islands are available on the 1,021-passenger ship the S.S. *Independence* and the 1,212-passenger M.S. *Patriot,* under the direction of American Hawai'i Cruises. Seven-day cruises originate from both Honolulu and Kahului Harbor in Maui, for visits to both these islands as well as ports of call on the Big Island and Kaua'i. To get the best deal on a cruise, **consult a cruise-only travel agency.**

Even if you choose, as most travelers do, to travel by air to the Islands, you can get the flavor of what the luxury-cruise era in Hawai'i was like by checking out Aloha Tower Marketplace's Boat Day Celebrations in Honolulu. Vessels stopping here are met upon arrival by hula dancers and the kind of entertainment and floral festivities that once greeted travelers almost a century ago. Contact the Aloha Tower Marketplace for a boat-day schedule upon arrival.

To learn how to plan, choose, and book a cruise-ship voyage, check out Cruise How-to's on www.fodors.com and consult *Fodor's FYI: Plan & Enjoy Your Cruise* (available in bookstores everywhere).

➤ CRUISE LINES: For details on cruises that pass through Honolulu: **American Hawai'i Cruises** (☎ 800/765–7000, WEB www.cruisehawaii.com). **Cunard** (☎ 800/221–4770, WEB www.cunard.com). **Holland America** (☎ 800/426–0327, WEB www.hollandamerica.com). **Princess** (☎ 800/421–0522, WEB www.princess.com). **Royal Caribbean Cruise Line** (☎ 800/327–6700, WEB www.rccl.com).

CUSTOMS & DUTIES

When shopping, **keep receipts** for all purchases. Upon reentering the country, **be ready to show customs officials what you've bought.** If you feel a duty is incorrect or object to the way your clearance was handled, note the inspector's badge number and ask to see a supervisor. If the problem isn't resolved, write to the appropriate authorities, beginning with the port director at your point of entry.

IN AUSTRALIA

Australian residents who are 18 or older may bring home $A400 worth of souvenirs and gifts (including jewelry), 250 cigarettes or 250 grams of tobacco, and 1,125 ml of alcohol (including wine, beer, and spirits). Residents under 18 may bring back $A200 worth of goods. Prohibited items include meat products. Seeds, plants, and fruits need to be declared upon arrival.

➤ INFORMATION: **Australian Customs Service** (Regional Director, ✉ Box 8, Sydney, NSW 2001, Australia, ☎ 02/9213–2000, FAX 02/9213–4000, WEB www.customs.gov.au).

IN CANADA

Canadian residents who have been out of Canada for at least seven days may bring home C$500 worth of goods duty-free. If you've been away fewer than seven days but more than 48 hours, the duty-free allowance drops to C$200; if your trip lasts 24–48 hours, the allowance is C$50. You may not pool allowances with family members. Goods claimed under the C$500 exemption may follow you by mail; those claimed under the lesser exemptions must accompany you. Alcohol and tobacco products may be included in the seven-day and 48-hour exemptions but not in the 24-hour exemption. If you meet the age requirements of the province or territory through which you reenter Canada, you may bring in, duty-free, 1.14 liters (40 imperial ounces) of wine or liquor *or* 24 12-ounce cans or bottles of beer or ale. If you are 16 or older you may bring in, duty-free, 200 cigarettes and 50 cigars. Check ahead of time with Revenue Canada or the Department of Agriculture for policies regarding meat products, seeds, plants, and fruits.

You may send an unlimited number of gifts worth up to C$60 each duty-free to Canada. Label the package UNSOLICITED GIFT—VALUE UNDER $60. Alcohol and tobacco are excluded.

➤ INFORMATION: **Revenue Canada** (✉ 2265 St. Laurent Blvd. S, Ottawa, Ontario K1G 4K3, Canada, ☎ 613/993–0534; 800/461–9999 in Canada, FAX 613/991–4126, WEB www.ccra-adrc.gc.ca).

IN HAWAI'I

Plants and plant products are subject to regulation by the Department of Agriculture, both on entering and leaving Hawai'i. Pineapples and coconuts with the packer's agricultural inspection stamp pass freely; papayas must be treated, inspected, and stamped. All other fruits are banned for export to the U.S. mainland. Flowers pass except for gardenia, rose leaves, jade vine, and mauna loa. Also banned are insects, snails, soil, cotton, cacti, sugarcane, and all berry plants.

You'll have to **leave dogs and other pets at home.** A strict six-month quarantine is imposed to keep out rabies, which is nonexistent in Hawai'i.

➤ INFORMATION: **U.S. Customs Service** (✉ 1300 Pennsylvania Ave. NW, Washington, DC 20229, WEB www.customs.gov; inquiries ☎ 202/354–1000; complaints c/o ✉ 1300 Pennsylvania Ave. NW, Room 5.4D, Washington, DC 20229; registration of equipment c/o ✉ Resource Management, ☎ 202/927–0540).

IN NEW ZEALAND

Homeward-bound residents 17 or older may bring back $700 worth of souvenirs and gifts. Your duty-free allowance also includes 4.5 liters of wine or beer; one 1,125-ml bottle of spirits; and either 200 cigarettes, 250 grams of tobacco, 50 cigars, or a combination of the three up to 250 grams. Prohibited items include meat products, seeds, plants, and fruits.

➤ INFORMATION: **New Zealand Customs** (Custom House, ✉ 50 Anzac Ave., Box 29, Auckland, New Zealand, ☎ 09/300–5399, ℻ 09/359–6730, WEB www.customs.govt.nz).

IN THE U.K.

From countries outside the EU, including the United States, you may bring home, duty-free, 200 cigarettes or 50 cigars; 1 liter of spirits or 2 liters of fortified or sparkling wine or liqueurs; 2 liters of still table wine; 60 ml of perfume; 250 ml of toilet water; plus £136 worth of other goods, including gifts and souvenirs. If returning from outside the EU, prohibited items include meat products, seeds, plants, and fruits.

➤ INFORMATION: **HM Customs and Excise** (✉ Dorset House, Stamford St., Bromley, Kent BR1 1XX, U.K., ☎ 020/7202–4227, WEB www.hmce.gov.uk).

DINING

Food in Hawai'i is a reflection of the state's diverse cultural makeup and tropical location. Fresh seafood is the hallmark of Hawai'i regional cuisine, and its preparations are drawn from across the Pacific Rim, including Japan, the Philippines, Korea, and Thailand. But Hawaiian food is a cuisine in its own right. Meals in resort areas are costly but often excellent.

The restaurants we list are the cream of the crop in each price category. Price categories are as follows:

CATEGORY	COST*
$$$$	over $45
$$$	$30–$45
$$	$15–$30
$	$5–$15

*per person for a main course at dinner

RESERVATIONS & DRESS

Hawai'i is decidedly casual. Aloha shirts and long pants for men and island-style dresses or casual resort wear for women are standard attire for evenings in most hotel restaurants and local eateries. T-shirts and shorts will do the trick for breakfast and lunch.

Reservations are always a good idea: we mention them only when they're essential or not accepted. Book as far ahead as you can, and reconfirm as soon as you arrive. We mention dress only when men are required to wear a jacket or a jacket and tie.

SPECIALTIES

Fish, fruit, and fresh island-grown produce are the base of Hawai'i regional cuisine. The "plate lunch" is the heart of most Hawaiians' days and usually consists of grilled teriyaki chicken, beef, or fish, served with two scoops of white rice and two side salads. Poke, pickled raw tuna, is a local hallmark.

WINE, BEER & SPIRITS

Hawai'i has a new generation of microbreweries that can be found throughout O'ahu, the Big Island, and Maui. Many restaurants also have on-site microbreweries. On Maui, check out the Tedeschi Vineyards, where you can tour a beautiful island estate and get a taste of sweet pineapple wine. The drinking age in Hawai'i is 21 years of age, and a photo ID must be presented to purchase alcoholic beverages. Bars are open until 2 AM; venues with a cabaret license can stay open until 4 AM. No matter what you might see in the local parks, drinking alcohol in public parks or on the beaches is illegal. It is also illegal to have open containers of alcohol in motor vehicles.

DISABILITIES & ACCESSIBILITY

The Society for the Advancement of Travel for the Handicapped has named Hawai'i the most accessible vacation spot for people with disabilities. Ramped visitor areas and specially equipped lodgings are relatively common. The Hawai'i Center for Independent Living publishes the "Aloha Guide to Accessibility," which lists addresses and telephone numbers for support-service organizations and rates the Islands' hotels, beaches, shopping and entertainment centers, and major attractions. The guide costs $15 but is available in sections for $3 to $5 per section. Part I (general information) is free. Travelers with vision impairments who use a guide dog don't have to worry about quarantine restrictions. All you need to do is present documentation that the animal is a trained guide dog and has a current inoculation record for rabies.

➤ LOCAL RESOURCES: **Hawai'i Center for Independent Living** (✉ 414 Kauwili St., Suite 102, Honolulu 96817, ☎ 808/522–5400). For accessibility information on Neighbor Islands: **Disability and Communications Access Board** offices on Kaua'i (✉ 3060 'Eiwa St., Room 207, Līhu'e 96766, ☎ 808/274–3308), and Maui (✉ 54 High St., Wailuku 96793, ☎ 808/984–8219).

LODGING

Travelers with disabilities and people using wheelchairs find it easy to get around Hawai'i's resorts and hotels, with indoor/outdoor layouts that are easily accommodated. If choosing a smaller hotel or a condo or apartment rental, inquire about ground-floor accommodations and **check to see if rooms will accommodate wheelchairs and if bathrooms are accessible.** Many hotels now offer special-needs rooms featuring larger living spaces and bathrooms equipped for guests who require additional assistance.

RESERVATIONS

When discussing accessibility with an operator or reservations agent, **ask hard questions.** Are there any stairs, inside *or* out? Are there grab bars next to the toilet *and* in the shower/tub? How wide is the doorway to the room? To the bathroom? For the most extensive facilities meeting the latest legal specifications, **opt for newer accommodations.**

SIGHTS & ATTRACTIONS

Many of Hawai'i's sights and attractions are accessible to travelers with disabilities. The state's number-one visitor attraction, Hawai'i Volcanoes National Park, includes a drive-through volcano. In Waikīkī, the Honolulu Department of Parks and Recreation can assist in obtaining an "all-terrain" wheelchair for strolls down the beach. Accessibility Vans of Hawaii can help travelers plan activities from snorkeling to whale-watching.

➤ INFORMATION: **Accessibility Vans of Hawaii** (☎ 800/303–3750, 🖳 www.accessiblevanshawaii.com). **Honolulu Department of Parks and Recreation** (Therapeutic Recreation Unit: ☎ 808/522–7034).

TRANSPORTATION

Paratransit Services (HandiVan) will take you to a specific destination on O'ahu—not on sightseeing outings—in vans with lifts and lock-downs. With a HandiVan Pass, one-way trips cost $1.50. Passes are free and can be obtained from the Department of Transportation Services, which is open weekdays from 7:45 to 4:30; you'll need a doctor's written confirmation of your disability or a paratransit ID card. Handi-Cabs of the Pacific also operates ramp-equipped vans with lock-downs in Honolulu. Fares are $9 plus $2.25 per mi for curbside service. Reservations at least one day in advance are required by both companies, so plan ahead.

Those who prefer to do their own driving may rent hand-controlled cars from Avis (reserve 24 hours ahead) and Hertz (24- to 72-hour notice required). You can use the windshield card from your own state to park in spaces reserved for people with disabilities.

➤ INFORMATION: **Avis** (☎ 800/331–1212). **Department of Transportation Services** (✉ 711 Kapi'olani Blvd., Honolulu 96819, ☎ 808/523–4083). **Handi-Cabs of the Pacific** (☎ 808/524–3866). **Hertz** (☎ 800/654–3131). **Paratransit Services** (HandiVan) (☎ 808/456–5555).

➤ COMPLAINTS: **Aviation Consumer Protection Division** (☞ Air Travel) for airline-related problems. **Civil Rights Office** (✉ U.S. Department of Transportation, Departmental Office of Civil Rights, S-30, 400 7th St. SW, Room 10215, Washington, DC 20590, ☎ 202/366–4648, 🖷 202/366–9371, 🖳 www.dot.gov/ost/docr/index.htm) for problems with surface transportation. **Disability Rights Section** (✉ U.S.

Department of Justice, Civil Rights Division, Box 66738, Washington, DC 20035-6738, ☎ 202/514–0301 or 800/514–0301; 202/514–0383 TTY; 800/514–0383 TTY, ℻ 202/307–1198, WEB www.usdoj.gov/crt/ada/adahom1.htm) for general complaints.

TRAVEL AGENCIES

In the United States, the Americans with Disabilities Act requires that travel firms serve the needs of all travelers. Some agencies specialize in working with people with disabilities.

➤ TRAVELERS WITH MOBILITY PROBLEMS: **Access Adventures** (⊠ 206 Chestnut Ridge Rd., Scottsville, NY 14624, ☎ 716/889–9096, dltravel@prodigy.net), run by a former physical-rehabilitation counselor. **Accessible Vans of America** (⊠ 9 Spielman Rd., Fairfield, NJ 07004, ☎ 877/282–8267, ℻ 973/808–9713, WEB www.accessiblevans.com). **Accessible Vans of Hawaii, Activity and Travel Agency** (⊠ 296 Alamaha St., Suite C, Kahului, HI 96732, ☎ 808/871–7785 or 800/303–3750, ℻ 808/871–7536, WEB www.accessiblevanshawaii.com). **CareVacations** (⊠ 5-5110 50th Ave., Leduc, Alberta T9E 6V4, Canada, ☎ 780/986–6404 or 877/478–7827, ℻ 780/986–8332, WEB www.carevacations.com), for group tours and cruise vacations. **Flying Wheels Travel** (⊠ 143 W. Bridge St., Box 382, Owatonna, MN 55060, ☎ 507/451–5005 or 800/535–6790, ℻ 507/451–1685, WEB www.flyingwheelstravel.com).

➤ TRAVELERS WITH DEVELOPMENTAL DISABILITIES: **New Directions** (⊠ 5276 Hollister Ave., Suite 207, Santa Barbara, CA 93111, ☎ 805/967–2841 or 888/967–2841, ℻ 805/964–7344, WEB www.newdirectionstravel.com).

DISCOUNTS & DEALS

Be a smart shopper and **compare all your options** before making decisions. A plane ticket bought with a promotional coupon from travel clubs, coupon books, and direct-mail offers or on the Internet may not be cheaper than the least expensive fare from a discount ticket agency. And always keep in mind that what you get is just as important as what you save.

DISCOUNT RESERVATIONS

To save money, **look into discount reservations services** with toll-free numbers, which use their buying power to get a better price on hotels, airline tickets, even car rentals. When booking a room, always **call the hotel's local toll-free number** (if one is available) rather than the central reservations number—you'll often get a better price. Always ask about special packages or corporate rates.

➤ AIRLINE TICKETS: ☎ **800/FLY–ASAP.**

➤ HOTEL ROOMS: **Players Express Vacations** (☎ 800/458–6161, WEB www.playersexpress.com). **RMC Travel** (☎ 800/245–5738, WEB www.rmcwebtravel.com). **Steigenberger Reservation Service** (☎ 800/223–5652, WEB www.srs-worldhotels.com). **Turbotrip.com** (☎ 800/473–7829, WEB www.turbotrip.com).

PACKAGE DEALS

Don't confuse packages and guided tours. When you buy a package, you travel on your own, just as though you had planned the trip yourself. Fly/drive packages, which combine airfare and car rental, are often a good deal.

ECOTOURISM

Hawai'i's connection to its environment is spiritual, cultural, and essential to its survival. You'll find a rainbow of natural attractions to explore, from the ribbon of beaches to volcanic peaks, where lava shows after dark are spectacular. There are 13 climatic regions in the world, and Maui and the Big Island offer ecotravelers a glimpse of 11 of them. Much of Kaua'i's natural beauty can only be seen on foot. Its Nā Pali Coast/Waimea Canyon/Koke'e trail network includes 28 trails totaling some 45 mi rich in endemic species of flora and fauna. Maui offers the exhilaration of a rain-forest hike in Hana, the cool Upcountry climes of Kula and the awe-inspiring Haleakalā Crater. Moloka'i and Lāna'i, two of the least-developed islands, hold adventures best experienced on foot and by four-wheel-drive vehicle, or even by mule. Eco-touring in Hawai'i gives visitors the opportunity to learn from local guides who are familiar with the *aina* (land) and Hawai'i's unique cultural heritage. Many of these tours take clients to locations less traveled, so it helps to **be in good physical shape.** The views at the ends of these roads are an exceedingly rich reward.

Nature is sacred to Hawaiians, so before taking pieces of lava rock home for souvenirs, listen to what residents (and some vacationers) will tell you: leave them here. Hapless travelers who take "souvenir" rocks speak of consequences in the form of stalled cars, bad luck, and bouts of illness. Park rangers spin tales about lava rocks being returned from around the world with notes telling tales of woe, begging for them to be put back. Believe it or not, but if nothing else, with millions of visitors a year, there aren't enough cool rocks to go around.

➤ LOCAL RESOURCES: **Hawai'i Ecotourism Association** (☎ 877/300–7058). **Alternative-Hawai'i** (WEB www.Alternative-Hawaii.com) offers an ecotravel cyberguide.

ETIQUETTE AND BEHAVIOR

In 2001, Hawai'i celebrated 42 years of statehood, so residents can be pretty sensitive to visitors who refer to their own hometowns "back in the States." Remember, **when in Hawai'i, refer to the contiguous 48 states as "the mainland" and not as the United States.** When you do, people will think of you as less of a *malahini* (newcomer).

GAY & LESBIAN TRAVEL

A few small hotels and some bed-and-breakfasts in Hawai'i are favored by gay and lesbian visitors. A computerized Gay Community listing compiled by GLEA (Gay & Lesbian Education Advocacy Foundation) is available. Pacific Ocean Holidays specializes in prearranging package tours for independent gay travelers; the organization also publishes the *Pocket Guide to Hawai'i*, distributed free in the state at gay-operated venues and available for $5 by mail for one issue. For details about the gay and lesbian scene, consult *Fodor's Gay Guide to the USA* (available in bookstores everywhere).

➤ LOCAL RESOURCES: **GLEA** (✉ Box 37083, Honolulu 96837, ☎ 808/532–9000). **Pacific Ocean Holidays**

(✉ Box 88245, Honolulu 96830, ☎ 808/923–2400 or 800/735–6600, WEB www.gayHawaii.com).

➤ GAY- & LESBIAN-FRIENDLY TRAVEL AGENCIES: **Different Roads Travel** (✉ 8383 Wilshire Blvd., Suite 902, Beverly Hills, CA 90211, ☎ 323/651–5557 or 800/429–8747, FAX 323/651–3678, lgernert@tzell.com). **Kennedy Travel** (✉ 314 Jericho Turnpike, Floral Park, NY 11001, ☎ 516/352–4888 or 800/237–7433, FAX 516/354–8849, WEB www.kennedytravel.com). **Now Voyager** (✉ 4406 18th St., San Francisco, CA 94114, ☎ 415/626–1169 or 800/255–6951, FAX 415/626–8626, WEB www.nowvoyager.com). **Skylink Travel and Tour** (✉ 1006 Mendocino Ave., Santa Rosa, CA 95401, ☎ 707/546–9888 or 800/225–5759, FAX 707/546–9891, WEB www.skylinktravel.com), serving lesbian travelers.

GUIDEBOOKS

Plan well and you won't be sorry. Guidebooks are excellent tools—and you can take them with you. You may want to check out *Fodor's Exploring Hawaii, Compass American Guide: Hawaii,* and *Escape to the Hawaiian Islands*—all in full color—and all available at on-line retailers and bookstores everywhere.

HEALTH

Hawai'i is known as the Health State. The life expectancy here is 79 years, the longest in the nation. Balmy weather makes it easy to remain active year-round, and the low-stress aloha attitude certainly contributes to general well-being. When visiting the Islands, however, there are a few health issues to keep in mind.

The Hawaii State Department of Health recommends that you **drink 4 ounces of water every 15 minutes to avoid dehydration when hiking or spending time in the sun.** Use sunblock, wear sunglasses, and protect your head with a visor or hat for shade. If you're not acclimated to warm, humid weather you should allow plenty of time for rest stops and refreshments. When visiting freshwater streams, be aware of the tropical disease leptospirosis, which is spread by animal urine and carried into streams and mud. Symptoms include fever, headache, nausea, and red eyes. If left untreated it can cause liver and kidney damage, respiratory failure, internal bleeding, and even death. To avoid this, don't swim or wade in freshwater streams or ponds if you have open sores and don't drink from any freshwater steams or ponds.

In the Islands, fog is a rare occurrence, but there can often be "vog," an airborne haze of gases released from volcanic vents. During certain weather conditions such as "Kona Winds," the vog can settle over the Islands and wreak havoc with respiratory and other health conditions, especially asthma or emphysema. If susceptible, stay indoors and get emergency assistance if needed.

DIVERS' ALERT

Do not fly for 24 hours after scuba diving.

PESTS & OTHER HAZARDS

The Islands have their share of bugs and insects that enjoy the tropical climate as much as visitors do. Most are harmless but annoying. When planning to spend time outdoors in hiking areas, **wear long-sleeved clothing and long pants** and **use mosquito repellant containing deet.** In very damp places you may encounter the dreaded local centipede. In the Islands they usually come in two colors, brown and blue, and they range from the size of a worm to an 8-inch cigar. Their sting is very painful, and the reaction is similar to bee- and wasp-sting reactions. When camping, **shake out your sleeping bag before climbing in, and check your shoes in the morning as the centipedes like cozy places.** If planning on hiking or traveling in remote areas, always **carry a first-aid kit and appropriate medications for sting reactions.**

HOLIDAYS

Major national holidays include New Year's Day (Jan. 1); Martin Luther King, Jr., Day (3rd Mon. in Jan.); President's Day (3rd Mon. in Feb.); Memorial Day (last Mon. in May); Independence Day (July 4); Labor Day (1st Mon. in Sept.); Thanksgiving Day (4th Thurs. in Nov.); Christmas Eve and Christmas Day (Dec. 24 and 25); and New Year's Eve (Dec. 31).

In addition, Hawai'i celebrates Prince Kuhio Day (Mar. 26); King Kamehameha Day (June 11); and Admission Day (3rd Fri. in Aug.). State, city, and county offices as well as many local companies are closed for business.

INSURANCE

The most useful travel-insurance plan is a comprehensive policy that includes coverage for trip cancellation and interruption, default, trip delay, and medical expenses (with a waiver for preexisting conditions).

Without insurance you will lose all or most of your money if you cancel your trip, regardless of the reason. Default insurance covers you if your tour operator, airline, or cruise line goes out of business. Trip-delay covers expenses that arise because of bad weather or mechanical delays. Study the fine print when comparing policies.

Always **buy travel policies directly from the insurance company;** if you buy them from a cruise line, airline, or tour operator that goes out of business you probably will not be covered for the agency or operator's default, a major risk. Before making any purchase, **review your existing health and home-owner's policies** to find what they cover away from home.

➤ TRAVEL INSURERS: In the U.S.: **Access America** (✉ 6600 W. Broad St., Richmond, VA 23230, ☎ 804/285–3300 or 800/284–8300, ℻ 804/673–1586, 🌐 www.previewtravel. com), **Travel Guard International** (✉ 1145 Clark St., Stevens Point, WI 54481, ☎ 715/345–0505 or 800/826–1300, ℻ 800/955–8785, 🌐 www.noelgroup.com).

FOR INTERNATIONAL TRAVELERS

For information on customs restrictions, *see* Customs & Duties, *above.*

CAR TRAVEL

Driving in the United States is on the right. Do **obey speed limits** posted along roads and highways. Watch for lower limits in small towns and on back roads. On weekdays between 6 and 10 AM and again between 4 and

7 PM **expect heavy traffic.** To encourage carpooling, some freeways have special lanes for so-called high-occupancy vehicles (HOV)—cars carrying more than one passenger. For more information on rules of the road, *see* Car Travel).

State police and tow trucks patrol major highways and lend assistance. If your car breaks down on an interstate, pull onto the shoulder and wait for help, or have your passengers wait while you walk to an emergency phone. If you carry a cell phone, dial *55, noting your location on the small green roadside mileage markers.

Bookstores, gas stations, convenience stores, and rest stops sell maps (about $3) and multiregion road atlases (about $10).

CURRENCY

The dollar is the basic unit of U.S. currency. It has 100 cents. Coins include the copper penny (1¢); the silvery nickel (5¢), dime (10¢), quarter (25¢), and half-dollar (50¢); and the golden $1 coin, replacing a now-rare silver dollar. Bills are denominated $1, $5, $10, $20, $50, and $100, all green and identical in size; designs vary. The exchange rate at press time was US$1.45 per British pound, 66¢ per Canadian dollar, 54¢ per Australian dollar, and 44¢ per New Zealand dollar.

ELECTRICITY

The U.S. standard is AC, 110 volts/60 cycles. Plugs have two flat pins set parallel to each other.

EMERGENCIES

For police, fire, or ambulance, **dial 911** (0 in rural areas).

INSURANCE

Britons and Australians need extra medical coverage when traveling overseas.

➤ INSURANCE INFORMATION: In the U.K.: **Association of British Insurers** (✉ 51–55 Gresham St., London EC2V 7HQ, U.K., ☎ 020/7600–3333, FAX 020/7696–8999, WEB www.abi.org.uk). In Australia: **Insurance Council of Australia** (✉ Level 3, 56 Pitt St., Sydney NSW 2000, ☎ 03/9614–1077, FAX 03/9614–7924). In Canada: **RBC Insurance** (✉ 6880 Financial Dr., Mississauga, Ontario L5N 7Y5, Canada, ☎ 905/816–2400 or 800/668–4342 in Canada, FAX 905/816–2498, WEB www.royalbank.com). In New Zealand: **Insurance Council of New Zealand** (✉ Box 474, Wellington, New Zealand, ☎ 04/472–5230, FAX 04/473–3011, WEB www.icnz.org.nz).

MAIL & SHIPPING

You can buy stamps and aerograms and send letters and parcels in post offices. Stamp-dispensing machines can occasionally be found in airports, bus and train stations, office buildings, drugstores, and the like. You can also deposit mail in the stout, dark-blue, steel bins at strategic locations everywhere and in the mail chutes of large buildings; pickup schedules are posted.

For mail sent within the United States, you need a 34¢ stamp for first-class letters weighing up to 1 ounce (21¢ for each additional ounce) and 20¢ for domestic postcards. For overseas mail, you pay 80¢ for 1-ounce airmail letters, 70¢ for airmail postcards, and 35¢ for surface-rate postcards. For Canada and Mexico you need a 60¢ stamp for a 1-ounce letter and 50¢ for a postcard. For 70¢ you can buy an aerogram—a single sheet of lightweight blue paper that folds into its own envelope, stamped for overseas airmail.

To receive mail on the road, have it sent c/o General Delivery at your destination's main post office (use the correct five-digit zip code). You must pick up mail in person within 30 days and show a driver's license or passport.

PASSPORTS & VISAS

When traveling internationally, **carry your passport** even if you don't need one (it's always the best form of I.D.) and **make two photocopies of the data page** (one for someone at home and another for you, carried separately from your passport). If you lose your passport, promptly call the nearest embassy or consulate and the local police.

Visitor visas are not necessary for Canadian citizens, or for citizens of Australia and the United Kingdom who are staying fewer than 90 days.

➤ AUSTRALIAN CITIZENS: **Australian Passport Office** (☎ 131–232). **U.S. Office of Australia Affairs** (✉ MLC Centre, 19-29 Martin Pl., 59th floor, Sydney NSW 2000, Australia).

➤ CANADIAN CITIZENS: **Passport Office** (☎ 819/994–3500; 800/567–6868 in Canada).

➤ NEW ZEALAND CITIZENS: **New Zealand Passport Office** (☎ 04/494–0700 for application procedures; 0800/225–050 in New Zealand for application-status updates). **U.S. Office of New Zealand Affairs** (✉ 29 Fitzherbert Terr., Thorndon, Wellington, New Zealand).

➤ U.K. CITIZENS: **London Passport Office** (☎ 0870/521–0410) for application procedures and emergency passports. **U.S. Embassy Visa Information Line** (☎ 01891/200–290). **U.S. Embassy Visa Branch** (✉ 5 Upper Grosvenor Sq., London W1A 1AE, U.K.); send a self-addressed, stamped envelope. **U.S. Consulate General** (✉ Queen's House, Queen St., Belfast BTI 6EO, Northern Ireland).

TELEPHONES

All U.S. telephone numbers consist of a three-digit area code and a seven-digit local number. Within most local calling areas, dial only the seven-digit number. Within the same area code, dial "1" first. To call between area-code regions, dial "1" then all 10 digits; the same goes for calls to numbers prefixed by "800," "888," and "877"—all toll-free. For calls to numbers preceded by "900" you must pay—usually dearly.

For international calls, dial "011" followed by the country code and the local number. For help, dial "0" and ask for an overseas operator. The country code is 61 for Australia, 64 for New Zealand, 44 for the United Kingdom. Calling Canada is the same as calling within the United States. Most local phone books list country codes and U.S. area codes. The country code for the United States is 1.

For operator assistance, dial "0". To obtain someone's phone number, call directory assistance, 555–1212 or occasionally 411 (free at public phones). To have the person you're calling foot the bill, phone collect; dial "0" instead of "1" before the 10-digit number.

At pay phones, instructions are usually posted. Usually you insert coins in a slot (10¢–35¢ for local calls) and wait for a steady tone before dialing. When you call long-distance, the operator will tell you how much to insert; prepaid phone cards, widely available in various denominations, are easier. Call the number on the back, punch in the card's personal identification number when prompted, then dial your number.

LANGUAGE

English is the primary language in the Islands, so you can get away without knowing much Hawaiian. Making the effort to learn some words of this lyrical language can be rewarding, however. Despite the length of many Hawaiian words, the Hawaiian alphabet is actually one of the world's shortest, with only 12 letters: the five vowels, *a, e, i, o, u,* and 7 consonants, *h, k, l, m, n, p, w.* Hawaiian words you are most likely to encounter during your visit to the Islands are *aloha, mahalo* (thank you), *keiki* (child), *haole* (Caucasian or foreigner), *mauka* (toward the mountains), *makai* (toward the ocean), and *pau* (finished, all done). Hawai'ian history includes waves of immigrants, each bringing their own language. To communicate with each other, they developed a sort of slang known as "pidgin." If you listen closely, you will know what is being said by the inflections and by the extensive use of body language. For example, when you know what you want to say, but don't know how to say it, just say "you know, da kine." For an informative and somewhat-hilarious view of things Hawaiian, check out Jerry Hopkins's series of books titled, *Pidgin to the Max* and *Fax to the Max,* available at most local bookstores in the Hawaiiana sections.

LEI GREETINGS

When you walk off a long flight, perhaps a bit groggy and stiff, nothing quite compares with a Hawaiian lei greeting. The casual ceremony ranks as one of the fastest ways to make the transition from the worries of home to the joys of your vacation.

Though the tradition has created an expectation that everyone receives this floral garland when they step off the plane, the state of Hawai'i cannot greet each of its nearly 7 million annual visitors.

Still, it's easy to **arrange for a lei ceremony for yourself or your companions before you arrive.** Contact one of the following companies if you have not signed up with a tour company that provides it. If you really want to be wowed by the experience, request a lei of tuberoses, some of the most divine-smelling blossoms on the planet. Aloha Lei Greeters charges $12 to $29 and needs at least one week's notice. Greeters of Hawai'i requires 48-hours' notice and charges $19.95 to $29.95 per person; add $10 for late notification. Kama'āina Ali'i, Flowers & Greeters charges $11.50 for a standard greeting on O'ahu, and $13.50 for the Neighbor Islands.

➤ LEI GREETERS: **Aloha Lei Greeters** (☎ 808/951–9990 or 800/367–5255, FAX 808/951–9992). **Greeters of Hawai'i** (☎ 808/836–0161; 808/834–7667 for airport desk, FAX 800/926–2644). **Kama'aina Ali'i, Flowers & Greeters** (☎ 808/836–3246 or 800/367–5183, FAX 808/836–1814).

LODGING

No matter what your budget, there is a place for you in Hawai'i. Large city-size resorts grace the Islands' most scenic shores. Family-style condominiums have many of the amenities of fine hotels, and it's possible to find some at reasonable prices. Vacation rentals and bed-and-breakfasts are becoming increasingly popular as visitors look for a real slice of Hawai'i away from the crowds. Often tucked into nooks of the Islands you would normally never see, they are competitively priced, highly personalized, and great for relaxing.

The lodgings we list are the cream of the crop in each price category. We always list the facilities that are available, but we don't specify whether they cost extra. When pricing accommodations, always ask what's included and what costs extra.

CATEGORY	COST*
$$$$	over $200
$$$	$125–$200
$$	$75–$125
$	under $75

All prices are for a standard double room, excluding 11.25% tax and service charges.

Assume that hotels operate on the **European Plan** (EP, with no meals) unless we specify that they use the **Continental Plan** (CP, with a Continental breakfast), **Breakfast Plan** (BP, with a full breakfast), **Modified American Plan** (MAP, with breakfast and dinner), or the **Full American Plan** (FAP, with all meals).

APARTMENT & VILLA RENTALS

If you want a home base that's roomy enough for a family and comes with cooking facilities, **consider a furnished rental.** There are Upcountry ranchland locations, private beachfront estates, as well as exclusive jungle hideaways and units on the resort strips. To get the real flavor of the Islands, **book a private, secluded location.** Most cost less than hotels and allow a relaxed and authentic experience, often providing personal chefs, massage, and arrangements for wedding ceremonies and activities. Many people switch to this option after a few days in the crowded resort areas, so think ahead.

➤ INTERNATIONAL AGENTS: **Hideaways International** (✉ 767 Islington St., Portsmouth, NH 03801, ☎ 603/430–4433 or 800/843–4433, FAX 603/430–4444, WEB www.hideaways.com; membership $129). **Hometours International** (✉ Box 11503, Knoxville, TN 37939, ☎ 865/690–8484 or 800/367–4668, WEB http://thor.he.net/~hometour/). **Vacation Home Rentals Worldwide** (✉ 235 Kensington Ave., Norwood, NJ 07648, ☎ 201/767–9393 or 800/633–3284, FAX 201/767–5510, WEB www.vhrww.com). **Villas and Apartments Abroad** (✉ 1270 Avenue of the Americas, 15th floor, New York, NY 10020, ☎ 212/897–5045 or 800/433–3020, FAX 212/897–5039, WEB www.vaanyc.com).

➤ LOCAL AGENTS: **My Maui Paradise** (✉ Box 790450, Paia 96779, ☎ 808/573–2986, WEB www.mymauiparadise.com) specializing in Maui accommodations.

B&BS

B&Bs offer visitors an accommodations alternative that is unique, charming, intimate, and often spotlights Hawai'i's diverse cultural melting pot. Tucked away from traditional resort areas, most are located on the Neighbor Islands, with only a select few on O'ahu due to government regulations. Before you choose this alternative, **decide exactly how much privacy you desire and what amenities you require** to be comfortable. Most of these accommodations book well in advance, require a 50% deposit prior to arrival, and do not accept credit cards. Utilizing a reservations service in the Islands can assist you in finding the B&B that will meet your personal expectations. Some require a small fee for these services, but they provide you a professional point of contact should something go wrong. These services can also assist with interisland travel and car-rental arrangements.

➤ RESERVATION SERVICES: **Bed and Breakfast Hawai'i** (⊠ Box 449, Kapa'a, 96746, ☎ 808/822–7771 or 800/733–1632, WEB www.bandb-hawaii. com). **Bed and Breakfast Honolulu** (statewide) (⊠ 3242 Kā'ohinani Dr., Honolulu 96817, ☎ 808/595–7533 or 800/288–4666, WEB www.hawaiibnb. com). **Go Native Hawai'i** (⊠ 2009 W. Holmes Rd., Suite #9, Lansing, MI 48910, ☎ 800/662–8483). **Hawai'i's Best B&Bs** (⊠ Box 563, Kamuela 96743, ☎ 808/885–0550 or 800/262–9912, WEB www.bestbnb.com) specializing in upscale properties. **My Maui Paradise** (⊠ Box 790450, Paia 96779, ☎ 808/573–2986, WEB www. mymauiparadise.com) specializing in Maui accommodations. **Pacific Hawai'i Bed and Breakfast** (⊠ 99-1661 Aiea Heights Dr., Aiea, 96701, ☎ 808/261–0532 or 800/999–6026). **Volcano Reservations** (⊠ Box 998, Volcano Village, 96785, ☎ 808/967–7244 or 800/937–7786, WEB www.volcano-hawaii. com) has listings in the Volcano area of the Big Island.

CAMPING

Several national, state, and county parks are available, some with bathroom and cooking facilities, others a bit more primitive. The National Park Service and State Parks Division of the Hawai'i Department of Land and Natural Resources (☞ National and State Parks) can provide more information; details on local camping are available from the individual counties.

The City and County of Honolulu can provide information about camping at county sites on O'ahu; the State Parks Division, Hawai'i State Department of Land and Natural Resources handles the same questions for state camping sites. You can pack up your own sleeping bag and bring it along, or you can rent camping equipment at companies such as Omar the Tent Man on O'ahu; Pacific Rent-All on the Big Island; and Pedal 'n' Paddle on Kaua'i.

➤ CAMPING AND RV FACILITIES: **City and County of Honolulu** (☎ 808/523–4525). **State Parks Division, Hawai'i State Department of Land and Natural Resources** (☎ 808/587–0300). **Omar the Tent Man** (⊠ 94-158 Leo'ole St., Waipahu, 96797, ☎ 808/677–8785). **Pacific Rent-All** (⊠ 1080 Kilauea Ave., Hilo, 96720, ☎ 808/935–2974). **Pedal 'n' Paddle** (⊠ Box 1413, Ching Young Village, Hānalei, 96714, ☎ 808/826–9069).

CONDOMINIUMS

Hawai'i is known for developing the resort condominium concept in the early 1970s and continues to maintain its status as a leader in the field. Besides large living areas and full kitchens, many condos now offer front-desk and daily maid services. Nearly 100 companies in Hawai'i and around the United States rent out condominium space in the Islands. Your travel agent will be the most helpful in finding the condo you desire.

➤ RESOURCES: **Castle Resorts and Hotels** (⊠ 1150 S. King St., Honolulu, 96814, ☎ 800/367–5004, FAX 800/477–2329). **Hawai'i Condo Exchange** (⊠ 1817 El Cerrito Pl., Los Angeles, CA 90068, ☎ 323/436–0300 or 800/442–0404, FAX 323/435–0331).

HOME EXCHANGES

If you would like to exchange your home for someone else's, **join a home-exchange organization,** which will send you its updated listings of available exchanges for a year and will include your own listing in at least one of them. It's up to you to make specific arrangements.

➤ EXCHANGE CLUBS: **HomeLink International** (✉ Box 47747, Tampa, FL 33647, ☎ 813/975–9825 or 800/638–3841, FAX 813/910–8144, WEB www. homelink.org; $98 per year). **Intervac U.S.** (✉ Box 590504, San Francisco, CA 94159, ☎ 800/756–4663, FAX 415/435–7440, WEB www.intervacus.com; $93 yearly fee includes one catalog and on-line access).

HOSTELS

No matter what your age, you can **save on lodging costs by staying at hostels.** In some 5,000 locations in more than 70 countries around the world, Hostelling International (HI), the umbrella group for a number of national youth-hostel associations, offers single-sex, dorm-style beds and, at many hostels, rooms for couples and family accommodations. Membership in any HI national hostel association, open to travelers of all ages, allows you to stay in HI-affiliated hostels at member rates; one-year membership is about $25 for adults (C$26.75 in Canada, £9.30 in the U.K., $30 in Australia, and $30 in New Zealand); hostels run about $10–$25 per night. Members have priority if the hostel is full; they're also eligible for discounts around the world, even on rail and bus travel in some countries.

➤ ORGANIZATIONS: **Hostelling International—American Youth Hostels** (✉ 733 15th St. NW, Suite 840, Washington, DC 20005, ☎ 202/783–6161, FAX 202/783–6171, WEB www.hiayh. org). **Hostelling International—Canada** (✉ 400–205 Catherine St., Ottawa, Ontario K2P 1C3, Canada, ☎ 613/237–7884, FAX 613/237–7868, WEB www.hostellingintl.ca). **Youth Hostel Association of England and Wales** (✉ Trevelyan House, 8 St. Stephen's Hill, St. Albans, Hertfordshire AL1 2DY, U.K., ☎ 0870/8708808, FAX 01727/844126, WEB www.yha.org.uk). **Australian Youth Hostel Association** (✉ 10 Mallett St., Camperdown, NSW 2050, Australia, ☎ 02/9565–1699, FAX 02/9565–1325, WEB www.yha.com.au). **Youth Hostels Association of New Zealand** (✉ Box 436, Christchurch, New Zealand, ☎ 03/379–9970, FAX 03/365–4476, WEB www.yha.org.nz).

HOTELS

You can find most major hotel brands in Hawai'i; large, locally based operators, such as Aston Hotels and Resorts and Outrigger Hotels Hawai'i; and a number of independents. The result is an extensive range of rooms, from rock-bottom economy units to luxurious suites.

➤ TOLL-FREE NUMBERS: **Best Western** (☎ 800/528–1234, WEB www. bestwestern.com). **Choice** (☎ 800/221–2222, WEB www.hotelchoice. com). **Clarion** (☎ 800/252–7466, WEB www.hotelchoice.com). **Colony** (☎ 800/777–1700, WEB www.colony. com). **Comfort** (☎ 800/228–5150, WEB www.comfortinn.com). **Days Inn** (☎ 800/325–2525, WEB www.daysinn. com). **Doubletree and Red Lion Hotels** (☎ 800/222–8733, WEB www. doubletree.com). **Embassy Suites** (☎ 800/362–2779, WEB www. embassysuites.com). **Fairfield Inn** (☎ 800/228–2800, WEB www.marriott. com). **Hilton** (☎ 800/445–8667, WEB www.hilton.com). **Holiday Inn** (☎ 800/465–4329, WEB www.basshotels. com). **Howard Johnson** (☎ 800/654–4656, WEB www.hojo.com). **Hyatt Hotels & Resorts** (☎ 800/233–1234, WEB www.hyatt.com). **La Quinta** (☎ 800/531–5900, WEB www.laquinta. com). **Marriott** (☎ 800/228–9290, WEB www.marriott.com). **Nikko Hotels International** (☎ 800/645–5687, WEB www.nikkohotels.com). **Radisson** (☎ 800/333–3333, WEB www.radisson. com). **Ramada** (☎ 800/228–2828, WEB www.ramada.com). **Renaissance Hotels & Resorts** (☎ 800/468–3571, WEB www.renaissancehotels.com). **Ritz-Carlton** (☎ 800/241–3333, WEB www. ritzcarlton.com). **Sheraton** (☎ 800/325–3535, WEB www.starwood.com). **Westin Hotels & Resorts** (☎ 800/228–3000, WEB www.westin.com).

MEDIA

Hawaii is wired to a variety of media, including network television, cable television, Web-based media, newspapers, magazines, and radio. Many of the resorts and hotels throughout the Islands include an additional **visitor-information channel on your in-room television.** Consult your in-room directory for channel and scheduling information and to find out the special activities or events that might be happening during your visit.

NEWSPAPERS & MAGAZINES

Each of the Islands has its own daily newspapers, available through many hotel bell desks, in sundry stores, restaurants, cafés, and at newspaper stands. Many hotels will deliver one to your room upon request. *The Honolulu Advertiser* is O'ahu's morning and Sunday paper; *The Honolulu Star-Bulletin* is O'ahu's evening paper. *West Hawai'i Today* is the Big Island's Kona Coast newspaper, and the *Hawai'i Tribune-Herald* serves the Hilo side of the island. On Maui, it's *The Maui News*. On Kaua'i, it's *The Garden Island* and *Kaua'i Times*. *The Honolulu Weekly* is a great guide for arts and alternative events, and the *Pacific Business News* provides the latest in business news. A variety of free visitor publications and guides is available throughout the Islands. In addition, the monthly *Honolulu Magazine* focuses on island issues and happenings. Check out local bookstores for Neighbor Island magazines, some of which publish on a quarterly schedule.

RADIO & TELEVISION

Radio airwaves on the Islands are affected by natural terrain, so don't expect to hear one radio station island-wide. For Hawaiian music, tune your FM radio dials to 105.7 KINE (O'ahu), 100 KINE (O'ahu), 97.9 KKBG (East Hawai'i), 106.1 KLEO (West Hawai'i), 93.5 KPOA (Maui), and 95.7 KSRF (Kaua'i). News junkies can get their fill of news and talk by tuning to the AM radio dial and the following island stations: 590 KSSK (O'ahu), 650 KHNR (O'ahu), 670 KPUA (East Hawai'i), 620 KIPA (West Hawai'i), 1110 KAOI or 1570 KUAU (Maui), 570 KONG (Kaua'i). National Public Radio enthusiasts can tune to the FM dial for NPR programming on 88.1 KHPR (O'ahu) and 90.7 KKUA (Maui). On Kaua'i you can listen to the only commercial-free public radio station in the Islands, KKCR, at 90.9 and 91.9 FM. They've got Hawaiian music, jazz, folk, and reggae as well as talk shows on local issues.

Many Hawaiians wake up with Perry and Price on KSSK AM 59 or FM 92. The lively duo provides news, traffic updates, and weather reports between "easy-listening music" and phone calls from listeners from 5 to 10 AM.

Television channels in the Islands are plentiful between network and cable channels. Channel allocation varies by island and location. On O'ahu, you can find the following network programming with its channel and local affiliate call sign: FOX (2) KHON, ABC (4) KITV, UPN/WB (5) KHVE, CBS (9) KGMB, PBS (10) KHET, and NBC (13) KHNL.

MONEY MATTERS

Many of the Islands' best attractions and activities, such as beaches and hiking, can be found in the form of natural beauty and cost nothing to view. You'll pay 50¢ for a daily newspaper, $1.50 to ride the bus anywhere on O'ahu, and from $45 on up to attend a lū'au. Large museums cost between $8 and $15 per entry, smaller ones can cost from $3 to $6. Prices throughout this guide are given for adults. Substantially reduced fees are almost always available for children, students, and senior citizens.

ATMS

Automatic teller machines for easy access to cash are everywhere on the Islands. ATMs can be found in shopping centers, small convenience and grocery stores, inside hotels and resorts, as well as outside most bank branches. For a directory of locations, call 800/424–7787 for the Cirrus network or 800/843–7587 for the Plus network.

CREDIT CARDS

Most major credit cards are accepted throughout the Islands and are required to rent a car. When making reservations, double-check to ensure that the lodging, restaurant, or attraction you are planning to visit accepts them. In smaller concessions, B&Bs, and fast-food outlets, expect to pay cash.

Throughout this guide, the following abbreviations are used: **AE**, American Express; **D**, Discover; **DC**, Diner's Club; **MC**, MasterCard; and **V**, Visa.

➤ REPORTING LOST CARDS: **American Express** (☎ 800/528–4800). **Discover** (☎ 800/347–2683). **Diner's Club** (☎ 800/234–6377). **MasterCard**

(☎ 800/307–7309). **Visa** (☎ 800/ 847–2911).

NATIONAL AND STATE PARKS

Hawai'i is home to seven national parks. On Maui is the summit and crater of the Haleakalā volcano, at Haleakalā National Park. Moloka'i's Kalaupapa National Historical Park was once a leper colony where victims of Hansen's disease were sent into exile in the late 1800s, and cared for by Father Damien, a Belgian missionary. On the island of O'ahu, the U.S.S. *Arizona* Memorial at Pearl Harbor is overseen by the National Park Service.

The Big Island, Hawai'i's largest island, has four national parks. Hawai'i Volcanoes National Park is the state's number-one visitor attraction, where vents have been spewing lava for nearly 20 years. The other three are Pu'uhonua O Hōnaunau National Historical Park, Pu'ukoholā Heiau National Historical Site, and Kaloko-Honokōhau National Historical Park, all of which give a glimpse into Hawai'i's rich cultural history.

Hawai'i's 52 state parks encompass more than 25,000 acres on five islands, and include many of its most beautiful beaches and coastal areas. The State Parks Division of the Hawai'i State Department of Land and Natural Resources can provide information on state parks and historic areas.

Look into discount passes to save money on park entrance fees. The National Parks Pass ($50) gets you and your companions free admission to all parks for one year. (Camping and parking are extra.) A percentage of the proceeds from sales of the pass will fund National Parks projects. Both the Golden Age Passport ($10), for those 62 and older, and the Golden Access Passport (free), for travelers with disabilities, entitle holders to free entry to all national parks, plus 50% off fees for the use of many park facilities and services. You must show proof of age and of U.S. citizenship or permanent residency (such as a U.S. passport, driver's license, or birth certificate, and, if requesting Golden Access, proof of disability). The Golden Age and Golden Access passes are available at all national parks wher-

ever entrance fees are charged. The National Parks Pass is available by mail or through the Internet.

➤ PASSES BY MAIL: **National Park Service** (✉ National Park Service/Department of Interior, 1849 C St. NW, Washington, DC 20240, ☎ 202/208–4747, WEB www.nps.gov). **National Parks Pass** (✉ 27540 Ave. Mentry, Valencia, CA 91355, ☎ 888/GO–PARKS, WEB www.nationalparks.org).

➤ STATE PARKS: **State Parks Division, Hawai'i State Department of Land and Natural Resources** (✉ 1151 Punchbowl St., Room 310, Honolulu, 96813, ☎ 808/587–0300, WEB www.hawaii.gov).

OUTDOORS & SPORTS

Outdoors enthusiasts are in their element in Hawai'i, where they can swim, hike, bike, scuba dive, and play golf, among other activities. Alternative Hawai'i's Web site provides detailed information on hiking, diving, camping, kayaking, and outfitters on each island. Whatever you do outdoors, don't forget to tread lightly.

➤ RESOURCE: **Alternative Hawai'i** (☎ 808/695–5113, WEB www.alternative-hawaii.com).

BEACHES

Hawai'i's beaches are the stuff of legend, with white sand wedged between palm trees and turquoise water, or even colorful black and green stretches of sand. All beaches are free and open to the public unless otherwise noted—even the most luxurious hotels have to share their beachfronts. Note that riptides and strong undertows can challenge even the strongest swimmers, so if you see a beach where no one is swimming, ask a local about its safety before diving in. Use care when diving into lagoons as well, as they often are not as deep as they appear. Alcohol is not permitted on most beaches.

GOLF

With many high-profile tournaments on TV each year, Hawai'i is known for its golf. To experience the glory for yourself, check with your hotel concierge or golf shop to arrange tee times, or call the courses listed in the chapters directly.

HIKING AND CAMPING

Hiking can be a wonderful way to explore the natural beauty of the Islands. **Don't stray off trails,** be sure to **wear sturdy hiking shoes,** especially if you're doing lava hikes, and **bring plenty of water** wherever you hike. When camping, **be prepared for radical weather shifts,** especially at high altitudes. Haleakalā National Park, for example, can reach 85°F by day, and 35 by night. Fog, wind, and rain can and do blow in with little or no warning.

KAYAKING

Kayaking is an excellent low-impact way to enjoy the scenery. Kayak rentals are available on each island, and you can arrange guided trips. **Remain close to shore** if you don't want to be whooshed away to another island in terrible seas. Check with the kayak rental shop for weather advisories.

SCUBA DIVING AND SNORKELING

Underwater Hawai'i is breathtaking, but diving tends to be pricey. You can arrange trips with countless outfitters, or rent equipment on your own. Whether snorkeling or diving, remember to **never go alone,** and be sure to ask at the dive shop about rip currents and places to avoid. Undersea life is extremely fragile, so don't touch (or take) the coral, and watch that your fins don't hit the reefs behind you.

PACKING

Hawai'i is casual: sandals, bathing suits, and comfortable, informal clothing are the norm. In summer synthetic slacks and shirts, although easy to care for, can be uncomfortably warm. You'll easily find a bathing suit in Hawai'i, but **bring a bathing cap with you if you wear one.** You can waste hours searching for one.

Probably the most important thing to tuck into your suitcase is sunscreen. This is the tropics, and the ultraviolet rays are powerful. Doctors advise putting on sunscreen when you get up in the morning. Don't forget to **reapply sunscreen periodically during the day,** since perspiration can wash it away. Consider using sunscreens with a sun protection factor (SPF) of 15 or higher. There are many tanning oils on the market in Hawai'i, including coconut and *kukui* (the nut from a local tree) oils, but doctors warn that they merely sauté your skin. Too many Hawaiian vacations have been spoiled by sunburn, and even sun poisoning. Hats and sunglasses offer important sun protection, too. Both are easy to find in island shops, but if you already have a favorite packable hat or sun visor, bring it with you, and don't forget to wear it. All major hotels in Hawai'i provide beach towels.

As for clothing in the Hawaiian Islands, there's a saying that when a man wears a suit during the day, he's either going for a loan or he's a lawyer trying a case. Only a few upscale restaurants require a jacket for dinner, and none require a tie. The aloha shirt is accepted dress in Hawai'i for business and most social occasions. Shorts are acceptable daytime attire, along with a T-shirt or polo shirt. There's no need to buy expensive sandals on the mainland—here you can get flip-flops for about a dollar and off-brand sandals for $10. Golfers should remember that many courses have dress codes requiring a collared shirt; call courses you're interested in for details. If you're not prepared, you can pick up appropriate clothing at resort pro shops. If you're visiting in winter or planning to visit a volcano area, **bring a sweater or light- to medium-weight jacket.** Trade winds cool things off when the sun goes down, and things get chilly above 10,000 ft.

In your carry-on luggage, **pack an extra pair of eyeglasses or contact lenses** and **enough of any medication you take** to last the entire trip. You may also ask your doctor to write a spare prescription using the drug's generic name, since brand names may vary from country to country. In luggage to be checked, **never pack prescription drugs or valuables.** To avoid customs delays, carry medications in their original packaging. And don't forget to carry with you the addresses of offices that handle refunds of lost traveler's checks. Check *Fodor's How to Pack* (available in bookstores everywhere) for more tips.

CHECKING LUGGAGE

How many carry-on bags you can bring with you is up to the airline. Most allow two, but not always, so make sure that everything you carry aboard will fit under your seat or in the overhead bin, and get to the gate early. Note that if you have a seat at the back of the plane, you'll probably board first, while the overhead bins are still empty.

If you are flying internationally, note that baggage allowances may be determined not by piece but by weight—generally 88 pounds (40 kilograms) in first class, 66 pounds (30 kilograms) in business class, and 44 pounds (20 kilograms) in economy.

Airline liability for baggage is limited to $1,250 per person on flights within the United States. On international flights it amounts to $9.07 per pound or $20 per kilogram for checked baggage (roughly $640 per 70-pound bag) and $400 per passenger for unchecked baggage. You can buy additional coverage at check-in for about $10 per $1,000 of coverage, but it excludes a rather extensive list of items, shown on your airline ticket.

Before departure, **itemize your bags' contents** and their worth, and label the bags with your name, address, and phone number. (If you use your home address, cover it so potential thieves can't see it readily.) Inside each bag, **pack a copy of your itinerary.** At check-in, **make sure that each bag is correctly tagged** with the destination airport's three-letter code. If your bags arrive damaged or fail to arrive at all, file a written report with the airline before leaving the airport.

SAFETY

Hawai'i is generally a safe tourist destination, but it's still wise to **follow the same common sense safety precautions you would normally follow** in your own hometown. There are some spots on every island that you might wish to avoid. Hotel and visitor center staff can provide information should you decide to head out on your own to more remote areas. Rental cars are magnets for break-ins, so don't leave any valuables in the car, not even in a locked trunk. Avoid poorly lit areas, beach parks, and isolated areas after

dark as a precaution. When hiking, **stay on marked trails,** no matter how alluring the temptation might be to stray. Weather conditions can cause landscapes to become muddy, slippery, and tenuous, so staying on marked trails will lessen the possibility of a fall or getting lost. Ocean safety is of utmost importance when visiting an island destination. **Don't swim alone, and follow the international signage posted at beaches that alerts swimmers** to strong currents, man-of-war jellyfish, sharp coral, high surf, sharks, and dangerous shorebreaks. At coastal lookouts along cliff tops, heed the signs indicating that waves can climb over the ledges. Check with lifeguards at each beach for current conditions, and **if the red flags are up, indicating swimming and surfing are not allowed, don't attempt to swim.** Waters that look calm on the surface can harbor strong currents and undertows.

LOCAL SCAMS

Be wary of those hawking "too good to be true" prices on everything from car rentals to visitor attractions. Many of these offers are just a lure to get you in the door for time-share presentations. When handed a flyer, read the fine print before you make your decision to participate.

WOMEN IN HAWAI'I

Women traveling alone are generally safe in the Islands, but always follow the safety precautions you would use in any major destination. When booking hotels, inquire about concierge or club floors that offer executive services, request rooms closest to the elevator, and always keep your hotel room door and balcony doors locked. Stay away from isolated areas after dark, and camping solo is not advisable. If you stay out late visiting nightclubs and bars, use caution when exiting the night spot and returning to your lodging.

SENIOR-CITIZEN TRAVEL

Hawai'i is steeped in a tradition that gives great respect to elders, or *kapuna,* and considers them "keepers of the wisdom." For seniors, traveling in Hawai'i offers special discounts, special senior-oriented activities, and easy access. Many lodging facilities have discounts for members of the American Association of Retired Persons (AARP). To qualify for age-related discounts, **mention your senior-citizen status up front** when booking hotel reservations (not when checking out) and before you're seated in restaurants (not when paying the bill). When renting a car, ask about promotional car-rental discounts, which can be cheaper than senior-citizen rates. Also, when visiting attractions, museums, or movie theaters, **inquire about their senior-citizen discounts.** They can save you a bundle.

➤ EDUCATIONAL PROGRAMS: **Elderhostel** (✉ 11 Ave. de Lafayette, Boston, MA 02111-1746, ☎ 877/426–8056, FAX 877/426–2166, WEB www.elderhostel. org). **Interhostel** (✉ University of New Hampshire, 6 Garrison Ave., Durham, NH 03824, ☎ 603/862–1147 or 800/733–9753, FAX 603/862–1113, WEB www. learn.unh.edu).

SHOPPING

KEY DESTINATIONS

On Oʻahu, Ala Moana Center is one of the largest shopping spots; it's within easy walking distance of the west end of Waikīkī. The Royal Hawaiian Shopping Center is centrally located in Waikīkī itself. Farther away, you'll find Ward Warehouse, Aloha Tower Marketplace, and the Kāhala Mall.

The Neighbor Islands offer more in the way of smaller strips of shops. Still, it's possible to find larger stores grouped in areas such as Kauaʻi's Kukui Grove Center in Līhuʻe, Maui's Kaʻahumanu Shopping Center, and the Big Island's Prince Kūhiō Shopping Plaza in Hilo, and Keauhou Shopping Village and Lanihau Center in Kailua-Kona. Exclusive shops can often be found in the lobbies of luxury hotels on all the Islands.

SMART SOUVENIRS

Aloha shirts and resort wear, Hawaiian-music recordings, shell leis, coral jewelry, traditional quilts, island foods, Kona coffee, and koa-wood products are just a few of the gifts that visitors to Hawaiʻi treasure. For the more elegant gift items, check out the Hawaiian boutiques located in major island shopping centers as well as those tucked away in smaller shopping areas in residential districts.

Island craft fairs and swap meets offer a bargain bazaar of standard items such as T-shirts and tiki statues as well as the original works of local artisans.

STUDENTS IN HAWAIʻI

Hawaiʻi is a popular destination for exchange students from around the world. Contact your hometown university about study and internship possibilities. To check out the student scene in the Islands, stop by any of the University of Hawaiʻi campuses, the community college campuses, and read the *Honolulu Weekly* upon arrival for club and event information. Be sure to ask about discounts for students at all museums and major attractions and be prepared to show ID to qualify.

➤ I.D.S & SERVICES: **Council Travel** (CIEE; ✉ 205 E. 42nd St., 15th floor, New York, NY 10017, ☎ 212/822–2700 or 888/268–6245, FAX 212/822–2699, WEB www.councilexchanges.org) for mail orders only, in the U.S. **Travel Cuts** (✉ 187 College St., Toronto, Ontario M5T 1P7, Canada, ☎ 416/979–2406 or 800/667–2887 in Canada, FAX 416/979–8167, WEB www. travelcuts.com).

TAXES

There is a 4% state sales tax on all purchases, including food. A hotel room tax of 7.25%, combined with the sales tax of 4%, equals an 11.25% rate added onto your hotel bill. A $2-per-day road tax is also assessed on each rental vehicle.

TIME

Hawaiʻi is on Hawaiian Standard Time, 5 hours behind New York, 2 hours behind Los Angeles, and 10 hours behind London.

When the U.S. mainland is on daylight savings time, Hawaiʻi is not, so add an extra hour of time difference between the Islands and U.S. mainland destinations. You may also find that things generally move more slowly here. That has nothing to do with your watch—it's just the laid-back way called Hawaiian time.

TIPPING

Tipping begins with your taxi ride from the airport. Tip cab drivers 15% of the fare. Standard tips for restaurants and bar tabs runs from 15% to 20% of the bill, depending on the standard of service. Bellhops at hotels usually receive $1 per bag, more if you have bulky items such as bicycles and surfboards. Tip the hotel-room maid $1 per night, paid daily. Tip doormen $1 for assistance with taxis; tips for concierge vary depending on the service. For example, tip more for "hard-to-get" event tickets or dining reservations.

TOURS & PACKAGES

Because everything is prearranged on a prepackaged tour or independent vacation, you spend less time planning—and often get it all at a good price.

Packages that include any combination of lodging, airfare, meals, sightseeing, car rental, and even sports activities and entertainment are popular in Hawai'i and are often considerably cheaper than piecing the vacation together à la carte. Just do your research, and make sure that the options offered (especially when it comes to lodging and meals) are really the ones you want. Honeymoon packages that include everything from the actual wedding ceremony to extras such as special suites, champagne, flowers, and romantic dinners are offered by some resorts and hotels. Again, **do some homework, ask questions, and make sure that the package suits your tastes and budget.**

BOOKING WITH AN AGENT

Travel agents are excellent resources. But it's a good idea to collect brochures from several agencies as some agents' suggestions may be influenced by relationships with tour and package firms that reward them for volume sales. If you have a special interest, **find an agent with expertise in that area**; ASTA (☞ Travel Agencies) has a database of specialists worldwide.

Make sure your travel agent knows the accommodations and other services of the place they're recommending. Ask about the hotel's location, room size, beds, and whether it has a pool, room service, or programs for children, if you care about these. Has

your agent been there in person or sent others whom you can contact?

Do some homework on your own, too: local tourism boards can provide information about lesser-known and small-niche operators, some of which may sell only direct.

BUYER BEWARE

Each year consumers are stranded or lose their money when tour operators—even large ones with excellent reputations—go out of business. So **check out the operator.** Ask several travel agents about its reputation, and try to **book with a company that has a consumer-protection program.** (Look for information in the company's brochure.) In the United States, members of the National Tour Association and the United States Tour Operators Association are required to set aside funds to cover your payments and travel arrangements in the event that the company defaults. It's also a good idea to choose a company that participates in the American Society of Travel Agents' Tour Operator Program (TOP); ASTA will act as mediator in any disputes between you and your tour operator.

Remember that the more your package or tour includes the better you can predict the ultimate cost of your vacation. Make sure you know exactly what is covered, and **beware of hidden costs.** Are taxes, tips, and transfers included? Entertainment and excursions? These can add up.

➤ TOUR-OPERATOR RECOMMENDATIONS: **American Society of Travel Agents** (☞ Travel Agencies). **National Tour Association** (NTA; ✉ 546 E. Main St., Lexington, KY 40508, ☎ 859/226–4444 or 800/682–8886, WEB www. ntaonline.com). **United States Tour Operators Association** (USTOA; ✉ 342 Madison Ave., Suite 1522, New York, NY 10173, ☎ 212/599–6599 or 800/ 468–7862, FAX 212/599–6744, WEB www. ustoa.com).

TRANSPORTATION AROUND
HAWAI'I

Renting a car is definitely recommended for those who plan to move beyond their hotel lounge chair. With the exception of O'ahu, public transportation is extremely limited, and even if you are staying in Honolulu or Waīkkī you may want a car if you plan to do any exploring or if you're short on time. **Reserve your vehicle in advance,** particularly during peak travel times and on the smaller islands, where the car-rental fleets are limited. Most major companies have airport counters and complimentary transportation for pickup/drop-off back at the airport upon departure.

Taxis can also be found at island airports, through your hotel doorman, in the more popular resort areas, or by contacting local taxi companies by telephone. Flag-down fees are $2, and each additional mile is $1.70. Most companies will also provide a car and driver for half-day or day-long island tours if you absolutely don't want to rent a car, and a number of companies also offer personal guides. Remember, however, that rates are quite steep for these services, ranging from $100 to $200 and up.

TRAVEL AGENCIES

A good travel agent puts your needs first. Look for an agency that has been in business at least five years, emphasizes customer service, and has someone on staff who specializes in your destination. In addition, **make sure the agency belongs to a professional trade organization.** The American Society of Travel Agents (ASTA), with more than 26,000 members in some 170 countries, is the largest and most influential in the field. Operating under the motto "Without a travel agent, you're on your own," it maintains and enforces a strict code of ethics and will step in to help mediate any agent-client disputes if necessary. ASTA also maintains a Web site that includes a directory of agents. (If a travel agency is also acting as your tour operator, *see* Buyer Beware *in* Tours & Packages.)

➤ LOCAL AGENT REFERRALS: **American Society of Travel Agents** (ASTA; ☎ 800/965–2782 24-hr hot line, FAX 703/739–7642, WEB www.astanet. com). **Association of British Travel Agents** (✉ 68–71 Newman St., London W1T 3AH, U.K., ☎ 020/7637–2444, FAX 020/7637–0713, WEB www.

abtanet.com). **Association of Canadian Travel Agents** (✉ 130 Albert St., Suite 1705, Ottawa, Ontario K1P 5G4, Canada, ☎ 613/237–3657, FAX 613/237–7502, WEB www.acta.net). **Australian Federation of Travel Agents** (✉ Level 3, 309 Pitt St., Sydney NSW 2000, Australia, ☎ 02/9264–3299, FAX 02/9264–1085, WEB www.afta.com. au). **Travel Agents' Association of New Zealand** (✉ Box 1888, Wellington 10033, New Zealand, ☎ 04/499–0104, FAX 04/499–0827, WEB www. taanz.org.nz).

VISITOR INFORMATION

Before you go, contact the Hawai'i Visitors & Convention Bureau for general information on each island, free brochures that include an accommodations and car-rental guide, and an entertainment and dining listing containing one-line descriptions of bureau members. Take a virtual visit to Hawai'i on the Web, which can be most helpful in planning your vacation. The HVCB site has a calendar section that allows you to see what local events are in place during the time of your stay.

➤ TOURIST INFORMATION: **Hawai'i Visitors & Convention Bureau** (✉ 2270 Kalakaua Ave., Suite 801, Honolulu, 96817, ☎ 808/923–1811; 800/464–2924 for brochures; WEB www. gohawaii.com). In the U.K. contact the **Hawai'i Visitors & Convention Bureau** (✉ Box 208, Sunbury, Middlesex, TW16 5RJ, ☎ 020/8941–4009, WEB www.gohawaii.com; send a £2 check or postal order for an information pack).

WEB SITES

Do check out the World Wide Web when planning your trip. You'll find everything from weather forecasts to virtual tours of famous cities. Be sure to **visit Fodors.com** (www.fodors.com), a complete travel-planning site. You can research prices and book plane tickets, hotel rooms, rental cars, vacation packages, and more. In addition, you can post your pressing questions in the Travel Talk section and, in the site's Rants & Raves section, read comments about some of the restaurants and hotels in this book—and chime in yourself. Other planning tools include a currency converter and weather reports, and there are loads of links to travel resources.

For more information on Hawai'i, visit WEB www.gohawaii.com, the official Web site of the Hawai'i Convention and Visitors Bureau.

Other sites to check out include www.bigisland.org (Big Island Visitors Bureau); www.visitmaui.com (Maui County Visitors Bureau); www.visit-Oahu.com (O'ahu Visitors Bureau); www.kauaivisitorsbureau. org (Kaua'i Visitors Bureau); www. molokai-hawaii.com (Moloka'i Visitor Information); www.cruisehawaii. com (for information on cruise vessels sailing interisland); www.thebus.org (O'ahu's public transportation system); and www.alohaboatdays.com (for a schedule and information about cruise-arrival celebrations at Aloha Tower, Honolulu Harbor).

www.hawaii.net has links to more than 100 Hawaiian sites (click on Visiting Hawai'i). www.search-hawaii.com has an engine that can search all linked Hawaiian Web pages by topic or word.

Visit www.hshawaii.com for the Hawai'i State vacation planner; www.kauai-hawaii.com for Kaua'i visitors information; www.honoluluweekly.com for a weekly guide to the arts, entertainment, and dining in Honolulu; www.hawaii.gov, the state's official Web site, for all information on the destination, including camping; and www.nps.gov for national parks information.

WHEN TO GO

Long days of sunshine and fairly mild year-round temperatures make Hawai'i an all-season destination. Most resort areas are at sea level, with average afternoon temperature

during the coldest winter months of December and January at 75°F; during the hottest months of August and September the temperature often reaches 92°F. Cold weather (30°F) can occur in Hawai'i in winter, but only near the summit of the Big Island's Mauna Ke'a crater, where skiing is possible.

Most travelers head to the Islands during winter. From mid-December through mid-April, visitors from the mainland and other areas covered with snow find Hawai'i's sun-splashed beaches and balmy trade winds appealing. This high season means that fewer travel bargains are available; room rates average 10%–15% higher during this season than the rest of the year.

Rainfall increases in winter, though it's rarely overcast for very long. Regardless of the season, the northern and eastern shores of each island usually receive more rain than those on the south. Kaua'i's and the Big Island's northern sections get more annual rainfall than the rest of Hawai'i, and so much rain falls on Kaua'i's Mount Wai'ale'ale (approximately 472 inches of rain, or 39 ft), that it's considered the wettest place on earth.

CLIMATE

The following are average maximum and minimum temperatures for Honolulu; the temperatures throughout the Hawaiian Islands are similar.

➤ FORECASTS: **Weather Channel Connection** (☎ 900/932–8437), 95¢ per minute from a Touch-Tone phone.

FESTIVALS AND SEASONAL EVENTS

➤ DEC.: **Triple Crown of Surfing** (O'ahu; ☎ 808/638–7266): The world's top pro surfers gather on the

Honolulu, O'ahu

Jan.	80F	27C	May	85F	29C	Sept.	88F	31C
	65	18		70	21		73	23
Feb.	80F	27C	June	86F	30C	Oct.	87F	31C
	65	18		72	22		72	22
Mar.	81F	27C	July	87F	31C	Nov.	84F	29C
	69	21		73	23		69	21
Apr.	83F	28C	Aug.	88F	31C	Dec.	81F	27C
	69	21		74	23		67	19

North Shore during November and December for the big winter waves and some tough competition. **Nā Mele O Maui** (Maui; ☎ 808/661–3271): The first week of December, this Hawaiiana festival at Kā'anapali features arts and crafts and schoolchildren competing in Hawaiian song and hula performances. **Honolulu Marathon** (O'ahu; ☎ 808/734–7200): Watch or run in one of the country's most popular marathons. **Bodhi Day** (all Islands; ☎ 808/536–7044): The traditional Buddhist Day of Enlightenment is celebrated in early December at temples statewide; visitors are welcome. **Kaua'i Products Fair** (Kaua'i; ☎ 808/246–0988): Locally made crafts, fruit, plants, clothes, wellness practitioners, and entertainment are all available at this monthlong outdoor market (weekends only). **Family Ocean Discovery Series: Turtle Hurdles** (Maui; ☎ 808/879–8860): Join with the Pacific Whale Foundation to learn about Hawai'i's rare resident turtles. **Pacific Master & and Senior Amateur Golf Championships** (O'ahu; ☎ 808/666–1125): This five-day tournament draws golfers from across North America. **Annual Kailua-Kona Community Christmas Parade** (Big Island; ☎ 808/326–4447): Marching bands, floats, and Santa make their way through town. **Jeep Aloha/Jeep O'ahu Bowls** (O'ahu; ☎ 808/947–4141): Four top college football squads meet in this annual football doubleheader held at Aloha Stadium on Christmas Day. **Festival of Lights** (all Islands; ☎ 808/523–4674 O'ahu, ☎ 808/828–0014 Kaua'i, ☎ 808/667–9175 Maui): Islands deck out the lights to celebrate December's holiday season, with electric light parades, decorated city buildings, and events that last throughout December. **Christmas** (all Islands): Hotels outdo each other in such extravagant exhibits and events as Santa arriving by outrigger canoe. **Christmas Lighting of the Banyan Tree** (Maui; ☎ 808/667–9193): Five thousand lights cover the historic banyan tree on Front Street. **Pacific Handcrafters Guild's Annual Christmas Festival of Art & Fine Crafts** (O'ahu; ☎ 808/637–1248): More than 100 craftspeople display their creations at this two-day event at Thomas Square Park; it also includes music, food, and activities for kids. **Rainbow Classic** (O'ahu; ☎ 808/956–6501): The UH Rainbows and seven top-ranked college basketball teams from the mainland compete at the University of Hawai'i between Christmas and New Year's Day. **First Night Maui** (Maui; ☎ 808/244–9166): An alcohol-free New Year's Eve street festival of arts and entertainment at dozens of downtown locations.

➤ JAN.: **Rivals.com Hula Bowl Game** (Maui; ☎ 808/947–4141): This annual college all-star football classic is followed by a Hawaiian-style concert. **Morey Boogie World Body Board Championships** (O'ahu; ☎ 808/396–2326): Competition days for the world's best body boarders are determined by the wave action at Banzai Pipeline. **Cherry Blossom Festival** (O'ahu; ☎ 808/949–2255): This popular celebration of all things Japanese includes a run, cultural displays, cooking demonstrations, music, and crafts. It runs through the end of March.

➤ JAN.–FEB.: **Chinese New Year Celebrations** (all Islands; ☎ 808/533–3181 O'ahu, 808/667–9175 Maui): The Chinese New Year is welcomed with a Narcissus Festival pageant, coronation ball, cooking demonstrations, fireworks, and lion dances. **Sony Open Golf in Hawai'i Tournament** (O'ahu; ☎ 808/734–2151): Top golf pros tee off at the Wai'alae Country Club.

➤ FEB.: **NFL Pro Bowl** (O'ahu; ☎ 808/486–9300): A week after the Super Bowl this annual pro-football all-star game is played at Aloha Stadium. It culminates in **NFL Week** (☎ 808/233–4635), with events on each island. **Punahou Carnival** (O'ahu; ☎ 808/944–5711): Hawai'i's most prestigious private school stages an annual two-day fund-raiser with rides, arts and crafts, local food, and a great white-elephant tent. **Sand-Castle Building Contest** (O'ahu; ☎ 808/956–7225): Students of the University of Hawai'i School of Architecture take on Hawai'i's professional architects in a friendly competition; the result is some amazing and unusual sand sculpture at Kailua Beach Park.

➤ FEB.–MAR.: **Buffalo's Annual Big Board Surfing Classic** (O'ahu; ☎ 808/696–3878): The event features surfing as it used to be, on old-fashioned 12- to 16-ft boards, plus food and entertainment.

➤ MAR.: **Opening Day of Polo Season** (O'ahu; ☎ 808/947–6511): Games are held every Sunday through August at 2 PM at Mokule'ia and Waimānalo. **O'ahu Kite Festival** (O'ahu; ☎ 808/ 735–9059): Kite-flying demonstrations, workshops, and competitions are held at Kapi'olani Park. **East Maui Taro Festival** (Maui; ☎ 808/248– 8972): Held in Hana, this three-day festival focuses on all things taro, including poi. **Twilight Tattoo** (O'ahu; ☎ 808/655–9759): Professional bands compete at Ft. DeRussy Park in Waikīkī.

➤ APR.: **Merrie Monarch Festival** (Big Island; ☎ 808/935–9168): A full week of ancient and modern hula competition begins with a parade the Saturday morning following Easter Sunday. Tickets must be purchased (and hotel rooms reserved) months in advance; the competition is held at the Edith Kanaka'ole Auditorium in Hilo. **Celebration of the Arts** (Maui; ☎ 808/669–6200): For three days the Ritz-Carlton, Kapalua pays tribute to Hawai'i's culture with hula and chanting demonstrations, art workshops, a lū'au, and Hawaiian music and dance concerts. Most activities are free. **Maui Country Fair** (Maui; ☎ 808/875–0457): This decades-old annual event is very popular. Rides, games, entertainment, and exhibits are at the War Memorial Complex, Kahului.

Maui Country Fair/The 'Ulupalakua Thing! (Maui; ☎ 808/875–0457): Maui County holds its annual agriculture trade show and sampling, hosted by Tedeschi Winery, on the lovely grounds of 'Ulupalakua Ranch. Rides, games, and entertainment take place. **Buddha Day** (all Islands; ☎ 808/536– 7044): Flower pageants are staged at Buddhist temples to celebrate Buddha's birth. **Honolulu International Bed Race and Parade** (O'ahu; ☎ 808/ 239–5546): Big names in town turn out for this wild event centered in Waikīkī. The race and after-dark electric light parade are part of a charity fund-raiser. **Great Keiki Fest** (O'ahu; ☎ 808/937–9800): This family event for kids at Ala Moana Beach Park

promotes health, education, ocean awareness, and conservation. **Hawai'ian Scottish Festival and Games** (O'ahu; ☎ 808/235–7605): Scottish songs, tartans, crafts, food, and traditional Highland athletic competitions make up this festival at Kapi'olani Park.

➤ MAY: **Lei Day** (all Islands; ☎ 808/ 547–7393): This annual flower-filled celebration on May 1 includes music, hula, food, and lei-making competitions, with lots of exquisite leis on exhibit and for sale. **Prince Lot Music Festival** (Kaua'i; ☎ 808/826–9644): Princeville's signature event attracts local musicians and distinguished American composers, plus there are hula performances and art and cultural exhibits. **Ka Hula Piko** (Moloka'i; ☎ 800/800–6367): A community celebration of the birth of hula is marked by performances, storytelling, Hawaiian food, crafts, and lectures. **Hawai'i Fisherman's Festival** (O'ahu; ☎ 808/ 254–3474): This two-day event includes exhibits, forums, demonstrations from both governmental and state agencies who play a role in the preservation of Hawai'i's fisheries. **Big Island Bounty Festival** (Big Island; ☎ 800/845–9905): Hawai'i's top chefs celebrate Hawai'i regional cuisine with cooking demonstrations, wine tastings, an outdoor market, dinners, and receptions at The Orchid at Mauna Lani.

➤ MAY–JUNE: **50th State Fair** (O'ahu; ☎ 808/682–5767): Produce exhibits, food stands, amusement rides, and live entertainment are at Aloha Stadium over several weekends. **Hawai'ian Airlines O'ahu Oceanfest** (O'ahu; ☎ 808/ 521–4322): This festival includes ocean-based competitions, entertainment, international lifeguard competitions, as well as beach sports. **Lantern Floating at Keahi Lagoon** (O'ahu; ☎ 808/947–2814): A Buddhist ceremony with 700 floating lanterns pays tribute to peace and departed ancestors at Keahi Lagoon Beach Park. **World Fire Knife Dance Competition** (O'ahu; ☎ 808/293–3333): This international competition of Samoan fire knife dancing takes place at the Polynesian Cultural Center.

➤ MAY–AUG.: **The Wildest Show in Town** (O'ahu; ☎ 808/971–7171): Popular local entertainers perform free early evening concerts Wednesday at the Honolulu Zoo.

➤ JUNE: **King Kamehameha Day** (all Islands; ☎ 808/586–0333): Parades and fairs abound, and twin statues of Hawai'i's first king—in Honolulu on O'ahu and in Kapa'au on the Big Island—are draped in giant leis. **Taste of Honolulu** (O'ahu; ☎ 808/536–1015): One of O'ahu's best food events, it features two days of sampling from the finest restaurants in town and entertainment outdoors on the grounds of the Honolulu Civic Center.

➤ JULY: **Pu'uhonua O Hōnunau Festival** (Big Island; ☎ 808/328–2288): Ancient Hawaiian games, hula performances, food tasting, and lau hala and coconut-frond weaving demonstrations take place at the historic City of Refuge. **Kapalua Wine and Food Symposium** (Maui; ☎ 800/669–0244): Wine and food experts and enthusiasts gather for tastings, discussions, and gourmet dinners at this four-day event at Kapalua Resort. **Makawao Statewide Rodeo** (Maui; ☎ 808/871–7711): This old-time Upcountry rodeo, held at the Oskie Rice Arena in Makawao on the July 4th weekend, includes a parade and three days of festivities. **Parker Ranch Rodeo** (Big Island; ☎ 808/885–7311): In beautiful Waimea, see how the Hawaiian cowboy, the *paniolo,* works the circuit. **Independence Day** (all Islands): The national holiday on July 4 is celebrated with fairs, parades, and fireworks. Special activities include an outrigger canoe regatta with 30 events held on and off Waikīkī Beach. **Prince Lot Hula Festival** (O'ahu; ☎ 808/839–5334): A whole day of hula unfolds beneath the towering trees of O'ahu's Moanalua Gardens. **Kīlauea Volcano Wilderness Marathon and Rim Runs** (Big Island; ☎ 808/329–1758): More than 1,000 athletes from Hawai'i, the mainland, and Japan run 26.2 mi across Ka'ū desert, 5 mi around the Kīlauea Caldera rim, and 5.5 mi into Kīlauea Iki Crater. The event takes place in Hawai'i Volcanoes National Park. **Cuisines of the Sun** (Big Island; ☎ 808/885–6622): Well-known guest chefs present imaginative cuisine paired with fine wines at cooking classes and evening galas during a five-day celebration of food at the Mauna Lani Bay Hotel & Bungalows. **Kane'ohe BayFest** (O'ahu; ☎ 808/254–7679): This event is the largest military festival of its kind in Hawai'i—with rides, contests, food, and entertainment. **Queen Lili'uokalani Keiki Hula Competition** (O'ahu; ☎ 808/521–6905): Tickets for this popular children's hula competition, held over three days, are usually available at the end of June and sell out soon after.

➤ JULY–AUG.: **Bon Odori Season** (all Islands; ☎ 808/661–4304): Buddhist temples invite everyone to festivals that honor ancestors and feature Japanese *o-bon* dancing. **Hawai'i State Farm Fair** (O'ahu; ☎ 808/848–2074): This 10-day fair with farm products, agricultural exhibits, crafts, a petting zoo, contests, and a country market is held at Aloha Stadium.

➤ JULY–SEPT.: **International Festival of the Pacific** (Big Island; ☎ 808/934–0177): Music; dance; a lantern parade; floats; sporting events; and food from Japan, China, Korea, Portugal, Tahiti, New Zealand, and the Philippines round out this event spanning July, August, and September.

➤ AUG.: **Hawaiian International Billfish Tournament** (Big Island; ☎ 808/329–6155): This international marlin fishing tournament, held in Kailua-Kona, includes a parade with amusing entries. **Made In Hawai'i Festival** (O'ahu; ☎ 808/533–1292): A three-day showcase of all products made in Hawai'i gives visitors an overview of what is available in the Islands. The **Maui Onion Festival** (Maui; ☎ 808/661–4567): This lighthearted and food-filled celebration of Maui's most famous crop takes place at Whalers Village, Kā'napali. **Admission Day** (all Islands): The state holiday, the third Friday in August, recognizes Hawai'i's attainment of statehood in 1959. **Poke Contest** (Maui; ☎ 808/874–1111): Chefs from throughout the Islands convene at the Maui Prince Hotel to compare renditions of this prized local raw-tuna specialty.

➤ SEPT.: **Maui Music Festival** (Maui; ☎ 808/661–3271 or 800/245–9229): On Labor Day weekend, well-known contemporary jazz, Hawaiian, and other musicians converge on the Kā'anapali Beach Resort for two days of nonstop music on several outdoor stages. **Maui Writers Conference** (Maui; ☎ 808/879–0061): Best-selling authors and powerhouse agents and publishers offer advice—and a few contracts—to aspiring authors and screenwriters at this Labor Day Weekend gathering. **Taste of Lahaina** (Maui; ☎ 808/667–9175): Maui's best chefs compete for top cooking honors, and samples of their entries are sold at a lively open-air party with live entertainment. **Kaua'i Mokihana Festival** (Kaua'i; ☎ 808/822–2166): This two-day islandwide event combines music, crafts, dancing, and hula competitions.

➤ SEPT.–OCT.: **Aloha Festivals** (all Islands; ☎ 808/923–1811, WEB www. gohawaii.com): This traditional celebration, started in 1946, preserves Hawaiian native culture. Crafts, music, dance, pageantry, street parties, and canoe races are all part of the festival. **Bankoh Moloka'i Hoe** (Moloka'i and O'ahu; ☎ 808/259–7112): Two annual canoe races from Moloka'i to O'ahu finish in Waikīkī. The women's race is in September; the men's is in October.

➤ OCT.: **Talking Island Festival** (O'ahu; ☎ 808/923–1811, WEB www. gohawaii.com): Storytellers share legends and myths of Polynesia at Ala Moana Park's McCoy Pavilion. **Ironman Triathlon World Championships** (Big Island; ☎ 808/329–0063, WEB www.ironmanlive.com): This popular annual sporting event is limited to 1,250 competitors who swim, run, and bicycle. **Aloha Classic World Wavesailing Championships** (Maui; ☎ 808/923–1811, WEB www.gohawaii.com): Top windsurfers from around the globe gather at Ho'okipa Beach for this professional tour's final event of the season.

➤ NOV.: **King Kalakaua Kupuna and Keiki Hula Festival** (Big Island; ☎ 808/329–1532): Both children and *kupuna* (adults 55 years and older) compete at this popular hula contest. **Kona Coffee Cultural Festival** (Big Island; ☎ 808/326–7820): A week-long celebration, including two parades and a family day with ethnic foods and entertainment at Hale Halawai Recreation Pavilion, follows the coffee harvest. **Winter Wine Escape** (Big Island; ☎ 808/880–1111): Three days of food and wine pairings, cooking demonstrations, receptions, dinners, and a farmers' market showcase Hawai'i regional cuisine at the Hāpuna Beach Prince Hotel. **Mission Houses Museum Annual Christmas Fair** (O'ahu; ☎ 808/531–0481, WEB www.lava.net/~mhm): Artists and craftspeople sell their creations in an open market. **Hawai'i International Film Festival** (O'ahu and Neighbor Islands; ☎ 808/528–3456): The visual feast showcases films from the United States, Asia, and the Pacific and includes seminars with filmmakers and critics.

WORDS AND PHRASES

Although an understanding of Hawaiian is by no means required on a trip to the Aloha State, a *malihini*, or newcomer, will find plenty of opportunities to pick up a few of the local words and phrases. Traditional names and expressions are widely used in the Islands, thanks in part to legislation enacted in the early '90s to encourage the use of the Hawaiian language. You're likely to read or hear at least a few words each day of your stay. Such exposure enriches a trip to Hawai'i.

With a basic understanding and some uninhibited practice, anyone can have enough command of the local tongue to ask for directions and to order from a restaurant menu. One visitor announced she would not leave until she could pronounce the name of the state fish, the *humuhumunukunukuāpua'a*. Luckily, she had scheduled a nine-day stay.

Simplifying the learning process is the fact that the Hawaiian language contains only eight consonants—*H, K, L, M, N, P, W,* and the silent *'okina*, or glottal stop, written '—plus the five vowels. All syllables, and therefore all words, end in a vowel. Each vowel, with the exception of a few diphthongized double vowels such as *au* (pronounced "ow") or *ai* (pronounced "eye"), is pronounced separately. Thus *'Iolani* is four syllables (ee-oh-la-nee), not three (yo-la-nee). Although some Hawaiian words have only vowels, most also contain some consonants, but consonants are never doubled.

Pronunciation is simple. Pronounce *A* "ah" as father; *E* "ay" as in weigh; *I* "ee" as in marine; *O* "oh" as in no; *U* "oo" as in true.

Consonants mirror their English equivalents, with the exception of *W*. When the letter begins any syllable other than the first one in a word, it is usually pronounced as a *V*. *'Awa*, the Polynesian drink, is pronounced "ava"; *'ewa* is pronounced "eva."

Nearly all long Hawaiian words are combinations of shorter words; they are not difficult to pronounce if you segment them into shorter words. *Kalaniana'ole*, the highway running east from Honolulu, is easily understood as *Kalani ana 'ole*. Apply the standard pronunciation rules—the stress falls on the next-to-last syllable of most two- or three-syllable Hawaiian words—and Kalaniana'ole Highway is as easy to say as Main Street.

Now about that fish. Try *humu-humu nuku-nuku āpu a'a*.

The other unusual element in Hawaiian language is the *kahakō*, or macron, written as a short line (‾) placed over a vowel. Like the accent (´) in Spanish, the kahakō puts emphasis on a syllable that would normally not be stressed. The most familiar example is probably *Waikīkī*. With no macrons, the stress would fall on the middle syllable; with only one macron, on the last syllable, the stress would fall on the first and last syllables. Some words become plural with the addition of a macron, often on a syllable that would have been stressed anyway. No Hawaiian word becomes plural with the addition of an *S*, since that letter does not exist in the *'ōlelo Hawai'i* (which is Hawaiian for "Hawaiian language").

What follows is a glossary of some of the most commonly used Hawaiian words. Don't be afraid to give them a try. Hawaiian residents appreciate visitors who at least try to pick up the local language.

ʻaʻā: rough, crumbling lava, contrasting with *pāhoehoe,* which is smooth.

ʻae: yes.

aikane: friend.

āina: land.

akamai: smart, clever, possessing savoir faire.

akua: god.

ala: a road, path, or trail.

aliʻi: a Hawaiian chief, a member of the chiefly class.

aloha: love, affection, kindness. Also a salutation meaning both greetings and farewell.

ʻānuenue: rainbow.

ʻaʻole: no.

ʻapōpō: tomorrow.

ʻauwai: a ditch.

auwē: alas, woe is me!

ʻehu: a red-haired Hawaiian.

ʻewa: in the direction of ʻEwa plantation, west of Honolulu.

hala: the pandanus tree, whose leaves (*lau hala*) are used to make baskets and plaited mats.

hālau: school.

hale: a house.

hale pule: church, house of worship.

ha mea iki or **ha mea ʻole:** you're welcome.

hana: to work.

haole: ghost. Since the first foreigners were Caucasian, *haole* now means a Caucasian person.

hapa: a part, sometimes a half; often used as a short form of *hapa haole,* to mean a person who is part-Caucasian; thus, the name of a popular local band, whose members represent a variety of ethnicities.

hauʻoli: to rejoice. *Hauʻoli Makahiki Hou* means Happy New Year. *Hauʻoli lā hānau* means Happy Birthday.

heiau: an outdoor stone platform; an ancient Hawaiian place of worship.

holo: to run.

holoholo: to go for a walk, ride, or sail.

holokū: a long Hawaiian dress, somewhat fitted, with a yoke and a train. Influenced by European fashion, it was worn at court, and at least one local translates the word as "expensive muʻumuʻu."

holomū: a post–World War II cross between a *holokū* and a muʻumuʻu, less fitted than the former but less voluminous than the latter, and having no train.

honi: to kiss; a kiss. A phrase that some tourists may find useful, quoted from a popular hula, is *Honi Kaʻua Wikiwiki:* Kiss me quick!

honu: turtle.

hoʻomalimali: flattery, a deceptive "line," bunk, baloney, hooey.

huhū: angry.

hui: a group, club, or assembly. A church may refer to its congregation as a *hui* and a social club may be called a *hui.*

hukilau: a seine; a communal fishing party in which everyone helps to drive the fish into a huge net, pull it in, and divide the catch.

hula: the dance of Hawaiʻi.

iki: little.

ipo: sweetheart.

ka: the. This is the definite article for most singular words; for plural nouns, the definite article is usually *nā.* Since there is no *S* in Hawaiian, the article may be your only clue that a noun is plural.

kahuna: a priest, doctor, or other trained person of old Hawaiʻi, endowed with special professional skills that often included the gift of prophecy or other supernatural powers; plural: *kāhuna.*

kai: the sea, saltwater.

kalo: the taro plant from whose root poi is made.

kama'āina: literally, a child of the soil, it refers to people who were born in the Islands or have lived there for a long time.

kanaka: originally a man or humanity in general, it is now used to denote a male Hawaiian or part-Hawaiian, but is occasionally taken as a slur when used by non-Hawaiians. *Kanaka maoli,* originally a full-blooded Hawaiian person, is used by some native Hawaiian rights activists to embrace part-Hawaiians as well.

kāne: a man, a husband. If you see this word on a door, it's the men's room. If you see *kane* on a door, it's probably a misspelling; that is the Hawaiian name for the skin fungus, tinea.

kapa: also called by its Tahitian name, *tapa,* a cloth made of beaten bark and usually dyed and stamped with a repeat design.

kapakahi: crooked, cockeyed, uneven. You've got your hat on *kapakahi.*

kapu: keep out, prohibited. This is the Hawaiian version of the more widely known Tongan word *tabu* (taboo).

kapuna: grandparent; elder.

kēia lā: today.

keiki: a child; *keikikāne* is a boy, *keikiwahine* a girl.

kona: the leeward side of the Islands, the direction (south) from which the *kona* wind and *kona* rain come.

kula: upland.

kuleana: a homestead or small plot of ground on which a family has been installed for some generations without necessarily owning it. By extension, *kuleana* is used to denote any area or department in which one has a special interest or prerogative. You'll hear it used this way: If you want to hire a surfboard, see Moki; that's his *kuleana.* And conversely: I can't help you with that; that's not my *kuleana.*

lā: sun.

lamalama: to fish with a torch.

lānai: a porch, a balcony, an outdoor living room. Almost every house in Hawai'i has one. Don't confuse this two-syllable word with the three-syllable name of the island, Lāna'i.

lani: heaven, the sky.

lau hala: the leaf of the *hala* or pandanus tree, widely used in Hawaiian handicrafts.

lei: a garland of flowers.

limu: sun.

lolo: stupid.

luna: a plantation overseer or foreman.

mahalo: thank you.

makai: toward the ocean.

malihini: a newcomer to the Islands.

mana: the spiritual power that the Hawaiian believed inhabited all things and creatures.

manō: shark.

manuwahi: free, gratis.

mauka: toward the mountains.

mauna: mountain.

mele: a Hawaiian song or chant, often of epic proportions.

Mele Kalikimaka: Merry Christmas (a transliteration from the English phrase).

Menehune: a Hawaiian pixie. The *Menehune* were a legendary race of little people who accomplished prodigious work, such as building fishponds and temples in the course of a single night.

moana: the ocean.

mu'umu'u: the voluminous dress in which the missionaries enveloped Hawaiian women. Now made in bright printed cottons and silks, it is an indispensable garment in a Hawaiian woman's wardrobe. Culturally sensitive locals have embraced the Hawaiian spelling but often shorten the spoken word to "mu'u."

Most English dictionaries include the spelling "muumuu," and that version is a part of many apparel companies' names.

nani: beautiful.

nui: big.

ohana: family.

'ono: delicious.

pāhoehoe: smooth, unbroken, satiny lava.

Pākē: Chinese. This *Pākē* carver makes beautiful things.

palapala: document, printed matter.

pali: a cliff, precipice.

pānini: prickly pear cactus.

paniolo: a Hawaiian cowboy, a rough transliteration of *español*, the language of the Islands' earliest cowboys.

pau: finished, done.

pilikia: trouble. The Hawaiian word is much more widely used here than its English equivalent.

puka: a hole.

pupule: crazy, like the celebrated Princess Pupule. This word has replaced its English equivalent in local usage.

pu'u: volcanic cinder cone.

waha: mouth.

wahine: a female, a woman, a wife, and a sign on the ladies' roomdoor; plural: *wāhine*.

wai: freshwater, as opposed to saltwater, which is *kai*.

wailele: waterfall.

wikiwiki: to hurry, hurry up. (Since this is a reduplication of *wiki*, quick, neither *W* is pronounced as a *V*.)

Note: Pidgin is the unofficial language of Hawai'i. It is a Creole language, with its own grammar, evolved from the mixture of English, Hawaiian, Japanese, Portuguese, and other languages spoken in 19th-century Hawai'i, and it is heard everywhere: on ranches, in warehouses, on beaches, and in the hallowed halls (and occasionally in the classrooms) of the University of Hawai'i.

KEY WORDS
ON THE MENU

Much of the Hawaiian language encountered during a stay in the Islands will appear on restaurant menus and lists of lūʻau fare. Here's a quick primer.

ʻahi: yellowfin tuna.

aku: skipjack, bonito tuna.

ʻamaʻama: mullet; it's hard to get but tasty.

bento: a box lunch.

chicken lūʻau: a stew made from chicken, taro leaves, and coconut milk.

haupia: a light, gelatinlike dessert made from coconut.

imu: the underground ovens in which pigs are roasted for lūʻau.

kālua: to bake underground.

kaukau: food. The word comes from Chinese but is used in the Islands.

kimchee: Korean dish of pickled cabbage made with garlic and hot peppers.

Kona coffee: coffee grown in the Kona district of the Big Island.

laulau: literally, a bundle. *Laulau* are morsels of pork, butterfish, or other ingredients wrapped with young taro shoots in ti leaves for steaming.

lilikoʻi: passion fruit, a tart, seedy yellow fruit that makes delicious desserts, jellies, and sherbet.

lomilomi: to rub or massage; also a massage. *Lomilomi* salmon is fish that has been rubbed with onions and herbs, commonly served with minced onions and tomatoes.

lūʻau: a Hawaiian feast, also the leaf of the taro plant used in preparing such a feast.

lūʻau leaves: cooked taro tops with a taste similar to spinach.

mahimahi: mild-flavored dolphinfish, not the marine mammal.

mai tai: potent rum drink with orange and lime juice, from the Tahitian word for "good."

malasada: a Portuguese deep-fried doughnut without a hole, dipped in sugar.

manapua: dough wrapped around diced pork.

manō: shark.

niu: coconut.

ʻōkolehao: a liqueur distilled from the ti root.

onaga: pink or red snapper.

ono: a long, slender mackerel-like fish; also called wahoo.

ʻono: delicious; also hungry.

ʻopihi: a tiny shellfish, or mollusk, found on rocks; also called limpets.

pāpio: a young *ulua* or jack fish.

pohā: Cape gooseberry. Tasting a bit like honey, the pohā berry is often used in jams and desserts.

poi: a paste made from pounded taro root, a staple of the Hawaiian diet.

poke: chopped, pickled raw tuna, tossed with herbs and seasonings.

pūpū: Hawaiian hors d'oeuvre.

saimin: long thin noodles and vegetables in broth, often garnished with small pieces of fish cake, scrambled egg, luncheon meat, and green onion.

sashimi: raw fish thinly sliced and usually eaten with soy sauce.

ti leaves: a member of the agave family, used to wrap food in cooking and removed before eating.

uku: deep-sea snapper.

ulua: a member of the jack family that also includes pompano and amberjack. Also called crevalle, jack fish, and jack crevalle.

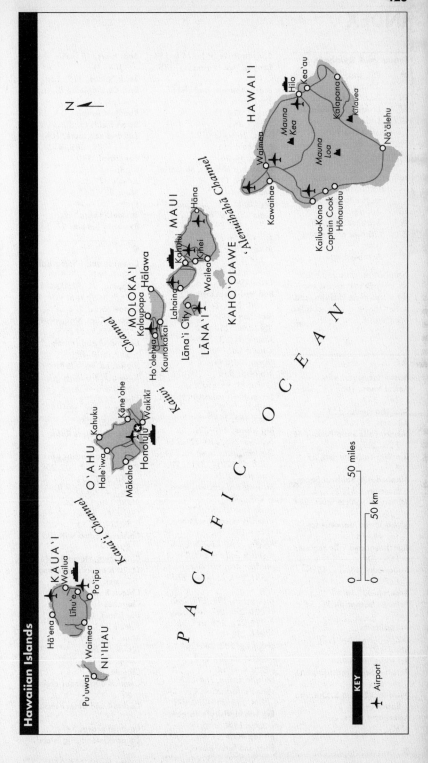

Hawaiian Islands

N

HAWAI'I

Kea'au
Hilo
Kalapana
Kīlauea
Mauna
Kea
Nā'ālehu
Mauna
Loa
Waimea
Kawaihae
Kailua-Kona
Captain Cook
Hōnaunau

'Alenuihāhā Channel

MAUI
Hāna
Ka'alui
Kīhei
Wailea
Hālawa

MOLOKA'I
Kalaupapa
Lahaina
Kaunakakai
Ho'olehua
Lāna'i City
LĀNA'I

KAHO'OLAWE

Pailolo Channel

Kaiwi

O'AHU
Kahuku
Kāne'ohe
Waikīkī
Hale'iwa
Mākaha
Honolulu

PACIFIC OCEAN

Kaua'i Channel

KAUA'I
Hā'ena
Wailua
Līhu'e
Po'ipū
Pu'uwai
Waimea
NI'IHAU

50 miles

50 km

0

KEY

✈ Airport

INDEX

FODOR'S HAWAI'I 2002

EDITOR: Deborah B. Kaufman

Editorial Contributors: Carissa Bluestone, DeSoto Brown, Gary Diedrichs, Betty Fullard-Leo, Sophia Schweitzer, Daniel Taras, Marty Wentzel, Kim Westerman, Marggie Wunsch

Editorial Production: Ira-Neil Dittersdorf

Maps: David Lindroth, *cartographer;* Rebecca Baer and Bob Blake, *map editors*

Design: Fabrizio La Rocca, *creative director;* Guido Caroti, *art director;* Jolie Novak, *senior picture editor;* Melanie Marin, *photo editor*

Cover Design: Pentagram

Production/Manufacturing: Angela L. McLean

COPYRIGHT

ISBN 0–679–00852–7

ISSN 0071–6421

Grateful acknowledgment is made to the following for permission to reprint previously published material: "The Aloha Shirt: A Colorful Swatch of Island History" by DeSoto Brown reprinted from *Aloha* magazine; copyright © October 1987 Davick Publications.

SPECIAL SALES

IMPORTANT TIP

Although all prices, opening times, and other details in this book are based on information supplied to us at press time, changes do occur all the time in the travel world, and Fodor's cannot accept responsibility for facts that become outdated or for inadvertent erros or omissions. So always confirm information when it matters, especially if you're making a detour to visit a specific place.

PHOTOGRAPHY

Catherine Karnow, *cover (Nā Pali Coast, Kaua`i).*

Alexander & Baldwin Sugar Museum, *p. 28 top.*

Big Island Visitors Bureau: *Bob Abraham, p. 2 top left. Robert Coello, p. 3 top right. Robert Miller, p. 3 center right. John Penisten, p. 2 top right, 30I. Red Sail Sports, p. 17H.*

Currents-Hawaii's Big Island, *p. 16E.*

John DeMello, *p. 23D, 30G.*

Dole Pineapple Plantation, *p. 2 bottom right.*

Sheila Donnelly & Associates: *Arnold Savrann, p. 30F.*

Robert Holmes, *15C.*

The Image Bank: *Alan Becker, p. 20 center, 20F. Andy Caulfield, p. 7D, 28 bottom. Angelo Cavalli, p. 15 bottom left, 16F, 29. David Hamilton, p. 1. Jeff Hunter, p. 15D. Marcel Isy-Schwart, p. 24 bottom right. John Kelly, p. 17I. Don King, p. 6A. A. Lanzellotto, 30H. Paul McCormick, p. 23E, 27 bottom. Michael Melford, p. 9H. Kaz Mori, p. 7C. Bernard Roussel, p. 11B. Joseph Szkodzinski, p. 8F, 20E, 30B. John Lewis Stage, p. 12G. Harald Sund, p. 7B, 11C. Cindy Turner, p. 17G. Pete Turner, p. 12E. Turner & De Vries, p. 9G, 13I, 19D, 21G, 27 top. Alvis Upitis, p. 16 top. Ulf Wallin, p. 13H. Stephen Wilkes, p. 30A.*

The Island of Lanai: *Jeffrey Asher, p. 25D, 30E.*

Kahala Mandarin Oriental, *p. 30C.*

Kaua'i Visitors Bureau: *David Boynton, p. 18A.*

Maui Ocean Center, *p. 13J.*

Maui Visitors Bureau: *William Waterfall, p. 3 bottom left, 3 bottom right. Phil Spalding III, p. 22B.*

Robert Miller, *p. 30J.*

PhotoDisc, *p. 26 bottom, 28 center.*

Photo Resource Hawaii: *David Boynton, p. 18C. John Callahan, p. 32. Jim Cazel, p. 4–5, 10A, 11D, 12F. Linny Morris Cunningham, p. 18B. Tammy Dawson, p. 21 bottom. Brad Lewis, p. 14A, 14B. Jon K. Ogata, p. 23C. Franco Salmoiraghi, p. 22A, 24A, 24B.*

Polynesian Cultural Center: *p. 2 bottom left, 3 top left, 8E, 9I. Dana Edmunds, p. 26 top.*

Princeville Resort: *Paul Barton, p. 21H, 30D.*

Trilogy Excursions: *Ron Dahlquist, p. 2 bottom center, 25C, 25E.*

ABOUT OUR WRITERS

The more you know before you go, the better your trip will be. Hawai'i's loveliest beach could be just around the corner from your hotel, but if you don't know it's there, it might as well be on the other side of the globe. That's where this book comes in. It's a great step toward making sure your next trip lives up to your expectations. As you plan, check out the Web as well. Guidebooks have been helping smart travelers find the special places for years; the Web is one more tool. Whatever reference you consult, be savvy about what you read, and always consider the source. Images and language can be massaged to make places appear better than they are. And one traveler's quaint is another's grimy. Here at Fodor's, and at our on-line arm, Fodors.com, our focus is on providing you with information that's not only useful but accurate and on target. Every day Fodor's editors put enormous effort into getting things right, beginning with the search for the right contributors—people who have objective judgment, broad travel experience, and the writing ability to put their insights into words. There's no substitute for advice from a like-minded friend who has just come back from where you're going, but our writers, having seen all corners of Hawai'i, are the next best thing. They're the kind of people you'd poll for tips yourself if you knew them.

Betty Fullard-Leo, a resident of the Islands since 1962, writes extensively about destinations, lifestyle, art, food, and culture in the Aloha State. Her work on *Fodor's Hawai'i* over the years has been invaluable. This year she was responsible for the Kaua'i and Moloka'i chapters. She's a contributing food editor for *Hawai'i* magazine, and previously she was editor of *Pacific Art & Travel* and associate editor of *ALOHA Magazine*. She has recently begun writing for travel sites on the Internet, including Insight2.com.

Big Island resident **Sophia Schweitzer** is our updater for that chapter as well as for Lāna'i. Sophia is a freelance food, wine, health and fitness, and travel writer whose work has appeared in magazines across the country. She is an educational writer for *Wine X*, a lifestyle magazine for the new generation, and has coauthored a book about the Big Island.

Geographer, photographer, writer, and chef **Daniel J. Taras** has crisscrossed the globe, with extended layovers in New York, Oregon, Mexico, and Hawai'i, where he owned and operated his own café and sushi bar in Upcountry Maui. Feeling overworked, Daniel retired from the restaurant business and took up travel writing, and now rarely works at all. He updated the Background and Essentials chapter.

Even though Maui updater **Kim Westerman** makes her home in the Sonoran Desert in Arizona, she is an island girl at heart. Her favorite restaurant on Maui is Sansei, in Kapalua, and she swears by the *mai tai* (rum drink with orange and lime juice) recipe at Mama's Fish House. Her favorite beach is a secret.

Maggie Wunsch, our O'ahu updater, is a 27-year resident of Hawai'i whose writings about the Islands have appeared on radio, local and national television, and in both consumer and travel-trade publications. Maggie grew up in Asia and Europe and fell in love with Hawai'i in 1961 when, at the age of 6, she first met the Pacific Ocean on the beach fronting the Halekūlani Hotel. Her fascination with Hawai'i and the Pacific continues to this day.

Don't Forget to Write

Your experiences—positive and negative—matter to us. If we have missed or misstated something, we want to hear about it. We follow up on all suggestions. Contact the Hawai'i editor at editors@fodors.com or c/o Fodor's, 280 Park Avenue, New York, New York 10017. And have a fabulous trip!

Karen Cure
Editorial Director